COLLINS

POSTCODE ATLAS
GREAT BRITAIN AND NORTHERN IRELAND

CONTENTS

Published by Collins
An imprint of HarperCollins*Publishers*
77-85 Fulham Palace Road, Hammersmith, London W6 8JB

Copyright © HarperCollins*Publishers* Ltd 2001
Mapping © Bartholomew Ltd 1999
Postcode Boundaries and Codes Copyright © The Post Office

Mapping generated from Bartholomew digital databases

Printed in Hong Kong   ISBN 0 00 448836 9   MV10118   CUNA

e-mail: roadcheck@harpercollins.co.uk   web site: www.bartholomewmaps.com

HarperCollins*Publishers*

Map of Postcode Areas

Postcode	Area	Postcode	Area	Postcode	Area
AB	Aberdeen	HG	Harrogate	PL	Plymouth
AL	St Albans	HP	Hemel	PO	Portsmouth
B	Birmingham		Hempstead	PR	Preston
BA	Bath	HR	Hereford	RG	Reading
BB	Blackburn	HS	Hebrides	RH	Redhill
BD	Bradford	HU	Kingston upon	RM	Romford
BH	Bournemouth		Hull	S	Sheffield
BL	Bolton	HX	Halifax	SA	Swansea
BN	Brighton	IG	Ilford	SE	London SE
BR	Bromley	IM	Isle of Man	SG	Stevenage
BS	Bristol	IP	Ipswich	SK	Stockport
BT	Belfast	IV	Inverness	SL	Slough
CA	Carlisle	KA	Kilmarnock	SM	Sutton
CB	Cambridge	KT	Kingston-upon-	SN	Swindon
CF	Cardiff		Thames	SO	Southampton
CH	Chester	KW	Kirkwall	SP	Salisbury
CM	Chelmsford	KY	Kirkcaldy	SR	Sunderland
CO	Colchester	L	Liverpool	SS	Southend-on-
CR	Croydon	LA	Lancaster		Sea
CT	Canterbury	LD	Llandrindod	ST	Stoke-on-Trent
CV	Coventry		Wells	SW	London SW
CW	Crewe	LE	Leicester	SY	Shrewsbury
DA	Dartford	LL	Llandudno	TA	Taunton
DD	Dundee	LN	Lincoln	TD	Galashiels
DE	Derby	LS	Leeds	TF	Telford
DG	Dumfries	LU	Luton	TN	Royal Tunbridge
DH	Durham	M	Manchester		Wells
DL	Darlington	ME	Medway	TQ	Torquay
DN	Doncaster	MK	Milton Keynes	TR	Truro
DT	Dorchester	ML	Motherwell	TS	Teesside
DY	Dudley	N	London N	TW	Twickenham
E	London E	NE	Newcastle upon	UB	Southall
EC	London EC		Tyne	W	London W
EH	Edinburgh	NG	Nottingham	WA	Warrington
EN	Enfield	NN	Northampton	WC	London WC
EX	Exeter	NP	Newport	WD	Watford
FK	Falkirk	NR	Norwich	WF	Wakefield
FY	Blackpool	NW	London NW	WN	Wigan
G	Glasgow	OL	Oldham	WR	Worcester
GL	Gloucester	OX	Oxford	WS	Walsall
GU	Guildford	PA	Paisley	WV	Wolverhampton
HA	Harrow	PE	Peterborough	YO	York
HD	Huddersfield	PH	Perth	ZE	Lerwick

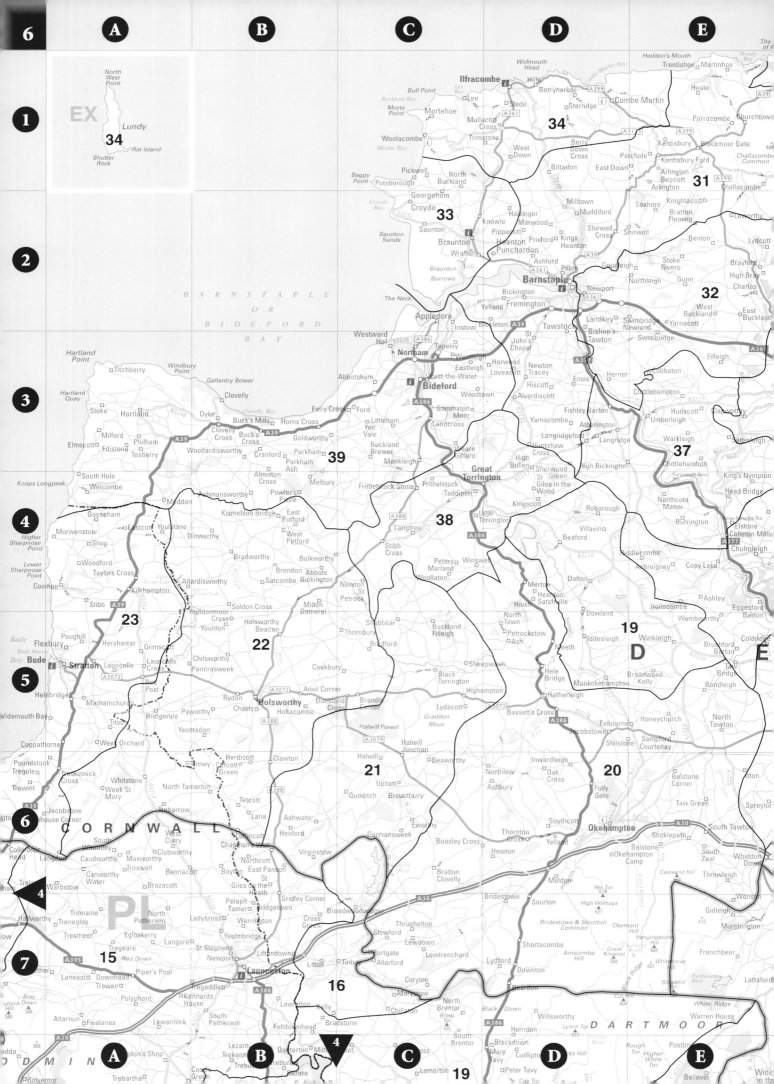

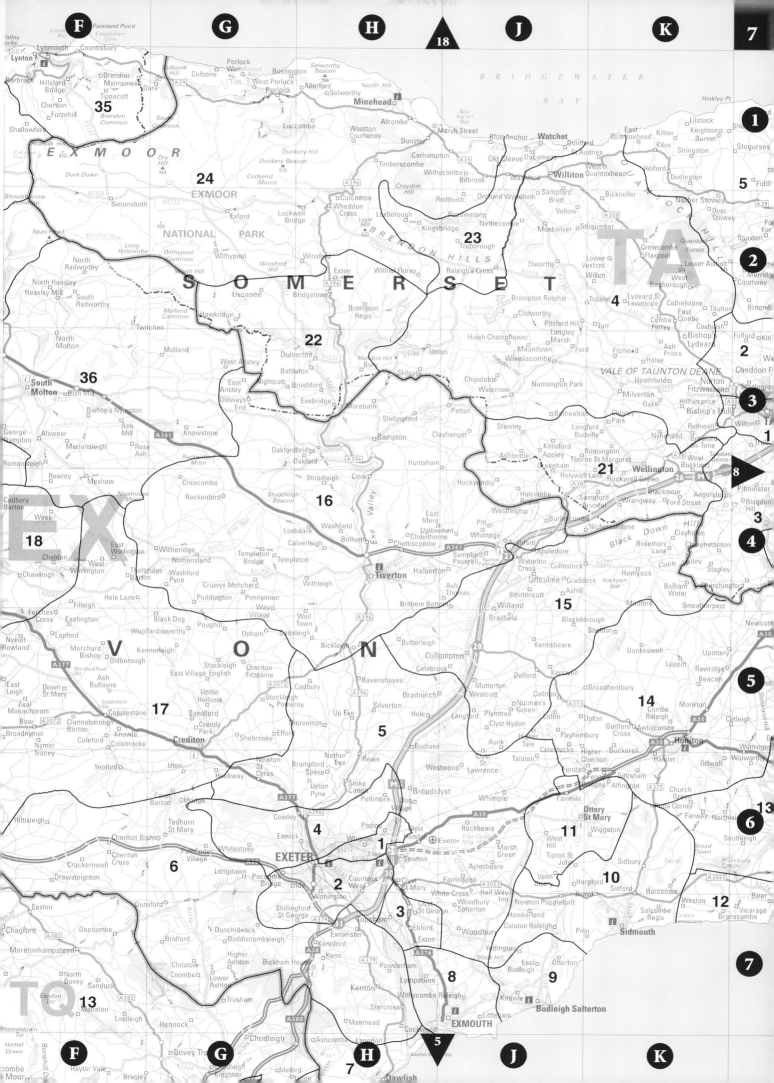

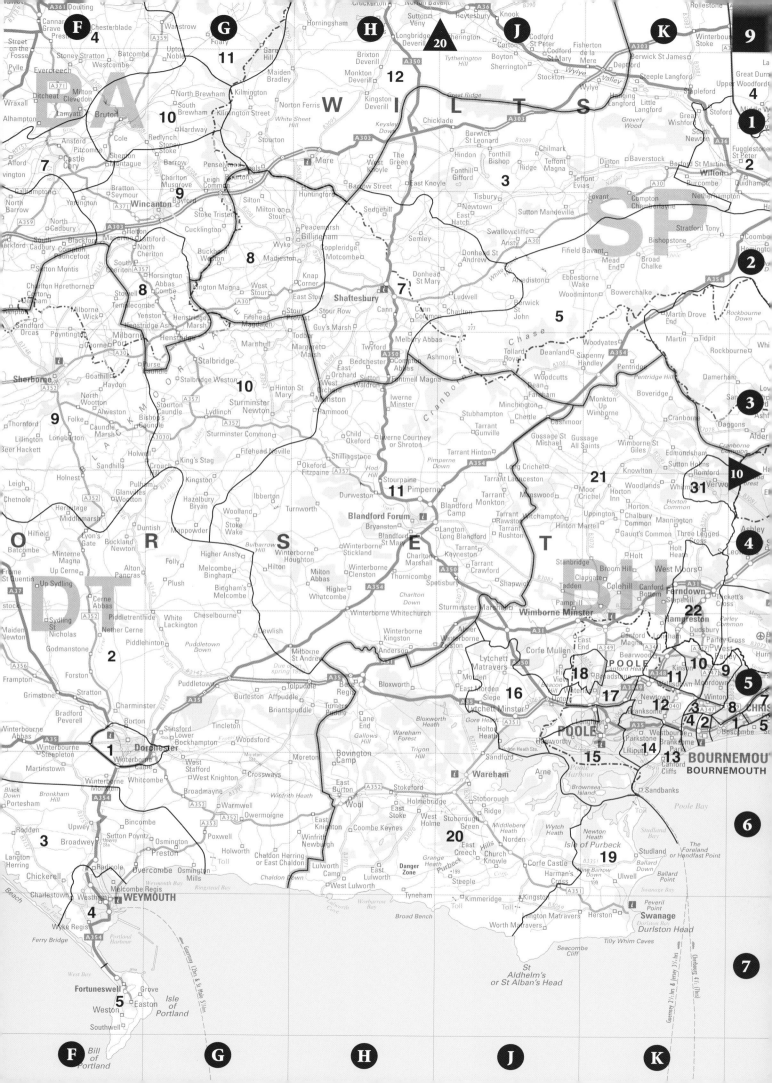

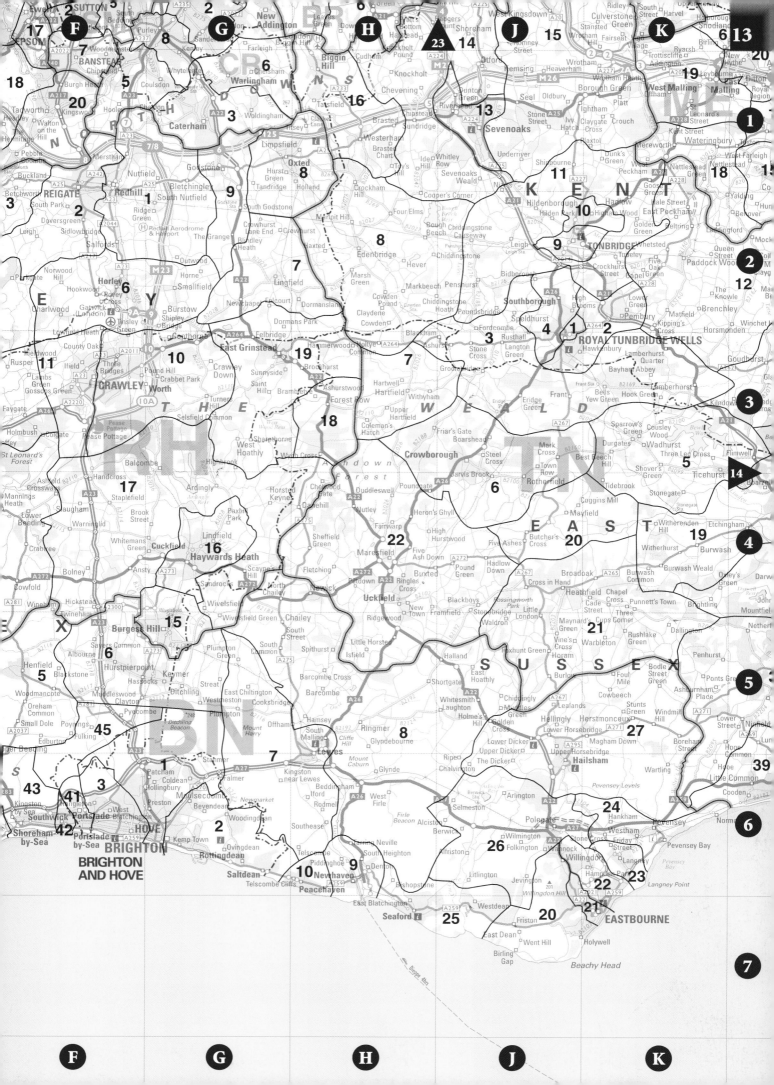

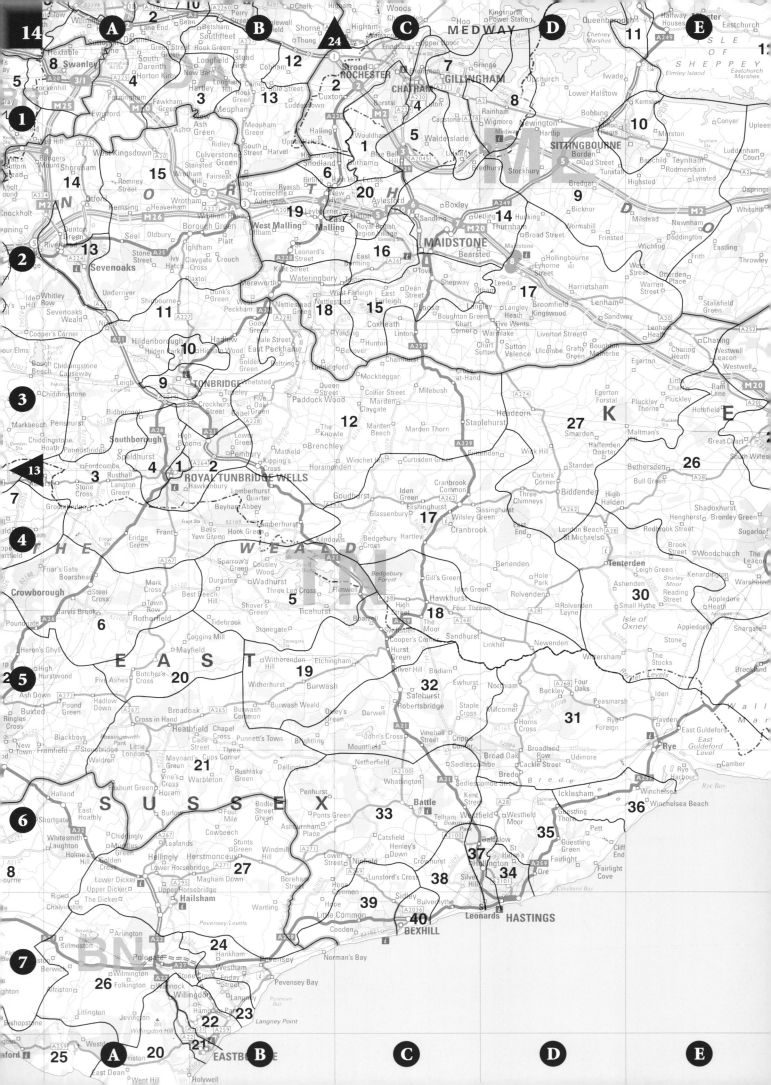

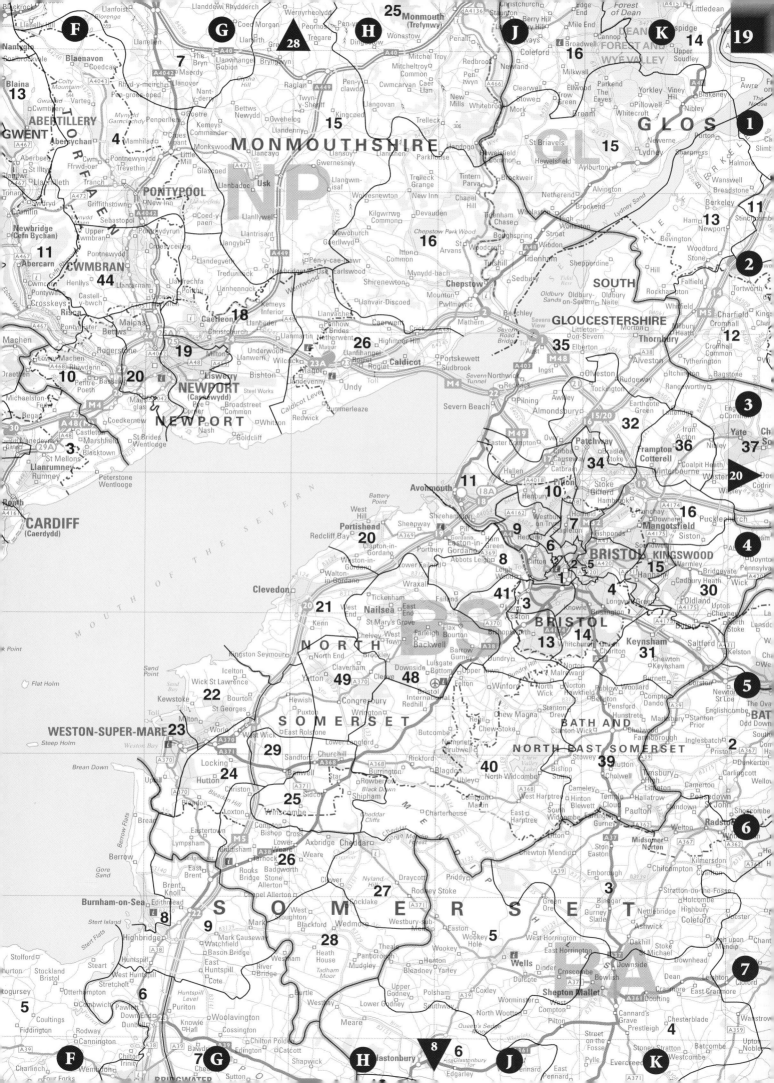

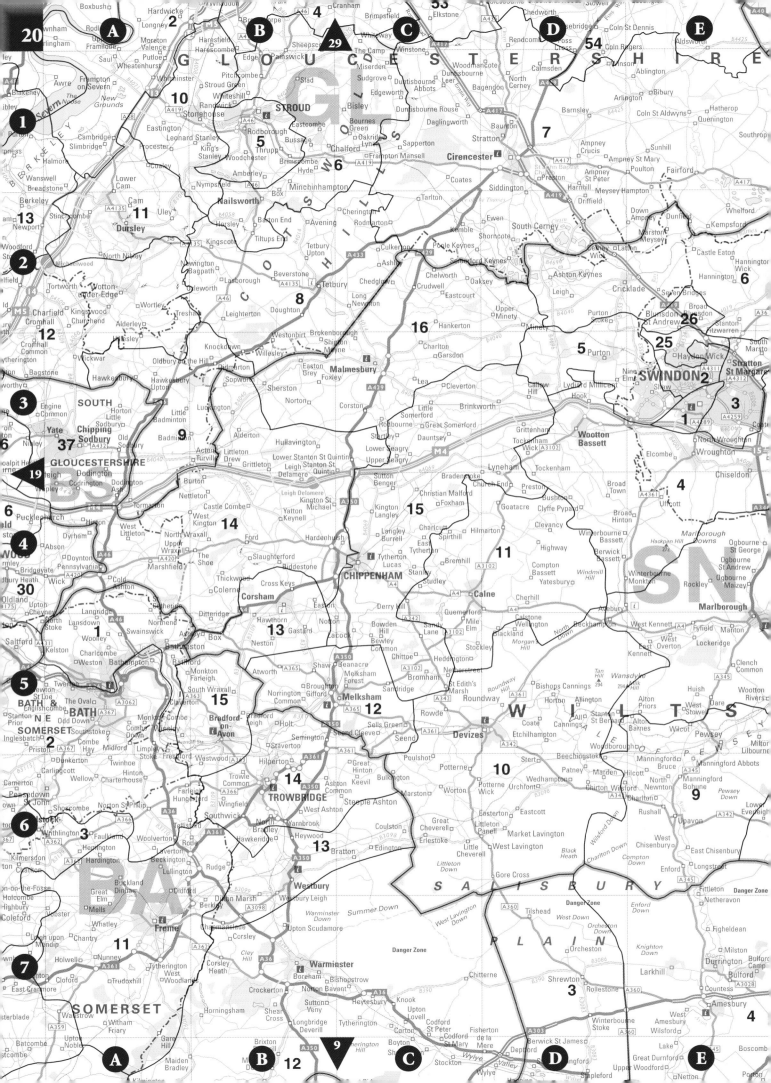

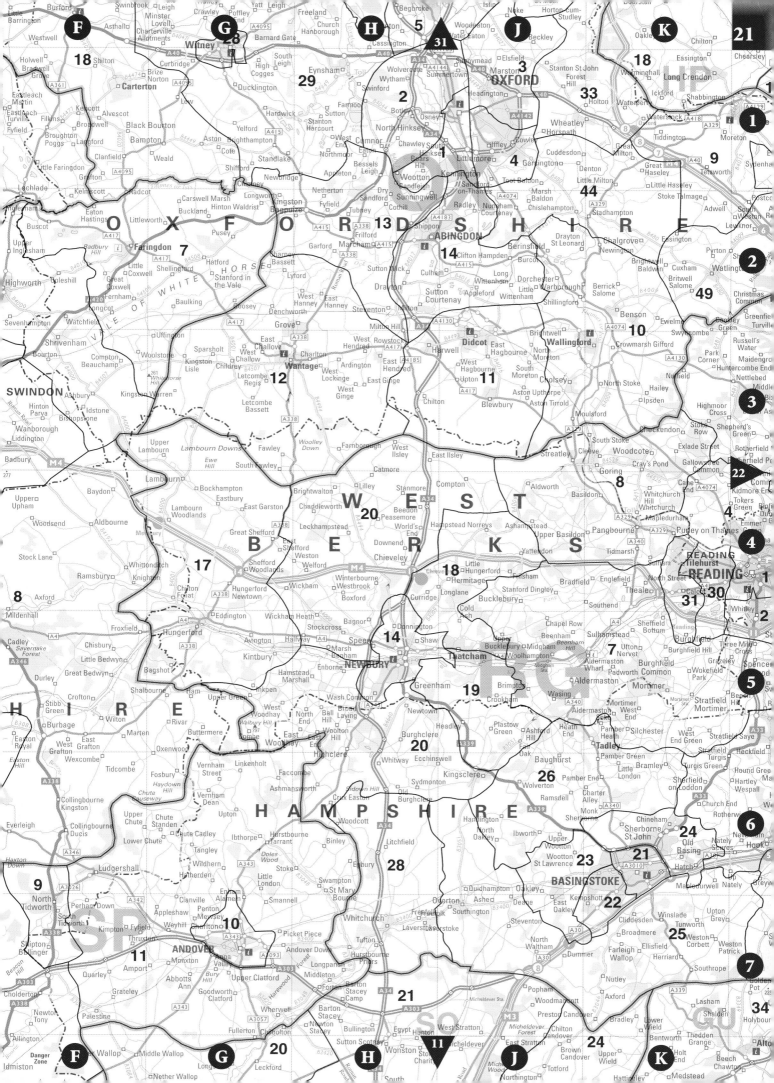

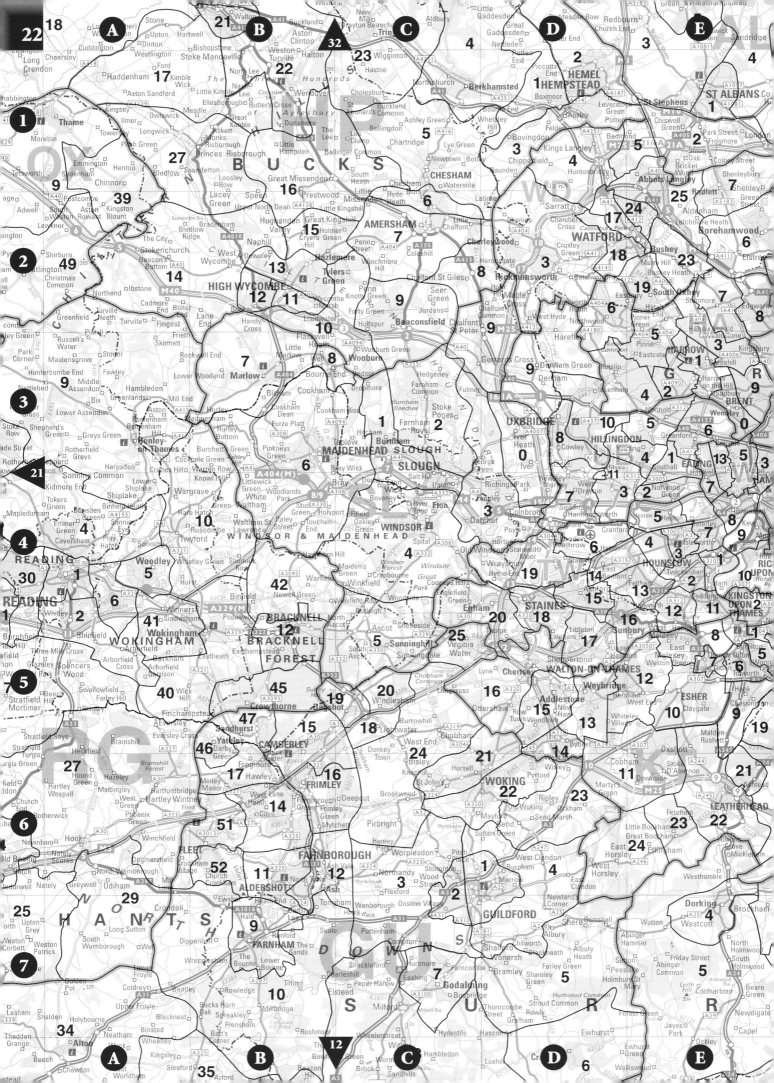

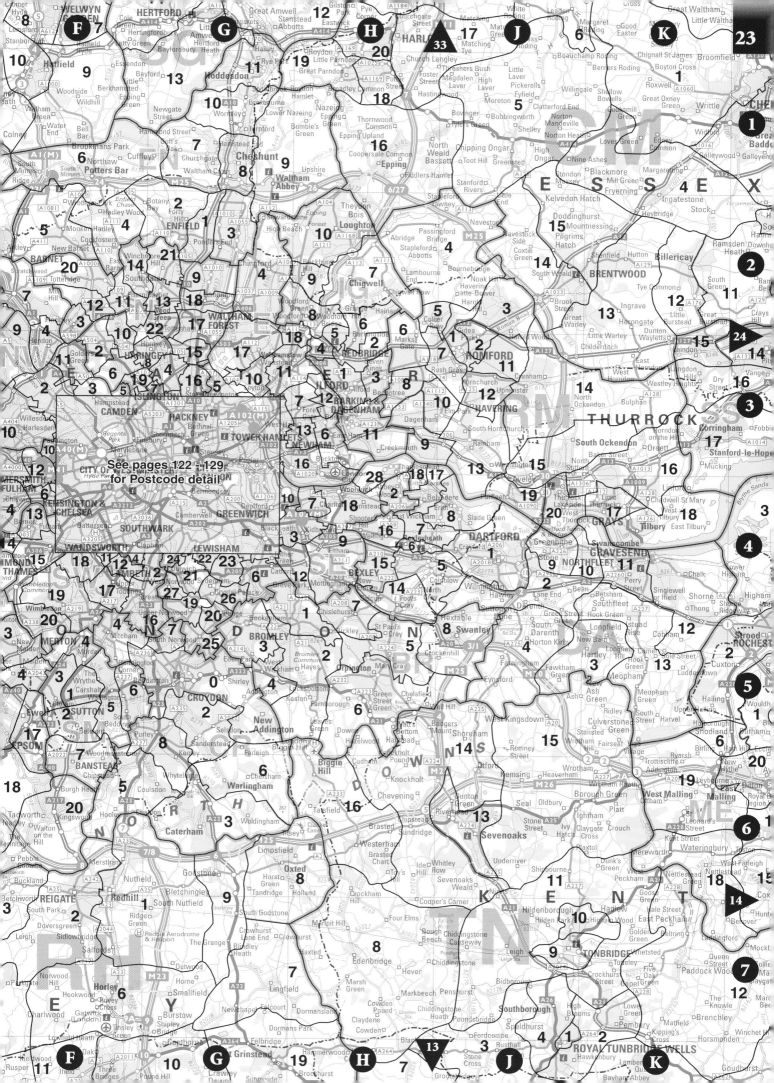

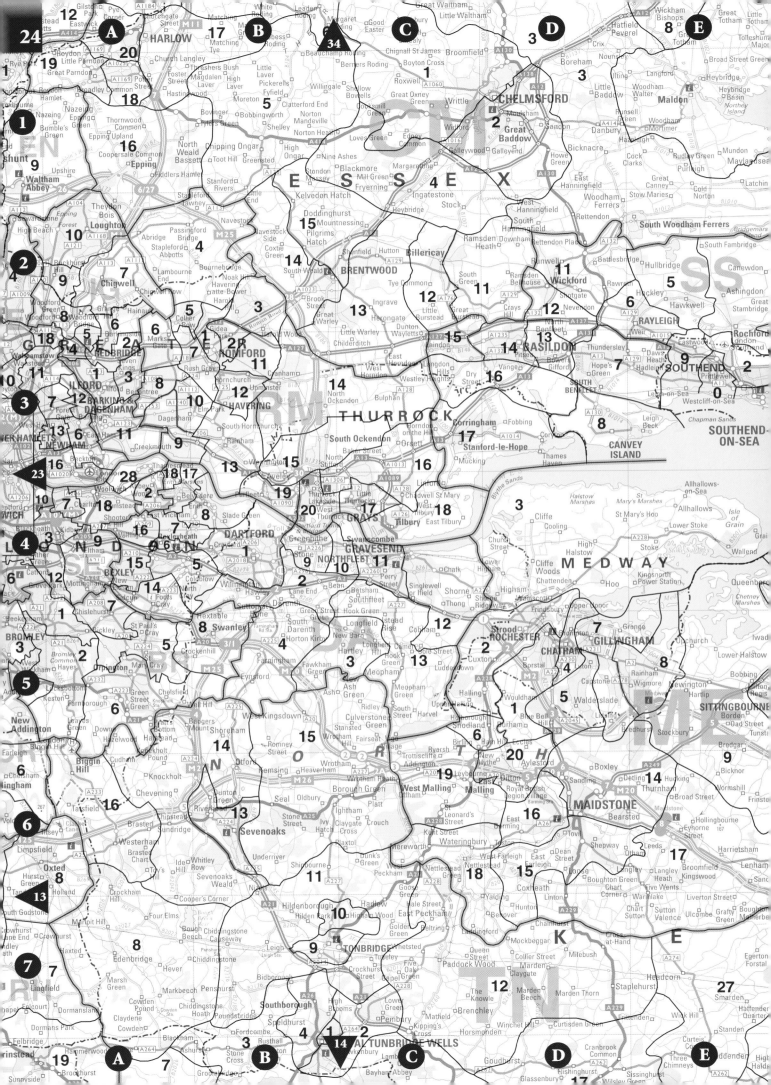

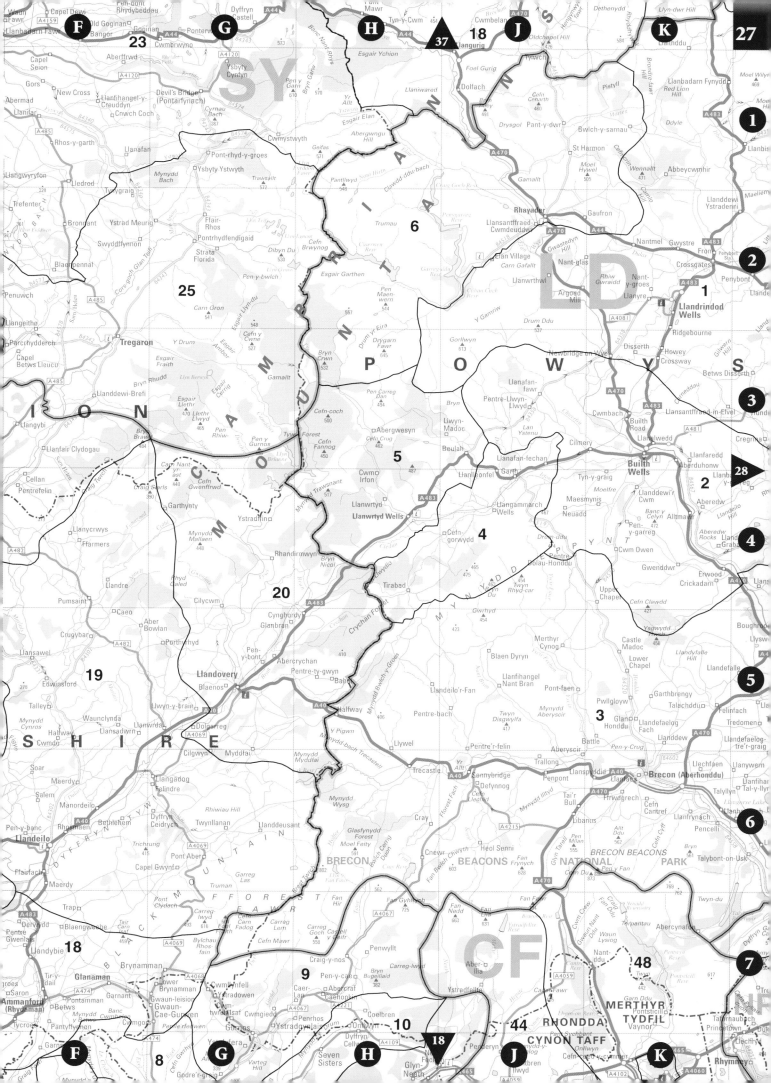

See page 112 - 113 for Postcode detail

See page 112 - 113 for Postcode detail

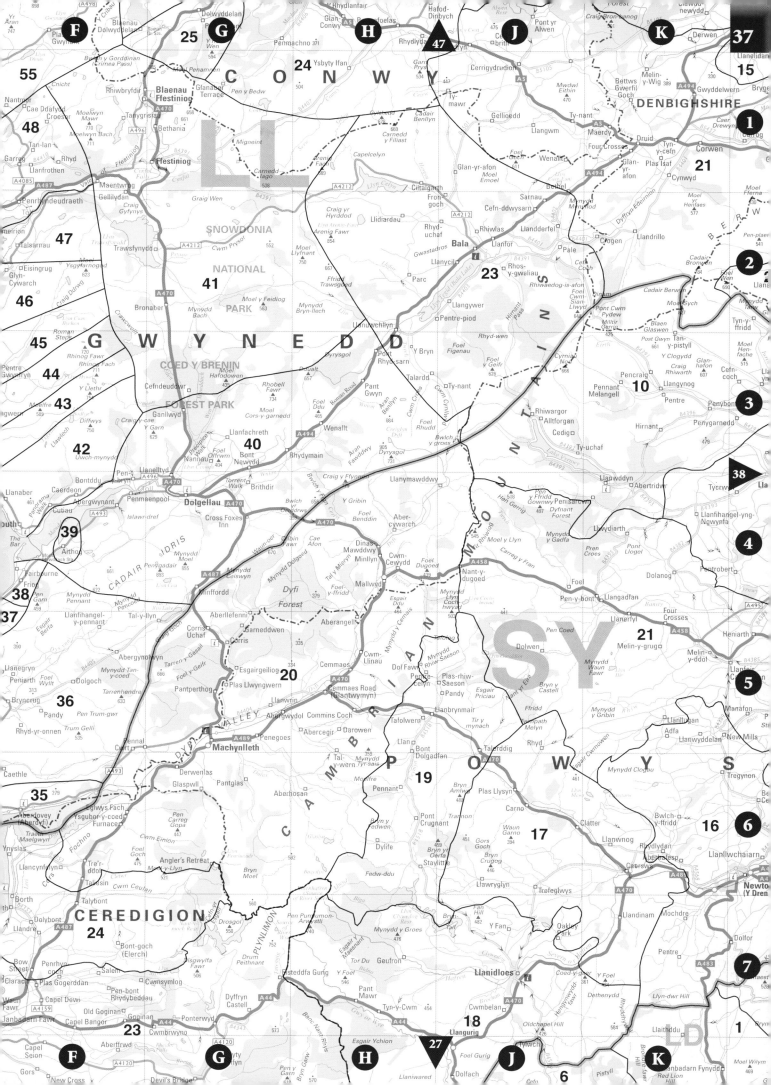

See page 112 - 113 for Postcode detail

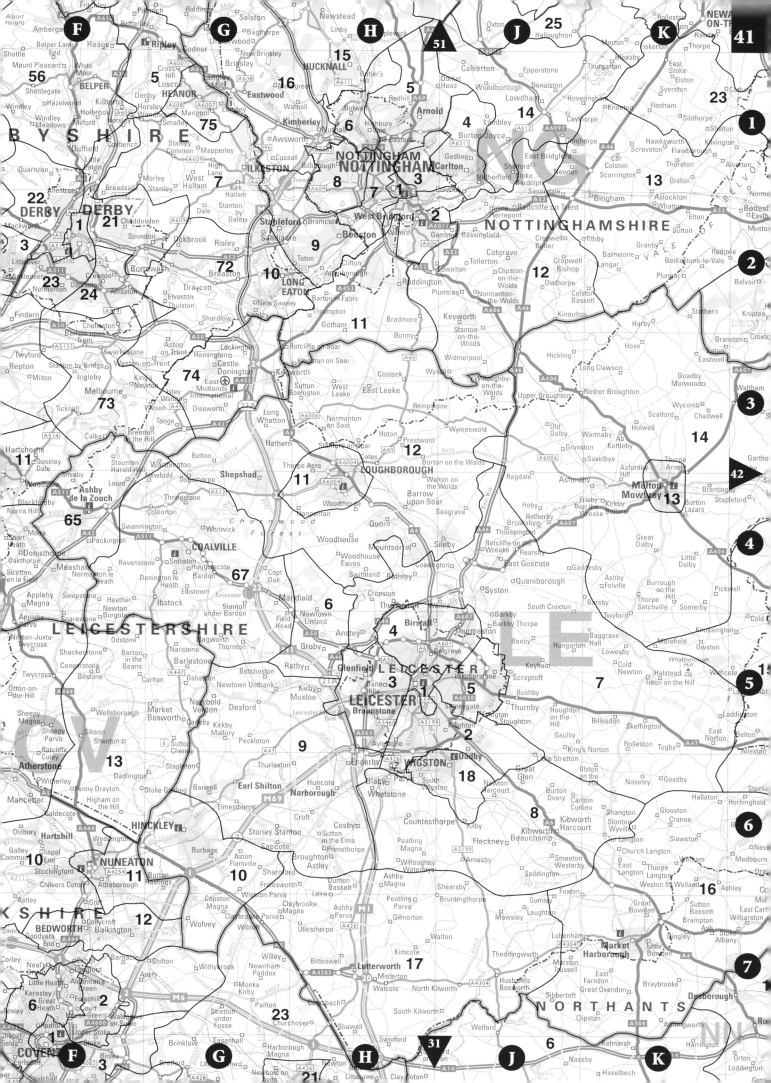

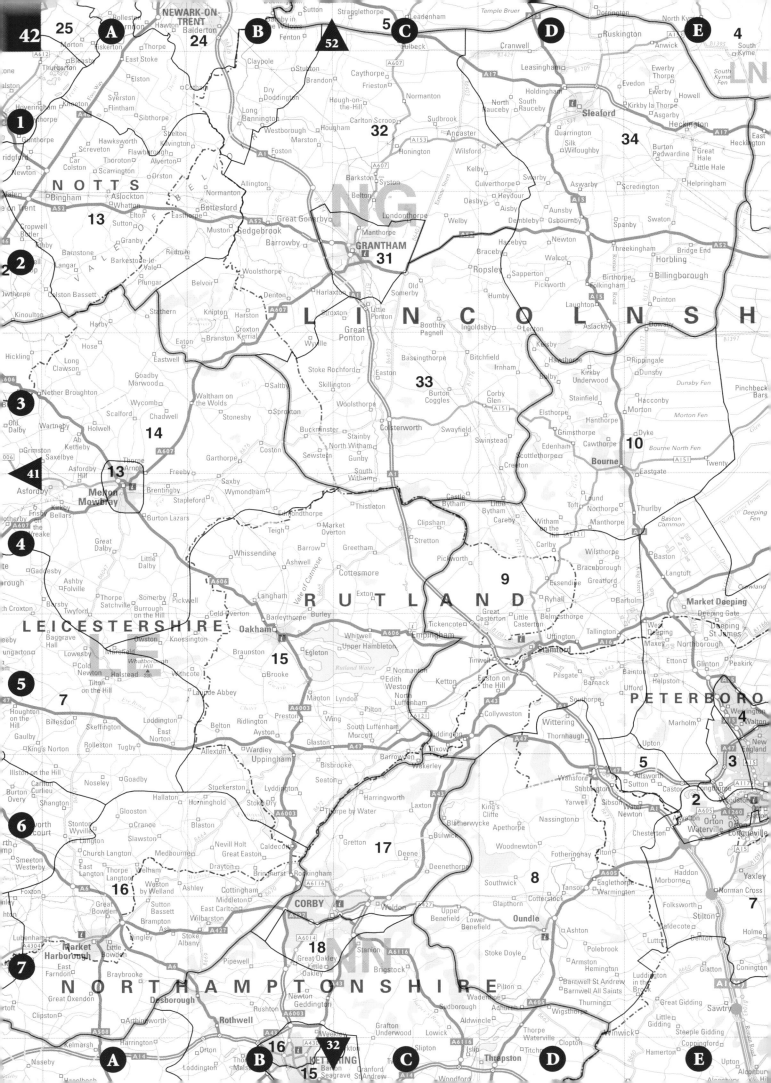

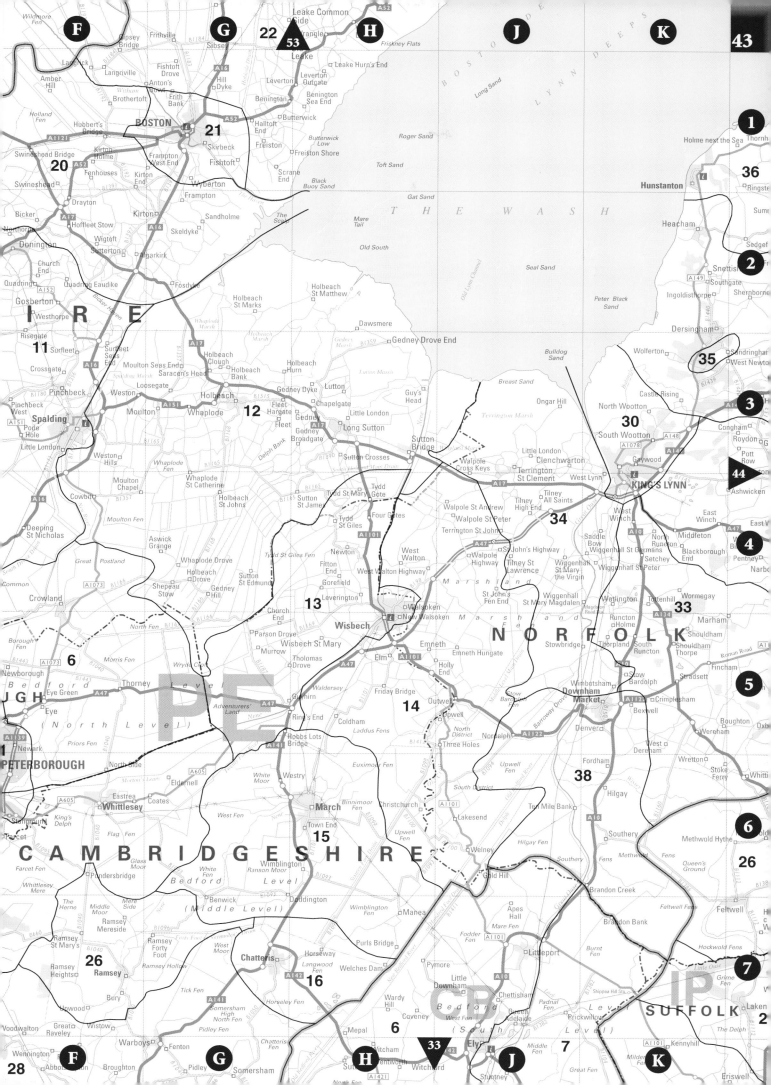

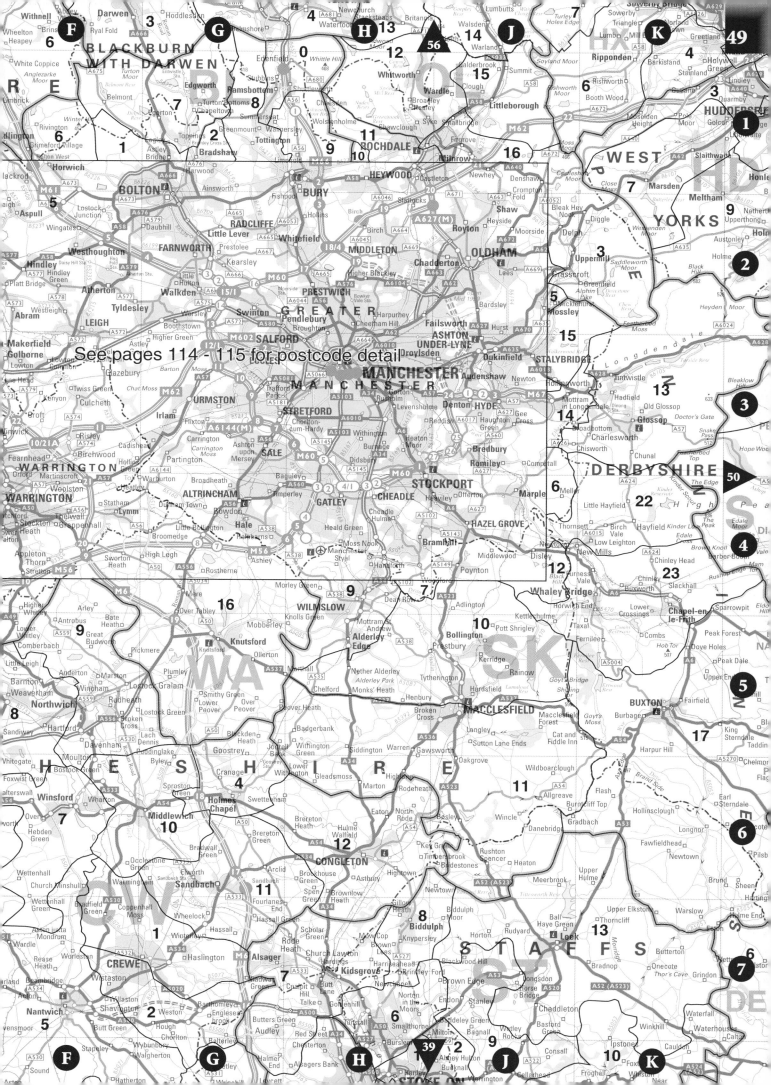

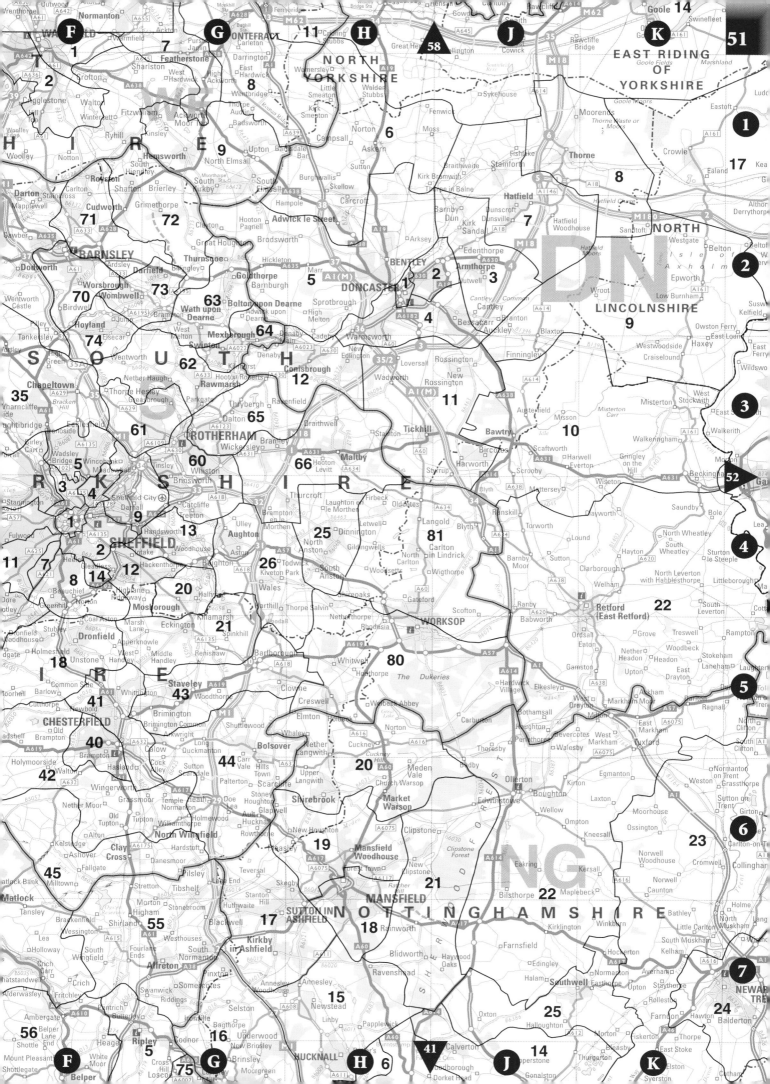

A   B   C   D   E

1

2

3

4

5

6

7

same scale as main map

ISLE
OF
MAN

IM

Lane End
Whitfell
Ulpha
Bigert Mire
Ulpha Park
Corney
Prion Park
19
Stub Place
LAKE DISTRICT
Stoneside Hill
Bank End
Hycemoor
Hyton
Bootle
Bootle Fell
NATIONAL
Duddon Bridge
Broadgate
Annaside
A595
Black Combe
600
PARK
White Combe
Lad Ha
Whitbeck
A595
18
Whicham
A5093
Silecroft
Kirksanton
Haverigg
Millom
Haverigg Point
Duddon Sands
North Scale
ISLE OF WALNEY
Vickerstown
A590
Tummer Hill Scar
Bigger

Point of Ayre
Rue Point
The Ayres
A16
The Lhen
Smeale
Glentruan
Cranstal
A10
Dhowin
A19
Bride
Sartfield
A10
Andreas
A9
A10
Jurby Head
Jurby East
B3
A17
Shellag Point
Jurby West
Sandygate
A17
B2
Ballasalla
A13
Regaby
Ramsey Bay
Crawyn
A14
St Judes
Dhoor
The Cronk
The Curraghs
A3
Sulby
B14
8
Ramsey
Orrisdale
A10
Ballaugh
Churchtown
Glen Auldyn
Port e Vullen
Orrisdale Head
Ravensdale
7
A15
Dreemskerry
Maughold Head
Kirk Michael
ISLE
Slieau Curn
A18
North Barrule
Maughold
Ballajora
Corrany
Port Mooar
Slieau Dhoo
Slieau Managh
Clagh Ouyr
Ballacarnane Beg
A3
Sileau Freoaghane
A14
Shaefell
621
Port Cornaa
Barregarrow
6
Sartfell
B10
Slieau Lhean
Dhoon
Gob y Deigan
Shoughlaige-e-Caine
Sulby Resr
Beinn-y-Phott
546
Slieau Ruy
Knocksharry
A4
Little London
Injebreck
Bulgham Bay
Cronk-y-Voddy
Injebreck Resr
OF
St Patrick's Isle
Ballagyr
Lambfell Moar
Colden
487
Laxey Head
Peel
A20
Ballig
Sileau Ruy
478
Laxey
Ballacannell
Contrary Head
Greeba Mountain
Baldwin
Laxey Bay
Knockaloe Moar
Patrick
A30
St John's
A1
A23
Hiflberry
Baldrine
Garwick Bay
5
333
A3
Crosby
A2
Clay Head
Glenmaye
Foxdale
Eairy
Garth
Glen Vine
Onchan
A11
Port Groudle
Dalby Point
Dalby
A24
Union Mills
Strang
3
Onchan Head
Niarbyl Island
Dalby Mountain
B35
2
Niarbyl Bay
South Barrule
483
Braaid
A34
1
Douglas
Belfast 2¾-4½ hrs (summer only)
Stroin Vuigh
341
A27
Close Clark
Stuggadhoo
Quine's Hill
Douglas Head
Heysham 3¾ hrs
Ballamodha
9
Newtown Hill
Douglas Bay
Lingague
Ronague
Grenaby
St Mark's
Ballaveare
Little Ness
Fleetwood 3½ hrs (summer only)
Fleshwick Bay
A36
A26
A5
A25
Liverpool 2½-4½ hrs
Bradda
Ballakilpheric
Ballabeg
Bradda Head
Colby
A7
Ballasalla
Ballafesson
A32
Croit e Caley
Port Grenaugh
Port Erin
Balladoole
A3
Santon Head
Calf of Man
Cregneish
The Howe
Port St Mary
Bay ny Carrickey
Isle of Man
Derbyhaven
Santon Head
A31
Castletown
St Michael's Island
Spanish Head
Perwick Bay
Castletown Bay
Langness
Dreswick Point
Chicken Rock
Dublin 2½ hrs (summer only)

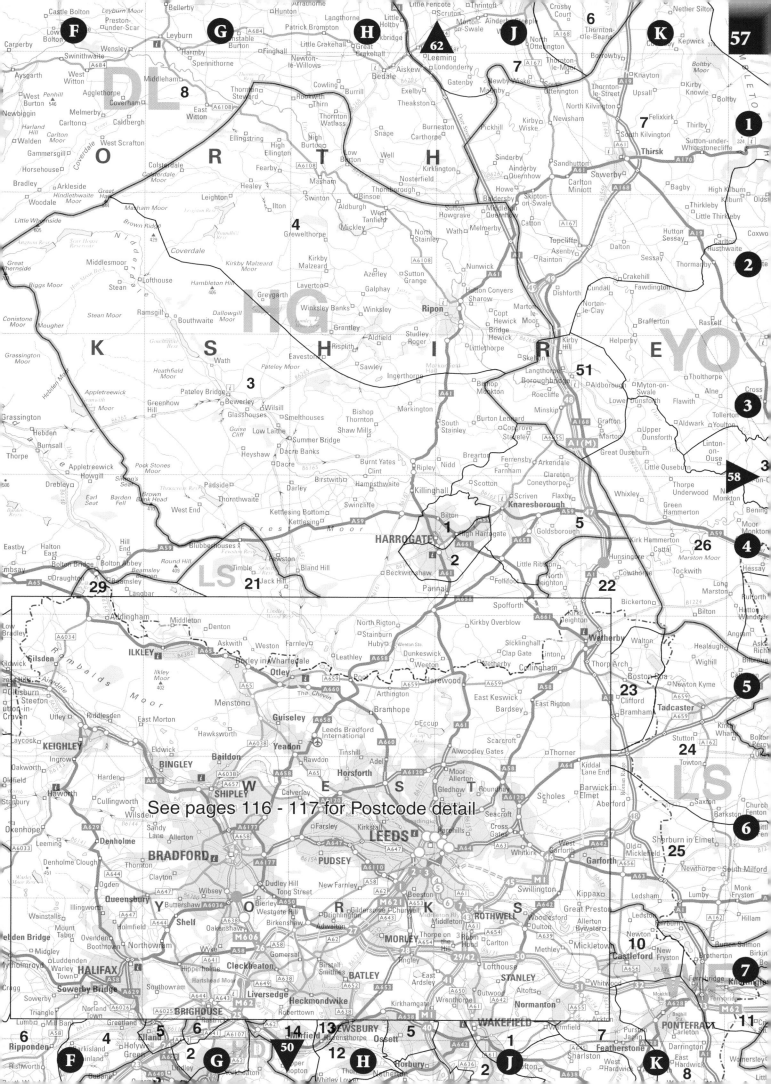

See pages 116 - 117 for Postcode detail

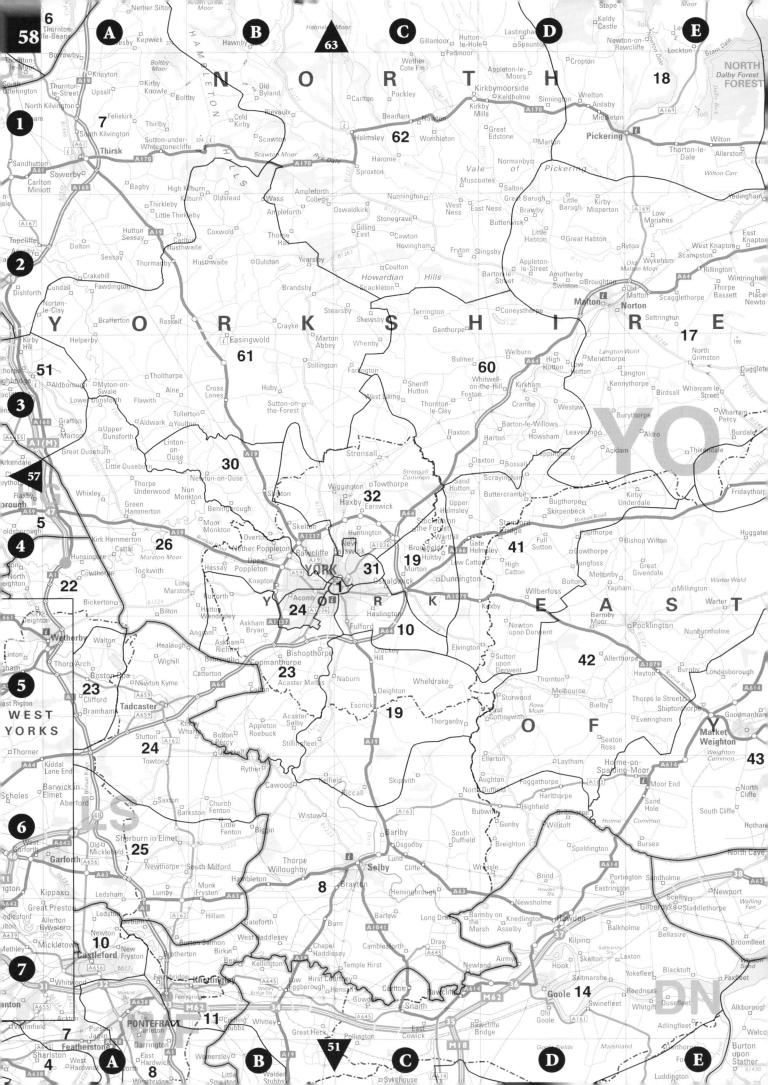

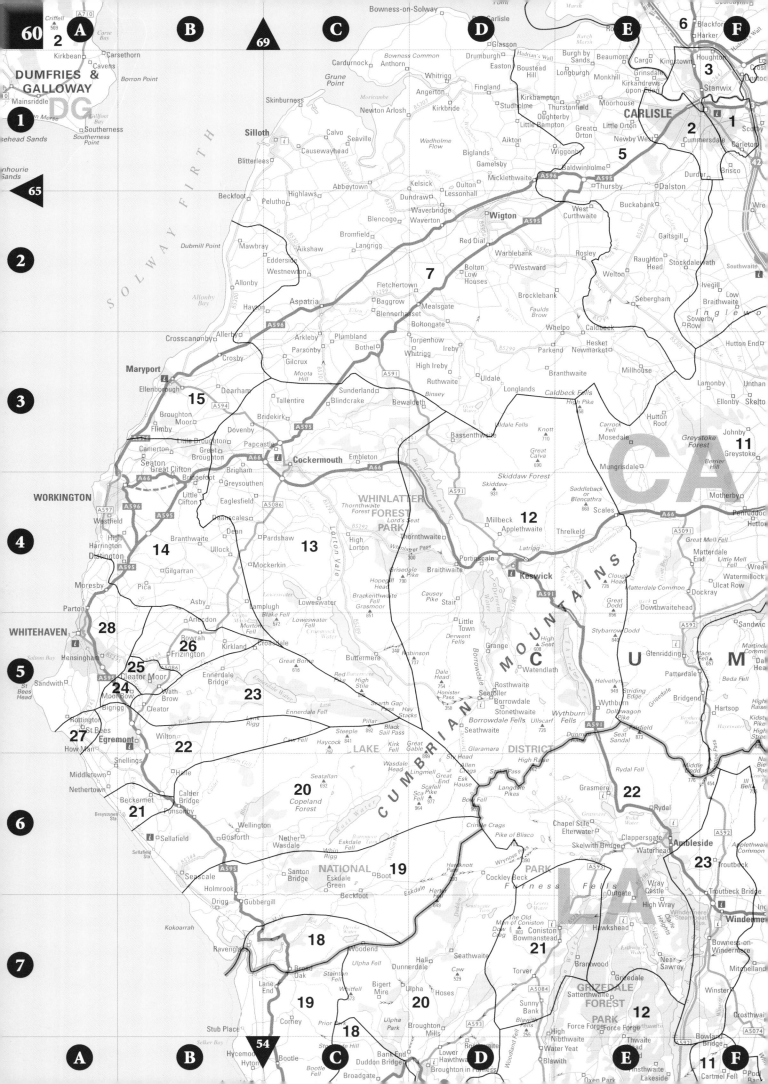

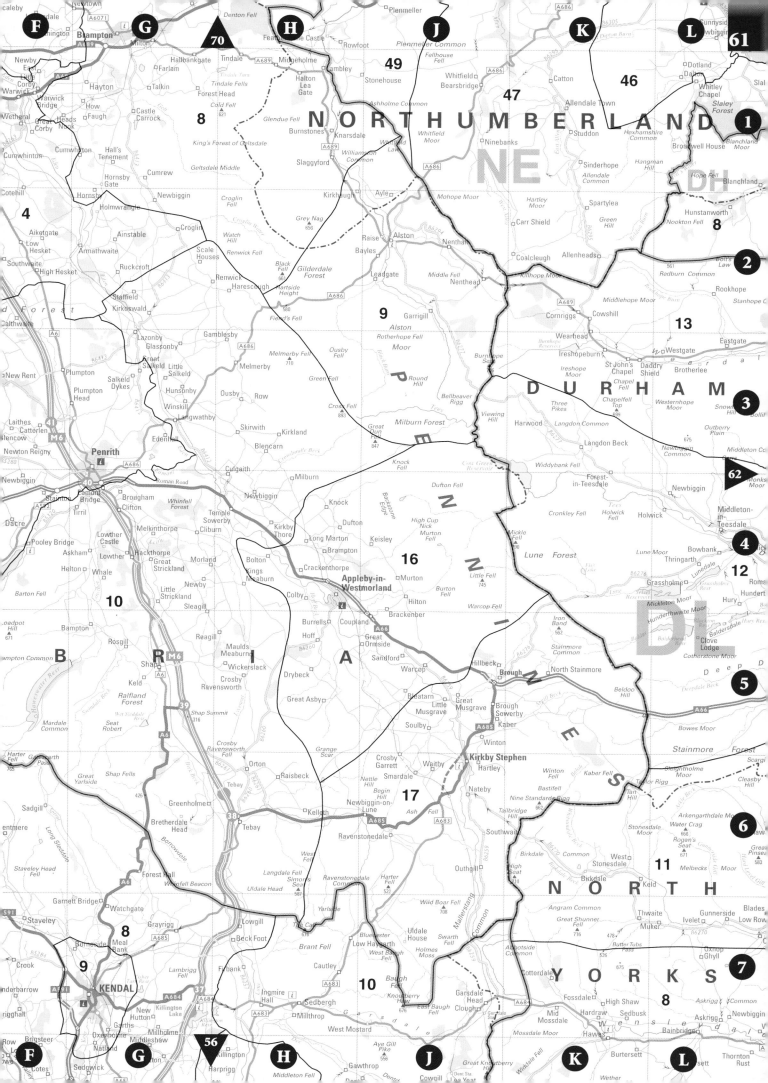

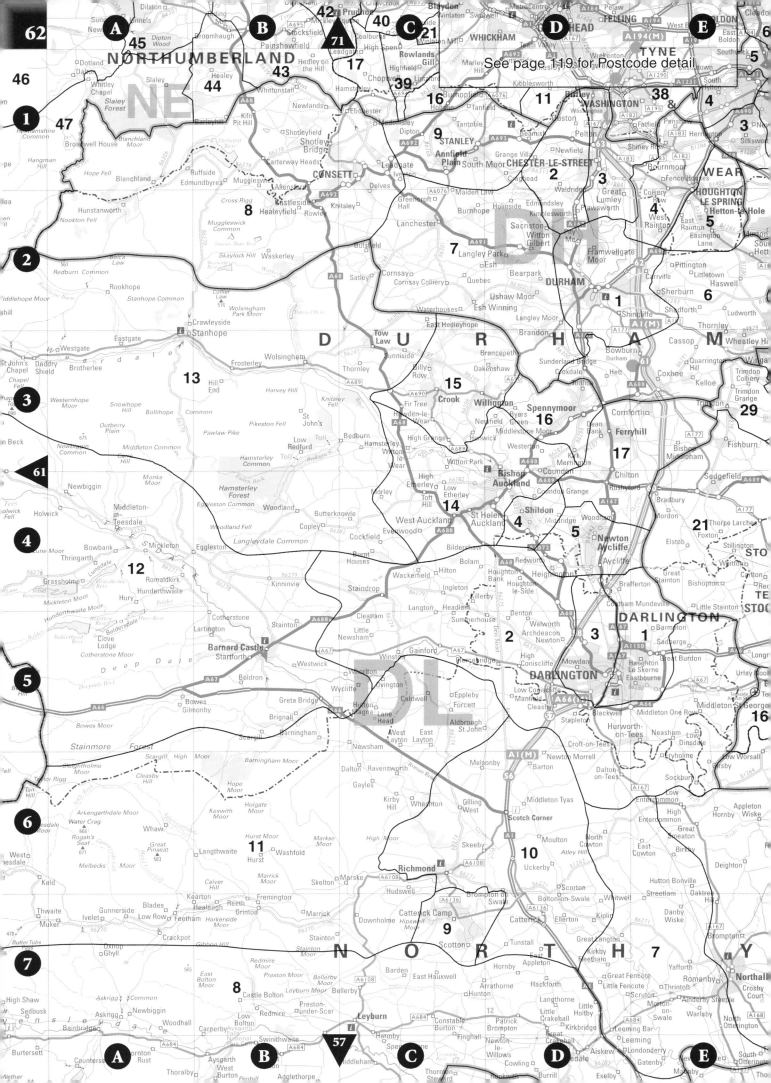

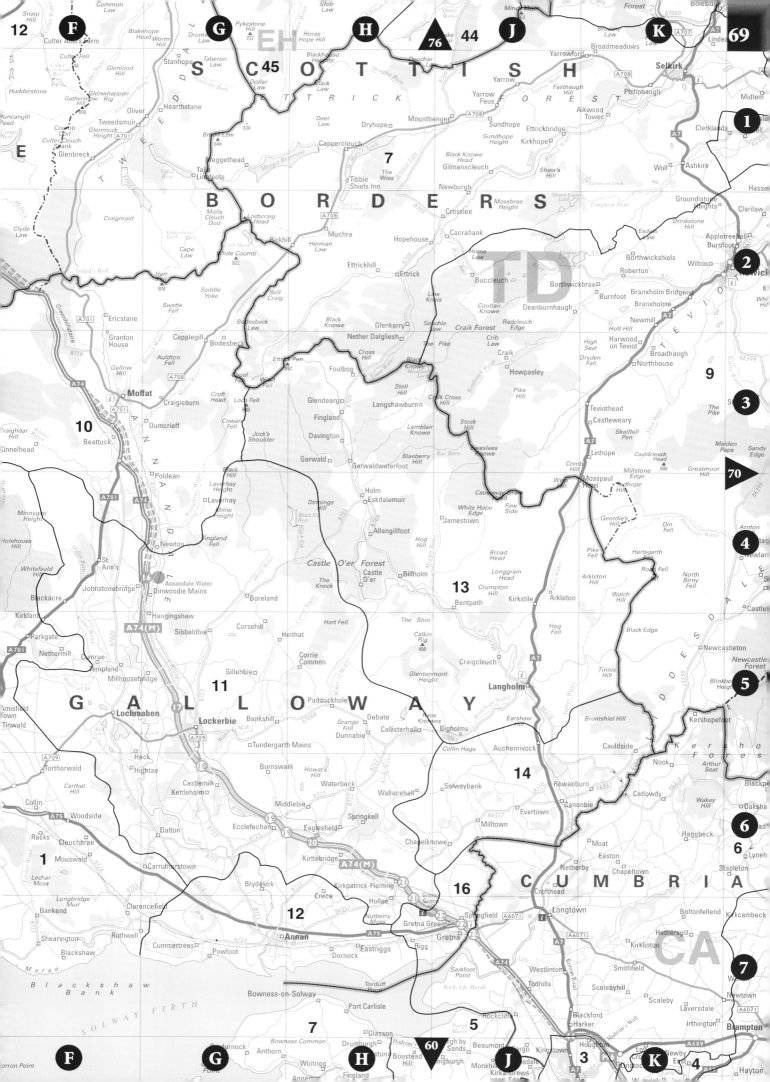

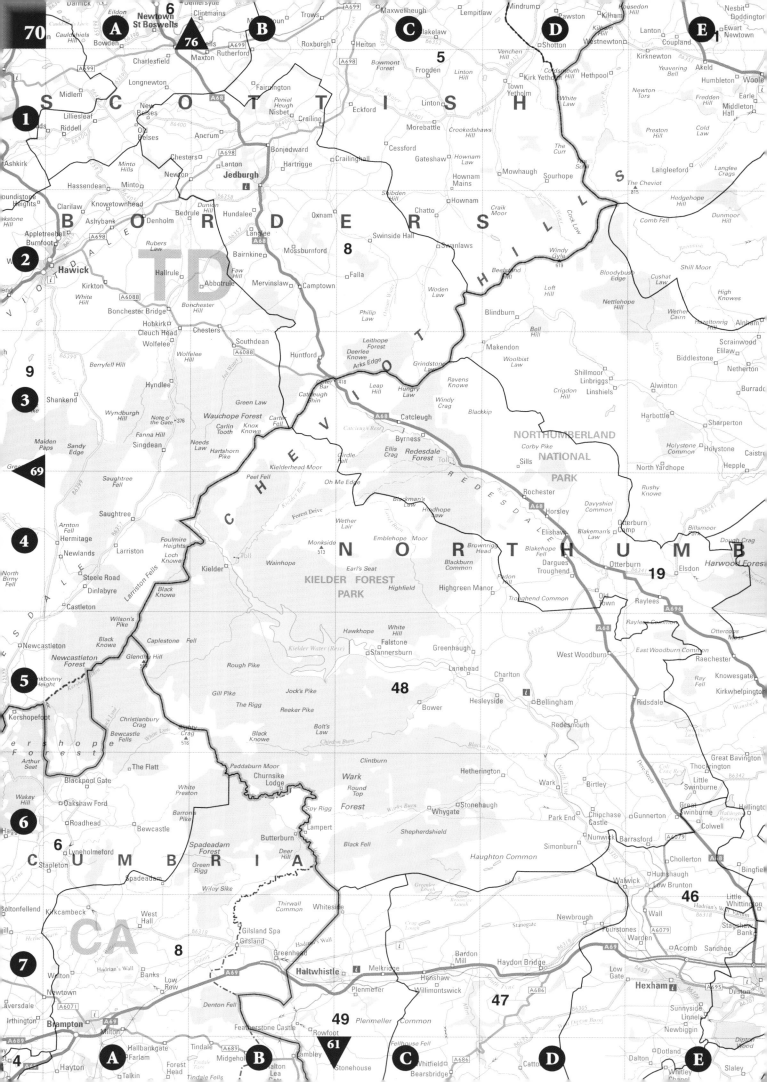

See page 119 for Postcode detail

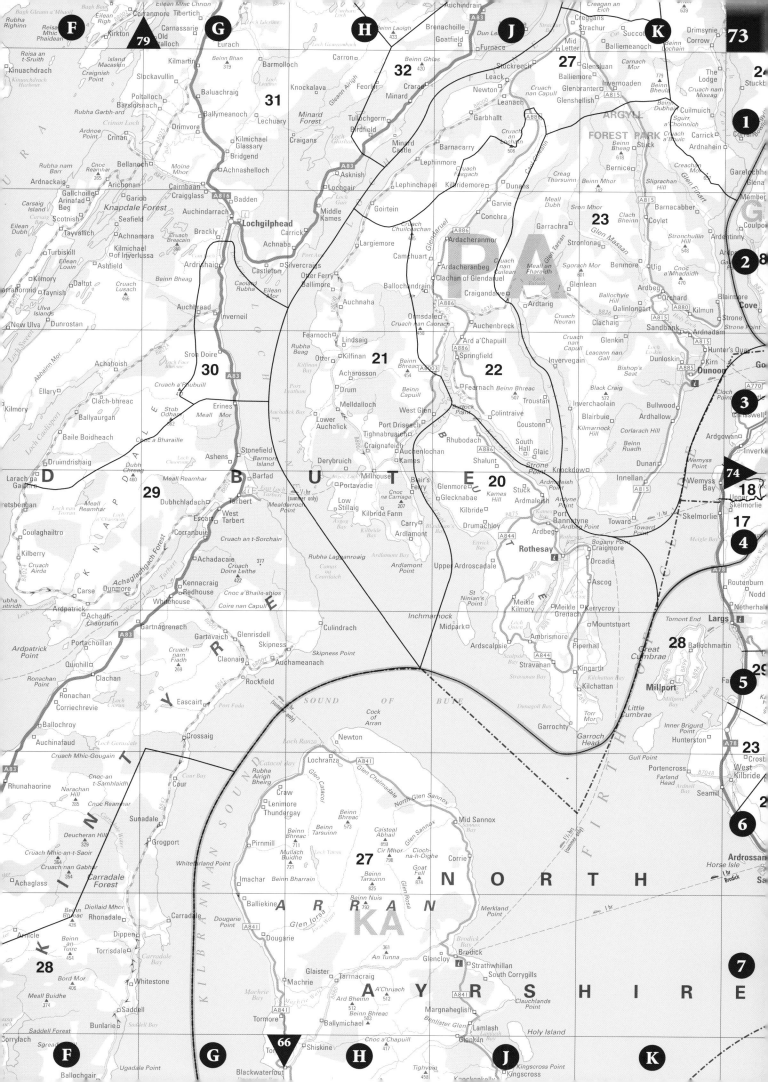

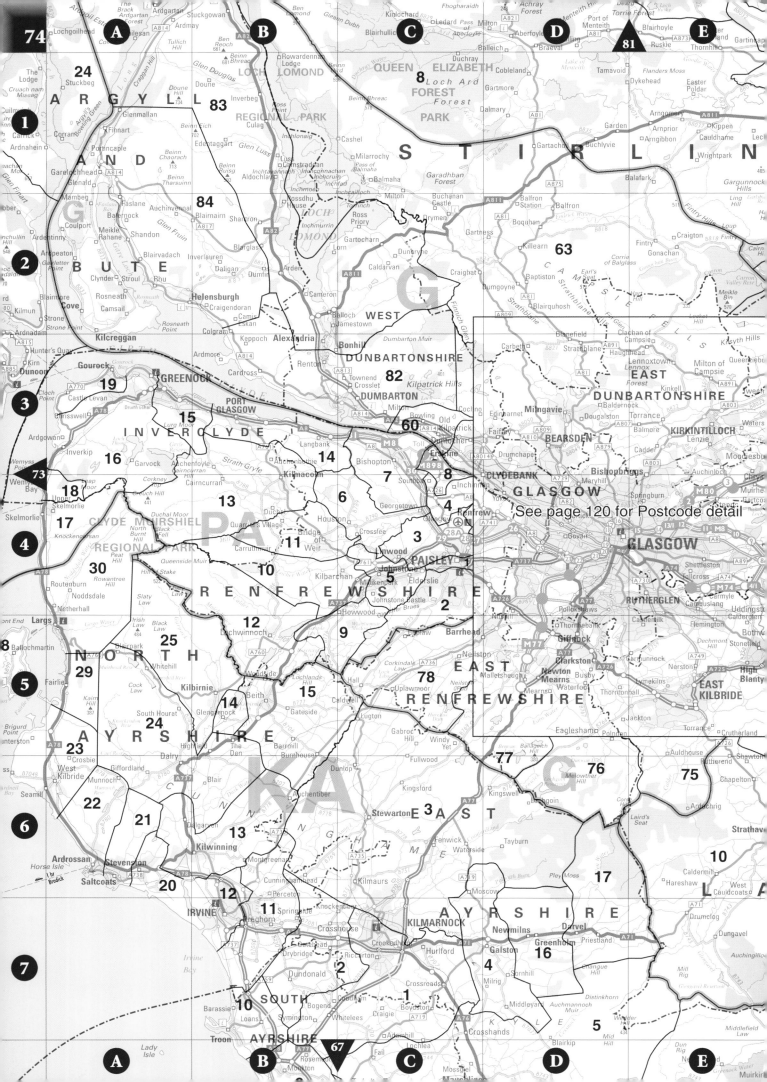

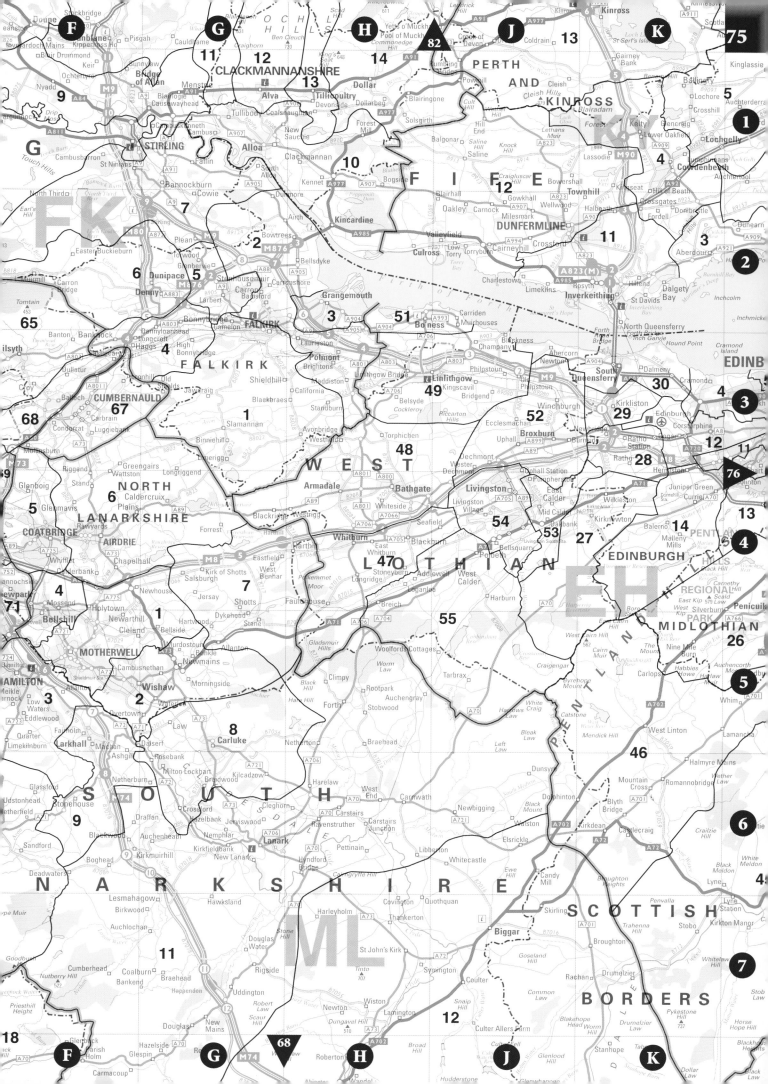

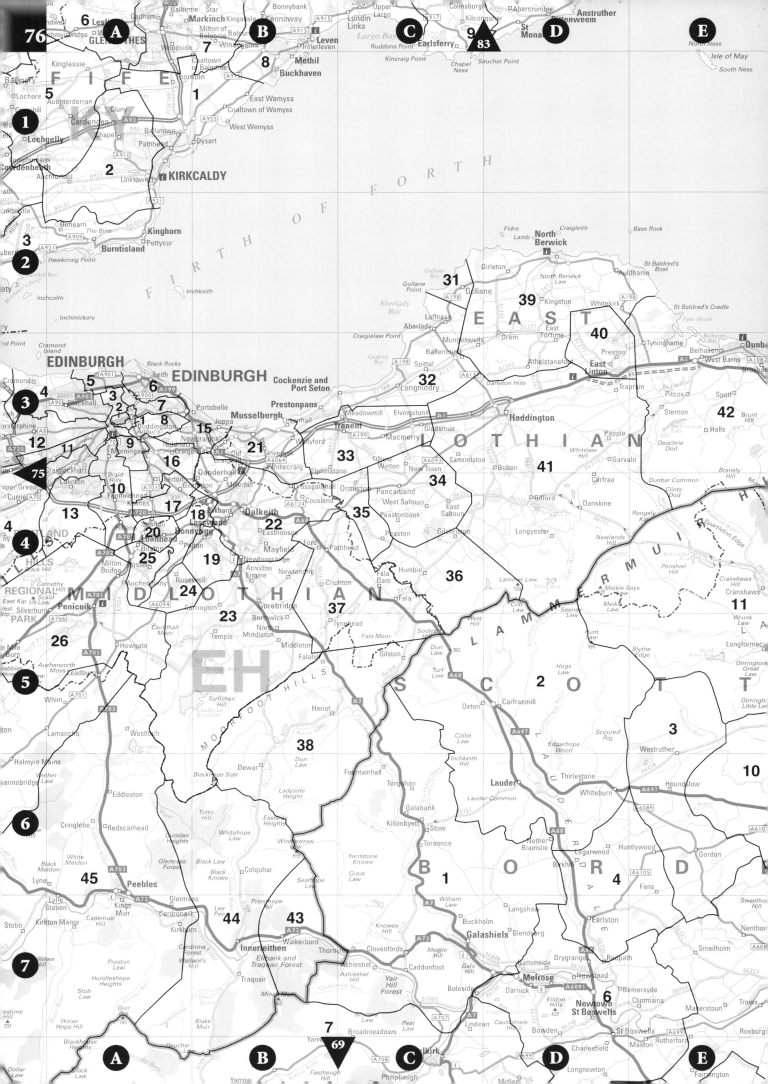

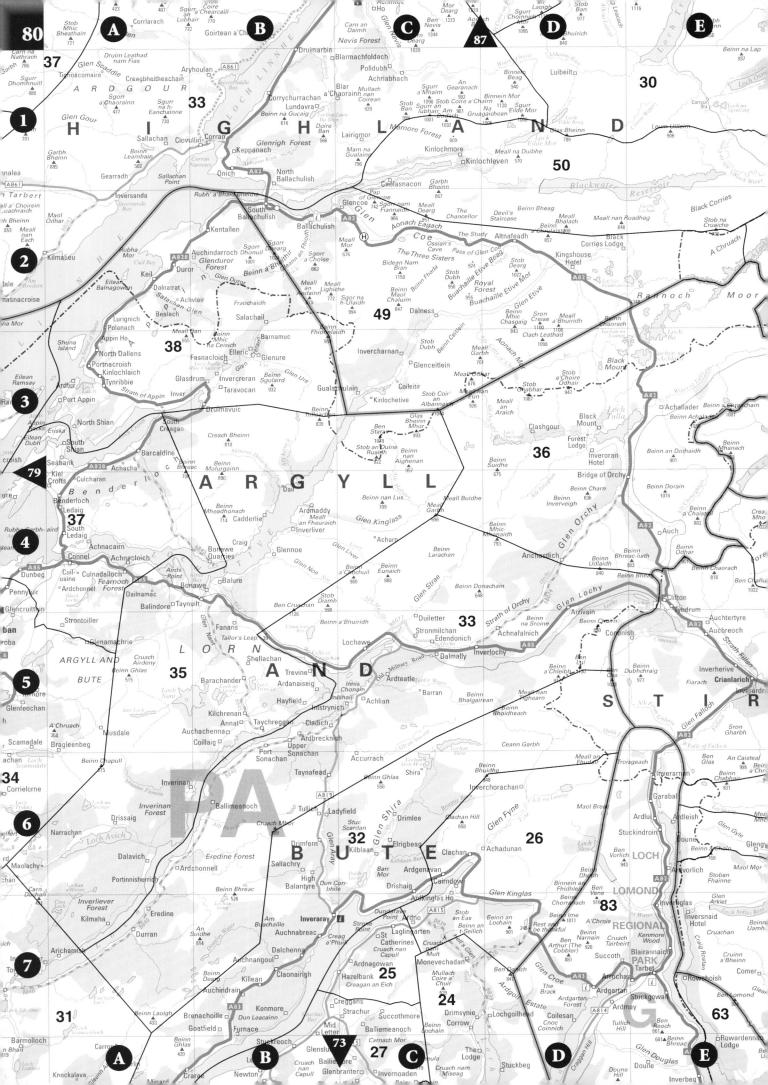

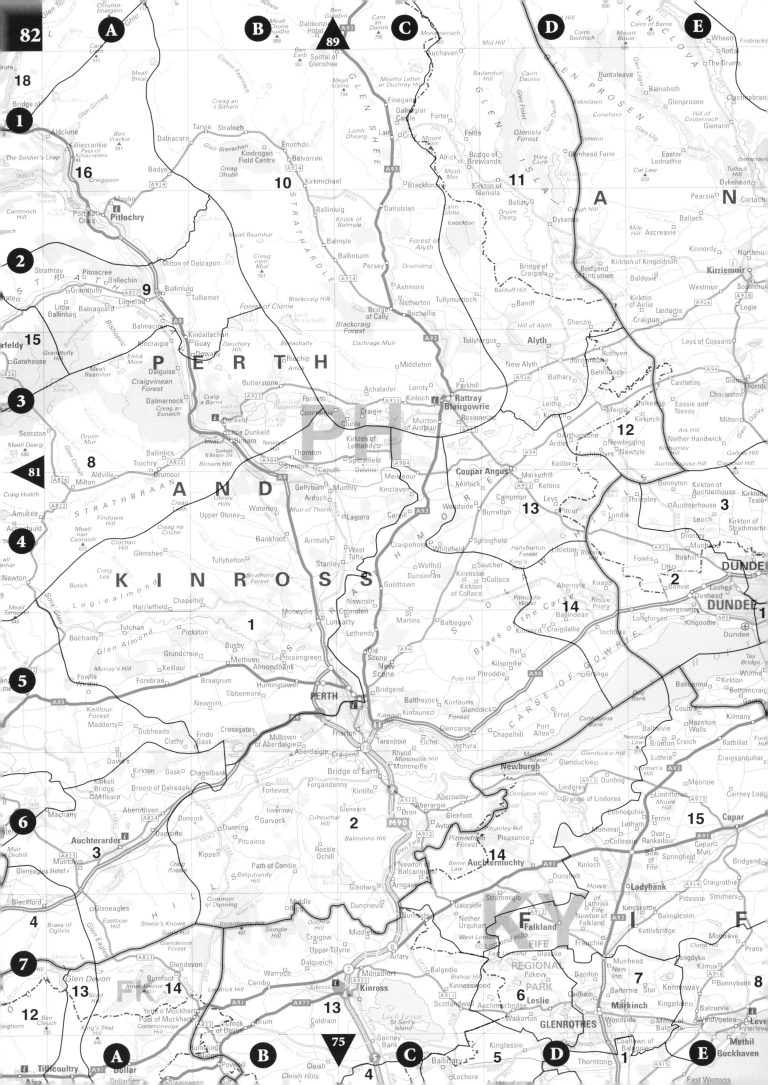

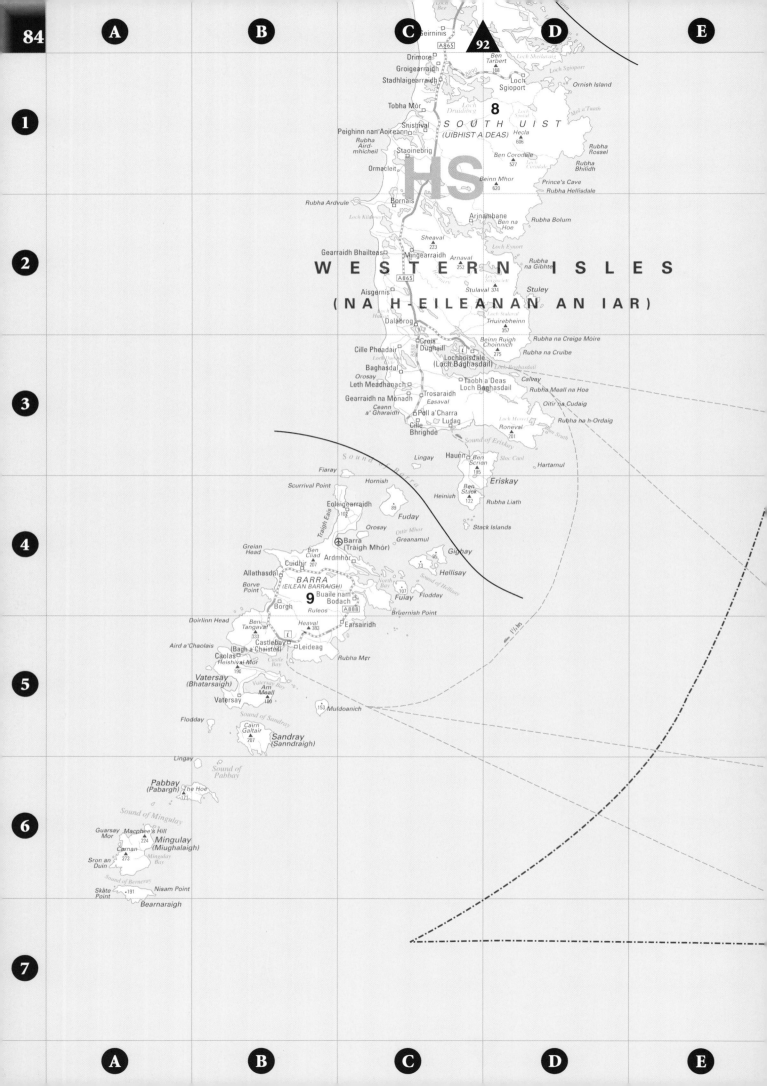

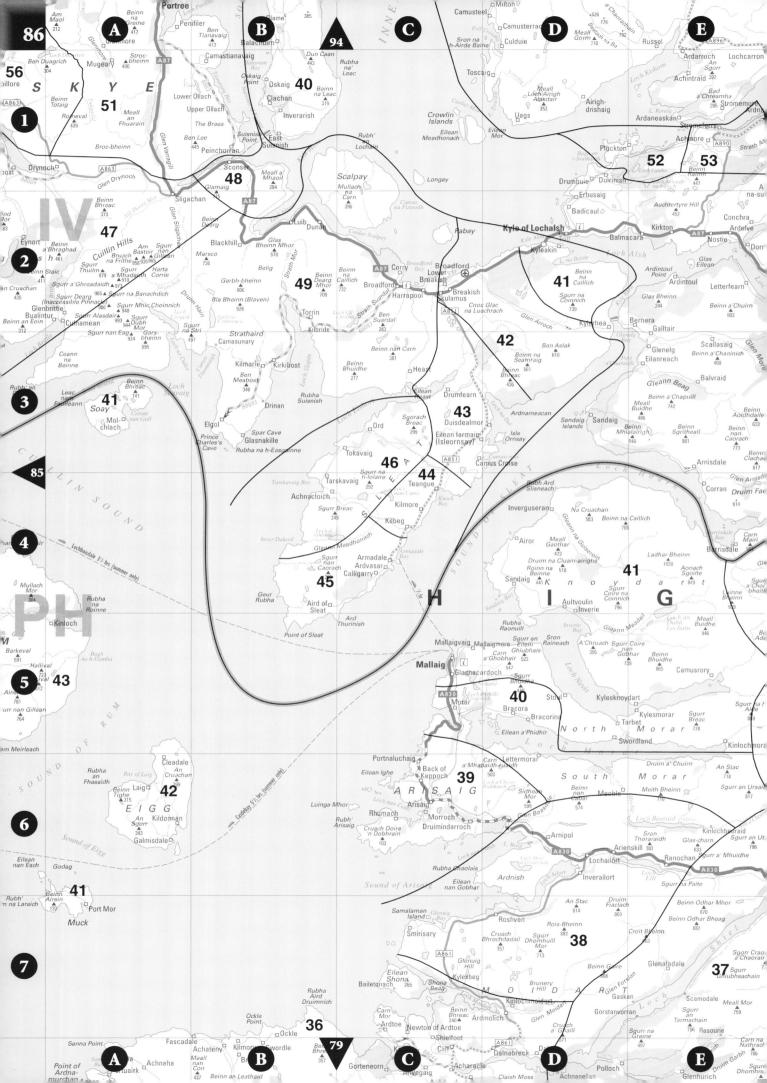

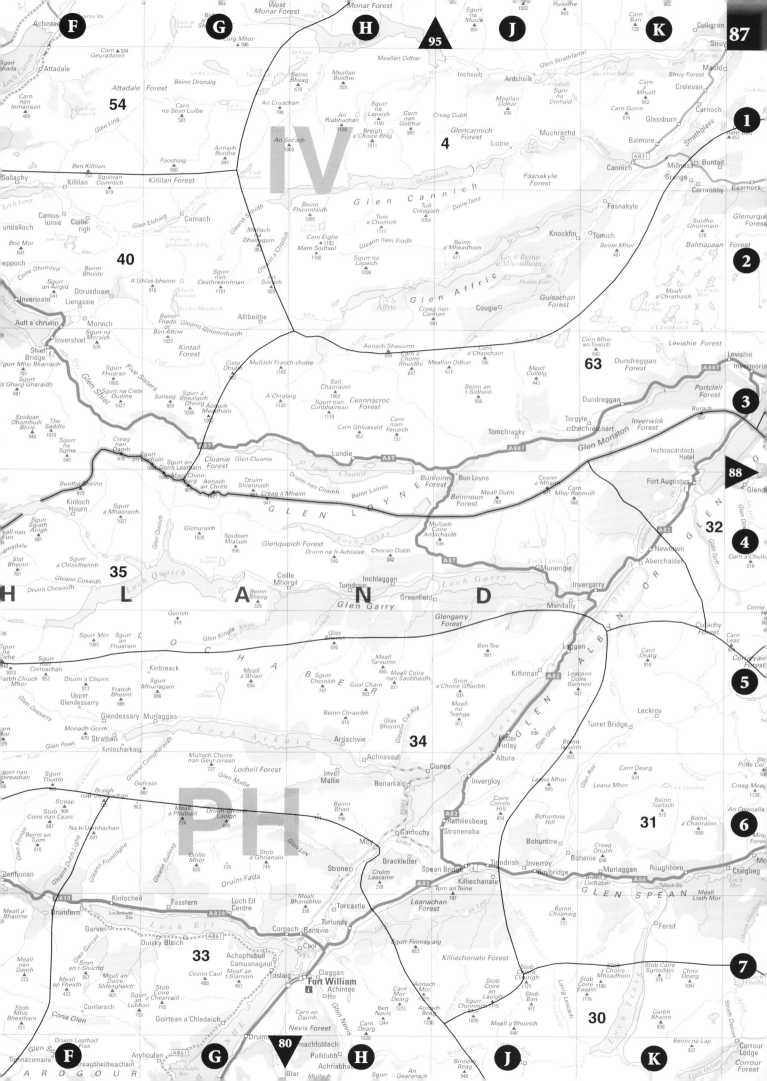

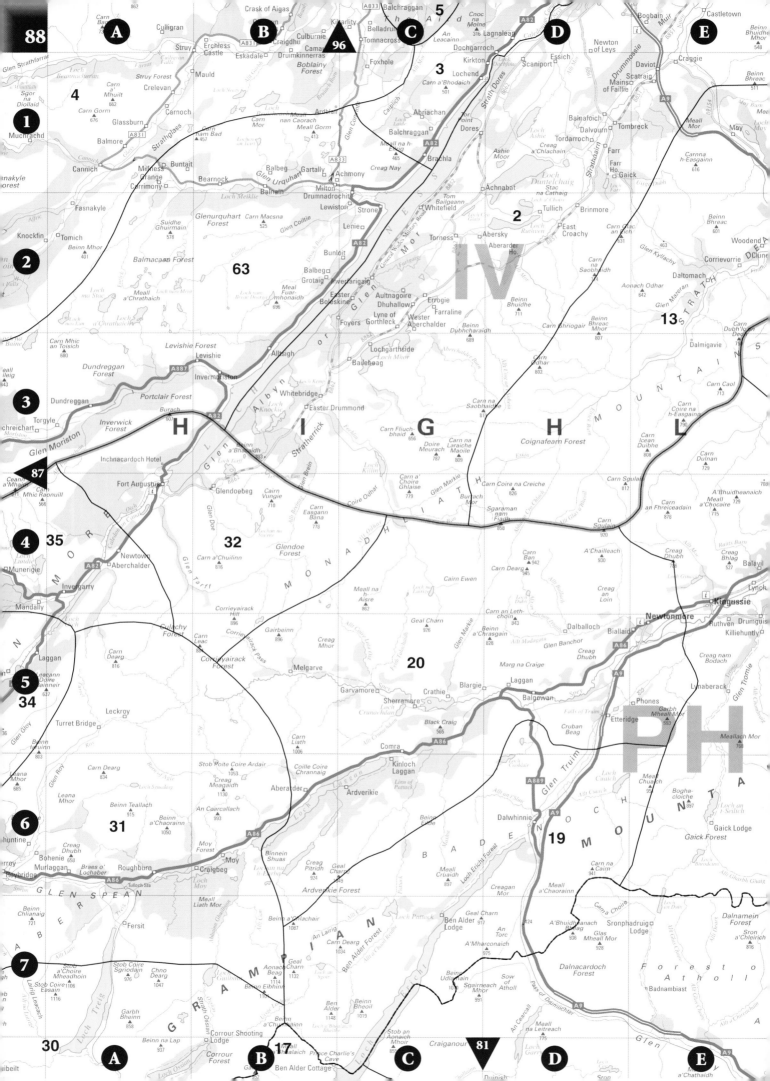

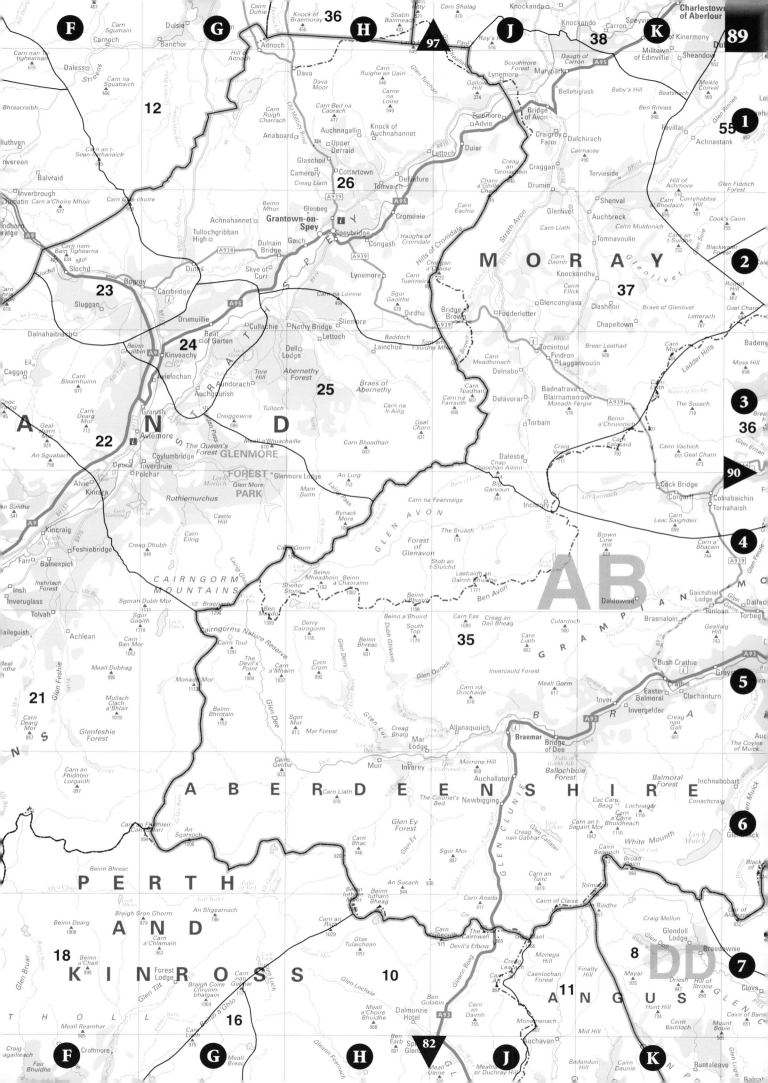

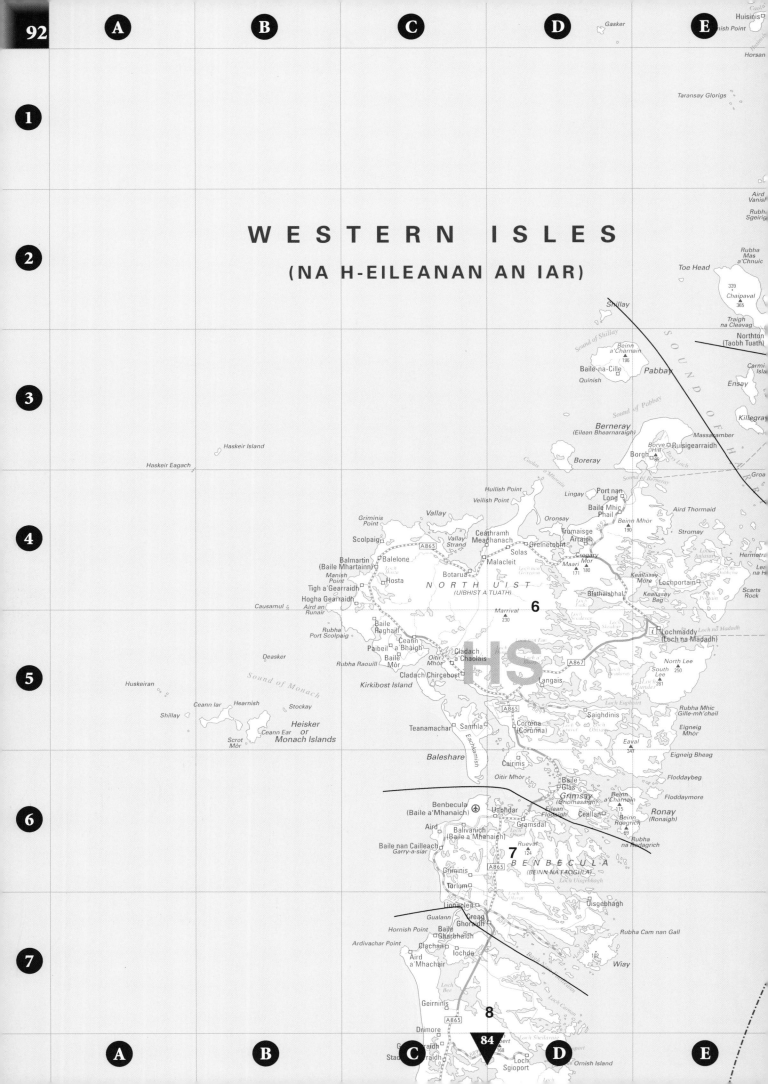

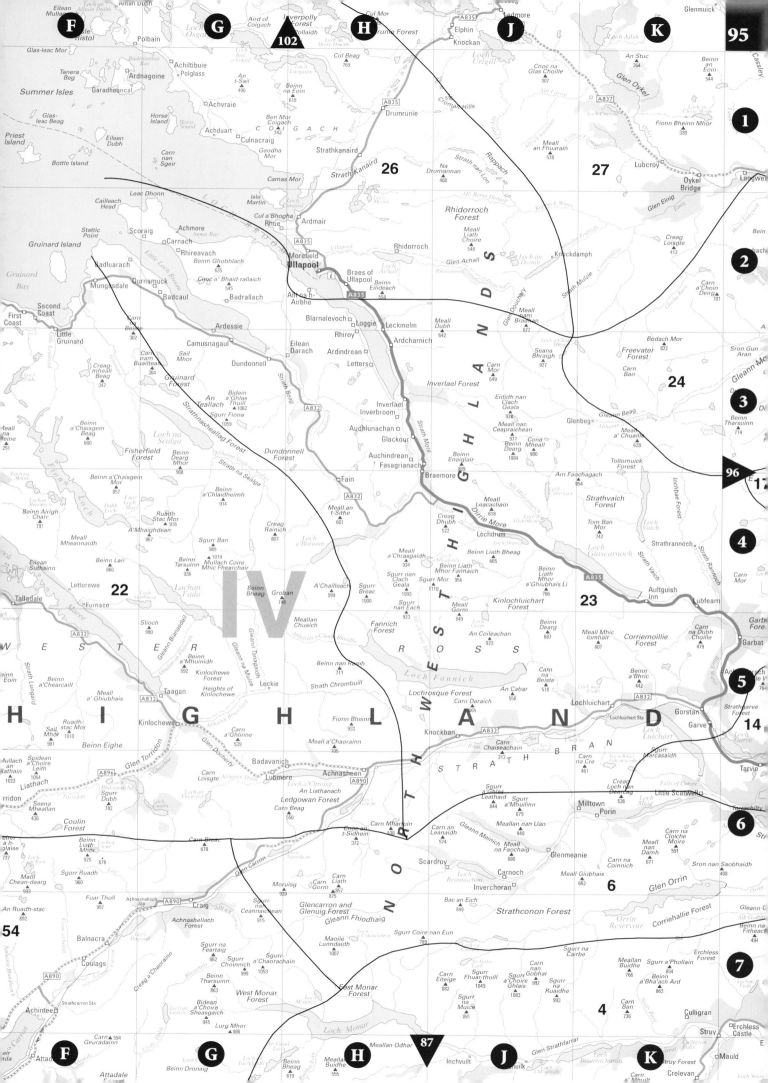

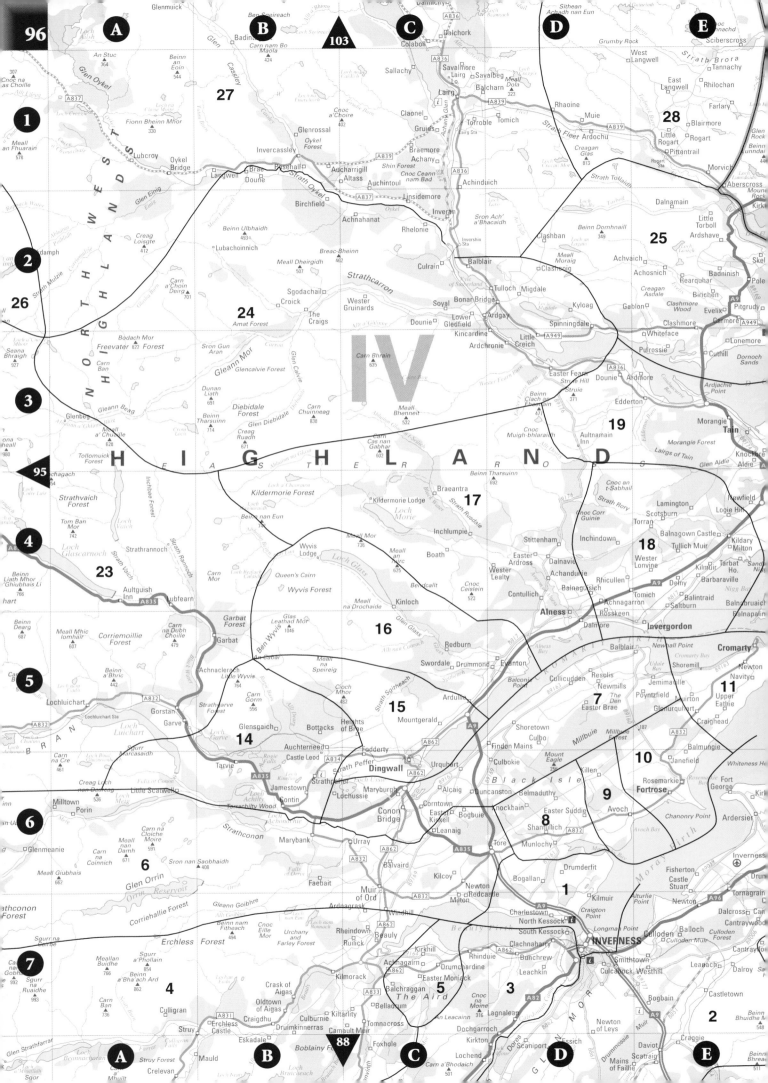

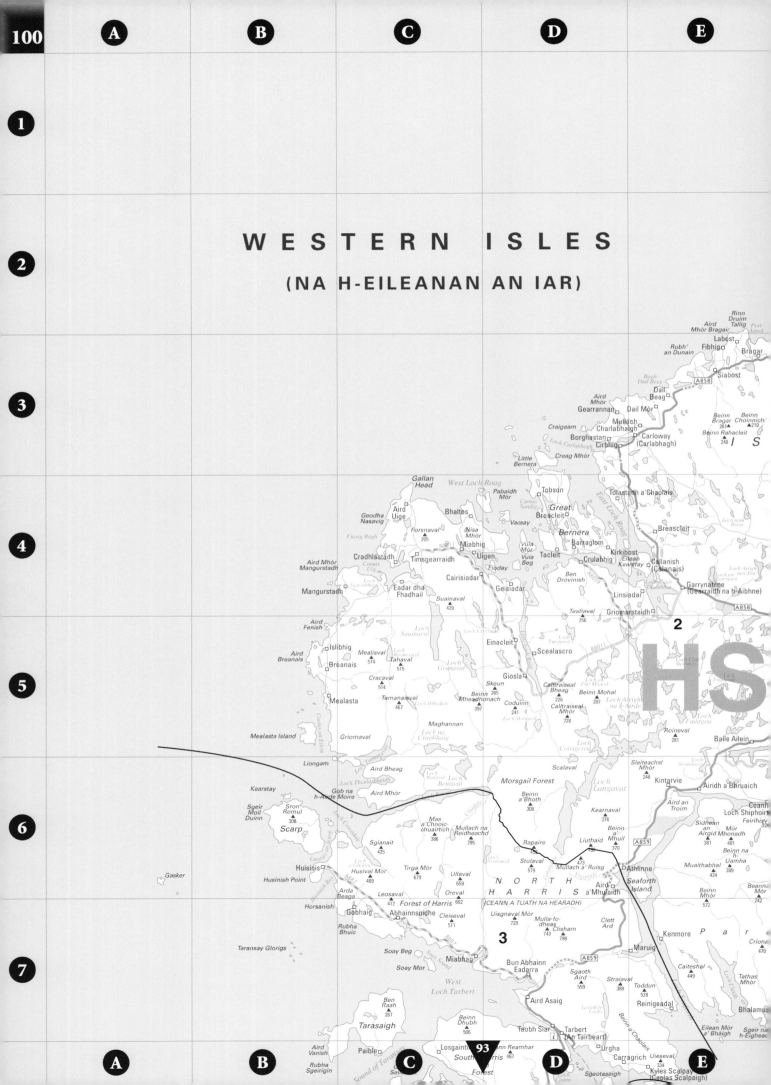

A **B** **C** **D** **E**

1

2

WESTERN ISLES
(NA H-EILEANAN AN IAR)

3

Rinn Druim Tallig
Port Arnol
Aird Mhòr Bragair
Labost
Rubh' an Dunain
Fibhig
Bragar
Siabost
Bagh Dail Beag
Dail Beag
Dail Mòr
Aird Mhòr Gearrannan
Mullach Charlabhaigh
Borghastan
Carloway (Carlabhagh)
Craigeam
Cirbhig
Loch Carlabhagh
Creag Mhòr
Beinn Bragar 261
Beinn Choinnich 210
Beinn Rahacleit 248
I S

4

Gallan Head
West Loch Roag
Pabaidh Mòr
Camus Sandig
Great Breacleit
Tolastadh a'Ghaolais
Geodha Nasavig
Aird Uige
Bhaltos
Vacsay
Tobson
Breascleit
Forsnaval 205
Nisa Mhòr
Bernera
Aird Mhòr Mangurstadh
Cradhlastadh
Timsgearraidh
Miabhig
Uigen
Vuia Mòr
Vuia Beg
Barraglom
Kirkibost
Eilean Kearstay
Tacleit
Crulabhig
Callanish (Calanais)
Fiuvig Bagh
Camas Uig
Eadar dha Fhadhail
Fioday
Ben Drovinish
Linsiadar
Loch Àirigh
Garrynahine (Gearraidh na h-Aibhne)
Mangurstadh
Cairisiadar
Geisiadar
Teahaval 256
Griomarstaidh
A858

5

Aird Fenish
Islibhig
Loch Suaineval
Suainaval 429
Einacleit
Ben Tungavat
2
HS
Aird Breanais
Mealisval 574
Tahaval 515
Loch Roinavat
Loch Grunavat
Scealascro
Breanais
Cracaval 514
Skeun
Giosla
Calltraiseal Bheag 226
Beinn Mohal 207
Loch Fuir Mhuad
Loch Àirigh na h-Àirde
Loch Faidagoa
Mealasta
Tamanaisval 467
Loch Dibadale
Beinn Mheadhonach 397
Coduinn 265
Calltraiseal Mhòr 228
Roineval 281
Baile Ailein
Loch Sheilavaig
Mealasta Island
Griomaval
Maghannan
Loch na Craobhag
Loch Coirgerod

6

Liongam
Aird Bheag
Scalaval
Sleiteachal Mhòr 248
Kintarvie
Airidh a'Bhruaich
Kearstay
Gob na h-Airde Moire
Loch Thealasbhaidh
Aird Mhòr
Morsgail Forest
Loch Langavat
Aird an Troim
Loch Shiphoirt
Ceann
Feirihisy
Sgeir Moil Duinn
Sron Romul 308
Loch Cravadale
Mas a'Chnoic-chuairtich 386
Beinn a'Bhoth 308
Kearnaval 378
Sidhean an Airgid Mhonaidh 381
Mòr 401
Scarp
Sgianait 425
Mullach na Reidheachd 295
Rapaire
Liuthaid
Beinn a' Mhuil 370
A859
Beinn na h- Uamha
Gasker
Huisinis
Husival Mòr 489
Tirga Mòr 679
Ullaval 659
Stulaval 473
Mullach a' Ruisg
Athlinne
Muaithabhal 424
Husinish Point
Arda Beaga
Leosaval 412
Forest of Harris 662
N O R T H
Aird a'Mhulaidh
Seaforth Island
Beanna Mòr 242
Horsanish
Gobhaig
Abhainnsuidhe
Cleiseval 511
H A R R I S
Beinn Mhòr 572
Kenmore
Par
Rubha Bhuic
(CEANN A TUATH NA HEARADH)
Uisgnaval Mòr 729
Mulla-fo-dheas 743
Clisham 799
Clett Ard
Maruig
Criona

7

Taransay Glorigs
Soay Beg
Soay Mòr
Miabhag
3
Bun Abhainn Eadarra
Sgaoth Aird 559
Straiaval 389
Toddun 528
Caiteshal 449
Tathas Mhòr
West Loch Tarbert
A859
Aird Asaig
Reinigeadal
Bhalamus
Ben Raah 267
Beinn Dhubh 506
Taobh Siar
Tarbert (An Tairbeart)
Urgha
Sgeir na h-Eigheac
Tarasaigh
Aird Vanish
Paible
Losgaintir
93
Beinn Reamhar 467
Carragrich
Uieseval 334
Eilean Mòr a' Bhàigh
Rubha Sgeirigin
South Harris Forest
Sound of Taransay
Sgeotasaigh
Kyles Scalpay (Caolas Scalpaigh)

A **B** **C** **D** **E**

Butt of Lewis
(Rubha Robhanais)

Port a' Stoth

Cunndal

Eoropaidh
Bad an
Fhithich
Tabost
Suainebost
Cros
Aird Dhail
Dail Bho Dheas
Dail Bho Thuath

Còig Peighinnean
Port Nis
Lional
Eorodal
Sgiogarstaigh

Port
Skigersta

Meall Geal

Toa Galson
Gabhsunn Bho Thuath
Gabhsunn Bho Dheas

A857

South Galson

Glen Cross

Ness

Port
Aluisdair

Cuidhaseadair

Laimhrig

Mealabost
Roinn a'
Bhuic

Airigh
na Glaice
Ben
Dell

Airighean
Beinn
nan Caorach

Cellar Head

Còig Peighinnean
Siadar Iarach
Siadar Uarach
Rubha Leathann
Baile an Truiseil

Airighean Loch
Breihavat

Diaval

Loch Mòr
Sandavat
Geiraha

Loch Langavat

Goile
Chròic
Loch Mòr
Bharabhais
Bru
Barvas
(Barabhas)

A857

Glen Shader

Loch Greas

Port Geiraha

LE OF LEWIS
(EILEAN LEODHAIS)

Gleann Mòr Bharabhais
Gleann Bhruthadail

Glen Bragar

Roishal
Mòr
174

Loch Breivat

Loch Urrahag

Beinn
Mholach
292

Loch an Tobair

Loch
Sgeireach Mòr

Muirneag
248

Tolastadh Ùr
Tolastadh

Tolsta
Head

Port nam Bothag

acasahl
16

Loch
Stiornag

Loch Mèr an Stairr

Gleann
Tholastaidh

Port Bun a' Ghlinne

Griais

Creag
Fhraoich

Beinn
Mholach
292

Bac

Col

Breibhig
Col Sands

Rubha Bhataisgeir

Tiumpan Head
(Rubha an t-Siumpain)

Portnaguran
(Port nan Giùran)

Rubha
Deas

A866

Aird Thunga
Tunga
Sron
Ruadh
Melbost Sands

Loch
a' Tuath

Siulaisiadar
Seisiadar

Rubha na
Gréine

Newmarket
Stornoway
(Steornabhagh)
Laxdale
(Lacasdal)
Stornoway

1

East
Roisnish
Melbost Pt
Melbost
Aignis
Cnoc
Suardail

Garrabost
Eye Peninsula
(An Rubha)

2

Rubha na
Bearnaich

A858

Sandwick
(Sanndabhaig)
Branahuie
Banks

Pabail
Uarach
Pabail
Iarach

Bagh Phabail

Loch a' Vanavist

Creed

Beinn
a'Bhuna
3 200

Arnish Pt
Arnish Moor

Rubh
a' Bhaigh
Uaine

Ceann na Circ

Achadh Mòr

A859

Loch Thota
Bhrionn
Loch nan
Eilean

Loch
Nisreavat

Loch
a'
Fada

Iurbost
Crosbost

Grimsiadar
Loch
Grimsiadar

Raerinish Point

A859

Ceos
Lacasaigh
Eilean Chaluim
Chille
Orasaigh
Gleann Ghrabhair

Tabhaigh
Mhor

Cearsiadar
Tabost
Gearraidh
Bhaird
Cabharstadh

Torraigh

Marthig

3060

Loch
Erisort

B8060

Calbost

Rubha
Iosal

Glen Ouirn
Loch
Shandabhaig

Grabhair
Loch Odhairn

Tom
an
Fhuadain

Kebock
Head

Leumrabhagh

Gob
na
Milaid

alasgair

Eisgean

Loch Shell

Eilean
Iubhard

Srianach

Cuddie a'Tuath

orlabhadh

Uisenis
371

Mulhagery

Mol Truisg

THE MINCH

Ullapool 2¼ hrs

Garbh
Eilean

Gob
Rubh'Uisenis

Rubha
Bhrollum

Rubh
a'
Bhaird

161

A　　B　　C　　D　　E

1

2

3

101

4

5

6

7

A　　B　　C　　D　　E

Cape Wrath
Duslic
Stac
Clo Kearv
Kearvaig
Geodha Ruadh
na Fola
Cnoc
a'Ghiubhais
797
Bay of Keisgais

Am
Balg
Am Buachaille
Beinn
Dearg
473
Sandwood
Loch
Creag
Riabhach
485
Rubh' an Fhir Leithe
Sandwood
Bay
An Grianan
467
Meall
na Moine
464
Strath Shinary

Sheigra
Blairmore
Balchrick
Oldshore Beg
Beinn
a'Chraisg
257
An Socach
358
Eilean
an Roin Mor
Oldshore
More
Kinlochbervie
Rubha na Leacaig
Bugh Loch
an Roin
Badcall
Achriesgill
Ardmore
Point
Achlyness
Rhiconich
Rubha Ruadh
Ceathramh
Garbh

Fanagmore
Tarbet
Foindle
Laxford
Bridge

Handa
Island
Badnabay
A894
A838
Loch
Stack
Scourie More
Scourie
Ben
Stack
721
Rubh' Aird
an t-Sionnaich
Strath Stack
Achfary
Badcall
Ben
Auskaird
386
Reay
Forest

Eilean
a'Bhreitheimh
Meall
Mor
Rubh'
a'Mhucard
A894
Ben Strome
426
Meall
Beag
Calbha Beag
Calbha
Mor

Point
of
Stoer
Rubha
nan Cosan
Sgeir
nan
Gall
Oldany Island
Eddrachillis
Bay
Ardvar
Kylestrome
Glendhu Forest
Ben
a'Bhu
Cirean Geardail
161
Culkein
Eilean
Chrona
Clashnessie
Bay
Drumbeg
Unapool
Ben Aird
da Loch
530
Cluas Deas
Raffin
Achnacarnin
Nedd
Newton
Clashnessie
Sail Gorm
776
Balchladich
Gleann Leireag
Quinag
808
Rubh'a'
Mhill Dheirg
Stoer
Bay
of
Stoer
Clachtoll
Spidean Coinich
764
A894
Rubha
Leumair
Glas Bheinn
776
Achmelvich
Bay
Rhicarn
Little
Assynt
A837
Loch Assynt
Beinn Uidhe
740
Achmelvich
Rubha Rodha
Ardroe
Inchnadamph
Inchnadamp
Fores
Gleann Dubh
Baddidarach
Lochinver
Beinn
Gharbh
540
Soyea Island
Loch Inver
Kirkaig Point
Badnaban
Strathan
A'Chleit
Glencanisp Forest
Stronechrubie
Rubha na
Breige
Inverkirkaig
Rubha
Coigeach
Eilean Mor
Rhegreanoch
Suilven
731
Canisp
846
A837
Feochag
Bay
Loch Sionascaig
Breabag
814
Camus
Eilean
Ghlais
Camus Coille
Eilard Bay
Rubh'
a'Choin
Polly Bay
Meall
Bhraghi
Rubha Mor
Reiff
Aird of
Coigach
Cul Mor
Ledbeg
A835
Ledmore
A837
Alltan Dubh
Inverpolly
Forest
Stac Pollaidh
613
Drumrunie Forest
Eilean
Mullagrach
Loch an
Alltain Duibh
Isle
Ristol
Polbain
Loch
Osgaig
Cul Beag
Elphin
Knockan
Loch
Urigill
Glas-leac Mor
Achiltibu
Polglass
An
t-Sail
490
Cnoc na
Glas Choille
307
Summer Isles
Ardvagoine
Garadheancal
Beinn
na Eoin

26
95
An
t-Sail

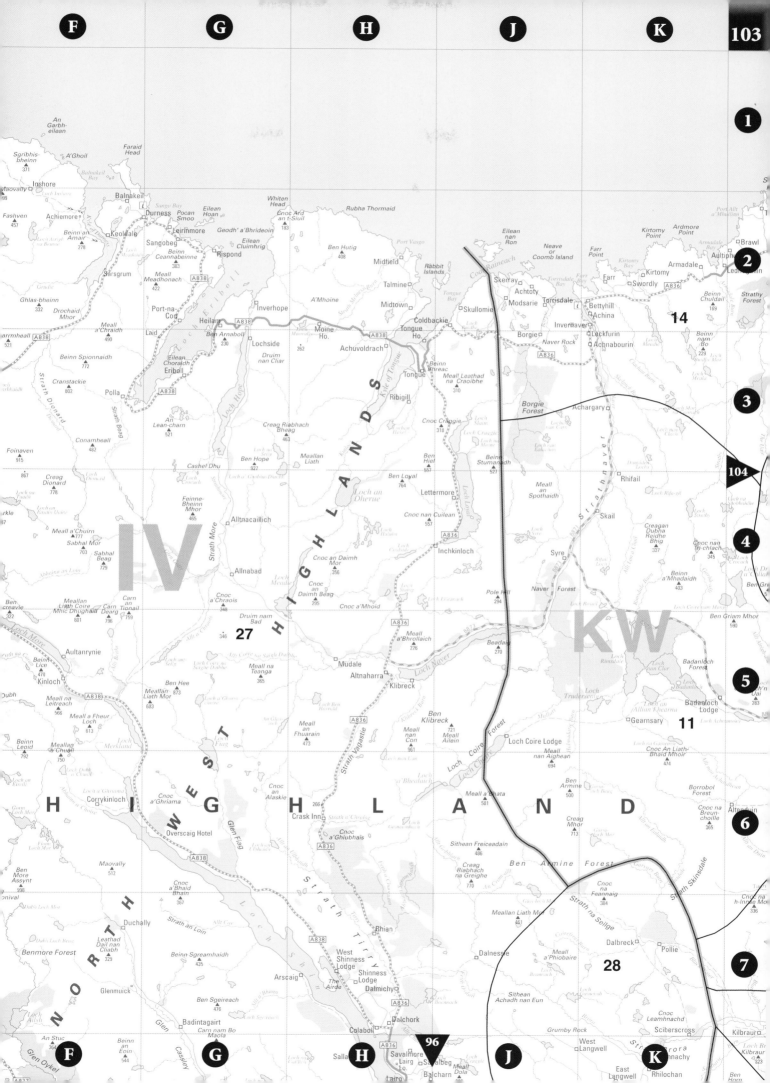

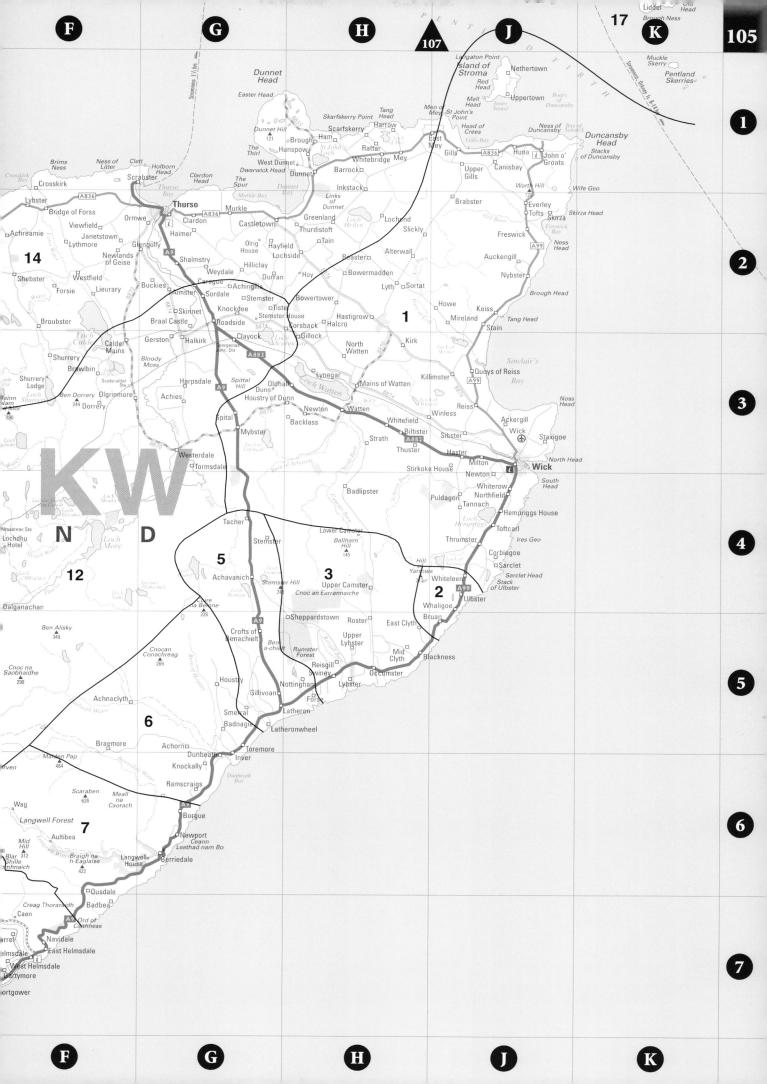

ZE

SHETLAND

MAINLAND

same scale as main map

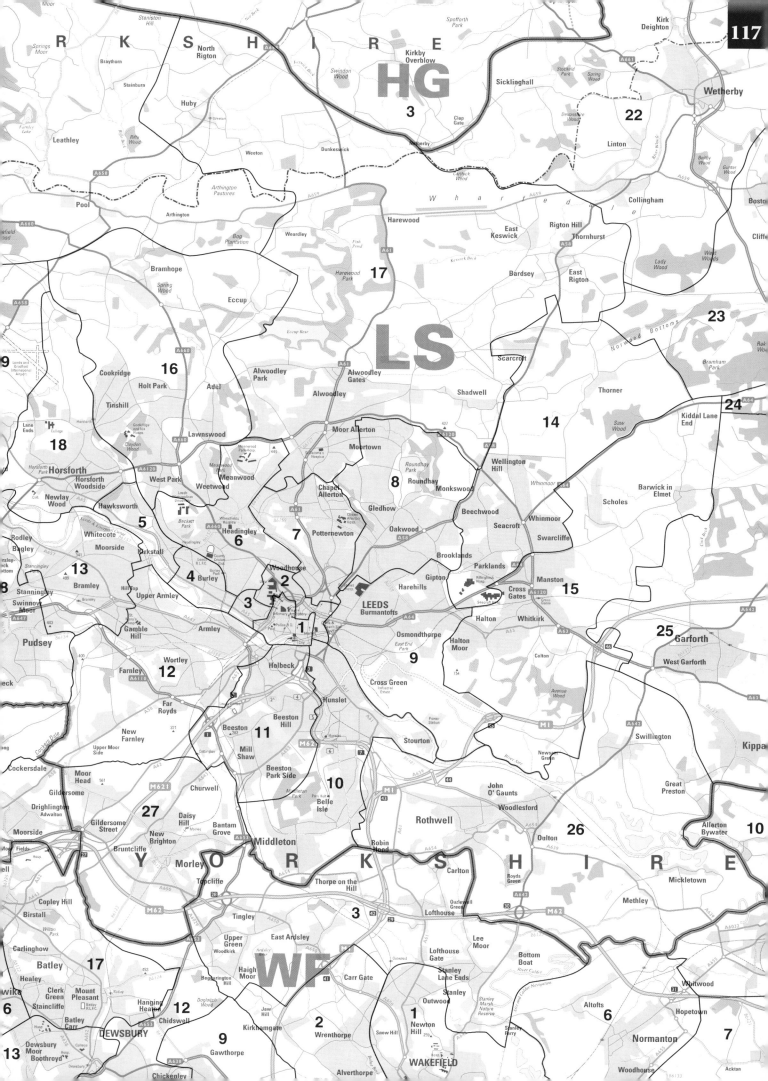

High Church
Morpeth
Stobhill
Tranwell

Sheepwash
Stakeford
Guide Post
Scotland Gate
62
63

East Sleekburn
Cambois

Bedlington Station
22

Cowpen

The Rockers

Blyth

Pier

Saltwick
61

Nedderton
BEDLINGTON

24

Seaton Sea Rocks

Stannington

East Hartford
Shankhouse

New Delaval
Newsham

NORTHUMBERLAND

Industrial Estate

Nelson Village
Eastfield

Beaconhill

Cramlington

New Hartley

Seaton Sluice

Whitelea
Mayfield

East Cramlington

Seaton Delaval
25

Seaton
Hartley

26

Collingwood
Southfield
23

Burnside Park
Seaton Burn

Moor Farm Roundabout

Seghill

Holywell

20

13

Prestwick Carr
Mason

Dinnington

Annitsford

Dudley

Burradon

Earsdon
Backworth

Monkseaton
West Monkseaton

Whitley Bay

Brown's Point

Prestwick

Brunswick Village
Hazlerigg

Wide Open

Camperdown

27
Shiremoor

Murton
New York

Saddle Rock
Cullercoats

Newcastle International Airport (Woolsington)

NE

Killingworth

Shiremoor

Marden

West Allotment

Woolsington
Woolsington Park

East Brunton

West Moor
12

Palmersville
Benton

Holystone
Benton Square

North Shields

30
Preston

Tynemouth

Black Callerton

Kenton Bank

Fawdon
Kingston Park

3

Gosforth Wood

Forest Hall

Balliol Business Park

Billy Mill
West Chirton

29

Callerton
North Walbottle

5

Newbiggin Hall Estate

Coxlodge
Gosforth

Longbenton

Battle Hill

Chirton

North Shields

South Shields

Chapel Park

Kenton Bar
Kenton

S. Gosforth
South Gosforth

High Heaton
7

Holy Cross
28
Willington

Howdon

Percy Main
Royal Quays

Westerhope

Blakelaw
Nuns Moor

NEWCASTLE UPON TYNE

Heaton

Wallsend

Rosehill
Willington Quay

Chapel House
West Denton

2 Jesmond

WALLSEND

33
West Park

NEWBURN
15
Lemington
Bell's Close
Denton Burn

East Denton

Cowgate

Fenham

Arthur's Hill

Sandyford

Byker

Walker
6

TYNE
Jarrow
32

West Harton

Benwell
4

Shieldfield
1

Brough Park
Walker Park

& WEAR
Hebburn
31

34

Scotswood

Elswick

Salt Meadows

St. Anthony's

Monkton
Primrose

Simonside

Stella

Blaydon

Derwent Haugh
Gateshead

Low Team
8

Felling Shore
Bill Quay
Pelaw

Felling

Wardley

Hedworth

Whiteleas

Winlaton
21

Swalwell

Dunston
Bensham

Mount Pleasant

Hewortth

Fellgate

Boldon Colliery

35

Winlaton Mill

Whickham Bank
Swalwell Bank

Dunston Hill

Gateshead

Carr Hill

High Felling
10

Boldon

West Boldon

East Boldon

39

Whickham

Team Valley

Windy Nook
High Fell

Wrekenton

37

Hylton Red House

5

Marley Hill

11

Harlow Green
9
Chowdene
Eighton Banks
Springwell

Stephenson

Town End Farm

Downhill

SR

Sunniside
16

Low Eighton

Blackhams Hill

Donwell Usworth
Sulgrave
Concord

Washington

38

Hylton Castle
Castletown

4

SUND

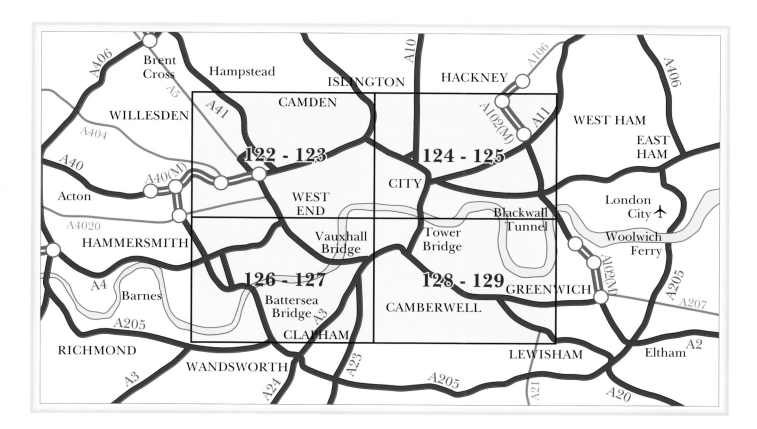

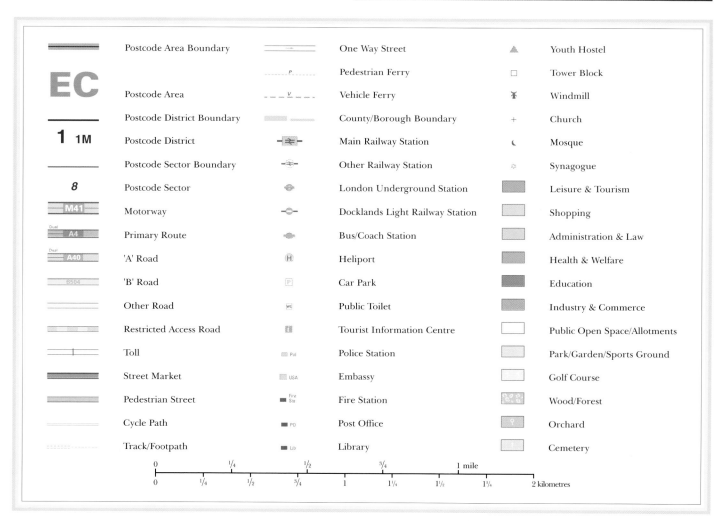

Postcode Area Boundary		One Way Street		Youth Hostel	
EC Postcode Area		Pedestrian Ferry		Tower Block	
		Vehicle Ferry		Windmill	
Postcode District Boundary		County/Borough Boundary		Church	
1 1M Postcode District		Main Railway Station		Mosque	
Postcode Sector Boundary		Other Railway Station		Synagogue	
8 Postcode Sector		London Underground Station		Leisure & Tourism	
M41 Motorway		Docklands Light Railway Station		Shopping	
Dual A4 Primary Route		Bus/Coach Station		Administration & Law	
Dual A40 'A' Road		Heliport		Health & Welfare	
B504 'B' Road		Car Park		Education	
Other Road		Public Toilet		Industry & Commerce	
Restricted Access Road		Tourist Information Centre		Public Open Space/Allotments	
Toll		Police Station		Park/Garden/Sports Ground	
Street Market		Embassy		Golf Course	
Pedestrian Street		Fire Station		Wood/Forest	
Cycle Path		Post Office		Orchard	
Track/Footpath		Library		Cemetery	

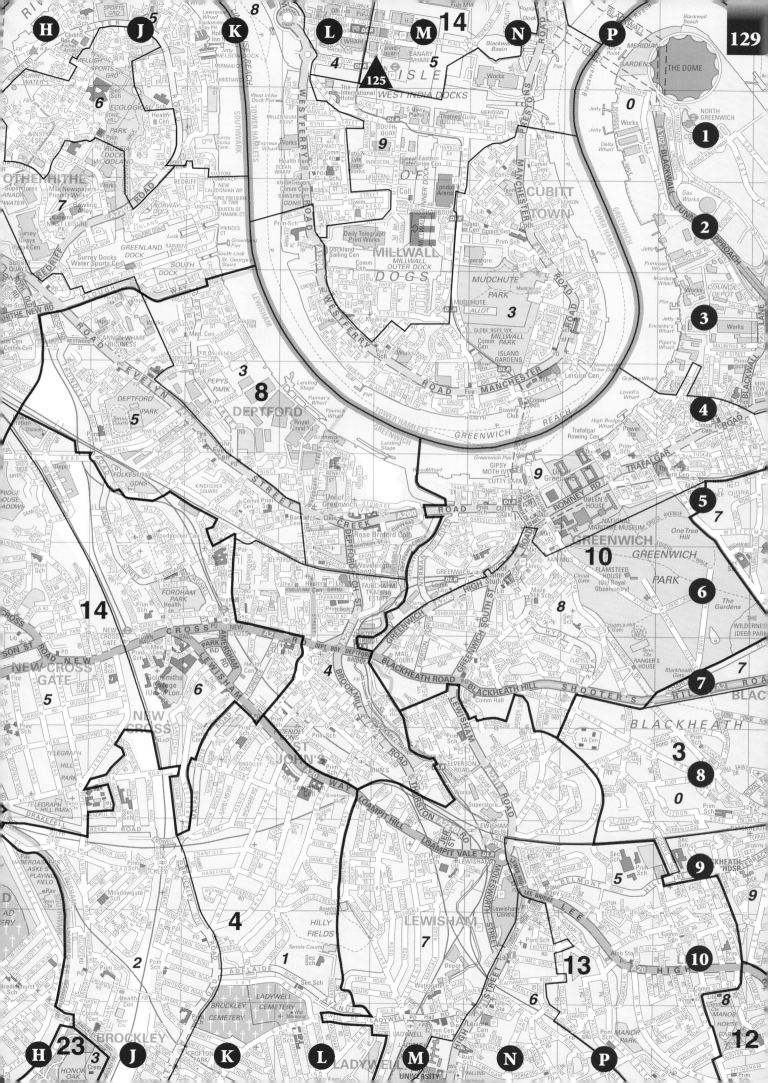

Notes: Listed below are the administrative areas for Great Britain and Isle of Man used in this Postcode Atlas. Where an area is dual language, the English form is given first, followed by the alternative in parenthesis. Each entry includes its standard abbreviation in *italics* which will appear in the index. Population figures are derived from 1991 Census information, or mid Census estimates, with modifications to allow for the newly created unitary authorities. A brief description of the area then follows, which includes: adjoining administrative areas; main centres (based on descending order of population); historical, physical and economic characteristics. For English counties or former Metropolitan counties, each district, city or borough authority is listed under the heading, **Districts**. A selection of the most visited tourist attractions then follows under the heading, **Places of interest**.

Aberdeen *Aberdeen* Population: 219,120.
Unitary authority surrounding Aberdeen, Scotland's third largest city, on the NE coast and neighbouring Aberdeenshire. Aberdeen is the major commercial and administrative centre for N Scotland. It is the second largest fishing port in Scotland, with docks at the mouth of the River Dee, and is the oil and gas capital of Europe.
Places of interest: Aberdeen Art Gallery; Aberdeen Exhibition and Conference Centre; Duthie Park & Winter Gardens; Provost Skene's House.

Aberdeenshire *Aber.* Population: 226,530.
Unitary authority on the NE coast of Scotland neighbouring Aberdeen, Angus, Highland, Moray and Perth & Kinross. Main centres are Peterhead, Fraserburgh, Inverurie, Stonehaven, Ellon, Banchory, Portlethan and Huntly. Aberdeenshire is split geographically into two main areas. The W is dominated by the Grampian Mountains and is largely unpopulated. The undulating lowlands of the E are mainly rural and are populated by farming and fishing communities. The major rivers are the Dee, which flows through Royal Deeside, and the Don.
Places of interest: Aden Country Park, Mintlaw; Balmedie Country Park; Balmoral Castle, Crathie; Crathes Castle (NTS); Haddo House Country Park (NTS); Storybook Glen, Maryculter.

Angus *Angus* Population: 111,329.
Unitary authority on the E coast of Scotland neighbouring Aberdeenshire, Dundee and Perth & Kinross. The chief centres are Arbroath, Forfar, Montrose, Carnoustie, the ancient cathedral city of Brechin, Kirriemuir and Monifieth. Angus occupies an area of 2200 square km and is an important agricultural area. It combines ancient relics and castles with highland terrain and market towns. Rivers include the North Esk, Isla and Prosen Water.
Places of interest: Glamis Castle; Monikie Country Park.

Argyll & Bute *Arg. & B.* Population: 90,550.
Unitary authority on the W coast of Scotland combining mainland and island life and neighbouring Highland, Inverclyde, North Ayrshire, Perth & Kinross, Stirling and West Dunbartonshire. The main towns are Helensburgh, Dunoon, Oban, Campbeltown, Rothesay and Lochgilphead. It includes the former districts of Argyll and Bute as well as the islands of Islay, Jura, Colonsay and Mull. The main industries are fishing, agriculture, whisky production and tourism.
Places of interest: Inveraray Castle; Inveraray Jail; Iona Abbey; Loch Lomond Park Centre, Luss.

Bath & North East Somerset *B. & N.E.Som.* Population: 158,692.
Unitary authority in SW England neighbouring Bristol, North Somerset, Somerset, South Gloucestershire and Wiltshire. It surrounds the city of Bath, and includes the towns of Keynsham, Radstock and Midsomer Norton. The Georgian spa of Bath is considered to be one of the most beautiful cities in Britain, and is an important commercial and ecclesiastical centre popular with tourists. The River Avon flows through the area.
Places of interest: Bath Abbey; Museum of Costume, Bath; Roman Baths & Pump Room, Bath.

Bedfordshire *Beds.* Population: 352,434.
S midland county of England bounded by Buckinghamshire, Cambridgeshire, Hertfordshire, Luton, Milton Keynes and Northamptonshire. Main centres are the county town of Bedford, Dunstable, Leighton Buzzard, Kempston and Biggleswade. The N end of the Chiltern Hills runs through the S and SE of the county, which is otherwise mostly flat. Most of Bedfordshire is rural, and includes many stately homes. Industries include light engineering, brick manufacture, mineral extraction and vegetable growing. Chief river is the Great Ouse.

Districts: Bedford; Mid Bedfordshire; South Bedfordshire.
Places of interest: Dunstable Downs; Harrold-Odell Country Park; Stockgrove Country Park, Leighton Buzzard; Sundon Hills Country Park, Upper Sundon; Whipsnade Wild Animal Park, Dunstable; Woburn Safari Park.

Blackburn with Darwen *B'burn.* Population: 136,612.
Unitary authority in NW England surrounding Blackburn and Darwen and neighbouring Greater Manchester and Lancashire. Blackburn is a market and retail centre with a wide spread of industry including textiles, brewing and electronic engineering.
Places of interest: Blackburn Museum; Witton Country Park Visitor Centre, Blackburn.

Blackpool *B'pool* Population: 146,069.
Unitary authority on the NW coast of England surrounding Blackpool and neighbouring Lancashire. Blackpool receives around 7.2 million visitors each year, making it the most popular seaside resort in Europe. Attractions including the Tower, Pleasure Beach, Winter Gardens and Illuminations.
Places of interest: Blackpool Pleasure Beach; Blackpool Tower; Blackpool Zoo; Louis Tussaud's Waxworks; Sea Life Centre; South Pier; The Magic of Coronation Street; Winter Gardens.

Blaenau Gwent *B.Gwent* Population: 73,000.
Unitary authority in S Wales bounded by Caerphilly, Monmouthshire, Powys and Torfaen. The chief towns are Ebbw Vale, Tredegar, Bryn-mawr and Abertillery. The area was previously dependent upon coal, iron and steel industries but has since developed a broader industrial base. Part of the Brecon Beacons are in the N of the area.
Places of interest: Bryn Bach Country Park, Tredgar; Festival Park Visitor Centre, Ebbw Vale.

Bournemouth *Bourne.* Population: 151,302.
Unitary authority on the S coast of England surrounding Bournemouth and neighbouring Dorset and Poole. Bournemouth is a major resort, conference and commercial centre.
Places of interest: Bournemouth International Centre & Pavilion; Russell-Cotes Art Gallery & Museum.

Bracknell Forest *Brack.F.* Population: 95,949.
Unitary authority to the W of Greater London and bounded by Hampshire, Surrey, Windsor & Maidenhead and Wokingham. Bracknell is the chief town, while to the N of the area there are the villages of Winkfield and Binfield. To the S lies forest and heathland, and the towns of Crowthorne and Sandhurst. Bracknell has many hi-tech industries, and is a shopping and leisure centre.
Places of interest: Look Out Discovery Park & Visitor Centre, Bracknell.

Bridgend (Pen-y-Bont ar Ogwr). *Bridgend* Population: 128,340.
Unitary authority in S Wales bounded by Neath Port Talbot, Rhondda Cynon Taff, Vale of Glamorgan and the sea. Main centres are Bridgend, Maesteg and Porthcawl. The area is mountainous to the N, having ribbon development along river valleys; there is greater urbanisation in the S.
Places of interest: Bryngarw Country Park; Coity Castle.

Brighton & Hove *B. & H.* Population: 155,000.
Unitary authority on the S coast of England neighbouring East Sussex and West Sussex. It encompasses the seaside resort of Brighton, which is a major commercial and conference centre, and the surrounding area which includes Hove, Portslade-by-Sea, Portslade, Rottingdean, Saltdean and part of the South Downs.
Places of interest: Brighton Centre; Brighton Museum & Art Gallery; Royal Pavilion, Brighton; Sea Life Centre, Brighton; The Palace Pier, Brighton.

Bristol *Bristol* Population: 374,000.
Unitary authority in SW England neighbouring Bath & North East Somerset, North Somerset, South Gloucestershire and the Bristol Channel. The area includes the city of Bristol and surrounding urban area, including Avonmouth. Bristol is an important industrial and commercial centre of W England. A former major port, its character varies from docks and a busy city centre, to parks and gardens and Georgian terracing. The city hosts the Balloon Fiesta and Harbour Regatta. River Avon forms part of the W border of the area.
Places of interest: Arnolfini Gallery; Ashton Court Estate; Bristol Cathedral; Bristol City Museum & Art Gallery; Bristol Zoo; Colston Hall; Maritime Heritage Centre; S.S. Great Britain; The Exploratory.

Buckinghamshire *Bucks.* Population: 432,487.
S midland county of England bounded by Bedfordshire, Greater London, Hertfordshire, Northamptonshire, Oxfordshire, Surrey, Windsor & Maidenhead and Wokingham. Chief towns are High Wycombe, the county town of Aylesbury, Amersham, Chesham, Marlow and Beaconsfield, around which, and other smaller towns, is a variety of light industry, as well as extensive residential areas. The chalk downs of the Chiltern Hills traverse the S part of the county, which is otherwise mostly flat. The River Thames flows along its S border.
Districts: Aylesbury Vale; Chiltern; South Bucks; Wycombe.
Places of interest: Bekonscot Model Village, Beaconsfield; Black Park, Wexham; Cliveden (NT); Langley Park; Odd Farm Park, Woburn Common; Waddesdon Manor (NT), Aylesbury.

Caerphilly (Caerffili). *Caerp.* Population: 172,000.
Unitary authority in S Wales bordered by Blaenau Gwent, Cardiff, Merthyr Tydfil, Rhondda Cynon Taff and Torfaen. The chief centres are Caerphilly, Gelligaer, Risca, Bargoed, Blackwood and Bedwas. The geography of the area varies from open moorland to busy market towns. The former mining industry has been replaced by electronics and automotive companies, with tourism also being important to the local economy. Rivers include the Rhymney and Sirhowy.
Places of interest: Caerphilly Castle; Sirhowy Valley Country Park, Cross Keys.

Cambridgeshire *Cambs.* Population: 491,959.
County of E England bounded by Bedfordshire, Essex, Hertfordshire, Lincolnshire, Norfolk, Northamptonshire, Peterborough and Suffolk. Cambridgeshire is mostly flat, with fenland to N and E, although there are low chalk hills in the S and SE. Chief centres are the city and county town of Cambridge, Wisbech, St. Ives, March, Huntingdon, St. Neots and the cathedral city of Ely. Agriculture is a major industry with sugar beet, potatoes and corn all important crops; soft fruit and vegetable cultivation and canning are also significant rural industries. There has been recent growth of medical, pharmaceutical and hi-tech industries around Cambridge. Rivers include the Cam, Nene, and Great Ouse.
Districts: Cambridge; East Cambridgeshire; Fenland; Huntingdonshire; South Cambridgeshire.
Places of interest: Anglesey Abbey (NT), Lode; Corn Exchange, Cambridge; Ely Cathedral; Fitzwilliam Museum, Cambridge; Grafham Water, Huntingdon; Great St. Mary, Cambridge; Holy Sepulchre, Cambridge; Imperial War Museum, Duxford; King's College Chapel, Cambridge; Linton Zoo & Gardens; Wandlebury Country Park, Cambridge; Wimpole Home Farm (NT), Arrington; Wood Green Animal Shelter, Godmanchester.

Cardiff (Caerdydd). *Cardiff* Population: 315,000.
Unitary authority in S Wales surrounding the city of Cardiff and bordered by Caerphilly, Newport, Rhondda Cynon Taff, Vale of Glamorgan and the Bristol Channel. Cardiff, the capital of Wales, is a major administrative, commercial, cultural and tourism centre. It contains the Welsh Office, Welsh National Stadium, remains of medieval castle, cathedral at Llandarff and university. Cardiff docks, which were formerly used to export Welsh coal, are part of an ongoing major redevelopment. The city has excellent shopping facilities, notably at the St. David's Centre. There are associations with Roald Dahl.
Places of interest: Cardiff Bay Visitor Centre; Cardiff Castle; Museum of Welsh Life; National Museum of Wales; St. David's Hall; Techniquest.

Carmarthenshire (Sir Gaerfyrddin). *Carmar.* Population: 68,900.
Unitary authority in S Wales bounded by Ceredigion, Neath Port Talbot, Pembrokeshire, Powys, Swansea and the sea. The chief towns are Llanelli, Carmarthen and Ammanford. The geography varies from the Brecon Beacons in the E, to the river valleys in the N, and the fishing villages, beaches and coastal towns in the S. The 50m coastline runs along the S of the area. Rivers include the Tywi, Cothi, Gwendaeth Fach and Gwendaeth Fawr.
Places of interest: Pembrey Country Park.

Ceredigion *Cere.* Population: 68,900.
Unitary authority in W Wales bounded by Carmarthenshire, Gwynedd, Pembrokeshire, Powys and the sea at Cardigan Bay. The main towns are Aberystwyth, Cardigan, Aberaeron, Lampeter, Tregaron and Llandysul. Part of the Cambrian Mountains lie in the E of the area and the 50m coast has many sandy beaches. Tourism and agriculture are the most important industries. The main river is the Teifi.
Places of interest: Ceredigion Museum, Aberystwyth; Vale of Rheidol Railway, Aberystwyth.

Cheshire *Ches.* Population: 639,900.
County of NW England bounded by Derbyshire, Greater Manchester, Halton, Merseyside, Staffordshire, Shropshire, Warrington and the Welsh authorities of Flintshire and Wrexham. Chief centres are the cathedral city of Chester and the towns of Ellesmere Port, Crewe, Macclesfield, Northwich, Wilmslow, Winsford and Congleton. The country is mainly flat, except in the NE, where the foothills of The Pennines enter the county. The rural areas, which are mostly in the S and W, are noted for dairy products. Much of the county is industrialised; there are large salt mines with an associated chemicals industry in the N, silk and cotton mills, and engineering. Chief rivers are the Dane, Dee, and Weaver. In the NW the county reaches the estuaries of the River Dee and River Mersey.
Districts: Chester; Congleton; Crewe & Nantwich; Ellesmere Port & Neston; Macclesfield; Vale Royal.
Places of interest: Blakemere Craft Centre, Northwich; Brookside Miniature Railway, Poynton; Cheshire Candle Workshops Ltd., Burwardsley; Cheshire Ice Cream Farm, Tattenhall; Chester Cathedral; Chester Visitor Centre; Chester Zoo; Grosvenor Museum, Chester; Jodrell Bank Science Centre & Arboretum, Macclesfield; Lyme Hall (NT); Lyme Park (NT); Marbury Country Park; Ness Gardens, Neston; Palms Tropical Oasis (Stapeley Water Gardens), Stapeley; Quarry Bank Mill (NT), Styal; Styal Country Park, Wilmslow; Tatton Park (NT); Tatton Park, Knutsford; Tegg's Nose Country Park.

Clackmannanshire *Clack.* Population: 47,679.
Unitary authority in central Scotland neighbouring Fife, Perth & Kinross and Stirling. The N includes the Ochil Hills, while the lowland surrounding the Forth estuary contains the chief towns which are Alloa, Tullibody, Tillicoultry and Alva. Clackmannanshire has over 50 sites of nature conservation and five historic castles and towers. The main rivers are the Devon and the Forth.
Places of interest: Gartmorn Dam Country Park, Coalsnaughton; Mill Trail Visitor Centre, Alva.

Conwy *Conwy* Population: 113,000.
Unitary authority in N Wales bordered by Denbighshire, Gwynedd and the sea. The chief towns are Colwyn Bay, Llandudno, Abergele, Rhôs-on-Sea and Conwy. Around 40 per cent of Conwy is within Snowdonia National Park and there are 29m of coastline. The coastal resorts attract tourism which is a key industry, but agriculture and light manufacturing are also important to the local economy. The main river is the Conwy.
Places of interest: Bodnant Gardens (NT), Tal-y-Cafn; Conwy Castle; Great Orme Tramway; North Wales Theatre, Llandudno; Swallow Falls, Betws-y-Coed.

Cornwall *Cornw.* Population: 468,425.
South-westernmost county of England bounded by Devon and the sea. Chief centres are St. Austell, Falmouth, Penzance, the cathedral city and administrative centre of Truro, Redruth, Camborne and Newquay. The coastline is wild and rocky; headlands and cliffs are interspersed with large sandy beaches in the N, and deeply indented with river estuaries in the S. The interior is dominated by areas of moorland, notably the granite mass of Bodmin Moor in the NE. There are also farmlands

providing rich cattle-grazing, and deep river valleys. The climate is mild, and flower cultivation is carried on extensively. The many derelict tin mines are witness to the former importance of this industry; there has recently been a partial revival. The chief industry is tourism. China clay is produced in large quantities in the St. Austell area, and there is some fishing. Rivers include the Tamar, forming the boundary with Devon; Fowey, East and West Looe, Fal, Camel, and Lynher.

Districts: Caradon; Carrick; Kerrier; North Cornwall; Penwith; Restormel.

Places of interest: Boscastle Pottery; Callestock Cider Farm, Truro; Camel Trail, Bodmin; Cornish Goldsmiths, Portreath; Cornish Seal Sanctuary, Gweek; Dobwalls Family Adventure Park; Flambards Village Theme Park, Helston; Holywell Bay Fun Park, Newquay; Land's End; Lanhydrock (NT), Bodmin; Lost Gardens of Heligan, St. Austell; Mount Edgcumbe Country Park, Torpoint; Newquay Pearl; Newquay Zoo; St. Just in Roseland; St. Michael's Mount (NT), Marazion; St. Winwaloe, Gunwalloe; Sea Life Centre, Newquay; Tate Gallery, St. Ives; Tehidy Country Park, Coombe; Tintagel Castle; Trebah Garden, Mawnan Smith; Trelissick (NT), Feock; Truro Cathedral.

Cumbria *Cumb.* Population: 483,163.

County of NW England bounded by Durham, Lancashire, Northumberland and North Yorkshire; the Scottish authorities of Dumfries & Galloway and Scottish Borders; and the Solway Firth and Irish Sea. Chief centres are the city of Carlisle and the towns of Barrow-in-Furness, Whitehaven, Workington, Kendal, Penrith and Ulverston. A narrow strip of flat country along the coast widens to a plain in the N and around Carlisle. Otherwise the county is composed of mountains, moorland and lakes, and includes the scenically famous Lake District. Cumbria is mostly rural and uncultivated, with industry centred on Carlisle and the urban centres. Whitehaven, Workington, and Maryport all once relied on coal, while Barrow-in-Furness developed due to shipbuilding and heavy industry. There are links with nuclear technology: Calder Hall, N of Seascale, was Britain's first atomic power station, Sellafield is the site of a nuclear reprocessing plant and Trident submarines were built at Barrow-in-Furness. Tourism in the Lake District and sheep farming are also important industries. The area is noted for its radial drainage, with Windermere and Ullswater being the largest of the lakes and the River Eden being the chief of many rivers.

Districts: Allerdale; Barrow-in-Furness; Carlisle; Copeland; Eden; South Lakeland.

Places of interest: Adrian Sankey Glass Makers, Ambleside; Carlisle Cathedral; Colony Gift Corporation, Lindal-in-Furness; Cumberland Pencil Museum, Keswick; Dock Museum, Barrow-in-Furness; Fell Foot Park (NT), Staveley-in-Cartmel; Grizedale Forest Park; Lakeside & Haverthwaite Railway, Lakeside; National Park Visitor Centre, Brockhole; Ravenglass & Eskdale Railway, Ravenglass; Sellafield Visitors Centre; South Lakes Wild Animal Park, Dalton-in-Furness; Talkin Tarn Country Park, Farlam; Tullie House, Carlisle; Ullswater Steamers, Kendal; Whinlatter Forest; Windermere Lake Cruises; World of Beatrix Potter Exhibition, Bowness-on-Windermere.

Darlington *Darl.* Population: 98,906.

Unitary authority in NE England surrounding Darlington and neighbouring Durham, North Yorkshire and Stockton-on-Tees. Darlington has a variety of industries, including iron, steel and textiles. The River Tees forms the S border.

Denbighshire (Sir Ddinbych). *Denb.* Population: 91,000.

Unitary authority in N Wales neighbouring Conwy, Flintshire, Gwynedd, Powys, Wrexham and the sea. The chief towns are Rhyl, Prestatyn, Denbigh, Ruthin, the ancient city of St. Asaph, and Llangollen. Main industries are tourism, centred on the coastal resorts of Rhyl and Prestatyn, and agriculture. Rivers include the Morwynion.

Places of interest: Llangollen Railway; Llyn Brenig Visitor Centre, near Corwen; Loggerheads Country Park; Moel Famau Country Park; Ocean Beach Amusement Park, Rhyl; Ruthin Craft Centre; Sea Life Centre, Rhyl; Sky Tower, Rhyl.

Derby *Derby* Population: 218,802.

Unitary authority in central England surrounding the city of Derby and bordered by Derbyshire. Derby has a history dating back to Roman times and is now important in the rail industry; other key industries are manufacturing and aerospace engineering. The River Derwent passes through the area.

Places of interest: Derby Industrial Museum; Pickfords House Museum.

Derbyshire *Derbys.* Population: 709,834.

Midland county of England bounded by Cheshire, Derby, Greater Manchester, Leicestershire, Nottinghamshire, South Yorkshire, Staffordshire and West Yorkshire. Chief towns are Chesterfield, Long Eaton, Swadlincote, Ilkeston, Staveley, Dronfield, Alfreton, Heanor and Buxton. The high steep hills in the N, which include the dramatic scenery of The Peak, are the S extremity of The Pennines, and provide grazing for sheep and cattle. There is some textile industry in the towns of the N and W, while the S of the county is dominated by heavy industry, mining, and quarrying. Tourism is based on the scenic Peak District National Park, most of which falls in the county. Principal rivers are the Dove, forming much of the boundary with Staffordshire and noted for its scenery and fishing, and the Derwent; the Trent flows through the S corner of the county.

Districts: Amber Valley; Bolsover; Chesterfield; Derbyshire Dales; Erewash; High Peak; North East Derbyshire; South Derbyshire.

Places of interest: Calke Abbey (NT), Ticknall; Carsington Water, Ashbourne; Caudwell's Mill, Matlock; Chatsworth Farmyard & Adventure Playground, Edensor; Chatsworth House, Bakewell; Denby Pottery; Elvaston Castle Country Park; Ferrers Centre for Arts & Crafts, Staunton Harold; Foremark Reservoir, Milton; Haddon Hall, Bakewell; Linacre Reservoirs, Cutthorpe; Midland Railway, Butterley; National Tramway Museum, Matlock; Ogston Reservoir, Clay Cross; St. Lawrence, Eyam; St. Michael, Hathersage; Shipley Country Park, Heanor; Staunton Harold Reservoir, Melbourne; The American Adventure Theme Park, Shipley; Upper Derwent Reservoirs, Bamford.

Devon *Devon* Population: 646,903.

Large county in SW peninsula of England bounded by Cornwall, Dorset, Plymouth, Somerset, Torbay and the Bristol and English Channels. The chief centres are the city of Exeter, Exmouth, Barnstaple, Newton Abbot, Tiverton, Bideford and Teignmouth. The county includes the W end of Exmoor and the whole of the granite mass of Dartmoor, whose summit, High Willhays, is the highest point in S England. Moorland areas apart, the county is largely given over to agriculture, and on the coast, to fishing and tourism. On Dartmoor there are quarries and a military training area; there are china clay workings in the S. Daffodils are grown commercially in River Tamar valley. Chief rivers are Exe, Teign, Dart, Avon, Erme, Tamar and Tavy in the S; and Taw and Torridge in the N. The granite island of Lundy is included in the county for administrative purposes.

Districts: East Devon; Exeter; Mid Devon; North Devon; South Hams; Teignbridge; Torridge; West Devon.

Places of interest: Bicton Park Gardens, East Budleigh; Big Sheep, Bideford; Buckfast Abbey; Canonteign Falls, Exeter; Cardew Design, Bovey Tracey; Castle Drogo (NT), Chagford; Clovelly Village, Clovelly; Combe Martin Wildlife & Dinosaur Park; Crealy Park, Exeter; Dartington Crystal and Cider Press Centre; Dartington Crystal Ltd., Great Torrington; Donkey Sanctuary, Sidmouth; Exeter Cathedral; Grand Western Canal Country Park, Tiverton; High Moorland Visitor Centre, Princetown; Killerton (NT); Lynton & Lynmouth Cliff Railway; Morwellham Quay Museum; National Shire Horse Centre; Northam Burrows Country Park, Bideford; Paignton & Dartmouth Steam Railway, Paignton; Quince Honey Farm, South Molton; River Dart (Dart Pleasure Craft), Dartmouth; Rosemoor, Torrington; Royal Albert Memorial Museum, Exeter; South Devon Railway, Buckfastleigh; Stuart Line Cruises, Exmouth; The Grand Pier, Teignmouth; Trago Mills, Newton Abbot; Watermouth Castle, Ilfracombe; Westpoint Exhibition Centre, Exeter; Woodlands Leisure Park, Totnes.

Dorset *Dorset* Population: 360,814.

County in SW England bounded by Bournemouth, Devon, Hampshire, Poole, Somerset, Wiltshire and the English Channel. The chief towns are Weymouth, Christchurch, Wimborne Minster, the county town of Dorchester, Bridport, Swanage and Blandford Forum. The county is hilly, with chalk downs and impressive geological formations along the coastline. Sand, gravel, stone and oil extraction takes place around the Isle of Portland and the Isle of Purbeck. Dorset is also noted for its agricultural and dairy produce. Tourism is an important industry due to the beautiful scenery, the proliferation of prehistoric and Roman remains, and the connection with Thomas Hardy's Wessex. Among numerous minor rivers are the Stour, Frome, and Piddle or Trent.

Districts: Christchurch; East Dorset; North Dorset; Purbeck; West Dorset; Weymouth & Portland.

Places of interest: Abbotsbury Swannery & Sub-Tropical Gardens, Weymouth; Avon Heath Country Park, St. Leonards; Brownsea Island; Christchurch Priory; Corfe Castle (NT); Corfe Castle Museum; Dinosaur Museum, Dorchester; Durlston Country Park Visitor Centre, Swanage; Durlston Country Park, Swanage; Kingston Lacy (NT), Wimborne Minster;

Monkey World, Wareham; Moors Valley Country Park, Ringwood; Sea Life Centre, Weymouth; Stapehill Abbey Crafts & Garden, Wimborne Minster; Swanage Railway; Tank Museum, Bovington Camp; The Tutankhamun Exhibition, Dorchester; Wimborne Minster.

Dumfries & Galloway *D. & G.* Population: 147,900.
Unitary authority in SW Scotland neighbouring East Ayrshire, Scottish Borders, South Ayrshire, South Lanarkshire, the English county of Cumbria and the sea. It comprises the former counties of Dumfries, Kirkcudbright, and Wigtown. Chief towns are Dumfries, Stranraer, Annan, Dalbeattie, Lockerbie, Castle Douglas, Newton Stewart and Kirkcudbright. The hilly area to the N is largely given over to sheep-grazing and afforestation, while farther S there is some good-quality arable farmland. At the extreme W of the area is the peninsula known as the Rinns of Galloway, and the port of Stranraer, which provides passenger and car ferry services to Larne in Northern Ireland. Main rivers are the Esk, Annan, Nith, Dee and Cree which descend S to the Solway Firth from the Tweedsmuir Hills, Lowther Hills and the Rhinns of Kells in the N.
Places of interest: Blacksmith's Shop, Gretna Green; Threave Gardens (NTS), Castle Douglas.

Dundee *Dundee* Population: 155,000.
Unitary authority on the E coast of Scotland surrounding the city of Dundee and neighbouring Angus and Perth & Kinross. Dundee is Scotland's fourth largest city and is a centre of excellence in a variety of areas from telecommunications to medical research. The Firth of Tay borders Dundee to the S.
Places of interest: Discovery Point & R.R.S. Discovery; McManus Galleries.

Durham *Dur.* Population: 494,524.
County in NE England bounded by Cumbria, Darlington, Hartlepool, Northumberland, North Yorkshire, Stockton-on-Tees, Tyne & Wear and the North Sea. Chief centres are the cathedral city and county town of Durham; and the towns of Chester-le-Street, Peterlee, Newton Aycliffe, Bishop Auckland, Seaham and Consett. The W part of the county includes The Pennines and consists mostly of open moorlands which provide rough sheep-grazing and water for the urban areas from a number of large reservoirs. Economic activity is concentrated on the lowland in the E which is more heavily populated, and was formerly a centre for coal-mining and heavy industry. Diversification has since provided a broad industrial base. The principal rivers are the Tees and the Wear.
Districts: Chester-le-Street; Derwentside; Durham; Easington; Sedgefield; Teesdale; Wear Valley.
Places of interest: Allensford Country Park; Beamish Open Air Museum; Bowlees Picnic Area, Middleton-in-Teesdale; Brandon/Bishop Auckland Walk; Consett & Sunderland Railway Path, Stanley; Deerness Valley Walk; Derwent Walk Country Park, Consett; Derwent Walk; Durham Cathedral; Hamsterley Forest; Hardwick Hall Country Park, Sedgefield; Lanchester Valley Walk; Pow Hill Country Park, Edmundbyers.

East Ayrshire *E.Ayr.* Population: 124,000.
Unitary authority in SW Scotland bounded by Dumfries & Galloway, East Renfrewshire, North Ayrshire, South Ayrshire and South Lanarkshire. The principal towns are Kilmarnock, Cumnock, Stewarton, Galston and Auchinleck. Traditional industries centred on textiles and lace in the Irvine valley, coal mining and engineering. Dairy farming is also an important industry, particularly beef and sheep production. The area is a popular tourist destination, with several castles, battle sites and associations with Robert Burns and Keir Hardie. Rivers include the Irvine, Annick and Cessnock.
Places of interest: Blackshaw Farm Park Ltd., Kilmarnock; Loudon Castle Park, Galston.

East Dunbartonshire *E.Dun.* Population: 110,220.
Unitary authority in central Scotland bounded by Glasgow, North Lanarkshire, Stirling and West Dunbartonshire. The chief centres are Bearsden, Bishopbriggs, Kirkintilloch and Milngavie. Much of the urban and industrial development occurs on the N periphery of Greater Glasgow. The Campsie Fells lie in the N of the area.
Places of interest: Lillie Art Gallery.

East Lothian *E.Loth.* Population: 85,500.
Unitary authority in central Scotland neighbouring Edinburgh,

Midlothian, Scottish Borders and the North Sea. The main towns are Musselburgh, Haddington, Tranent, Prestonpans, Dunbar, North Berwick and Cockenzie and Port Seton. There are 43m of varied coastline and the topography includes the Lammermuir Hills in the S, and the ancient volcanoes at North Berwick and Traprain. Much of the urban and industrial development is in the NW and N of the area. Rivers include Whitehead Water, the Tyne, Peffer Burn and Gifford Water.
Places of interest: Gullane Bents; John Muir Country Park; Longniddry Bents; Yellowcraig, Dirleton.

East Renfrewshire *E.Renf.* Population: 86,780.
Unitary authority in SW Scotland bounded by East Ayrshire, Glasgow, Inverclyde, North Ayrshire, Renfrewshire and South Lanarkshire. The principal centres are Newton Mearns, Clarkston, Barrhead and Giffnock, which lie on the S periphery of Greater Glasgow. Over two-thirds of East Renfrewshire is farmland; the rest being mostly residential, with some light industry.

East Riding of Yorkshire *E.Riding* Population: 310,000.
Unitary authority on the E coast of England neighbouring Kingston upon Hull, North Lincolnshire, North Yorkshire, South Yorkshire and York. The chief centres are Bridlington, Beverley, Goole, Great Driffield, Hornsea, Brough, Hedon and Withernsea. The area is mostly low-lying, except for the central ridge which forms part of The Wolds. The coastline is subject to much erosion, with material being moved from Flamborough Head to the large spit of Spurn Head, at the mouth of the River Humber. Key industries in the area include agriculture, aerospace, gas and oil industries.
Places of interest: Beverley Minster; Hornsea Freeport; Park Rose Pottery & Leisure Park, Bridlington; Sewerby Hall; Wolds Village, Great Driffield.

East Sussex *E.Suss.* Population: 535,447.
County of SE England bounded by Brighton & Hove, Kent, Surrey, West Sussex and the English Channel. Main towns are Eastbourne, Hastings, Bexhill, Seaford, Crowborough, Hailsham, Peacehaven and the county town of Lewes; Rye is a small historic town in the E of the county. In the W, the coast is backed by the chalk ridge of the South Downs, ending with the white cliffs of the Seven Sisters and Beachy Head, just W of Eastbourne. E of this point, there are extensive areas of reclaimed marshland, which provide good sheep-grazing. Inland is the heavily wooded Weald, a former centre of the iron industry, interspersed with hill ridges, the largest being the open heathland of Ashdown Forest. Rivers, none large, include the Cuckmere, Ouse, Rother, and upper reaches of the Medway.
Districts: Eastbourne; Hastings; Lewes; Rother; Wealden.
Places of interest: Battle Abbey; Bewl Water, Lamberhurst; Bodiam Castle (NT); Buckleys Yesterday's World, Battle; Clambers Play Centre, Hastings; Drusillas Park, Alfriston; Eastbourne Pier; Filching Manor, Polegate; Fort Fun, Eastbourne; Glass Studio, Eastbourne; Hastings Castle (Ruins); Hastings Fishermen's Museum; Middle Farm & English Farm Cider Centre, West Firle; Paradise Family Leisure Park, Newhaven; St. Mary the Virgin, Rye; Sea Life Centre, Hastings; Sheffield Park (NT), Uckfield; Smugglers Adventure, Hastings; Volks Electric Railway.

Edinburgh *Edin.* Population: 447,550.
Unitary authority on the E coast of central Scotland surrounding the city of Edinburgh and neighbouring East Lothian, Midlothian, West Lothian and the sea at the Firth of Forth. Edinburgh as the capital of Scotland, is a major administrative, cultural, commercial and tourist centre. It contains most of Scotland's national and cultural institutions. Its historic core is centred around Edinburgh Castle and the Royal Mile, attracting much tourism. The city is also a centre for education and scientific research; other important industries are electronics and food and drink production. The river Water of Leith runs through the city to the docks at Leith.
Places of interest: City Art Centre; Edinburgh Castle; Edinburgh Zoo; Gorgie City Farm; Museum of Antiquities; Museum of Childhood; National Gallery of Scotland; Palace of Holyroodhouse; People's Story Museum; Queen's Hall; Royal Botanic Garden; Royal Highland Centre; Royal Museum of Scotland; St. Giles Cathedral; Scotch Whisky Heritage Centre; Scottish National Gallery of Modern Art; Scottish National Portrait Gallery; Scottish United Services Museum, Edinburgh Castle; The Royal Scots Regimental Museum; Tron Kirk; Usher Hall.

Essex *Essex* Population: 1,228,209.

County of SE England bounded by Cambridgeshire, Greater London, Hertfordshire, Southend, Suffolk, Thurrock and the sea at the Thames estuary and North Sea. Chief towns are Basildon, the county town of Chelmsford, Colchester, Harlow, Brentwood, Clacton-on-Sea, Loughton, Canvey Island, Billericay and Braintree. The landscape is mostly flat or gently undulating, and the low-lying coast is deeply indented with river estuaries. Along the county's S and W sides, there is a concentration of urban development, with a mixture of light engineering and service industries. In the N and central parts are farmlands, orchards, market and nursery gardens. The NE coast has the busy passenger and container port of Harwich, and the popular seaside resort of Clacton-on-Sea. Rivers include the Stour, forming part of the boundary with Suffolk, the Lea, forming part of the boundary with Hertfordshire, and the Blackwater.

Districts: Basildon; Braintree; Brentwood; Castle Point; Chelmsford; Colchester; Epping Forest; Harlow; Maldon; Rochford; Tendring; Uttlesford.

Places of interest: Audley End, Saffron Walden; Clacton Pier; Colchester Castle; Colchester Zoo; Hainault Forest Country Park; High Woods Country Park, Colchester; Lee Valley Country Park, Waltham Abbey; Marsh Farm Country Park, Chelmsford; New Walton Pier, Walton on the Naze; North Weald Airfield, Epping; Pitsea Hall Country Park.

Falkirk *Falk.* Population: 142,530.

Unitary authority in central Scotland surrounding Falkirk and neighbouring Clackmannanshire, Fife, North Lanarkshire, Stirling and West Lothian. Main towns are Falkirk, Grangemouth, Polmont, Stenhousemuir and Bo'ness. Petrochemical and chemical industries are important to the local economy, as well as bus manufacturing, toffees and paper-making. The Firth of Forth borders Falkirk to the N. Other rivers include the Carron and Pow Burn.

Places of interest: Blackness Castle, Linlithgow; Bo'ness & Kinneil Railway.

Fife *Fife* Population: 351,200.

Unitary authority in E Scotland neighbouring Clackmannanshire and Perth & Kinross, and lying between the Firth of Tay and Firth of Forth. Main towns are Dunfermline, Kirkcaldy, Glenrothes, Buckhaven, Cowdenbeath and St. Andrews. Fife comprises the former county of the same name, known since ancient times as the Kingdom of Fife, and is noted for its fine coastline with many distinctive small towns and fishing ports. The historic town of St. Andrews, on the coast between the two firths, is a university town, and the home of the world's premier golf club. Inland, the area is outstandingly fertile, with agriculture being an important industry. The SW of the area is a former coal-mining area.

Places of interest: Craigtoun Country Park, near St. Andrews; Deep Sea World, North Queensferry; Lochore Meadows Country Park, Crosshill; Sea Life Centre, St. Andrews.

Flintshire (Sir y Fflint). *Flints.* Population: 144,000.

Unitary authority in N Wales neighbouring Conwy, Denbighshire, Wrexham, the English county of Cheshire and the mouth of the River Dee. Main towns are Buckley, Connah's Quay, Flint, Hawarden, Shotton, Queensferry, Mold and Holywell. Known as the Gateway to N Wales, the landscape varies from the mountains which form the Clwydian Range, to small villages and woodlands.

Places of interest: Wepre Country Park, Connah's Quay.

Glasgow *Glas.* Population: 618,430.

Unitary authority in SW Scotland surrounding Glasgow and bounded by East Dunbartonshire, East Renfrewshire, North Lanarkshire, Renfrewshire, South Lanarkshire and West Dunbartonshire. Glasgow is Scotland's largest city and its principal industrial and shopping centre. The city developed significantly due to heavy industry, notably shipbuilding, being centred on the Clyde. While such industry has declined, Glasgow has emerged as a major cultural centre of Europe, due to its impressive arts and cultural scene. The River Clyde runs through the city.

Places of interest: Burrell Collection; Gallery of Modern Art; Glasgow Botanic Garden; Glasgow Cathedral; Hunterian Museum & Art Gallery; Kelvingrove Art Gallery & Museum; McLellan Galleries; Museum of Transport, Kelvin Hall; People's Palace Museum; Royal Concert Hall; St. Mungo's Museum; Scottish Exhibition & Conference Centre (S.E.C.C.).

Gloucestershire *Glos.* Population: 528,370.

County of W England bounded by Herefordshire, Oxfordshire, South Gloucestershire, Swindon, Warwickshire, Wiltshire, Worcestershire and the Welsh authority of Monmouthshire. Main centres are the cathedral city and county town of Gloucester and the towns of Cheltenham, Stroud, Cirencester and Dursley. The limestone mass of the Cotswold Hills dominates the centre of the county, and provides the characteristic pale golden stone of many of its buildings. The River Severn forms a wide valley to the W, ending in a long tidal estuary, beyond which are the hills of the Forest of Dean. Industry is centred on the fertile Severn Vale, with aerospace, light engineering, food production, and service industries in and around the towns; in rural areas market gardening and orchards dominate. The River Thames rises in the county, and forms part of its S boundary in the vicinity of Lechlade. Apart from the Severn and the Thames, there is the River Wye, which forms part of the boundary with Monmouthshire, and many smaller rivers, among them the Chelt, Coln, Evenlode, Leach, Leadon, and Windrush.

Districts: Cheltenham; Cotswold; Forest of Dean; Gloucester; Stroud; Tewkesbury.

Places of interest: Birdland, Bourton on the Water; Crickley Hill Country Park, Birdlip; Gloucester Cathedral; Gloucestershire & Warwickshire Railway, Toddington; Hidcote Manor (NT), Chipping Campden; Historic Gloucester Docks; Prinknash Abbey Pottery, Gloucester; St. John Baptist, Cirencester; Slimbridge Wildfowl & Wetlands Trust; Snowshill Manor (NT); Sudeley Castle, Winchcombe; Tewkesbury Abbey; Westonbirt Arboretum, Tetbury.

Greater London *Gt.Lon.* Population: 6,675,557.

Former metropolitan county of 32 boroughs and the City of London which together form the conurbation of London, the capital of the UK. Greater London is the largest financial, commercial, cultural, distribution and communications centre in the country, including all but primary industrial sectors. London developed from the City of London, a walled Roman settlement on the Thames, and Westminster, which was a Saxon religious settlement and later a Norman seat of government. The Great Fire of 1666 destroyed most of the medieval city, and was followed by a period of rebuilding and rapid, unplanned expansion. Industrialisation and improved public transport over the last two centuries have caused major suburban growth, and the absorption of most of the surrounding settlements and countryside. Tourism is a major industry, with most attractions situated in and around the historic core, and along the Thames bankside. Other notable tourist areas include Greenwich, Hampstead, Kew and Richmond. Industrial activity is widespread, with major concentrations in the E along the Thames. Leisure facilities include national and major sports stadiums, and many big parks and gardens. Airports at Heathrow and docklands. The main river is the Thames.

Districts: Barking & Dagenham; Barnet; Bexley; Brent; Bromley; Camden; City of London; City of Westminster; Croydon; Ealing; Enfield; Greenwich; Hackney; Hammersmith & Fulham; Haringey; Harrow; Havering; Hillingdon; Hounslow; Islington; Kensington & Chelsea; Kingston upon Thames; Lambeth; Lewisham; Merton; Newham; Redbridge; Richmond upon Thames; Southwark; Sutton; Tower Hamlets; Waltham Forest; Wandsworth.

Places of interest: Albert Memorial Visitor Centre; Alexandra Palace Exhibition Centre; Baden-Powell House; Bank of England Museum; Barbican Art Gallery; Barbican Centre; Battersea Park Children's Zoo; Bethnal Green Museum of Childhood; Brass Rubbing Centre (Westminster Abbey); British Museum; Buckingham Palace; Business Design Centre; Cabaret Mechanical Theatre (Covent Garden); Cabinet War Rooms; Central Criminal Court (Old Bailey); Chapter House (Westminster Abbey); Chessington World of Adventure; Commonwealth Institute; Courtauld Institute Gallery; Crystal Palace Park Farmyard; Cutty Sark; Design Museum; Earl's Court; Fairfield Halls, Croydon; Funland & Laserbowl, Trocadero; H.M.S. Belfast; Hampton Court Garden and Maze; Hampton Court Palace; Harrow Museum, Harrow; Hayward Gallery; Heathrow Roof Garden; Heathrow Visitor Centre; Horniman Museum; Hounslow Urban Farm; Imperial War Museum; Kensington Palace; Kenwood House; Kew Gardens; Labatt's Apollo; London Arena; London Docklands Visitor Centre; London Dungeon; London Transport Museum; London Zoo; Lord's Cricket Ground; Madame Tussaud's; Morden Hall Park, Morden; Museum of London; Museum of the Moving Image; National Army Museum; National Gallery; National Maritime Museum; National Portrait Gallery; Natural History Museum; Old Royal Observatory; Olympia; Osterley Park (NT), Isleworth; Queen Elizabeth Hall; Queen Elizabeth II Conference Centre; Queen's Gallery; Rock Circus; Royal Academy of Arts; Royal Air Force Museum; Royal Albert Hall; Royal Festival Hall Complex; Royal Horticultural Halls; Royal Opera House; St. Martin in-the-Fields; St. Paul's

Cathedral; Science Museum; Serpentine Gallery; Sir John Soane's Museum; Southwark Cathedral; Tate Gallery; The Photographer's Gallery; Theatre Museum; Tower Bridge; Tower Hill Pageant; Tower of London; Twickenham Rugby Football Ground; Victoria & Albert Museum; Wallace Collection; Wembley Stadium Complex; Westminster Abbey; Westminster Cathedral; Whitechapel Art Gallery; Wimbledon Lawn Tennis Club; Winston Churchill's Britain At War Experience.

Greater Manchester *Gt.Man.* Population: 2,499,441.
Former metropolitan county of NW England neighbouring Blackburn with Darwen, Cheshire, Derbyshire, Lancashire, Merseyside, Warrington and West Yorkshire. It comprises the near-continuous urban complex which includes the adjoining cities of Manchester and Salford; and towns including Bolton, Stockport, Oldham, Rochdale, Wigan, Bury and Sale. The conurbation is framed by the wild moorland of The Pennines to the N and the Peak District and Cheshire Plain to the S. Development occurred during the 18c and 19c, creating a series of cotton producing textile towns, while Manchester established itself as the commercial and trading hub, later becoming an inland port linked to Liverpool via the canal network. As textile production declined, the industrial base of the area broadened to include brewing, food production, electronics, plastics, printing, light engineering, financial, leisure and service sectors. Retail is based on town shopping centres and malls such as the Arndale and Trafford Centres. There are many major sporting venues in the area, and cultural facilities include the G-MEX centre, numerous universities, museums and galleries and a diverse nightlife. The area is served by Manchester Airport. Main rivers are Irwell and Mersey.
Districts: Bolton; Bury; Manchester; Oldham; Rochdale; Salford; Stockport; Tameside; Trafford; Wigan.
Places of interest: Animal World, Bolton; Aviation Viewing Park, Manchester; Bolton Museum & Art Gallery; Dunham Massey Country Park, Altrincham; Etherow Country Park, Compstall; G-MEX Centre, Manchester; Granada Studios Tour, Salford; Haigh Hall Country Park, Wigan; Heaton Park, Manchester; Hollingworth Lake Country Park Visitor Centre, Rochdale; Hollingworth Lake Country Park, Littleborough; Labatt's Apollo, Manchester; Manchester City Art Galleries; Manchester Museum; Manchester United Museum & Tour Centre; Museum of Science & Industry, Manchester; Pennington Flash Country Park, Leigh; Whitworth Art Gallery, Manchester; Wigan Pier.

Gwynedd *Gwyn.* Population: 116,000.
Unitary authority in NW Wales bounded by Ceredigion, Conwy, Denbighshire, Isle of Anglesey, Powys and the sea. Main centres are the cathedral city of Bangor, Caernarfon, Ffestiniog, Blaenau Ffestiniog, Llanddeiniolen, Pwllheli, Llanllynfi, Bethesda and Porthmadog. The whole mainland area, except the Lleyn Peninsula in the NW, is extremely mountainous and contains the scenically famous Snowdonia National Park. There is slate-quarrying in the Ffestiniog valley, otherwise sheep-farming and tourism are the principal occupations; the coastline has been much developed for the holiday trade. The area contains many lakes and reservoirs, among them are Llyn Trawsfynedd, Llyn Celyn and Llyn Tegid. Of the many rivers, the Wnion and the Dyfi, which flows through part of the area, are most significant.
Places of interest: Butlin's Starcoast World, Pwllheli; Caernarfon Castle; Ffestiniog Railway, Porthmadog; Llechwedd Slate Caverns, Blaenau Ffestiniog; Padarn Country Park; Penrhyn Castle (NT), Bangor; Portmeirion Village, Penrhyndeudraeth; Royal Welch Fusiliers Regiment Museum, Caernarfon; Snowdon Mountain Railway.

Halton *Halton* Population: 123,716.
Unitary authority in NW England neighbouring Cheshire, Merseyside and Warrington. The principal towns are Runcorn and Widnes, separated by the River Mersey. The area is industrialised, being dominated by petro-chemicals and chemicals industries due to the nearby salt mines and port facilities.
Places of interest: Catalyst Museum, Widnes; Norton Priory & Museum, Runcorn.

Hampshire *Hants.* Population: 1,169,986.
County of S England bounded by Bracknell Forest, Dorset, Portsmouth, Southampton, Surrey, West Berkshire, West Sussex, Wiltshire, Wokingham and the English Channel. Main towns are Basingstoke, Gosport, Waterlooville, Farnborough, Aldershot, Eastleigh, Havant, the ancient city and county town of Winchester, Andover and Fleet. The centre of the county consists largely of chalk downs interspersed with fertile valleys. In the SW is the New Forest, while in the NE is the military area centred on Aldershot. The much indented coastline borders The Solent and looks across to the Isle of Wight. Main industries are in the service sector, with chemicals and pharmaceuticals also important. The chief rivers are the Itchen and Test, both chalk streams flowing into Southampton Water, and the Meon flowing into The Solent.
Districts: Basingstoke & Deane; East Hampshire; Eastleigh; Fareham; Gosport; Hart; Havant; New Forest; Rushmoor; Test Valley; Winchester.
Places of interest: Beaulieu Abbey; Beaulieu House; Birdworld, Holt Pound; Buckler's Hard Maritime Museum, Beaulieu; Eling Tide Mill, Totton; Exbury Gardens, Exbury; Finkley Down Farm Park, Andover; Manor Farm Country Park, Bursledon; Marwell Zoo, Colden Common; Mottisfont Abbey Gardens (NT); National Motor Museum, Beaulieu; Paulton's Park, Ower; Queen Elizabeth Country Park, Horndean; The Great Hall, Winchester; Winchester Cathedral.

Hartlepool *Hart.* Population: 90,409.
Unitary authority on the NE coast of England surrounding Hartlepool and bordering Darlington, Durham, Stockton-on-Tees and the North Sea. Fishing is a major industry and a marina has been created from part of the old docks. The mouth of the River Tees forms part of the E border.
Places of interest: Hartlepool Power Station Visitor Centre; Museum of Hartlepool.

Herefordshire *Here.* Population: 164,700.
Unitary authority in W England bounded by Gloucestershire, Shropshire, Worcestershire and the Welsh authorities of Monmouthshire and Powys. Main centres are the cathedral city of Hereford and the towns of Ross-on-Wye, Leominster and Ledbury. Herefordshire lies between the Malvern Hills to the E and the Black Mountains to the W. It is mainly rural, with dairy farming, orchards and market gardening in evidence. The main river is the Wye, which provides excellent fishing.
Places of interest: Hereford Cathedral; Queenswood Country Park, Leominster.

Hertfordshire *Herts.* Population: 975,829.
S midland county of England bounded by Bedfordshire, Buckinghamshire, Cambridgeshire, Essex, Greater London and Luton. Chief centres are Watford, the cathedral city of St. Albans, Hemel Hempstead, Stevenage, Cheshunt, Welwyn Garden City, Hoddesdon, Hitchin, Letchworth and Hatfield; the county town is Hertford. The Chilterns rise along the W border, and there are chalk hills in the N around Royston; otherwise the landscape is mostly flat or gently undulating. There is a mixture of rural and urban life, with agricultural and hi-tech industries represented. While the urban centres in the S lie on the N periphery of the Greater London conurbation, there are many villages with the traditional large green or common. The more urban S part of the county includes a dense network of major roads bypassing, and leading N from London. Rivers include the Colne, Ivel, and Lee.
Districts: Broxbourne; Dacorum; East Herts; Hertsmere; North Hertfordshire; St. Albans; Stevenage; Three Rivers; Watford; Welwyn Hatfield.
Places of interest: Adventure Island Playbarn, Sawbridgeworth; Aldenham Reservoir Country Park, Elstree; Bowmans Farm, London Colney; Hatfield House; Knebworth House; Paradise Wildlife Park, Broxbourne; St. Albans Cathedral; Standalone Farm, Letchworth.

Highland *High.* Population: 207,500.
Unitary authority covering a large part of N Scotland and neighbouring Aberdeenshire, Argyll & Bute, Moray and Perth & Kinross. It contains a mixture of mainland and island life, comprising the former districts of Badenoch and Strathspey, Caithness, Inverness, Lochaber, Nairn, Ross and Cromarty, Skye and Lochalsh and Sutherland. Main towns are Inverness, Fort William, Thurso, Nairn, Wick, Alness and Dingwall. Overall, Highland is very sparsely inhabited, being wild and remote in character. It is scenically outstanding, containing as it does part of the Cairngorm Mountains, Ben Nevis, and the North West Highlands. Many of the finest sea and inland lochs in Scotland are also here, such as Loch Ness, Loch Linnhe, Loch Torridon and Loch Broom. The discovery of North Sea oil has made an impact on the towns and villages around the Moray Firth. Elsewhere, tourism, crofting, fishing and skiing are important locally.

Places of interest: Aonach Mhor Mountain Gondola Lift & Nevis Range Ski Centre, Fort William; Ben Nevis, Fort William; Bught Floral Hall and Visitor Centre, Inverness; Culloden Visitor Centre, near Inverness; Dunvegan Castle; Fort Augustus Abbey Visitor Centre; Glencoe Visitor Centre (NTS); Inverewe Gardens (NTS), Londubh; Loch Ness Monster Exhibition Centre, Drumnadrochit; Rothiemurchus Visitor Centre & Forest Trail; Shin Falls; Speyside Heather Centre, Dulnain Bridge; Urquhart Castle, Drumnadrochit.

Inverclyde *Inclyde* Population: 89,990.
Unitary authority on the W coast of central Scotland, on the S bank of the River Clyde. It is bordered by North Ayrshire, Renfrewshire and the Firth of Clyde. The chief towns are Greenock, Port Glasgow, Gourock and Kilmacolm.
Places of interest: Lunderston Bay, Gourock; McLean Museum & Art Gallery, Greenock.

Isle of Anglesey (Sir Ynys Môn). *I.o.A.* Population: 71,000.
Unitary authority island of NW Wales divided from Gwynedd and the mainland by the Menai Strait, and with Holy Island lying to the W. Main towns are Holyhead, Llangefni, Amlwch and Menai Bridge. Anglesey has 125m of coastline and 16 beaches. Agriculture is an important industry to the island, with other industries including aluminium smelting and food processing. Holyhead is an important port terminus for the Republic of Ireland. Rivers include the Braint and Cefni.
Places of interest: Anglesey Sea Zoo, Brynsiencyn; Beaumaris Castle.

Isle of Man *I.o.M.* Population: 69,788.
Self-governing island in the Irish Sea, situated in the centre of the British Isles. The chief towns are Douglas, Ramsey, Peel, Castletown, Port St. Mary, Port Erin and Laxey. Apart from the N tip, the topography is generally mountainous, rising to a peak at Snaefell. The main industries are agriculture, fishing and tourism as well as financial services and manufacturing. The island is synonymous with motorsport, being the home of the internationally renowned Tourist Trophy Circuit. Rivers include the Glen Auldyn and Neb.
Places of interest: Ballachurry Fort; Ballaheannagh.

Isle of Wight *I.o.W.* Population: 130,000.
County and island with an area of 147 square miles or 381 square km, separated from the S coast of England by The Solent. Chief towns are the capital, Newport, Ryde, Cowes, Shanklin, Sandown, Ventnor and Yarmouth. The island is geologically diverse, composed of sedimentary rocks and contains many important fossil remains. Tourism flourishes owing to the mild climate and the natural beauty of the island. There are Royal associations as Queen Victoria lived and died at Osborne House in the N of the island. There is a strong naval tradition, with the island historically acting as a defence for Portsmouth. Cowes is internationally famous for yachting. There are ferry and hovercraft connections at Cowes, Ryde, and Yarmouth (ferry to Lymington). Chief river is the Medina.
Places of interest: All Saints, Godshill; Blackgang Chine; Brickfields Horse Country, Binstead; Carisbrooke Castle & Museum; Flamingo Park; Isle of Wight Pearl, Brighstone; Isle of Wight Zoo, Sandown; Museum of Isle of Wight Geology, Sandown; Needles Pleasure Park; Osborne House; St. Mildred, Whippingham; Shanklin Chine; Ventnor Botanic Gardens.

Isles of Scilly *I.o.S.* Population: 1964.
Group of some 140 islands 48m/45km SW of Land's End, Cornwall, of which five are inhabited: Bryher, St. Agnes, St. Martin's, St. Mary's and Tresco. Chief industries are fishing, and the growing of early flowers and vegetables due to the exceptionally mild climate.
Places of interest: Isles of Scilly Museum, St. Mary's; Tresco Abbey Gardens.

Kent *Kent* Population: 1,268,052.
South-easternmost county of England bounded by East Sussex, Greater London, Medway, Surrey and the sea at the Thames estuary and the Strait of Dover. Chief centres are the county town of Maidstone, Royal Tunbridge Wells, Dartford, Margate, Ashford, Gravesend, Folkestone, Sittingbourne, Ramsgate, the cathedral city of Canterbury, Tonbridge and Dover. The chalk ridge of the North Downs runs along the N side, then SE to Folkestone and Dover. The River Medway cuts through the chalk in the vicinity of Maidstone, and there are low lying areas to the E of Canterbury

and of Tonbridge, on Romney Marsh in the S, and bordering the Thames estuary in the N. Chief industrial areas are around Maidstone, Ashford and Tonbridge; Dover and Folkestone are major ports, with the Channel Tunnel terminus to the N of Folkestone; Sheerness is a port of growing importance and Ramsgate is a hovercraft terminal. Industrial activity includes mineral extraction, cement manufacture and papermaking. On the highly productive agricultural land, Kent's reputation as the Garden of England is earned, with market gardening, fruit and hop production. Romney Marsh is used for extensive sheep-grazing. Rivers include the Medway, Stour, and Beult.
Districts: Ashford; Canterbury; Dartford; Dover; Gravesham; Maidstone; Sevenoaks; Shepway; Swale; Thanet; Tonbridge & Malling; Tunbridge Wells.
Places of interest: Brogdale Horticultural Trust, Faversham; Canterbury Cathedral; Chartwell (NT), Westerham; Dover Castle; Dover Museum; Dreamland Theme Park, Margate; Eastbridge Hospital, Canterbury; Hever Castle Gardens; Hever Castle; Howletts Wildlife Park; Ightham Mote (NT), Sevenoaks; Kent & East Sussex Railway; Knole (NT), Sevenoaks; Leeds Castle Gardens; Leeds Castle; M.V. Princess Pocahontas, Northfleet; Port Lympne Zoo Park; R.A.F. Manston Spitfire & Hurricane Memorial Building, Manston; Romney, Hythe & Dymchurch Railway, Romney; Rotunda Amusement Park, Folkestone; St. Mary in Castro, Dover; Scotney Castle Garden (NT), Lamberhurst; Sissinghurst Castle (NT), Cranbrook; The Canterbury Tales, Canterbury; The Friars; Whitbread Hop Farm, Beltring; White Cliffs Experience, Dover.

Kingston upon Hull *Hull* Population: 265,000.
Unitary authority on the E coast of England surrounding the city of Kingston upon Hull and bounded by East Riding of Yorkshire and the mouth of the River Humber. Kingston upon Hull is a major sea port and a great industrial city, with key industries including chemicals, food processing, pharmaceuticals and engineering. The River Hull passes through the area, and the River Humber forms the S border.
Places of interest: Ferens Art Gallery; Humber Bridge Country Park.

Lancashire *Lancs.* Population: 1,101,317.
County of NW England bounded by Blackburn with Darwen, Cumbria, Greater Manchester, Merseyside, North Yorkshire, West Yorkshire and the Irish Sea. Chief towns are the administrative centre of Preston, Burnley, Morecambe, the historic county town of Lancaster, Skelmersdale, Lytham St. Anne's, Leyland, Accrington and Chorley; Fleetwood and Heysham are ports. The inland side of the county is hilly and includes the wild and impressive Forest of Bowland. The W side contains the coastal plain, where vegetables are extensively cultivated. The S is largely urban; industries include cotton spinning and weaving, chemicals, glass, rubber, electrical goods, and motor vehicles. The principal rivers are the Lune and the Ribble.
Districts: Burnley; Chorley; Fylde; Hyndburn; Lancaster; Pendle; Preston; Ribble Valley; Rossendale; South Ribble; West Lancashire; Wyre.
Places of interest: Beacon Fell Country Park, White Chapel; Beacon Park, Upholland; Camelot Theme Park; East Lancashire Railway, Waterfoot; Frontierland, Morecambe; Harris Museum & Art Gallery, Preston; Lancaster Leisure Park; Leighton Moss, Carnforth; Martin Mere; St. Mary, Lancaster; Towneley Hall Art Gallery & Museum, Burnley; Williamson Park, Lancaster; Wycoller Country Park.

Leicester *Leic.* Population: 270,493.
Unitary authority in central England surrounding Leicester and bounded by Leicestershire. It is one of the leading shopping regions in the Midlands. Traditional industries such as hosiery and footwear, as well as hi-tech industries, are important to the local economy. Leicester is aiming to be one of the most environmentally-friendly cities in Europe. It is involved in pioneering electronic toll road schemes in order to encourage the use of public transport. The Rivers Sence and Soar run through the area.
Places of interest: Gorse Hill City Farm; Leicester Guildhall.

Leicestershire *Leics.* Population: 565,539.
Midland county of England bounded by Derbyshire, Leicester, Lincolnshire, Northamptonshire, Nottinghamshire, Rutland, Staffordshire and Warwickshire. Chief towns are Loughborough, Hinckley, Wigston, Coalville, Melton Mowbray, Oadby, Market Harborough, Shepshed and Ashby de la Zouch. The landscape is mostly of low, rolling hills. E and W of Leicester are areas of higher ground, notably Charnwood Forest. The W is largely industrial; industries include light engineering, hosiery, and

footwear. The E is rural, with large fields and scattered woods, and is noted for field sports and food production. Part of the legacy left by the Roman occupation of Leicestershire are the Great North Road, Watling Street and Fosse Way which dissect the county. River Soar traverses the county from S to N, while River Welland forms part of the boundary with Northamptonshire to the S.

Districts: Blaby; Charnwood; Harborough; Hinckley & Bosworth; Melton; North West Leicestershire; Oadby & Wigston.

Places of interest: Beacon Hill Country Park; Bosworth Battlefield Country Park; Bradgate Park, Newtown Linford; Broombriggs Farm, Loughborough; Burbage Common, Hinckley; Farmworld, Oadby; Foxton Canal, Market Harborough; Queen's Royal Lancers Regiment Museum, Belvoir; Snibston Discovery Park, Coalville; Twycross Zoo, Atherstone.

Lincolnshire *Lincs.* Population: 584,534.

County of E England bounded by Cambridgeshire, Leicestershire, Norfolk, Northamptonshire, North East Lincolnshire, North Lincolnshire, Nottinghamshire, Peterborough, Rutland and the North Sea. Main towns are the cathedral city and county town of Lincoln and the towns of Boston, Grantham, Gainsborough, Spalding, Stamford, Skegness and Louth. Much of the county is flat and includes a large area of The Fens in the S. This reclaimed marshland is richly fertile, producing large crops of peas (for canning), sugar beet, potatoes, corn, and around Spalding, flower bulbs. Two ranges of hills traverse the county N and S: the narrow limestone ridge, a continuation of the Cotswold Hills, running from Grantham to Scunthorpe, and the chalk Wolds, about 12m/20km wide, running N from Spilsby and Horncastle. Apart from agriculture, industries include manufacture of agricultural machinery and tourism, which is centred on historic Lincoln, and the coastal resorts of Skegness and Mablethorpe. The rivers, of which the chief are the Witham and Welland, are largely incorporated into the extensive land-drainage system, and scarcely distinguishable from man-made channels.

Districts: Boston; East Lindsey; Lincoln; North Kesteven; South Holland; South Kesteven; West Lindsey.

Places of interest: Belton House (NT); Gibraltar Point, Skegness; Grimsthorpe Castle; Hartsholme Country Park, Lincoln; Lincoln Castle; Lincoln Cathedral; St. Botolph, Boston; Skegness Natureland Seal Sanctuary; The Lawn, Lincoln.

Luton *Luton* Population: 171,671.

Unitary authority in SE England surrounding Luton and bounded by Bedfordshire and Hertfordshire. Luton is one of the major centres of employment and manufacturing in SE England, with automotive, electrical and retail industries among the most important. The production and export of high fashion and straw hats remains a feature of the local economy. London Luton Airport is situated in the SE of the area, and the River Lea rises nearby.

Places of interest: Stockwood Craft Museum & Gardens; Woodside Farm.

Medway *Med.* Population: 240,821.

Unitary authority on SE coast of England S of the River Thames estuary and neighbouring Kent. The chief centres are Gillingham, the naval base of Chatham, Strood and the cathedral city of Rochester. The S part of the area, surrounding the River Medway, is largely urban and industrialised. The marshland to the N includes Kingsnorth Power Station and the Isle of Grain, but is mostly rural, and contains Northward Hill Nature Reserve which is a haven for birds.

Places of interest: Chatham Historic Dockyard & Lifeboat Collection; Guildhall Museum, Rochester; Rochester Castle; Rochester Cathedral.

Merseyside *Mersey.* Population: 1,403,642.

Former metropolitan county of NW England. It neighbours Cheshire, Greater Manchester, Halton, Lancashire, Warrington and the sea. It comprises the near-continuous urban complex which includes the city of Liverpool and the towns of St. Helens, Birkenhead, Southport, Bootle, Wallasey, Bebington, Huyton and Crosby. The county straddles the long, wide estuary of the River Mersey, which accounts for the development of the area. During the 18c, growing Imperial trade of goods and slaves, led to the explosion of urban development surrounding the docks at Liverpool, Birkenhead and Bootle. Liverpool went on to become Britain's premier transatlantic port and a significant terminus during the migration flows of the 19c, leading to an ethnically

diverse city culture. Over the last century the docks have declined, leaving behind an impressive waterfront and cityscape as testament to a mercantile and maritime heritage. Inland, the urban spread has reached the industrial town of St. Helens which is famed for glass production. To the N are the residential areas of Crosby, Formby and the coastal resort of Southport. The area includes race courses at Aintree and Haydock, and an airport at Speke.

Districts: Knowsley; Liverpool; St. Helens; Sefton; Wirral.

Places of interest: Albert Dock Village, Liverpool; Cavern Club, Liverpool; Croxteth Hall Country Park, Liverpool; Croxteth Hall, Liverpool; H.M. Customs National Museum, Liverpool; Knowsley Safari Park, Prescot; Liverpool Cathedral; Liverpool Metropolitan Cathedral (RC); Liverpool Museum; Maritime Museum, Liverpool; Mersey Ferries, Liverpool; Museum of Liverpool Life; Natural History Centre, Liverpool; New Palace and Adventureland, New Brighton; Philharmonic Hall, Liverpool; Pleasureland Amusement Park, Southport; St. George's Hall, Liverpool; Southport Pier; Tate Gallery, Liverpool; Voirrey Embroidery, Wirral; Walker Art Gallery, Liverpool.

Merthyr Tydfil *M.Tyd.* Population: 60,000.

Unitary authority in S Wales bounded by Caerphilly, Powys and Rhondda Cynon Taff. Main centres are the town of Merthyr Tydfil and the villages of Treharris, Abercanaid and Troedyrhiw. The area stretches from the Brecon Beacons, along the Taff Valley, to the centre of the former Welsh coal mining district. The local economy has diversified from primary industry, with Merthyr Tydfil being an important centre for public administration, shopping and employment for the region. The River Taff flows through the area.

Places of interest: Brecon Mountain Railway; Cyfarthfa Museum.

Middlesbrough *Middbro.* Population: 146,000.

Unitary authority in NE England surrounding Middlesbrough and bounded by North Yorkshire, Redcar & Cleveland and Stockton-on-Tees. Middlesbrough is an industrial town, with chemical and petro-chemical industries in evidence. It is also an important sub-regional shopping and entertainment centre between Leeds and Newcastle upon Tyne.

Places of interest: Albert Park; Captain Cook Birthplace Museum; Stewart Park, Marton.

Midlothian *Midloth.* Population: 79,901.

Unitary authority in central Scotland neighbouring East Lothian, Edinburgh and Scottish Borders. Main towns are Penicuik, Bonnyrigg, Dalkeith, Gorebridge and Loanhead. The area is mostly rural, including the rolling moorland of the Pentland Hills and Moorfoot Hills in the S. To the N, the urban area is comprised of satellite towns to the SE of Edinburgh. Rivers include Tyne Water and South Esk.

Places of interest: Edinburgh Crystal Visitor Centre, Penicuik; Vogrie Country Park, near Ford.

Milton Keynes *M.K.* Population: 200,000.

S midland unitary authority of England bounded by Bedfordshire, Buckinghamshire and Northamptonshire. The area includes the city of Milton Keynes, Bletchley, Newport Pagnell, Great Linford, Stony Stratford and Wolverton. Over the past 30 years, the area has undergone the fastest rate of growth in the country, attracting numerous industries. The Great Ouse and Ouzel rivers pass through the area.

Places of interest: Cowper & Newton Museum, Olney; Emberton Park.

Monmouthshire (Sir Fynwy). *Mon.* Population: 80,400.

Unitary authority in SE Wales bounded by Blaenau Gwent, Newport, Powys, Torfaen, the English areas of Gloucestershire, Herefordshire and the Bristol Channel. The main towns are Abergavenny, Caldicot, Chepstow and Monmouth. Part of the Brecon Beacons are found in NW Monmouthshire, whereas the SW area is mainly flat. Agriculture, mineral extraction and the service sector are important to the local economy. Rivers include the Wye, which forms part of E border, and the Usk, Trothy and Monnow.

Places of interest: Tintern Abbey (Ruin); The Old Station, Tintern.

Moray *Moray* Population: 85,000.

Unitary authority in N Scotland neighboured by Aberdeenshire, Highland and the sea. Main towns are Elgin, Forres, Buckie,

Lossiemouth and Keith. The area is mainly mountainous, including part of the Cairngorm Mountains in the S. It is dissected by many deep river valleys, most notably that of the River Spey. Along with the local grain and peat, the abundant waters provide the raw materials for half of Scotland's malt whisky distilleries, leading to the Whisky Trail and much tourism through Speyside.
Places of interest: Baxters Visitor Centre, Fochabers; Glenfiddich Distillery, Dufftown; Johnstons Cashmere Visitor Centre, Elgin.

Neath Port Talbot (Castell-nedd Port Talbot). *N.P.T.* Population: 139,650.
Unitary authority in S Wales neighbouring Bridgend, Powys, Rhondda Cynon Taff, Swansea and the sea. The chief centres are Neath, Port Talbot, Pontardawe, Baglan, Glyncorrwg and Briton Ferry. The area is mostly mountainous, divided up by the river valleys of the Tawe, Neath, Afan and Dulais, which all flow out to sea at Swansea Bay. The lower valley of the River Neath is heavily industrialised.
Places of interest: Afan Argoed Country Park, Cynonville; Margam Country Park; Penscynor Wildlife Park, Cilfrew.

Newport (Casnewydd). *Newport* Population: 137,700.
Unitary authority on the S coast of Wales, N of the mouth of the River Severn, and bounded by Caerphilly, Cardiff, Monmouthshire and Torfaen. Main centres are Newport, Liswerry, Malpas and Caerleon. Steel manufacturing and hi-tech industries are important to the local economy. The rivers Ebbw and Usk run through the area.
Places of interest: Caerleon Roman Fortress, Baths & Amphitheatre; Newport Museum & Art Gallery.

Norfolk *Norf.* Population: 745,613.
County of E England bounded by Cambridgeshire, Lincolnshire, Suffolk and the North Sea. Chief centres are the cathedral city and county town of Norwich, Great Yarmouth on the E coast, the expanding port of King's Lynn near the mouth of the Great Ouse and The Wash, Thetford, which is known as the Breckland 'capital', East Dereham and Wymondham. Norfolk is mainly flat or gently undulating, with fenland in the W characterised by large drainage channels emptying into The Wash. In the SW is Breckland, an expanse of heath and conifer forest used for military training; other afforested areas are near King's Lynn and North Walsham. NE of Norwich are The Broads, an area of meres and rivers popular for boating; reeds for thatching are grown here. The N Norfolk coastline is an Area of Outstanding Natural Beauty and Heritage Coast, and includes the popular resorts of Cromer and Sheringham. Otherwise the county is almost entirely agricultural, with farming an important activity; service and manufacturing industries are also significant. Rivers include the Great Ouse, Bure, Nar, Wensum, Wissey, and Yare; the Little Ouse and Waveney both enter the county briefly, but mainly form the boundary with Suffolk.
Districts: Breckland; Broadland; Great Yarmouth; King's Lynn & West Norfolk; North Norfolk; Norwich; South Norfolk.
Places of interest: Banham Zoo; Blickling Hall (NT); Bressingham Live Steam Museum; Mustard Shop, Norwich; Norfolk Lavender, Heacham; North Norfolk Railway, Sheringham; Norwich Castle Museum; Norwich Cathedral; Pettitts Animal Adventure Park, Reedham; Pleasure Beach, Great Yarmouth; St. Andrew's Hall, Norwich; St. Mary Magdalene Chapel, Sandringham; Sea Life Centre, Great Yarmouth; Sea Life Centre, Hunstanton; Shrine of Our Lady of Walsingham, Little Walsingham; The Thursford Collection Steam Museum, Fakenham; Thetford Forest Park; Wroxham Barns, Hoveton.

North Ayrshire *N.Ayr.* Population: 139,175.
Unitary authority in central Scotland including the islands of Arran, Great Cumbrae and Little Cumbrae. It is bounded by East Ayrshire, East Renfrewshire, Inverclyde, Renfrewshire, South Ayrshire and the sea. The principal towns are Irvine, Kilwinning, Saltcoats, Largs, Ardrossan, Stevenston and Kirbirnie. The area includes mountains and part of Clyde Muirshiel Regional Park in the N, and the lower lands of Cunninghame in the S. There is a maritime heritage to the area; ferry routes operate from Largs and Ardrossan. Rivers include the Garnock, Dusk Water and Noddsdale Water.
Places of interest: Brodick Castle (NTS); Kelburn Country Centre, near Largs.

North East Lincolnshire *N.E.Lincs.* Population: 164,000.
Unitary authority in NE England, S of the mouth of the River Humber and bounded by Lincolnshire, North Lincolnshire and the North Sea. Chief towns are Grimsby, Cleethorpes and Immingham. Grimsby and Cleethorpes together are the shopping and commercial centres of the area. Fishing, food, tourism, chemical and port industries are all important to the local economy. The main rivers are the Humber and Freshney.
Places of interest: Cleethorpes Discovery Centre; National Fishing Heritage Centre, Grimsby; Pleasure Island Theme Park, Cleethorpes.

North Lanarkshire *N.Lan.* Population: 326,750.
Unitary authority in central Scotland neighbouring East Dunbartonshire, Falkirk, Glasgow, South Lanarkshire, Stirling and West Lothian. The chief centres are Cumbernauld, Coatbridge, Airdrie, Motherwell, Wishaw and Bellshill. North Lanarkshsire contains a mixture of urban and rural areas, and formerly depended heavily upon the coal, engineering and steel industries. Regeneration and diversification have occurred in recent years.
Places of interest: Drumpellier Country Park, Coatbridge; Palacerigg Country Park, Cumbernauld; Strathclyde Country Park, Motherwell; Summerlee Heritage Trust, Coatbridge.

North Lincolnshire *N.Lincs.* Population: 153,000.
Unitary authority in NE England neighbouring East Riding of Yorkshire, Leicestershire, Norfolk, North East Lincolnshire, Nottinghamshire, Peterborough, Rutland, South Yorkshire and the River Humber. The main centres are Scunthorpe, Bottesford, Barton-upon-Humber and Brigg. The area is mainly rural, but does include oil refineries, steel and manufacturing industries; the River Humber provides pool and wharf facilities. Rivers include the Humber, Trent and the Old Ancholme.
Places of interest: Barton Clay Pits Project, Barton-upon-Humber; Normanby Hall Country Park.

North Somerset *N.Som.* Population: 177,000.
Unitary authority in W England, S of the mouth of the River Severn, and neighbouring Bath & North East Somerset, Bristol, Somerset and the Bristol Channel. Chief towns are Weston-super-Mare, Clevedon, Nailsea and Portishead. The area is largely rural with tourism, centred on the coastal resort of Weston-super-Mare, being a major industry. Bristol International Airport is located in the E of the area.
Places of interest: Clevedon Pier; Winter Gardens, Weston-super-Mare.

North Yorkshire *N.Yorks.* Population: 556,200.
Large county of N England bounded by Cumbria, Darlington, Durham, East Riding of Yorkshire, Lancashire, Middlesbrough, Redcar & Cleveland, South Yorkshire, Stockton-on-Tees, West Yorkshire, York and the North Sea. Main centres are Harrogate, Scarborough, Hetton, Selby, the cathedral city of Ripon, the county town of Northallerton, Whitby, Skipton and Knaresborough. Apart from the wide plain around York, through which flow River Ouse and its tributaries, and the smaller Vale of Pickering, watered by the Derwent and its tributary the Rye, the county is dominated by two ranges of hills; The Pennines in the W and the Cleveland Hills in the NE. The plains are pastoral and agricultural, while the hills provide rough sheep-grazing. The county includes the popular resorts of Scarborough and Whitby, and the majority of the North York Moors and Yorkshire Dales National Parks which promote tourism. Other economic activities include light engineering, service and hi-tech industries. Principal rivers are the Ouse, fed by the Derwent, Swale, Ure, Nidd and Wharfe, and draining into the Humber; the Esk, flowing into the North Sea at Whitby; and in the W, the Ribble, passing out into Lancashire and the Irish Sea.
Districts: Craven; Hambleton; Harrogate; Richmondshire; Ryedale; Scarborough; Selby.
Places of interest: Beningbrough Hall (NT); Bolton Abbey Estate, Skipton; Bolton Priory (Ruins); Brymor, High Jervaulx Farm, Masham; Castle Howard, Coneysthorpe; Eden Camp, Malton; Embsay Steam Railway, Skipton; Flamingo Land Theme Park, Malton; Fountains Abbey (NT), Ripon; Grassington National Park Centre; Harlow Carr, Harrogate; Harrogate International Centre; Holy Trinity, Skipton; Kinderland, Scarborough; Malham National Park Centre; Moors Centre, Danby; Mother Shipton's Cave, Knaresborough; Newby Hall, Skelton; North Riding Forest Park, Pickering; North York Moors Railway, Pickering; Ripon Cathedral; St. Mary, Whitby; Sea Life Centre, Scarborough; Skipton Castle; Spa Complex, Scarborough; W.R. Outhwaite & Son Ropemakers, Hawes; Watershed Mill

Visitor Centre, Settle; Whitby Abbey; Whitby Lifeboat Museum; Wyville Animal Farm, Slingsby.

Northamptonshire *Northants.* Population: 578,807.

Midland county of England bounded by Bedfordshire, Buckinghamshire, Cambridgeshire, Leicestershire, Lincolnshire, Milton Keynes, Oxfordshire, Peterborough, Rutland and Warwickshire. Chief towns are Northampton, Corby, Kettering, Wellingborough, Rushden and Daventry. The county consists largely of undulating agricultural country rising locally to low hills, especially along the W border. Large fields and scattered woods provide terrain for field sports. Northamptonshire still retains its rural and agricultural charm, despite undergoing rapid population growth recently. There are many villages of architectural, scenic and historic interest. Industrial development is modest, concentrating on the traditional footwear manufacture. Corby is undergoing regeneration following the decline of its steel industry. Tourism is set to increase due to the county's natural Middle England ambience, and the seasonal opening of the Althorp Estate, the family home and resting place of Diana, Princess of Wales. The principal rivers are the Nene and Welland.
Districts: Corby; Daventry; East Northamptonshire; Kettering; Northampton; South Northamptonshire; Wellingborough.
Places of interest: Barnwell Country Park, Oundle; Brampton Valley Way Country Park, Lamport; Brigstock Country Park, Kettering; Brixworth Country Park; Daventry Country Park; Irchester Country Park; Sywell Reservoir Country Park, Ecton; Wicksteed Park.

Northumberland *Northumb.* Population: 307,709.

Northernmost county of England bounded by Cumbria, Durham and Tyne & Wear, the Scottish authority of Scottish Borders and the North Sea. The principal towns are Blyth, Ashington, Cramlington, Bedlington, Morpeth, Berwick-upon-Tweed, Prudhoe and Hexham. There is some industry in the SE coastal area, otherwise the county is almost entirely rural, the greater part being high moorland, culminating in the Cheviot Hills along the Scottish border. The most spectacular stretches of Hadrian's Wall traverse the county to the N of Haltwhistle and Hexham. There is extensive afforestation, including Kielder Forest Park and part of the Northumberland National Park in the NW; parts of these forests are used for military training. The large reservoir, Kielder Water, also occurs in the NW of the area. Rivers include the Aln, Blyth, Breamish, Coquet, East and West Allen, North and South Tyne, Till, and Wansbeck. The Tweed forms part of the Scottish border and flows out to sea at Berwick-upon-Tweed.
Districts: Alnwick; Berwick-upon-Tweed; Blyth Valley; Castle Morpeth; Tynedale; Wansbeck.
Places of interest: Bamburgh Castle; Bedlington Country Park; Belsay Hall and Gardens; Bolam Lake Country Park; Cragside (NT), Rothbury; Cragside Country Park, Rothbury; Druridge Bay Country Park, Morpeth; Hexham Abbey; Housesteads (Vercovicivm), Bardon Mill; Kielder Forest; Kielder Water, Hexham; Morpeth Chantry; Northumbria Craft Centre, Morpeth; Once Brewed Visitor Centre, Bardon Mill; Plessey Woods Country Park, Bedlington; Queen Elizabeth II Country Park, Ashington; St. Mary, Holy Island; Tyne Green Country Park, Hexham; Wallington (NT), near Cambo; Wansbeck Country Park, near Stakeford.

Nottingham *Nott.* Population: 263,522.

Unitary authority in central England surrounding the city of Nottingham and bounded by Nottinghamshire. The city of Nottingham has a long history, having been granted many Royal Charters; Nottingham Castle and Wollaton Hall are among its many historical buildings. It is also an industrial and engineering centre, and a university city. Its main industries include the manufacture of chemicals, tobacco, cycles, lace and hosiery. The River Trent flows through the city.
Places of interest: Lace Centre; Nottingham Castle Museum; Royal Centre; Royal Concert Hall and Theatre Royal; Tales of Robin Hood; Wollaton Hall Natural History Museum.

Nottinghamshire *Notts.* Population: 730,260.

Midland county of England bounded by Derbyshire, Leicestershire, Lincolnshire, North Lincolnshire, Nottingham and South Yorkshire. Principal towns are Mansfield, Carlton, Sutton in Ashfield, Arnold, Worksop, Newark-on-Trent, West Bridgford, Beeston, Stapleford, Hucknall and Kirkby in Ashfield. Much of the county is rural, with extensive woodlands in the central area of The Dukeries, part of the larger Sherwood Forest. Cattle-grazing is the chief farming activity. Around the large towns there is much industry, including iron and steel, engineering, knitwear, pharmaceuticals, and coal-mining. The county has associations with Robin Hood, at Sherwood Forest, and D.H. Lawrence, at Eastwood. The most important river is the Trent.
Districts: Ashfield; Bassetlaw; Broxtowe; Gedling; Mansfield; Newark & Sherwood; Rushcliffe.
Places of interest: Bestwood Lodge Country Park, Bestwood Village; Clumber Country Park (NT), Hardwick Village; Newark Castle; Newstead Abbey Gardens, Linby; Patchings Farm Art Centre, Calverton; Rufford Country Park; Sherwood Country Park, Edwinstowe; Sherwood Forest Amusement Park, Edwinstowe; Sherwood Pines Forest Park, Edwinstowe; Southwell Minster; Sundown Kiddies Adventureland, Rampton; Watermead Country Park, Syston; White Post Modern Farm Centre, Farnsfield.

Orkney *Ork.* Population: 19,900.

Group of some fifteen main islands and numerous smaller islands, islets and rocks. Designated an Islands Area for administrative purposes, and lying N of the NE end of the Scottish mainland across the Pentland Firth. Kirkwall is the capital, situated on the island Mainland, 24m/38km N of Duncansby Head. Stromness is the only other town. About twenty of the islands are inhabited. In general the islands are low-lying but have steep, high cliffs on W side. The climate is generally mild for the latitude but storms are frequent. Fishing and farming (mainly cattle-rearing) are the chief industries. The oil industry is also represented, with an oil terminal on the island of Flotta, and oil service bases at Car Ness and Stromness, Mainland and at Lyness, Hoy. Lesser industries include whisky distilling, knitwear and tourism. The islands are noted for their unique prehistoric and archaeological remains. The main airport is at Grimsetter, near Kirkwall, with most of the populated islands being served by airstrips. Ferries also operate from the Scottish mainland, and between islands in the group.
Places of interest: Italian Chapel, Lambholm; Skara Brae.

Oxfordshire *Oxon.* Population: 547,584.

S midland county of England bounded by Buckinghamshire, Gloucestershire, Northamptonshire, Reading, Swindon, Warwickshire, West Berkshire, Wiltshire and Wokingham. Chief centres are the county town, cathedral and university city of Oxford and towns of Banbury, Abingdon, Bicester, Witney, Didcot, Thame and Henley-on-Thames. Burford and Chipping Norton are small Cotswold towns in the W and NW respectively. The landscape is predominantly flat or gently undulating, forming part of the Thames Valley. High ground occurs where the Chiltern Hills enter the county in the SE and the Cotswold Hills in the NW. The county is largely agricultural, with industries centred on the towns. Scientific, medical and research establishments are attracted by the proximity of Oxford's universities. Printing and publishing industries have their greatest concentration outside London. The motor industry is well represented with car manufacture at Cowley, Oxford, and the county has the world's largest concentration of performance car development and manufacturing. Tourism, attracted to stately homes, notably Blenheim Palace, and Oxford city centre, is also important. Chief rivers are the Thames (or Isis), Cherwell, Ock, Thame, and Windrush.
Districts: Cherwell; Oxford; South Oxfordshire; Vale of White Horse; West Oxfordshire.
Places of interest: Ashmolean Museum, Oxford; Blenheim Palace, Woodstock; Christ Church College, Oxford; Cotswold Wildlife Park, Burford; Museum of Modern Art, Oxford; Oxford Cathedral; Oxford Story; Oxford University Museum; Pitt Rivers Museum, Oxford; St. John the Baptist, Burford; St. Mary the Virgin, Oxford; Salter Bros. Passenger Boats, Oxford; University of Oxford Botanical Garden.

Pembrokeshire (Sir Benfro). *Pembs.* Population: 117,000.

Unitary authority in the SW corner of Wales neighbouring Carmarthenshire, Ceredigion and the sea. The chief centres are Haverfordwest, Pembroke Dock, Pembroke, Tenby, Saundersfoot, Neyland, Fishguard and the ancient cathedral city of St. David's. Key industries are tourism, agriculture and oil refining. The deep estuarial waters of Milford Haven provide a berth for oil tankers. A large part of Pembrokeshire's coastline forms Britain's only coastal National Park. Ferries from Fishguard and Pembroke Dock sail to Rosslare in the Republic of Ireland.
Places of interest: Canaston Centre, Narberth; Folly Farm, Kilgetty; Llys-y-Fran Reservoir Country Park; Oakwood Leisure Park, near Narberth; Pembroke Castle.

Perth & Kinross *P. & K.* Population: 131,780.
Unitary authority in Scotland bounded by Aberdeenshire, Angus, Argyll & Bute, Clackmannanshire, Fife, Highland and Stirling. Chief centres are the city of Perth, Blairgowrie, Crieff, Kinross, Auchterader and Pitlochry. The area is mountainous, containing large areas of remote open moorland, especially in the N and W; the vast upland expanses of Breadalbane, Rannoch and Atholl, form the S edge of the Grampian Mountains. The lower land of the S and E is more heavily populated and is dominated by the ancient city of Perth. The area is rich in history as it links the Highlands to the N with the central belt and lowlands to the S via important mountain passes, most notably the Pass of Dromochter. The area has many castles, and Scottish Kings were traditionally enthroned at Scone Abbey, to the N of Perth. There are many lochs, including Loch Rannoch and Loch Tay. Main industries are tourism and whisky production. The world famous Gleneagles golf course is in the S of the area. Rivers include the Tay, Almond and Earn.
Places of interest: Blair Castle, Blair Atholl; Crieff Visitor Centre; Edradour Distillery, Pitlochry; Glenturret Distillery, Hosh; Hydro-Electrical Visitor Centre & Fish Ladder, Pitlochry; Queen's View Centre, Loch Tummel; Scone Palace, Perth.

Peterborough *Peter.* Population: 153,166.
Unitary authority in E England neighbouring Cambridgeshire, Lincolnshire, Northamptonshire and Rutland. The area includes the city of Peterborough, which lies at the heart of an important agricultural area. Developing as a railway hub, it has become a major industrial, distribution and shopping centre. The River Nene passes through Peterborough.
Places of interest: Peakirk Wildfowl Refuge; Peterborough Cathedral.

Plymouth *Plym.* Population: 243,373.
Unitary authority on the SW coast of England surrounding the city of Plymouth and neighbouring Cornwall and Devon. Plymouth stands at the mouth of the River Tamar and is the largest city on the S coast of England. It has strong mercantile and naval traditions; it is closely linked with Sir Francis Drake, and has maintained a Royal Naval Dockyard for 300 years. Plymouth is a regional shopping centre and a popular resort.
Places of interest: Plymouth City Museum & Art Gallery; Plymouth Dome; Plymouth Pavilions.

Poole *Poole* Population: 133,050.
Unitary authority on S coast of England surrounding Poole and bordered by Bournemouth and Dorset. Poole Harbour is the second largest natural harbour in the world, which enabled Poole to prosper through trading, especially with Newfoundland. Poole has now attracted a variety of industries including boat-building, fishing, pottery, engineering and electronics. It is also the ferry terminus for the Channel Islands and Cherbourg.
Places of interest: Poole Pottery; Upton Park Country Park.

Portsmouth *Ports.* Population: 174,697.
Unitary authority on the S coast of England surrounding the city of Portsmouth and bordered by Hampshire. Portsmouth developed as a strategic port around Portsmouth Harbour, and it is still the home of the Royal Navy. It has become a culturally diverse centre, attracting a wide range of industries which include leisure, tourism, financial services, distribution, manufacturing and hi-tech industries.
Places of interest: H.M.S. Victory; H.M.S. Warrior; Mary Rose Exhibition; Mary Rose; Portsmouth Guildhall; Portsmouth Historic Dockyard; Royal Naval Museum; Sea Life Centre.

Powys *Powys* Population: 123,600.
Large unitary authority in central Wales bordering Blaenau Gwent, Caerphilly, Carmarthenshire, Ceredigion, Denbighshire, Gwynedd, Merthyr Tydfil, Monmouthshire, Neath Port Talbot, Rhondda Cynon Taff, Wrexham and the English areas of Herefordshire and Shropshire. Main centres are Newtown, Gurnos, Brecon, Welshpool, Ystradgynlais, Llanllwchaiarn, Llandrindod Wells, Knighton, Llanidloes, Builth Wells and Machynlleth. Powys is almost entirely rural, with mountainous terrain; most of the Brecon Beacons National Park falls within the S part of the area, while the Cambrian Mountains are in the W. There is considerable afforestation, and a number of large reservoirs, including Lake Vyrnwy. To the N of Brecon, on

Mynydd Eppynt, is an extensive military training area. Main economic activities are agriculture, which is predominantly based around hill farming. Tourism is significant, owing to the natural beauty of the area, and innovative attractions such as the Centre for Alternative Technology. Industrial development is gradually increasing. Among the many rivers, the largest are the Severn, Usk, and Wye.
Places of interest: Brecon Beacons Mountain Centre, Libanus; Centre For Alternative Technology, Machynlleth; Elan Valley Visitor Centre, Rhayader; Powis Castle (NT), Welshpool.

Reading *Read.* Population: 128,877.
Unitary authority in S England to W of Greater London, surrounding Reading and bordered by Oxfordshire, West Berkshire, Windsor & Maidenhead and Wokingham. Reading developed as a crossing point of the River Thames and River Kennet. Traditional industries include brewing and food production, notably biscuits. These are accompanied by an increasing sector of hi-tech and computer-based companies, attracted by Reading's location in the M4 corridor. Reading has also established itself as a major entertainments centre.
Places of interest: Blake's Lock Museum; Museum of Reading.

Redcar & Cleveland *R. & C.* Population: 144,000.
Unitary authority on the NE coast of England neighbouring Hartlepool, Middlesbrough and North Yorkshire. The main centres are Redcar, South Bank, Eston, Guisborough, Marske-by-the-Sea, Saltburn-by-the-Sea, Loftus and Skelton. The area is one of great contrasts. It combines rural villages, market towns and coastal resorts, along with heavily populated urban areas and industrialised port facilities. Industries include steel-making, due to the local ironstone, and chemicals, based around the River Tees to the NW of the area. The coastal towns attract some tourism. The River Tees forms part of the border to the W.
Places of interest: Flatts Lane Woodland Country Park, Eston; Kirkleatham Old Hall Museum.

Renfrewshire *Renf.* Population: 176,970.
Unitary authority in central Scotland bordering East Renfrewshire, Glasgow, Inverclyde, North Ayrshire, West Dunbartonshire and the Firth of Clyde. Main centres are Paisley, Renfrew, Johnstone, Erskine and Linwood. The area emerges W from the Greater Glasgow periphery into a contrasting countryside of highlands, lochs and glens. Industry is centred on the urban area and includes electronics, engineering, food and drink production and service sectors; in rural areas to the W, agriculture is still important. The W part of the area includes some of Clyde Muirshiels Regional Park; Glasgow Airport is in the E.
Places of interest: Castle Semple Country Park; Gleniffer Braes Country Park, Paisley.

Rhondda Cynon Taff (Rhondda Cynon Taf). *R.C.T.*
Population: 232,581.
Unitary authority in S Wales bounded by Bridgend, Caerphilly, Cardiff, Merthyr Tydfil, Neath Port Talbot, Powys and Vale of Glamorgan. The principal towns are Treorchy, Aberdare, Pontypridd, Ferndale and Mountain Ash. Rhondda Cynon Taff is a mountainous area, dissected by deep narrow valleys, with urbanisation typified by ribbon development. The area was the former heart of the Welsh coal mining industry, and has experienced a sharp economic decline as pits closed. Diversification into light engineering and service sectors are gradually improving the industrial base. Main rivers are the Rhondda and Cynon.
Places of interest: Dare Valley Country Park, Aberdare;

Rutland *Rut.* Population: 31,489.
Unitary authority in E England neighbouring Leicestershire, Lincolnshire, Northamptonshire and Peterborough. The main town is Oakham. Agriculture is the main industry; other important industries are engineering, cement-making, plastics, clothing and tourism. The area includes the large reservoir, Rutland Water, which is an important feature for leisure, tourism and wildlife.
Places of interest: East Carlton Countryside Park; Rutland Water, Empingham.

Scottish Borders *Sc.Bord.* Population: 105,300.
Administrative region of SE Scotland bordering Dumfries & Galloway, East Lothian, Midlothian, South Lanarkshire, West Lothian, the English counties of Cumbria and Northumberland and the North Sea. It comprises the former counties of Berwick, Peebles, Roxburgh and Selkirk. Main towns are Hawick, Galashiels, Peebles, Kelso, Selkirk and Jedburgh. It extends from the Tweedsmuir Hills in the W to the North Sea on either side of St. Abb's Head in the E, and from the Pentland, Moorfoot and Lammermuir Hills in the N to the Cheviot Hills and the English border in the S. The fertile area of rich farmland between the hills to N and S is known as The Merse. The area around Peebles and Galashiels is noted for woollen manufacture. Elsewhere, the electronics industry is of growing importance. The River Tweed rises in the extreme W and flows between Kelso and Coldstream, finally passing into England, 4m/6km W of Berwick-upon-Tweed.
Places of interest: Abbotsford House, Melrose; St. Abb's Head.

Shetland *Shet.* Population: 22,522.
Group of over 100 islands, lying beyond Orkney to the NE of the Scottish mainland; Sumburgh Head being about 100m/160km from Duncansby Head. Designated an Islands Area for administrative purposes, the chief islands are Mainland, on which the capital and chief port of Lerwick is situated, Unst and Yell. Some twenty of the islands are inhabited. The islands are mainly low-lying, the highest point being Ronas Hill, on Mainland. The oil industry has made an impact on Shetland, with oil service bases at Lerwick and Sandwick, and a large terminal at Sullom Voe. Other industries include cattle and sheep-rearing, knitwear and fishing. The climate is mild, considering the latitude, but severe storms are frequent. The islands are famous for the small Shetland breed of pony, which is renowned for its strength and hardiness. There is an airport at Sumburgh, on S part of Mainland.
Places of interest: Jarlshof, Sumburgh; Shetland Museum, Lerwick.

Shropshire *Shrop.* Population: 262,957.
W midland county of England bounded by Cheshire, Herefordshire, Staffordshire, Telford & Wrekin, Worcestershire and the Welsh authorities of Powys and Wrexham. Main towns are the county town of Shrewsbury, Oswestry, Bridgnorth, Market Drayton, Ludlow and Whitchurch. The S and W borders are hilly, with large areas of open moorland, including The Long Mynd and Wenlock Edge, which provide good sheep-grazing. Elsewhere the county undulates towards the Severn Valley, which provides fertile agricultural land served by prosperous market towns. Agricultural output includes dairy, poultry and pig farming, along with corn crops. As the former heart of the Marches of Wales, Shropshire contains the remains of numerous border defences. There are also the remains of several monasteries, for instance, at Much Wenlock and Buildwas. The most important river is the Severn, which flows across the county from W to SE; others include the Clun, Corve, Perry, Rea Brook, and Teme.
Districts: Bridgnorth; North Shropshire; Oswestry; Shrewsbury & Atcham; South Shropshire.
Places of interest: Aerospace Museum, Cosford; Bridgnorth Cliff Railway, Bridgnorth; Severn Valley Railway.

Slough *Slo.* Population: 107,000.
Unitary authority in SE England to the W of London, surrounding Slough and bordering Buckinghamshire, Greater London, Surrey and Windsor & Maidenhead. Slough has grown significantly over the past 30 years, and is a major regional shopping centre. Industry is centred on the large Slough Trading Estate, which was planned after World War I. Numerous sectors are represented in Slough, among them is confectionery.

Somerset *Som.* Population: 460,368.
County in SW England bounded by Bath & North East Somerset, Devon, Dorset, North Somerset, Wiltshire and the Bristol Channel. The chief centres are the county town of Taunton, Yeovil, Bridgwater, Frome, Chard, Street, Burnham-on-Sea, Highbridge, the small cathedral city of Wells, Wellington and Minehead. Somerset consists of several hill ranges, including the Mendip, Polden, Quantock, Brendon Hills, along with most of Exmoor. These uplands are separated by valleys, or, on either side of the River Parrett, by the extensive marshy flats of Sedgemoor.

Economic activity is mainly based on agriculture in the fertile vales, with manufacturing, distribution and service industries centred on the urban areas. Tourism is important with attractions including Exmoor National Park, a holiday complex at Minehead and the county's natural rural charm. Somerset also holds one of Europe's largest music festivals at Glastonbury. The chief rivers are Axe, Brue, Parrett, and Tone, draining into the Bristol Channel; and Barle and Exe, rising on Exmoor and flowing into Devon and the English Channel.
Districts: Mendip; Sedgemoor; South Somerset; Taunton Deane; West Somerset.
Places of interest: Black Swan Guild, Frome; Butlin's Somerwest World, Minehead; Cheddar Caves; Cheddar Gorge Cheese Co.; Crinkley Bottom, Cricket St. Thomas; Dunster Castle (NT); Fleet Air Arm Museum, Yeovilton; Glastonbury Abbey; Montacute House (NT); Royal Bath & Wells Showground, Shepton Mallet; Wells Cathedral; West Somerset Railway, Minehead; Wookey Hole Caves & Paper Mill, Wells.

South Ayrshire *S.Ayr.* Population: 114,000.
Unitary authority in SW Scotland bounded by Dumfries & Galloway, East Ayrshire, North Ayrshire and the sea. The chief towns are Ayr, Troon, Prestwick, Girvan and Maybole. The area consists of a long coastline, with lowlands surrounding Ayr Bay and higher ground to the S. Agriculture is a major economic activity on the uplands. To the N, aerospace and hi-tech industries are located near Prestwick International Airport and Ayr, the main retail centre. Notable sporting venues include a race course at Ayr and open championship golf courses at Troon and Turnberry. Tourism is a major feature of the local economy. The area was the birthplace of Robert the Bruce and Robert Burns; it contains Scotland's first country park at Culzean Castle; and it has a holiday camp on the coast near Ayr. Rivers include the Ayr, Water of Girvan and Stinchar.
Places of interest: Butlin's Wonderwest World, Ayr; Culzean Castle (NTS); Culzean Country Park (NTS); Tam o'Shanter Experience, Alloway.

South Gloucestershire *S.Glos.* Population: 235,000.
Unitary authority in SW England neighbouring Bath & North East Somerset, Bristol, Gloucestershire and Wiltshire. The chief centres are Kingswood, Chipping Sodbury, Mangotsfield, Frampton Cotterell, Yate, Thornbury, Patchway and Filton. The S part of the area lies on the N and E fringes of Bristol. The Cotswold hills are in the E, and the Severn Vale in the W. Main industries are in the S, and include aerospace engineering; the N is mainly agricultural. South Gloucestershire includes the English side of both Severn road bridges. Badminton Park in the E of the area, is the location for the Badminton Horse Trials. The River Severn borders the area to the NW.
Places of interest: Dyrham Park (NT); Oldown, Thornbury.

South Lanarkshire *S.Lan.* Population: 307,400.
Unitary authority in central Scotland bordering Dumfries & Galloway, East Ayrshire, East Renfrewshire, Glasgow, North Lanarkshire, Scottish Borders and West Lothian. The main towns are East Kilbride, Hamilton, Blantyre, Larkhall, Carluke, Lanark and Bothwell. Urban development is mainly in the N, merging with the SE periphery of Greater Glasgow. The S part is mostly farmland and not highly populated. Tourism is mainly centred on the picturesque valley of the upper Clyde; there is a race course at Hamilton. The area has associations with the industrial philanthropist, Robert Owen, who built a model village at New Lanark. Rivers include the Clyde, Avon and Dippool Water.
Places of interest: Calder Glen Country Park, East Kilbride; Chatelherault Country Park, Hamilton; New Lanark World Heritage Village.

South Yorkshire *S.Yorks.* Population: 1,262,630.
Former metropolitan county of N England bordered by Derbyshire, East Riding of Yorkshire, North Lincolnshire, North Yorkshire, Nottinghamshire and West Yorkshire. It comprises the industrial and urban area around the city of Sheffield and the towns of Rotherham, Barnsley and Doncaster. Located at the heart of a major coalfield, South Yorkshire prospered through the development of heavy industry. Barnsley and Rotherham were coal mining towns, with steel and fine cutlery centred on Sheffield. The decline of these industries has led to the area redefining itself. Sheffield has become a centre of learning, tourism and conferences, aided by its environmental improvements. Barnsley, Rotherham and Doncaster have increased their industrial base,

especially via light industries. Leisure and recreation are an important feature of the area, with venues including Barnsley's Metrodome, Doncaster's race course and Dome, and Sheffield's Arena and Don Valley Stadium. Retail has increased with city and town centre redevelopment, and the Meadowhall complex. The surrounding countryside includes country parks at Rother Valley and Thrybergh, with part of the Peak District National Park W and NW of Sheffield. The chief river is the Don.

Districts: Barnsley; Doncaster; Rotherham; Sheffield.

Places of interest: Cannon Hall Country Park, Cawthorne; Cannon Hall Farm, Barnsley; Doncaster Racecourse Exhibition Centre; Elsecar Discovery Centre, Barnsley; Graves Art Gallery, Sheffield; Heeley City Farm, Sheffield; Rother Valley Country Park, Beighton; Sheffield City Museum & Mappin Art Gallery; Thrybergh Country Park; Ulley Reservoir Country Park; Worsbrough Mill Country Park.

Southampton *S'ham.* Population: 196,864.

Unitary authority on the S coast of England surrounding the city of Southampton, and bordered by Hampshire. Southampton owes much to the deep waters of Southampton Water, which have enabled the development of Europe's busiest cruise port. Water and the waterfront remain very important to the local economy, with marine technology, oceanography, boat shows and yacht races all prominent. The city is also a leading media, recreational, entertainment and retail centre. The chief river is the Itchen.

Places of interest: Itchen Valley Country Park; Royal Victoria Country Park.

Southend *S'end* Population: 169,000.

Unitary authority in SE England, N of the mouth of the River Thames, surrounding Southend-on-Sea and bordering Essex. Southend is a commerical, residential, shopping and holiday centre, with tourism among its main industries. It includes a 7m shoreline from Leigh-on-Sea to Shoeburyness, a famous pier and a sea life centre.

Places of interest: Sea Life Centre; Southend Pier.

Staffordshire *Staffs.* Population: 786,498.

Midland county of England bounded by Cheshire, Derbyshire, Leicestershire, Shropshire, Stoke-on-Trent, Telford & Wrekin, Warwickshire, West Midlands and Worcestershire. Chief centres are Newcastle-under-Lyme, Tamworth, the county town of Stafford, Burton upon Trent, Cannock, Burntwood, the cathedral city of Lichfield, Kidsgrove, Rugeley and Leek. The urban development occurs around the West Midlands conurbation in the S, where main industries include engineering, iron and steel, rubber goods and leather production, while to the N, there is an urban concentration around Stoke-on-Trent. Burton upon Trent is noted for brewing. The ancient hunting forest and former mining district of Cannock Chase is in the centre of the county and contains preserved tracts of moorland. In the NE lies part of the Peak District National Park. The rest of the county is predominantly agricultural, with milk, wheat and sugar beet produced. To the E of Leek, moorland broken up by limestone walls extends across the Manifold valley to the Derbyshire border. In additon to the Trent, which dominates much of the county, rivers include the Blithe, Manifold, Sow and Tame. River Dove forms the boundary with Derbyshire.

Districts: Cannock Chase; East Staffordshire; Lichfield; Newcastle-under-Lyme; South Staffordshire; Stafford; Staffordshire Moorlands; Tamworth.

Places of interest: Alton Towers Leisure Park; Amerton Working Farm, Stowe-by-Chartley; Bass Museum of Brewing, Burton upon Trent; Branston Water Park, Burton upon Trent; Drayton Manor Park, Tamworth; Heart of the Country Centre, Lichfield; Lichfield Cathedral; Rudyard Lake, Leek; Shire Hall Gallery, Stafford; Shugborough Estate (NT), Milford; The Children's Farm, Middleton; Tittesworth Reservoir, Leek; Wedgwood Visitor Centre, Barlaston; Weston Park.

Stirling *Stir.* Population: 82,000.

Unitary authority in central Scotland neighbouring Argyll & Bute, Clackmannanshire, East Dunbartonshire, Falkirk, North Lanarkshire, Perth & Kinross and West Dunbartonshire. The chief centres are Stirling, the ancient cathedral city of Dunblane, Bannockburn, Bridge of Allan and Callander. The fertile agricultural lands of the Forth valley are in the centre of the area, bounded by mountains: The Trossachs and the mountain peaks of Ben Lomond, Ben More and Ben Lui in the N, while in the S are the Campsie Fells. Tourism is an important industry with Stirling including many sites of historical significance to Scotland,

particularly during the struggle to retain independence. There are associations with Rob Roy, and the battle site of Bannockburn. Other features include The Trossachs, part of the Loch Lomond Regional Park and the Queen Elizabeth Forest Park. There are several lochs, including Loch Lomond, which forms part of the W border, and Loch Katrine. Scotland's only lake named as such, Lake of Menteith, is also in Stirling. The main river is the Forth.

Places of interest: Argyll & Sutherland Highlanders Museum; Bannockburn Heritage Centre; Blair Drummond Safari Park; Breadalbane Folklore Centre, Killin; Mugdock Country Park, Milngavie; Queen Elizabeth Forest Park, Aberfoyle; Rob Roy & Trossachs Visitor Centre, Callander; Royal Burgh of Stirling Visitor Centre; Stirling Castle; Wallace Monument, Causewayhead.

Stockton-on-Tees *Stock.* Population: 178,000.

Unitary authority in NE England neighbouring Darlington, Durham, Hartlepool, Middlesbrough, North Yorkshire and Redcar & Cleveland. The main centres are Stockton-on-Tees, Billingham, Thornaby-on-Tees, Eaglescliffe, Egglescliffe and Yarm. The area has a diverse mix of picturesque villages, large-scale urbanisation and heavy industry. The area has recently undergone major renewal and regeneration, with industries now including electronics, food technology and chemical production. Stockton is the main shopping centre for the area, and includes the Teesside Retail Park. The main river is the Tees, which is controlled by the Tees Barrage. This has created Britain's largest purpose-built whitewater canoeing course.

Places of interest: Billingham Beck Valley Country Park; Castle Eden Walkway Country Park; Preston Hall Museum, Eaglescliffe.

Stoke-on-Trent *Stoke* Population: 244,637.

Unitary authority in England surrounding the city of Stoke-on-Trent and neighbouring Staffordshire. The city has six town centres: Burslem, Fenton, Hanley, Longton, Stoke-upon-Trent and Tunstall. Hanley is where most current city centre activities are located. The area forms The Potteries, and is the largest claywear producer in the world, although now it is largely a finishing centre for imported pottery. There are a wide variety of other industries, including steel, engineering, paper, glass and furniture. Stoke-on-Trent is a centre of employment, leisure and shopping for the surrounding areas. It is noted for its environmental approach, particularly with land reclamation which accounts for around 10 per cent of the city area; sites include Festival Park, Central Forest Park and Westport Lake. The River Trent flows through the area.

Places of interest: Stoke-on-Trent Museum & Art Gallery, Hanley; W. Moorcroft plc, Burslem.

Suffolk *Suff.* Population: 636,266.

Easternmost county of England bounded by Cambridgeshire, Essex, Norfolk and the North Sea. Main towns are the county town of Ipswich, Lowestoft, Bury St. Edmunds, Felixstowe, Sudbury, Haverhill, Newmarket, Stowmarket and Woodbridge. The county is low-lying and gently undulating. It is almost entirely agricultural, with cereal crops and oil seed rape in abundance. The low coastline, behind which are areas of heath and marsh, afforested in places, is subject to much erosion; it is deeply indented with long river estuaries which provide good sailing. The NW corner of the county forms part of Breckland. The central region includes many notable historic Wool Towns, for instance, Lavenham. Apart from agriculture, industries include electronics, telecommunications, printing and port facilities. Lowestoft is a prominent fishing port and Felixstowe is a container port of growing importance. River Stour forms the S boundary with Essex, and the Little Ouse and Waveney form most of the N boundary with Norfolk. The many other small rivers include the Alde with its estuary the Ore, Deben, and Gipping with its estuary the Orwell, in the E and Lark in the W.

Districts: Babergh; Forest Heath; Ipswich; Mid Suffolk; St. Edmundsbury; Suffolk Coastal; Waveney.

Places of interest: Alton Water, Ipswich; Clare Castle Country Park; East Point Pavilion, Lowestoft; Fritton Lake & Gardens Country Park; High Lodge Forest Centre, Brandon; Ickworth (NT), Bury St. Edmunds; Knettishall Heath Country Park; Manning's Amusement Park, Felixstowe; Pleasurewood Hills Theme Park; Stonham Barns Craft Centre, Stowmarket; Suffolk Country Park; Suffolk Wildlife Park, Kessingland; West Stow Country Park.

Surrey *Surr.* Population: 1,018,003.
County of SE England bounded by Bracknell Forest, East Sussex, Greater London, Hampshire, Kent, Slough, West Sussex and Windsor & Maidenhead. The prinicpal towns are Woking, the cathedral and university town of Guildford, Staines, Leatherhead, Farnham, Epsom, Ewell, Sunbury, Walton-on-Thames, Weybridge, Egham, Redhill, Reigate, Esher, Camberley, Frimley and Godalming. The chalk ridge of the North Downs, gently sloping on the N side but forming a steep escarpment on the S, traverses the county from E to W. Extensive sandy heaths in the W are much used for military training. The county is heavily wooded, and contains many traces of the former iron industry in the predominantly rural S. Much of the urbanised E and N areas include commuter or dormitory towns which form the residential outskirts of the Greater London conurbation. Industries include the agricultural activites of dairy farming and horticulture. Tourism and recreation are also important, with Surrey including numerous stately homes, Wentworth golf course, four race courses, and a theme park at Thorpe Park. The chief river is the Thames, into which flow the Wey and the Mole.
Districts: Elmbridge; Epsom & Ewell; Guildford; Mole Valley; Reigate & Banstead; Runnymede; Spelthorne; Surrey Heath; Tandridge; Waverley; Woking.
Places of interest: Bocketts Farm Park, Fetcham; Chapel Farm Animal Trail, West Humble; Claremont Landscape Garden (NT), Esher; Denbies Wine Centre, Dorking; Godstone Farm; Guildford House Gallery; Horton Park Farm, Epsom; Loseley House; Polesden Lacey (NT), Dorking; Sandown Exhibition Centre, Esher; Thorpe Park, Chertsey; Wisley R.H.S. Gardens, Woking.

Swansea (Abertawe). *Swan.* Population: 232,000.
Unitary authority in S Wales bordering Carmarthenshire, Neath Port Talbot and the sea. Main centres are the city of Swansea, Gorseinon, The Mumbles, Sketty, Cockett and Clydach. The area includes mountains in the N, the urban centre surrounding Swansea, and the Gower peninsula in the S. Swansea originally developed as a port serving the W coalfield of S Wales. The area gained an international reputation for tin-plating and copper and nickel production. Swansea is now a regional shopping and commercial centre, including a university and marina development. The Gower peninsula attracts many tourists with its fine beaches and cliff scenery; hang-gliding is popular at Rhossili Down, and there are associations with Dylan Thomas. The Mumbles is a popular resort, formerly connected to Swansea via a tramway. The chief river is the Tawe.
Places of interest: Glynn Vivian Art Gallery & Museum; Swansea Maritime & Industrial Museum.

Swindon *Swin.* Population: 177,271.
Unitary authority in SW England neighbouring Gloucestershire, Oxfordshire and Wiltshire. Main centres are Swindon, Stratton St. Margaret, Highworth and Wroughton. The area is located between the Cotswold Hills and Wiltshire Downs, on the fringes of the Thames Valley. Originally a railway town, Swindon has experienced rapid recent growth and is now a centre for car manufacture and central commercial operations. The town is a regional shopping centre with a redeveloped town centre and the Designer Outlet Village. The River Thames borders the area to the N and the River Cole to the E.
Places of interest: Great Western Railway Museum; Swindon Museum & Art Gallery.

Telford & Wrekin *Tel. & W.* Population: 143,430.
Unitary authority in W England bordered by Shropshire and Staffordshire. Main centres are Telford, Wellington, Madeley, Donnington, Oakengates, Hadley and Newport. The area was the cradle of the Industrial Revolution, with notable firsts including Darby's discovery of the iron smelting process at Coalbrookdale, the casting and construction of the first cold blast iron bridge at Ironbridge, and the construction of the first iron ship. The new town of Telford, named after the famous engineer, surveyor and road builder, Thomas Telford, is the major commercial centre. The River Severn runs S through the area.
Places of interest: Ironbridge Gorge Museum; Telford International Centre.

Thurrock *Thur.* Population: 131,368.
Unitary authority in SE England, N of the mouth of the River Thames. It is bounded by Essex and Greater London. The main centres are Grays, South Ockendon, Stanford-le-Hope, Corringham and Tilbury. The area is a mix of old and modern, rural and urban. In the N there are historic villages set in agricultural land, while in the S, there are the modern urban developments, and industrial activities surrounding oil refining and the container port of Tilbury. Grays is the commercial centre of Thurrock, with the major retail centre being Thurrock Lakeside. The area includes the N stretch of the Dartford Tunnel and Queen Elizabeth II Bridge, both of which cross the River Thames.
Places of interest: Tilbury Fort; Westley Heights Country Park.

Torbay *Torbay* Population: 119,674.
Unitary authority located on the SW coast of England neighbouring Devon. The major towns are Torquay, Paignton and Brixham. The area, situated on Tor Bay, is among Britain's main holiday resorts, and is widely regarded as the English Riviera. Tourism is the main industry, with Torbay receiving over 1.5 million visitors per year. Excellent leisure, recreation and conference facilities are added attractions.
Places of interest: Babbacombe Model Village; Cockington Court, Torquay; English Riviera Centre, Torquay; Paignton Pier; Paignton Zoo.

Torfaen (Tor-faen). *Torfaen* Population: 90,700.
Unitary authority in S Wales bounded by Blaenau Gwent, Caerphilly, Monmouthshire and Newport. The principal towns are Cwmbran, Pontypool and Blaenavon. Torfaen contains rugged mountains with a 12-mile-long valley running N to S from Blaenavon to Cwmbran. The area is a manufacturing centre which includes electronics, engineering and automotive companies. The industrial past of the area has led to the growth of tourist attractions, with notable sites including The Valley Inheritance at Pontypool, and Big Pit Mining Museum and 19c ironworks at Blaenavon. The river Afon Llwyd runs through the area.
Places of interest: Big Pit Mining Museum, Blaenafon; Greenmeadow Community Farm, Cwmbran.

Tyne & Wear *T. & W.* Population: 1,095,152.
Maritime county of NE England bordered by Durham and Northumberland. It comprises the urban complex around the cities of Newcastle upon Tyne and Sunderland, South Shields, Gateshead, Washington and Wallsend. Named after its two important rivers, the area developed largely through the coal mining and ship-building industries. As these industries declined, the area has undergone urban and industrial regeneration. Newcastle upon Tyne is now a commercial, university and cultural centre, with a historic heart including a cathedral, 12c castle and the Tyne Bridge; the historic Quayside has recently been developed. Sunderland gained city status in 1992, and is now a centre for car manufacture, with recreational facilities including the Crowtree Leisure Complex and the National Glass Centre. Elsewhere, Wallsend has hi-tech and off-shore industries; South Tyneside has electronics industries, and tourism, via its Catherine Cookson links. Gateshead has an international athletics stadium, Europe's largest undercover shopping centre, the Metrocentre, and the modern symbol of renewal, the Angel of the North. The area is served by the Port of Tyne and Newcastle International Airport.
Districts: Gateshead; Newcastle upon Tyne; North Tyneside; South Tyneside; Sunderland.
Places of interest: Hancock Museum, Newcastle upon Tyne; Laing Art Gallery, Newcastle upon Tyne; Metroland, Gateshead; Newcastle Discovery; People's Museum of Memorabilia, Newcastle upon Tyne; Saltwell Park, Gateshead; Sea Life Centre, Tynemouth; South Shields Museum & Art Gallery; Spanish City, Whitley Bay; Sunderland Museum & Art Gallery.

Vale of Glamorgan (Bro Morgannwg). *V. of Glam.*
Population: 119,500.
Unitary authority on the S coast of Wales neighbouring Bridgend, Cardiff and Rhondda Cynon Taff. The chief towns are Barry, Penarth and Llantwit Major. Vale of Glamorgan is a lowland area between Cardiff and Bridgend, with some agricultural activities, and tourism at the resorts of Barry and Penarth. Cardiff International Airport is situated in the SE near Rhoose. Main river is the Ely, which passes through the area.
Places of interest: Barry Island Pleasure Park; Cosmeston Country Park;

Pleasure Steamers Waverley and Balmoral, Penarth; Porthkerry Country Park, Barry.

Warrington *Warr.* Population: 193,000.
Unitary authority in NW England surrounding Warrington and bounded by Cheshire, Greater Manchester, Halton and Merseyside. The area developed as a main crossing point of the River Mersey and latterly the Manchester Ship Canal. During industrialisation it became an important strategic trading centre for the NW region. In 1968, Warrington was granted New Town status, leading to traditional industries such as chemicals, brewing and food processing being joined by hi-tech industries and research and development facilities. Warrington retains its importance as a regional shopping, leisure and commercial centre. The River Mersey flows through the area.
Places of interest: Mount Pleasant Farm Craft Centre; Walton Hall Gardens.

Warwickshire *Warks.* Population: 484,247.
Midland county of England bounded by Gloucestershire, Leicestershire, Northamptonshire, Oxfordshire, Staffordshire, West Midlands and Worcestershire. Chief towns are Nuneaton, Rugby, Royal Leamington Spa, Bedworth, the county town of Warwick, Stratford-upon-Avon and Kenilworth. Warwickshire consists of mostly flat or undulating farmland, although the foothills of the Cotswold Hills spill over the SW border. Main manufacturing activites occur in an industrial belt extending NW from Rugby to the boundary with Staffordshire. They include motor and component industries, service sectors, electrical and general engineering. Tourism is centred on the historic town of Warwick with its medieval castle, and Stratford-upon-Avon with its Shakespeare associations. The principal river is the Avon.
Districts: North Warwickshire; Nuneaton & Bedworth; Rugby; Stratford-on-Avon; Warwick.
Places of interest: Anne Hathaway's Cottage; Baddesley Clinton (NT), Lapworth; Charlecote Park (NT), Wellesbourne; Hall's Croft, Stratford-upon-Avon; Hatton Country World, Warwick; Holy Trinity, Stratford-upon-Avon; Kenilworth Castle; Mary Arden's House; National Agricultural Centre, Stoneleigh; New Place Museum, Stratford-upon-Avon; St. Mary, Warwick; Shakespeare's Birthplace, Stratford-upon-Avon; Stratford-upon-Avon Shire Horse Centre; Warwick Castle; Warwickshire County Museum, Warwick.

West Berkshire *W.Berks.* Population: 136,700.
Unitary authority in S England bordered by Hampshire, Oxfordshire, Reading, Wiltshire and Wokingham. The chief centres are Newbury, Thatcham and Hungerford. West Berkshire is a mixture of old market towns, historic buildings and waterways, and includes the famous Newbury racecourse. Rivers include the Kennet and the Pang.
Places of interest: Beale Park; Newbury Conference & Exhibition Centre.

West Dunbartonshire *W.Dun.* Population: 97,790.
Unitary authority in central Scotland bordered by Argyll & Bute, East Dunbartonshire, Glasgow, Inverclyde, Renfrewshire and Stirling. The chief towns are Clydebank, Dumbarton, Alexandria and Bonhill. The area is mountainous, containing the Kilpatrick Hills, and is bounded by Loch Lomond in the N and the Firth of Clyde in the S. The urban SE area of West Dunbartonshire forms part of the NW periphery of Greater Glasgow. There is a broad base of light manufacturing and service sector industries. Tourism and leisure are a feature, with the SE tip of Loch Lomond Regional Park and the whole of Balloch Castle Country Park falling within the area. West Dunbartonshire includes the Erskine Bridge which spans the River Clyde, other rivers include the Leven.
Places of interest: Balloch Castle Country Park; Dumbarton Castle.

West Lothian *W.Loth.* Population: 147,870.
Unitary authority in central Scotland neighbouring Edinburgh, Falkirk, Midlothian, North Lanarkshire, Scottish Borders and South Lanarkshire. The chief towns are Livingston, Bathgate, Linlithgow, Broxburn, Whitburn and Armadale. The area undulates to the S of the Firth of Forth, and rises to moorland at the foot of the Pentland Hills in the S. The main urban areas are situated along commuter corridors between Glasgow, Edinburgh and Falkirk; elsewhere the area is mostly rural. Hi-tech and computing industries are in evidence.

Places of interest: Almondell & Calderwood Country Park, East Calder; Beecraigs Country Park, Linlithgow; Muiravonside Country Park, Linlithgow; Polkemmet Country Park, Whitburn.

West Midlands *W.Mid.* Population: 2,552,205.
Former metropolitan county of central England bordered by Staffordshire, Warwickshire and Worcestershire. It comprises the urban complex around the cities of Birmingham and Coventry, and the towns of Wolverhampton, Dudley, Walsall, West Bromwich, Sutton Coldfield and Solihull. The West Midlands developed as a manufacturing and engineering centre which specialised in the metalworking and motor trades. The area around Dudley, Walsall and Wolverhampton became known as the Black Country, with heavy industry centred on the local deposits of coal, iron ore and limestone. Other local trades included glassware, saddlery and lock-making. Birmingham became Britain's second city by specialising in 1001 trades from confectionery to cars, and has developed into the major business, industrial, commercial and cultural centre for the area. As the traditional industries have declined, there has been a shift towards service, leisure and recreation sectors of the economy; several significant corporate service centres and venues, such as the National Exhibition Centre and the Indoor Arena, are in the West Midlands. The area is served by Birmingham International Airport. Rivers include the Tame and the Cole.
Districts: Birmingham; Coventry; Dudley; Sandwell; Solihull; Walsall; Wolverhampton.
Places of interest: Birmingham Botanical Gardens; Birmingham City Museum & Art Gallery; Birmingham International Airport Visitor Centre; Birmingham Museum of Science & Technology; Birmingham Nature Centre; Black Country World, Dudley; Cadbury World, Birmingham; Cannon Hill Park, Birmingham; Coombe Abbey Country Park; Cotwall End Nature Centre, Sedgley; Coventry Cathedral; Dudley Canal Tunnel & Singing Cavern; Dudley Zoo & Castle; Himley Country Park, Dudley; National Exhibition Centre, Birmingham; National Indoor Arena, Birmingham; National Motorcycle Museum, Solihull; National Sea Life Centre, Birmingham; Ryton Gardens, Coventry; Sandwell Park Farm, West Bromwich; Sandwell Priory, West Bromwich; Sandwell Valley Country Park, West Bromwich; Walsall Arboretum Illuminations; Wolverhampton Art Gallery.

West Sussex *W.Suss.* Population: 702,290.
County of S England bounded by Brighton & Hove, East Sussex, Hampshire, Surrey and the English Channel. Main towns are Worthing, Crawley, Bognor Regis, Littlehampton, Horsham, Haywards Heath, East Grinstead, the cathedral city and county town of Chichester, Burgess Hill and Shoreham-by-Sea. N of a level coastal strip run the South Downs, a steep-sided chalk ridge which is thickly wooded in parts. The remaining inland area, The Weald, is largely well-wooded farmland, although there is industrial development around Crawley, Gatwick (London) Airport, Horsham, and Haywards Heath, as well as among the predominantly residential towns on the coast. Tourism is a major activity throughout the county. There are many castles and stately homes, such as Arundel Castle and Goodwood House, the popular seaside resorts of Bognor Regis and Worthing, race courses at Goodwood and Fontwell, Chichester Harbour, which is a centre for yachtsmen and wildfowl, historic Chichester itself, and numerous picturesque villages. The N of the county includes Gatwick (London) Airport. The rivers, none large, include the Adur and Arun, with its tributary the Rother; the Medway rises in the E of the county.
Districts: Adur; Arun; Chichester; Crawley; Horsham; Mid Sussex; Worthing.
Places of interest: Arundel Castle; Arundel Cathedral (RC); Arundel Wildfowl & Wetlands Trust; Bluebell Railway; Body Shop Visitor Centre, Littlehampton; Chichester Cathedral; Fishbourne Roman Palace; Gatwick Skyview; Nymans (NT), Handcross; Petworth House (NT); Pulborough Brooks R.S.P.B. Nature Reserve; Smarts Amusement Park, Littlehampton; Tilgate Forest Country Park, Crawley; Wakehurst Place (NT), Ardingley; Weald & Downland Open Air Museum, Chichester.

West Yorkshire *W.Yorks.* Population: 2,013,693.
Former metropolitan county of N England bordering Derbyshire, Greater Manchester, Lancashire, North Yorkshire and South Yorkshire. It comprises the area around the cities of Leeds, Bradford and Wakefield, and the towns of Huddersfield, Halifax, Dewsbury, Keighley, Batley, Morley, Castleford, Brighouse, Pudsey, Pontefract and Shipley. West Yorkshire developed as a centre for wool and textiles, manufacturing and engineering, creating an

industrial urban landscape set against rural moorland. As the traditional industries have declined, the area has undergone regeneration and diversification, moving towards tertiary economic sectors. Leeds is the industrial, administrative, commercial and cultural centre of the area, containing regional government offices and many corporate service centres and head offices. Emerging economic activities across West Yorkshire have included printing, distribution, chemicals, food and drink production, hi-tech industries and financial services. Haworth with its Brontë associations, Holmfirth and the moorlands are the centres of tourism. The area includes Leeds Bradford International Airport. The chief rivers are the Aire and the Calder, while the Wharfe forms its N boundary below Addingham.

Districts: Bradford; Calderdale; Kirklees; Leeds; Wakefield.

Places of interest: 1853 Gallery, Saltaire; Bradford Cathedral; Brontë Parsonage, Haworth; Brontë Weaving Shed, Haworth; Cartwright Hall Art Gallery, Bradford; Cliffe Castle Art Gallery & Museum, Keighley; Dean Clough Galleries, Halifax; Eureka, The Museum for Children; Golden Acre Park, Leeds; Harewood House; Hemsworth Water Park, Pontefract; Keighley & Worth Valley Railway, Keighley; Leeds City Art Gallery and Museum; Lotherton Hall Country Park, Old Mickleford; National Museum of Photography, Bradford; Newmillerdam Country Park; Oakwell Hall Country Park, Batley; Ogden Water, Illingworth; Piece Hall, Halifax; Pugneys Country Park, Wakefield; Royal Armouries Museum, Leeds; Temple Newsam Country Park, Whitkirk; Transperience Centre, Bradford; Tropical World, Leeds; Walkley Clogs, Hebden Bridge; Yorkshire Sculpture Park, Bretton.

Western Isles (Na h-Eileanan an Iar. Also known as Outer Hebrides.) *W.Isles* Population: 27,815.

String of islands off the W coast of Scotland and separated from Skye and the mainland by The Minch. They extend for some 130m/209km from Butt of Lewis in the N, to Barra Head in the S. Stornoway, situated on the Isle of Lewis, is the main town; elsewhere, there are mainly scattered coastal villages and settlements. The chief islands are Isle of Lewis, North Uist, Benbecula, South Uist and Barra. North Harris and South Harris form significant areas in the S part of the Isle of Lewis. The topography of the islands consists of undulating moorland, mountains and lochs. The main industries are fishing, grazing and, on the Isle of Lewis, tweed manufacture. There are airfields with scheduled passenger flights on the Isle of Lewis, Benbecula and Barra.

Places of interest: An Lanntair Gallery, Stornoway; Calanais Standing Stones.

Wiltshire *Wilts.* Population: 387,200.

County of S England bounded by Bath & North East Somerset, Dorset, Gloucestershire, Hampshire, Oxfordshire, Somerset, South Gloucestershire, Swindon and West Berkshire. Main centres are the cathedral city of Salisbury, the county town of Trowbridge, Chippenham, Warminster, Devizes and Melksham. Wiltshire consists of extensive chalk uplands scattered with prehistoric remains, notably at Avebury and Stonehenge, and interspersed with wide, well-watered valleys. The N of the county is dominated by the Marlborough Downs which are much used for racehorse training, while in the S, the chalk plateau of Salisbury Plain is an important military training area. Between these two upland areas lies the fertile Vale of Pewsey where dairy production and bacon-curing are important agricultural activities. Other industries include electronics, computing, pharmaceuticals, plastics, telecommunications and service sector activities. Wiltshire attracts tourism with its prehistoric remains, stately houses and picturesque market towns and villages. Rivers include the so-called Bristol and Wiltshire Avons, Ebble, Kennet, Nadder, Wylye, and the upper reaches of the Thames.

Districts: Kennet; North Wiltshire; Salisbury; West Wiltshire.

Places of interest: Bowood, Calne; Keynes Park; Longleat House; Longleat Safari Park; Salisbury Cathedral; Stonehenge; Stourhead (NT), Stourton; Wilton House.

Windsor & Maidenhead *W. & M.* Population: 132,465.

Unitary authority in SE England to the W of Greater London, and bounded by Bracknell Forest, Buckinghamshire, Slough, Surrey and Wokingham. The towns of Maidenhead and Windsor are the main centres for industry, leisure and recreation. The area is particularly noted for its strong Royal connections as it includes Windsor Castle and the former Royal hunting estate of Windsor Great Park. Other popular tourist attractions include Ascot race course, Windsor Legoland and Eton College. The River Thames forms the N boundary.

Places of interest: Legoland, Windsor; Queen Mary's Dolls' House, Windsor; Windsor Castle.

Wokingham *W'ham* Population: 139,189.

Unitary authority in SE England, to the W of Greater London. The area encompasses Wokingham and is bordered by Bracknell Forest, Buckinghamshire, Hampshire, Oxfordshire, Reading, West Berkshire and Windsor & Maidenhead. The area includes riverside villages in the N, with undulating ridges covered by woodlands and commons in the S. Wokingham is a growing centre for hi-tech and computer industries. The River Thames forms the N border, and the River Blackwater forms the border to the S.

Places of interest: California Country Park; Dinton Pastures Country Park.

Worcestershire *Worcs.* Population: 534,285.

S midland county of England neighbouring Gloucestershire, Herefordshire, Shropshire, Warwickshire and West Midlands. Main centres are the cathedral city and the county town of Worcester, and the towns of Redditch, Kidderminster, Great Malvern, Bromsgrove, Droitwich Spa, Stourport-on-Severn and Evesham. The urban areas in the N of the county form part of the periphery and commuter belt of the West Midlands conurbation, and attract much of the industrial development. The central and S sections of the county are largely rural, containing the fertile Severn Valley and Vale of Evesham, with market gardening and orchard-growing being the main agricultural activities. Tourism is an important industry, much of it being centred on historic Worcester, with its cathedral, the triennial Three Choirs Festival, Worcester Sauce and china factories. Other popular attractions include boating on the River Severn and visiting the Vale of Evesham whilst the flowers are in full bloom. The main river is the Severn.

Districts: Bromsgrove; Malvern Hills; Redditch; Worcester; Wychavon; Wyre Forest.

Places of interest: Clent Hills Country Park; Kingsford Country Park; Leapgate Country Park, Stourport; Lickey Hills Country Park, Rednal; Pershore Bridge Picnic Site; Ragley Hall, Alcester; Royal Worcester; Shatterford Fishery & Wildlife Sanctuary; Three Counties Showground, Great Malvern; Waseley Hills Country Park, Rubery; Worcester Cathedral; Worcester Woods Country Park, Worcester.

Wrexham (Wrecsam). *Wrex.* Population: 123,500.

Unitary authority in NE Wales bordering Denbighshire, Flintshire, Powys and the English counties of Cheshire and Shropshire. Main centres are Wrexham, Rhosllanerchrugog, Gwersyllt, Cefn-mawr and Coedpoeth. The area is mountainous in the SW, containing part of the Berwyn range; the Dee valley lies in the NE. The area was formerly dominated by the iron, coal and limestone industries. Food manufacture, brewing, plastics and hi-tech industries are now important to the local economy. Wrexham is the largest commercial and shopping centre in N Wales. The River Dee flows through the area.

Places of interest: Chirk Castle (NT); Erddig Hall.

York *York* Population: 174,760.

Unitary authority in N England surrounding the historic cathedral city of York and bordered by East Riding of Yorkshire and North Yorkshire. York is a major archaeological, episcopal, industrial, commercial and cultural centre, situated at the confluence of the River Foss and the River Ouse. The city has a unique history dating from the original Roman military camp, which has led to it becoming one of the main museum and tourist centres in the country. The historic core, situated around the centrepiece of the medieval Minster, is well preserved. Other major attractions include the Jorvik Viking Centre, the medieval city walls and the National Railway Museum. Economic sectors include the confectionery industry, company head offices, Government departmental offices, and research and development establishments. The main river is the Ouse.

Places of interest: Castle Museum; Clifford's Tower; Impressions Gallery; Jorvik Viking Centre; Museum of Automata; National Railway Museum; York City Art Gallery; York Dungeon; York Minster; Yorkshire Museum.

WALES Counties

BLAENAU GWENT
BRIDGEND
CAERPHILLY
CARDIFF
CARMARTHENSHIRE
CEREDIGION
CONWY
DENBIGHSHIRE
FLINTSHIRE
GWYNEDD
ISLE OF ANGLESEY
MERTHYR TYDFIL
MONMOUTHSHIRE
NEATH PORT TALBOT
NEWPORT
PEMBROKESHIRE
POWYS
RHONDDA CYNON TAFF
SWANSEA
TORFAEN
VALE OF GLAMORGAN
WREXHAM

Scale 1:1,250,000

0   10   20   30   40 kilometres
0   10   20   30 miles

ENGLAND
Counties & Districts

BATH AND NORTH
EAST SOMERSET

BEDFORDSHIRE
1 North Bedfordshire
2 Mid Bedfordshire
3 South Bedfordshire

BOURNEMOUTH

BRACKNELL FOREST

BRIGHTON & HOVE

BRISTOL

BUCKINGHAMSHIRE
1 Aylesbury Vale
2 Wycombe
3 Chiltern
4 South Buckinghamshire

CAMBRIDGESHIRE
1 Fenland
2 Huntingdonshire
3 East Cambridgeshire
4 South Cambridgeshire
5 Cambridge

CORNWALL
1 North Cornwall
2 Caradon
3 Restormel
4 Carrick
5 Kerrier
6 Penwith

DEVON
1 North Devon
2 Torridge
3 Mid Devon
4 East Devon

5 Exeter
6 Teignbridge
7 West Devon
8 South Hams

DORSET
1 North Dorset
2 East Dorset
3 Christchurch
4 Purbeck
5 West Dorset
6 Weymouth & Portland

EAST SUSSEX
1 Lewes
2 Wealden
3 Eastbourne
4 Rother
5 Hastings

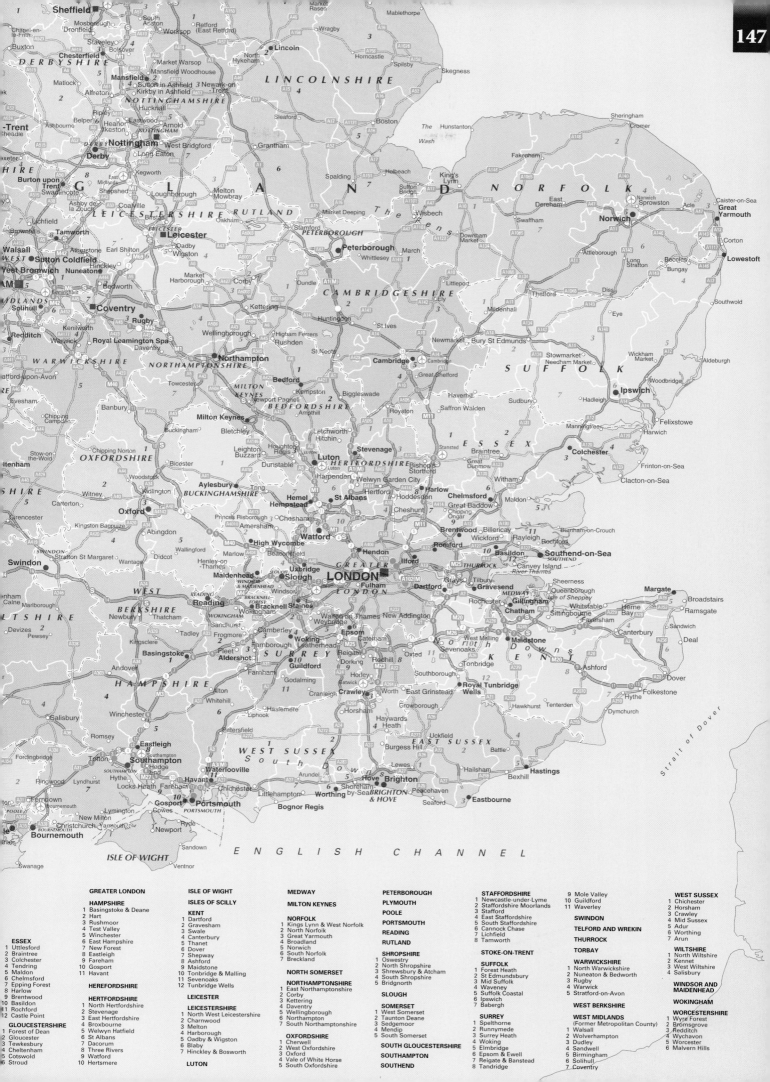

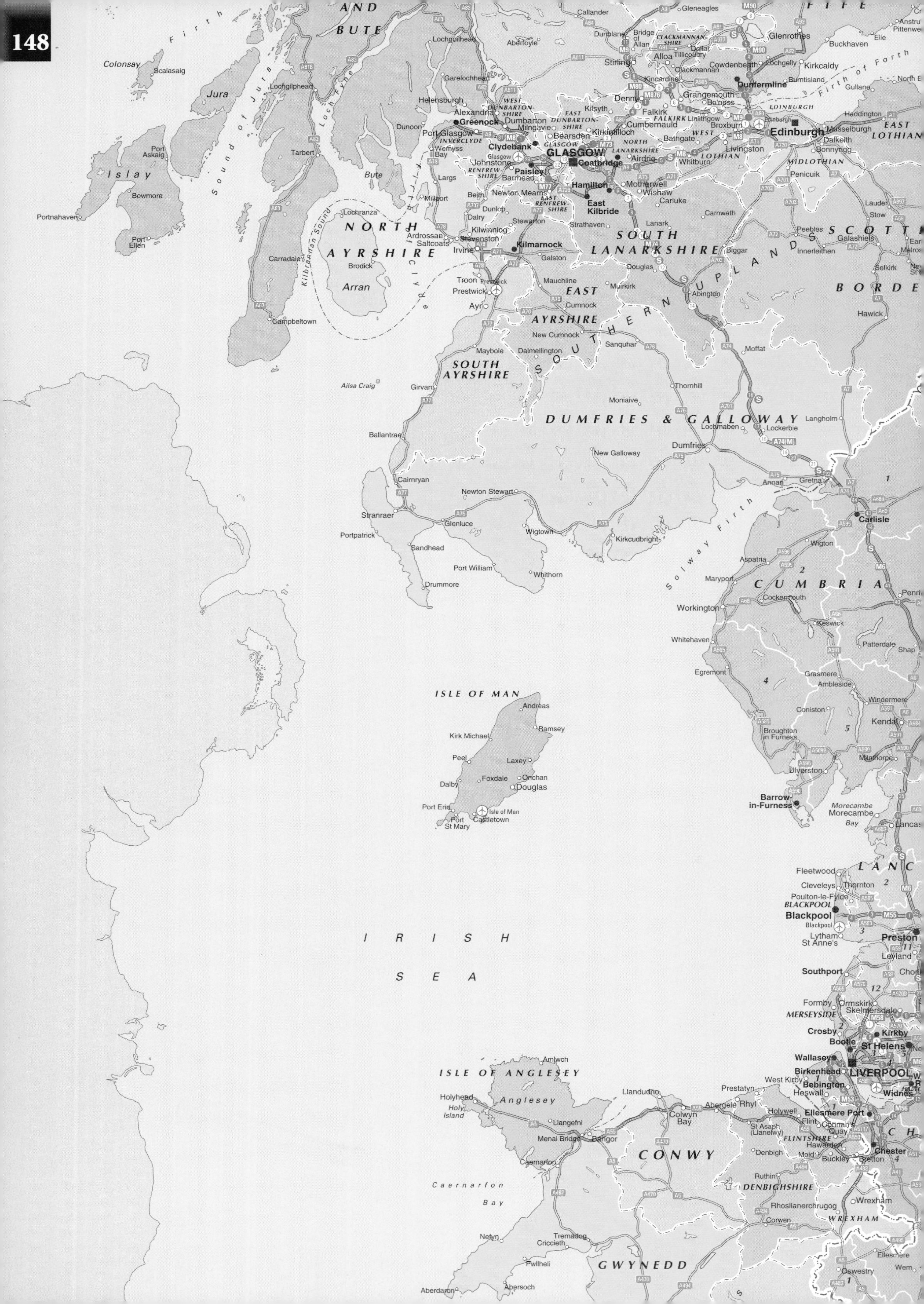

AND BUTE

Firth

Colonsay
Scalasaig

Jura

Sound of Jura

Lochgilphead

Tarbert

Port Askaig

Islay

Bowmore

Portnahaven

Port Ellen

Carradale

Campbeltown

Lochgoilhead
Callander
Aberfoyle
Gleneagles
Dunblane
Bridge of Allan
Stirling
Alloa
Tillicoultry
Dollar
CLACKMANNAN-SHIRE
Kincardine
Cowdenbeath
Kinross
Lochgelly
Kirkcaldy
Glenrothes
FIFE
Buckhaven
Elie
Anstruther
Pittenweem
Burntisland
Dunfermline
North Berwick
Gullane

Garelochhead
Helensburgh
Alexandria
WEST DUNBARTON-SHIRE
Dumbarton
Milngavie
EAST DUNBARTON-SHIRE
Kilsyth
Kirkintilloch
Cumbernauld
Denny
Falkirk
FALKIRK
Linlithgow
Bo'ness
Grangemouth
Bathgate
WEST LOTHIAN
Broxburn
Livingston
EDINBURGH
Edinburgh
Musselburgh
Dalkeith
Haddington
EAST LOTHIAN
Lauder
Dunoon
Port Glasgow
INVERCLYDE
Greenock
Wemyss Bay
Clydebank
Bearsden
GLASGOW
Glasgow
Paisley
Johnstone
Barrhead
RENFREW-SHIRE
EAST RENFREW-SHIRE
Newton Mearns
Coatbridge
Airdrie
Whitburn
Whitburn
Whitburn
MIDLOTHIAN
Penicuik
Peebles
Galashiels
SCOTT
BORDE
Selkirk
Hawick
Bonnyrigg
Stow
Earl
Melro
Innerleithen

Largs
Millport
Beith
Dunlop
Stewarton
NORTH AYRSHIRE
Lochranza
Brodick
Arran
Kilbirnie Sound
Firth of Clyde
Bute

Ardrossan
Stevenston
Saltcoats
Irvine
Kilwinning
Kilmarnock
Galston
Mauchline
Hamilton
East Kilbride
Motherwell
Wishaw
Carluke
Lanark
Carnwath
SOUTH LANARKSHIRE
Strathaven
Douglas
Biggar
Abington
SOUTHERN UPLANDS
Moffat
Langholm
Lockerbie

EAST AYRSHIRE
Cumnock
Muirkirk
New Cumnock
Sanquhar
Troon
Prestwick
Ayr
Maybole
Dalmellington
Thornhill
Moniaive
DUMFRIES & GALLOWAY
Thornhill
Lochmaben
Dumfries
A74(M)
Annan
Gretna

SOUTH AYRSHIRE
Ailsa Craig
Girvan
Ballantrae
New Galloway
Cairnryan
Stranraer
Portpatrick
Newton Stewart
Wigtown
Kirkcudbright
Sandhead
Port William
Whithorn
Drummore

Solway Firth
Carlisle
Wigton
Aspatria
CUMBRIA
Maryport
Cockermouth
Penri
Workington
Keswick
Whitehaven
Patterdale
Shap
Egremont
Grasmere
Ambleside
Windermere
Coniston
Kendal
Broughton in Furness
Milnthorpe
Ulverston
Barrow-in-Furness
Morecambe
Morecambe Bay
Lancas

ISLE OF MAN
Andreas
Ramsey
Kirk Michael
Peel
Laxey
Onchan
Dalby
Foxdale
Douglas
Port Erin
Isle of Man
Castletown
Port St Mary

IRISH SEA

Fleetwood
Cleveleys
Thornton
Poulton-le-Fylde
BLACKPOOL
Blackpool
LANC
Lytham St Anne's
Preston
Leyland
Southport
Chor
Formby
Ormskirk
Skelmersdale
MERSEYSIDE
Crosby
Kirkby
Bootle
St Helens
Wallasey
Birkenhead
LIVERPOOL
Bebington
Widnes
West Kirby
Heswall
Ellesmere Port
CH

ISLE OF ANGLESEY
Amlwch
Holyhead
Holy Island
Anglesey
Llanfairfechan
Llandudno
Llangefni
Menai Bridge
Bangor
Caernarfon
Colwyn Bay
Abergele
Rhyl
Prestatyn
Holywell
St Asaph (Llanelwy)
Flint
Mold
Denbigh
FLINTSHIRE
Hawarden
Buckley
Chester
CONWY
Nefyn
DENBIGHSHIRE
Ruthin
Trefriw
Criccieth
Tremadog
Corwen
Rhosllanerchrugog
WREXHAM
Wrexham
Pwllheli
GWYNEDD
Caernarfon Bay
Aberdaron
Abersoch
Oswestry

I R I S H
S E A

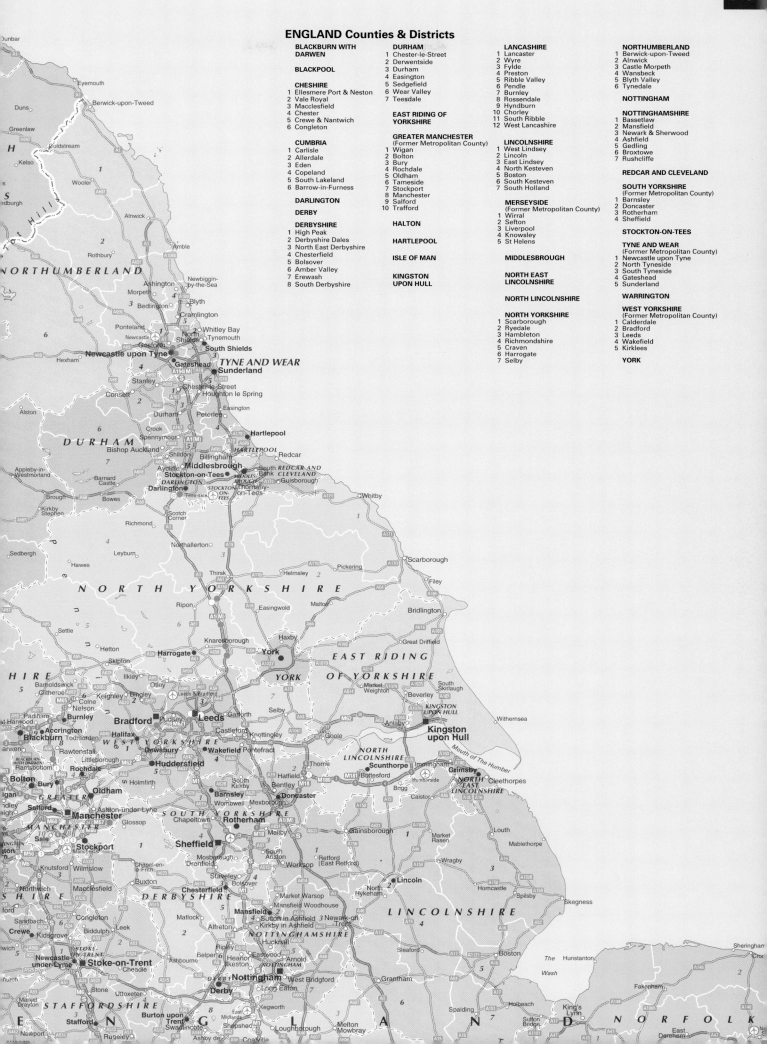

Pentla

Scrabster
Thurso
Halki

Durness
Bettyhill
Tongue

Caith

Rhiconich
Laxford
Bridge
Scourie

S u t h e r l a n d

Kinbrace

Lochinver
Ledmore

Helms

Summer
Isles

Brora

Ullapool

Golspie

E a s t e r
R o s s

Bonar
Bridge

Dornoch Firth

Portmahomack

Aultbea

Burghe

Poolewe

Moray Firth

Gairloch

H I G H L A N D

A835

Garve

Invergordon

W e s t e r
R o s s

Kinlochewe

Cromarty Firth
Cromarty

Shieldaig

Strathpeffer

Dingwall

Fortrose

Nairn

M O

Kinlochewe
Achnasheen

Muir of Ord
Beauly

Inverness

Inverness

Lochcarron

Stromeferry

Drumnadrochit

Grantown
-on-Spey

Carrbridge

Kyle of Lochalsh

Invermoriston

Aviemore

Kyleakin

Fort Augustus

G l e n   M o r e

A87

Kingussie
Newtonmore

A9

Broadford

Invergarry

Elgol

Ardvasar

A82

Spean
Bridge

Dalwhinnie

Glenfinnan

G r a m p i a n   M o u

Fort William

Blair Atholl

Kinlochleven

Rannoch
Sta

Kinloch
Rannoch

Pitlochry

Ballachulish

A82

Aberfeldy

P E R T H   A N

Bridge of Orchy

S C O T L A N D

K I N R O S

Crieff

Tyndrum

Killin

Dalmally

Crianlarich

Lochearnhead

Auchtera
Gleneagle

A85

Taynuilt

A82

Callander

Dunblane

Bridge
of
Allan

CLACKMANNAN-
SHIRE

A R G Y L L

A N D

B U T E

Lochgoilhead

Aberfoyle

Stirling

Alloa
Tillicoultry

Dollar

Clackmanna

A811

Kincardine

M9

Lochgoilhead

Garelochhead

WEST
DUNBARTON-
SHIRE

Kilsyth

Denny
M80

Grangen
Bo

Helensburgh

Alexandria

Dumbarton

DUNBARTON-
SHIRE

Falkirk

FALKIRK

Linlithgow

Dunoon

Port Glasgow

Milngavie

Cumbernauld

Bathgate

WEST

Greenock

INVERCLYDE

Bearsden

Kirkintilloch

NORTH
LANARKSHIRE

Wemyss
Bay

Clydebank

Airdrie

Whitburn

Johnstone

GLASGOW

Coatbridge

Largs

RENFREW-
SHIRE

Paisley

Barrhead

M77

Hamilton

Motherwell
Wishaw

Carluke

Beith

Newton Mearns

EAST
RENFREW-
SHIRE

East
Kilbride

Millport

Lochranza

N O R T H

Dalry

Stewarton

Strathaven

Lanark

A Y R S H I R E

Kilwinning

Dunlop

Kilmarnock

Brodick

Ardrossan
Saltcoats

Stevenston

Irvine

SOUTH
LANARKSHIRE

Arran

Galston

Douglas

Carradale

Troon
Prestwick

Mauchline

Muirkirk

Abingto

Prestwick

Ayr

EAST

New Cumnock

Sanquhar

Campbeltown

Maybole

Dalmellington

SOUTH
AYRSHIRE

A Y R S H I R E

Cumnock

S O U T H E R N   U

DUMFRIES &

Western Isles / Islands (left side):

Port Nis

Steòrnabhagh
(Stornoway)

Port nan
Giuran

Gearraidh na h-Aibhne

Eilean Leòdhais
(Lewis)

WESTERN ISLES
(NA H-EILEANAN AN IAR)

An Tàirbeart

South
Harris

Roghadal

Uibhist a' Tuath
(North Uist)

Loch na Madadh
(Lochmaddy)

Uig

T h e   M i n c h

Beinn na Faoghla
(Benbecula)

Dunvegan

S k y e

Portree

Raasay

I n n e r   S o u n d

L i t t l e   M i n c h

Uibhist a' Deas
(South Uist)

Sligachan

Loch Baghasdail (Lochboisdale)

Canna

Eilean Barraigh
(Barra)

Rum
(Rhum)

S o u n d   o f   S l e a t

Mallaig

Bàgh a' Chaisteil
(Castlebay)

Bhatarsaigh
(Vatersay)

Eigg

Arisaig

Coll

Salen

Tiree

Tobermory

Lochaline

L o c h   L i n n h e

M u l l

Craignure

Oban

Taynuilt

Iona

Fionnphort

S T I R L I N G

F i r t h   o f   L o r n

Colonsay

Scalasaig

A816

Jura

S o u n d   o f   J u r a

Lochgilphead

L o c h   F y n e

Islay

Tarbert

Bute

Port
Askaig

Bowmore

Portnahaven

K i l b r a n n a n   S o u n d

Port
Ellen

C l y d e

ORKNEY

John o'Groats
North Ronaldsay
Papa Westray
Westray
Sanday
Rousay
Eday
Stronsay
Mainland
Shapinsay
Kirkwall
Stromness
ORKNEY
Hoy
Lyness
St Margaret's Hope
South Ronaldsay
Pentland Firth
Scrabster
John o'Groats
Thurso

SHETLAND

Unst
Yell
Fetlar
Whalsay
Mainland
SHETLAND
Bressay
Lerwick
Scalloway
Sumburgh
Fair Isle

Firth
John o'Groats
Wick
ness
A882
A9
A99

Lossiemouth
Portknockie
Portsoy
Macduff
Fraserburgh
Elgin
Buckie
Banff
MRAY
Dufftown
Turriff
New Deer
Peterhead
A95
A96
Strathbogie
A96
A952
Huntly
A90
Oldmeldrum
Ellon
A96
Inverurie
Newburgh
A93
Dyce
ABERDEEN
Aberdeen
ABERDEENSHIRE
Aboyne
A92
Ballater
Banchory
Stonehaven
A90
tains
mar
Clova
A93
ANGUS
Brechin
Montrose
Kirriemuir
Forfar
Arbroath
A90
Coupar Angus
Carnoustie
DUNDEE
Broughty Ferry
Dundee
A92
Perth
Newburgh
St Andrews
Fife Ness
Auchtermuchty
Cupar
A91
FIFE
Crail
Anstruther
Pittenweem
Glenrothes
Buckhaven
Elie
Lochgelly
Kirkcaldy
nbeath
Burntisland
North Berwick
Dunfermline
Firth of Forth
Dunbar
Gullane
EDINBURGH
M9
Haddington
M8
Edinburgh
Musselburgh
EAST LOTHIAN
vingston
Bonnyrigg
Dalkeith
Eyemouth
A1
MIDLOTHIAN
Penicuik
A7
Duns
Berwick-upon-Tweed
A68
A703
Lauder
Greenlaw
Coldstream
ggar
Peebles
Stow
1
A72
Earlston
Innerleithen
Melrose
Kelso
SCOTTISH
Galashiels
Wooler
LAND
Selkirk
Newtown
St Boswells
A697
BORDERS
Jedburgh
Alnwick
Moffat
Hawick
2
A1
LOWAY
Rothbury
Amble
NORTHUMBERLAND

N O R T H S E A

SCOTLAND Councils

ABERDEEN
ABERDEENSHIRE
ANGUS
ARGYLL AND BUTE
CLACKMANNANSHIRE
DUMFRIES AND GALLOWAY
DUNDEE
EAST AYRSHIRE
EAST DUNBARTONSHIRE
EAST LOTHIAN
EAST RENFREWSHIRE
EDINBURGH
FALKIRK
FIFE
GLASGOW
HIGHLAND
INVERCLYDE
MIDLOTHIAN
MORAY
NORTH AYRSHIRE
NORTH LANARKSHIRE
ORKNEY
PERTH AND KINROSS
RENFREWSHIRE
SCOTTISH BORDERS
SHETLAND
SOUTH AYRSHIRE
SOUTH LANARKSHIRE
STIRLING
WEST DUNBARTONSHIRE
WEST LOTHIAN
WESTERN ISLES (NA
   H-EILEANAN AN IAR)

DACORUM

ST. ALBANS

WELWYN
HATFIELD BR

THREE

RIVERS

WATFORD

HERTSMERE

Watford

CHILTERN

Barnet

ENF

BARNET

HARROW

Finchley

HARING

Harrow

Tott

SOUTH
BUCKS

HILLINGDON

BRENT

Hampstead

ISLINGTON

CAMDEN

Wembley

Uxbridge

Islingto

EALING

WESTMINSTER

Ealing

KENSINGTON &
CHELSEA

SLOUGH

HAMMERSMITH &
FULHAM

C

WINDSOR &
MAIDENHEAD

Heathrow
✈ Airport

HOUNSLOW

LAMBETH

Richmond
upon
Thames

Wandsworth

Brixto

Hounslow

SPELTHORNE

RICHMOND

WANDSWORTH

UPON THAMES

RUNNYMEDE

Wimbledon

Kingston
upon Thames

MERTON

KINGSTON
UPON THAMES

ELMBRIDGE

SUTTON

Sutton

EPSOM
& EWELL

Woking

WOKING

REIGATE &

GUILDFORD

MOLE VALLEY

BANSTEAD

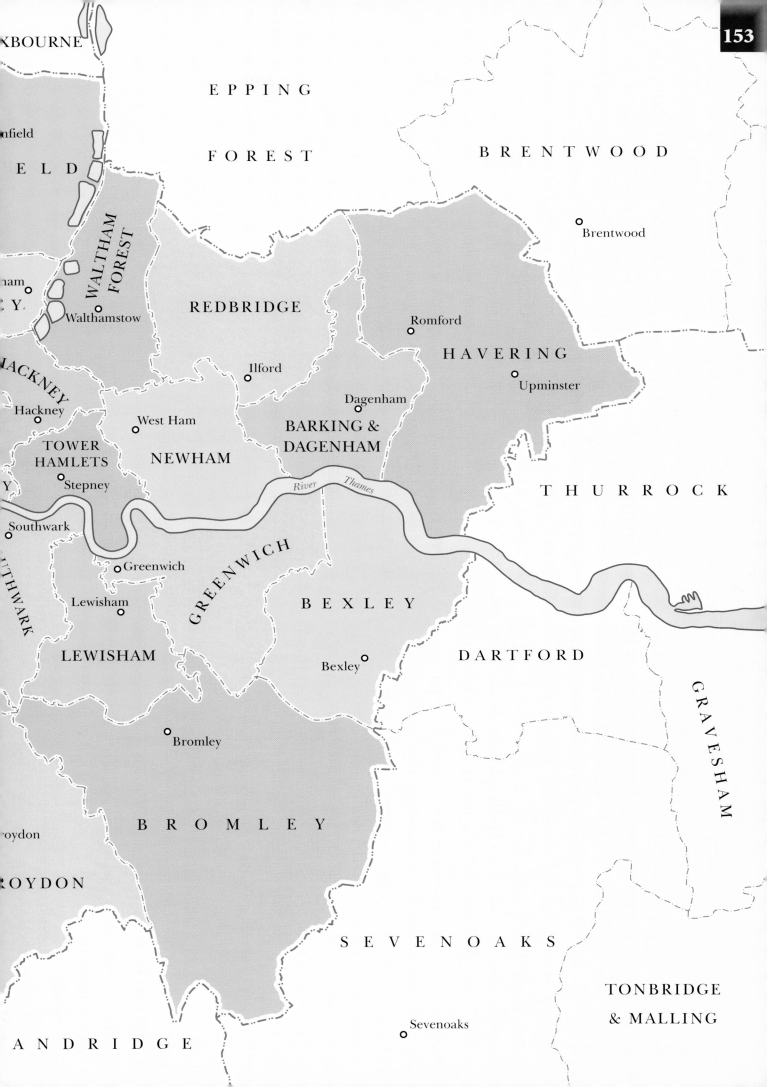

INDEX TO CENTRAL LONDON

General Abbreviations

All	Alley
Allot	Allotments
Amb	Ambulance
App	Approach
Arc	Arcade
Av/Ave	Avenue
Bdy	Broadway
Bk	Bank
Bldgs	Buildings
Boul	Boulevard
Bowl	Bowling
Br/Bri	Bridge
Bus	Business
C of E	Church of England
Cath	Cathedral
Cem	Cemetery
Cen	Central, Centre
Cft	Croft
Cfts	Crofts
Ch	Church
Chyd	Churchyard
Cin	Cinema
Circ	Circus
Cl/Clo	Close
Co	County
Coll	College
Comm	Community
Conv	Convent
Cor	Corner
Coron	Coroners
Cors	Corners
Cotts	Cottages
Cov	Covered
Crem	Crematorium
Cres	Crescent
Ct	Court
Cts	Courts
Ctyd	Courtyard
Dep	Depot
Dev	Development
Dr	Drive
Dws	Dwellings
E	East
Ed	Education
Elec	Electricity
Embk	Embankment
Est	Estate
Ex	Exchange
Exhib	Exhibition
FB	Footbridge
FC	Football Club
Fld	Field
Flds	Fields
Fm	Farm
Gall	Gallery
Gar	Garage
Gdn	Garden
Gdns	Gardens
Govt	Government
Gra	Grange
Grd	Ground
Grds	Grounds
Grn	Green
Grns	Greens
Gro	Grove
Gros	Groves
Gt	Great
Ho	House
Hos	Houses
Hosp	Hospital
Hts	Heights
Ind	Industrial
Int	International
Junct	Junction
La	Lane
Las	Lanes
Lib	Library
Lo	Lodge
Lwr	Lower
Mag	Magistrates
Mans	Mansions
Mem	Memorial
Mkt	Market
Mkts	Markets
Ms	Mews
Mt	Mount
Mus	Museum
N	North
NT	National Trust
Nat	National
PH	Public House
PO	Post Office
Par	Parade
Pas	Passage
Pav	Pavilion
Pk	Park
Pl	Place
Pol	Police
Prec	Precinct
Prim	Primary
Prom	Promenade
Pt	Point
Quad	Quadrant
RC	Roman Catholic
Rd	Road
Rds	Roads
Rec	Recreation
Res	Reservoir
Ri	Rise
S	South
Sch	School
Sec	Secondary
Shop	Shopping
Sq	Square
St.	Saint
St	Street
Sta	Station
Sts	Streets
Sub	Subway
Swim	Swimming
TA	Territorial Army
TH	Town Hall
Tenn	Tennis
Ter	Terrace
Thea	Theatre
Trd	Trading
Twr	Tower
Twrs	Towers
Uni	University
Vil	Villa, Villas
Vw	View
W	West
Wd	Wood
Wds	Woods
Wf	Wharf
Wk	Walk
Wks	Works
Yd	Yard

A

Abbey Gdns **NW8** 122 C4
Abbey La **E15** 125 N4
Abbey Orchard St **SW1** 127 K2
Abbey Rd **NW6** 122 B2
Abbey Rd **NW8** 122 C4
Abbey Rd Est **NW8** 122 B3
Abbey St **SE1** 128 C2
Abbeyfield Est **SE16** 128 G3
Abbeyfield Rd **SE16** 128 G3
Abbot St **E8** 124 D1
Abbots Manor Est **SW1** 127 H3
Abbot's Pl **NW6** 122 B3
Abbotsbury Cl **E15** 125 N4
Abbotsbury Ms **SE15** 128 G9
Abbotshade Rd **SE16** 125 H10
Abbotswood Rd **SE22** 128 C10
Abbott Rd **E14** 125 N7
Abchurch La **EC4** 124 B9
Aberavon Rd **E3** 125 J5
Abercorn Cl **NW8** 122 C5
Abercorn Pl **NW8** 122 C5
Abercorn Way **SE1** 128 E4
Abercrombie St **SW11** 126 E8
Aberdare Gdns **NW6** 122 B2
Aberdeen Pl **NW8** 122 D6
Aberdeen Ter **SE3** 129 P8
Aberdour St **SE1** 128 C3
Aberfeldy St **E14** 125 N8
Abingdon Rd **W8** 126 A2
Abingdon St **SW1** 127 L2
Abingdon Vil **W8** 126 A2
Abinger Gro **SE8** 129 K5
Ablett St **SE16** 128 G4
Acacia Cl **SE8** 129 J3
Acacia Pl **NW8** 122 D4
Acacia Rd **NW8** 122 D4
Acanthus Dr **SE1** 128 E4
Acanthus Rd **SW11** 126 G9
Acfold Rd **SW6** 126 B7
Achilles Cl **SE1** 128 E4
Achilles St **SE14** 129 J6
Ackmar Rd **SW6** 126 A7
Ackroyd Dr **E3** 125 K7
Acland Cres **SE5** 128 B10
Acol Rd **NW6** 122 A2
Acorn Wk **SE16** 125 J10
Acre Dr **SE22** 128 E10
Acre La **SW2** 127 L10
Acton Ms **E8** 124 D3
Acton St **WC1** 123 M5
Ada Gdns **E14** 125 P8
Ada Pl **E2** 124 E3
Ada Rd **SE5** 128 C6
Ada St **E8** 124 F3
Adam & Eve Ms **W8** 126 A2
Adam St **WC2** 123 L9
Adams Row **W1** 122 G9
Adamson Rd **NW3** 122 D2
Adderley St **E14** 125 N8
Addington Rd **E3** 125 L5
Addington Sq **SE5** 128 A5
Adelaide Av **SE4** 129 K10
Adelaide Rd **NW3** 122 D2
Adelina Gro **E1** 124 G7
Adeline Pl **WC1** 123 K7
Adler St **E1** 124 E8
Admiral Pl **SE16** 125 J10
Admiral Sq **SW10** 126 D7
Admiral St **SE8** 129 L7
Admiral Wk **W9** 122 A7
Admirals Way **E14** 129 L1
Adolphus St **SE8** 129 K6
Adpar St **W2** 122 D6
Adrian Ms **SW10** 126 B5
Adys Rd **SE15** 128 D9
Afghan Rd **SW11** 126 E8
Agar Gro **NW1** 123 J2
Agar Gro Est **NW1** 123 K2
Agar Pl **NW1** 123 J2
Agar St **WC2** 123 L9
Agdon St **EC1** 123 P6
Agnes St **E14** 125 K8
Ailsa St **E14** 125 N7
Ainger Rd **NW3** 122 F2
Ainsdale Dr **SE1** 128 E4
Ainsley St **E2** 124 F5
Ainsty Est **SE16** 129 H1
Ainsworth Rd **E9** 124 G2
Ainsworth Way **NW8** 122 C3
Air St **W1** 123 J9
Airdrie Cl **N1** 123 M2
Airlie Gdns **W8** 126 A1
Akerman Rd **SW9** 127 P8
Albany Mans **SW11** 126 E6
Albany Rd **SE5** 128 B5
Albany St **NW1** 123 H4
Albatross Way **SE16** 129 H1
Albemarle St **W1** 123 H9
Albert Av **SW8** 127 M6
Albert Br **SW3** 126 E5
Albert Br **SW11** 126 E5
Albert Br Rd **SW11** 126 E6
Albert Ct **SW7** 126 D1
Albert Embk **SE1** 127 L4
Albert Gdns **E1** 125 H8
Albert Gate **SW1** 126 F1
Albert Pl **W8** 126 B1
Albert Sq **SW8** 127 M6
Albert St **NW1** 123 H3
Albert Ter **NW1** 122 G3
Albert Way **SE15** 128 F6
Alberta Est **SE17** 127 P4
Alberta St **SE17** 127 P4
Albion Av **SW8** 127 K8
Albion Dr **E8** 124 D2
Albion Est **SE16** 129 H1
Albion Hill **SE13** 129 M8
Albion Ms **N1** 123 N3
Albion Ms **W2** 122 E8
Albion Pl **EC1** 123 P7
Albion Sq **E8** 124 D2
Albion St **SE16** 128 G1
Albion St **W2** 122 E8
Albion Ter **E8** 124 D2
Albion Way **SE13** 129 N10
Albrighton Rd **SE22** 128 C9
Albury St **SE8** 129 L5
Albyn Rd **SE8** 129 L7
Aldbridge St **SE17** 128 C4
Aldebert Ter **SW8** 127 L6
Aldenham St **NW1** 123 K4
Alder Cl **SE15** 128 D5
Aldermanbury **EC2** 124 A8
Alderney Rd **E1** 125 H6
Alderney St **SW1** 127 H3
Aldersgate St **EC1** 124 A7
Alderton Rd **SE24** 128 A9
Aldford St **W1** 122 G10
Aldgate **EC3** 124 D8
Aldgate High St **EC3** 124 D8
Aldsworth Cl **W9** 122 B6
Aldwych **WC2** 123 M9
Alexander Pl **SW7** 126 E3
Alexander Sq **SW3** 126 E3
Alexander St **W2** 122 A8
Alexandra Av **SW11** 126 G7
Alexandra Cotts **SE14** 129 K7
Alexandra Pl **NW8** 122 C3
Alexandra Rd **NW8** 122 C2
Alexandra St **SE14** 129 J6
Alexis St **SE16** 128 E3
Alford Rd **SW8** 127 K7
Alfred Ms **W1** 123 K7
Alfred Pl **WC1** 123 K7
Alfred Rd **W2** 122 A7
Alfred St **E3** 125 K5
Alfreda St **SW11** 127 H7
Algernon Rd **NW6** 122 A3
Algernon Rd **SE13** 129 M10
Algiers Rd **SE13** 129 L10
Alice La **E3** 125 K3
Alice St **SE1** 128 C2
Alie St **E1** 124 D8
Aliwal Rd **SW11** 126 E10
All Saints St **N1** 123 M4
Allardyce St **SW4** 127 M10
Allen Edwards Dr **SW8** 127 L7
Allen Rd **E3** 125 K4
Allen St **W8** 126 A2
Allensbury Pl **NW1** 123 K2
Allingham St **N1** 124 A4
Allington St **SW1** 127 H2
Allitsen Rd **NW8** 122 E4
Alloa Rd **SE8** 129 H4
Alloway Rd **E3** 125 J5
Allsop Pl **NW1** 122 F6
Alma Gro **SE1** 128 D3
Alma Sq **NW8** 122 C5
Alma St **E15** 125 P1
Alma St **NW5** 123 H1
Almeida St **N1** 123 P2
Almeric Rd **SW11** 126 F10
Almond Cl **SE15** 128 E8
Almond Rd **SE16** 128 F3
Almorah Rd **N1** 124 B2
Alpha Gro **E14** 129 L1
Alpha Pl **NW6** 122 A4
Alpha Pl **SW3** 126 E5
Alpha Rd **SE14** 129 K7
Alpha St **SE15** 128 E8
Alpine Gro **E9** 124 G2
Alpine Rd **SE16** 128 G3
Alsace Rd **SE17** 128 C4
Alscot Rd **SE1** 128 D3
Alscot Way **SE1** 128 D3
Altenburg Gdns **SW11** 126 F10
Althea St **SW6** 126 B9
Alton St **E14** 125 M7
Alverton St **SE8** 129 K4
Alvey Est **SE17** 128 C3
Alvey St **SE17** 128 C4
Alwyne Pl **N1** 124 A1
Alwyne Rd **N1** 124 A2
Alwyne Sq **N1** 124 A1
Alwyne Vil **N1** 123 P2
Alzette Ho **E2** 125 H5
Ambassador Sq **E14** 129 M3
Ambergate St **SE17** 127 P4
Amberley Rd **W9** 122 A7
Ambrosden Av **SW1** 127 J2
Ambrose Ms **SW11** 126 E8
Ambrose St **SE16** 128 F3
Amelia St **SE17** 127 P4
Amersham Gro **SE14** 129 K6
Amersham Rd **SE14** 129 K7
Amersham Vale **SE14** 129 K6
Amiel St **E1** 124 G6
Amies St **SW11** 126 F9
Amott Rd **SE15** 128 E9
Amoy Pl **E14** 125 L8
Ampton St **WC1** 123 M5
Amsterdam Rd **E14** 129 N2
Amwell St **EC1** 123 N5
Anchor St **SE16** 128 F3
Andalus Rd **SW9** 127 L9
Anderson Rd **E9** 125 H1
Anderson St **SW3** 126 F4
Anderton Cl **SE5** 128 B9
Andover Pl **NW6** 122 B4
Andrew St **E14** 125 N8
Andrew's Rd **E8** 124 F3
Anerley St **SW11** 126 F8
Angel Ct **EC2** 124 B8
Angel La **E15** 125 P1
Angel Ms **N1** 123 N4
Angel St **EC1** 124 A8
Angell Pk Gdns **SW9** 127 N9
Angell Rd **SW9** 127 N9
Angler's La **NW5** 123 H1
Anglia Ho **E14** 125 J8
Anglo Rd **E3** 125 K4
Angrave Ct **E8** 124 D3
Angus St **SE14** 129 J6
Anhalt Rd **SW11** 126 E6
Ann La **SW10** 126 D6
Ann Moss Way **SE16** 128 G2
Anna Cl **E8** 124 D3
Annabel Cl **E14** 125 M8
Annie Besant Cl **E3** 125 K3
Annis Rd **E9** 125 J1
Ansdell Rd **SE15** 128 G8
Ansdell St **W8** 126 B2
Anselm Rd **SW6** 126 A5
Anstey Rd **SE15** 128 E9
Antill Rd **E3** 125 J5
Antill Ter **E1** 125 H8
Antrim Gro **NW3** 122 F1
Antrim Mans **NW3** 122 E1
Antrim Rd **NW3** 122 F1
Apollo Pl **SW10** 126 D6
Appleby Rd **E8** 124 E2
Appleby St **E2** 124 D4
Appold St **EC2** 124 C7
Approach Rd **E2** 124 G4
Aquila St **NW8** 122 D4
Arabin Rd **SE4** 129 J10
Arbery Rd **E3** 125 J5
Arbour Sq **E1** 125 H8
Arbuthnot Rd **SE14** 129 H8
Arbutus St **E8** 124 C3
Arcadia St **E14** 125 L8
Arch St **SE1** 128 A2
Archangel St **SE16** 129 H1
Archery Cl **W2** 122 E8
Archibald Ms **W1** 122 G10
Archibald St **E3** 125 L5
Arden Cres **E14** 129 L3
Arden Est **N1** 124 C4
Ardleigh Rd **N1** 124 B1
Argon Ms **SW6** 126 A6
Argyle Rd **E1** 125 H6
Argyle Sq **WC1** 123 L5
Argyle St **WC1** 123 L5
Argyle Way **SE16** 128 E4
Argyll Rd **W8** 126 A1
Argyll St **W1** 123 J8
Arica Rd **SE4** 129 J10
Ariel Rd **NW6** 122 A1
Aristotle Rd **SW4** 127 K9
Arklow Rd **SE14** 129 K5
Arlesford Rd **SW9** 127 L9
Arlington Av **N1** 124 A4
Arlington Lo **SW2** 127 M10
Arlington Rd **NW1** 123 H3
Arlington Sq **N1** 124 A3
Arlington St **SW1** 123 J10
Arlington Way **EC1** 123 N5
Armada St **SE8** 129 L5
Armadale Rd **SW6** 126 A6
Armagh Rd **E3** 125 K3
Armoury Rd **SE8** 129 M8
Armstrong Rd **SW7** 126 D2
Arne St **WC2** 123 L8
Arnhem Pl **E14** 129 L2
Arnold Circ **E2** 124 D5
Arnold Est **SE1** 128 D1
Arnold Rd **E3** 125 L5
Arnould Av **SE5** 128 B10
Arnside St **SE17** 128 A5
Arran Wk **N1** 124 A2
Arrow Rd **E3** 125 M5
Artesian Rd **W2** 122 A8
Artillery La **E1** 124 C7
Artillery Row **SW1** 127 K2
Arundel Pl **N1** 123 N1
Arundel Sq **N7** 123 N1
Arundel St **WC2** 123 M9
Ascalon St **SW8** 127 J6
Ash Gro **E8** 124 F3
Ashbridge St **NW8** 122 E6
Ashburn Gdns **SW7** 126 C3
Ashburn Pl **SW7** 126 C3
Ashburnham Gro **SE10** 129 M6
Ashburnham Pl **SE10** 129 M6
Ashburnham Retreat **SE10** 129 M6
Ashburnham Rd **SW10** 126 C6
Ashbury Rd **SW11** 126 F9
Ashby Gro **N1** 124 A2
Ashby Ms **SE4** 129 K8
Ashby Rd **SE4** 129 K8
Ashcombe St **SW6** 126 B8
Ashcroft Rd **E3** 125 J5
Ashdene **SE15** 128 F7
Ashdown Wk **E14** 129 L3
Asher Way **E1** 124 E9
Ashfield St **E1** 124 F7
Ashland Pl **W1** 122 G7
Ashley Cres **SW11** 126 G9
Ashley Gdns **SW1** 127 J2
Ashley Pl **SW1** 127 J2
Ashmead Rd **SE8** 129 L8
Ashmere Gro **SW2** 127 L10
Ashmill St **NW1** 122 E7
Ashmole Pl **SW8** 127 M5
Ashmole St **SW8** 127 M5
Ashton St **E14** 125 N9
Ashwin St **E8** 124 D1
Ashworth Rd **W9** 122 B5
Aspen Way **E14** 125 M9
Aspinall Rd **SE4** 129 H9
Aspinden Rd **SE16** 128 F3
Assembly Pas **E1** 124 G7
Astbury Rd **SE15** 128 G7
Aste St **E14** 129 N1
Astell St **SW3** 126 E4
Astle St **SW11** 126 G8
Aston St **E14** 125 J8
Astoria Wk **SW9** 127 N9
Astwood Ms **SW7** 126 B3
Asylum Rd **SE15** 128 F6
Athelstane Gro **E3** 125 K4
Atherfold Rd **SW9** 127 L9
Atherstone Ms **SW7** 126 C3
Atherton St **SW11** 126 E8
Athlone St **NW5** 122 G1
Athol Sq **E14** 125 N8
Atlantic Rd **SW9** 127 N10
Atlas Ms **N7** 123 M1
Atley Rd **E3** 125 L3
Atterbury St **SW1** 127 L3
Auckland Rd **SW11** 126 E10
Auden Pl **NW1** 122 G3
Audley Cl **SW11** 126 G9
Audrey St **E2** 124 E4
Augusta St **E14** 125 M8
Augustus St **NW1** 123 H4
Aulton Pl **SE11** 127 N4
Austen Ho **NW6** 122 A5
Austin Friars **EC2** 124 B8
Austin Rd **SW11** 126 G7
Austin St **E2** 124 D5
Austral St **SE11** 127 P3
Autumn St **E3** 125 L3
Avalon Rd **SW6** 126 B7
Ave Maria La **EC4** 123 P8
Aveline St **SE11** 127 N4
Avenue, The **SE10** 129 P6
Avenue Cl **NW8** 122 E3
Avenue Rd **NW3** 122 D2
Avenue Rd **NW8** 122 D3
Avery Row **W1** 123 H9
Avignon Rd **SE4** 129 H9
Avis Sq **E1** 125 H8
Avon Rd **SE4** 129 L9
Avondale Ri **SE15** 128 D9
Avondale Sq **SE1** 128 E4
Avonley Rd **SE14** 128 G6
Avonmouth St **SE1** 128 A2
Aybrook St **W1** 122 G7
Aylesbury Rd **SE17** 128 B4
Aylesbury St **EC1** 123 P6
Aylesford St **SW1** 127 K4
Aylward St **E1** 124 G8
Aylwyn Est **SE1** 128 C2
Ayres St **SE1** 128 A1
Aytoun Pl **SW9** 127 M8
Aytoun Rd **SW9** 127 M8

Bronti Cl

Bronti Cl **SE17** 128 A4
Bronze St **SE8** 129 L6
Brook Dr **SE11** 127 N3
Brook Gate **W1** 122 F9
Brook St **W1** 123 H8
Brook St **W2** 122 D9
Brookbank Rd **SE13** 129 L9
Brooke St **EC1** 123 N7
Brookfield Rd **E9** 125 J1
Brookmill Rd **SE8** 129 L7
Brook's Ms **W1** 123 H9
Brooksbank St **E9** 125 H1
Brooksby St **N1** 123 N2
Broome Way **SE5** 128 A6
Broomfield St **E14** 125 L7
Broomgrove Rd **SW9** 127 M8
Broomhouse La **SW6** 126 A8
Broomhouse Rd **SW6** 126 A8
Brougham Rd **E8** 124 E3
Brougham St **SW11** 126 F8
Broughton Dr **SW9** 127 N10
Broughton Rd **SW6** 126 B8
Broughton St **SW8** 126 G8
Brown Hart Gdns **W1** 122 G9
Brown St **W1** 122 F8
Brownfield St **E14** 125 M8
Browning Est **SE17** 128 A4
Browning St **SE17** 128 A4
Brownlow Ms **WC1** 123 M6
Brownlow Rd **E8** 124 D3
Brown's Bldgs **EC3** 124 C8
Broxwood Way **NW8** 122 E3
Bruce Rd **E3** 125 M5
Brune St **E1** 124 D7
Brunel Est **W2** 122 A7
Brunel Rd **SE16** 128 G1
Brunswick Ct **SE1** 128 C1
Brunswick Gdns **W8** 122 A10
Brunswick Pk **SE5** 128 B7
Brunswick Pl **N1** 124 B5
Brunswick Quay **SE16** 129 H2
Brunswick Sq **WC1** 123 L6
Brunswick Vil **SE5** 128 C7
Brunton Pl **E14** 125 J8
Brushfield St **E1** 124 C7
Brussels Rd **SW11** 126 D10
Bruton La **W1** 123 H9
Bruton Pl **W1** 123 H9
Bruton St **W1** 123 H9
Bryan Rd **SE16** 129 K1
Bryanston Pl **W1** 122 F7
Bryanston Sq **W1** 122 F7
Bryanston St **W1** 122 F8
Bryant Ct **E2** 124 D4
Bryant St **E15** 125 P2
Brymay Cl **E3** 125 L4
Brynmaer Rd **SW11** 126 F7
Buchan Rd **SE15** 128 G9
Buck St **NW1** 123 H2
Buckfast St **E2** 124 E5
Buckhurst St **E1** 124 F6
Buckingham Gate **SW1** 127 J2
Buckingham Palace Rd **SW1** 127 H3
Buckingham Rd **N1** 124 C1
Buckland Cres **NW3** 122 D2
Buckland St **N1** 124 B4
Bucklersbury **EC4** 124 B8
Buckmaster Rd **SW11** 126 E10
Bucknall St **WC2** 123 K8
Bucknell Cl **SW2** 127 M10
Buckner Rd **SW2** 127 M10
Buckters Rents **SE16** 125 J10
Budge's Wk **W2** 122 C9
Bulinga St **SW1** 127 K3
Bullards Pl **E2** 125 H5
Bullen St **SW11** 126 E8
Buller Cl **SE15** 128 E6
Bullivant St **E14** 125 N9
Bulmer Pl **W11** 122 A10
Bulstrode St **W1** 122 G8
Bunhill Row **EC1** 124 B6
Bunhouse Pl **SW1** 126 G4
Bunning Way **N7** 123 L2
Burbage Cl **SE1** 128 B2
Burcham St **E14** 125 M8
Burchell Rd **SE15** 128 F7
Burder Cl **N1** 124 C1
Burdett Rd **E3** 125 K6
Burdett Rd **E14** 125 K6
Burford Rd **E15** 125 P2
Burge St **SE1** 128 B2
Burgess St **E14** 125 L7
Burgh St **N1** 123 P4
Burgos Gro **SE10** 129 M7
Burgoyne Rd **SW9** 127 M9
Burlington Arc **W1** 123 J9
Burlington Gdns **W1** 123 J9
Burnaby St **SW10** 126 C6
Burne St **NW1** 122 E7
Burney St **SE10** 129 N6
Burnham **NW3** 122 E2
Burnham St **E2** 124 G5
Burnley Rd **SW9** 127 M8
Burns Rd **SW11** 126 F8
Burnsall St **SW3** 126 E4
Burnside Cl **SE16** 125 H10
Burnthwaite Rd **SW6** 126 A6
Burr Cl **E1** 124 E10
Burrell St **SE1** 123 P10
Burrells Wf Sq **E14** 129 M4
Burrow Rd **SE22** 128 C10
Burslem St **E1** 124 E8
Burton La **SW9** 127 N8
Burton Rd **SW9** 127 P8
Burton St **WC1** 123 K5
Burwell Wk **E3** 125 L6
Burwood Pl **W2** 122 E8
Bury Pl **WC1** 123 L7
Bury St **EC3** 124 C8
Bury St **SW1** 123 J10
Bury Wk **SW3** 126 E4
Busby Pl **NW5** 123 K1
Bush Rd **E8** 124 F3
Bush Rd **SE8** 129 H3
Bushberry Rd **E9** 125 J1
Bushey Hill Rd **SE5** 128 C7
Bushwood Dr **SE1** 128 D3
Butcher Row **E1** 125 H9
Butcher Row **E14** 125 H9
Bute St **SW7** 126 D3
Butlers Wf **SE1** 124 D10
Buttermere Wk **E8** 124 D1
Buttesland St **N1** 124 B5
Buxted Rd **E8** 124 D2
Buxted Rd **SE22** 128 C10
Buxton St **E1** 124 D6
Byam St **SW6** 126 C8
Byfield Cl **SE16** 129 J1
Bygrove St **E14** 125 M8
Byng Pl **WC1** 123 K6
Byng St **E14** 129 L1
Byron Cl **E8** 124 E3
Bythorn St **SW9** 127 M9
Byward St **EC3** 124 C9
Bywater Pl **SE16** 125 J10
Bywater St **SW3** 126 F4

C

Cabbell St **NW1** 122 E7
Cable St **E1** 124 E9
Cabot Sq **E14** 125 L10
Cabul Rd **SW11** 126 E8
Cade Rd **SE10** 129 P7
Cadet Dr **SE1** 128 D3
Cadiz St **SE17** 128 A4
Cadogan Gdns **SW3** 126 F3
Cadogan Gate **SW1** 126 F3
Cadogan La **SW1** 126 G2
Cadogan Pl **SW1** 126 F2
Cadogan Sq **SW1** 126 F2
Cadogan St **SW3** 126 F3
Cadogan Ter **E9** 125 K1
Cahir St **E14** 129 M3
Calabria Rd **N5** 123 P1
Calais St **SE5** 127 P7
Caldecot Rd **SE5** 128 A8
Caldwell St **SW9** 127 M6
Cale St **SW3** 126 E4
Caledonia St **N1** 123 L4
Caledonian Rd **N1** 123 M4
Caledonian Wf **E14** 129 P3
Callendar Rd **SW7** 126 D2
Callow St **SW3** 126 D5
Calshot St **N1** 123 M4
Calthorpe St **WC1** 123 M6
Calvert Av **E2** 124 C5
Calvin St **E1** 124 D6
Calypso Way **SE16** 129 K2
Cam Rd **E15** 125 P3
Camberwell Ch St **SE5** 128 B7
Camberwell Glebe **SE5** 128 B7
Camberwell Grn **SE5** 128 B7
Camberwell Gro **SE5** 128 B7
Camberwell New Rd **SE5** 127 N6
Camberwell Rd **SE5** 128 A5
Camberwell Sta Rd **SE5** 128 A7
Cambria Rd **SE5** 128 A9
Cambria St **SW6** 126 B6
Cambridge Av **NW6** 122 A4
Cambridge Circ **WC2** 123 K8
Cambridge Cres **E2** 124 F4
Cambridge Gdns **NW6** 122 A4
Cambridge Heath Rd **E1** 124 F4
Cambridge Heath Rd **E2** 124 F4
Cambridge Pl **W8** 126 B1
Cambridge Rd **NW6** 122 A5
Cambridge Rd **SW11** 126 F7
Cambridge Sq **W2** 122 E8
Cambridge St **SW1** 127 H4
Camden High St **NW1** 123 H3
Camden Ms **NW1** 123 K1
Camden Pk Rd **NW1** 123 K1
Camden Pas **N1** 123 P3
Camden Rd **NW1** 123 J2
Camden Sq **NW1** 123 K1
Camden St **NW1** 123 J2
Camden Wk **N1** 123 P3
Camdenhurst St **E14** 125 J8
Camellia St **SW8** 127 L6
Camera Pl **SW10** 126 D5
Camilla Rd **SE16** 128 F3
Camlet St **E2** 124 D6
Camley St **NW1** 123 K2
Camomile St **EC3** 124 C8
Campana Rd **SW6** 126 A7
Campbell Rd **E3** 125 L5
Campden Gro **W8** 126 A1
Campden Hill Gdns **W8** 122 A10
Campden Hill Rd **W8** 122 A10
Campden St **W8** 122 A10
Camplin St **SE14** 129 H6
Canada Est **SE16** 128 G2
Canada Sq **E14** 125 M10
Canada St **SE16** 129 H1
Canal App **SE8** 129 J4
Canal Cl **E1** 125 J6
Canal Gro **SE15** 128 E5
Canal Path **E2** 124 D3
Canal Rd **E3** 125 J6
Canal St **SE5** 128 B5
Canal Wk **N1** 124 B3
Cancell Rd **SW9** 127 N7
Candahar Rd **SW11** 126 E8
Candy St **E3** 125 K3
Canfield Gdns **NW6** 122 C2
Canning Cross **SE5** 128 C8
Canning Pas **W8** 126 C2
Canning Pl **W8** 126 C2
Cannon Dr **E14** 125 L9
Cannon St **EC4** 124 A8
Cannon St Rd **E1** 124 F8
Cannon Wf Business Cen **SE8** 129 J3
Canon Beck Rd **SE16** 128 G1
Canon Row **SW1** 127 L1
Canon St **N1** 124 A3
Canonbury Cres **N1** 124 A2
Canonbury Gro **N1** 124 A2
Canonbury La **N1** 123 P2
Canonbury Pk N **N1** 124 A1
Canonbury Pk S **N1** 124 A1
Canonbury Pl **N1** 123 P1
Canonbury Rd **N1** 123 P1
Canonbury Sq **N1** 123 P2
Canonbury St **N1** 124 A2
Canonbury Vil **N1** 123 P2
Canrobert St **E2** 124 F5
Cantelowes Rd **NW1** 123 K1
Canterbury Cres **SW9** 127 N9
Canterbury Pl **SE17** 127 P3
Canterbury Rd **NW6** 122 A4
Canterbury Ter **NW6** 122 A4
Canton St **E14** 125 L8
Cantrell Rd **E3** 125 K6
Canute Gdns **SE16** 129 H3
Capland St **NW8** 122 D6
Capper St **WC1** 123 J6
Capstan Rd **SE8** 129 K3
Capstan Sq **E14** 129 N1
Capstan Way **SE16** 125 J10
Caradoc Cl **W2** 122 A8
Carbis Rd **E14** 125 K8
Carburton St **W1** 123 H7
Carden Rd **SE15** 128 F9
Cardigan Rd **E3** 125 K4
Cardigan St **SE11** 127 N4
Cardinal Bourne St **SE1** 128 B2
Cardine Ms **SE15** 128 F6
Cardington St **NW1** 123 J5
Carew St **SE5** 128 A8
Carey Gdns **SW8** 127 J7
Carey St **WC2** 123 M8
Carlile Cl **E3** 125 K4
Carlisle La **SE1** 127 M2
Carlisle Ms **NW8** 122 D7
Carlisle Pl **SW1** 127 J2
Carlos Pl **W1** 122 G9
Carlton Ct **SW9** 127 P7
Carlton Gdns **SW1** 123 K10
Carlton Gro **SE15** 128 F7
Carlton Hill **NW8** 122 B4
Carlton Ho Ter **SW1** 123 K10
Carlton Twr Pl **SW1** 126 F2
Carlton Vale **NW6** 122 B4
Carlyle Sq **SW3** 126 D4
Carmelite St **EC4** 123 N9
Carmen St **E14** 125 M8
Carnaby St **W1** 123 J8
Carnegie St **N1** 123 M3
Carnoustie Dr **N1** 123 M2
Carnwath Rd **SW6** 126 A9
Carol St **NW1** 123 J3
Caroline Gdns **SE15** 128 F6
Caroline Pl **SW11** 126 G8
Caroline Pl **W2** 122 B9
Caroline St **E1** 125 H8
Caroline Ter **SW1** 126 G3
Carpenters Pl **SW4** 127 K10
Carpenters Rd **E15** 125 M1
Carr St **E14** 125 J7
Carriage Dr E **SW11** 126 G6
Carriage Dr N **SW11** 126 G5
Carriage Dr S **SW11** 126 F7
Carriage Dr W **SW11** 126 F6
Carron Cl **E14** 125 M8
Carroun Rd **SW8** 127 M6
Carter La **EC4** 123 P8
Carter Pl **SE17** 128 A4
Carter St **SE17** 128 A5
Carteret St **SW1** 127 K1
Carteret Way **SE8** 129 J3
Carthusian St **EC1** 124 A7
Cartier Circle **E14** 125 M10
Carting La **WC2** 123 L9
Cartwright Gdns **WC1** 123 L5
Cartwright St **E1** 124 D9
Casella Rd **SE14** 129 H6
Caspian St **SE5** 128 B6
Cassidy Rd **SW6** 126 A6
Cassland Rd **E9** 124 G2
Casson St **E1** 124 E7
Castellain Rd **W9** 122 B6
Casterbridge **NW6** 122 B3
Castle La **SW1** 127 J2
Castle Pl **NW1** 123 H1
Castle Rd **NW1** 123 H1
Castlebrook Cl **SE11** 127 P3
Castlehaven Rd **NW1** 123 H2
Castlemaine Twr **SW11** 126 F7
Castor La **E14** 125 M9
Caterham Rd **SE13** 129 N9
Catesby St **SE17** 128 B3
Cathay St **SE16** 128 F1
Cathcart Rd **SW10** 126 C5
Cathcart St **NW5** 123 H1
Cathedral St **SE1** 124 B10
Catherine Gro **SE10** 129 M7
Catherine Pl **SW1** 127 J2
Catherine St **WC2** 123 M9
Catlin St **SE16** 128 E4
Cato Rd **SW4** 127 K9
Cato St **W1** 122 E7
Cator St **SE15** 128 D5
Catton St **WC1** 123 M7
Caulfield Rd **SE15** 128 F8
Causeway, The **SW18** 126 B10
Causton St **SW1** 127 K3
Cavell St **E1** 124 F7
Cavendish Av **NW8** 122 D4
Cavendish Cl **NW8** 122 D5
Cavendish Pl **W1** 123 H8
Cavendish Sq **W1** 123 H8
Cavendish St **N1** 124 B4
Caversham Rd **NW5** 123 J1
Caversham St **SW3** 126 F5
Caxton Gro **E3** 125 L5
Caxton St **SW1** 127 J2
Cedar Ct **E8** 124 D2
Cedar Way **NW1** 123 K2
Cedarne Rd **SW6** 126 B6
Cedars Rd **SW4** 127 H9
Celandine Cl **E14** 125 L7
Celestial Gdns **SE13** 129 P10
Celtic St **E14** 125 M7
Centaur St **SE1** 127 M2
Central Av **SW11** 126 F6
Central Mkts **EC1** 123 P7
Central St **EC1** 124 A5
Centre St **E2** 124 F4
Centrepoint **WC2** 123 K8
Centurion Cl **N7** 123 M2
Cephas Av **E1** 124 G6
Cephas St **E1** 124 G6
Cerise Rd **SE15** 128 E7
Chadbourn St **E14** 125 M7
Chadwell St **EC1** 123 N5
Chadwick Rd **SE15** 128 D8
Chadwick St **SW1** 127 K2
Chagford St **NW1** 122 F6
Chalbury Wk **N1** 123 M4
Chalcot Cres **NW1** 122 F3
Chalcot Gdns **NW3** 122 F1
Chalcot Rd **NW1** 122 G2
Chalcot Sq **NW1** 122 G2
Chalk Fm Rd **NW1** 122 G2
Chalsey Rd **SE4** 129 K10
Chalton St **NW1** 123 K4
Chamber St **E1** 124 D9
Chambers St **SE16** 128 E1
Chambord St **E2** 124 D5
Champion Gro **SE5** 128 B9
Champion Hill **SE5** 128 B9
Champion Hill Est **SE5** 128 C9
Champion Pk **SE5** 128 B8
Chance St **E1** 124 D6
Chance St **E2** 124 D6
Chancel St **SE1** 123 P10
Chancery La **WC2** 123 N7
Chandler Way **SE15** 128 D6
Chandlers Ms **E14** 129 L1
Chandos Pl **WC2** 123 L9
Chandos St **W1** 123 H7
Channelsea Rd **E15** 125 P3
Chant Sq **E15** 125 P2
Chant St **E15** 125 P2
Chantrey Rd **SW9** 127 M9
Chantry St **N1** 123 P3
Chapel Ho St **E14** 129 M4
Chapel Mkt **N1** 123 N4
Chapel Pl **W1** 123 H8
Chapel Side **W2** 122 B9
Chapel St **NW1** 122 E7
Chapel St **SW1** 126 G2
Chaplin Cl **SE1** 127 N1
Chapman Rd **E9** 125 K1
Chapman St **E1** 124 F9
Chapter Rd **SE17** 127 P4
Chapter St **SW1** 127 K3
Charing Cross Rd **WC2** 123 K8
Charlbert St **NW8** 122 E4
Charles Barry Cl **SW4** 127 J9
Charles Coveney Rd **SE15** 128 D7
Charles Dickens Ho **E2** 124 F5
Charles II St **SW1** 123 K10
Charles Sq **N1** 124 B5
Charles St **W1** 123 H10
Charleston St **SE17** 128 A3
Charlotte Despard Av **SW11** 126 G7
Charlotte Rd **EC2** 124 C6
Charlotte St **W1** 123 J7
Charlotte Ter **N1** 123 M3
Charlton Pl **N1** 123 P4
Charlwood Pl **SW1** 127 J3
Charlwood St **SW1** 127 J4
Charnwood Gdns **E14** 129 L3
Charrington St **NW1** 123 K4
Chart St **N1** 124 B5
Charterhouse Sq **EC1** 123 P7
Charterhouse St **EC1** 123 P7
Chase, The **SW4** 127 H9
Chaseley St **E14** 125 J8
Chatfield Rd **SW11** 126 C9
Chatham Pl **E9** 124 G1
Chatham St **SE17** 128 B3
Chatsworth Ct **W8** 126 A3
Chaucer Dr **SE1** 128 D3
Cheapside **EC2** 124 A8
Chelsea Br **SW1** 127 H5
Chelsea Br **SW8** 127 H5
Chelsea Br Rd **SW1** 126 G4
Chelsea Embk **SW3** 126 E5
Chelsea Harbour **SW10** 126 D7
Chelsea Harbour Dr **SW10** 126 C7
Chelsea Manor Gdns **SW3** 126 E5
Chelsea Manor St **SW3** 126 E4
Chelsea Pk Gdns **SW3** 126 D5
Chelsea Sq **SW3** 126 D4
Chelsea Wf **SW10** 126 D6
Chelsham Rd **SW4** 127 K9
Cheltenham Rd **SE15** 128 G10
Cheltenham Ter **SW3** 126 F4
Chelwood Wk **SE4** 129 J10
Cheney Rd **NW1** 123 L4
Chenies Pl **NW1** 123 K4
Chenies St **WC1** 123 K7
Cheniston Gdns **W8** 126 B2
Chepstow Cres **W11** 122 A9
Chepstow Pl **W2** 122 A8
Chepstow Rd **W2** 122 A8
Chepstow Way **SE15** 128 D7
Cherbury St **N1** 124 B4
Cherry Gdn St **SE16** 128 F1
Cherrywood Cl **E3** 125 J5
Cheryls Cl **SW6** 126 B7
Chesham Ms **SW1** 126 G2
Chesham Pl **SW1** 126 G2
Chesham St **SW1** 126 G2
Cheshire Cl **SE4** 129 K8
Cheshire St **E2** 124 D6
Chesil Ct **E2** 124 F4
Chesney St **SW11** 126 G7
Chester Cl **SW1** 126 G1
Chester Ct **SE5** 128 B6
Chester Gate **NW1** 123 H5
Chester Ms **SW1** 127 H2
Chester Rd **NW1** 122 G5
Chester Row **SW1** 126 G3
Chester Sq **SW1** 127 H2
Chester St **E2** 124 E6
Chester St **SW1** 126 G2
Chester Way **SE11** 127 N3
Chesterfield Gdns **W1** 123 H10
Chesterfield Hill **W1** 123 H9
Chesterfield St **W1** 123 H10
Chesterfield Wk **SE10** 129 P7
Chesterfield Way **SE15** 128 G6
Chestnuts, The **SE14** 129 K7
Cheval Pl **SW7** 126 E2
Cheval St **E14** 129 L2
Cheyne Gdns **SW3** 126 E5
Cheyne Ms **SW3** 126 E5
Cheyne Pl **SW3** 126 F5
Cheyne Row **SW3** 126 E5
Cheyne Wk **SW3** 126 E5
Cheyne Wk **SW10** 126 D6
Chicheley St **SE1** 127 M1
Chichester Rd **NW6** 122 A4
Chichester Rd **W2** 122 B7
Chichester St **SW1** 127 J4
Chichester Way **E14** 129 P3
Chicksand St **E1** 124 D7
Chiddingstone St **SW6** 126 A8
Childeric Rd **SE14** 129 J6
Childers St **SE8** 129 J5
Child's Pl **SW5** 126 A3
Child's St **SW5** 126 A3
Chiltern Rd **E3** 125 L6
Chiltern St **W1** 122 G7
Chilton Gro **SE8** 129 H3
Chilton St **E2** 124 D6
Chilworth Ms **W2** 122 C8
Chilworth St **W2** 122 C8
Chip St **SW4** 127 K10
Chipka St **E14** 129 N1
Chipley St **SE14** 129 J5
Chippenham Gdns **NW6** 122 A5
Chippenham Ms **W9** 122 A6
Chippenham Rd **W9** 122 A6
Chipstead St **SW6** 126 A7
Chisenhale Rd **E3** 125 J4
Chiswell St **EC1** 124 A7
Chitty St **W1** 123 J7
Choumert Gro **SE15** 128 E8
Choumert Rd **SE15** 128 D9
Choumert Sq **SE15** 128 E8
Chrisp St **E14** 125 M7
Christchurch St **SW3** 126 F5
Christian Ct **SE16** 125 K10
Christian St **E1** 124 E8
Christie Rd **E9** 125 J1
Christopher Cl **SE16** 129 H1
Christopher St **EC2** 124 B6
Chryssell Rd **SW9** 127 N6
Chubworthy St **SE14** 129 J5
Chudleigh St **E1** 125 H8
Chumleigh St **SE5** 128 C5
Church Cres **E9** 125 H2
Church Gro **SE13** 129 M10
Church St **NW8** 122 D6
Church St **W2** 122 D7
Church St Est **NW8** 122 D6
Church Ter **SW8** 127 K8
Churchill Gdns **SW1** 127 J4
Churchill Gdns Rd **SW1** 127 H4
Churchill Pl **E14** 125 M10
Churchway **NW1** 123 K5
Churton Pl **SW1** 127 J3
Churton St **SW1** 127 J3
Cicely Rd **SE15** 128 E7
Cinnamon Row **SW11** 126 C9
Cinnamon St **E1** 124 F10
Circus Rd **NW8** 122 D5
Circus St **SE10** 129 N6
Cirencester St **W2** 122 B7
City Gdn Row **N1** 123 P4
City Rd **EC1** 123 P4
Clabon Ms **SW1** 126 F2
Clack St **SE16** 128 G1
Claire Pl **E14** 129 L2
Clancarty Rd **SW6** 126 A8
Clandon St **SE8** 129 L8
Clanricarde Gdns **W2** 122 A9
Clapham Common N Side **SW4** 127 H10
Clapham Common W Side **SW4** 126 G10
Clapham Cres **SW4** 127 K10
Clapham High St **SW4** 127 K10
Clapham Junct Est **SW11** 126 E10
Clapham Manor St **SW4** 127 J9
Clapham Pk Rd **SW4** 127 K10
Clapham Rd **SW9** 127 L9
Clapham Rd Est **SW4** 127 K9
Clare La **N1** 124 A2
Clare Rd **SE14** 129 K7
Clare St **E2** 124 F4
Claredale St **E2** 124 E4
Claremont Cl **N1** 123 N4
Claremont Sq **N1** 123 N4
Claremont St **SE10** 129 M5
Clarence Gdns **NW1** 123 H5
Clarence Ms **SE16** 125 H10
Clarence Wk **SW4** 127 L8
Clarence Way **NW1** 123 H2
Clarence Way Est **NW1** 123 H2
Clarendon Cl **E9** 124 G2
Clarendon Gdns **W9** 122 C6
Clarendon Pl **W2** 122 E9

Dock Hill Av

Clarendon Ri SE13 129 N9
Clarendon St SW1 127 H4
Clareville Gro SW7 126 C3
Clareville St SW7 126 C3
Clarges Ms W1 123 H10
Clarges St W1 123 H10
Claribel Rd SW9 127 P8
Clarissa St E8 124 D3
Clark St E1 124 F7
Clarkson Row NW1 123 H4
Clarkson St E2 124 F5
Claude Rd SE15 128 F8
Claude St E14 129 L3
Clavell St SE10 129 N5
Claverton St SW1 127 J4
Claylands Pl SW8 127 N6
Claylands Rd SW8 127 M5
Claypole Rd E15 125 N4
Clayton Ms SE10 129 P7
Clayton Rd SE15 128 E7
Clayton St SE11 127 N5
Clearwell Dr W9 122 B6
Cleaver Sq SE11 127 N4
Cleaver St SE11 127 N4
Clemence St E14 125 K7
Clement Av SW4 127 K10
Clement's Inn WC2 123 M8
Clements La EC4 124 B9
Clements Rd SE16 128 E2
Clephane Rd N1 124 B1
Clerkenwell Cl EC1 123 N6
Clerkenwell Grn EC1 123 P6
Clerkenwell Rd EC1 123 N6
Clermont Rd E9 124 G3
Cleve Rd NW6 122 A2
Cleveland Gdns W2 122 C8
Cleveland Rd N1 124 B2
Cleveland Row SW1 123 J10
Cleveland Sq W2 122 C8
Cleveland St W1 123 H6
Cleveland Ter W2 122 C8
Cleveland Way E1 124 G6
Clichy Est E1 124 G7
Cliff Rd NW1 123 K1
Cliff Ter SE8 129 L8
Cliff Vil NW1 123 K1
Clifford Dr SW9 127 P10
Clifford St W1 123 J9
Cliffview Rd SE13 129 L9
Clifton Cres SE15 128 F6
Clifton Gdns W9 122 C6
Clifton Gro E8 124 E1
Clifton Hill NW8 122 B4
Clifton Pl W2 122 D9
Clifton Ri SE14 129 J6
Clifton Rd W9 122 C6
Clifton St EC2 124 C6
Clifton Vil W9 122 B7
Clifton Way SE15 128 G6
Clink St SE1 124 B10
Clinton Rd E3 125 J5
Clipper Way SE13 129 N10
Clipstone Ms W1 123 J6
Clipstone St W1 123 J7
Clitheroe Rd SW9 127 L8
Cliveden Pl SW1 126 G3
Cloak La EC4 124 A9
Clock Twr Pl N7 123 L1
Cloth Fair EC1 123 P7
Cloudesley Pl N1 123 N3
Cloudesley Rd N1 123 N3
Cloudesley Sq N1 123 N3
Cloudesley St N1 123 N3
Clove Cres E14 125 P9
Clove Hitch Quay SW11 126 C9
Cloysters Grn E1 124 E10
Club Row E1 124 D6
Club Row E2 124 D6
Cluny Ms SW5 126 A3
Clutton St E14 125 M7
Clyde St SE8 129 K5
Clyston St SW8 127 J8
Coate St E2 124 E4
Cobb St E1 124 D7
Cobbett St SW8 127 M6
Coborn Rd E3 125 K5
Coborn St E3 125 K5
Cobourg Rd SE5 128 D5
Cobourg St NW1 123 J5
Cochrane St NW8 122 D4
Cock La EC1 123 P7
Cockayne Way SE8 129 J4
Cockspur St SW1 123 K10
Code St E1 124 D6
Cody Rd E16 125 P6
Cody Rd Business Cen E16 125 P6
Coin St SE1 123 N10
Coity Rd NW5 122 G1
Coke St E1 124 E8
Colbeck Ms SW7 126 B3
Cold Blow La SE14 129 H6
Cold Harbour E14 129 N1
Coldbath St SE13 129 M7
Coldharbour La SE5 127 N10
Coldharbour La SW9 127 N10
Cole St SE1 128 A1
Colebeck Ms N1 123 P1
Colebert Av E1 124 G6
Colebrooke Row N1 123 P4
Colegrove Rd SE15 128 D6
Coleherne Ct SW5 126 B4
Coleherne Ms SW10 126 B4
Coleherne Rd SW10 126 B4
Coleman Flds N1 124 A3
Coleman Rd SE5 128 C6
Coleman St EC2 124 B8
Coleridge Cl SW8 127 H8
Colestown St SW11 126 E8
Coley St WC1 123 M6
College App SE10 129 N5
College Cres NW3 122 D1
College Cross N1 123 N2
College Pk Cl SE13 129 P10
College Pl NW1 123 J3
College Ter E3 125 K5
Collent St E9 124 G1
Collett Rd SE16 128 E2
Collier St N1 123 M4
Collingham Gdns SW5 126 B3
Collingham Pl SW5 126 B3
Collingham Rd SW5 126 B3
Collingwood St E1 124 F6
Colls Rd SE15 128 G7
Colmore Ms SE15 128 F7
Colnbrook St SE1 127 P2
Cologne Rd SW11 126 D10
Colombo St SE1 123 P10
Colonnade WC1 123 L6
Colonnades, The W2 122 B8
Columbia Rd E2 124 D5
Columbine Way SE13 129 N8
Colville Est N1 124 C3
Colyer Cl N1 123 M4
Comber Gro SE5 128 A7
Combermere Rd SW9 127 M9
Comerford Rd SE4 129 J10
Comet Pl SE8 129 L6
Comet St SE8 129 L6
Commercial Rd E1 124 E8
Commercial Rd E14 124 G8
Commercial St E1 124 D6
Commercial Way SE15 128 D6
Commodore Sq SW10 126 D7
Commodore St E1 125 J6
Compayne Gdns NW6 122 B2
Compton Av N1 123 P1
Compton Cl E3 125 L7
Compton Rd N1 123 P1
Compton St EC1 123 P6
Compton Ter N1 123 P1
Comus Pl SE17 128 C3
Comyn Rd SW11 126 E10
Concanon Rd SW2 127 M10
Concert Hall App SE1 123 M10
Condell Rd SW8 127 J7
Conderton Rd SE5 128 A9
Condray Pl SW11 126 E6
Conduit Ms W2 122 D8
Conduit Pl W2 122 D8
Conduit St W1 123 H9
Coney Way SW8 127 M5
Congreve St SE17 128 C3
Coniger Rd SW6 126 A8
Conington Rd SE13 129 M8
Coniston Ho SE5 128 A6
Conistone Way N7 123 L2
Connaught Pl W2 122 F9
Connaught Sq W2 122 F8
Connaught St W2 122 E8
Consort Rd SE15 128 F7
Constitution Hill SW1 127 H1
Content St SE17 128 B3
Conway St W1 123 J7
Conyer St E3 125 J4
Cook's Rd E15 125 M4
Cooks Rd SE17 127 P5
Coombs St N1 123 P4
Coopers Cl E1 124 G6
Coopers La NW1 123 K4
Coopers Rd SE1 128 D4
Cope Pl W8 126 A2
Cope St SE16 129 H3
Copeland Dr E14 129 L3
Copeland Rd SE15 128 E8
Copenhagen Pl E14 125 K8
Copenhagen St N1 123 L3
Copleston Pas SE15 128 D9
Copleston Rd SE15 128 D9
Copper Row SE1 124 D10
Copperas St SE8 129 M5
Copperfield Rd E3 125 J6
Copperfield St SE1 127 P1
Coppock Cl SW11 126 E8
Copthall Av EC2 124 B8
Copthall Ct EC2 124 B8
Coptic St WC1 123 L7
Coral St SE1 127 N1
Coram St WC1 123 L6
Corbiere Ho N1 124 C3
Corbridge Cres E2 124 F4
Cordelia Cl SE24 127 P10
Cordelia St E14 125 M8
Cordova Rd E3 125 J5
Corfield St E2 124 F5
Coriander Av E14 125 P8
Cork St W1 123 J9
Corlett St NW1 122 E7
Cormont Rd SE5 127 P7
Cornelia St N7 123 M1
Cornhill EC3 124 B8
Cornmill La SE13 129 M9
Cornwall Av E2 124 G5
Cornwall Gdns SW7 126 C2
Cornwall Ms S SW7 126 C2
Cornwall Rd SE1 123 N10
Cornwood Dr E1 124 G8
Coronet St N1 124 C5
Corporation Row EC1 123 N6
Corrance Rd SW2 127 L10
Corsham St N1 124 B5
Corsica St N5 123 P1
Corunna Rd SW8 127 J7
Corunna Ter SW8 127 J7
Cossall Wk SE15 128 F7
Cosser St SE1 127 N2
Costa St SE15 128 E8
Cosway St NW1 122 E7
Cotall St E14 125 L8
Cotleigh Rd NW6 122 A2
Cottage Grn SE5 128 B6
Cottage Gro SW9 127 L9
Cottage Pl SW3 126 E2
Cottage St E14 125 M9
Cottesmore Gdns W8 126 B2
Cottingham Rd SW8 127 M6
Cotton Row SW11 126 C9
Cotton St E14 125 N9
Coulgate St SE4 129 J9
Coulson St SW3 126 F3
Councillor St SE5 128 A6
County Gro SE5 128 A7
County St SE1 128 B2
Courland Gro SW8 127 K7
Courland St SW8 127 K7
Court Gdns N7 123 N1
Courtenay St SE11 127 N4
Courtfield Gdns SW5 126 B3
Courtfield Rd SW7 126 B3
Courthill Rd SE13 129 N10
Courtnell St W2 122 A8
Courtyard, The N1 123 M2
Covent Gdn WC2 123 L9
Coventry Rd E1 124 F6
Coventry Rd E2 124 F6
Coventry St W1 123 K9
Coverley Cl E1 124 E7
Cowcross St EC1 123 P7
Cowdenbeath Path N1 123 M3
Cowley Rd SW9 127 N7
Cowper St EC2 124 B6
Cowthorpe Rd SW8 127 K7
Crabtree Cl E2 124 D4
Crampton St SE17 128 A3
Cranbourn St WC2 123 K9
Cranbrook Rd SE8 129 L7
Cranbury Rd SW6 126 B8
Crane Gro N7 123 N1
Crane Mead SE16 129 H3
Crane St SE10 129 P4
Crane St SE15 128 D7
Cranfield Rd SE4 129 K9
Cranford St E1 125 H9
Cranleigh Ms SW11 126 E8
Cranleigh St NW1 123 J4
Cranley Gdns SW7 126 C4
Cranley Ms SW7 126 C4
Cranley Pl SW7 126 D3
Cranmer Ct SW4 127 K9
Cranmer Rd SW9 127 N6
Cranston Est N1 124 B4
Cranswick Rd SE16 128 F4
Cranwell Cl E3 125 M6
Cranwood St EC1 124 B5
Cranworth Gdns SW9 127 N7
Craven Hill W2 122 C9
Craven Hill Gdns W2 122 C9
Craven Hill Ms W2 122 C9
Craven Pas WC2 123 L10
Craven Rd W2 122 C9
Craven St WC2 123 L10
Craven Ter W2 122 C9
Crawford Est SE5 128 A8
Crawford Pl W1 122 E8
Crawford Rd SE5 128 A7
Crawford St W1 122 F7
Crawthew Gro SE22 128 D10
Creasy Est SE1 128 C2
Credon Rd SE16 128 F4
Creechurch La EC3 124 C8
Creek Rd SE8 129 L5
Creek Rd SE10 129 L5
Creekside SE8 129 M6
Cremer St E2 124 D4
Cremorne Rd SW10 126 C6
Crescent Gro SW4 127 J10
Crescent Pl SW3 126 E3
Crescent St N1 123 M2
Crescent Way SE4 129 L9
Cresford Rd SW6 126 B7
Cresset Rd E9 124 G1
Cresset St SW4 127 K9
Cressingham Rd SE13 129 N9
Cresswell Gdns SW5 126 C4
Cresswell Pl SW10 126 C4
Cressy Pl E1 124 G7
Crestfield St WC1 123 L5
Crewdson Rd SW9 127 N6
Crews St E14 129 L3
Crewys Rd SE15 128 F8
Cricketers Ct SE11 127 P3
Crimscott St SE1 128 C2
Crimsworth Rd SW8 127 K7
Crinan St N1 123 L4
Cringle St SW8 127 J6
Crispin St E1 124 D7
Croft St SE8 129 J3
Crofters Way NW1 123 K3
Crofton Rd SE5 128 C7
Crofts St E1 124 E9
Crogsland Rd NW1 122 G2
Cromer St WC1 123 L5
Crompton St W2 122 D6
Cromwell Cres SW5 126 A3
Cromwell Gdns SW7 126 D2
Cromwell Ms SW7 126 D3
Cromwell Pl SW7 126 D3
Cromwell Rd SW5 126 B3
Cromwell Rd SW7 126 B3
Cromwell Rd SW9 127 P7
Crondace Rd SW6 126 A7
Crondall St N1 124 B4
Cronin St SE15 128 D6
Crooke Rd SE8 129 J4
Crooms Hill SE10 129 P6
Crooms Hill Gro SE10 129 N6
Cropley St N1 124 B4
Crosby Row SE1 128 B1
Cross Av SE10 129 P5
Cross Rd SE5 128 C8
Cross St N1 123 P3
Crossfield Rd NW3 122 D2
Crossfield St SE8 129 L6
Crossford St SW9 127 M8
Crossley St N7 123 N1
Crossmount Ho SE5 128 A6
Crossthwaite Av SE5 128 B10
Crosswall EC3 124 D9
Croston St E8 124 E3
Crowder St E1 124 F9
Crowhurst Cl SW9 127 N8
Crowland Ter N1 124 B2
Crown Cl E3 125 L3
Crown Cl NW6 122 B1
Crown Pas SW1 123 J10
Crown Pl EC2 124 C7
Crown St SE5 128 A6
Crowndale Rd NW1 123 J4
Crows Rd E15 125 P5
Crucifix La SE1 128 C1
Cruden St N1 123 P3
Cruikshank St WC1 123 N5
Crutched Friars EC3 124 C9
Crystal Palace Rd SE22 128 E10
Cuba St E14 129 L1
Cubitt St WC1 123 M5
Cubitt Ter SW4 127 J9
Cudworth St E1 124 F6
Cuff Pt E2 124 D5
Culford Gdns SW3 126 F3
Culford Gro N1 124 C1
Culford Rd N1 124 C2
Culloden Cl SE16 128 E4
Culloden St E14 125 N8
Culmore Rd SE15 128 F6
Culross St W1 122 G9
Culvert Pl SW11 126 G8
Culvert Rd SW11 126 F8
Cumberland Cl E8 124 D1
Cumberland Gate W1 122 F9
Cumberland Mkt NW1 123 H5
Cumberland St SW1 127 H4
Cumming St N1 123 M4
Cunard Wk SE16 129 J3
Cundy St SW1 126 G3
Cunningham Pl NW8 122 D6
Cupar Rd SW11 126 G7
Cureton St SW1 127 K3
Curlew St SE1 128 D1
Cursitor St EC4 123 N8
Curtain Rd EC2 124 C6
Curtis St SE1 128 D3
Curtis Way SE1 128 D3
Curzon Gate W1 122 G10
Curzon St W1 122 G10
Custom Ho Reach SE16 129 K1
Custom Ho Wk EC3 124 C9
Cut, The SE1 127 N1
Cutcombe Rd SE5 128 A8
Cuthbert St W2 122 D6
Cuthill Wk SE5 128 B7
Cutler St E1 124 C8
Cyclops Ms E14 129 L3
Cynthia St N1 123 M4
Cyprus Pl E2 124 G4
Cyprus St E2 124 G4
Cyril Mans SW11 126 F7
Cyrus St EC1 123 P6
Czar St SE8 129 L5

D

Dabin Cres SE10 129 N7
Dacca St SE8 129 K5
Dace Rd E3 125 L2
Dacre St SW1 127 K2
Dagmar Rd SE5 128 C7
Dagmar Ter N1 123 P3
Dagnall St SW11 126 F8
Dairy Ms SW9 127 L9
Daisy La SW6 126 A9
Dalby Rd SW18 126 C10
Dalby St NW5 123 H1
Dale Rd SE17 127 P5
Daleham Ms NW3 122 D1
Dalehead NW1 123 J4
Daley St E9 125 H1
Daley Thompson Way SW8 127 H8
Dalgleish St E14 125 J8
Daling Way E3 125 J3
Dallington St EC1 123 P6
Dalrymple Rd SE4 129 J10
Dalston Cross Shop Cen E8 124 D1
Dalston La E8 124 D1
Dalwood St SE5 128 C7
Dalyell Rd SW9 127 M9
Dame St N1 124 A4
Damien St E1 124 F8
Danbury St N1 123 P4
Danby St SE15 128 D9
Danesdale Rd E9 125 J1
Daneville Rd SE5 128 B7
Daniel Gdns SE15 128 D6
Daniels Ms SE4 129 K10
Daniels Rd SE15 128 G9
Dante Rd SE11 127 P3
Danvers St SW3 126 D5
D'Arblay St W1 123 J8
Darien Rd SW11 126 D9
Darling Rd SE4 129 L9
Darling Row E1 124 F6
Darnley Ho E14 125 J8
Darnley Rd E9 124 F1
Darsley Dr SW8 127 L7
Dartford St SE17 128 A5
Dartmouth Gro SE10 129 N7
Dartmouth Hill SE10 129 N7
Dartmouth Row SE10 129 N7
Dartmouth St SW1 127 K1
Dartmouth Ter SE10 129 P7
Darwin St SE17 128 B3
Datchelor Pl SE5 128 B7
Date St SE17 128 A4
Daubeney Twr SE8 129 K3
Davenant St E1 124 E7
Daventry St NW1 122 E7
Davey Cl N7 123 M1
Davey Rd E9 125 L2
Davey St SE15 128 D5
David St E15 125 P1
Davidge St SE1 127 P1
Davidson Gdns SW8 127 L6
Davies St W1 123 H9
Dawes St SE17 128 B4
Dawson Pl W2 122 A9
Dawson St E2 124 D4
Dayton Gro SE15 128 G7
De Beauvoir Cres N1 124 C3
De Beauvoir Est N1 124 B3
De Beauvoir Rd N1 124 C3
De Beauvoir Sq N1 124 C2
De Crespigny Pk SE5 128 B8
De Laune St SE17 127 P4
De Morgan Rd SW6 126 B9
De Vere Gdns W8 126 C1
Deacon Ms N1 124 B2
Deacon Way SE17 128 A3
Deal Porters Way SE16 128 G2
Deal St E1 124 E7
Dean Bradley St SW1 127 L2
Dean Farrar St SW1 127 K2
Dean Ryle St SW1 127 L3
Dean Stanley St SW1 127 L2
Dean St W1 123 K8
Dean Trench St SW1 127 L2
Deancross St E1 124 G8
Deanery St W1 122 G10
Deans Bldgs SE17 128 B3
Dean's Pl SW1 127 K4
Decima St SE1 128 C2
Dee St E14 125 N8
Deeley Rd SW8 127 K7
Deepdene Rd SE5 128 B10
Deerdale Rd SE24 128 A10
Delaford Rd SE16 128 F4
Delamere Ter W2 122 B7
Delancey St NW1 123 H3
Delaware Rd W9 122 B6
Delhi St N1 123 L3
Delius Gro E15 125 P4
Dell Cl E15 125 P3
Dellow St E1 124 F9
Deloraine St SE8 129 L7
Delverton Rd SE17 127 P4
Delvino Rd SW6 126 A7
Denbigh Pl SW1 127 J4
Denbigh St SW1 127 J3
Dene Cl SE4 129 J9
Denman Rd SE15 128 D7
Denmark Gro N1 123 N4
Denmark Hill SE5 128 B7
Denmark Hill Est SE5 128 B10
Denmark Rd SE5 128 A7
Denmark St WC2 123 K8
Denne Ter E8 124 D3
Dennetts Rd SE14 128 G7
Denning Cl NW8 122 C5
Dennington Pk Rd NW6 122 A1
Dennison Pt E15 125 N2
Denny St SE11 127 N4
Denyer St SW3 126 E3
Deptford Br SE8 129 L7
Deptford Bdy SE8 129 L7
Deptford Ch St SE8 129 L5
Deptford Ferry Rd E14 129 L3
Deptford Grn SE8 129 L5
Deptford High St SE8 129 L5
Deptford Strand SE8 129 K3
Deptford Wf SE8 129 K3
Derby Rd E9 125 H3
Derbyshire St E2 124 E5
Dericote St E8 124 E3
Dering St W1 123 H8
Derry St W8 126 B1
Derwent Gro SE22 128 D10
Desmond St SE14 129 J5
Devas St E3 125 M6
Deverell St SE1 128 B2
Devon St SE15 128 F5
Devonia Rd N1 123 P4
Devonport St E1 124 G8
Devons Est E3 125 M5
Devons Rd E3 125 L7
Devonshire Cl W1 123 H7
Devonshire Dr SE10 129 M6
Devonshire Gro SE15 128 F5
Devonshire Ms S W1 123 H7
Devonshire Ms W W1 123 H7
Devonshire Pl W1 122 G6
Devonshire St W1 123 H7
Devonshire Ter W2 122 C8
Dewar St SE15 128 E9
Dewberry St E14 125 N7
Dewey Rd N1 123 N4
D'Eynsford Rd SE5 128 B7
Dial Wk, The W8 126 B1
Diamond St SE15 128 C6
Diamond Ter SE10 129 N7
Diana Pl NW1 123 H6
Dibden St N1 124 A3
Dickens Est SE1 128 E1
Dickens Est SE16 128 E1
Dickens Sq SE1 128 A2
Dickens St SW8 127 H8
Digby Rd E9 125 H1
Digby St E2 124 G5
Dighton Ct SE5 128 A5
Dilke St SW3 126 F5
Dimson Cres E3 125 L6
Dingle Gdns E14 125 L9
Dingley Pl EC1 124 A5
Dingley Rd EC1 124 A5
Discovery Wk E1 124 F10
Diss St E2 124 D5
Distaff La EC4 124 A9
Distin St SE11 127 N3
Ditch All SE10 129 M7
Ditchburn St E14 125 N9
Dixon Rd SE14 129 J7
Dixon's All SE16 128 F1
Dobson Cl NW6 122 D2
Dock Hill Av SE16 129 H1

Dock St

Dock St E1 124 E9
Dockers Tanner Rd E14 129 L2
Dockhead SE1 128 D1
Dockley Rd SE16 128 E2
Docwra's Bldgs N1 124 C1
Dod St E14 125 L8
Doddington Gro SE17 127 P5
Doddington Pl SE17 127 P5
Dodson St SE1 127 N1
Dog Kennel Hill SE22 128 C9
Dog Kennel Hill Est SE22 128 C9
Dolben St SE1 123 P10
Dolland St SE11 127 M4
Dolman St SW4 127 M10
Dolphin La E14 125 M9
Dolphin Sq SW1 127 J4
Dombey St WC1 123 M7
Domett Cl SE5 128 B10
Don Phelan Cl SE5 128 B7
Donegal St N1 123 M4
Donne Pl SW3 126 E3
Dora St E14 125 K8
Doran Wk E15 125 N2
Doric Way NW1 123 K5
Dorking Cl SE8 129 K5
Dorman Way NW8 122 D3
Dorney NW3 122 E2
Dorothy Rd SW11 126 F9
Dorrington St EC1 123 N7
Dorset Est E2 124 D5
Dorset Pl E15 125 P1
Dorset Ri EC4 123 P8
Dorset Rd SW8 127 M6
Dorset Sq NW1 122 F6
Dorset St W1 122 G7
Doughty Ms WC1 123 M6
Doughty St WC1 123 M6
Douglas Est N1 124 A1
Douglas Rd N1 124 A2
Douglas St SW1 127 K3
Douglas Way SE8 129 K6
Douro Pl W8 126 B2
Douro St E3 125 L4
Dove Ms SW5 126 C3
Dove Rd N1 124 B1
Dove Row E2 124 E3
Dovehouse St SW3 126 D4
Dover St W1 123 H9
Dovercourt Est N1 124 B1
Dove's Yd N1 123 N3
Dowgate Hill EC4 124 B9
Dowlas St SE5 128 C6
Down St W1 123 H10
Downfield Cl W9 122 B6
Downham Rd N1 124 B2
Downing St SW1 127 L1
Downtown Rd SE16 129 J1
Dowson Cl SE5 128 B10
D'Oyley St SW1 126 G3
Draco St SE17 128 A5
Dragon Rd SE15 128 C5
Dragoon Rd SE8 129 K4
Drake Rd SE4 129 L9
Drakefell Rd SE4 129 H8
Drakefell Rd SE14 129 H8
Drawdock Rd SE10 125 P10
Draycott Av SW3 126 E3
Draycott Pl SW3 126 F3
Draycott Ter SW3 126 F3
Drayson Ms W8 126 A1
Drayton Gdns SW10 126 C4
Dresden Cl NW6 122 B1
Driffield Rd E3 125 J4
Drover La SE15 128 F6
Drovers Pl SE15 128 F6
Druid St SE1 128 C1
Drummond Cres NW1 123 K5
Drummond Gate SW1 127 K4
Drummond Rd SE16 128 F2
Drummond St NW1 123 J6
Drury La WC2 123 L8
Dryden Ct SE11 127 N3
Drysdale St N1 124 C5
Dublin Av E8 124 E3
Duchess of Bedford's Wk W8 126 A1
Duchess St W1 123 H7
Duchy St SE1 123 N10
Ducie St SW4 127 M10
Duckett St E1 125 H7
Dudley St W2 122 D7
Duff St E14 125 M8
Dufferin St EC1 124 A6
Dugard Way SE11 127 P3
Duke of Wellington Pl SW1 126 G1
Duke of York St SW1 123 J10
Duke St SW1 123 J10
Duke St W1 122 G8
Dukes La W8 126 A1
Dukes Pl EC3 124 C8
Duke's Rd WC1 123 K5
Dunbridge St E2 124 E6
Duncan Rd E8 124 F3
Duncan St N1 123 P4
Duncan Ter N1 123 P4
Duncannon St WC2 123 L9
Dundalk Rd SE4 129 J9
Dundas Rd SE15 128 G8
Dundee St E1 124 F10
Dunelm St E1 125 H8
Dunloe St E2 124 D4
Dunston Rd E8 124 D3
Dunston Rd SW11 126 G8
Dunston St E8 124 D3
Dunton Rd SE1 128 D4
Durand Gdns SW9 127 M7
Durands Wk SE16 129 K1
Durant St E2 124 E5
Durham Row E1 125 J7
Durham St SE11 127 M4
Durham Ter W2 122 B8
Durward St E1 124 F7
Durweston St W1 122 F7
Dutton St SE10 129 N7
Dye Ho La E3 125 L3
Dylan Rd SE24 127 P10
Dylways SE5 128 B10
Dymock St SW6 126 B9
Dynham Rd NW6 122 A2
Dyott St WC1 123 K8

E

Eagle Ct EC1 123 P7
Eagle St WC1 123 M7
Eagle Wf Rd N1 124 A4
Eamont St NW8 122 E4
Eardley Cres SW5 126 A4
Earl St EC2 124 B7
Earlham St WC2 123 K8
Earls Ct Gdns SW5 126 B3
Earls Ct Rd SW5 126 A3
Earls Ct Rd W8 126 A2
Earls Ct Sq SW5 126 B4
Earls Wk W8 126 A2
Earlsferry Way N1 123 M3
Earlston Gro E9 124 F3
Earnshaw St WC2 123 K8
East Arbour St E1 125 H8
East Cross Route E3 125 L3
East Dulwich Rd SE15 128 D10
East Dulwich Rd SE22 128 D10
East Ferry Rd E14 129 M2
East India Dock Rd E14 125 P8
East La SE16 128 E1
East Mt St E1 124 F7
East Rd N1 124 B5
East Smithfield E1 124 D9
East St SE17 128 A4
East Surrey Gro SE15 128 D6
East Tenter St E1 124 D8
Eastbourne Ms W2 122 C8
Eastbourne Ter W2 122 C8
Eastbury Ter E1 125 H6
Eastcastle St W1 123 J8
Eastcheap EC3 124 B9
Eastcote St SW9 127 M8
Eastdown Pk SE13 129 P10
Eastern Rd SE4 129 L10
Eastlake Rd SE5 127 P8
Eastney St SE10 129 P4
Eastway E9 125 K1
Eaton Cl SW1 126 G3
Eaton Dr SW9 127 P10
Eaton Gate SW1 126 G3
Eaton La SW1 127 H2
Eaton Ms N SW1 126 G2
Eaton Ms S SW1 127 H2
Eaton Ms W SW1 126 G3
Eaton Pl SW1 126 G2
Eaton Row SW1 127 H2
Eaton Sq SW1 126 G3
Eaton Ter SW1 126 G3
Ebbisham Dr SW8 127 M5
Ebenezer St N1 124 B5
Ebley Cl SE15 128 D5
Ebor St E1 124 D6
Ebury Br SW1 127 H4
Ebury Br Est SW1 127 H4
Ebury Br Rd SW1 126 G4
Ebury Ms SW1 127 H3
Ebury Sq SW1 126 G3
Ebury St SW1 126 G3
Eccles Rd SW11 126 F10
Ecclesbourne Rd N1 124 A2
Eccleston Br SW1 127 H3
Eccleston Ms SW1 126 G2
Eccleston Pl SW1 127 H3
Eccleston Sq SW1 127 H3
Eccleston St SW1 126 G2
Eckford St N1 123 N4
Eckstein Rd SW11 126 E10
Edbrooke Rd W9 122 A6
Edenbridge Rd E9 125 H2
Edenvale St SW6 126 B8
Edgar Kail Way SE22 128 C10
Edgar Rd E3 125 M5
Edgeley Rd SW4 127 K9
Edgware Rd W2 122 E8
Edinburgh Gate SW1 126 F1
Edinburgh Ho W9 122 C5
Edis St NW1 122 G3
Edith Gro SW10 126 C5
Edith Row SW6 126 B7
Edith St E2 124 E4
Edith Ter SW10 126 C6
Edithna St SW9 127 L9
Edmeston Cl E9 125 J1
Edmund St SE5 128 B6
Edna St SW11 126 E7
Edric Rd SE14 129 H6
Edrich Ho SW4 127 L7
Edward Pl SE8 129 K5
Edward St SE8 129 K5
Edward St SE14 129 J6
Edwardes Sq W8 126 A2
Edwards Ms N1 123 N2
Edwards Ms W1 122 G8
Edwin St E1 124 G6
Effie Pl SW6 126 A6
Effie Rd SW6 126 A6
Effra Rd SW2 127 N10
Egbert St NW1 122 G3
Egerton Cres SW3 126 E3
Egerton Dr SE10 129 M7
Egerton Gdns SW3 126 E2
Egerton Gdns Ms SW3 126 E2
Egerton Pl SW3 126 E2
Egerton Ter SW3 126 E2
Egmont St SE14 129 H6
Elam Cl SE5 127 P8
Elam St SE5 127 P8
Eland Rd SW11 126 F9
Elbe St SW6 126 C8
Elcho St SW11 126 E6
Elcot Av SE15 128 F6
Elder St E1 124 D7
Eldon Rd W8 126 B2
Eldon St EC2 124 B7
Eleanor Cl SE16 129 H1
Eleanor Rd E8 124 F2
Eleanor St E3 125 L5
Electric Av SW9 127 N10
Electric La SW9 127 N10
Elephant & Castle SE1 127 P3
Elephant La SE16 128 G1
Elephant Rd SE17 128 A3
Elf Row E1 124 G9
Elgar St SE16 129 J2
Elgin Av W9 122 B5
Elia Ms N1 123 P4
Elia St N1 123 P4
Elias Pl SW8 127 N5
Elim Est SE1 128 C2
Eliot Hill SE13 129 N8
Eliot Ms NW8 122 C4
Eliot Pk SE13 129 N9
Eliot Vale SE3 129 P8
Elizabeth Av N1 124 A2
Elizabeth Br SW1 127 H3
Elizabeth Est SE17 128 B5
Elizabeth Ms NW3 122 E1
Elizabeth St SW1 126 G3
Elland Rd SE15 128 G10
Ellen St E1 124 E8
Ellerdale St SE13 129 M10
Ellery St SE15 128 F8
Ellesmere Rd E3 125 J4
Ellesmere St E14 125 M8
Ellingfort Rd E8 124 F2
Ellington St N7 123 N1
Elliott Rd SW9 127 P6
Elliott Sq NW3 122 E2
Elliotts Row SE11 127 P3
Ellis St SW1 126 F3
Ellsworth St E2 124 F5
Elm Friars Wk NW1 123 K2
Elm Gro SE15 128 D8
Elm Pk Gdns SW10 126 D4
Elm Pk La SW3 126 D4
Elm Pk Rd SW3 126 D5
Elm Pl SW7 126 D4
Elm Quay Ct SW8 127 K5
Elm St WC1 123 M6
Elm Tree Cl NW8 122 D5
Elm Tree Rd NW8 122 D5
Elmfield Way W9 122 A7
Elmhurst St SW4 127 K9
Elmington Est SE5 128 B6
Elmington Rd SE5 128 B7
Elmira St SE13 129 M9
Elmore St N1 124 A2
Elms Ms W2 122 D9
Elmslie Pt E3 125 K7
Elmstone Rd SW6 126 A7
Elrington Rd E8 124 E1
Elsa St E1 125 J7
Elsdale St E9 124 G1
Elsie Rd SE22 128 D10
Elsley Rd SW11 126 F9
Elspeth Rd SW11 126 F10
Elsted St SE17 128 B3
Elswick Rd SE13 129 M8
Elswick St SW6 126 C8
Elsworthy Ri NW3 122 E2
Elsworthy Rd NW3 122 E3
Elsworthy Ter NW3 122 E2
Elthiron Rd SW6 126 A7
Elton Ho E3 125 K3
Eltringham St SW18 126 C10
Elvaston Ms SW7 126 C2
Elvaston Pl SW7 126 C2
Elverson Rd SE8 129 M8
Elverton St SW1 127 K3
Elwin St E2 124 E5
Elystan Pl SW3 126 E4
Elystan St SW3 126 E3
Emba St SE16 128 E1
Embankment Gdns SW3 126 F5
Embankment Pl WC2 123 L10
Embleton Rd SE13 129 M9
Emden St SW6 126 B7
Emerald St WC1 123 M7
Emerson St SE1 124 A10
Emery Hill St SW1 127 J2
Emma St E2 124 F4
Emmott Cl E1 125 J6
Emperor's Gate SW7 126 B2
Empire Wf Rd E14 129 P3
Empress Pl SW6 126 A4
Empress St SE17 128 A5
Empson St E3 125 M6
Emu Rd SW8 127 H8
Endell St WC2 123 L8
Endsleigh Gdns WC1 123 K6
Endsleigh Pl WC1 123 K6
Endsleigh St WC1 123 K6
Endwell Rd SE4 129 J8
Enfield Rd N1 124 C2
Enford St W1 122 F7
Engate St SE13 129 N10
Englands La NW3 122 F1
Englefield Rd N1 124 B1
English St E3 125 K6
Enid St SE16 128 D2
Ennerdale Ho E3 125 K6
Ennismore Gdns SW7 126 E1
Ennismore Gdns Ms SW7 126 E2
Ennismore Ms SW7 126 E1
Ennismore St SW7 126 E2
Ensign St E1 124 E9
Enterprise Way SW18 126 A10
Enterprize Way SE8 129 K3
Epirus Ms SW6 126 A6
Epping Cl E14 129 L3
Epworth St EC2 124 B6
Erasmus St SW1 127 K3
Eresby Pl NW6 122 A2
Eric St E3 125 K6
Erlanger Rd SE14 129 H7
Ermine Rd SE13 129 M9
Ernest St E1 125 H6
Errol St EC1 124 A6
Erskine Rd NW3 122 F2
Esmeralda Rd SE1 128 E3
Essendine Rd W9 122 A6
Essex Rd N1 123 P3
Essex Vil W8 126 A1
Essian St E1 125 J7
Este Rd SW11 126 E9
Esterbrooke St SW1 127 K3
Ethelburga St SW11 126 E7
Ethnard Rd SE15 128 F5
Eton Av NW3 122 D2
Eton College Rd NW3 122 F1
Eton Rd NW3 122 F2
Eton Vil NW3 122 F1
Etta St SE8 129 J5
Ettrick St E14 125 N8
Eugenia Rd SE16 128 G3
Eustace Rd SW6 126 A6
Euston Gro NW1 123 K5
Euston Rd N1 123 K6
Euston Rd NW1 123 H6
Euston Sq NW1 123 K5
Euston St NW1 123 J5
Evandale Rd SW9 127 N8
Evelina Rd SE15 128 G9
Eveline Lowe Est SE16 128 E2
Evelyn Gdns SW7 126 D4
Evelyn St SE8 129 J4
Evelyn Wk N1 124 B4
Everest Pl E14 125 N7
Everilda St N1 123 M3
Eversholt St NW1 123 J4
Eversleigh Rd SW11 126 G8
Everthorpe Rd SE15 128 D9
Evesham Wk SW9 127 N8
Evesham Way SW11 126 G9
Ewart Pl E3 125 K4
Ewe Cl N7 123 L1
Ewer St SE1 124 A10
Ewhurst Ho E1 124 G7
Excelsior Gdns SE13 129 N8
Exchange Sq EC2 124 C7
Exeter St WC2 123 L9
Exeter Way SE14 129 K6
Exhibition Rd SW7 126 D1
Exmouth Mkt EC1 123 N6
Exmouth Pl E8 124 F2
Exon St SE17 128 C4
Exton St SE1 123 N10
Eythorne Rd SW9 127 N7
Ezra St E2 124 D5

F

Fairbairn Grn SW9 127 N7
Faircharm Trd Est SE8 129 M6
Fairclough St E1 124 E8
Fairfax Pl NW6 122 C2
Fairfax Rd NW6 122 C2
Fairfield Rd E3 125 L4
Fairfoot Rd E3 125 L6
Fairhazel Gdns NW6 122 B1
Fakruddin St E1 124 E6
Falcon Ct EC4 123 N8
Falcon Gro SW11 126 E9
Falcon La SW11 126 E9
Falcon Rd SW11 126 E8
Falcon Ter SW11 126 E9
Falcon Way E14 129 M3
Falkirk Ho W9 122 B5
Falkirk St N1 124 C4
Falmouth Rd SE1 128 A2
Fann St EC1 124 A6
Fann St EC2 124 A6
Fanshaw St N1 124 C5
Farm La SW6 126 A5
Farm St W1 123 H9
Farmers Rd SE5 127 P6
Farncombe St SE16 128 E1
Farnham Royal SE11 127 M4
Farrance St E14 125 K8
Farrell Ho E1 124 G8
Farrier St NW1 123 H2
Farrier Wk SW10 126 C5
Farringdon La EC1 123 N6
Farringdon Rd EC1 123 N6
Farringdon St EC4 123 P7
Farrins Rents SE16 125 J10
Farrow La SE14 128 G6
Farthingale Wk E15 125 P2
Fashion St E1 124 D7
Fassett Rd E8 124 E1
Fassett Sq E8 124 E1
Faulkner St SE14 128 G7
Favart Rd SW6 126 A7
Fawcett Cl SW11 126 D8
Fawcett St SW10 126 C5
Fawe St E14 125 M7
Feathers Pl SE10 129 P5
Featherstone St EC1 124 B6
Featley Rd SW9 127 P9
Fellows Ct E2 124 D4
Fellows Rd NW3 122 D2
Felstead St E9 125 K1
Felton St N1 124 B3
Fenchurch Av EC3 124 C8
Fenchurch St EC3 124 C9
Fendall St SE1 128 C2
Fenham Rd SE15 128 E6
Fentiman Rd SW8 127 L5
Fenton Cl SW9 127 M8
Fenwick Gro SE15 128 E9
Fenwick Pl SW9 127 L9
Fenwick Rd SE15 128 E9
Ferdinand St NW1 122 G1
Ferguson Cl E14 129 L3
Fern St E3 125 L6
Ferndale Rd SW4 127 L10
Ferndale Rd SW9 127 M9
Ferndene Rd SE24 128 A10
Fernshaw Rd SW10 126 C5
Ferrier St SW18 126 B10
Ferris Rd SE22 128 E10
Ferry St E14 129 N4
Fetter La EC4 123 N8
Ffinch St SE8 129 L6
Field St WC1 123 M5
Fieldgate St E1 124 E7
Fielding Ho NW6 122 A5
Fielding St SE17 128 A5
Fields Est E8 124 E2
Fife Ter N1 123 M4
Finborough Rd SW10 126 B4
Finch Ms SE15 128 D6
Finchley Pl NW8 122 D4
Finchley Rd NW3 122 C1
Finchley Rd NW8 122 D3
Findhorn St E14 125 N8
Finland Quay SE16 129 J2
Finland Rd SE4 129 J9
Finland St SE16 129 J2
Finnis St E2 124 F5
Finsbury Circ EC2 124 B7
Finsbury Est EC1 123 N5
Finsbury Mkt EC2 124 C6
Finsbury Pavement EC2 124 B7
Finsbury Sq EC2 124 B7
Finsbury St EC2 124 B7
Finsen Rd SE5 128 A9
Fir Trees Cl SE16 125 J10
Firbank Rd SE15 128 F8
First St SW3 126 E3
Fish St Hill EC3 124 B9
Fisher St WC1 123 M7
Fishermans Dr SE16 129 H1
Fisherman's Wk E14 125 L10
Fisherton St NW8 122 D6
Fitzalan St SE11 127 M3
Fitzgerald Ho E14 125 M8
Fitzhardinge St W1 122 G8
Fitzmaurice Pl W1 123 H9
Fitzroy Rd NW1 122 G3
Fitzroy Sq W1 123 J6
Fitzroy St W1 123 J6
Fitzwilliam Rd SW4 127 J9
Fiveways Rd SW9 127 P8
Flamborough St E14 125 J8
Flanders Way E9 125 H1
Flaxman Rd SE5 127 P8
Flaxman Ter WC1 123 K5
Fleet St EC4 123 N8
Fleming Rd SE17 127 P5
Fleur de Lis St E1 124 C6
Flint St SE17 128 B3
Flinton St SE17 128 C4
Flodden Rd SE5 128 A7
Flood St SW3 126 E4
Flood Wk SW3 126 E5
Flora Cl E14 125 M8
Floral St WC2 123 L9
Florence Rd SE14 129 K7
Florence St N1 123 P2
Florence Ter SE14 129 K7
Florida St E2 124 E5
Flower Wk, The SW7 126 C1
Foley St W1 123 J7
Folgate St E1 124 C7
Follett St E14 125 N8
Folly Wall E14 129 N1
Fontarabia Rd SW11 126 G10
Ford Rd E3 125 J3
Ford Sq E1 124 F7
Ford St E3 125 J3
Fordham St E1 124 E8
Fore St EC2 124 A7
Foreshore SE8 129 K3
Forest Gro E8 124 D2
Forest Rd E8 124 D1
Forester Rd SE15 128 F10
Forfar Rd SW11 126 G7
Formosa St W9 122 B6
Forset St W1 122 E8
Forsyth Gdns SE17 127 P5
Fort Rd SE1 128 D3
Forthbridge Rd SW11 126 G10
Fortune St EC1 124 A6
Fossil Rd SE13 129 L9
Foster La EC2 124 A8
Foubert's Pl W1 123 J8
Foulis Ter SW7 126 D4
Foundry Cl SE16 125 J10
Fount St SW8 127 K6
Fountain Pl SW9 127 N7
Fountain Sq SW1 127 H3
Four Seasons Cl E3 125 L4
Fournier St E1 124 D7
Fowler Cl SW11 126 D9
Fownes St SW11 126 E9
Fox Cl E1 124 G6
Foxberry Rd SE4 129 J9
Foxcote SE5 128 C4
Foxley Rd SW9 127 N6
Foxmore St SW11 126 F7
Foxwell St SE4 129 J9
Frampton Pk Rd E9 124 G1
Frampton St NW8 122 D6
Francis Chichester Way SW11 126 G7
Francis St SW1 127 J3
Frankham St SE8 129 L6
Frankland Cl SE16 128 G3
Frankland Rd SW7 126 D2
Franklin Cl SE13 129 M7
Franklin's Row SW3 126 F4
Frazier St SE1 127 N1
Frean St SE16 128 E2
Frederick Cl W2 122 E9
Frederick Cres SW9 127 P6
Frederick St WC1 123 M5

Hedgers Gro

Freedom St SW11 126 F8
Freemantle St SE17 128 C4
Freke Rd SW11 126 G9
Fremont St E9 124 G3
Frendsbury Rd SE4 129 J10
Frensham St SE15 128 E5
Frere St SW11 126 E8
Freshfield Av E8 124 D2
Friars Mead E14 129 N2
Friary Est SE15 128 E5
Friary Rd SE15 128 E6
Friday St EC4 124 A8
Friend St EC1 123 P5
Friendly St SE8 129 L7
Frimley Way E1 125 H6
Friston St SW6 126 B8
Frith St W1 123 K8
Frogley Rd SE22 128 D10
Frognal Ct NW3 122 C1
Frome St N1 124 A4
Frostic Wk E1 124 D7
Froude St SW8 127 H8
Fulford St SE16 128 F1
Fulham Bdy SW6 126 A6
Fulham Rd SW3 126 C5
Fulham Rd SW10 126 B6
Fulmead St SW6 126 B7
Fulwood Pl WC1 123 M7
Furley Rd SE15 128 E6
Furlong Rd N7 123 N1
Furness Rd SW6 126 B8
Furnival St EC4 123 N8
Furze St E3 125 L7
Fyfield Rd SW9 127 N9
Fynes St SW1 127 K3

G

Gables Cl SE5 128 C7
Gabrielle Ct NW3 122 D1
Gainsford St SE1 128 D1
Gairloch Rd SE5 128 C8
Gaisford St NW5 123 J1
Galbraith St E14 129 N2
Gale St E3 125 L7
Gales Gdns E2 124 F5
Galleywall Rd SE16 128 F3
Galway St EC1 124 A5
Gambetta St SW8 127 H8
Garden Rd NW8 122 C5
Garden Row SE1 127 P2
Garden St E1 125 H7
Gardens, The SE22 128 E10
Garfield Rd SW11 126 G9
Garford St E14 125 L9
Garlick Hill EC4 124 A9
Garnet St E1 124 G9
Garnies Cl SE15 128 D6
Garrick Cl SW18 126 C10
Garrick St WC2 123 L9
Garsington Ms SE4 129 K9
Gartons Way SW11 126 C9
Garway Rd W2 122 B8
Gascoigne Pl E2 124 D5
Gascony Av NW6 122 A2
Gascoyne Rd E9 125 H2
Gaselee St E14 125 N9
Gaskell St SW4 127 L8
Gaskin St N1 123 P3
Gataker St SE16 128 F2
Gate Ms SW7 126 E1
Gateforth St NW8 122 E6
Gateley Rd SW9 127 M9
Gateway SE17 128 A5
Gateways, The SW3 126 F3
Gatliff Rd SW1 127 H4
Gauden Cl SW4 127 K9
Gauden Rd SW4 127 K8
Gautrey Rd SE15 128 G8
Gawber St E2 124 G5
Gay Rd E15 125 P4
Gaydon Ho W2 122 B7
Gayfere St SW1 127 L2
Gayhurst Rd E8 124 E2
Gaywood Est SE1 127 P2
Gedling Pl SE1 128 D1
Gee St EC1 124 A6
Geffrye St E2 124 D4
Geldart Rd SE15 128 F6
Gellatly Rd SE14 128 G8
General Wolfe Rd SE10 129 P7
Geneva Dr SW9 127 N10
Geoffrey Cl SE5 128 A8
Geoffrey Rd SE4 129 K9
George Beard Rd SE8 129 K3
George Mathers Rd SE11 127 P3
George Row SE16 128 E1
George St W1 122 G8
George Yd W1 122 G9
Georgiana St NW1 123 J3
Gerald Rd SW1 126 G3
Geraldine St SE11 127 P2
Gerards Cl SE16 128 G4
Gernon Rd E3 125 J4
Gerrard Rd N1 123 P4
Gerrard St W1 123 K9
Gerridge St SE1 127 N2
Gertrude St SW10 126 C5
Gervase St SE15 128 F6
Gibbins Rd E15 125 N2
Gibbon Rd SE15 128 G8
Gibraltar Wk E2 124 D5
Gibson Rd SE11 127 M3
Gibson Sq N1 123 N3
Gideon Rd SW11 126 G9
Giffin St SE8 129 L6
Gifford St N1 123 L2
Gilbert Rd SE11 127 N3
Gilbert St W1 122 G8
Gill St E14 125 K8
Gillender St E3 125 N6
Gillender St E14 125 N6
Gillfoot NW1 123 J4
Gilling Ct NW3 122 E1
Gillingham St SW1 127 H3
Gilmore Rd SE13 129 P10
Gilstead Rd SW6 126 B8
Gilston Rd SW10 126 C4
Giltspur St EC1 123 P8
Giraud St E14 125 M8
Gladstone St SE1 127 P2
Gladstone Ter SW8 127 H7
Gladys Rd NW6 122 A2
Glamis Pl E1 124 G9
Glamis Rd E1 124 G9
Glasgow Ho W9 122 B4
Glasgow Ter SW1 127 J4
Glasshill St SE1 127 P1
Glasshouse Flds E1 125 H9
Glasshouse St W1 123 J9
Glasshouse Wk SE11 127 L4
Glaucus St E3 125 M7
Glebe Pl SW3 126 E5
Gledhow Gdns SW5 126 C3
Glenaffric Av E14 129 P3
Glendall St SW9 127 M10
Glendower Pl SW7 126 D3
Glenfinlas Way SE5 127 P6
Glengall Causeway E14 129 L2
Glengall Gro E14 129 N2
Glengall Rd SE15 128 D5
Glengall Ter SE15 128 D5
Glengarnock Av E14 129 N3
Glenilla Rd NW3 122 E1
Glenloch Rd NW3 122 E1
Glenmore Rd NW3 122 E1
Glenrosa St SW6 126 C8
Glensdale Rd SE4 129 K9
Glentworth St NW1 122 F6
Glenville Gro SE8 129 K6
Glenworth Av E14 129 P3
Globe Pond Rd SE16 125 J10
Globe Rd E1 124 G5
Globe Rd E2 124 G5
Globe Rope Wk E14 129 N3
Globe St SE1 128 B2
Gloucester Av NW1 122 G2
Gloucester Circ SE10 129 N6
Gloucester Cres NW1 123 H3
Gloucester Gate NW1 123 H4
Gloucester Gro Est SE15 128 C5
Gloucester Ho NW6 122 A4
Gloucester Ms W2 122 C8
Gloucester Pl NW1 122 F6
Gloucester Pl W1 122 F7
Gloucester Rd SW7 126 C3
Gloucester Sq W2 122 D8
Gloucester St SW1 127 J4
Gloucester Ter W2 122 D9
Gloucester Wk W8 126 A1
Gloucester Way EC1 123 N5
Glycena Rd SW11 126 F9
Godalming Rd E14 125 M7
Godfrey St E15 125 N4
Godfrey St SW3 126 E4
Goding St SE11 127 L4
Godliman St EC4 124 A8
Godman Rd SE15 128 F8
Godson St N1 123 N4
Goffers Rd SE3 129 P7
Golden La EC1 124 A6
Golden Sq W1 123 J9
Goldhurst Ter NW6 122 B2
Golding St E1 124 E8
Goldington Cres NW1 123 K4
Goldington St NW1 123 K4
Goldman Cl E2 124 E6
Goldney Rd W9 122 A6
Goldsboro Rd SW8 127 K7
Goldsmith Rd SE15 128 E7
Goldsmith's Row E2 124 E4
Goldsmith's Sq E2 124 E4
Goldsworthy Gdns SE16 128 G3
Goldwin Cl SE14 128 G7
Gomm Rd SE16 128 G2
Gonson Pl SE8 129 L5
Gonson St SE8 129 M5
Goodge St W1 123 J7
Goodhart Pl E14 125 J9
Goodinge Cl N7 123 L1
Goodman's Stile E1 124 E8
Goodmans Yd E1 124 D9
Goods Way NW1 123 L4
Goodway Gdns E14 125 P8
Goodwin Cl SE16 128 E2
Goodwood Rd SE14 129 J6
Gopsall St N1 124 B3
Gordon Gro SE5 127 P8
Gordon Pl W8 126 A1
Gordon Rd SE15 128 F8
Gordon Sq WC1 123 K6
Gordon St WC1 123 K6
Gore Rd E9 124 G3
Gore St SW7 126 C2
Gorefield Pl NW6 122 A4
Goring St EC3 124 C8
Gorsuch St E2 124 D5
Gosfield St W1 123 J7
Gosling Way SW9 127 N7
Gosset St E2 124 D5
Gosterwood St SE8 129 J5
Goswell Rd EC1 123 P5
Gough Sq EC4 123 N8
Gough St WC1 123 M6
Goulston St E1 124 D8
Gower Ms WC1 123 K7
Gower Pl WC1 123 J6
Gower St WC1 123 J6
Gower's Wk E1 124 E8
Gowlett Rd SE15 128 E9
Gowrie Rd SW11 126 G9
Grace St E3 125 M5
Gracechurch St EC3 124 B9
Grace's All E1 124 E9
Graces Ms SE5 128 C8
Graces Rd SE5 128 C8
Grafton Cres NW1 123 H1
Grafton Ho E3 125 L5
Grafton Pl NW1 123 K5
Grafton Sq SW4 127 J9
Grafton St W1 123 H9
Grafton Way W1 123 J6
Grafton Way WC1 123 J6
Graham Rd E8 124 E1
Graham St N1 123 P4
Graham Ter SW1 126 G3
Granary Rd E1 124 F6
Granary St NW1 123 K3
Granby St E2 124 D6
Granby Ter NW1 123 J4
Grand Junct Wf N1 124 A4
Grand Union Cres E8 124 E2
Grand Union Wk NW1 123 H2
Granfield St SW11 126 D7
Grange, The SE1 128 D2
Grange Ct E8 124 D2
Grange Gro N1 124 A1
Grange Pl NW6 122 A2
Grange Rd SE1 128 C2
Grange St N1 124 B3
Grange Wk SE1 128 C2
Grange Yd SE1 128 D2
Gransden Av E8 124 F2
Grant Rd SW11 126 D10
Grantbridge St N1 123 P4
Grantham Rd SW9 127 L8
Grantley St E1 125 H5
Grantully Rd W9 122 B5
Granville Ct N1 124 B3
Granville Gro SE13 129 N9
Granville Pk SE13 129 N9
Granville Pl W1 122 G8
Granville Rd NW6 122 A4
Granville Sq SE15 128 C6
Granville Sq WC1 123 M5
Grayling Sq E2 124 E5
Gray's Inn WC1 123 N7
Gray's Inn Rd WC1 123 M6
Grayshott Rd SW11 126 G8
Great Castle St W1 123 J8
Great Cen St NW1 122 F7
Great Chapel St W1 123 K8
Great College St SW1 127 L2
Great Cumberland Pl W1 122 F8
Great Dover St SE1 128 B1
Great Eastern Rd E15 125 P2
Great Eastern St EC2 124 C5
Great George St SW1 127 K1
Great Guildford St SE1 124 A10
Great James St WC1 123 M7
Great Marlborough St W1 123 J8
Great Maze Pond SE1 128 B1
Great Ormond St WC1 123 L7
Great Percy St WC1 123 M5
Great Peter St SW1 127 K2
Great Portland St W1 123 H7
Great Pulteney St W1 123 J9
Great Queen St WC2 123 L8
Great Russell St WC1 123 L7
Great St. Helens EC3 124 C8
Great Scotland Yd SW1 123 L10
Great Smith St SW1 127 K2
Great Suffolk St SE1 127 P1
Great Sutton St EC1 123 P6
Great Titchfield St W1 123 J8
Great Twr St EC3 124 C9
Great Winchester St EC2 124 B8
Great Windmill St W1 123 K9
Greatfield Cl SE4 129 L10
Greatorex St E1 124 E7
Greek St W1 123 K8
Green Bk E1 124 F10
Green Dale SE5 128 B10
Green Hundred Rd SE15 128 E5
Green St W1 122 G9
Greenberry St NW8 122 E4
Greencoat Pl SW1 127 J3
Greencroft Gdns NW6 122 B2
Greenfield Rd E1 124 E7
Greenham Cl SE1 127 N1
Greenland Quay SE16 129 H3
Greenland Rd NW1 123 J3
Greenman St N1 124 A2
Greenwell St W1 123 H6
Greenwich Ch St SE10 129 N5
Greenwich Foot Tunnel E14 129 N4
Greenwich Foot Tunnel SE10 129 N4
Greenwich High Rd SE10 129 M7
Greenwich Mkt SE10 129 N5
Greenwich Pk St SE10 129 P4
Greenwich S St SE10 129 M7
Greenwich Vw Pl E14 129 M2
Greenwood Ct SW1 127 J4
Greenwood Rd E8 124 E1
Greet St SE1 123 N10
Gregory Pl W8 126 B1
Grenade St E14 125 K9
Grendon St NW8 122 E6
Grenville Ms SW7 126 C3
Grenville Pl SW7 126 C2
Grenville St WC1 123 L6
Gresham Rd SW9 127 N9
Gresham St EC2 124 A8
Gresse St W1 123 K7
Greville Hall NW6 122 B4
Greville Pl NW6 122 B4
Greville Rd NW6 122 B3
Greville St EC1 123 N7
Grey Eagle St E1 124 D7
Greycoat Pl SW1 127 K2
Greycoat St SW1 127 K2
Grimwade Cl SE15 128 G9
Grinling Pl SE8 129 L5
Grinstead Rd SE8 129 J4
Grittleton Rd W9 122 A6
Groom Pl SW1 126 G2
Groombridge Rd E9 125 H2
Grosvenor Cres SW1 126 G1
Grosvenor Cres Ms SW1 126 G1
Grosvenor Est SW1 127 K3
Grosvenor Gdns SW1 127 H2
Grosvenor Gate W1 122 F9
Grosvenor Hill W1 123 H9
Grosvenor Pk SE5 128 A5
Grosvenor Pl SW1 126 G1
Grosvenor Rd SW1 127 H5
Grosvenor Sq W1 122 G9
Grosvenor St W1 123 H9
Grosvenor Ter SE5 127 P6
Grosvenor Wf Rd E14 129 P3
Grove Cotts SW3 126 E5
Grove Cres SE5 128 C8
Grove Cres Rd E15 125 P1
Grove End Rd NW8 122 D5
Grove Hill Rd SE5 128 C9
Grove La SE5 128 B7
Grove Pk SE5 128 C8
Grove Pas E2 124 F4
Grove Rd E3 125 H3
Grove St SE8 129 K3
Grove Vale SE22 128 D10
Grove Vil E14 125 M9
Grovelands Cl SE5 128 C8
Groveway SW9 127 M7
Grummant Rd SE15 128 D7
Grundy St E14 125 M8
Guildford Gro SE10 129 M7
Guildford Rd SW8 127 L7
Guildhouse St SW1 127 J3
Guilford Pl WC1 123 M6
Guilford St WC1 123 L6
Guinness Bldgs SE1 128 C3
Guinness Cl E9 125 J2
Guinness Trust Bldgs SE11 127 P4
Guinness Trust Bldgs SW9 127 P10
Gulliver St SE16 129 K2
Gun St E1 124 D7
Gunmakers La E3 125 J3
Gunter Gro SW10 126 C5
Gunthorpe St E1 124 D8
Gunwhale Cl SE16 125 H10
Gutter La EC2 124 A8
Guy St SE1 128 B1
Gwyn Cl SW6 126 C6
Gwynne Rd SW11 126 D8
Gylcote Cl SE5 128 B10

H

Haberdasher St N1 124 B5
Hackford Rd SW9 127 M7
Hackney Rd E2 124 D5
Haddo St SE10 129 M5
Haddonfield SE8 129 H3
Hadleigh St E2 124 G6
Hadley St NW1 123 H1
Hadrian Est E2 124 E4
Hafer Rd SW11 126 F10
Haggerston Rd E8 124 D2
Hainford Cl SE4 129 H10
Hainton Cl E1 124 F8
Halcomb St N1 124 C3
Hale St E14 125 M9
Halesworth Rd SE13 129 M9
Half Moon Cres N1 123 M4
Half Moon St W1 123 H10
Halford Rd SW6 126 A5
Halkin Arc SW1 126 G2
Halkin Pl SW1 126 G2
Halkin St SW1 126 G1
Hall Pl W2 122 D6
Hall Rd NW8 122 C5
Hall St EC1 123 P5
Hallam St W1 123 H7
Halley Gdns SE13 129 P10
Halley St E14 125 J7
Hallfield Est W2 122 C8
Halliford St N1 124 A2
Halsey St SW3 126 F3
Halsmere Rd SE5 127 P7
Halton Cross St N1 123 P3
Halton Rd N1 123 P2
Hamble St SW6 126 B9
Hamilton Cl NW8 122 D5
Hamilton Gdns NW8 122 C5
Hamilton Pl W1 122 G10
Hamilton Ter NW8 122 B4
Hamlet, The SE5 128 B9
Hamlets Way E3 125 K6
Hammond St NW5 123 J1
Hampson Way SW8 127 M7
Hampstead Rd NW1 123 J4
Hampton Cl NW6 122 A5
Hampton St SE1 127 P3
Hampton St SE17 127 P3
Hanbury St E1 124 D7
Hancock Rd E3 125 N5
Hand Ct WC1 123 M7
Handel St WC1 123 L6
Handforth Rd SW9 127 N6
Handley Rd E9 124 G2
Hankey Pl SE1 128 B1
Hannibal Rd E1 124 G7
Hannington Rd SW4 127 H9
Hanover Gdns SE11 127 N5
Hanover Gate NW1 122 E5
Hanover Pk SE15 128 E7
Hanover Sq W1 123 H8
Hanover St W1 123 H8
Hanover Ter NW1 122 E5
Hans Cres SW1 126 F2
Hans Pl SW1 126 F2
Hans Rd SW3 126 F2
Hanson St W1 123 J7
Hanway St W1 123 K8
Harben Rd NW6 122 C2
Harbet Rd W2 122 D7
Harbinger Rd E14 129 M3
Harbledown Rd SW6 126 A7
Harbour Av SW10 126 C7
Harbour Ex Sq E14 129 M1
Harbour Rd SE5 128 A9
Harbut Rd SW11 126 D10
Harcourt Rd SE4 129 J10
Harcourt St W1 122 E7
Harcourt Ter SW10 126 B4
Harders Rd SE15 128 F8
Hardinge St E1 124 G8
Hardwick St EC1 123 N5
Hare & Billet Rd SE3 129 P7
Hare Row E2 124 F4
Hare Wk N1 124 C4
Harecourt Rd N1 124 A1
Haredale Rd SE24 128 A10
Harefield Ms SE4 129 K9
Harefield Rd SE4 129 K9
Harewood Av NW1 122 E6
Harfield Gdns SE5 128 C9
Harford St E1 125 J6
Hargwyne St SW9 127 M9
Harlescott Rd SE15 129 H10
Harley Gdns SW10 126 C4
Harley Gro E3 125 K5
Harley Pl W1 123 H7
Harley Rd NW3 122 D2
Harley St W1 123 H6
Harleyford Rd SE11 127 M5
Harleyford St SE11 127 N5
Harmood St NW1 123 H2
Harmsworth St SE17 127 P4
Harold Est SE1 128 C2
Harold Pl SE11 127 N4
Harper Rd SE1 128 A2
Harpley Sq E1 124 G5
Harpsden St SW11 126 G7
Harpur St WC1 123 M7
Harrap St E14 125 N9
Harriet Cl E8 124 E3
Harriet Wk SW1 126 F1
Harrington Gdns SW7 126 B3
Harrington Rd SW7 126 D3
Harrington Sq NW1 123 J4
Harrington St NW1 123 J5
Harris St SE5 128 B6
Harrison St WC1 123 L5
Harrow La E14 125 N9
Harrow Pl E1 124 C8
Harroway Rd SW11 126 D8
Harrowby St W1 122 E8
Harrowgate Rd E9 125 J1
Hartfield Ter E3 125 L4
Hartington Rd SW8 127 L7
Hartlake Rd E9 125 H1
Hartland Rd NW1 123 H2
Hartley St E2 124 G5
Harton St SE8 129 L7
Harts La SE14 129 J6
Harvey Rd SE5 128 B7
Harvey St N1 124 B3
Harwich La EC2 124 C7
Harwood Rd SW6 126 A6
Harwood Ter SW6 126 B7
Hascombe Ter SE5 128 B8
Haselrigge Rd SW4 127 K10
Hasker St SW3 126 E3
Haslam Cl N1 123 N2
Haslam St SE15 128 D6
Hassett Rd E9 125 H1
Hastings Cl SE15 128 E6
Hastings St WC1 123 L5
Hatcham Pk Rd SE14 129 H7
Hatcham Rd SE15 128 G5
Hatfields SE1 123 P10
Hatherley Gro W2 122 B8
Hathorne Cl SE15 128 F8
Hatton Gdn EC1 123 N7
Hatton Pl EC1 123 N6
Hatton Wall EC1 123 N7
Havannah St E14 129 L1
Havelock St N1 123 L3
Havelock Ter SW8 127 H6
Haverfield Rd E3 125 J5
Haverstock St N1 123 P4
Havil St SE5 128 C6
Hawes St N1 123 P2
Hawgood St E3 125 L7
Hawkstone Rd SE16 128 G3
Hawley Cres NW1 123 H2
Hawley Rd NW1 123 H2
Hawley St NW1 123 H2
Hawthorne Cl N1 124 C1
Hawtrey Rd NW3 122 E2
Hay Currie St E14 125 M8
Hay Hill W1 123 H9
Hay St E2 124 E3
Hayles St SE11 127 P3
Haymarket SW1 123 K9
Haymerle Rd SE15 128 E5
Hay's Ms W1 123 H9
Hazel Cl SE15 128 E8
Hazelmere Rd NW6 122 A3
Hazlebury Rd SW6 126 B8
Head St E1 125 H8
Headfort Pl SW1 126 G1
Headlam St E1 124 F6
Heald St SE14 129 K7
Healey St NW1 123 H1
Hearn St EC2 124 C6
Heath La SE3 129 P8
Heath Rd SW8 127 H8
Heathcote St WC1 123 M6
Heather Cl SW8 127 H9
Heathwall St SW11 126 F9
Heaton Rd SE15 128 E9
Heddon St W1 123 J9
Hedgers Gro E9 125 J1

Heiron St

Heiron St SE17 127 P5
Helmet Row EC1 124 A6
Helmsley Pl E8 124 F2
Hemans St SW8 127 K6
Hemberton Rd SW9 127 L9
Hemingford Rd N1 123 M3
Hemming St E1 124 E6
Hemp Wk SE17 128 B3
Hemstal Rd NW6 122 A2
Hemsworth St N1 124 C4
Heneage St E1 124 D7
Henley Dr SE1 128 D3
Henley St SW11 126 G8
Henning St SW11 126 E7
Henrietta Cl SE8 129 L5
Henrietta Pl W1 123 H8
Henrietta St WC2 123 L9
Henriques St E1 124 E8
Henshall St N1 124 B1
Henshaw St SE17 128 B3
Henstridge Pl NW8 122 E4
Henty Cl SW11 126 E6
Hepscott Rd E9 125 L2
Herbal Hill EC1 123 N6
Herbert St NW5 122 G1
Herbrand St WC1 123 L6
Hercules Rd SE1 127 M2
Hereford Ho NW6 122 A4
Hereford Pl SE14 129 K6
Hereford Rd W2 122 A8
Hereford Sq SW7 126 C3
Hereford St E2 124 E6
Heritage Cl SW9 127 P9
Hermes Pt W9 122 A6
Hermit St EC1 123 P5
Hermitage St W2 122 D7
Hermitage Wall E1 124 E10
Herne Hill Rd SE24 128 A9
Heron Pl SE16 125 J10
Heron Quay E14 125 L10
Heron Rd SE24 128 A10
Herrick St SW1 127 K3
Hertford Rd N1 124 C3
Hertford St W1 123 H10
Hertsmere Rd E14 125 L9
Hesper Ms SW5 126 B4
Hesperus Cres E14 129 M3
Hessel St E1 124 F8
Hester Rd SW11 126 E6
Heston St SE14 129 K7
Hetherington Rd SW4 127 L10
Hewison St E3 125 K4
Hewlett Rd E3 125 J4
Heyford Av SW8 127 L6
Heygate St SE17 128 A3
Hibbert St SW11 126 D9
Hickmore Wk SW4 127 J9
Hicks Cl SW11 126 E9
Hicks St SE8 129 J4
Hide Pl SW1 127 K3
High Br SE10 129 P4
High Br Wf SE10 129 P4
High Holborn WC1 123 L8
High St E15 125 N4
High Timber St EC4 124 A9
Highbury Cor N5 123 N1
Highbury Gro N5 123 P1
Highbury Pl N5 123 P1
Highbury Sta Rd N1 123 N1
Highshore Rd SE15 128 D8
Highway, The E1 124 F9
Highway, The E14 124 F9
Hilary Cl SW6 126 B6
Hilda Ter SW9 127 N8
Hildyard Rd SW6 126 A5
Hilgrove Rd NW6 122 C2
Hill Rd NW8 122 C4
Hill St W1 123 H10
Hillbeck Cl SE15 128 G6
Hillgate Pl W8 122 A10
Hillgate St W8 122 A10
Hillingdon St SE5 127 P5
Hillingdon St SE17 127 P5
Hillman St E8 124 F1
Hillmead Dr SW9 127 P10
Hillside Cl NW8 122 B4
Hilltop Rd NW6 122 A2
Hilly Flds Cres SE4 129 L9
Hillyard St SW9 127 N7
Hinckley Rd SE15 128 E10
Hind Gro E14 125 L8
Hinde St W1 122 G8
Hinton Rd SE24 127 P9
Hitchin Sq E3 125 J4
Hobart Pl SW1 127 H2
Hobday St E14 125 M7
Hobury St SW10 126 C5
Hockett Cl SE8 129 J3
Hodnet Gro SE16 129 H3
Hogarth Rd SW5 126 B3
Holbeck Row SE15 128 E6
Holbein Ms SW1 126 G4
Holbein Pl SW1 126 G3
Holborn EC1 123 N7
Holborn Viaduct EC1 123 N7
Holcroft Rd E9 124 G2
Holden St SW11 126 G8
Holford St WC1 123 N5
Holgate Av SW11 126 D9
Holland Gro SW9 127 N6
Holland St SE1 123 P10
Holland St W8 126 A1
Hollen St W1 123 J8
Holles St W1 123 H8
Holloway Rd N7 123 N1
Holly Gro SE15 128 D8
Holly St E8 124 D1
Holly St Est E8 124 D2
Hollybush Gdns E2 124 F5
Hollybush Wk SW9 127 P10
Hollydale Rd SE15 128 G7
Hollydene SE15 128 F7
Hollymount Cl SE10 129 N7
Hollywood Rd SW10 126 C5
Holman Rd SW11 126 D8
Holmead Rd SW6 126 B6
Holmefield Ct NW3 122 E1
Holmes Ter SE1 127 N1
Holms St E2 124 E4
Holton St E1 125 H6
Holwood Pl SW4 127 K10
Holyhead Cl E3 125 L5
Holywell La EC2 124 C6
Holywell Row EC2 124 C6
Home Rd SW11 126 E8
Homefield St N1 124 C4
Homer Dr E14 129 L3
Homer Rd E9 125 J1
Homer Row W1 122 E7
Homer St W1 122 E7
Hooper St E1 124 E8
Hope St SW11 126 D9
Hopewell St SE5 128 B6
Hopton Gdns SE1 123 P10
Hopton St SE1 123 P10
Hopwood Rd SE17 128 B5
Horatio St E2 124 D4
Horbury Cres W11 122 A9
Hornby Cl NW3 122 D2
Hornshay St SE15 128 G5
Hornton Pl W8 126 A1
Hornton St W8 126 A1
Horse Guards Av SW1 123 L10
Horse Guards Rd SW1 123 K10
Horse Ride SW1 123 J10
Horseferry Pl SE10 129 N5
Horseferry Rd E14 125 J9
Horseferry Rd SW1 127 K3
Horselydown La SE1 128 D1
Horsley St SE17 128 B5
Hortensia Rd SW10 126 C6
Horton Rd E8 124 F1
Horton St SE13 129 M9
Hosier La EC1 123 P7
Hoskins St SE10 129 P4
Hotspur St SE11 127 N4
Houndsditch EC3 124 C8
Howbury Rd SE15 128 G9
Howden St SE15 128 E9
Howick Pl SW1 127 J2
Howie St SW11 126 E6
Howitt Rd NW3 122 E1
Howland Est SE16 128 G2
Howland St W1 123 J7
Howland Way SE16 129 J1
Howley Pl W2 122 C7
Hows St E2 124 D4
Howson Rd SE4 129 J10
Hoxton Sq N1 124 C5
Hoxton St N1 124 C3
Hubert Gro SW9 127 L9
Huddart St E3 125 L7
Huddleston Cl E2 124 G4
Hugh St SW1 127 H3
Hugon Rd SW6 126 B9
Huguenot Pl E1 124 D7
Hull Cl SE16 129 H1
Humphrey St SE1 128 D4
Hungerford Br SE1 123 L10
Hungerford Br WC2 123 L10
Hunsdon Rd SE14 129 H5
Hunter St WC1 123 L6
Huntingdon St N1 123 M2
Huntley St WC1 123 J6
Hunton St E1 124 E6
Hunts La E15 125 N4
Huntsman St SE17 128 B3
Hurley Rd SE11 127 N3
Huson Cl NW3 122 E2
Hutchings St E14 129 L1
Hyde Pk SW7 122 F10
Hyde Pk W1 122 F10
Hyde Pk W2 122 F10
Hyde Pk Cor W1 126 G1
Hyde Pk Cres W2 122 E8
Hyde Pk Gdns W2 122 D9
Hyde Pk Gate SW7 126 C1
Hyde Pk Pl W2 122 E9
Hyde Pk Sq W2 122 E8
Hyde Pk St W2 122 E8
Hyde Rd N1 124 B3
Hyde Vale SE10 129 N6
Hyndman St SE15 128 F5

I

Iceland Rd E3 125 L3
Ida St E14 125 N8
Idonia St SE8 129 K6
Ifield Rd SW10 126 B5
Ilchester Gdns W2 122 B9
Ilderton Rd SE15 128 G6
Ilderton Rd SE16 128 F4
Iliffe St SE17 127 P4
Ilminster Gdns SW11 126 E10
Imber St N1 124 B3
Imperial College Rd SW7 126 D2
Imperial Rd SW6 126 C7
Imperial Sq SW6 126 B7
Imperial St E3 125 N5
Indescon Ct E14 129 M1
Ingate Pl SW8 127 H7
Ingelow Rd SW8 127 H8
Ingleborough St SW9 127 N8
Inglesham Wk E9 125 K1
Ingleton St SW9 127 N8
Inglewood Cl E14 129 L3
Inglis St SE5 127 P7
Ingrave St SW11 126 D9
Inkerman Rd NW5 123 H1
Inner Circle NW1 122 G5
Inverness Pl W2 122 B9
Inverness St NW1 123 H3
Inverness Ter W2 122 B9
Inverton Rd SE15 129 H10
Inville Rd SE17 128 B4
Inwen Ct SE8 129 J4
Inworth St SW11 126 E8
Ireland Yd EC4 123 P8
Irene Rd SW6 126 A7
Ironmonger Row EC1 124 A5
Irving Gro SW9 127 M8
Irving St WC2 123 K9
Isabel St SW9 127 M7
Isabella St SE1 123 P10
Isambard Ms E14 129 N2
Islington Grn N1 123 P3
Islington High St N1 123 P4
Islington Pk St N1 123 N2
Ivanhoe Rd SE5 128 D9
Iveagh Cl E9 125 H3
Iveley Rd SW4 127 J8
Iverna Ct W8 126 A2
Iverna Gdns W8 126 A2
Ives St SW3 126 E3
Ivimey St E2 124 E5
Ivor Pl NW1 122 F6
Ivor St NW1 123 J2
Ivy Rd SE4 129 K10
Ivy St N1 124 C4
Ivydale Rd SE15 129 H9
Ixworth Pl SW3 126 E4

J

Jackman St E8 124 F3
Jackson Cl E9 124 G2
Jacob St SE1 128 E1
Jago Wk SE5 128 B6
Jamaica Rd SE1 128 E1
Jamaica Rd SE16 128 F1
Jamaica St E1 124 G8
James St W1 122 G8
Jameson St W8 122 A10
Jamestown Rd NW1 123 H3
Jamestown Way E14 125 P9
Janet St E14 129 L2
Janeway St SE16 128 E1
Jardine Rd E1 125 H9
Jarrow Rd SE16 128 G3
Jay Ms SW7 126 C1
Jebb St E3 125 L4
Jedburgh St SW11 126 G10
Jeffreys Rd SW4 127 L8
Jeffreys St NW1 123 H2
Jeffreys Wk SW4 127 L8
Jeger Av E2 124 D3
Jerdan Pl SW6 126 A6
Jeremiah St E14 125 M8
Jermyn St SW1 123 K9
Jerningham Rd SE14 129 J8
Jerome Cres NW8 122 E6
Jerrard St SE13 129 M9
Jewry St EC3 124 D8
Jew's Row SW18 126 C10
Joan St SE1 123 P10
Jocelyn St SE15 128 E7
Jockey's Flds WC1 123 M7
Jodane St SE8 129 K3
Jodrell Rd E3 125 K3
John Adam St WC2 123 L9
John Aird Ct W2 122 C7
John Carpenter St EC4 123 P9
John Felton Rd SE16 128 E1
John Fisher St E1 124 E9
John Islip St SW1 127 L3
John Maurice Cl SE17 128 B3
John Penn St SE13 129 M7
John Princes St W1 123 H8
John Roll Way SE16 128 E2
John Ruskin St SE5 127 P6
John Silkin La SE8 129 H3
John Spencer Sq N1 123 P1
John St WC1 123 M6
John Williams Cl SE14 129 H5
John's Ms WC1 123 M6
Johnson Cl E8 124 E3
Johnson's Pl SW1 127 J4
Jonathan St SE11 127 M4
Joseph St E3 125 K6
Joubert St SW11 126 F8
Jowett St SE15 128 D6
Jubilee Cres E14 129 N2
Jubilee Pl SW3 126 E4
Jubilee St E1 124 G8
Judd St WC1 123 L5
Juer St SW11 126 E6
Julian Pl E14 129 M4
Junction App SE13 129 N9
Junction App SW11 126 E9
Juniper Cres NW1 122 G2
Juniper St E1 124 G9
Juno Way SE14 129 H5
Jupiter Way N7 123 M1
Jupp Rd E15 125 P2
Jupp Rd W E15 125 N3
Juxon St SE11 127 M3

K

Kambala Rd SW11 126 D9
Kassala Rd SW11 126 F7
Kathleen Rd SW11 126 F9
Kay Rd SW9 127 L8
Kay St E2 124 E4
Kay St E15 125 P2
Kean St WC2 123 M8
Keel Cl SE16 125 H10
Keeley St WC2 123 M8
Keesey St SE17 128 B5
Keetons Rd SE16 128 F2
Keildon Rd SW11 126 F10
Kellett Rd SW2 127 N10
Kelly Av SE15 128 D6
Kelly St NW1 123 H1
Kelman Cl SW4 127 K8
Kelmore Gro SE22 128 E10
Kelsey St E2 124 F6
Kelso Pl W8 126 B2
Kelson Ho E14 129 N2
Kemble St WC2 123 M8
Kemerton Rd SE5 128 A9
Kempsford Gdns SW5 126 A4
Kempsford Rd SE11 127 N3
Kempson Rd SW6 126 A7
Kempthorne Rd SE8 129 J3
Kenbury St SE5 128 A8
Kenchester Cl SW8 127 L6
Kendal Cl SW9 127 P6
Kendal St W2 122 E8
Kender St SE14 128 G6
Kendoa Rd SW4 127 K10
Kendrick Pl SW7 126 D3
Kenilworth Rd E3 125 J4
Kennard Rd E15 125 P2
Kennard St SW11 126 G8
Kennet St E1 124 E10
Kenning Ter N1 124 C3
Kennings Way SE11 127 N4
Kennington La SE11 127 M4
Kennington Oval SE11 127 M5
Kennington Pk Gdns SE11 127 P5
Kennington Pk Pl SE11 127 N5
Kennington Pk Rd SE11 127 N5
Kennington Rd SE1 127 N2
Kennington Rd SE11 127 N3
Kensington Ch Ct W8 126 B1
Kensington Ch St W8 122 A10
Kensington Ch Wk W8 126 B1
Kensington Ct W8 126 B1
Kensington Ct Pl W8 126 B2
Kensington Gdns W2 122 C10
Kensington Gdns Sq W2 122 B8
Kensington Gate W8 126 C2
Kensington Gore SW7 126 D1
Kensington High St W8 126 A2
Kensington Mall W8 122 A10
Kensington Palace Gdns W8 122 B10
Kensington Pl W8 122 A10
Kensington Rd SW7 126 D1
Kensington Rd W8 126 B1
Kensington Sq W8 126 B1
Kent Pas NW1 122 F5
Kent St E2 124 D4
Kent Ter NW1 122 E5
Kentish Town Rd NW1 123 H2
Kentish Town Rd NW5 123 H2
Kenton Rd E9 125 H1
Kenton St WC1 123 L6
Kenway Rd SW5 126 B3
Kenwyn Rd SW4 127 K10
Kepler Rd SW4 127 L10
Keppel St WC1 123 K7
Kerbey St E14 125 M8
Kerfield Cres SE5 128 B7
Kerfield Pl SE5 128 B7
Kerridge Ct N1 124 C1
Kerrison Rd E15 125 P3
Kerrison Rd SW11 126 E9
Kerry Rd SE14 129 K5
Kersley Ms SW11 126 F8
Kersley St SW11 126 F8
Keston Rd SE15 128 E9
Kestrel Ho EC1 123 P5
Kevan Ho SE5 128 A6
Key Cl E1 124 F6
Keybridge Ho SW8 127 L5
Keyworth St SE1 127 P2
Khyber Rd SW11 126 E8
Kibworth St SW8 127 M6
Kilburn Pk Rd NW6 122 A5
Kilburn Pl NW6 122 A3
Kilburn Priory NW6 122 B3
Kildare Gdns W2 122 A8
Kildare Ter W2 122 A8
Kilkie St SW6 126 C8
Killick St N1 123 M4
Killowen Rd E9 125 H1
Killyon Rd SW8 127 J8
Killyon Ter SW8 127 J8
Kilner St E14 125 L7
Kimberley Av SE15 128 F8
Kimberley Rd SW9 127 L8
Kimpton Rd SE5 128 B7
Kinburn St SE16 129 H1
Kincaid Rd SE15 128 F6
King & Queen St SE17 128 A4
King Arthur Cl SE15 128 G6
King Charles St SW1 127 K1
King David La E1 124 G9
King Edward St EC1 124 A8
King Edward Wk SE1 127 N2
King Edwards Rd E9 124 F3
King Frederik IX Twr SE16 129 K2
King George St SE10 129 N6
King Henry's Rd NW3 122 E2
King Henry's Wk N1 124 C1
King James St SE1 127 P1
King John St E1 125 H7
King St EC2 124 A8
King St SW1 123 J10
King St WC2 123 L9
King William St EC4 124 B9
King William Wk SE10 129 N5
Kingdon Rd NW6 122 A1
Kingfield St E14 129 N3
Kingfisher Sq SE8 129 K5
Kinglake St SE17 128 C4
Kingly St W1 123 J8
Kings College Rd NW3 122 E2
King's Cross Rd WC1 123 M5
Kings Gro SE15 128 F6
King's Ms WC1 123 M7
King's Reach Twr SE1 123 N10
King's Rd SW1 126 F4
King's Rd SW3 126 F4
King's Rd SW6 126 B7
King's Rd SW10 126 B7
Kingsbury Rd N1 124 C1
Kingsbury Ter N1 124 C1
Kingsgate Pl NW6 122 A2
Kingsgate Rd NW6 122 A2
Kingshold Rd E9 124 G2
Kingsland Grn E8 124 C1
Kingsland Rd E2 124 C4
Kingsland Rd E8 124 C4
Kingsley St SW11 126 F9
Kingsmill Ter NW8 122 D4
Kingstown St NW1 122 G3
Kingsway WC2 123 M8
Kingswood Cl SW8 127 L6
Kinnerton St SW1 126 G1
Kinsale Rd SE15 128 E9
Kipling Est SE1 128 B1
Kipling St SE1 128 B1
Kirby Est SE16 128 F2
Kirby Gro SE1 128 C1
Kirkland Wk E8 124 D1
Kirkwall Pl E2 124 G5
Kirkwood Rd SE15 128 F8
Kirtling St SW8 127 J6
Kirwyn Way SE5 127 P6
Kitcat Ter E3 125 L5
Kitson Rd SE5 128 B6
Kitto Rd SE14 129 H8
Knapp Rd E3 125 L6
Knaresborough Pl SW5 126 B3
Knatchbull Rd SE5 128 A7
Kneller Rd SE4 129 J10
Knighten St E1 124 E10
Knightsbridge SW1 126 F1
Knightsbridge SW7 126 E1
Knightsbridge Grn SW1 126 F1
Knivet Rd SW6 126 A5
Knobs Hill Rd E15 125 M3
Knottisford St E2 124 G5
Knowle Cl SW9 127 N9
Knowles Wk SW4 127 J9
Knowsley Rd SW11 126 F8
Knox St W1 122 F7
Kylemore Rd NW6 122 A2
Kynance Ms SW7 126 B2
Kynance Pl SW7 126 C2

L

Laburnum St E2 124 D3
Lacey Wk E3 125 L4
Lackington St EC2 124 B7
Lacon Rd SE22 128 E10
Ladycroft Rd SE13 129 M9
Lafone St SE1 128 D1
Lagado Ms SE16 125 H10
Laird Ho SE5 128 A6
Lamb La E8 124 F2
Lamb St E1 124 D7
Lambert St N1 123 N2
Lambeth Br SE1 127 L3
Lambeth Br SW1 127 L3
Lambeth High St SE1 127 M3
Lambeth Hill EC4 124 A9
Lambeth Palace Rd SE1 127 M2
Lambeth Rd SE1 127 M3
Lambeth Rd SE11 127 M3
Lambeth Wk SE11 127 M3
Lambolle Pl NW3 122 E1
Lambolle Rd NW3 122 E1
Lambourn Rd SW4 127 H9
Lamb's Conduit St WC1 123 M6
Lamb's Pas EC1 124 B7
Lamerton St SE8 129 L5
Lammas Rd E9 125 H2
Lamont Rd SW10 126 C5
Lanark Pl W9 122 C6
Lanark Rd W9 122 B4
Lanark Sq E14 129 M2
Lanbury Rd SE15 129 H10
Lancaster Dr NW3 122 E1
Lancaster Gate W2 122 C9
Lancaster Gro NW3 122 D1
Lancaster Ms W2 122 C9
Lancaster Pl WC2 123 M9
Lancaster St SE1 127 P1
Lancaster Ter W2 122 D9
Lancaster Wk W2 122 C10
Lancelot Pl SW7 126 F1
Lancresse Ct N1 124 C3
Landmann Way SE14 129 H4
Landon Pl SW1 126 F2
Landons Cl E14 125 N10
Landor Rd SW9 127 L9
Lanfranc Rd E3 125 J4
Lang St E1 124 G6
Langbourne Pl E14 129 M4
Langdale Cl SE17 128 A5
Langdale Rd SE10 129 N6
Langford Ct NW8 122 C4
Langford Grn SE5 128 C9
Langford Pl NW8 122 C4
Langford Rd SW6 126 B8
Langham Pl W1 123 H7
Langham St W1 123 H7
Langley La SW8 127 M5
Langley St WC2 123 L8
Langton Rd SW9 127 P6
Langton St SW10 126 C5
Langtry Rd NW8 122 B3
Lanhill Rd W9 122 A6
Lanrick Rd E14 125 P8
Lansbury Est E14 125 M8
Lansbury Gdns E14 125 P8
Lanscombe Wk SW8 127 L7
Lansdowne Dr E8 124 E1
Lansdowne Gdns SW8 127 L7
Lansdowne Ter WC1 123 L6
Lansdowne Way SW8 127 L7
Lant St SE1 128 A1
Lanterns Ct E14 129 L1

Mews St

Lanvanor Rd **SE15** 128 G8
Larcom St **SE17** 128 A3
Lark Row **E2** 124 G3
Larkhall La **SW4** 127 K8
Larkhall Ri **SW4** 127 J9
Lassell St **SE10** 129 P4
Latchmere Rd **SW11** 126 F8
Latchmere St **SW11** 126 F8
Latham Ho **E1** 125 H8
Latona Rd **SE15** 128 E5
Lauderdale Rd **W9** 122 B5
Launceston Pl **W8** 126 C2
Launch St **E14** 129 N2
Laurel St **E8** 124 D1
Laurie Gro **SE14** 129 J7
Lauriston Rd **E9** 125 H3
Lausanne Rd **SE15** 128 G7
Lavender Gdns **SW11** 126 F10
Lavender Gro **E8** 124 D2
Lavender Hill **SW11** 126 E10
Lavender Rd **SE16** 125 J10
Lavender Rd **SW11** 126 D9
Lavender Sweep **SW11** 126 F10
Lavender Wk **SW11** 126 F10
Laverton Pl **SW5** 126 B3
Lavington St **SE1** 123 P10
Law St **SE1** 128 B2
Lawford Rd **N1** 124 C2
Lawford Rd **NW5** 123 J1
Lawless St **E14** 125 M9
Lawn Ho Cl **E14** 129 N1
Lawn La **SW8** 127 L5
Lawrence Cl **E3** 125 L4
Lawrence St **SW3** 126 E5
Lawson Est **SE1** 128 B2
Lawton Rd **E3** 125 J5
Laxley Cl **SE5** 127 P6
Layard Rd **SE16** 128 F3
Layard Sq **SE16** 128 F3
Laycock St **N1** 123 N1
Laystall St **EC1** 123 N6
Leabank Sq **E9** 125 L1
Leadenhall St **EC3** 124 C8
Leake St **SE1** 127 M1
Leamouth Rd **E14** 125 P8
Leander Ct **SE8** 129 L7
Leather La **EC1** 123 N7
Leathermarket Ct **SE1** 128 C1
Leathermarket St **SE1** 128 C1
Leathwaite Rd **SW11** 126 F10
Leathwell Rd **SE8** 129 M8
Lecky St **SW7** 126 D4
Ledbury Est **SE15** 128 F6
Ledbury St **SE15** 128 E6
Lee Br **SE13** 129 N9
Lee High Rd **SE12** 129 P9
Lee High Rd **SE13** 129 P9
Lee St **E8** 124 D3
Leeke St **WC1** 123 M5
Leerdam Dr **E14** 129 N2
Lees Pl **W1** 122 G9
Leeson Rd **SE24** 127 N10
Leeway **SE8** 129 K4
Lefevre Wk **E3** 125 L3
Leggatt Rd **E15** 125 N4
Legion Cl **N1** 123 N1
Leicester Sq **WC2** 123 K9
Leigh St **WC1** 123 L6
Leinster Gdns **W2** 122 C8
Leinster Ms **W2** 122 C9
Leinster Pl **W2** 122 C8
Leinster Sq **W2** 122 A8
Leinster Ter **W2** 122 C9
Leman St **E1** 124 D8
Lendal Ter **SW4** 127 K9
Lennox Gdns **SW1** 126 F2
Lennox Gdns Ms **SW1** 126 F2
Lenthall Rd **E8** 124 E2
Leo St **SE15** 128 F6
Leonard St **EC2** 124 B6
Leontine Cl **SE15** 128 E6
Leopold St **E3** 125 K7
Leroy St **SE1** 128 C3
Lethbridge Cl **SE13** 129 N7
Lett Rd **E15** 125 P2
Lettsom St **SE5** 128 C8
Levehurst Way **SW4** 127 L8
Leven Rd **E14** 125 N7
Lever St **EC1** 123 P5
Lewey Ho **E3** 125 K6
Lewis Gro **SE13** 129 N9
Lewis St **NW1** 123 H2
Lewisham High St **SE13** 129 N9
Lewisham Hill **SE13** 129 N8
Lewisham Rd **SE13** 129 M7
Lewisham Way **SE4** 129 K7
Lewisham Way **SE14** 129 K7
Lexham Gdns **W8** 126 B2
Lexham Gdns Ms **W8** 126 B2
Lexham Ms **W8** 126 A3
Lexington St **W1** 123 J8
Leybourne Rd **NW1** 123 H2
Leylang Rd **SE14** 129 H6
Liardet St **SE14** 129 J5
Liberia Rd **N5** 123 P1
Liberty St **SW9** 127 M7
Libra Rd **E3** 125 K3
Library St **SE1** 127 P1
Lichfield Rd **E3** 125 J5
Lidcote Gdns **SW9** 127 N8
Liddell Rd **NW6** 122 A1
Lidlington Pl **NW1** 123 J4
Lighter Cl **SE16** 129 J3
Lighterman Ms **E1** 125 H8
Lightermans Rd **E14** 129 L1
Lightermans Wk **SW18** 126 A10
Lilac Pl **SE11** 127 M3
Lilestone St **NW8** 122 E6
Lilford Rd **SE5** 127 P8
Lillie Yd **SW6** 126 A5
Lillieshall Rd **SW4** 127 H9
Lily Pl **EC1** 123 N7
Limburg Rd **SW11** 126 F10
Lime Cl **E1** 124 E10
Lime St **EC3** 124 C9
Limeburner La **EC4** 123 P8
Limeharbour **E14** 129 M2
Limehouse Causeway **E14** 125 K9
Limehouse Flds Est **E14** 125 J7
Limehouse Link **E14** 125 J9
Limerston St **SW10** 126 C5
Limes Gro **SE13** 129 N10
Limes Wk **SE15** 128 F10
Limesford Rd **SE15** 129 H10
Linberry Wk **SE8** 129 K3
Lincoln St **SW3** 126 F3
Lincoln's Inn **WC2** 123 N8
Lincoln's Inn Flds **WC2** 123 M8
Lind St **SE8** 129 M8
Linden Gdns **W2** 122 A9
Linden Gro **SE15** 128 G9
Lindfield St **E14** 125 L8
Lindley St **E1** 124 G7
Lindore Rd **SW11** 126 F10
Lindrop St **SW6** 126 C8
Lindsay Sq **SW1** 127 K4
Lindsell St **SE10** 129 N7
Lindsey Ms **N1** 124 A2
Lindsey St **EC1** 123 P7
Linford St **SW8** 127 J7
Lingards Rd **SE13** 129 N10
Lingham St **SW9** 127 L8
Linhope St **NW1** 122 F6
Link St **E9** 124 G1
Linnell Rd **SE5** 128 C8
Linom Rd **SW4** 127 L10
Linsey St **SE16** 128 E3
Linstead St **NW6** 122 A2
Linton St **N1** 124 A3
Linver Rd **SW6** 126 A8
Linwood Cl **SE5** 128 D8
Lisford St **SE15** 128 D7
Lisle St **WC2** 123 K9
Lisson Grn Est **NW8** 122 E5
Lisson Gro **NW1** 122 E6
Lisson Gro **NW8** 122 D5
Lisson St **NW1** 122 E7
Liston Rd **SW4** 127 J9
Litchfield St **WC2** 123 K9
Lithos Rd **NW3** 122 B1
Little Boltons, The **SW5** 126 B4
Little Boltons, The **SW10** 126 B4
Little Britain **EC1** 123 P7
Little Chester St **SW1** 127 H2
Little Dorrit Ct **SE1** 128 A1
Little Newport St **WC2** 123 K9
Little Portland St **W1** 123 H8
Little Russell St **WC1** 123 L7
Little St. James's St **SW1** 123 J10
Littlebury Rd **SW4** 127 K9
Livermere Rd **E8** 124 D3
Liverpool Gro **SE17** 128 B4
Liverpool Rd **N1** 123 N4
Liverpool St **EC2** 124 C7
Livingstone Rd **E15** 125 N3
Livingstone Wk **SW11** 126 D9
Lizard St **EC1** 124 A5
Lloyd Baker St **WC1** 123 M5
Lloyd Sq **WC1** 123 N5
Lloyd St **WC1** 123 N5
Lloyd's Av **EC3** 124 C8
Loampit Hill **SE13** 129 L8
Loampit Vale **SE13** 129 M9
Lochnagar St **E14** 125 N7
Lockesfield Pl **E14** 129 M4
Lockhart Cl **N7** 123 M1
Lockhart St **E3** 125 K6
Lockington Rd **SW8** 127 H7
Lockmead Rd **SE13** 129 N9
Locksley Est **E14** 125 K8
Locksley St **E14** 125 K7
Lockwood Sq **SE16** 128 F2
Loddiges Rd **E9** 124 G2
Loder St **SE15** 128 G7
Lodge Rd **NW8** 122 D5
Lodore St **E14** 125 N8
Loftie St **SE16** 128 E1
Lofting Rd **N1** 123 M2
Logan Ms **W8** 126 A3
Logan Pl **W8** 126 A3
Lollard St **SE11** 127 M3
Loman St **SE1** 127 P1
Lomas Ct **E8** 124 D2
Lomas St **E1** 124 E7
Lombard Rd **SW11** 126 D8
Lombard St **EC3** 124 B8
Lomond Gro **SE5** 128 B6
Loncroft Rd **SE5** 128 C5
London Br **EC4** 124 B10
London Br **SE1** 124 B10
London Br St **SE1** 124 B10
London Br Wk **SE1** 124 C10
London Flds **E8** 124 F2
London Flds E Side **E8** 124 F2
London Flds W Side **E8** 124 E2
London La **E8** 124 F2
London Rd **SE1** 127 P2
London St **W2** 122 D8
London Wall **EC2** 124 A7
Long Acre **WC2** 123 L9
Long La **EC1** 123 P7
Long La **SE1** 128 B1
Long Rd **SW4** 127 J10
Long St **E2** 124 D5
Long Yd **WC1** 123 M6
Longbeach Rd **SW11** 126 F9
Longfield Est **SE1** 128 D3
Longford St **NW1** 123 H6
Longhedge St **SW11** 126 G8
Longhope Cl **SE15** 128 C5
Longley St **SE1** 128 E3
Longmoore St **SW1** 127 J3
Longnor Rd **E1** 125 H5
Longridge Rd **SW5** 126 A3
Long's Ct **WC2** 123 K9
Longshore **SE8** 129 K3
Lonsdale Sq **N1** 123 N2
Lord Amory Way **E14** 129 N1
Lord Hills Rd **W2** 122 B7
Lord N St **SW1** 127 L2
Lorden Wk **E2** 124 E5
Lorenzo St **WC1** 123 M5
Lorn Ct **SW9** 127 N8
Lorn Rd **SW9** 127 M8
Lorrimore Rd **SE17** 127 P5
Lorrimore Sq **SE17** 127 P5
Lothbury **EC2** 124 B8
Lothian Rd **SW9** 127 P7
Lots Rd **SW10** 126 C6
Loudoun Rd **NW8** 122 C2
Lough Rd **N7** 123 M1
Loughborough Pk **SW9** 127 P10
Loughborough Rd **SW9** 127 N8
Loughborough St **SE11** 127 M4
Louisa St **E1** 125 H6
Louvaine Rd **SW11** 126 D10
Love La **EC2** 124 A8
Love Wk **SE5** 128 B8
Lovegrove St **SE1** 128 E4
Lovegrove Wk **E14** 125 N10
Lovelinch Cl **SE15** 128 G5
Lovell Ho **E8** 124 E3
Lover's Wk **W1** 122 G10
Lowden Rd **SE24** 127 P10
Lowell St **E14** 125 J8
Lower Aberdeen Wf **E14** 125 K10
Lower Belgrave St **SW1** 127 H2
Lower Grosvenor Pl **SW1** 127 H2
Lower Marsh **SE1** 127 N1
Lower Merton Ri **NW3** 122 E2
Lower Rd **SE8** 128 G2
Lower Rd **SE16** 128 G2
Lower Sloane St **SW1** 126 G3
Lower Thames St **EC3** 124 B9
Lowfield Rd **NW6** 122 A2
Lowndes Cl **SW1** 126 G2
Lowndes Pl **SW1** 126 G2
Lowndes Sq **SW1** 126 F1
Lowndes St **SW1** 126 G2
Lowth Rd **SE5** 128 A8
Lowther Gdns **SW7** 126 D1
Lubbock St **SE14** 128 G6
Lucan Pl **SW3** 126 E3
Lucas St **SE8** 129 L7
Lucey Rd **SE16** 128 E2
Ludgate Hill **EC4** 123 P8
Ludwick Ms **SE14** 129 J6
Lugard Rd **SE15** 128 F8
Luke Ho **E1** 124 F8
Luke St **EC2** 124 C6
Lukin St **E1** 124 G8
Lulworth Rd **SE15** 128 F8
Lupus St **SW1** 127 H5
Lurline Gdns **SW11** 126 G7
Luscombe Way **SW8** 127 L6
Luton Pl **SE10** 129 N6
Luton St **NW8** 122 D6
Luxborough St **W1** 122 G6
Luxford St **SE16** 129 H3
Luxmore St **SE4** 129 K7
Luxor St **SE5** 128 A9
Lyal Rd **E3** 125 J4
Lyall Ms **SW1** 126 G2
Lyall St **SW1** 126 G2
Lydney Cl **SE15** 128 C6
Lydon Rd **SW4** 127 J9
Lyme St **NW1** 123 J2
Lymington Rd **NW6** 122 B1
Lympstone Gdns **SE15** 128 E6
Lyncott Cres **SW4** 127 H10
Lyndhurst Gro **SE15** 128 C8
Lyndhurst Sq **SE15** 128 D7
Lyndhurst Way **SE15** 128 D7
Lynton Rd **SE1** 128 D3
Lyons Pl **NW8** 122 D6
Lytham St **SE17** 128 B4
Lyttelton Cl **NW3** 122 E2

M

Mabledon Pl **WC1** 123 K5
Mabley St **E9** 125 J1
Macaulay Ct **SW4** 127 H9
Macaulay Rd **SW4** 127 H9
Macaulay Sq **SW4** 127 H10
Macauley Ms **SE13** 129 N8
Macclesfield Br **NW1** 122 E4
Macclesfield Rd **EC1** 124 A5
Macclesfield St **W1** 123 K9
Macduff Rd **SW11** 126 G7
Mace St **E2** 125 H4
Machell Rd **SE15** 128 G9
Mackay Rd **SW4** 127 H9
Mackennal St **NW8** 122 E4
Mackenzie Rd **N7** 123 M1
Mackenzie Wk **E14** 125 L10
Macklin St **WC2** 123 L8
Macks Rd **SE16** 128 E3
Mackworth St **NW1** 123 J5
Macleod St **SE17** 128 A4
Maconochies Rd **E14** 129 M4
Macquarie Way **E14** 129 M3
Maddams St **E3** 125 M6
Maddock Way **SE17** 127 P5
Maddox St **W1** 123 H9
Madinah Rd **E8** 124 E1
Madras Pl **N7** 123 N1
Madrigal La **SE5** 127 P6
Madron St **SE17** 128 C4
Magdalen St **SE1** 124 C10
Magee St **SE11** 127 N5
Maguire St **SE1** 128 D1
Mahogany Cl **SE16** 125 J10
Maida Av **W2** 122 C7
Maida Vale **W9** 122 B4
Maiden La **NW1** 123 K2
Maiden La **WC2** 123 L9
Maidenstone Hill **SE10** 129 N7
Maitland Cl **SE10** 129 M6
Maitland Pk Est **NW3** 122 F1
Maitland Pk Rd **NW3** 122 F1
Maitland Pk Vil **NW3** 122 F1
Makins St **SW3** 126 E3
Malabar St **E14** 129 L1
Malcolm Pl **E2** 124 G6
Malcolm Rd **E1** 124 G6
Malden Cres **NW1** 122 G1
Maldon Cl **N1** 124 A3
Maldon Cl **SE5** 128 C9
Malet Pl **WC1** 123 K6
Malet St **WC1** 123 K6
Malfort Rd **SE5** 128 C9
Mall, The **E15** 125 P2
Mall, The **SW1** 127 J1
Mallard Cl **E9** 125 K1
Mallard Cl **NW6** 122 A4
Mallord St **SW3** 126 D5
Mallory Cl **SE4** 129 J10
Mallory St **NW8** 122 E6
Malmesbury Rd **E3** 125 K5
Malpas Rd **E8** 124 F1
Malpas Rd **SE4** 129 K8
Malt St **SE1** 128 E5
Maltby St **SE1** 128 D1
Malting Ho **E14** 125 K9
Maltings Pl **SW6** 126 C7
Malvern Ct **SW7** 126 D3
Malvern Rd **E8** 124 E2
Malvern Rd **NW6** 122 A5
Malvern Ter **N1** 123 N3
Manaton Cl **SE15** 128 F9
Manchester Gro **E14** 129 N4
Manchester Rd **E14** 129 N4
Manchester Sq **W1** 122 G8
Manchester St **W1** 122 G7
Manciple St **SE1** 128 B2
Mandela St **NW1** 123 J3
Mandela St **SW9** 127 N6
Mandela Way **SE1** 128 C3
Mandeville Pl **W1** 122 G8
Manette St **W1** 123 K8
Manger Rd **N7** 123 L1
Manilla St **E14** 129 L1
Manley St **NW1** 122 G3
Manor Av **SE4** 129 K8
Manor Est **SE16** 128 F3
Manor Gro **SE15** 128 G5
Manor Ms **SE4** 129 L8
Manor Pk **SE13** 129 P10
Manor Pl **SE17** 127 P4
Manresa Rd **SW3** 126 E4
Mansell St **E1** 124 D8
Mansfield St **W1** 123 H7
Mansford St **E2** 124 E4
Mansion Ho **EC4** 124 B8
Manson Ms **SW7** 126 C3
Manson Pl **SW7** 126 D3
Mantle Rd **SE4** 129 J9
Mantua St **SW11** 126 D9
Mantus Rd **E1** 124 G6
Mape St **E2** 124 F6
Maple St **W1** 123 J7
Mapledene Rd **E8** 124 D2
Maplin St **E3** 125 K5
Marble Arch **W1** 122 F9
Marble Quay **E1** 124 E10
Marchmont St **WC1** 123 L6
Marchwood Cl **SE5** 128 C6
Marcia Rd **SE1** 128 C3
Marcon Pl **E8** 124 F1
Marcus Garvey Way **SE24** 127 N10
Marden Sq **SE16** 128 F2
Mare St **E8** 124 F3
Margaret St **W1** 123 H8
Margaretta Ter **SW3** 126 E5
Margery St **WC1** 123 N5
Maria Ter **E1** 125 H6
Marian Pl **E2** 124 F4
Marigold St **SE16** 128 F1
Marinefield Rd **SW6** 126 B8
Mariners Ms **E14** 129 P3
Marischal Rd **SE13** 129 P9
Maritime Quay **E14** 129 L4
Maritime St **E3** 125 K6
Marjorie Gro **SW11** 126 F10
Mark La **EC3** 124 C9
Market Est **N7** 123 L1
Market Ms **W1** 123 H10
Market Pl **W1** 123 J8
Market Rd **N7** 123 L1
Markham Sq **SW3** 126 F4
Markham St **SW3** 126 E4
Marl Rd **SW18** 126 B10
Marlborough Av **E8** 124 E3
Marlborough Bldgs **SW3** 126 E3
Marlborough Ct **W8** 126 A3
Marlborough Gro **SE1** 128 E4
Marlborough Hill **NW8** 122 C3
Marlborough Pl **NW8** 122 C4
Marlborough Rd **SW1** 123 J10
Marlborough St **SW3** 126 E3
Marloes Rd **W8** 126 B2
Marlow Way **SE16** 129 H1
Marlowes, The **NW8** 122 D3
Marmion Rd **SW11** 126 G10
Marmont Rd **SE15** 128 E7
Marney Rd **SW11** 126 G10
Maroon St **E14** 125 J7
Marquess Rd **N1** 124 B1
Marquis Rd **NW1** 123 K1
Marsala Rd **SE13** 129 M10
Marsden Rd **SE15** 128 D9
Marsden St **NW5** 122 G1
Marsh Wall **E14** 125 L10
Marshall St **W1** 123 J8
Marshalsea Rd **SE1** 128 A1
Marsham St **SW1** 127 K2
Marshfield St **E14** 129 N2
Marshgate La **E15** 125 M3
Marsland Cl **SE17** 127 P4
Martello St **E8** 124 F2
Martello Ter **E8** 124 F2
Martha St **E1** 124 F8
Martineau St **E1** 124 G9
Mary Ann Gdns **SE8** 129 L5
Mary Datchelor Cl **SE5** 128 B7
Mary Grn **NW8** 122 B3
Mary St **N1** 124 A3
Mary Ter **NW1** 123 H3
Marylands Rd **W9** 122 A6
Marylebone High St **W1** 122 G7
Marylebone La **W1** 122 G8
Marylebone Ms **W1** 123 H7
Marylebone Rd **NW1** 122 E7
Marylebone St **W1** 122 G7
Marylee Way **SE11** 127 M3
Maskelyne Cl **SW11** 126 E7
Mason St **SE17** 128 B3
Mason's Pl **EC1** 123 P5
Massingham St **E1** 125 H6
Mast Ho Ter **E14** 129 L3
Mast Leisure Pk **SE16** 129 H2
Masterman Ho **SE5** 128 B6
Masters Dr **SE16** 128 F4
Masters St **E1** 125 H7
Mastmaker Rd **E14** 129 L1
Matham Gro **SE22** 128 D10
Matilda St **N1** 123 M3
Matlock Cl **SE24** 128 A10
Matlock St **E14** 125 J8
Matrimony Pl **SW8** 127 J8
Matthew Parker St **SW1** 127 K1
Matthews St **SW11** 126 F8
Maude Rd **SE5** 128 C7
Maunsel St **SW1** 127 K3
Maverton Rd **E3** 125 L3
Mawbey Est **SE1** 128 E4
Mawbey Pl **SE1** 128 D4
Mawbey St **SW8** 127 L6
Maxted Rd **SE15** 128 D9
Maxwell Rd **SW6** 126 B6
Mayfair Pl **W1** 123 H10
Mayfield Rd **E8** 124 D2
Mayflower Rd **SW9** 127 L9
Mayflower St **SE16** 128 G1
Maygood St **N1** 123 M4
Maysoule Rd **SW11** 126 D10
Mazenod Av **NW6** 122 A2
McAuley Cl **SE1** 127 N2
McCullum Rd **E3** 125 K3
McDermott Cl **SW11** 126 E9
McDermott Rd **SE15** 128 E9
McDowall Rd **SE5** 128 A7
McEwen Way **E15** 125 P3
McKerrell Rd **SE15** 128 E7
McLeod's Ms **SW7** 126 B3
McMillan St **SE8** 129 L5
McNeil Rd **SE5** 128 C8
Mead Pl **E9** 124 G1
Meadcroft Rd **SE11** 127 P5
Meadow Ms **SW8** 127 M5
Meadow Pl **SW8** 127 L6
Meadow Rd **SW8** 127 M5
Meadow Row **SE1** 128 A2
Meadowbank **NW3** 122 F2
Meakin Est **SE1** 128 C2
Meard St **W1** 123 K8
Meath St **SW11** 127 H7
Mecklenburgh Pl **WC1** 123 M6
Mecklenburgh Sq **WC1** 123 M6
Medburn St **NW1** 123 K4
Medlar St **SE5** 128 A7
Medley Rd **NW6** 122 A1
Medway Rd **E3** 125 J4
Medway St **SW1** 127 K2
Medwin St **SW4** 127 M10
Meeting Ho La **SE15** 128 F7
Mehetabel Rd **E9** 124 G1
Melba Way **SE13** 129 M7
Melbourne Gro **SE22** 128 C10
Melbourne Ms **SW9** 127 N7
Melbourne Pl **WC2** 123 M8
Melbury Ter **NW1** 122 E6
Melcombe Pl **NW1** 122 F7
Melcombe St **NW1** 122 F6
Melina Pl **NW8** 122 D5
Melior St **SE1** 128 B1
Mellish St **E14** 129 L2
Melon Rd **SE15** 128 E7
Melton Ct **SW7** 126 D3
Melton St **NW1** 123 K5
Mendip Rd **SW11** 126 C9
Mentmore Ter **E8** 124 F2
Mepham St **SE1** 123 M10
Mercator Rd **SE13** 129 P10
Mercer St **WC2** 123 L8
Merceron St **E1** 124 F6
Merchant St **E3** 125 K5
Mercia Gro **SE13** 129 N10
Mercury Way **SE14** 129 H5
Mercy Ter **SE13** 129 M10
Meretone Cl **SE4** 129 J10
Meridian Gate **E14** 129 N1
Meridian Pl **E14** 129 M1
Mermaid Ct **SE1** 128 B1
Mermaid Ct **SE16** 125 K10
Merrick Sq **SE1** 128 A2
Merrington Rd **SW6** 126 A5
Merrow St **SE17** 128 A5
Merton Ri **NW3** 122 E2
Mervan Rd **SW2** 127 N10
Messina Av **NW6** 122 A2
Meteor St **SW11** 126 G10
Methley St **SE11** 127 N4
Mews Deck **E1** 124 F9
Mews St **E1** 124 E10

Meymott St

Meymott St **SE1** 123 P10
Meynell Cres **E9** 125 H2
Meynell Gdns **E9** 125 H2
Meynell Rd **E9** 125 H2
Meyrick Rd **SW11** 126 D9
Micawber St **N1** 124 A5
Michael Rd **SW6** 126 B7
Micklethwaite Rd **SW6** 126 A5
Middle Fld **NW8** 122 D3
Middle Temple La **EC4** 123 N8
Middlesex St **E1** 124 C7
Middleton Dr **SE16** 129 H1
Middleton Rd **E8** 124 D2
Middleton St **E2** 124 F5
Middleton Way **SE13** 129 P10
Midland Rd **NW1** 123 K4
Midlothian Rd **E3** 125 K7
Midship Pt **E14** 129 L1
Milborne Gro **SW10** 126 C4
Milborne St **E9** 124 G1
Milcote St **SE1** 127 P1
Mildmay Av **N1** 124 B1
Mildmay St **N1** 124 B1
Mile End Pl **E1** 125 H6
Mile End Rd **E1** 124 G7
Mile End Rd **E3** 124 G7
Miles St **SW8** 127 L5
Milford La **WC2** 123 M9
Milk Yd **E1** 124 G9
Milkwell Yd **SE5** 128 A7
Mill Row **N1** 124 C3
Mill St **SE1** 128 D1
Mill St **W1** 123 J9
Millbank **SW1** 127 L2
Millbank Twr **SW1** 127 L3
Millbrook Rd **SW9** 127 P9
Millender Wk **SE16** 128 G3
Millennium Dr **E14** 129 P3
Millennium Mile **SE1** 123 P9
Millennium Pl **E2** 124 F4
Millennium Pt **E14** 129 L1
Miller St **NW1** 123 J4
Miller Wk **SE1** 123 N10
Millgrove St **SW11** 126 G8
Millharbour **E14** 129 M2
Milligan St **E14** 125 K9
Millman Ms **WC1** 123 M6
Millman St **WC1** 123 M6
Millmark Gro **SE14** 129 J8
Millstream Rd **SE1** 128 D1
Millwall Dock Rd **E14** 129 L2
Milman's St **SW10** 126 D5
Milner Pl **N1** 123 N3
Milner Sq **N1** 123 P2
Milner St **SW3** 126 F3
Milton Cl **SE1** 128 D3
Milton Ct Rd **SE14** 129 J5
Milton St **EC2** 124 B7
Milverton St **SE11** 127 N4
Mina Rd **SE17** 128 C4
Mincing La **EC3** 124 C9
Minera Ms **SW1** 126 G3
Minerva Cl **SW9** 127 N6
Minerva St **E2** 124 F4
Minet Rd **SW9** 127 P8
Ming St **E14** 125 L9
Minories **EC3** 124 D8
Minson Rd **E9** 125 H3
Mintern St **N1** 124 B4
Mission Pl **SE15** 128 E7
Mitchell St **EC1** 124 A6
Mitchison Rd **N1** 124 B1
Mitre Rd **SE1** 127 N1
Mitre St **EC3** 124 C8
Moat Pl **SW9** 127 M9
Modling Ho **E2** 125 H4
Molesford Rd **SW6** 126 A7
Molesworth St **SE13** 129 N9
Molyneux St **W1** 122 E7
Mona Rd **SE15** 128 G8
Monck St **SW1** 127 K2
Monclar Rd **SE5** 128 B10
Moncrieff St **SE15** 128 E8
Monier Rd **E3** 125 L2
Monkton St **SE11** 127 N3
Monmouth Rd **W2** 122 B8
Monmouth St **WC2** 123 L9
Monnow Rd **SE1** 128 E3
Monson Rd **SE14** 129 H6
Montagu Ms N **W1** 122 F7
Montagu Pl **W1** 122 F7
Montagu Sq **W1** 122 F7
Montagu St **W1** 122 F8
Montague Av **SE4** 129 K10
Montague Cl **SE1** 124 B10
Montague Pl **WC1** 123 K7
Montague St **EC1** 124 A7
Montague St **WC1** 123 L7
Monteagle Way **SE15** 128 F9
Montefiore St **SW8** 127 H8
Monteith Rd **E3** 125 K3
Montford Pl **SE11** 127 N4
Montpelier Pl **E1** 124 G8
Montpelier Pl **SW7** 126 E2
Montpelier Rd **SE15** 128 F7
Montpelier Sq **SW7** 126 E1
Montpelier St **SW7** 126 E1
Montpelier Wk **SW7** 126 E2
Montrose Ct **SW7** 126 D1
Montrose Pl **SW1** 126 G1
Monument St **EC3** 124 B9
Monza St **E1** 124 G9
Moodkee St **SE16** 128 G2
Moody Rd **SE15** 128 D7
Moody St **E1** 125 H5
Moon St **N1** 123 P3
Moor La **EC2** 124 B7
Moore Pk Rd **SW6** 126 B6
Moore St **SW3** 126 F3
Moorfields **EC2** 124 B7
Moorgate **EC2** 124 B8
Moorhouse Rd **W2** 122 A8
Moorland Rd **SW9** 127 P10
Moorlands Est **SW9** 127 N10
Mora St **EC1** 124 A5
Morant St **E14** 125 L9
Morat St **SW9** 127 M7
Moravian St **E2** 124 G5
Mordaunt St **SW9** 127 M9
Morden Cl **SE13** 129 N8
Morden Hill **SE13** 129 N8
Morden La **SE13** 129 N7
Morden St **SE13** 129 M7
Morecambe Cl **E1** 125 H7
Morecambe St **SE17** 128 A3
Moreland St **EC1** 123 P5
Moresby Wk **SW8** 127 J8
Moreton Pl **SW1** 127 J4
Moreton St **SW1** 127 K4
Moreton Ter **SW1** 127 J4
Morgan St **E3** 125 J5
Morgans La **SE1** 124 C10
Morley Rd **SE13** 129 N10
Morley St **SE1** 127 N1
Morna Rd **SE5** 128 A8
Morning La **E9** 124 G1
Mornington Cres **NW1** 123 J4
Mornington Gro **E3** 125 L5
Mornington Ms **SE5** 128 A7
Mornington Rd **SE8** 129 K6
Mornington St **NW1** 123 H4
Mornington Ter **NW1** 123 H3
Morocco St **SE1** 128 C1
Morpeth Gro **E9** 125 H3
Morpeth Rd **E9** 124 G3
Morpeth St **E2** 125 H5
Morpeth Ter **SW1** 127 J2
Morris Rd **E14** 125 M7
Morris St **E1** 124 F8
Morrison St **SW11** 126 G9
Morshead Rd **W9** 122 A5
Mortimer Cres **NW6** 122 B3
Mortimer Est **NW6** 122 B3
Mortimer Pl **NW6** 122 B3
Mortimer Rd **N1** 124 C2
Mortimer St **W1** 123 J8
Morton Rd **N1** 124 A2
Morville St **E3** 125 L4
Moscow Rd **W2** 122 A9
Mossbury Rd **SW11** 126 E9
Mossford St **E3** 125 K6
Mossop St **SW3** 126 E3
Mostyn Gro **E3** 125 K4
Mostyn Rd **SW9** 127 N7
Motcomb St **SW1** 126 G2
Moulins Rd **E9** 124 G3
Mount Pleasant **WC1** 123 N6
Mount Row **W1** 123 H9
Mount St **W1** 122 G9
Mountague Pl **E14** 125 N9
Mounts Pond Rd **SE3** 129 P8
Mowlem St **E2** 124 F4
Mowll St **SW9** 127 N6
Moxon St **W1** 122 G7
Mozart Ter **SW1** 126 G3
Mulberry Rd **E8** 124 D2
Mulberry Wk **SW3** 126 D5
Mulvaney Way **SE1** 128 B1
Mundy St **N1** 124 C5
Munro Ter **SW10** 126 D6
Munster Sq **NW1** 123 H5
Munton Rd **SE17** 128 A3
Murdock St **SE15** 128 F5
Muriel St **N1** 123 M4
Murillo Rd **SE13** 129 P10
Murphy St **SE1** 127 N1
Murray Gro **N1** 124 A4
Murray Ms **NW1** 123 K2
Murray St **NW1** 123 K2
Mursell Est **SW8** 127 M7
Musbury St **E1** 124 G8
Muschamp Rd **SE15** 128 D9
Museum St **WC1** 123 L8
Musgrave Cres **SW6** 126 A7
Musgrove Rd **SE14** 129 H7
Mutrix Rd **NW6** 122 A3
Myatt Rd **SW9** 127 P7
Myatt's Flds S **SW9** 127 N8
Myddelton Sq **EC1** 123 N5
Myddelton St **EC1** 123 N5
Myers La **SE14** 129 H5
Mylne St **EC1** 123 N5
Myrdle St **E1** 124 E7
Myron Pl **SE13** 129 N9
Myrtle Wk **N1** 124 C4
Mysore Rd **SW11** 126 F9

N

Nairn St **E14** 125 N7
Naish Ct **N1** 123 L3
Nankin St **E14** 125 L8
Nansen Rd **SW11** 126 G10
Nantes Cl **SW18** 126 C10
Napier Av **E14** 129 L4
Napier Gro **N1** 124 A4
Napier Ter **N1** 123 P2
Narborough St **SW6** 126 B8
Narrow St **E14** 125 J9
Nash Rd **SE4** 129 J10
Nassau St **W1** 123 J7
Naval Row **E14** 125 N9
Navarino Gro **E8** 124 E1
Navarino Rd **E8** 124 E1
Navarre St **E2** 124 D6
Navy St **SW4** 127 K9
Naylor Rd **SE15** 128 F6
Nazareth Gdns **SE15** 128 F8
Nazrul St **E2** 124 D5
Neal St **WC2** 123 L8
Nealden St **SW9** 127 M9
Neate St **SE5** 128 D5
Nebraska St **SE1** 128 B1
Neckinger **SE16** 128 D2
Neckinger Est **SE16** 128 D2
Neckinger St **SE1** 128 D1
Nectarine Way **SE13** 129 M8
Needleman St **SE16** 129 H1
Nelldale Rd **SE16** 128 G3
Nelson Gdns **E2** 124 E5
Nelson Pl **N1** 123 P4
Nelson Rd **SE10** 129 N5
Nelson Sq **SE1** 127 P1
Nelson St **E1** 124 F8
Nelson Ter **N1** 123 P4
Nelson's Row **SW4** 127 K10
Nepaul Rd **SW11** 126 E8
Neptune St **SE16** 128 G2
Nesham St **E1** 124 E10
Netherford Rd **SW4** 127 J8
Netherhall Gdns **NW3** 122 C1
Netherton Gro **SW10** 126 C5
Nettleton Rd **SE14** 129 H7
Nevada St **SE10** 129 N5
Nevern Pl **SW5** 126 A3
Nevern Rd **SW5** 126 A3
Nevern Sq **SW5** 126 A4
Neville Cl **SE15** 128 E6
Neville St **SW7** 126 D4
Neville Ter **SW7** 126 D4
New Bond St **W1** 123 H9
New Br St **EC4** 123 P8
New Broad St **EC2** 124 C7
New Burlington St **W1** 123 J9
New Butt La **SE8** 129 L6
New Caledonian Wf **SE16** 129 K2
New Cavendish St **W1** 122 G7
New Change **EC4** 124 A8
New Ch Rd **SE5** 128 A6
New Compton St **WC2** 123 K8
New Covent Gdn Mkt **SW8** 127 K6
New Cross Rd **SE14** 128 G6
New Fetter La **EC4** 123 N8
New Globe Wk **SE1** 124 A10
New Inn Yd **EC2** 124 C6
New Kent Rd **SE1** 128 A2
New King St **SE8** 129 L5
New N Rd **N1** 124 B4
New N St **WC1** 123 M7
New Oxford St **WC1** 123 K8
New Pl Sq **SE16** 128 F2
New Quebec St **W1** 122 F8
New Ride **SW7** 126 E1
New River Wk **N1** 124 A1
New Rd **E1** 124 F7
New Row **WC2** 123 L9
New Sq **WC2** 123 M8
New St **EC2** 124 C7
New Union Cl **E14** 129 N2
New Union St **EC2** 124 B7
New Wf Rd **N1** 123 L4
Newark St **E1** 124 F7
Newburgh St **W1** 123 J8
Newburn St **SE11** 127 M4
Newby Pl **E14** 125 N9
Newby St **SW8** 127 H9
Newcastle Pl **W2** 122 D7
Newcomen Rd **SW11** 126 D9
Newcomen St **SE1** 128 B1
Newcourt St **NW8** 122 E4
Newell St **E14** 125 K8
Newent Cl **SE15** 128 C6
Newgate St **EC1** 123 P8
Newington Butts **SE1** 127 P3
Newington Butts **SE11** 127 P3
Newington Causeway **SE1** 127 P2
Newington Grn Rd **N1** 124 B1
Newlands Quay **E1** 124 G9
Newman St **W1** 123 J7
Newport Av **E14** 125 P9
Newport Pl **WC2** 123 K9
Newport St **SE11** 127 M3
Newton Rd **W2** 122 A8
Newton St **WC2** 123 L8
Nicholas Rd **E1** 124 G6
Nicholl St **E2** 124 E3
Nicholson St **SE1** 123 P10
Nigel Rd **SE15** 128 E9
Nile St **N1** 124 B5
Nile Ter **SE15** 128 D4
Nine Elms La **SW8** 127 J5
Noble St **EC2** 124 A8
Noel Rd **N1** 123 P4
Noel St **W1** 123 J8
Norbiton Rd **E14** 125 K8
Norfolk Cres **W2** 122 E8
Norfolk Pl **W2** 122 D8
Norfolk Rd **NW8** 122 D3
Norfolk Sq **W2** 122 D8
Norman Gro **E3** 125 J4
Norman Rd **SE10** 129 M6
Normandy Rd **SW9** 127 N7
North Audley St **W1** 122 G8
North Bk **NW8** 122 E5
North Carriage Dr **W2** 122 D9
North Colonnade **E14** 125 L10
North Cres **E16** 125 P6
North Cres **WC1** 123 K7
North Gower St **NW1** 123 J5
North Ms **WC1** 123 M6
North Pas **SW18** 126 A10
North Peckham Est **SE15** 128 D6
North Ride **W2** 122 E9
North Rd **N7** 123 L1
North Row **W1** 122 F9
North St **SW4** 127 J9
North Tenter St **E1** 124 D8
North Ter **SW3** 126 E2
North Vil **NW1** 123 K1
North Wf Rd **W2** 122 D7
Northampton Pk **N1** 124 A1
Northampton Rd **EC1** 123 N6
Northampton Sq **EC1** 123 P5
Northampton St **N1** 124 A2
Northbourne Rd **SW4** 127 K10
Northburgh St **EC1** 123 P6
Northchurch Rd **N1** 124 B2
Northchurch Ter **N1** 124 C2
Northcote Rd **SW11** 126 E10
Northdown St **N1** 123 M4
Northey St **E14** 125 J9
Northfields **SW18** 126 A10
Northiam St **E9** 124 F3
Northington St **WC1** 123 M6
Northlands St **SE5** 128 A8
Northport St **N1** 124 B3
Northumberland All **EC3** 124 C8
Northumberland Av **WC2** 123 L10
Northumberland Pl **W2** 122 A8
Northumberland St **WC2** 123 L10
Northumbria St **E14** 125 L8
Northway Rd **SE5** 128 A9
Northwick Ter **NW8** 122 D6
Norton Folgate **E1** 124 C7
Norway Gate **SE16** 129 J2
Norway St **SE10** 129 M5
Norwich St **EC4** 123 N8
Notley St **SE5** 128 B6
Notre Dame Est **SW4** 127 J10
Notting Hill Gate **W11** 122 A10
Nottingham Pl **W1** 122 G6
Nottingham St **W1** 122 G7
Novello St **SW6** 126 A7
Nuding Cl **SE13** 129 L9
Nugent Ter **NW8** 122 C4
Nunhead Cres **SE15** 128 F9
Nunhead Est **SE15** 128 F9
Nunhead Grn **SE15** 128 F9
Nunhead Gro **SE15** 128 F9
Nunhead La **SE15** 128 F9
Nursery Cl **SE4** 129 K8
Nursery La **E2** 124 D3
Nursery Rd **SW9** 127 M10
Nursery Row **SE17** 128 B3
Nutbrook St **SE15** 128 E9
Nutcroft Rd **SE15** 128 F6
Nutford Pl **W1** 122 F8
Nutley Ter **NW3** 122 C1
Nutmeg La **E14** 125 P8
Nutt St **SE15** 128 D6
Nuttall St **N1** 124 C4
Nynehead St **SE14** 129 J6

O

Oak La **E14** 125 K9
Oak Tree Rd **NW8** 122 E5
Oakbank Gro **SE24** 128 A10
Oakbury Rd **SW6** 126 B8
Oakcroft Rd **SE13** 129 P8
Oakdale Rd **SE15** 128 G9
Oakden St **SE11** 127 N3
Oakey La **SE1** 127 N2
Oakfield St **SW10** 126 C5
Oakhurst Gro **SE22** 128 E10
Oakington Rd **W9** 122 A6
Oakley Gdns **SW3** 126 E5
Oakley Pl **SE1** 128 D4
Oakley Rd **N1** 124 B2
Oakley Sq **NW1** 123 J4
Oakley St **SW3** 126 E5
Oat La **EC2** 124 A8
Oban St **E14** 125 P8
Oberstein Rd **SW11** 126 D10
Observatory Gdns **W8** 126 A1
Occupation Rd **SE17** 128 A4
Ocean Est **E1** 125 H6
Ocean St **E1** 125 H7
Ocean Wf **E14** 129 L1
Ockendon Rd **N1** 124 B1
Octavia St **SW11** 126 E7
Octavius St **SE8** 129 L6
Odessa St **SE16** 129 K1
Odger St **SW11** 126 F8
Offenbach Ho **E2** 125 H4
Offerton Rd **SW4** 127 J9
Offley Rd **SW9** 127 N6
Offord Rd **N1** 123 M2
Offord St **N1** 123 M2
Oglander Rd **SE15** 128 D10
Ogle St **W1** 123 J7
Old Bailey **EC4** 123 P8
Old Bellgate Wf **E14** 129 L2
Old Bethnal Grn Rd **E2** 124 E5
Old Bond St **W1** 123 J9
Old Broad St **EC2** 124 B8
Old Brompton Rd **SW5** 126 A4
Old Brompton Rd **SW7** 126 A4
Old Burlington St **W1** 123 J9
Old Castle St **E1** 124 D8
Old Cavendish St **W1** 123 H8
Old Ch Rd **E1** 125 H8
Old Ch St **SW3** 126 D4
Old Compton St **W1** 123 K9
Old Ct Pl **W8** 126 B1
Old Ford Rd **E2** 124 G4
Old Ford Rd **E3** 125 J4
Old Gloucester St **WC1** 123 L7
Old Jamaica Rd **SE16** 128 E2
Old James St **SE15** 128 F9
Old Jewry **EC2** 124 B8
Old Kent Rd **SE1** 128 C3
Old Kent Rd **SE15** 128 C3
Old Marylebone Rd **NW1** 122 E7
Old Montague St **E1** 124 E7
Old Nichol St **E2** 124 D6
Old Palace Yd **SW1** 127 L2
Old Paradise St **SE11** 127 M3
Old Pk La **W1** 122 G10
Old Pye St **SW1** 127 K2
Old Quebec St **W1** 122 F8
Old Queen St **SW1** 127 K1
Old Royal Free Sq **N1** 123 N3
Old S Lambeth Rd **SW8** 127 L6
Old Spitalfields Mkt **E1** 124 D7
Old Sq **WC2** 123 M8
Old St **EC1** 124 A6
Old Town **SW4** 127 J9
Old Woolwich Rd **SE10** 129 P5
Oldbury Pl **W1** 122 G6
Oldfield Gro **SE16** 129 H3
O'Leary Sq **E1** 124 G7
Oliver-Goldsmith Est **SE15** 128 E7
Ollerton Grn **E3** 125 K3
Olliffe St **E14** 129 N2
Olmar St **SE1** 128 E5
Olney Rd **SE17** 127 P5
O'Meara St **SE1** 124 A10
Omega St **SE14** 129 L7
Ommaney Rd **SE14** 129 H7
Ondine Rd **SE15** 128 D10
Onega Gate **SE16** 129 J2
Ongar Rd **SW6** 126 A5
Onslow Gdns **SW7** 126 D4
Onslow Sq **SW7** 126 D3
Ontario St **SE1** 127 P2
Ontario Way **E14** 125 L9
Opal St **SE11** 127 P3
Ophir Ter **SE15** 128 E7
Oppenheim Rd **SE13** 129 N8
Oppidans Rd **NW3** 122 F2
Orange St **WC2** 123 K9
Orb St **SE17** 128 B3
Orbel St **SW11** 126 E7
Orchard, The **SE3** 129 P8
Orchard St **W1** 122 G8
Orchardson St **NW8** 122 D6
Orde Hall St **WC1** 123 M6
Ordell Rd **E3** 125 K4
Ordnance Cres **SE10** 129 P1
Ordnance Hill **NW8** 122 D3
Oregano Dr **E14** 125 P8
Oriel Rd **E9** 125 H1
Orkney St **SW11** 126 G8
Orlando Rd **SW4** 127 J9
Orleston Ms **N7** 123 N1
Orleston Rd **N7** 123 N1
Orme Ct **W2** 122 B9
Orme La **W2** 122 B9
Ormonde Gate **SW3** 126 F4
Ormonde Ter **NW8** 122 F3
Ormsby St **E2** 124 D4
Ormside St **SE15** 128 G5
Orpheus St **SE5** 128 B7
Orsett St **SE11** 127 M4
Orsett Ter **W2** 122 C8
Orsman Rd **N1** 124 C3
Orville Rd **SW11** 126 D8
Osborn Cl **E8** 124 E3
Osborn St **E1** 124 D7
Osborne Rd **E9** 125 K1
Oscar St **SE8** 129 L7
Oseney Cres **NW5** 123 J1
O'Shea Gro **E3** 125 K3
Osier St **E1** 124 G6
Osiers Rd **SW18** 126 A10
Osnaburgh St **NW1** 123 H6
Osric Path **N1** 124 C4
Ossington St **W2** 122 B9
Ossory Rd **SE1** 128 E4
Ossulston St **NW1** 123 K5
Oswell Ho **E1** 124 F10
Oswin St **SE11** 127 P3
Oswyth Rd **SE5** 128 C8
Otis St **E3** 125 N5
Otterburn Ho **SE5** 128 A6
Otto St **SE17** 127 P5
Outer Circle **NW1** 123 H4
Outram Pl **N1** 123 L3
Oval, The **E2** 124 F4
Oval Pl **SW8** 127 M6
Oval Rd **NW1** 123 H3
Oval Way **SE11** 127 M4
Overcliff Rd **SE13** 129 L9
Oversley Ho **W2** 122 A7
Overton Rd **SW9** 127 N8
Ovex Cl **E14** 129 N1
Ovington Gdns **SW3** 126 E2
Ovington Ms **SW3** 126 E2
Ovington Sq **SW3** 126 E2
Ovington St **SW3** 126 E2
Oxendon St **SW1** 123 K9
Oxenford St **SE15** 128 D9
Oxenholme **NW1** 123 J4
Oxestalls Rd **SE8** 129 J4
Oxford Rd **E15** 125 P1
Oxford Rd **NW6** 122 A4
Oxford Sq **W2** 122 E8
Oxford St **W1** 123 H8
Oxley Cl **SE1** 128 D4
Oxonian St **SE22** 128 D10

P

Packington Sq **N1** 124 A3
Packington St **N1** 123 P3
Padbury **SE17** 128 C4
Padbury Ct **E2** 124 D5
Paddington Grn **W2** 122 D7
Paddington St **W1** 122 G7
Padfield Rd **SE5** 128 A9
Pagden St **SW8** 127 H7
Page St **SW1** 127 L3
Pages Wk **SE1** 128 C3
Pagnell St **SE14** 129 K6
Pagoda Gdns **SE3** 129 P8
Pakenham St **WC1** 123 M5
Palace Av **W8** 122 B10
Palace Ct **W2** 122 B9
Palace Gdns Ms **W8** 122 A10
Palace Gdns Ter **W8** 122 A10
Palace Gate **W8** 126 C1
Palace Grn **W8** 126 B1
Palace St **SW1** 127 J2

Roan St

Palfrey Pl **SW8** 127 M6
Pall Mall **SW1** 123 J10
Pall Mall E **SW1** 123 K10
Pall Mall Pl **SW1** 123 J10
Palmer St **SW1** 127 K2
Palmers Rd **E2** 125 H4
Palmerston Rd **NW6** 122 A2
Pancras Rd **NW1** 123 K4
Pandora Rd **NW6** 122 A1
Parade, The **SW11** 126 F6
Paradise Rd **SW4** 127 L8
Paradise St **SE16** 128 F1
Paradise Wk **SW3** 126 F5
Paragon Rd **E9** 124 F1
Pardoner St **SE1** 128 B2
Parfett St **E1** 124 E7
Paris Gdn **SE1** 123 P10
Park Cl **E9** 124 G3
Park Cl **SW1** 126 F1
Park Cres **W1** 123 H6
Park La **W1** 122 G9
Park Pl **E14** 125 L10
Park Pl **SW1** 123 J10
Park Pl Vil **W2** 122 C7
Park Rd **NW1** 122 E5
Park Rd **NW8** 122 E5
Park Row **SE10** 129 P5
Park Sq E **NW1** 123 H6
Park Sq Ms **NW1** 123 H6
Park Sq W **NW1** 123 H6
Park St **SE1** 124 A10
Park St **W1** 122 G9
Park Vw Est **E2** 125 H4
Park Village E **NW1** 123 H4
Park Village W **NW1** 123 H4
Park Vista **SE10** 129 P5
Park Wk **SW10** 126 C5
Parker St **WC2** 123 L8
Parkfield Rd **SE14** 129 K7
Parkfield St **N1** 123 N4
Parkgate Rd **SW11** 126 E6
Parkham St **SW11** 126 E7
Parkholme Rd **E8** 124 D1
Parkhouse St **SE5** 128 B6
Parkside Rd **SW11** 126 G7
Parkway **NW1** 123 H3
Parliament Sq **SW1** 127 L1
Parliament St **SW1** 127 L1
Parma Cres **SW11** 126 F10
Parmiter St **E2** 124 F4
Parnell Rd **E3** 125 K3
Parr St **N1** 124 B4
Parry St **SW8** 127 L5
Parsonage St **E14** 129 N3
Parsons Grn **SW6** 126 A7
Parsons Grn La **SW6** 126 A7
Parson's Ho **W2** 122 D6
Parthenia Rd **SW6** 126 A7
Parvin St **SW8** 127 K7
Pascal St **SW8** 127 K6
Passmore St **SW1** 126 G3
Pastor St **SE11** 127 P3
Patcham Ter **SW8** 127 H7
Pater St **W8** 126 A2
Patience Rd **SW11** 126 E8
Patmore Est **SW8** 127 J7
Patmore St **SW8** 127 J7
Patmos Rd **SW9** 127 P6
Paton Cl **E3** 125 L5
Patrick Pas **SW11** 126 E8
Patriot Sq **E2** 124 F4
Patshull Rd **NW5** 123 J1
Patterdale Rd **SE15** 128 G6
Pattina Wk **SE16** 125 K10
Paul Julius Cl **E14** 125 P9
Paul St **E15** 125 P3
Paul St **EC2** 124 B6
Paulet Rd **SE5** 127 P8
Paul's Wk **EC4** 124 A9
Paultons Sq **SW3** 126 D5
Paultons St **SW3** 126 D5
Paveley Dr **SW11** 126 E6
Paveley St **NW8** 122 E5
Pavement, The **SW4** 127 J10
Pavilion Rd **SW1** 126 F1
Paxton Ter **SW1** 127 H5
Payne Rd **E3** 125 M4
Payne St **SE8** 129 K5
Peabody Sq **SE1** 127 P1
Peabody Trust **SE1** 124 A10
Pear Tree Cl **E2** 124 D3
Pear Tree Ct **EC1** 123 N6
Pear Tree St **EC1** 123 P6
Peardon St **SW8** 127 H8
Pearman St **SE1** 127 N1
Pearscroft Ct **SW6** 126 B7
Pearscroft Rd **SW6** 126 B7
Pearson St **E2** 124 D4
Peckford Pl **SW9** 127 N8
Peckham Gro **SE15** 128 C6
Peckham High St **SE15** 128 E7
Peckham Hill St **SE15** 128 E6
Peckham Pk Rd **SE15** 128 E6
Peckham Rd **SE5** 128 C7
Peckham Rd **SE15** 128 C7
Peckham Rye **SE15** 128 E9
Peckham Rye **SE22** 128 E10
Pedlars Wk **N7** 123 L1
Pedley St **E1** 124 D6
Peel Gro **E2** 124 G4
Peel Prec **NW6** 122 A4
Peel St **W8** 122 A10
Peerless St **EC1** 124 B5
Pekin St **E14** 125 L8
Pelham Cl **SE5** 128 C8
Pelham Cres **SW7** 126 E3
Pelham Pl **SW7** 126 E3
Pelham St **SW7** 126 E3
Pelican Est **SE15** 128 D7
Pelling St **E14** 125 L8
Pelter St **E2** 124 D5
Pembridge Cres **W11** 122 A9
Pembridge Gdns **W2** 122 A9
Pembridge Ms **W11** 122 A9
Pembridge Pl **W2** 122 A9
Pembridge Rd **W11** 122 A9
Pembridge Sq **W2** 122 A9
Pembridge Vil **W2** 122 A9
Pembridge Vil **W11** 122 A9
Pembroke Cl **SW1** 126 G1
Pembroke Gdns Cl **W8** 126 A2
Pembroke Pl **W8** 126 A2
Pembroke Rd **W8** 126 A3
Pembroke Sq **W8** 126 A2
Pembroke St **N1** 123 L2
Pembroke Vil **W8** 126 A3
Pembroke Wk **W8** 126 A3
Penang St **E1** 124 F10
Penarth St **SE15** 128 G5
Pencraig Way **SE15** 128 F5
Pendrell Rd **SE4** 129 J8
Penfold Pl **NW1** 122 E7
Penfold St **NW1** 122 D6
Penfold St **NW8** 122 D6
Penford St **SE5** 127 P8
Penn St **N1** 124 B3
Pennack Rd **SE15** 128 D5
Pennant Ms **W8** 126 B3
Pennethorne Rd **SE15** 128 F6
Pennington St **E1** 124 E9
Pennyfields **E14** 125 L9
Penpoll Rd **E8** 124 F1
Penrose Gro **SE17** 128 A4
Penrose Ho **SE17** 128 A4
Penrose St **SE17** 128 A4
Penryn St **NW1** 123 K4
Pensbury Pl **SW8** 127 J8
Pensbury St **SW8** 127 J8
Penshurst Rd **E9** 125 H2
Penton Pl **SE17** 127 P4
Penton Ri **WC1** 123 M5
Penton St **N1** 123 N4
Pentonville Rd **N1** 123 M4
Pentridge St **SE15** 128 D6
Penywern Rd **SW5** 126 A4
Pepper St **E14** 129 M2
Pepys Rd **SE14** 129 H7
Pepys St **EC3** 124 C9
Percival St **EC1** 123 P6
Percy Circ **WC1** 123 M5
Percy St **W1** 123 K7
Peregrine Ho **EC1** 123 P5
Perkin's Rents **SW1** 127 K2
Perrymead St **SW6** 126 A7
Perseverance Pl **SW9** 127 N6
Peter St **W1** 123 K9
Peterborough Ms **SW6** 126 A8
Peterborough Rd **SW6** 126 A8
Peterborough Vil **SW6** 126 B7
Petergate **SW11** 126 C10
Petersham La **SW7** 126 C2
Petersham Ms **SW7** 126 C2
Petersham Pl **SW7** 126 C2
Peto Pl **NW1** 123 H6
Petticoat La **E1** 124 C7
Petticoat Sq **E1** 124 D8
Petty France **SW1** 127 J2
Petworth St **SW11** 126 E7
Petyward **SW3** 126 E3
Peyton Pl **SE10** 129 N6
Phelp St **SE17** 128 B5
Phene St **SW3** 126 E5
Philbeach Gdns **SW5** 126 A4
Philip Wk **SE15** 128 E9
Phillimore Gdns **W8** 126 A1
Phillimore Pl **W8** 126 A1
Phillimore Wk **W8** 126 A2
Phillipp St **N1** 124 C3
Philpot St **E1** 124 F8
Phipp St **EC2** 124 C6
Phoenix Pl **WC1** 123 M6
Phoenix Rd **NW1** 123 K5
Piccadilly **W1** 123 H10
Piccadilly Circ **W1** 123 K9
Pickfords Wf **N1** 124 A4
Picton St **SE5** 128 B6
Pier St **E14** 129 N3
Pigott St **E14** 125 L8
Pilgrimage St **SE1** 128 B1
Pilkington Rd **SE15** 128 F8
Pilton Pl **SE17** 128 A4
Pimlico Rd **SW1** 126 G4
Pinchin St **E1** 124 E9
Pindar St **EC2** 124 C7
Pine St **EC1** 123 N6
Pinefield Cl **E14** 125 L9
Pioneer St **SE15** 128 E7
Pitchford St **E15** 125 P2
Pitfield Est **N1** 124 B5
Pitfield St **N1** 124 C5
Pitman St **SE5** 128 A6
Pitsea St **E1** 125 H8
Pitt St **W8** 126 A1
Pitt's Head Ms **W1** 122 G10
Pixley St **E14** 125 K8
Plantation Wf **SW11** 126 C9
Plato Rd **SW2** 127 L10
Platt St **NW1** 123 K4
Pleasant Pl **N1** 123 P2
Pleasant Row **NW1** 123 H3
Plender St **NW1** 123 J3
Plevna St **E14** 129 N2
Plough Rd **SW11** 126 D9
Plough Ter **SW11** 126 D10
Plough Way **SE16** 129 H3
Plough Yd **EC2** 124 C6
Plover Way **SE16** 129 J2
Plumbers Row **E1** 124 E7
Plymouth Wf **E14** 129 P3
Plympton St **NW8** 122 E6
Pocock St **SE1** 127 P1
Podmore Rd **SW18** 126 C10
Point Hill **SE10** 129 N6
Point Pleasant **SW18** 126 A10
Pointers Cl **E14** 129 M4
Poland St **W1** 123 J8
Polesworth Ho **W2** 122 A7
Pollard Row **E2** 124 E5
Pollard St **E2** 124 E5
Polygon Rd **NW1** 123 K4
Pomeroy St **SE14** 128 G7
Pond Pl **SW3** 126 E3
Ponder St **N7** 123 M2
Ponler St **E1** 124 F8
Ponsford St **E9** 124 G1
Ponsonby Pl **SW1** 127 K4
Ponsonby Ter **SW1** 127 K4
Pont St **SW1** 126 F2
Pont St Ms **SW1** 126 F2
Ponton Rd **SW8** 127 K5
Poole Rd **E9** 125 H1
Poole St **N1** 124 B3
Poolmans St **SE16** 129 H1
Pope St **SE1** 128 C1
Popes Rd **SW9** 127 N9
Popham Rd **N1** 124 A3
Popham St **N1** 123 P3
Poplar Business Pk **E14** 125 N9
Poplar High St **E14** 125 L9
Poplar Pl **W2** 122 B9
Poplar Rd **SE24** 128 A10
Poplar Wk **SE24** 128 A10
Porchester Cl **SE5** 128 A10
Porchester Gdns **W2** 122 B9
Porchester Ms **W2** 122 B8
Porchester Pl **W2** 122 E8
Porchester Rd **W2** 122 B8
Porchester Sq **W2** 122 B8
Porchester Ter **W2** 122 C9
Porchester Ter N **W2** 122 B8
Porden Rd **SW2** 127 M10
Porlock St **SE1** 128 B1
Portelet Rd **E1** 125 H5
Porteus Rd **W2** 122 C7
Portia Way **E3** 125 K6
Portland Gro **SW8** 127 M7
Portland Pl **W1** 123 H7
Portland St **SE17** 128 B4
Portman Cl **W1** 122 F8
Portman Ms S **W1** 122 G8
Portman Pl **E2** 124 G5
Portman Sq **W1** 122 F8
Portman St **W1** 122 G8
Portpool La **EC1** 123 N7
Portree St **E14** 125 P8
Portslade Rd **SW8** 127 J8
Portsoken St **E1** 124 D9
Portugal St **WC2** 123 M8
Post Office Way **SW8** 127 K6
Potier St **SE1** 128 B2
Pott St **E2** 124 F5
Potters Rd **SW6** 126 C8
Pottery St **SE16** 128 F1
Poultry **EC2** 124 B8
Pountney Rd **SW11** 126 G9
Powis Pl **WC1** 123 L6
Powis Rd **E3** 125 M5
Pownall Rd **E8** 124 D3
Poyntz Rd **SW11** 126 F8
Poyser St **E2** 124 F4
Praed St **W2** 122 D8
Prairie St **SW8** 126 G8
Pratt St **NW1** 123 J3
Pratt Wk **SE11** 127 M3
Prebend St **N1** 124 A3
Prescot St **E1** 124 D9
Prescott Pl **SW4** 127 K9
Prestage Way **E14** 125 N9
Prestons Rd **E14** 129 N1
Price's Yd **N1** 123 M3
Prideaux Pl **WC1** 123 M5
Prideaux Rd **SW9** 127 L9
Prima Rd **SW9** 127 N6
Primrose Gdns **NW3** 122 E1
Primrose Hill Ct **NW3** 122 F2
Primrose Hill Rd **NW3** 122 E2
Primrose Sq **E9** 124 G2
Primrose St **EC2** 124 C7
Prince Albert Rd **NW1** 122 E4
Prince Albert Rd **NW8** 122 E4
Prince Consort Rd **SW7** 126 C2
Prince Edward Rd **E9** 125 K1
Prince of Wales Dr **SW8** 127 H6
Prince of Wales Dr **SW11** 126 F7
Prince of Wales Gate **SW7** 126 E1
Prince of Wales Rd **NW5** 122 G1
Prince St **SE8** 129 K5
Princelet St **E1** 124 D7
Princes Ct **E1** 124 F9
Princes Ct **SE16** 129 K2
Princes Gdns **SW7** 126 D2
Princes Gate **SW7** 126 E1
Princes Gate Ms **SW7** 126 D2
Princes Ri **SE13** 129 N8
Princes Riverside Rd **SE16** 125 H10
Princes Sq **W2** 122 B9
Princes St **EC2** 124 B8
Princes St **W1** 123 H8
Princess Rd **NW1** 122 G3
Princess Rd **NW6** 122 A4
Princess St **SE1** 127 P2
Princethorpe Ho **W2** 122 B7
Princeton St **WC1** 123 M7
Prior Bolton St **N1** 123 P1
Prior St **SE10** 129 N6
Prioress St **SE1** 128 B2
Priory Ct **SW8** 127 K7
Priory Grn Est **N1** 123 M4
Priory Gro **SW8** 127 L7
Priory Ms **SW8** 127 K7
Priory Rd **NW6** 122 B3
Priory Ter **NW6** 122 B3
Priory Wk **SW10** 126 C4
Pritchard's Rd **E2** 124 E3
Priter Rd **SE16** 128 E2
Procter St **WC1** 123 M7
Prospect Pl **E1** 124 G10
Providence Ct **W1** 122 G9
Provost Est **N1** 124 B4
Provost Rd **NW3** 122 F2
Provost St **N1** 124 B5
Prusom St **E1** 124 F10
Pudding La **EC3** 124 B9
Pudding Mill La **E15** 125 M3
Pulross Rd **SW9** 127 M9
Pulteney Cl **E3** 125 K3
Pulteney Ter **N1** 123 M3
Pulton Pl **SW6** 126 A6
Pundersons Gdns **E2** 124 F5
Purbrook St **SE1** 128 C2
Purcell St **N1** 124 C4
Purchese St **NW1** 123 K4
Purdy St **E3** 125 M6
Purelake Ms **SE13** 129 P9
Puteaux Ho **E2** 125 H4
Pytchley Rd **SE22** 128 C9

Q

Quaker St **E1** 124 D6
Quality Ct **WC2** 123 N8
Quarrendon St **SW6** 126 A8
Quarterdeck, The **E14** 129 L1
Quebec Way **SE16** 129 H1
Queen Anne Rd **E9** 125 H1
Queen Anne St **W1** 123 H8
Queen Anne's Gate **SW1** 127 K1
Queen Elizabeth St **SE1** 128 D1
Queen of Denmark Ct **SE16** 129 K2
Queen Sq **WC1** 123 L6
Queen St **EC4** 124 A9
Queen St **W1** 123 H10
Queen Victoria St **EC4** 123 P9
Queenhithe **EC4** 124 A9
Queens Cres **NW5** 122 G1
Queens Gdns **W2** 122 C9
Queen's Gate **SW7** 126 C2
Queen's Gate Gdns **SW7** 126 C2
Queen's Gate Ms **SW7** 126 C1
Queen's Gate Pl **SW7** 126 C2
Queen's Gate Pl Ms **SW7** 126 C2
Queen's Gate Ter **SW7** 126 C2
Queen's Gro **NW8** 122 D3
Queen's Gro Ms **NW8** 122 D3
Queen's Head St **N1** 123 P3
Queens Ms **W2** 122 B9
Queens Rd **SE14** 128 F7
Queens Rd **SE15** 128 F7
Queen's Row **SE17** 128 B5
Queen's Ter **NW8** 122 D4
Queen's Wk **SW1** 123 J10
Queen's Wk, The **SE1** 124 C10
Queensberry Pl **SW7** 126 D3
Queensborough Ter **W2** 122 B9
Queensbridge Rd **E2** 124 D3
Queensbridge Rd **E8** 124 D2
Queensbury St **N1** 124 A2
Queensgate Pl **NW6** 122 A2
Queensmead **NW8** 122 D3
Queenstown Rd **SW8** 127 H5
Queensway **W2** 122 B8
Querrin St **SW6** 126 C8
Quex Rd **NW6** 122 A3
Quick Pl **N1** 123 P3
Quick St **N1** 123 P4
Quilter St **E2** 124 E5
Quixley St **E14** 125 P9
Quorn Rd **SE22** 128 C10

R

Racton Rd **SW6** 126 A5
Radcot St **SE11** 127 N4
Radlett Pl **NW8** 122 E3
Radley Ms **W8** 126 A2
Radnor Pl **W2** 122 E8
Radnor Rd **SE15** 128 E6
Radnor St **EC1** 124 A5
Radnor Wk **SW3** 126 E4
Radstock St **SW11** 126 E6
Raeburn St **SW2** 127 L10
Raglan St **NW5** 123 H1
Railway App **SE1** 124 B10
Railway Av **SE16** 128 G1
Railway St **N1** 123 L4
Rainbow Av **E14** 129 M4
Rainbow Quay **SE16** 129 J2
Rainbow St **SE5** 128 C6
Raine St **E1** 124 F10
Rainhill Way **E3** 125 L5
Rainsborough Av **SE8** 129 J3
Raleana Rd **E14** 125 N10
Raleigh St **N1** 123 P3
Ramillies Pl **W1** 123 J8
Rampayne St **SW1** 127 K4
Ramsey St **E2** 124 E6
Randall Cl **SW11** 126 E7
Randall Pl **SE10** 129 N6
Randall Rd **SE11** 127 M3
Randell's Rd **N1** 123 L3
Randolph Av **W9** 122 C6
Randolph Cres **W9** 122 C6
Randolph Gdns **NW6** 122 B4
Randolph Ms **W9** 122 C6
Randolph Rd **W9** 122 C6
Randolph St **NW1** 123 J2
Ranelagh Gro **SW1** 126 G4
Rangers Sq **SE10** 129 P7
Ranwell St **E3** 125 K3
Raphael St **SW7** 126 F1
Ratcliffe Cross St **E1** 125 H8
Ratcliffe La **E14** 125 J8
Ratcliffe Orchard **E1** 125 H9
Rathbone Pl **W1** 123 K8
Rathbone St **W1** 123 J7
Rattray Rd **SW2** 127 N10
Raul Rd **SE15** 128 E7
Raven Row **E1** 124 F7
Ravensbourne Pl **SE13** 129 M8
Ravenscroft St **E2** 124 D4
Ravensdon St **SE11** 127 N4
Ravenstone **SE17** 128 C4
Ravent Rd **SE11** 127 M3
Rawlings St **SW3** 126 F3
Rawstorne St **EC1** 123 P5
Ray St **EC1** 123 N6
Raymouth Rd **SE16** 128 F3
Reading La **E8** 124 F1
Reardon Path **E1** 124 F10
Reardon St **E1** 124 F10
Reaston St **SE14** 129 H6
Record St **SE15** 128 G5
Rector St **N1** 124 A3
Rectory Gdns **SW4** 127 J9
Rectory Gro **SW4** 127 J9
Rectory Sq **E1** 125 H7
Reculver Rd **SE16** 129 H4
Red Lion Row **SE17** 128 A5
Red Lion Sq **WC1** 123 M7
Red Lion St **WC1** 123 M7
Red Path **E9** 125 K1
Red Post Hill **SE24** 128 B10
Redan Pl **W2** 122 B8
Redbridge Gdns **SE5** 128 C6
Redburn St **SW3** 126 F5
Redcar St **SE5** 128 A6
Redcastle Cl **E1** 124 G9
Redchurch St **E2** 124 D6
Redcliffe Gdns **SW5** 126 B4
Redcliffe Gdns **SW10** 126 B4
Redcliffe Ms **SW10** 126 B4
Redcliffe Pl **SW10** 126 C5
Redcliffe Rd **SW10** 126 C4
Redcliffe Sq **SW10** 126 B4
Redcliffe St **SW10** 126 B5
Redcross Way **SE1** 128 A1
Reddins Rd **SE15** 128 E5
Redesdale St **SW3** 126 F5
Redfield La **SW5** 126 A3
Redhill St **NW1** 123 H4
Redman's Rd **E1** 124 G7
Redriff Est **SE16** 129 K2
Redriff Rd **SE16** 129 H3
Redruth Rd **E9** 125 H3
Redwood Cl **SE16** 125 J10
Reece Ms **SW7** 126 D3
Reedham St **SE15** 128 E8
Reedworth St **SE11** 127 N3
Rees St **N1** 124 A3
Reeves Ms **W1** 122 G9
Reeves Rd **E3** 125 M6
Reform St **SW11** 126 F8
Regan Way **N1** 124 C4
Regency St **SW1** 127 K3
Regent Sq **E3** 125 M5
Regent Sq **WC1** 123 L5
Regent St **SW1** 123 K9
Regent St **W1** 123 H8
Regents Br Gdns **SW8** 127 L6
Regent's Pk **NW1** 122 G4
Regents Pk Rd **NW1** 122 F3
Regent's Pl **NW1** 123 J6
Regents Row **E8** 124 E3
Reginald Rd **SE8** 129 L6
Reginald Sq **SE8** 129 L6
Regis Pl **SW2** 127 M10
Relf Rd **SE15** 128 E9
Rembrandt Cl **E14** 129 P2
Remington St **N1** 123 P4
Renforth St **SE16** 128 G1
Renfrew Rd **SE11** 127 P3
Rennell St **SE13** 129 N9
Rennie Est **SE16** 128 F3
Rennie St **SE1** 123 P10
Repton St **E14** 125 J8
Reservoir Rd **SE4** 129 J8
Retreat Pl **E9** 124 G1
Revelon Rd **SE4** 129 J10
Reverdy Rd **SE1** 128 E3
Rewell St **SW6** 126 C6
Rheidol Ter **N1** 123 P4
Rhodesia Rd **SW9** 127 L8
Rhodeswell Rd **E14** 125 K8
Rhondda Gro **E3** 125 J5
Rhyl St **NW5** 122 G1
Ricardo St **E14** 125 M8
Rich St **E14** 125 K9
Richborne Ter **SW8** 127 M6
Richmond Av **N1** 123 M3
Richmond Cres **N1** 123 M3
Richmond Gro **N1** 123 P2
Richmond Rd **E8** 124 D2
Richmond Ter **SW1** 127 L1
Rick Roberts Way **E15** 125 N3
Rickett St **SW6** 126 A5
Ridgdale St **E3** 125 M4
Ridgeway Rd **SW9** 127 P9
Riding Ho St **W1** 123 H7
Rifle Pl **SE11** 127 N5
Rifle St **E14** 125 M7
Rigden St **E14** 125 M8
Rigge Pl **SW4** 127 K10
Riley Rd **SE1** 128 D2
Riley St **SW10** 126 D5
Ring, The **W2** 122 D9
Ripplevale Gro **N1** 123 M2
Risinghill St **N1** 123 M4
Rita Rd **SW8** 127 L6
Ritchie St **N1** 123 N4
Ritson Rd **E8** 124 E1
Rivaz Pl **E9** 124 G1
River Pl **N1** 124 A2
River St **EC1** 123 N5
Riverside Ct **SW8** 127 K5
Riverside Rd **E15** 125 N4
Riverside Wk **SE1** 123 M10
Rivington St **EC2** 124 C5
Roach Rd **E3** 125 L2
Roan St **SE10** 129 N5

Robert Adam St

Robert Adam St **W1**	122	G8
Robert Dashwood Way **SE17**	128	A3
Robert Lowe Cl **SE14**	129	H6
Robert St **NW1**	123	H5
Roberta St **E2**	124	E5
Robertson Rd **E15**	125	N3
Robertson St **SW8**	127	H8
Robin Ct **SE16**	128	E3
Robin Hood La **E14**	125	N9
Robinson Rd **E2**	124	G4
Robsart St **SW9**	127	M8
Rochelle Cl **SW11**	126	D10
Rochester Ms **NW1**	123	J2
Rochester Pl **NW1**	123	J1
Rochester Rd **NW1**	123	J1
Rochester Row **SW1**	127	J3
Rochester Sq **NW1**	123	J2
Rochester St **SW1**	127	K2
Rochester Ter **NW1**	123	J1
Rockingham Est **SE1**	128	A2
Rockingham St **SE1**	128	A2
Rodmarton St **W1**	122	F7
Rodney Pl **SE17**	128	A3
Rodney Rd **SE17**	128	B3
Rodney St **N1**	123	M4
Roffey St **E14**	129	N1
Roger St **WC1**	123	M6
Rokeby Rd **SE4**	129	K8
Roland Gdns **SW7**	126	C4
Roland Way **SE17**	128	B4
Rollins St **SE15**	128	G5
Rolls Rd **SE1**	128	D4
Rolt St **SE8**	129	J5
Roman Rd **E2**	124	G5
Roman Rd **E3**	125	J4
Roman Way **N7**	123	M1
Romford St **E1**	124	E7
Romilly St **W1**	123	K9
Romney Rd **SE10**	129	N5
Romney St **SW1**	127	L2
Rood La **EC3**	124	C9
Rookery Rd **SW4**	127	J10
Rope St **SE16**	129	J3
Ropemaker Rd **SE16**	129	J2
Ropemaker St **EC2**	124	B7
Ropery St **E3**	125	K6
Ropley St **E2**	124	E4
Rosary Gdns **SW7**	126	C3
Rose All **SE1**	124	A10
Rose Sq **SW3**	126	D4
Rosebank Gdns **E3**	125	K4
Roseberry Pl **E8**	124	D1
Roseberry St **SE16**	128	F3
Rosebery Av **EC1**	123	N6
Rosebury Rd **SW6**	126	B8
Rosefield Gdns **E14**	125	L9
Rosemary Dr **E14**	125	P8
Rosemary Rd **SE15**	128	D6
Rosemont Rd **NW3**	122	C1
Rosemoor St **SW3**	126	F3
Rosenau Cres **SW11**	126	E7
Rosenau Rd **SW11**	126	E7
Roserton St **E14**	129	N1
Rosetta Cl **SW8**	127	L6
Rosher Cl **E15**	125	P2
Rosoman St **EC1**	123	N5
Rossendale Way **NW1**	123	J2
Rossetti Rd **SE16**	128	F4
Rossmore Rd **NW1**	122	E6
Rothbury Rd **E9**	125	K2
Rotherfield St **N1**	124	A2
Rotherhithe New Rd **SE16**	128	E4
Rotherhithe Old Rd **SE16**	129	H3
Rotherhithe St **SE16**	128	G1
Rotherhithe Tunnel **E1**	124	G10
Rotherhithe Tunnel App **E14**	128	G1
Rotherhithe Tunnel App **SE16**	128	G1
Rothery Ter **SW9**	127	P6
Rothsay St **SE1**	128	C2
Rothwell St **NW1**	122	F3
Rotten Row **SW1**	126	F1
Rotten Row **SW7**	126	E1
Rotterdam Dr **E14**	129	N2
Rouel Rd **SE16**	128	E2
Rounton Rd **E3**	125	L6
Roupell St **SE1**	123	N10
Rousden St **NW1**	123	J2
Rowcross St **SE1**	128	D4
Rowditch La **SW11**	126	G8
Rowena Cres **SW11**	126	E8
Rowington Cl **W2**	122	B7
Rowley Way **NW8**	122	B3
Rowse Cl **E15**	125	N2
Roxby Pl **SW6**	126	A5
Royal Av **SW3**	126	F4
Royal College St **NW1**	123	J2
Royal Ct **SE16**	129	K2
Royal Ex **EC3**	124	B8
Royal Hill **SE10**	129	N6
Royal Hospital Rd **SW3**	126	F5
Royal Ms, The **SW1**	127	H2
Royal Mint Ct **EC3**	124	D9
Royal Mint St **E1**	124	D9
Royal Naval Pl **SE14**	129	K6
Royal Oak Rd **E8**	124	F1
Royal Opera Arc **SW1**	123	K10
Royal Pl **SE10**	129	N6
Royal Rd **SE17**	127	P5
Royal St **SE1**	127	M2
Royal Victor Pl **E3**	125	H4
Royston St **E2**	124	G4
Rozel Ct **N1**	124	C3
Rozel Rd **SW4**	127	J8
Ruby St **SE15**	128	F5
Rudolph Rd **NW6**	122	A4
Rufford St **N1**	123	L3
Rugby St **WC1**	123	M6
Rugg St **E14**	125	L9
Rum Cl **E1**	124	G9
Rumbold Rd **SW6**	126	B6
Rumsey Rd **SW9**	127	M9
Rupert Gdns **SW9**	127	P8
Rupert St **W1**	123	K9
Rush Hill Rd **SW11**	126	G9
Rushcroft Rd **SW2**	127	N10
Rushton St **N1**	124	B4
Rushworth St **SE1**	127	P1
Ruskin Pk Ho **SE5**	128	B9
Russell Gro **SW9**	127	N6
Russell Sq **WC1**	123	K7
Russell St **WC2**	123	M8
Russia Dock Rd **SE16**	125	J10
Russia La **E2**	124	G4
Russia Wk **SE16**	129	J1
Rust Sq **SE5**	128	B6
Ruston St **E3**	125	K3
Rutherford St **SW1**	127	K3
Rutland Gdns **SW7**	126	E1
Rutland Gate **SW7**	126	E1
Rutland Rd **E9**	124	G3
Rutland St **SW7**	126	E2
Rutts Ter **SE14**	129	H7
Ryder Dr **SE16**	128	F4
Ryder St **SW1**	123	J10
Rye Hill Pk **SE15**	128	G10
Rye La **SE15**	128	E7
Rye Pas **SE15**	128	E9
Rye Rd **SE15**	129	H10
Ryecroft St **SW6**	126	B7
Ryland Rd **NW5**	123	H1
Rysbrack St **SW3**	126	F2
S		
Sabella Ct **E3**	125	K4
Sabine Rd **SW11**	126	F9
Sackville St **W1**	123	J9
Saffron Av **E14**	125	P9
Saffron Hill **EC1**	123	N6
Sail St **SE11**	127	M3
St. Agnes Pl **SE11**	127	N5
St. Albans Gro **W8**	126	B2
St. Albans Ms **W2**	122	D7
St. Alban's Pl **N1**	123	P3
St. Alfege Pas **SE10**	129	N5
St. Alphonsus Rd **SW4**	127	J10
St. Andrew St **EC4**	123	N7
St. Andrew's Hill **EC4**	123	P9
St. Andrews Pl **NW1**	123	H6
St. Andrews Way **E3**	125	M6
St. Ann's St **SW1**	127	K2
St. Ann's Ter **NW8**	122	D4
St. Anthonys Cl **E1**	124	E10
St. Asaph Rd **SE4**	129	H9
St. Augustines Rd **NW1**	123	K2
St. Austell Rd **SE13**	129	N8
St. Barnabas St **SW1**	126	G4
St. Barnabas Vil **SW8**	127	L7
St. Botolph St **EC3**	124	D8
St. Bride St **EC4**	123	P8
St. Chad's Pl **WC1**	123	L5
St. Chad's St **WC1**	123	L5
St. Clements St **N7**	123	N1
St. Cross St **EC1**	123	N7
St. Davids Sq **E14**	129	M4
St. Donatts Rd **SE14**	129	K7
St. Dunstan's Hill **EC3**	124	C9
St. Edmunds Ter **NW8**	122	E3
St. Elmos Rd **SE16**	129	J1
St. Francis Rd **SE22**	128	C10
St. George St **W1**	123	H8
St. Georges Circ **SE1**	127	P2
St. George's Dr **SW1**	127	H3
St. Georges Flds **W2**	122	E8
St. Georges Rd **SE1**	127	N2
St. Georges Sq **SE8**	129	K3
St. George's Sq **SW1**	127	K4
St. George's Sq Ms **SW1**	127	K4
St. Georges Way **SE15**	128	C5
St. Giles High St **WC2**	123	K8
St. Giles Rd **SE5**	128	C6
St. Gilles Ho **E2**	125	H4
St. Helena Rd **SE16**	129	H3
St. James Ms **E14**	129	N2
St. James's **SE14**	129	J7
St. James's Av **E2**	124	G4
St. James's Ct **SW1**	127	J2
St. James's Cres **SW9**	127	N9
St. James's Palace **SW1**	123	J10
St. James's Pk **SW1**	127	K1
St. James's Pl **SW1**	123	J10
St. James's Rd **SE1**	128	E4
St. James's Rd **SE16**	128	E2
St. James's Sq **SW1**	123	J10
St. James's St **SW1**	123	J10
St. James's Ter Ms **NW8**	122	F3
St. James's Wk **EC1**	123	P6
St. John St **EC1**	123	P6
St. John's Cres **SW9**	127	N9
St. John's Est **N1**	124	B4
St. John's Hill **SW11**	126	D10
St. John's Hill Gro **SW11**	126	D10
St. John's La **EC1**	123	P6
St. John's Rd **SW11**	126	E10
St. Johns Vale **SE8**	129	L8
St. John's Wd High St **NW8**	122	D4
St. John's Wd Pk **NW8**	122	D3
St. John's Wd Rd **NW8**	122	D6
St. John's Wd Ter **NW8**	122	D4
St. Joseph's Vale **SE3**	129	P8
St. Jude's Rd **E2**	124	F4
St. Katharine's Way **E1**	124	D10
St. Lawrence St **E14**	125	N10
St. Lawrence Way **SW9**	127	N8
St. Leonards Ct **N1**	124	B5
St. Leonards Rd **E14**	125	M7
St. Leonards Sq **NW5**	122	G1
St. Leonards St **E3**	125	M5
St. Leonard's Ter **SW3**	126	F4
St. Loo Av **SW3**	126	E5
St. Luke's Av **SW4**	127	K10
St. Luke's Est **EC1**	124	B5
St. Luke's St **SW3**	126	E4
St. Margarets La **W8**	126	B2
St. Margarets Rd **SE4**	129	K10
St. Margaret's St **SW1**	127	K3
St. Mark St **E1**	124	D8
St. Marks Cres **NW1**	122	G3
St. Mark's Gro **SW10**	126	B5
St. Marks Sq **NW1**	122	G3
St. Martins Cl **NW1**	123	J3
St. Martin's La **WC2**	123	L9
St. Martin's Pl **WC2**	123	L9
St. Martin's Rd **SW9**	127	M8
St. Martin's-le-Grand **EC1**	124	A8
St. Mary at Hill **EC3**	124	C9
St. Mary Axe **EC3**	124	C8
St. Marychurch St **SE16**	128	G1
St. Mary's Gdns **SE11**	127	N3
St. Mary's Gate **W8**	126	B2
St. Mary's Gro **N1**	123	P1
St. Marys Mans **W2**	122	C7
St. Marys Path **N1**	123	P3
St. Mary's Pl **W8**	126	B2
St. Mary's Rd **SE15**	128	G7
St. Marys Sq **W2**	122	D7
St. Marys Ter **W2**	122	D7
St. Mary's Wk **SE11**	127	N3
St. Matthew's Rd **SW2**	127	M10
St. Matthew's Row **E2**	124	E5
St. Michael's Rd **SW9**	127	M8
St. Michaels St **W2**	122	E7
St. Norbert Grn **SE4**	129	J10
St. Norbert Rd **SE4**	129	J10
St. Olav's Sq **SE16**	128	G2
St. Oswald's Pl **SE11**	127	M4
St. Pancras Way **NW1**	123	J2
St. Paul St **N1**	124	A3
St. Paul's Av **SE16**	125	H10
St. Paul's Chyd **EC4**	123	P8
St. Paul's Cres **NW1**	123	K2
St. Paul's Pl **N1**	124	B1
St. Paul's Rd **N1**	123	P1
St. Paul's Shrubbery **N1**	124	B1
St. Paul's Way **E3**	125	K7
St. Paul's Way **E14**	125	K7
St. Peter's Cl **E2**	124	E4
St. Peters St **N1**	123	P3
St. Peter's Way **N1**	124	C2
St. Petersburgh Ms **W2**	122	B9
St. Petersburgh Pl **W2**	122	B9
St. Philip Sq **SW8**	127	H8
St. Philip St **SW8**	127	H8
St. Philip's Rd **E8**	124	E1
St. Rule St **SW8**	127	J8
St. Saviour's Est **SE1**	128	D2
St. Silas Pl **NW5**	122	G1
St. Silas St Est **NW5**	122	G1
St. Stephens Cl **NW8**	122	E3
St. Stephens Cres **W2**	122	A8
St. Stephens Gdns **W2**	122	A8
St. Stephens Gro **SE13**	129	N9
St. Stephen's Rd **E3**	125	K4
St. Stephens Ter **SW8**	127	M6
St. Stephen's Wk **SW7**	126	C3
St. Swithin's La **EC4**	124	B9
St. Thomas Pl **NW1**	123	K2
St. Thomas St **SE1**	124	B10
St. Thomas's Pl **E9**	124	G2
St. Thomas's Sq **E9**	124	F2
Salamanca St **SE1**	127	M3
Sale Pl **W2**	122	E7
Salem Rd **W2**	122	B9
Salisbury Ct **EC4**	123	P8
Salisbury Pl **SW9**	127	P6
Salisbury Pl **W1**	122	F7
Salisbury St **NW8**	122	E6
Salisbury Ter **SE15**	128	G9
Salmon La **E14**	125	J8
Salter Rd **SE16**	125	H10
Salter St **E14**	125	L9
Saltoun Rd **SW2**	127	N10
Saltwell St **E14**	125	L9
Salway Rd **E15**	125	P1
Samford St **NW8**	122	D6
Sampson St **E1**	124	E10
Samuel Cl **SE14**	129	H5
Samuel Lewis Trust Dws **SW6**	126	A6
Samuel St **SE15**	128	D6
Sancroft St **SE11**	127	M4
Sandall Rd **NW5**	123	J1
Sandbourne Rd **SE4**	129	J8
Sandgate St **SE15**	128	F5
Sandilands Rd **SW6**	126	B7
Sandison St **SE15**	128	D9
Sandland St **WC1**	123	M7
Sandmere Rd **SW4**	127	L10
Sandpiper Cl **SE16**	129	K1
Sandrock Rd **SE13**	129	L9
Sand's End La **SW6**	126	B7
Sandwell Cres **NW6**	122	A1
Sandwich St **WC1**	123	L5
Sandy's Row **E1**	124	C7
Sanford St **SE14**	129	J5
Sangora Rd **SW11**	126	D10
Sans Wk **EC1**	123	N6
Sansom St **SE5**	128	B6
Santley St **SW4**	127	M10
Saperton Wk **SE11**	127	M3
Sapphire Rd **SE8**	129	J3
Saracen St **E14**	125	L8
Sartor Rd **SE15**	129	H10
Sarum Ter **E3**	125	K6
Satchwell Rd **E2**	124	E5
Saunders Ness Rd **E14**	129	N4
Saunders St **SE11**	127	N3
Savile Row **W1**	123	J9
Savona Est **SW8**	127	J6
Savona St **SW8**	127	J6
Savoy Pl **WC2**	123	L9
Savoy St **WC2**	123	M9
Sawyer St **SE1**	128	A1
Saxon Rd **E3**	125	K4
Saxton Cl **SE13**	129	P9
Sayes Ct St **SE8**	129	K5
Scala St **W1**	123	J7
Scandrett St **E1**	124	F10
Scarsdale Vil **W8**	126	A2
Scawen Rd **SE8**	129	J4
Scawfell St **E2**	124	D4
Sceaux Est **SE5**	128	C7
Sceaux Gdns **SE5**	128	D7
Sceptre Rd **E2**	124	G5
Schoolhouse La **E1**	125	H9
Schooner Cl **E14**	129	P2
Sclater St **E1**	124	D6
Scoresby St **SE1**	123	P10
Scott Ellis Gdns **NW8**	122	D5
Scott Lidgett Cres **SE16**	128	E1
Scott St **E1**	124	F6
Scriven St **E8**	124	D3
Scrutton St **EC2**	124	C6
Scylla Rd **SE15**	128	F9
Seaford St **WC1**	123	L5
Seagrave Rd **SW6**	126	A5
Searles Cl **SW11**	126	E6
Searles Rd **SE1**	128	B3
Sears St **SE5**	128	B6
Seaton Cl **SE11**	127	N4
Sebastian St **EC1**	123	P5
Sebbon St **N1**	123	P2
Sedding St **SW1**	126	G3
Sedgmoor Pl **SE5**	128	C6
Seething La **EC3**	124	C9
Sekforde St **EC1**	123	P6
Selby St **E1**	124	E6
Selden Rd **SE15**	128	G8
Selsdon Way **E14**	129	M2
Selsey St **E14**	125	L7
Selwood Pl **SW7**	126	D4
Selwyn Rd **E3**	125	K4
Semley Pl **SW1**	126	G3
Senate St **SE15**	128	G8
Senior St **W2**	122	B7
Senrab St **E1**	125	H8
Serle St **WC2**	123	M8
Serpentine Rd **W2**	122	F10
Settles St **E1**	124	E7
Settrington Rd **SW6**	126	B8
Severnake Cl **E14**	129	L3
Severus Rd **SW11**	126	E10
Seville Ms **N1**	124	C2
Seville St **SW1**	126	F1
Sevington St **W9**	122	B6
Seward St **EC1**	124	A5
Sewardstone Rd **E2**	124	G4
Sextant Av **E14**	129	P3
Seymour Gdns **SE4**	129	J9
Seymour Ms **W1**	122	G8
Seymour Pl **W1**	122	E7
Seymour St **W1**	122	F8
Seymour St **W2**	122	F8
Seymour Wk **SW10**	126	C5
Seyssel St **E14**	129	N3
Shacklewell St **E2**	124	D6
Shad Thames **SE1**	124	D10
Shaftesbury Av **W1**	123	K9
Shaftesbury Av **WC2**	123	K9
Shaftesbury St **N1**	124	A4
Shafton Rd **E9**	125	H3
Shalcomb St **SW10**	126	C5
Shamrock St **SW4**	127	K9
Shand St **SE1**	128	C1
Shandy St **E1**	125	H7
Shannon Gro **SW9**	127	M10
Shardeloes Rd **SE14**	129	K8
Sharon Gdns **E9**	124	G3
Sharpleshall St **NW1**	122	F2
Sharratt St **SE15**	128	G5
Sharsted St **SE17**	127	P4
Shaw Rd **SE22**	128	C10
Shawfield St **SW3**	126	E4
Shearling Way **N7**	123	L1
Sheep La **E8**	124	F3
Sheepcote La **SW11**	126	F8
Sheffield Ter **W8**	122	A10
Shell Rd **SE13**	129	M9
Shelley Cl **SE15**	128	F8
Shellwood Rd **SW11**	126	F8
Shelmerdine Cl **E3**	125	L7
Shelton St **WC2**	123	L8
Shenfield St **N1**	124	C4
Shenley Rd **SE5**	128	C7
Shepherdess Wk **N1**	124	A4
Shepherds Pl **W1**	122	G9
Sheppard Dr **SE16**	128	F4
Shepperton Rd **N1**	124	A3
Sherborne St **N1**	124	B3
Sheringham Rd **N7**	123	M1
Sherriff Rd **NW6**	122	A1
Sherwin Rd **SE14**	129	H7
Sherwood Gdns **E14**	129	L3
Sherwood Gdns **SE16**	128	E4
Shetland Rd **E3**	125	K4
Ship St **SE8**	129	L7
Shipton St **E2**	124	D5
Shipwright Rd **SE16**	129	J1
Shirbutt St **E14**	125	M9
Shirland Rd **W9**	122	A6
Shirley Gro **SW11**	126	G9
Shoe La **EC4**	123	N8
Shooter's Hill Rd **SE10**	129	P7
Shore Pl **E9**	124	G2
Shore Rd **E9**	124	G2
Shoreditch High St **E1**	124	C6
Shorncliffe Rd **SE1**	128	D4
Short Rd **E15**	125	P3
Short Wall **E15**	125	N5
Shorter St **E1**	124	D9
Shorts Gdns **WC2**	123	L8
Shottendane Rd **SW6**	126	A7
Shouldham St **W1**	122	E7
Shrewsbury Rd **W2**	122	A8
Shroton St **NW1**	122	E7
Shrubland Rd **E8**	124	E3
Shuttleworth Rd **SW11**	126	E8
Sibella Rd **SW4**	127	K8
Sidmouth Rd **SE15**	128	D7
Sidmouth St **WC1**	123	L5
Sidney Rd **SW9**	127	M8
Sidney Sq **E1**	124	G8
Sidney St **E1**	124	F7
Sidworth St **E8**	124	F2
Silex St **SE1**	127	P1
Silk St **EC2**	124	A7
Silkmills Sq **E9**	125	K1
Silver Wk **SE16**	125	K10
Silverthorne Rd **SW8**	127	H8
Silvocea Way **E14**	125	P8
Silwood Est **SE16**	128	G3
Silwood St **SE16**	128	G3
Simla Cl **SE14**	129	J5
Simms Rd **SE1**	128	E3
Simpson St **SW11**	126	D8
Simpsons Rd **E14**	125	M9
Sirinham Pt **SW8**	127	M5
Sisters Av **SW11**	126	F10
Sisulu Pl **SW9**	127	N9
Sivill Ho **E2**	124	D5
Six Bridges Trd Est **SE1**	128	E4
Sketchley Gdns **SE16**	129	H4
Skinner St **EC1**	123	N5
Skipworth Rd **E9**	124	G3
Slaidburn St **SW10**	126	C5
Slaithwaite Rd **SE13**	129	N10
Sleaford St **SW8**	127	J6
Slippers Pl **SE16**	128	F2
Sloane Av **SW3**	126	E3
Sloane Ct W **SW3**	126	G4
Sloane Gdns **SW1**	126	G3
Sloane Sq **SW1**	126	F3
Sloane St **SW1**	126	F1
Sloane Ter **SW1**	126	F3
Smart St **E2**	125	H5
Smeaton St **E1**	124	F10
Smedley St **SW4**	127	K8
Smedley St **SW8**	127	K8
Smeed Rd **E3**	125	L2
Smiles Pl **SE13**	129	N8
Smith Cl **SE16**	125	H10
Smith Sq **SW1**	127	L2
Smith St **SW3**	126	F4
Smith Ter **SW3**	126	F4
Smithy St **E1**	124	G7
Smokehouse Yd **EC1**	123	P7
Smugglers Way **SW18**	126	B10
Smyrks Rd **SE17**	128	C4
Smyrna Rd **NW6**	122	A2
Smythe St **E14**	125	M9
Snow Hill **EC1**	123	P7
Snowbury Rd **SW6**	126	B8
Snowden St **EC2**	124	C6
Snowman Ho **NW6**	122	B3
Snowsfields **SE1**	128	B1
Soames St **SE15**	128	D9
Soho Sq **W1**	123	K8
Solebay St **E1**	125	J6
Solomon's Pas **SE15**	128	F10
Solon New Rd **SW4**	127	L10
Solon Rd **SW2**	127	L10
Solway Rd **SE22**	128	E10
Somerford St **E1**	124	F6
Somerford Way **SE16**	129	J1
Somerleyton Pas **SW9**	127	P10
Somerleyton Rd **SW9**	127	N10
Somers Cres **W2**	122	E8
Somerset Est **SW11**	126	D7
Somerset Gdns **SE13**	129	M8
Somerton Rd **SE15**	128	F10
Sondes St **SE17**	128	B5
Sopwith Way **SW8**	127	H6
Sorrel La **E14**	125	P8
Sotheran Cl **E8**	124	E3
Sotheron Rd **SW6**	126	B6
Soudan Rd **SW11**	126	F7
South Audley St **W1**	122	G9
South Bolton Gdns **SW5**	126	B4
South Carriage Dr **SW1**	126	E1
South Carriage Dr **SW7**	126	E1
South Colonnade **E14**	125	L10
South Cres **E16**	125	P6
South Cres **WC1**	123	K7
South Eaton Pl **SW1**	126	G3
South End Row **W8**	126	B2
South Island Pl **SW9**	127	M6
South Lambeth Pl **SW8**	127	L5
South Lambeth Rd **SW8**	127	L6
South Molton La **W1**	123	H8
South Molton St **W1**	123	H8
South Par **SW3**	126	D4
South Pk **SW6**	126	A8
South Pk Ms **SW6**	126	B9
South Pl **EC2**	124	B7
South Sea St **SE16**	129	K2
South St **W1**	122	G10
South Tenter St **E1**	124	D9
South Ter **SW7**	126	E3
South Vil **NW1**	123	K1
South Wf Rd **W2**	122	D8
Southall Pl **SE1**	128	B1
Southampton Pl **WC1**	123	L7
Southampton Row **WC1**	123	L7
Southampton St **WC2**	123	L9
Southampton Way **SE5**	128	B6
Southborough Rd **E9**	124	G3
Southern Gro **E3**	125	K5
Southern St **N1**	123	M4
Southerngate Way **SE14**	129	J6
Southey Rd **SW9**	127	N7
Southgate Gro **N1**	124	B2
Southgate Rd **N1**	124	B2
Southmoor Way **E9**	125	K1
Southolm St **SW11**	127	H7
Southville **SW8**	127	K7
Southwark Br **EC4**	124	A10
Southwark Br **SE1**	124	A10
Southwark Br Rd **SE1**	127	P2
Southwark Pk Est **SE16**	128	F3

Valentine Pl

Southwark Pk Rd **SE16** 128 D3
Southwark St **SE1** 123 P10
Southwater Cl **E14** 125 K8
Southwell Gdns **SW7** 126 C3
Southwell Rd **SE5** 128 A9
Southwick Pl **W2** 122 E8
Southwick St **W2** 122 E8
Sovereign Cl **E1** 124 F9
Spa Grn Est **EC1** 123 N5
Spa Rd **SE16** 128 D2
Spanby Rd **E3** 125 L6
Spanish Pl **W1** 122 G8
Sparta St **SE10** 129 M7
Spear Ms **SW5** 126 A3
Speke Ho **SE5** 128 A6
Speldhurst Rd **E9** 125 H2
Spelman St **E1** 124 E7
Spencer Rd **SW18** 126 D10
Spencer St **EC1** 123 P5
Spenser St **SW1** 127 J2
Spert St **E14** 125 J9
Spey St **E14** 125 N7
Spicer Cl **SW9** 127 P8
Spindrift Av **E14** 129 M3
Spital Sq **E1** 124 C7
Spital St **E1** 124 E6
Sprimont Pl **SW3** 126 F4
Spring St **W2** 122 D8
Springall St **SE15** 128 F6
Springfield La **NW6** 122 B3
Springfield Rd **NW8** 122 C3
Springfield Wk **NW6** 122 B3
Springhill Cl **SE5** 128 B9
Sprules Rd **SE4** 129 J8
Spur Rd **SE1** 127 N1
Spur Rd **SW1** 127 J1
Spurgeon St **SE1** 128 B2
Spurling Rd **SE22** 128 D10
Squirries St **E2** 124 E5
Stable Yd Rd **SW1** 123 J10
Stables Way **SE11** 127 N4
Stacey St **WC2** 123 K8
Stadium St **SW10** 126 C6
Stafford Cl **NW6** 122 A5
Stafford Ct **W8** 126 A2
Stafford Pl **SW1** 127 J2
Stafford Rd **E3** 125 K4
Stafford Rd **NW6** 122 A5
Stafford St **W1** 123 J10
Stafford Ter **W8** 126 A2
Staffordshire St **SE15** 128 E7
Stag Pl **SW1** 127 J2
Stainer St **SE1** 124 B10
Staining La **EC2** 124 A8
Stainsby Rd **E14** 125 L8
Stalham St **SE16** 128 F2
Stamford Rd **N1** 124 C2
Stamford St **SE1** 123 N10
Stamp Pl **E2** 124 D5
Stanbury Rd **SE15** 128 F7
Stanfield Rd **E3** 125 J4
Stanford Rd **W8** 126 B2
Stanhope Gdns **SW7** 126 C3
Stanhope Gate **W1** 122 G10
Stanhope Ms E **SW7** 126 C3
Stanhope Ms W **SW7** 126 C3
Stanhope Pl **W2** 122 F8
Stanhope St **NW1** 123 J5
Stanhope Ter **W2** 122 D9
Stanley Cl **SW8** 127 M5
Stanley Gro **SW8** 126 G8
Stanley Rd **E15** 125 P3
Stanley St **SE8** 129 K6
Stanmer St **SW11** 126 E7
Stannard Ms **E8** 124 E1
Stannard Rd **E8** 124 E1
Stannary Pl **SE11** 127 N4
Stannary St **SE11** 127 N5
Stansfield Rd **SW9** 127 M9
Stanway St **N1** 124 C4
Stanworth St **SE1** 128 D1
Staple Inn Bldgs **WC1** 123 N7
Staple St **SE1** 128 B1
Staples Cl **SE16** 125 J10
Star St **W2** 122 E7
Starboard Way **E14** 129 L2
Starcross St **NW1** 123 J5
Station App **SE1** 127 N1
Station Rd **SE13** 129 N9
Station St **E15** 125 P2
Station Ter **SE5** 128 A7
Staunton St **SE8** 129 K5
Stave Yd Rd **SE16** 125 J10
Stayner's Rd **E1** 125 H6
Stead St **SE17** 128 B3
Stean St **E8** 124 D3
Stebondale St **E14** 129 N4
Steeles Rd **NW3** 122 F1
Steers Way **SE16** 129 J1
Stephan Cl **E8** 124 E3
Stephen St **W1** 123 K7
Stephendale Rd **SW6** 126 B8
Stephenson Way **NW1** 123 J6
Stepney Causeway **E1** 125 H8
Stepney Grn **E1** 124 G7
Stepney High St **E1** 125 H7
Stepney Way **E1** 124 F7
Sterling Gdns **SE14** 129 J5
Sternhall La **SE15** 128 E9
Sterry St **SE1** 128 B1
Stevens Av **E9** 124 G1
Stevenson Cres **SE16** 128 F4
Steward St **E1** 124 C7
Stewart St **E14** 129 N1
Stewart's Gro **SW3** 126 D3
Stewart's Rd **SW8** 127 J6
Stillington St **SW1** 127 J3
Stirling Rd **SW9** 127 L8
Stockholm Rd **SE16** 128 G4
Stockholm Way **E1** 124 E10
Stockwell Av **SW9** 127 M9
Stockwell Gdns **SW9** 127 M8
Stockwell Gdns Est **SW9** 127 L8
Stockwell Grn **SW9** 127 M8
Stockwell La **SW9** 127 M8
Stockwell Pk Cres **SW9** 127 M8
Stockwell Pk Est **SW9** 127 N8
Stockwell Pk Rd **SW9** 127 M7
Stockwell Pk Wk **SW9** 127 M9
Stockwell Rd **SW9** 127 M8
Stockwell St **SE10** 129 N5
Stockwell Ter **SW9** 127 M7
Stokenchurch St **SW6** 126 B7
Stone Bldgs **WC2** 123 M7
Stonecutter St **EC4** 123 P8
Stonefield St **N1** 123 N3
Stones End St **SE1** 128 A1
Stoney St **SE1** 124 B10
Stonhouse St **SW4** 127 K9
Stopes St **SE15** 128 D6
Stopford Rd **SE17** 127 P4
Store St **WC1** 123 K7
Storers Quay **E14** 129 P3
Storey's Gate **SW1** 127 K1
Stories Ms **SE5** 128 C8
Stories Rd **SE5** 128 C9
Storks Rd **SE16** 128 E2
Stormont Rd **SW11** 126 G9
Stour Rd **E3** 125 L2
Stourcliffe St **W1** 122 F8
Stowage **SE8** 129 L5
Strafford St **E14** 129 L1
Strahan Rd **E3** 125 J5
Straightsmouth **SE10** 129 N6
Straker's Rd **SE15** 128 F10
Strand **WC2** 123 L9
Stranraer Way **N1** 123 L2
Strasburg Rd **SW11** 127 H7
Stratford Cen, The **E15** 125 P2
Stratford Pl **W1** 123 H8
Stratford Rd **W8** 126 A2
Stratford Vil **NW1** 123 J2
Strath Ter **SW11** 126 E10
Strathblaine Rd **SW11** 126 D10
Strathearn Pl **W2** 122 E9
Strathnairn St **SE1** 128 E3
Strathray Gdns **NW3** 122 E1
Stratton St **W1** 123 H10
Strattondale St **E14** 129 N2
Streatham St **WC1** 123 K8
Streimer Rd **E15** 125 N4
Strickland St **SE8** 129 L8
Stroudley Wk **E3** 125 M5
Strutton Grd **SW1** 127 K2
Stuart Rd **NW6** 122 A5
Stuart Rd **SE15** 128 G10
Stuart Twr **W9** 122 C5
Stubbs Dr **SE16** 128 F4
Studd St **N1** 123 P3
Studdridge St **SW6** 126 A8
Studholme St **SE15** 128 F6
Studley Est **SW4** 127 L7
Studley Rd **SW4** 127 L7
Stukeley St **WC2** 123 L8
Sturdy Rd **SE15** 128 F8
Sturgeon Rd **SE17** 128 A4
Sturry St **E14** 125 M8
Sturt St **N1** 124 A4
Stutfield St **E1** 124 E8
Styles Gdns **SW9** 127 P9
Sudeley St **N1** 123 P4
Sudlow Rd **SW18** 126 A10
Sugar Ho La **E15** 125 N4
Sugar Quay Wk **EC3** 124 C9
Sugden Rd **SW11** 126 G9
Sulivan Ct **SW6** 126 A9
Sulivan Rd **SW6** 126 A9
Sullivan Cl **SW11** 126 E9
Sullivan Rd **SE11** 127 P3
Sultan St **SE5** 128 A6
Summercourt Rd **E1** 124 G8
Sumner Est **SE15** 128 D6
Sumner Pl **SW7** 126 D3
Sumner Rd **SE15** 128 D6
Sumner St **SE1** 124 A10
Sumpter Cl **NW3** 122 C1
Sun St **EC2** 124 B7
Sunbury La **SW11** 126 D7
Sunderland Ter **W2** 122 B8
Sunlight Sq **E2** 124 F5
Sunninghill Rd **SE13** 129 M8
Sunray Av **SE24** 128 B10
Sunset Rd **SE5** 128 A10
Surma Cl **E1** 124 F6
Surrendale Pl **W9** 122 A6
Surrey Canal Rd **SE14** 128 G5
Surrey Canal Rd **SE15** 128 G5
Surrey La **SW11** 126 E7
Surrey La Est **SW11** 126 E7
Surrey Quays Rd **SE16** 129 H1
Surrey Row **SE1** 127 P1
Surrey Sq **SE17** 128 C4
Surrey St **WC2** 123 M9
Surrey Ter **SE17** 128 C4
Surrey Water Rd **SE16** 125 H10
Susannah St **E14** 125 M8
Sussex Gdns **W2** 122 D8
Sussex Pl **NW1** 122 F6
Sussex Pl **W2** 122 D8
Sussex Sq **W2** 122 D9
Sussex St **SW1** 127 H4
Sussex Wk **SW9** 127 P10
Sutherland Av **W9** 122 C5
Sutherland Pl **W2** 122 A8
Sutherland Row **SW1** 127 H4
Sutherland Sq **SE17** 128 A4
Sutherland St **SW1** 127 H4
Sutherland Wk **SE17** 128 A4
Sutterton St **N7** 123 M1
Sutton Est **SW3** 126 E4
Sutton Est, The **N1** 123 P2
Sutton Row **W1** 123 K8
Sutton St **E1** 124 G8
Swallow Cl **SE14** 128 G7
Swan Mead **SE1** 128 C2
Swan Rd **SE16** 128 G1
Swan St **SE1** 128 A2
Swan Wk **SW3** 126 F5
Swandon Way **SW18** 126 B10
Swanfield St **E2** 124 D5
Swaton Rd **E3** 125 L6
Sweden Gate **SE16** 129 J2
Swedenborg Gdns **E1** 124 E9
Sweeney Cres **SE1** 128 D1
Swinford Gdns **SW9** 127 P9
Swinton Pl **WC1** 123 M5
Swinton St **WC1** 123 M5
Swiss Ter **NW6** 122 D2
Sybil Phoenix Cl **SE8** 129 H4
Sycamore Ms **SW4** 127 J9
Sydney Cl **SW3** 126 D3
Sydney Ms **SW3** 126 D3
Sydney Pl **SW7** 126 D3
Sydney St **SW3** 126 E3
Sylvan Gro **SE15** 128 F5
Sylvester Rd **E8** 124 F1
Symons St **SW3** 126 F3

T

Tabard Gdn Est **SE1** 128 B1
Tabard St **SE1** 128 B1
Tabernacle St **EC2** 124 B6
Tachbrook Est **SW1** 127 K4
Tachbrook St **SW1** 127 J3
Tack Ms **SE4** 129 L9
Tadema Rd **SW10** 126 C6
Taeping St **E14** 129 M3
Talacre Rd **NW5** 122 G1
Talbot Rd **SE22** 128 C10
Talbot Sq **W2** 122 D8
Talfourd Pl **SE15** 128 D7
Talfourd Rd **SE15** 128 D7
Tallis St **EC4** 123 N9
Talma Rd **SW2** 127 N10
Talwin St **E3** 125 M5
Tamworth St **SW6** 126 A5
Tanner St **SE1** 128 C1
Tanners Hill **SE8** 129 K7
Taplow **NW3** 122 D2
Taplow St **N1** 124 A4
Tapp St **E1** 124 F6
Tappesfield Rd **SE15** 128 G9
Tariff Cres **SE8** 129 K3
Tarling St **E1** 124 F8
Tarling St Est **E1** 124 G8
Tarragon Cl **SE14** 129 J6
Tarry La **SE8** 129 J3
Tarver Rd **SE17** 127 P4
Tarves Way **SE10** 129 M6
Tasman Rd **SW9** 127 L9
Tatum St **SE17** 128 B3
Taunton Pl **NW1** 122 F6
Tavern La **SW9** 127 N8
Tavistock Pl **WC1** 123 L6
Tavistock Sq **WC1** 123 K6
Tavistock St **WC2** 123 L9
Taviton St **WC1** 123 K6
Tavy Cl **SE11** 127 N4
Tawny Way **SE16** 129 H3
Taybridge Rd **SW11** 126 G9
Tayburn Cl **E14** 125 N8
Tayport Cl **N1** 123 L2
Teak Cl **SE16** 125 J10
Teale St **E2** 124 E4
Tedworth Sq **SW3** 126 F4
Teesdale Cl **E2** 124 F4
Teesdale St **E2** 124 F4
Teignmouth Cl **SW4** 127 K10
Telegraph Pl **E14** 129 M3
Telford Ter **SW1** 127 J5
Tell Gro **SE22** 128 D10
Templar St **SE5** 127 P8
Temple **EC4** 123 N9
Temple Av **EC4** 123 N9
Temple Pl **WC2** 123 M9
Temple St **E2** 124 F4
Temple W Ms **SE11** 127 P2
Templecombe Rd **E9** 124 G3
Templeton Pl **SW5** 126 A3
Tench St **E1** 124 F10
Tenison Way **SE1** 123 M10
Tennis St **SE1** 128 B1
Tennyson St **SW8** 127 H8
Tent St **E1** 124 F6
Tenterden St **W1** 123 H8
Teredo St **SE16** 129 H2
Terminus Pl **SW1** 127 H2
Terrace, The **NW6** 122 A3
Terrace Rd **E9** 124 G2
Tessa Sanderson Pl **SW8** 127 H9
Tetcott Rd **SW10** 126 C6
Teversham La **SW8** 127 L7
Teviot St **E14** 125 N7
Thackeray Rd **SW8** 127 H8
Thackeray St **W8** 126 B1
Thalia Cl **SE10** 129 P5
Thame Rd **SE16** 129 H1
Thames Av **SW10** 126 C7
Thames Path **SE1** 123 N9
Thames St **SE10** 129 M5
Thanet St **WC1** 123 L5
Thayer St **W1** 122 G7
Theatre St **SW11** 126 F9
Theberton St **N1** 123 N3
Theed St **SE1** 123 N10
Theobald's Rd **WC1** 123 M7
Thermopylae Gate **E14** 129 M3
Thessaly Rd **SW8** 127 J6
Thirleby Rd **SW1** 127 J2
Thirsk Rd **SW11** 126 G9
Thistle Gro **SW10** 126 C4
Thomas Baines Rd **SW11** 126 D9
Thomas Doyle St **SE1** 127 P2
Thomas More St **E1** 124 E9
Thomas Rd **E14** 125 K8
Thompson's Av **SE5** 128 A6
Thorburn Sq **SE1** 128 E3
Thoresby St **N1** 124 A5
Thorncroft St **SW8** 127 L6
Thorndike Cl **SW10** 126 C6
Thorndike St **SW1** 127 J3
Thorne Rd **SW8** 127 L6
Thorney Cres **SW11** 126 D6
Thorney St **SW1** 127 L3
Thorngate Rd **W9** 122 A6
Thornham St **SE10** 129 M5
Thornhaugh St **WC1** 123 K6
Thornhill Cres **N1** 123 M2
Thornhill Rd **N1** 123 N2
Thornhill Sq **N1** 123 M2
Thornton Pl **W1** 122 F7
Thornton St **SW9** 127 N8
Thornville St **SE8** 129 L7
Thorparch Rd **SW8** 127 K7
Thoydon Rd **E3** 125 J4
Thrale St **SE1** 124 A10
Thrawl St **E1** 124 D7
Threadneedle St **EC2** 124 B8
Three Colt St **E14** 125 K9
Three Colts La **E2** 124 F6
Three Kings Yd **W1** 123 H9
Three Mill La **E3** 125 N5
Throgmorton Av **EC2** 124 B8
Throgmorton St **EC2** 124 B8
Thurland Rd **SE16** 128 E2
Thurloe Cl **SW7** 126 E2
Thurloe Pl **SW7** 126 D3
Thurloe Sq **SW7** 126 E3
Thurloe St **SW7** 126 D3
Thurlow St **SE17** 128 B4
Thurston Rd **SE13** 129 M8
Thurtle Rd **E2** 124 D3
Tibbatts Rd **E3** 125 M6
Tidey St **E3** 125 L7
Tidworth Rd **E3** 125 L6
Tileyard Rd **N7** 123 L2
Tiller Rd **E14** 129 L2
Tilney Gdns **N1** 124 B1
Tilney St **W1** 122 G10
Timber Mill Way **SW4** 127 K9
Timber Pond Rd **SE16** 129 H1
Timberland Rd **E1** 124 F8
Timothy Rd **E3** 125 K7
Tindal St **SW9** 127 P7
Tinsley Rd **E1** 124 G7
Tintagel Cres **SE22** 128 D10
Tintern St **SW4** 127 L10
Tinworth St **SE11** 127 M4
Tipthorpe Rd **SW11** 126 G9
Tisdall Pl **SE17** 128 B3
Titchfield Rd **NW8** 122 F3
Tite St **SW3** 126 F4
Tiverton St **SE1** 128 A2
Tivoli Ct **SE16** 129 K1
Tobin Cl **NW3** 122 E2
Toby La **E1** 125 J6
Tollet St **E1** 125 H6
Tollgate Gdns **NW6** 122 B4
Tolpuddle St **N1** 123 N4
Tomlins Gro **E3** 125 L5
Tomlinson Cl **E2** 124 D5
Tonbridge St **WC1** 123 L5
Tooley St **SE1** 124 B10
Topmast Pt **E14** 129 L1
Tor Gdns **W8** 126 A1
Torrens St **EC1** 123 N4
Torridge Gdns **SE15** 128 G10
Torrington Pl **E1** 124 E10
Torrington Pl **WC1** 123 K7
Torrington Sq **WC1** 123 K6
Tothill St **SW1** 127 K1
Tottan Ter **E1** 125 H8
Tottenham Ct Rd **W1** 123 J6
Tottenham Rd **N1** 124 C1
Tottenham St **W1** 123 J7
Toulmin St **SE1** 128 A1
Toulon St **SE5** 128 A6
Towcester Rd **E3** 125 M6
Tower Br **E1** 124 D10
Tower Br **SE1** 124 D10
Tower Br App **E1** 124 D10
Tower Br Rd **SE1** 128 C2
Tower Hill **EC3** 124 C9
Tower Pier **EC3** 124 D10
Tower St **WC2** 123 K8
Town Hall Rd **SW11** 126 F9
Townmead Rd **SW6** 126 C8
Townsend St **SE17** 128 B3
Townshend Est **NW8** 122 E4
Townshend Rd **NW8** 122 E3
Toynbee St **E1** 124 D7
Tradescant Rd **SW8** 127 L6
Trafalgar Av **SE15** 128 D4
Trafalgar Gdns **E1** 125 H7
Trafalgar Gro **SE10** 129 P5
Trafalgar Rd **SE10** 129 P5
Trafalgar Sq **SW1** 123 K10
Trafalgar Sq **WC2** 123 K10
Trafalgar St **SE17** 128 B4
Trafalgar Way **E14** 125 N10
Transept St **NW1** 122 E7
Transom Sq **E14** 129 M4
Tranton Rd **SE16** 128 E2
Treadway St **E2** 124 F4
Treaty St **N1** 123 M3
Trebovir Rd **SW5** 126 A4
Treby St **E3** 125 K6
Tredegar Rd **E3** 125 K4
Tredegar Sq **E3** 125 K5
Tredegar Ter **E3** 125 K5
Trederwen Rd **E8** 124 E3
Tregarvon Rd **SW11** 126 G10
Trego Rd **E9** 125 L2
Tregothnan Rd **SW9** 127 L9
Tregunter Rd **SW10** 126 C5
Trelawney Est **E9** 124 G1
Tremadoc Rd **SW4** 127 K10
Tremaine Cl **SE4** 129 L8
Trenchard St **SE10** 129 P4
Trenchold St **SW8** 127 L5
Tresco Rd **SE15** 128 F10
Tresham Cres **NW8** 122 E6
Tressillian Cres **SE4** 129 L9
Tressillian Rd **SE4** 129 K10
Trevithick St **SE8** 129 L4
Trevor Pl **SW7** 126 E1
Trevor Sq **SW7** 126 F1
Trevor St **SW7** 126 E1
Triangle Pl **SW4** 127 K10
Triangle Rd **E8** 124 F3
Trident St **SE16** 129 H3
Trigon Rd **SW8** 127 M6
Trim St **SE14** 129 K5
Trinidad St **E14** 125 K9
Trinity Ch Sq **SE1** 128 A2
Trinity Cl **E8** 124 D1
Trinity Gdns **SW9** 127 M10
Trinity Gro **SE10** 129 N7
Trinity Sq **EC3** 124 C9
Trinity St **SE1** 128 A1
Trinity Wk **NW3** 122 C1
Triton Sq **NW1** 123 J6
Troon St **E1** 125 J8
Trott St **SW11** 126 E7
Troutbeck Rd **SE14** 129 J7
Trowbridge Rd **E9** 125 K1
Troy Town **SE15** 128 E9
Trundleys Rd **SE8** 129 H4
Trundleys Ter **SE8** 129 H3
Truro St **NW5** 122 G1
Tryon St **SW3** 126 F4
Tudor Gro **E9** 124 G2
Tudor Rd **E9** 124 F3
Tudor St **EC4** 123 N9
Tufton St **SW1** 127 K2
Tuilerie St **E2** 124 E4
Tunnel Av **SE10** 129 P1
Tunstall Rd **SW9** 127 M10
Turenne Cl **SW18** 126 C10
Turin St **E2** 124 E5
Turks Row **SW3** 126 F4
Turner St **E1** 124 F7
Turners Rd **E3** 125 K7
Turnmill St **EC1** 123 N6
Turnpike Ho **EC1** 123 P5
Turnpin La **SE10** 129 N5
Turret Gro **SW4** 127 J9
Tustin Est **SE15** 128 G5
Twelvetrees Cres **E3** 125 N6
Twine Ct **E1** 124 G9
Twyford St **N1** 123 M3
Tyburn Way **W1** 122 F9
Tyers Est **SE1** 128 C1
Tyers St **SE11** 127 M4
Tyers Ter **SE11** 127 M4
Tyler Cl **E2** 124 D4
Tyndale Ct **E14** 129 M3
Tyneham Rd **SW11** 126 G8
Tynemouth St **SW6** 126 C8
Type St **E2** 125 H4
Tyrawley Rd **SW6** 126 B7
Tyrrell Rd **SE22** 128 E10
Tyrwhitt Rd **SE4** 129 L9
Tyssen Pas **E8** 124 D1
Tyssen St **E8** 124 D1

U

Uamvar St **E14** 125 M7
Ufford St **SE1** 127 N1
Ufton Gro **N1** 124 B2
Ufton Rd **N1** 124 C2
Undercliff Rd **SE13** 129 L9
Undershaft **EC3** 124 C8
Underwood Rd **E1** 124 E6
Underwood Row **N1** 124 A5
Underwood St **N1** 124 A5
Undine Rd **E14** 129 M3
Union Gro **SW8** 127 K8
Union Rd **SW4** 127 K8
Union Rd **SW8** 127 K8
Union Sq **N1** 124 A3
Union St **E15** 125 N3
Union St **SE1** 123 P10
University St **WC1** 123 J6
Unwin Cl **SE15** 128 E5
Upcerne Rd **SW10** 126 C6
Upper Belgrave St **SW1** 126 G2
Upper Berkeley St **W1** 122 F8
Upper Brockley Rd **SE4** 129 K8
Upper Brook St **W1** 122 G9
Upper Cheyne Row **SW3** 126 E5
Upper Grosvenor St **W1** 122 G9
Upper Grd **SE1** 123 P10
Upper Harley St **NW1** 122 G6
Upper Marsh **SE1** 127 M2
Upper Montagu St **W1** 122 F7
Upper N St **E14** 125 L7
Upper Phillimore Gdns **W8** 126 A1
Upper St **N1** 123 N4
Upper Tachbrook St **SW1** 127 J3
Upper Thames St **EC4** 124 A9
Upper Wimpole St **W1** 122 G7
Upper Woburn Pl **WC1** 123 K5
Upstall St **SE5** 127 P7
Urlwin St **SE5** 128 A5
Urlwin Wk **SW9** 127 N8
Ursula St **SW11** 126 E7
Usborne Ms **SW8** 127 M6
Usher Rd **E3** 125 K4
Usk Rd **SW11** 126 C10
Usk St **E2** 125 H5
Uverdale Rd **SW10** 126 C6
Uxbridge St **W8** 122 A10

V

Vale, The **SW3** 126 D5
Vale Royal **N7** 123 L2
Valentine Pl **SE1** 127 P1

Valentine Rd

Valentine Rd E9 125 H1
Valentine Row SE1 127 P1
Valette St E9 124 F1
Vallance Rd E1 124 E6
Vallance Rd E2 124 E5
Valmar Rd SE5 128 A7
Vandon St SW1 127 J2
Vanguard St SE8 129 L7
Vansittart St SE14 129 J6
Vanston Pl SW6 126 A6
Varcoe Rd SE16 128 F4
Varden St E1 124 F8
Vardens Rd SW11 126 D10
Varndell St NW1 123 J5
Vassall Rd SW9 127 N6
Vauban Est SE16 128 E2
Vauban St SE16 128 D2
Vaughan Rd SE5 128 A9
Vaughan St SE16 129 K1
Vaughan Way E1 124 E9
Vauxhall Br SE1 127 L4
Vauxhall Br SW1 127 L4
Vauxhall Br Rd SW1 127 J3
Vauxhall Gro SW8 127 M5
Vauxhall St SE11 127 M4
Vauxhall Wk SE11 127 M4
Vawdrey Cl E1 124 G6
Veda Rd SE13 129 L10
Velletri Ho E2 125 H4
Venables St NW8 122 D6
Venetian Rd SE5 128 A8
Venn St SW4 127 J10
Ventnor Rd SE14 129 H6
Venue St E14 125 N7
Vere St W1 123 H8
Verney Rd SE16 128 E5
Verney Way SE16 128 F4
Vernon Pl WC1 123 L7
Vernon Ri WC1 123 M5
Vernon Rd E3 125 K4
Vesta Rd SE4 129 J8
Vestry Ms SE5 128 C7
Vestry Rd SE5 128 C7
Vestry St N1 124 B5
Viaduct St E2 124 F5
Vian St SE13 129 M9
Vicarage Cres SW11 126 D7
Vicarage Gdns W8 122 A10
Vicarage Gate W8 126 B1
Vicarage Gro SE5 128 B7
Vicars Hill SE13 129 M10
Viceroy Rd SW8 127 L7
Victoria Embk EC4 123 M9
Victoria Embk SW1 127 L1
Victoria Embk WC2 127 L1
Victoria Gdns W11 122 A10
Victoria Gro W8 126 C2
Victoria Ms NW6 122 A3
Victoria Pk E9 125 J2
Victoria Pk Rd E9 124 G3
Victoria Pk Sq E2 124 G5
Victoria Ri SW4 127 H9
Victoria Rd W8 126 C2
Victoria Sta SW1 127 H3
Victoria St SW1 127 J2
Victoria Wf E14 125 J9
Victory Pl SE17 128 A3
Victory Way SE16 129 J1
Vigo St W1 123 J9
Viking Ct SW6 126 A5
Villa Rd SW9 127 N9
Villa St SE17 128 B4
Villiers St WC2 123 L9
Vince St EC1 124 B5
Vincent Cl SE16 129 J1
Vincent Ms E3 125 L4
Vincent Sq SW1 127 J3
Vincent St SW1 127 K3
Vincent Ter N1 123 P4
Vine St Br EC1 123 N6
Viney Rd SE13 129 M9
Vineyard Wk EC1 123 N6
Vining St SW9 127 N10
Violet Hill NW8 122 C4
Violet Rd E3 125 M6
Virgil St SE1 127 M2
Virginia Rd E2 124 D5
Virginia St E1 124 E9
Vivian Rd E3 125 J4
Voltaire Rd SW4 127 K9
Voss St E2 124 E5
Vulcan Rd SE4 129 K8
Vulcan Ter SE4 129 K8
Vulcan Way N7 123 M1
Vyner St E2 124 F3

W

Wadding St SE17 128 B3
Waddington St E15 125 P1
Wades Pl E14 125 M9
Wadeson St E2 124 F4
Wadham Gdns NW3 122 E3
Wadhurst Rd SW8 127 J7
Wager St E3 125 K6
Waghorn St SE15 128 E9
Wagner St SE15 128 G6
Waite St SE15 128 D5
Wakefield St WC1 123 L5
Wakeham St N1 124 B1
Wakeling St E14 125 J8
Wakley St EC1 123 P4
Walberswick St SW8 127 L6
Walbrook EC4 124 B9
Walcot Sq SE11 127 N3
Walden St E1 124 F8
Walerand Rd SE13 129 N8
Wales Cl SE15 128 F6
Waley St E1 125 H7
Walham Gro SW6 126 A6
Wall St N1 124 B1
Wallace Rd N1 124 A1
Wallbutton Rd SE4 129 J8
Waller Rd SE14 129 H7
Wallgrave Rd SW5 126 B3
Wallis Cl SW11 126 D9
Wallis Rd E9 125 K1
Wallwood St E14 125 K7
Walnut Tree Wk SE11 127 N3
Walpole St SW3 126 F4
Walsham Rd SE14 129 H8
Walter St E2 125 H5
Walter Ter E1 125 H8
Walton Cl SW8 127 L6
Walton Pl SW3 126 F2
Walton St SW3 126 E3
Walworth Pl SE17 128 A4
Walworth Rd SE1 128 A3
Walworth Rd SE17 128 A3
Wandon Rd SW6 126 B6
Wandsworth Br SW6 126 B9
Wandsworth Br SW18 126 B9
Wandsworth Br Rd SW6 126 B7
Wandsworth Rd SW8 127 K6
Wanless Rd SE24 128 A9
Wanley Rd SE5 128 B10
Wansbeck Rd E9 125 K2
Wansey St SE17 128 A3
Wapping High St E1 124 E10
Wapping La E1 124 F9
Wapping Wall E1 124 G10
Warburton Rd E8 124 F2
Ward Rd E15 125 P3
Wardalls Gro SE14 128 G6
Warden Rd NW5 122 G1
Wardour St W1 123 K9
Warham St SE5 127 P6
Warley St E2 125 H5
Warlock Rd W9 122 A6
Warndon St SE16 129 H3
Warneford St E9 124 F3
Warner Pl E2 124 E4
Warner Rd SE5 128 A7
Warner St EC1 123 N6
Warren St W1 123 J6
Warriner Gdns SW11 126 F7
Warrington Cres W9 122 C6
Warton Rd E15 125 N2
Warwick Av W2 122 C6
Warwick Av W9 122 B6
Warwick Ct SE15 128 E8
Warwick Cres W2 122 C7
Warwick Est W2 122 B7
Warwick Ho St SW1 123 K10
Warwick La EC4 123 P8
Warwick Pl W9 122 C7
Warwick Pl N SW1 127 J3
Warwick Row SW1 127 H2
Warwick Sq SW1 127 J4
Warwick Sq Ms SW1 127 J3
Warwick St W1 123 J9
Warwick Way SW1 127 J3
Warwickshire Path SE8 129 K6
Washington Cl E3 125 N8
Wat Tyler Rd SE3 129 N8
Wat Tyler Rd SE10 129 N8
Water La SE14 128 G6
Water Ms SE15 128 G10
Waterford Rd SW6 126 B7
Watergate St SE8 129 L5
Waterhouse Sq EC1 123 N7
Waterloo Br SE1 123 M9
Waterloo Br WC2 123 M9
Waterloo Est E2 124 G4
Waterloo Gdns E2 124 G4
Waterloo Pas NW6 122 A2
Waterloo Pl SW1 123 K10
Waterloo Rd SE1 127 N1
Waterloo Ter N1 123 P2
Waterman Way E1 124 F10
Watermans Wk SE16 129 J2
Watermeadow La SW6 126 C8
Waterside Cl E3 125 K3
Waterside Pt SW11 126 E6
Waterson St E2 124 C5
Waterview Ho E14 125 J7
Watkinson Rd N7 123 M1
Watling St EC4 124 A8
Watney St E1 124 F8
Watson's St SE8 129 L6
Watts Gro E3 125 M7
Watts St E1 124 F10
Watts St SE15 128 D7
Waveney Av SE15 128 F10
Waverley Pl NW8 122 D4
Waverley Wk W2 122 A7
Waverton Ho E3 125 K3
Waverton St W1 122 G10
Wayford St SW11 126 E8
Wayman Ct E8 124 F1
Wear Pl E2 124 F5
Weardale Rd SE13 129 P10
Wearside Rd SE13 129 M10
Weatherley Cl E3 125 K7
Weaver St E1 124 E6
Weavers Ter SW6 126 A5
Weavers Way NW1 123 K3
Webb St SE1 128 C2
Webber Row SE1 127 P1
Webber St SE1 127 P1
Webster Rd SE16 128 E2
Weighhouse St W1 122 G8
Weir's Pas NW1 123 K5
Welbeck St W1 122 G7
Welbeck Way W1 123 H8
Welby St SE5 127 P7
Well St E9 124 G2
Welland St SE10 129 N5
Wellclose Sq E1 124 E9
Wellesley St E1 125 H7
Wellesley Ter N1 124 A5
Wellington Pl NW8 122 E4
Wellington Rd NW8 122 D4
Wellington Row E2 124 D5
Wellington Sq SW3 126 F4
Wellington St WC2 123 L9
Wellington Ter E1 124 F10
Wellington Way E3 125 L5
Wells Ri NW8 122 F3
Wells St W1 123 J8
Wells Way SE5 128 C5
Wells Way SW7 126 D2
Welsford St SE1 128 E4
Wendle Ct SW8 127 L5
Wendon St E3 125 K3
Wendover SE17 128 C4
Wenlock Rd N1 124 A4
Wenlock St N1 124 A4
Wennington Rd E3 125 H4
Wentworth Cres SE15 128 E6
Wentworth St E1 124 D8
Werrington St NW1 123 J4
Wesley Cl SE17 127 P3
Wessex St E2 124 G5
West Arbour St E1 125 H8
West Carriage Dr W2 122 D9
West Eaton Pl SW1 126 G3
West End La NW6 122 A3
West Gdns E1 124 F9
West Gro SE10 129 N7
West Halkin St SW1 126 G2
West Hampstead Ms NW6 122 B1
West India Av E14 125 L10
West India Dock Rd E14 125 K8
West La SE16 128 F1
West Rd SW3 126 F5
West Smithfield EC1 123 P7
West Sq SE11 127 P2
West St E2 124 F4
West Tenter St E1 124 D8
West Warwick Pl SW1 127 H3
Westbourne Br W2 122 C7
Westbourne Cres W2 122 D9
Westbourne Gdns W2 122 B8
Westbourne Gro W2 122 A8
Westbourne Gro Ter W2 122 B8
Westbourne Pk Rd W2 122 A7
Westbourne Pk Vil W2 122 A7
Westbourne Rd N7 123 N1
Westbourne St W2 122 D9
Westbourne Ter W2 122 D8
Westbourne Ter Ms W2 122 C8
Westbourne Ter Rd W2 122 C7
Westbridge Rd SW11 126 D7
Westbury St SW8 127 J8
Westcott Rd SE17 127 P5
Western Rd SW9 127 N9
Westferry Circ E14 125 K10
Westferry Rd E14 125 L10
Westfield Cl SW10 126 C6
Westfield Way E1 125 J5
Westgate St E8 124 F3
Westgate Ter SW10 126 B4
Westgrove La SE10 129 N7
Westminster Br SE1 127 L1
Westminster Br SW1 127 L1
Westminster Br Rd SE1 127 N2
Westmoreland Pl SW1 127 H4
Westmoreland Rd SE17 128 B5
Westmoreland St W1 122 G7
Westmoreland Ter SW1 127 H4
Weston Ri WC1 123 M4
Weston St SE1 128 B2
Westport St E1 125 H8
Westway W2 122 A7
Westway W9 122 A7
Wetherby Gdns SW5 126 C3
Wetherby Pl SW7 126 C3
Wetherell Rd E9 125 H3
Weybridge Pt SW11 126 G8
Weymouth Ms W1 123 H7
Weymouth St W1 123 H7
Weymouth Ter E2 124 D4
Wharf Pl E2 124 E3
Wharf Rd E15 125 P3
Wharf Rd N1 124 A4
Wharfdale Rd N1 123 L4
Wharfedale St SW10 126 B4
Wharton St WC1 123 M5
Wheat Sheaf Cl E14 129 M3
Wheatsheaf La SW8 127 L6
Wheelwright St N7 123 M2
Wheler St E1 124 D6
Whidborne St WC1 123 L5
Whiskin St EC1 123 P5
Whistlers Av SW11 126 D6
Whiston Rd E2 124 D4
Whitbread Rd SE4 129 J10
Whitburn Rd SE13 129 M10
Whitcher Cl SE14 129 J5
Whitcomb St WC2 123 K9
White Ch La E1 124 E8
White Hart St SE11 127 N4
White Horse La E1 125 H6
White Horse Rd E1 125 J8
White Horse St W1 123 H10
White Lion Hill EC4 123 P9
White Lion St N1 123 N4
White Post La E9 125 K2
White Post La SE13 129 L9
White Post St SE15 128 G6
Whiteadder Way E14 129 M3
Whitear Wk E15 125 P1
Whitechapel High St E1 124 D8
Whitechapel Rd E1 124 E7
Whitecross St EC1 124 A6
Whitefriars St EC4 123 N8
Whitehall SW1 123 L10
Whitehall Ct SW1 123 L10
Whitehall Pl SW1 123 L10
Whitehead's Gro SW3 126 E4
Whites Grds SE1 128 C1
White's Row E1 124 D7
Whitethorn St E3 125 L6
Whitfield Rd SE3 129 P7
Whitfield St W1 123 K7
Whitgift St SE11 127 M3
Whitman Rd E3 125 J6
Whitmore Est N1 124 C3
Whitmore Rd N1 124 C3
Whittaker St SW1 126 G3
Whitton Wk E3 125 L4
Whorlton Rd SE15 128 F9
Wick La E3 125 L4
Wick Rd E9 125 H1
Wickersley Rd SW11 126 G8
Wickford St E1 124 G6
Wickham Gdns SE4 129 K9
Wickham Ho E1 125 H7
Wickham Ms SE4 129 K8
Wickham Rd SE4 129 K9
Wickham St SE11 127 M4
Wicklow St WC1 123 M5
Wickwood St SE5 127 P8
Widdin St E15 125 P2
Widley Rd W9 122 A5
Wigmore Pl W1 123 H8
Wigmore St W1 122 G8
Wilbraham Pl SW1 126 F3
Wilcox Cl SW8 127 L6
Wilcox Rd SW8 127 L6
Wild Ct WC2 123 M8
Wild Goose Dr SE14 128 G7
Wild St WC2 123 L8
Wilde Cl E8 124 E3
Wild's Rents SE1 128 C2
Wilfred St SW1 127 J2
Wilkes St E1 124 D7
Wilkin St NW5 123 H1
Wilkinson St SW8 127 M6
Willard St SW8 127 H9
Willes Rd NW5 123 H1
William Bonney Est SW4 127 K10
William IV St WC2 123 L9
William Morris Way SW6 126 C9
William Rd NW1 123 H5
William St SW1 126 F1
Williams Bldgs E2 124 G6
Willington Rd SW9 127 L9
Willis St E14 125 M8
Willoughby Pas E14 125 L10
Willow Br Rd N1 124 A1
Willow Pl SW1 127 J3
Willow St EC2 124 C6
Willow Wk SE1 128 C3
Willowbrook Rd SE15 128 D5
Wilman Gro E8 124 E2
Wilmcote Ho W2 122 B7
Wilmer Gdns N1 124 C3
Wilmer Lea Cl E15 125 P2
Wilmington Sq WC1 123 N5
Wilmington St WC1 123 N5
Wilmot Cl SE15 128 E6
Wilmot Pl NW1 123 J2
Wilmot St E2 124 F6
Wilshaw St SE14 129 L7
Wilson Gro SE16 128 F1
Wilson Rd SE5 128 C7
Wilson St EC2 124 B7
Wilton Cres SW1 126 G1
Wilton Ms SW1 126 G2
Wilton Pl SW1 126 G1
Wilton Rd SW1 127 J2
Wilton Row SW1 126 G1
Wilton Sq N1 124 B3
Wilton St SW1 127 H2
Wilton Ter SW1 126 G2
Wilton Vil N1 124 B3
Wilton Way E8 124 E1
Wiltshire Rd SW9 127 N9
Wiltshire Row N1 124 B3
Wimbolt St E2 124 E5
Wimbourne St N1 124 B4
Wimpole Ms W1 123 H7
Wimpole St W1 123 H8
Winans Wk SW9 127 N8
Winchester Cl SE17 127 P3
Winchester Rd NW3 122 D2
Winchester Sq SE1 124 B10
Winchester St SW1 127 H4
Winchester Wk SE1 124 B10
Wincott St SE11 127 N3
Winders Rd SW11 126 E8
Windlass Pl SE8 129 J3
Windmill Cl SE13 129 N8
Windmill La E15 125 P1
Windmill Row SE11 127 N4
Windmill St W1 123 K7
Windmill Wk SE1 123 N10
Windrose Cl SE16 129 H1
Windsock Cl SE16 129 K3
Windsor Gdns W9 122 A7
Windsor St N1 123 P3
Windsor Ter N1 124 A5
Windsor Wk SE5 128 B8
Wine Cl E1 124 G9
Winford Ho E3 125 K2
Winforton St SE10 129 N7
Wingfield St SE15 128 E9
Wingmore Rd SE24 128 A9
Winifred Gro SW11 126 F10
Winkley St E2 124 F4
Winsland St W2 122 D8
Winsley St W1 123 J8
Winslow SE17 128 C4
Winstanley Est SW11 126 D9
Winstanley Rd SW11 126 D9
Winterton Ho E1 124 F8
Winthrop St E1 124 F7
Wise Rd E15 125 P3
Wisteria Rd SE13 129 P10
Witan St E2 124 F5
Wivenhoe Cl SE15 128 F9
Wixs La SW4 127 H10
Woburn Pl WC1 123 L6
Woburn Sq WC1 123 K6
Woburn Wk WC1 123 K5
Wodehouse Av SE5 128 D7
Wolfe Cres SE16 129 H1
Wolftencroft Cl SW11 126 D9
Wolseley St SE1 128 D1
Wolsey Ms NW5 123 J1
Wood Cl E2 124 E6
Wood St EC2 124 A8
Wood Wf SE10 129 M5
Woodbridge St EC1 123 P6
Woodchester Sq W2 122 B7
Woodchurch Rd NW6 122 A2
Woodfall St SW3 126 F4
Woodfarrs SE5 128 B10
Woodison St E3 125 J6
Woodland Cres SE16 129 H1
Woodpecker Rd SE14 129 J5
Woods Ms W1 122 G9
Woods Rd SE15 128 F7
Woodseer St E1 124 D7
Woodstock Ter E14 125 M9
Wooler St SE17 128 B4
Woolmore St E14 125 N9
Woolneigh St SW6 126 B9
Woolstaplers Way SE16 128 E3
Wooster Gdns E14 125 P8
Wootton St SE1 123 N10
Worfield St SW11 126 E6
Worgan St SE11 127 M4
Worgan St SE16 129 H2
World's End Est SW10 126 D6
Worlingham Rd SE22 128 D10
Wormwood St EC2 124 C8
Woronzow Rd NW8 122 D3
Worship St EC2 124 B6
Wotton Rd SE8 129 K5
Wren Rd SE5 128 B7
Wren St WC1 123 M6
Wrexham Rd E3 125 L4
Wrigglesworth St SE14 129 H6
Wrights La W8 126 B2
Wrights Rd E3 125 K4
Wroxton Rd SE15 128 F8
Wyatt Cl SE16 129 K1
Wycliffe Rd SW11 126 G8
Wye St SW11 126 D8
Wyke Rd E3 125 L2
Wyllen Cl E1 124 G6
Wymering Rd W9 122 A5
Wynan Rd E14 129 M4
Wyndham Est SE5 128 A6
Wyndham Pl W1 122 F7
Wyndham Rd SE5 127 P6
Wyndham St W1 122 F7
Wynford Rd N1 123 M4
Wynne Rd SW9 127 N8
Wynnstay Gdns W8 126 A2
Wynter St SW11 126 C10
Wynyard Ter SE11 127 M4
Wyvil Rd SW8 127 L5
Wyvis St E14 125 M7

Y

Yabsley St E14 125 N10
Yalding Rd SE16 128 E2
Yardley St WC1 123 N5
Yeate St N1 124 B2
Yelverton Rd SW11 126 D8
Yeo St E3 125 M7
Yeoman St SE8 129 J3
Yeoman's Row SW3 126 E2
York Br NW1 122 G6
York Gate NW1 122 G6
York Gro SE15 128 G7
York Ho Pl W8 126 B1
York Pl SW11 126 D9
York Rd SE1 127 M1
York Rd SW11 126 C9
York Rd SW18 126 C9
York Sq E14 125 J8
York St W1 122 F7
York Ter E NW1 122 G6
York Ter W NW1 122 G6
York Way N1 123 L3
York Way N7 123 K1
York Way Ct N1 123 L3
Yorkshire Rd E14 125 J8
Yorkton St E2 124 E4
Young St W8 126 B1

Z

Zampa Rd SE16 128 G4
Zealand Rd E3 125 J4
Zenoria St SE22 128 D10
Zetland St E14 125 M7

INDEX TO GREAT BRITAIN

Administrative Area Abbreviations

Aber.	Aberdeenshire	E.Ayr.	East Ayrshire	Lancs.	Lancashire	P. & K.	Perth & Kinross	Suff.	Suffolk
Arg. & B.	Argyll & Bute	E.Dun.	East Dunbartonshire	Leic.	Leicester	Pembs.	Pembrokeshire	Surr.	Surrey
B'burn.	Blackburn with Darwen	E.Loth.	East Lothian	Leics.	Leicestershire	Peter.	Peterborough	Swan.	Swansea
B. & H.	Brighton & Hove	E.Renf.	East Renfrewshire	Lincs.	Lincolnshire	Plym.	Plymouth	Swin.	Swindon
B. & N.E.Som.	Bath & North East Somerset	E.Riding	East Riding of Yorkshire	M.K.	Milton Keynes	Ports.	Portsmouth	T. & W.	Tyne & Wear
B.Gwent	Blaenau Gwent	E.Suss.	East Sussex	M.Tyd.	Merthyr Tydfil	R. & C.	Redcar & Cleveland	Tel. & W.	Telford & Wrekin
Beds.	Bedfordshire	Edin.	Edinburgh	Med.	Medway	R.C.T.	Rhondda Cynon Taff	Thur.	Thurrock
Bourne.	Bournemouth	Falk.	Falkirk	Mersey.	Merseyside	Read.	Reading	V. of Glam.	Vale of Glamorgan
Brack.F.	Bracknell Forest	Flints.	Flintshire	Middbro.	Middlesbrough	Renf.	Renfrewshire	W'ham	Wokingham
Bucks.	Buckinghamshire	Glas.	Glasgow	Midloth.	Midlothian	Rut.	Rutland	W. & M.	Windsor & Maidenhead
Caerp.	Caerphilly	Glos.	Gloucestershire	Mon.	Monmouthshire	S'end	Southend	W.Berks.	West Berkshire
Cambs.	Cambridgeshire	Gt.Lon.	Greater London	N.Ayr.	North Ayrshire	S'ham.	Southampton	W.Dun.	West Dunbartonshire
Carmar.	Carmarthenshire	Gt.Man.	Greater Manchester	N.E.Lincs.	North East Lincolnshire	S.Ayr.	South Ayrshire	W.Isles	Western Isles (Na h-Eileanan anlar)
Cere.	Ceredigion	Gwyn.	Gwynedd	N.Lan.	North Lanarkshire	S.Glos.	South Gloucestershire	W.Loth.	West Lothian
Ches.	Cheshire	Hants.	Hampshire	N.Lincs.	North Lincolnshire	S.Lan.	South Lanarkshire	W.Mid.	West Midlands
Cornw.	Cornwall	Hart.	Hartlepool	N.P.T.	Neath Port Talbot	S.Yorks.	South Yorkshire	W.Suss.	West Sussex
Cumb.	Cumbria	Here.	Herefordshire	N.Som.	North Somerset	Sc.Bord.	Scottish Borders	W.Yorks.	West Yorkshire
D. & G.	Dumfries & Galloway	Herts.	Hertfordshire	N.Yorks.	North Yorkshire	Shet.	Shetland	Warks.	Warwickshire
Darl.	Darlington	High.	Highland	Norf.	Norfolk	Shrop.	Shropshire	Warr.	Warrington
Denb.	Denbighshire	I.o.A.	Isle of Anglesey	Northants.	Northamptonshire	Slo.	Slough	Wilts.	Wiltshire
Derbys.	Derbyshire	I.o.M.	Isle of Man	Northumb.	Northumberland	Som.	Somerset	Worcs.	Worcestershire
Dur.	Durham	I.o.S.	Isles of Scilly	Nott.	Nottingham	Staffs.	Staffordshire	Wrex.	Wrexham
		I.o.W.	Isle of Wight	Notts.	Nottinghamshire	Stir.	Stirling		
		Inclyde	Inverclyde	Ork.	Orkney	Stock.	Stockton-on-Tees		
				Oxon.	Oxfordshire	Stoke	Stoke-on-Trent		

Notes

This index reads in the sequence: Place Name / Postal District / Map Page Number / Grid Reference.

Example: Cheltenham **GL52**   **29** J6

Where there is more than one place with the same name, the index reads in the sequence:
Place Name / Administrative Area / Postal District / Map Page Number / Grid Reference.

Example: Prestbury, *Ches.* **SK10**   **49** H5
Prestbury, *Glos.* **GL52**   **29** J6

Entries in the index shown in **BOLD CAPITALS** indicate a post town.

Example: **GLOUCESTER GL**   **29 H7**

A

Ab Kettleby **LE14** 42 A3
Abbas Combe **BA8** 9 G2
Abberley **WR6** 29 G2
Abberton, *Essex* **CO5** 34 E7
Abberton, *Worcs.* **WR10** 29 J3
Abberwick **NE66** 71 G2
Abbess Roding **CM5** 33 J7
Abbey Dore **HR2** 28 C5
Abbey Hulton **ST2** 40 B1
Abbey St. Bathans **TD11** 77 F4
Abbey Village **PR6** 56 B7
Abbey Wood **SE2** 23 H4
Abbeycwmhir **LD1** 27 K1
Abbeystead **LA2** 55 J4
Abbeytown **CA7** 60 C1
Abbotrule **TD9** 70 B2
Abbots Bickington **EX22** 6 B4
Abbots Bromley **WS15** 40 C3
Abbots Langley **WD25** 22 E1
Abbots Leigh **BS8** 19 J4
Abbots Morton **WR7** 30 B3
Abbots Ripton **PE28** 33 F1
Abbot's Salford **WR11** 30 B3
Abbotsbury **DT3** 8 E6
Abbotsham **EX39** 6 C3
Abbotskerswell **TQ12** 5 J4
Abbotsley **PE19** 33 F3
Abbotts Ann **SP11** 21 G7
Abbottswood **SO51** 10 E2
Abdon **SY7** 38 E7
Aber, *Cere.* **SA40** 26 D4
Aber, *Gwyn.* **LL53** 36 B2
Aber Bargoed **CF81** 18 E1
Aber Bowlan **SA19** 17 K1
Aber-banc **SA44** 26 C4
Aber-cywarch **SY20** 37 H4
Aber-Ilia **CF44** 27 J7
Aber-Naint **SY22** 38 A3
Aber-nant **CF44** 18 D1
Aber-pergwm **SA11** 18 B1
Aberaeron **SA46** 26 D2
Aberaman **CF44** 18 D1
Aberangell **SY20** 37 H5
Aberarad **SA38** 17 G1
Aberarder **PH20** 88 B6
Aberarder Ho. **IV2** 88 D2
Aberargie **PH2** 82 C6
Aberarth **SA46** 26 D2
Aberavon **SA12** 18 A3
Aberbeeg **NP13** 19 F1
Abercanaid **CF48** 18 D1
Abercarn **NP11** 19 F2
Abercastle **SA62** 16 B1
Abercegir **SY20** 37 H5
Aberchalder **PH35** 87 K4
Aberchirder **AB54** 98 E5
Abercorn **EH30** 75 J3
Abercraf **SA9** 27 H7
Abercrombie **KY10** 83 G7
Abercrychan **SA20** 27 G5
Abercwmboi **CF44** 18 D1
Abercych **SA37** 26 B4
Abercynafon **LD3** 27 K7
Abercynon **CF45** 18 D2
Aberdalgie **PH2** 82 B5
Aberdaron **LL53** 36 A3
Aberdaugleddau (Milford Haven) **SA73** 16 C4
ABERDEEN AB 91 H4
Aberdeen Airport **AB21** 91 G3
Aberdesach **LL54** 46 C7
Aberdour **KY3** 75 K2
Aberdovey (Aberdyfi) **LL35** 37 F6
Aberdulais **SA10** 18 A2
Aberdyfi (Aberdovey) **LL35** 37 F6
Aberedw **LD2** 27 K4
Abereiddy **SA62** 16 B1
Abererch **LL53** 36 D2
Aberfan **CF48** 18 D1
Aberfeldy **PH15** 81 K3
Aberffraw **LL62** 46 B6
Aberffrwd **SY23** 27 F1
Aberford **LS25** 57 K6
Aberfoyle **FK8** 81 G7
Abergarw **CF32** 18 C3
Abergavenny (Y Fenni) **NP7** 28 C7
Abergele **LL22** 47 H5
Abergiar **SA40** 26 E4
Abergorlech **SA32** 17 J1
Abergwesyn **LD5** 27 H3
Abergwili **SA31** 17 H2
Abergwuan (Fishguard) **SA65** 16 C1
Abergwydol **SY20** 37 G5
Abergwynant **LL40** 37 F4
Abergwynfi **SA13** 18 B2
Abergwyngregyn **LL33** 46 E5
Abergynolwyn **LL36** 37 F5
Aberhafesp **SY16** 37 K6
Aberhonddu (Brecon) **LD3** 27 K6
Aberhosan **SY20** 37 H6
Aberlady **EH32** 76 C2
Aberlemno **DD8** 83 G2
Aberllefenni **SY20** 37 G5
Abermad **SY23** 26 E1
Abermeurig **SA48** 26 E3
Abermule **SY15** 38 A6
Abernant **SA33** 17 G2
Abernethy **PH2** 82 C6
Abernyte **PH14** 82 D4
Aberporth **SA43** 26 B3
Aberriw (Berriew) **SY21** 38 A5
Aberscross **KW10** 96 E1
Abersky **IV2** 88 C2
Abersoch **LL53** 36 C3
Abersychan **NP4** 19 F1
ABERTAWE (SWANSEA) SA 17 K5
Aberteifi (Cardigan) **SA43** 26 A4
Aberthin **CF71** 18 D4
Abertillery **NP13** 19 F1
Abertridwr, *Caerp.* **CF83** 18 E3
Abertridwr, *Powys* **SY10** 37 K4
Abertysswg **NP22** 18 E1
Aberuthven **PH3** 82 A6
Aberyscir **LD3** 27 J6
Aberystwyth **SY23** 36 E7
Abhainnsuidhe **HS3** 100 C7
Abingdon **OX14** 21 H2
Abinger Common **RH5** 22 E7
Abinger Hammer **RH5** 22 D7
Abington **ML12** 68 E1
Abington Pigotts **SG8** 33 G4
Abingworth **RH20** 12 E5
Ablington **GL7** 20 E1
Abney **S32** 50 E5
Aboyne **AB34** 90 D5
Abram **WN2** 49 F2
Abriachan **IV3** 88 C1
Abridge **RM4** 23 H2
Abronhill **G67** 75 F3
Abson **BS30** 19 K4
Abthorpe **NN12** 31 H4
Abune-the-Hill **KW17** 106 B5
Aby **LN13** 53 H5
Acaster Malbis **YO23** 58 B5
Acaster Selby **YO23** 58 B5
Accrington **BB5** 56 C7
Accurrach **PA33** 80 C6
Acha **PA78** 78 C2
Achacha **PA37** 80 A3
Achadacaie **PA29** 73 G4
Achadh Mòr **HS2** 101 F5
Achadh-chaorrunn **PA29** 73 F5
Achadunan **PA26** 80 C6
Achagavel **PH33** 79 J2
Achaglass **PA29** 73 F6
Achahoish **PA31** 73 F3
Achalader **PH10** 82 C3
Achallader **PA36** 80 E3
Achamore **PA60** 72 D3
Achandunie **IV17** 96 D4
Achany **IV27** 96 C1
Achaphubuil **PH33** 87 G7
Acharacle **PH36** 79 H1
Achargary **KW14** 104 C3
Acharn, *Arg. & B.* **PA35** 80 C4
Acharn, *P. & K.* **PH15** 81 J3
Acharosson **PA21** 73 H3
Achateny **PH36** 79 G1
Achath **AB32** 91 F3
Achavanich **KW5** 105 G4
Achduart **IV26** 95 G1
Achentoul **KW11** 104 D5
Achfary **IV27** 102 E4
Achgarve **IV22** 94 E2
Achiemore, *High.* **IV27** 103 F2
Achiemore, *High.* **KW13** 104 D3
Achies **KW12** 105 G3
A'Chill **PH44** 85 H4
Achiltibuie **IV26** 95 G1
Achina **KW14** 104 C2
Achindown **IV12** 97 F7
Achinduich **IV27** 96 C1
Achingills **KW12** 105 G2
Achintee **IV54** 95 F7
Achintee Ho **PH33** 87 H7
Achintraid **IV54** 86 E1
Achlean **PH21** 89 F5
Achleanan **PA34** 79 G2
Achleek **PH33** 79 J2
Achlian **PA33** 80 C5
Achlyness **IV27** 102 E3
Achmelvich **IV27** 102 C6
Achmony **IV63** 88 B1
Achmore, *High.* **IV23** 95 G2
Achmore, *High.* **IV53** 86 E1
Achmore, *Stir.* **FK21** 81 G4
Achnaba **PA31** 73 H2
Achnabat **IV2** 88 C1
Achnabourin **KW14** 104 C3
Achnacairn **PA37** 80 A4
Achnacarnin **IV27** 102 C5
Achnaclerach **IV23** 96 B5
Achnacloich, *Arg. & B.* **PA37** 80 A4
Achnacloich, *High.* **IV46** 86 B4
Achnaclyth **KW6** 105 F5
Achnacraig **PA73** 79 F3
Achnacroish **PA34** 79 K3
Achnadrish **PA75** 79 F2
Achnafalnich **PA33** 80 D5
Achnafauld **PH8** 81 K4
Achnagarron **IV5** 96 C1
Achnagarron **IV18** 96 D4
Achnaha, *High.* **PH36** 79 F1
Achnaha, *High.* **PA34** 79 H3
Achnahanat **IV24** 96 C2
Achnahannet **PH26** 89 G2
Achnalea **PH33** 79 K1
Achnamara **PA31** 73 F2
Achnanellan **PH37** 79 J1
Achnasaul **PH34** 87 H6
Achnasheen **IV22** 95 H6
Achnashellach **PA31** 73 G1
Achnastank **AB55** 89 K1
Achosnich, *High.* **IV25** 96 E2
Achosnich, *High.* **PH36** 79 F1
Achreamie **KW14** 105 F2
Achriabhach **PH33** 80 C1
Achriesgill **IV27** 102 E3
Achrimsdale **KW9** 97 G1
Achronich **PA73** 79 F4
Achtoty **KW14** 103 J2
Achurch **PE8** 42 D7
Achuvoldrach **IV27** 103 H3
Achvaich **IV25** 96 E2
Achvarasdal **KW14** 104 E2
Achvlair **PA38** 80 A2
Achvraie **IV26** 95 G1
Ackergill **KW1** 105 J3
Acklam, *Middbro.* **TS5** 63 F5
Acklam, *N.Yorks.* **YO17** 58 D3
Ackleton **WV6** 39 G6
Acklington **NE65** 71 H3
Ackton **WF7** 57 K7
Ackworth Moor Top **WF7** 51 G1
Acle **NR13** 45 J4
Acock's Green **B27** 40 D7
Acol **CT7** 25 J5
Acomb, *Northumb.* **NE46** 70 E7
Acomb, *York* **YO24** 58 B4
Aconbury **HR2** 28 E5
Acre **BB5** 56 C7
Acrefair **LL14** 38 B1
Acrise Place **CT18** 15 G3
Acton, *Ches.* **CW5** 49 F7
Acton, *Gt.Lon.* **W3** 22 E4
Acton, *Shrop.* **SY9** 38 C7
Acton, *Suff.* **CO10** 34 C4
Acton, *Worcs.* **DY13** 29 H2
Acton Beauchamp **WR6** 29 F3
Acton Bridge **CW8** 48 E5
Acton Burnell **SY5** 38 E5
Acton Green **WR6** 29 F3
Acton Pigott **SY5** 38 E5
Acton Round **WV16** 39 F6
Acton Scott **SY6** 38 D7
Acton Trussell **ST18** 40 B4
Acton Turville **GL9** 20 B3
Adamhill **KA1** 74 C7
Adbaston **ST20** 39 G3
Adber **DT9** 8 E2
Adderbury **OX17** 31 F5
Adderley **TF9** 39 F2
Adderstone **NE70** 77 K7
Addiewell **EH55** 75 H4
Addingham **LS29** 57 F5
Addington, *Bucks.* **MK18** 31 J6
Addington, *Gt.Lon.* **CR0** 23 G5
Addington, *Kent* **ME19** 23 K6
Addlestone **KT15** 22 D5
Addlethorpe **PE24** 53 J6
Adel **LS16** 57 H6
Adeney **TF10** 39 F4
Adfa **SY16** 37 K5
Adforton **SY7** 28 C1
Adisham **CT3** 15 H2
Adlestrop **GL56** 30 D6
Adlingfleet **DN14** 58 E7
Adlington, *Ches.* **SK10** 49 J4
Adlington, *Lancs.* **BL6** 49 F1
Admaston, *Staffs.* **WS15** 40 C3
Admaston, *Tel. & W.* **TF5** 39 F4
Admington **CV36** 30 C4
Adsborough **TA2** 8 B2

Adstock

Adstock **MK18** 31 J5
Adstone **NN12** 31 G3
Adversane **RH14** 12 D4
Advie **PH26** 89 J1
Adwalton **BD11** 57 H7
Adwell **OX9** 21 K2
Adwick le Street **DN6** 51 H2
Adwick upon Dearne **S64** 51 G2
Ae Village **DG1** 68 E5
Affleck, *Aber.* **AB21** 91 G2
Affleck, *Angus* **DD5** 83 F4
Affpuddle **DT2** 9 H5
Afon-wen **CH7** 47 K5
Afton Bridgend **KA18** 68 B2
Agglethorpe **DL8** 57 F1
Aigburth **L17** 48 C4
Aignis **HS2** 101 G4
Aike **YO25** 59 G5
Aikerness **KW17** 106 D2
Aikers **KW17** 107 D8
Aiketgate **CA4** 61 F2
Aikshaw **CA7** 60 C2
Aikton **CA7** 60 D1
Aikwood Tower **TD7** 69 K1
Ailey **HR3** 28 C4
Ailsworth **PE5** 42 E6
Aimster **KW14** 105 G2
Ainderby Quernhow **YO7** 57 J1
Ainderby Steeple **DL7** 62 E7
Aingers Green **CO7** 35 F7
Ainsdale **PR8** 48 C1
Ainstable **CA4** 61 G2
Ainsworth **BL2** 49 G1
Ainthorpe **YO21** 63 J6
Aintree **L10** 48 C3
Aird **HS7** 92 C6
Aird a' Mhachair **HS8** 92 C7
Aird a' Mhulaidh **HS3** 100 D6
Aird Asaig **HS3** 100 D7
Aird Dhail **HS2** 101 G1
Aird Leimhe **HS3** 93 G3
Aird Mhige **HS3** 93 G2
Aird Mhighe **HS3** 93 F3
Aird of Sleat **IV45** 86 B4
Aird Thunga **HS2** 101 G4
Aird Uige **HS2** 100 C4
Airdrie, *Fife* **KY10** 83 G7
Airdrie, *N.Lan.* **ML6** 75 F4
Airidh a' Bhruaich **HS2** 100 E6
Airieland **DG7** 65 H5
Airies **DG9** 66 D7
Airigh-drishaig **IV54** 86 D1
Airmyn **DN14** 58 D7
Airntully **PH1** 82 B4
Airor **PH41** 86 D4
Airth **FK2** 75 G2
Airton **BD23** 56 E4
Airyhassen **DG8** 64 D6
Aisby, *Lincs.* **DN21** 52 B3
Aisby, *Lincs.* **NG32** 42 D2
Aisgernis **HS8** 84 C2
Aiskew **DL8** 57 H1
Aislaby, *N.Yorks.* **YO21** 63 K6
Aislaby, *N.Yorks.* **YO18** 58 D1
Aislaby, *Stock.* **TS16** 63 F5
Aisthorpe **LN1** 52 C4
Aith, *Ork.* **KW17** 106 F5
Aith, *Ork.* **KW16** 107 B6
Aith, *Shet.* **ZE2** 108 F3
Aith, *Shet.* **ZE2** 109 C7
Aitnoch **PH26** 89 G1
Akeld **NE71** 70 E1
Akeley **MK18** 31 J5
Akenham **IP1** 35 F4
Albaston **PL18** 4 E3
Alberbury **SY5** 38 C4
Albourne **BN6** 13 F5
Albrighton, *Shrop.* **SY4** 38 D4
Albrighton, *Shrop.* **WV7** 40 A5
Alburgh **IP20** 45 G7
Albury, *Herts.* **SG11** 33 H6
Albury, *Surr.* **GU5** 22 D7
Albury Heath **GU5** 22 D7
Alby Hill **NR11** 45 F2
Alcaig **IV7** 96 C6
Alcaston **SY6** 38 D7
Alcester **B49** 30 B3
Alciston **BN26** 13 J6
Alcombe **TA24** 7 H1
Alconbury **PE28** 32 E1
Alconbury Hill **PE28** 32 E1
Alconbury Weston **PE28** 32 E1
Aldborough, *N.Yorks.* **YO51** 57 K3
Aldborough, *Norf.* **NR11** 45 F2
Aldbourne **SN8** 21 F4
Aldbrough **HU11** 59 J6
Aldbrough St. John **DL11** 62 C5
Aldburgh **HG4** 57 H2
Aldbury **HP23** 32 C7
Aldclune **PH16** 82 A1
Aldeburgh **IP15** 35 J3
Aldeby **NR34** 45 J6
Aldenham **WD25** 22 E2
Alderbury **SP5** 10 C2
Alderford **NR9** 45 F4
Alderholt **SP6** 10 C3
Alderley **GL12** 20 A2
Alderley Edge **SK9** 49 H5
Alderman's Green **CV2** 41 F7
Aldermaston **RG7** 21 J5
Aldermaston Soke **RG7** 21 K5
Aldermaston Wharf **RG7** 21 K5
Alderminster **CV37** 30 D4
Aldersey Green **CH3** 48 D7
Aldershot **GU11** 22 B6
Alderton, *Glos.* **GL20** 29 J5
Alderton, *Northants.* **NN12** 31 J4
Alderton, *Shrop.* **SY4** 38 D3
Alderton, *Suff.* **IP12** 35 H4
Alderton, *Wilts.* **SN14** 20 B3
Alderwasley **DE56** 51 F7
Aldfield **HG4** 57 H3
Aldford **CH3** 48 D7
Aldham, *Essex* **CO6** 34 D6
Aldham, *Suff.* **IP7** 34 E4
Aldie, *Aber.* **AB42** 91 J1
Aldie, *High.* **IV19** 96 E3
Aldingbourne **PO20** 12 C6
Aldingham **LA12** 55 F2
Aldington, *Kent* **TN25** 15 F4
Aldington, *Worcs.* **WR11** 30 B4
Aldivalloch **AB54** 90 B2
Aldochlay **G83** 74 B1
Aldons **KA26** 67 F5
Aldreth **CB6** 33 H1
Aldridge **WS9** 40 C5
Aldringham **IP16** 35 J2
Aldro **YO17** 58 E3
Aldsworth **GL54** 30 C7
Aldunie **AB54** 90 B2
Aldville **PH8** 82 A4
Aldwark, *Derbys.* **DE4** 50 E7
Aldwark, *N.Yorks.* **YO61** 57 K3
Aldwick **PO21** 12 C7
Aldwincle **NN14** 42 D7
Aldworth **RG8** 21 J4
Alexandria **G83** 74 B3
Alfardisworthy **EX22** 6 A4
Alfington **EX11** 7 K6
Alfold **GU6** 12 D3
Alfold Crossways **GU6** 12 D3
Alford, *Aber.* **AB33** 90 D3
Alford, *Lincs.* **LN13** 53 H5
Alford, *Som.* **BA7** 9 F1
Alfreton **DE55** 51 G7
Alfrick **WR6** 29 G3
Alfriston **BN26** 13 J6
Algarkirk **PE20** 43 F2
Alhampton **BA4** 9 F1
Alkborough **DN15** 58 E7
Alkerton **OX15** 30 E4
Alkham **CT15** 15 H3
Alkington **SY13** 38 E2
Alkmonton **DE6** 40 D2
All Cannings **SN10** 20 D5
All Saints South Elmham **IP19** 45 H7
All Stretton **SY6** 38 D6
Allaleigh **TQ9** 5 J5
Allanaquoich **AB35** 89 J5
Allancreich **AB34** 90 D5
Allangillfoot **DG13** 69 H4
Allanton, *D. & G.* **DG2** 68 E5
Allanton, *N.Lan.* **ML7** 75 G5
Allanton, *S.Lan.* **ML3** 75 F5
Allanton, *Sc.Bord.* **TD11** 77 G5
Allardice **DD10** 91 G7
Allathasdal **HS9** 84 B4
Allendale Town **NE47** 61 K1
Allenheads **NE47** 61 K2
Allen's Green **CM21** 33 H7
Allensford **DH8** 62 B1
Allensmore **HR2** 28 D5
Aller **TA10** 8 C2
Allerby **CA7** 60 B3
Allerford, *Devon* **EX20** 6 C7
Allerford, *Som.* **TA24** 7 H1
Allerston **YO18** 58 E1
Allerthorpe **YO42** 58 D5
Allerton, *Mersey.* **L18** 48 D4
Allerton, *W.Yorks.* **BD15** 57 G6
Allerton Bywater **WF10** 57 K7
Allesley **CV5** 40 E7
Allestree **DE22** 41 F2
Allexton **LE15** 42 B5
Allgreave **SK11** 49 J6
Allhallows **ME3** 24 E4
Allhallows-on-Sea **ME3** 24 E4
Alligin Shuas **IV22** 94 E6
Allimore Green **ST18** 40 A4
Allington, *Lincs.* **NG32** 42 B1
Allington, *Wilts.* **SN10** 20 D5
Allington, *Wilts.* **SP4** 10 D1
Allithwaite **LA11** 55 G2
Allnabad **IV27** 103 G4
Alloa **FK10** 75 G1
Allonby **CA15** 60 B2
Alloway **KA7** 67 H2
Allscot **WV15** 39 G6
Allt na h-Airbhe **IV26** 95 H2
Allt-na-subh **IV40** 87 F2
Alltachonaich **PA34** 79 J2
Alltan Dubh **IV26** 102 B7
Alltbeithe **IV40** 87 G2
Alltforgan **SY10** 37 J3
Alltmawr **LD2** 27 K4
Alltnacaillich **IV27** 103 G4
Alltsigh **IV63** 88 B3
Alltwalis **SA33** 17 H1
Alltwen **SA8** 18 A1
Alltyblaca **SA40** 26 E4
Almeley **HR3** 28 C3
Almer **DT11** 9 J5
Almington **TF9** 39 F2
Almiston Cross **EX39** 6 B3
Almondbank **PH1** 82 B5
Almondbury **HD4** 50 D1
Almondsbury **BS32** 19 J3
Alne **YO61** 57 K3
Alness **IV17** 96 D5
Alnham **NE65** 70 E2
Alnmouth **NE66** 71 H2
Alnwick **NE66** 71 G2
Alphamstone **CO8** 34 C5
Alpheton **CO10** 34 C3
Alphington **EX2** 7 H6
Alpington **NR14** 45 G5
Alport **DE45** 50 E6
Alpraham **CW6** 48 E7
Alresford **CO7** 34 E6
Alrewas **DE13** 40 D4
Alrick **PH11** 82 C1
Alsager **ST7** 49 G7
Alsagers Bank **ST7** 40 A1
Alsop en le Dale **DE6** 50 D7
Alston, *Cumb.* **CA9** 61 J2
Alston, *Devon* **EX13** 8 C4
Alstone **GL20** 29 J5
Alstonefield **DE6** 50 D7
Alswear **EX36** 7 F3
Altanduin **KW11** 104 D6
Altarnun **PL15** 4 C2
Altass **IV27** 96 C1
Altens **AB12** 91 H4
Alterwall **KW1** 105 H2
Altham **BB5** 56 C6
Althorne **CM3** 25 F2
Althorpe **DN17** 52 B2
Alticry **DG8** 64 C5
Altnafeadh **PH49** 80 D2
Altnaharra **IV27** 103 H5
Altofts **WF6** 57 J7
Alton, *Derbys.* **S42** 51 F6
Alton, *Hants.* **GU34** 11 J1
Alton, *Staffs.* **ST10** 40 C1
Alton Barnes **SN9** 20 E5
Alton Pancras **DT2** 9 F4
Alton Priors **SN8** 20 E5
Altonside **IV30** 97 K6
Altrincham **WA14** 49 G4
Altura **PH34** 87 J6
Alva **FK12** 75 G1
Alvanley **WA6** 48 D5
Alvaston **DE24** 41 F2
Alvechurch **B48** 30 B1
Alvecote **B79** 40 E5
Alvediston **SP5** 9 J2
Alveley **WV15** 39 G7
Alverdiscott **EX31** 6 D3
Alverstoke **PO12** 11 H5
Alverstone **PO36** 11 G6
Alverton **NG13** 42 A1
Alves **IV30** 97 J5
Alvescot **OX18** 21 F1
Alveston, *S.Glos.* **BS35** 19 K3
Alveston, *Warks.* **CV37** 30 D3
Alvie **PH21** 89 F4
Alvingham **LN11** 53 G3
Alvington **GL15** 19 K1
Alwalton **PE2** 42 E6
Alweston **DT9** 9 F3
Alwinton **NE65** 70 E3
Alwoodley Gates **LS17** 57 J5
Alyth **PH11** 82 D3
Amalebra **TR20** 2 B5
Amber Hill **PE20** 43 F1
Ambergate **DE56** 51 F7
Amberley, *Glos.* **GL5** 20 B1
Amberley, *W.Suss.* **BN18** 12 D5
Amble **NE65** 71 H3
Amblecote **DY8** 40 A7
Ambleside **LA22** 60 E6
Ambleston **SA62** 16 D2
Ambrismore **PA20** 73 J5
Ambrosden **OX25** 31 H7
Amcotts **DN17** 52 B1
Amersham **HP7** 22 C2
Amesbury **SP4** 20 E7
Amington **B77** 40 E5
Amisfield Town **DG1** 69 F5
Amlwch **LL68** 46 C3
Amlwch Port **LL68** 46 C3
Ammanford (Rhydaman) **SA18** 17 K3
Amotherby **YO17** 58 D2
Ampfield **SO51** 10 E2
Ampleforth **YO62** 58 B2
Ampleforth College **YO62** 58 B2
Ampney Crucis **GL7** 20 D1
Ampney St. Mary **GL7** 20 D1
Ampney St. Peter **GL7** 20 D1
Amport **SP11** 21 G7
Ampthill **MK45** 32 D5
Ampton **IP31** 34 C1
Amroth **SA67** 16 E4
Amulree **PH8** 81 K4
An T-òb (Leverburgh) **HS5** 93 F3
An Tairbeart (Tarbert) **HS3** 100 D7
Anaboard **PH26** 89 H1
Anaheilt **PH36** 79 K1
Ancaster **NG32** 42 C1
Anchor **SY7** 38 A7
Ancroft **TD15** 77 H6
Ancrum **TD8** 70 B1
Ancton **PO22** 12 C6
Anderby **PE24** 53 J5
Anderson **DT11** 9 H5
Anderton **CW8** 49 F5
Andover **SP10** 21 G7
Andover Down **SP11** 21 G7
Andoversford **GL54** 30 B6
Andreas **IM7** 54 D4
Anelog **LL53** 36 A3
Angarrack **TR27** 2 C5
Angersleigh **TA3** 7 K4
Angerton **CA7** 60 D1
Angle **SA71** 16 B4
Angler's Retreat **SY20** 37 G6
Angmering **BN16** 12 D6
Angram **YO23** 58 B5
Anie **FK17** 81 G6
Ankerville **IV19** 97 F4
Anlaby **HU10** 59 G7
Anmer **PE31** 44 B3
Anna Valley **SP11** 21 G7
Annan **DG12** 69 G7
Annaside **LA19** 54 D1
Annat, *Arg. & B.* **PA35** 80 B5
Annat, *High.* **IV22** 94 E6
Annbank **KA6** 67 J1
Annesley **NG15** 51 H7
Annesley Woodhouse **NG15** 51 H7
Annfield Plain **DH9** 62 C1
Annscroft **SY5** 38 D5
Ansdell **FY8** 55 G7
Ansford **BA7** 9 F1
Ansley **CV10** 40 E6
Anslow **DE13** 40 E3
Anslow Gate **DE13** 40 D3
Anstey, *Herts.* **SG9** 33 H5
Anstey, *Leics.* **LE7** 41 H5
Anstruther **KY10** 83 G7
Ansty, *W.Suss.* **RH17** 13 F4
Ansty, *Warks.* **CV7** 41 F7
Ansty, *Wilts.* **SP3** 9 J2
Anthill Common **PO7** 11 H3
Anthorn **CA7** 60 C1
Antingham **NR28** 45 G2
Anton's Gowt **PE22** 43 F1
Antony **PL11** 4 D5
Antrobus **CW9** 49 F5
Anvil Corner **EX22** 6 B5
Anwick **NG34** 52 E7
Anwoth **DG7** 65 F5
Aoradh **PA44** 72 A4
Apes Hall **CB6** 43 J7
Apethorpe **PE8** 42 D6
Apley **LN8** 52 E5
Apperknowle **S18** 51 F5
Apperley **GL19** 29 H6
Appin Ho. **PA38** 80 A3
Appleby **DN15** 52 C1
Appleby Magna **DE12** 41 F4
Appleby Parva **DE12** 41 F5
Appleby-in-Westmorland **CA16** 61 H4
Applecross **IV54** 94 D7
Appledore, *Devon* **EX39** 6 C2
Appledore, *Devon* **EX16** 7 J4
Appledore, *Kent* **TN26** 14 E5
Appledore Heath **TN26** 14 E4
Appleford **OX14** 21 J2
Appleshaw **SP11** 21 G7
Applethwaite **CA12** 60 D4
Appleton **OX13** 21 H1
Appleton Roebuck **YO23** 58 B5
Appleton Thorn **WA4** 49 F4
Appleton Wiske **DL6** 62 E6
Appleton-le-Moors **YO62** 58 D1
Appleton-le-Street **YO17** 58 D2
Appletreehall **TD9** 70 A2
Appletreewick **BD23** 57 F3
Appley **TA21** 7 J3
Appley Bridge **WN6** 48 E1
Apse Heath **PO36** 11 G6
Apsley **HP3** 22 D1
Apsley End **SG5** 32 E5
Apuldram **PO20** 12 B6
Arberth (Narberth) **SA67** 16 E3
Arbirlot **DD11** 83 G3
Arborfield **RG2** 22 A5
Arborfield Cross **RG2** 22 A5
Arborfield Garrison **RG2** 22 A5
Arbroath **DD11** 83 H3
Arbuthnott **AB30** 91 G7
Archdeacon Newton **DL2** 62 D5
Archiestown **AB38** 97 K7
Arclid **CW11** 49 G6
Ard a' Chapuill **PA22** 73 J3
Ardacheranbeg **PA22** 73 J2
Ardacheranmor **PA22** 73 J2
Ardachoil **PA65** 79 J4
Ardachvie **PH34** 87 H5
Ardailly **PA41** 72 E5
Ardalanish **PA67** 78 E6
Ardallie **AB42** 91 J1
Ardanaiseig **PA35** 80 B5
Ardaneaskan **IV54** 86 E1
Ardanstur **PA34** 79 K6
Ardantiobairt **PA34** 79 H2
Ardantrive **PA34** 79 K5
Ardarroch **IV54** 86 E1
Ardbeg, *Arg. & B.* **PA23** 73 K2
Ardbeg, *Arg. & B.* **PA20** 73 J4
Ardbeg, *Arg. & B.* **PA42** 72 C6
Ardblair **IV4** 88 B1
Ardbrecknish **PA33** 80 B5
Ardcharnich **IV23** 95 H3
Ardchiavaig **PA67** 78 E6
Ardchonnel **PA37** 80 A4
Ardchonnell **PA33** 80 A6
Ardchrishnish **PA70** 79 F5
Ardchronie **IV24** 96 D3
Ardchuilk **IV4** 87 J1
Ardchullarie More **FK18** 81 G6
Ardchyle **FK20** 81 G5
Arddlin **SY22** 38 B4
Ardeley **SG2** 33 G6
Ardelve **IV40** 86 E2
Arden **G83** 74 B2
Ardencaple **PA34** 79 J6
Ardens Grafton **B49** 30 C3
Ardentallan **PA34** 79 K5
Ardentinny **PA23** 73 K2
Ardeonaig **FK21** 81 H4
Ardersier **IV2** 96 E6
Ardery **PH36** 79 J1
Ardessie **IV23** 95 G3
Ardfad **PA34** 79 J6
Ardfern **PA31** 79 K7
Ardfin **PA60** 72 C4
Ardgartan **G83** 80 D7
Ardgay **IV24** 96 C2
Ardgenavan **PA26** 80 C6
Ardgowan **PA16** 74 A3
Ardgowse **AB33** 90 E3
Ardgye **IV30** 97 J5
Ardhallow **PA23** 73 K3
Ardheslaig **IV54** 94 D6
Ardiecow **AB45** 98 D4
Ardinamar **PA34** 79 J6
Ardindrean **IV23** 95 H3
Ardingly **RH17** 13 G4
Ardington **OX12** 21 H3
Ardintoul **IV40** 86 E2
Ardkinglas Ho **PA26** 80 C6
Ardlair **AB52** 90 D2
Ardlamont **PA21** 73 H4
Ardleigh **CO7** 34 E6
Ardleish **G83** 80 E6
Ardler **PH12** 82 D3
Ardley **OX27** 31 G6
Ardlui **G83** 80 E6
Ardlussa **PA60** 72 E2
Ardmaddy **PA35** 80 B4
Ardmair **IV26** 95 H2
Ardmaleish **PA20** 73 J4
Ardmay **G83** 80 D7
Ardmenish **PA60** 72 D3
Ardmhòr **HS9** 84 C4
Ardminish **PA41** 72 E6
Ardmolich **PH36** 86 D7
Ardmore, *Arg. & B.* **PA34** 79 J5
Ardmore, *Arg. & B.* **G82** 74 B3
Ardmore, *Arg. & B.* **PA42** 72 C6
Ardmore, *High.* **IV19** 96 E3
Ardnackaig **PA31** 73 F1
Ardnacross **PA72** 79 G3
Ardnadam **PA23** 73 K3
Ardnadrochet **PA64** 79 J4
Ardnagoine **IV26** 95 F1
Ardnagowan **PA25** 80 C7
Ardnagrask **IV4** 96 C7
Ardnahein **PA24** 74 A1
Ardnahoe **PA46** 72 C3
Ardnarff **IV54** 86 E1
Ardnastang **PH36** 79 K1
Ardnave **PA44** 72 A3
Ardno **PA26** 80 C7
Ardo **AB41** 91 G1
Ardoch, *D. & G.* **DG3** 68 D3
Ardoch, *Moray* **IV36** 97 J6
Ardoch, *P. & K.* **PH1** 82 B4
Ardochrig **G75** 74 E6
Ardochu **IV28** 96 D1
Ardoyne **AB52** 90 E2
Ardpatrick **PA29** 73 F4
Ardpeaton **G84** 74 A2
Ardradnaig **PH15** 81 J3
Ardrishaig **PA30** 73 G2
Ardroe **IV27** 102 C6
Ardrossan **KA22** 74 A6
Ardscalpsie **PA20** 73 J5
Ardshave **IV25** 96 E2
Ardshealach **PH36** 79 H1
Ardshellach **PA34** 79 J6
Ardsley **S71** 51 F2
Ardslignish **PH36** 79 G1
Ardtalla **PA42** 72 C5
Ardtalnaig **PH15** 81 H4
Ardtarig **PA23** 73 J2
Ardteatle **PA33** 80 C5
Ardtoe **PH36** 86 C7
Ardtornish **PA34** 79 J3
Ardtrostan **PH6** 81 H5
Ardtur **PA38** 80 A3
Arduaine **PA34** 79 K7
Ardullie **IV16** 96 C5
Ardura **PA65** 79 H4
Ardvar **IV27** 102 D5
Ardvasar **IV45** 86 C4
Ardveich **FK19** 81 H5
Ardverikie **PH20** 88 C6
Ardvorlich, *Arg. & B.* **G83** 80 E6
Ardvorlich, *P. & K.* **FK19** 81 H5
Ardwall **DG7** 65 F5
Ardwell, *D. & G.* **DG9** 64 B6
Ardwell, *Moray* **AB54** 90 B1
Ardwell, *S.Ayr.* **KA26** 67 F4
Areley Kings **DY13** 29 G1
Arford **GU35** 12 B3
Argaty **FK16** 81 J7
Argoed **NP12** 18 E2
Argoed Mill **LD1** 27 J2
Argrennan **DG7** 65 H5
Arichamish **PA31** 80 A7
Arichastlich **PA36** 80 D4
Arichonan **PA31** 73 F1
Aridhglas **PA66** 78 E5
Arienskill **PH38** 86 D6
Arileod **PA78** 78 C2
Arinacrinachd **IV54** 94 D6
Arinafad Beg **PA31** 73 F2
Arinagour **PA78** 78 D2

B

Baguley

Baguley **M23** 49 H4
Bagworth **LE67** 41 G5
Bagwyllydiart **HR2** 28 D6
Baildon **BD17** 57 G6
Baile Ailein **HS2** 100 E5
Baile a' Mhanaich (Balivanich) **HS7** 92 C6
Baile an Truiseil **HS2** 101 F2
Baile Boidheach **PA31** 73 F3
Baile Gharbhaidh **HS8** 92 C7
Baile Glas **HS6** 92 D6
Baile Mhartainn (Balmartin) **HS6** 92 C4
Baile Mhic Phail **HS6** 92 D4
Baile Mòr **HS6** 92 C5
Baile nan Cailleach **HS7** 92 C6
Baile Raghaill **HS6** 92 C5
Baile-na-Cille **HS6** 92 D3
Bailebeag **IV2** 88 C3
Baileguish **PH21** 89 F5
Bailemeonach **PA65** 79 H3
Bailetonach **PH36** 86 C7
Bailliesward **AB54** 90 C1
Bainbridge **DL8** 62 A7
Bainsford **FK2** 75 G2
Bainshole **AB54** 90 E1
Bainton, *E.Riding* **YO25** 59 F4
Bainton, *Peter.* **PE9** 42 D5
Bairnkine **TD8** 70 B2
Bakebare **AB55** 90 B1
Baker Street **RM16** 24 C3
Baker's End **SG12** 33 G7
Bakewell **DE45** 50 E6
Bala **LL23** 37 J2
Balachuirn **IV40** 94 B7
Balafark **G63** 74 E1
Balaldie **IV20** 97 F4
Balavil **PH21** 88 E4
Balbeg, *High.* **IV63** 88 B1
Balbeg, *High.* **IV63** 88 B2
Balbeggie **PH2** 82 C5
Balbirnie **KY7** 82 D7
Balbithan **AB51** 91 F3
Balblair, *High.* **IV24** 96 C2
Balblair, *High.* **IV7** 96 E5
Balcharn **IV27** 96 C1
Balcherry **IV19** 97 F3
Balchers **AB45** 99 F5
Balchladich **IV27** 102 C5
Balchraggan, *High.* **IV5** 96 C7
Balchraggan, *High.* **IV3** 88 C1
Balchrick **IV27** 102 D2
Balcombe **RH17** 13 G3
Balcurvie **KY8** 82 E7
Baldernock **G62** 74 D3
Baldersby **YO7** 57 J2
Balderstone **BB2** 56 B6
Balderton **NG24** 52 B7
Baldhu **TR3** 2 E4
Baldinnie **KY15** 83 F6
Baldock **SG7** 33 F5
Baldovie, *Angus* **DD8** 82 E2
Baldovie, *Dundee* **DD5** 83 F4
Baldrine **IM4** 54 D5
Baldslow **TN37** 14 C6
Baldwin **IM4** 54 C5
Baldwinholme **CA5** 60 E1
Baldwin's Gate **ST5** 39 G1
Bale **NR21** 44 E2
Balelone **HS6** 92 C4
Balemartine **PA77** 78 A3
Balendoch **PH12** 82 D3
Balephuil **PA77** 78 A3
Balerno **EH14** 75 K4
Balernock **G84** 74 A2
Baleromindubh **PA61** 72 B1
Balerominmore **PA61** 72 B1
Balevulin **PA69** 79 F5
Balfield **DD9** 83 G1
Balfour, *Aber.* **AB34** 90 D5
Balfour, *Ork.* **KW17** 107 D6
Balfron **G63** 74 D2
Balfron Station **G63** 74 D2
Balgavies **DD8** 83 G2
Balgedie **KY13** 82 C7
Balgonar **KY12** 75 J1
Balgove **AB51** 91 G1
Balgowan, *D. & G.* **DG9** 64 B6
Balgowan, *High.* **PH20** 88 D5
Balgown **IV51** 93 J5
Balgray **DD4** 83 F4
Balgreen **AB45** 99 F5
Balgreggan **DG9** 64 A5
Balgy **IV54** 94 E6
Balhaldie **FK15** 81 K7
Balhalgardy **AB51** 91 F2
Balhary **PH11** 82 D3
Balhelvie **KY14** 82 E5
Balhousie **KY8** 83 F7
Baliasta **ZE2** 108 F2
Baligill **KW14** 104 D2
Baligrundle **PA34** 79 K4
Balindore **PA35** 80 A4
Balintore **IV20** 97 F4
Balintraid **IV18** 96 E4
Balintyre **PH15** 81 H3
Balivanich (Baile a' Mhanaich) **HS7** 92 C6
Balkeerie **DD8** 82 E3
Balkholme **DN14** 58 D7
Balkissock **KA26** 67 F5
Ball **SY10** 38 C3
Ball Haye Green **ST13** 49 J7
Ball Hill **RG20** 21 H5
Ballabeg **IM9** 54 B6
Ballacannell **IM4** 54 D5
Ballacarnane Beg **IM6** 54 C5
Ballachulish **PH49** 80 B2
Balladoole **IM9** 54 B7
Ballafesson **IM9** 54 B6
Ballagyr **IM5** 54 B5
Ballajora **IM7** 54 D4
Ballakilpheric **IM9** 54 B6
Ballamodha **IM9** 54 B6
Ballantrae **KA26** 66 E5
Ballards Gore **SS4** 25 F2
Ballasalla, *I.o.M.* **IM7** 54 C4
Ballasalla, *I.o.M.* **IM9** 54 B6
Ballater **AB35** 90 B5
Ballaterach **AB34** 90 C5
Ballaugh **IM7** 54 C4
Ballaveare **IM4** 54 C6
Ballechin **PH9** 82 A2
Balleich **FK8** 81 G7
Ballencrieff **EH32** 76 C3
Ballidon **DE6** 50 E7
Balliekine **KA27** 73 G7
Balliemeanoch **PA27** 80 C7
Balliemore, *Arg. & B.* **PA34** 79 K5
Balliemore, *Arg. & B.* **PA27** 73 K1
Balliemore, *P. & K.* **PH16** 81 J2
Ballig **IM4** 54 B5
Ballimeanoch **PA33** 80 B6
Ballimore, *Arg. & B.* **PA21** 73 H2
Ballimore, *Stir.* **FK19** 81 G6
Ballinaby **PA44** 72 A4
Ballindean **PH14** 82 D5
Ballingdon **CO10** 34 C4
Ballinger Common **HP16** 22 C1
Ballingham **HR2** 28 E5
Ballingry **KY5** 75 K1
Ballinlick **PH8** 82 A3
Ballinluig, *P. & K.* **PH10** 82 B2
Ballinluig, *P. & K.* **PH9** 82 A2
Ballintuim **PH10** 82 C2
Balloch, *Angus* **DD8** 82 E2
Balloch, *High.* **IV2** 96 E7
Balloch, *N.Lan.* **G68** 75 F3
Balloch, *P. & K.* **PH7** 81 K6
Balloch, *W.Dun.* **G83** 74 B2
Ballochan **AB31** 90 D5
Ballochandrain **PA22** 73 H2
Ballochford **AB54** 90 B1
Ballochgair **PA28** 66 B1
Ballochmartin **KA28** 73 K5
Ballochmorrie **KA26** 67 G5
Ballochmyle **KA5** 67 K1
Ballochroy **PA29** 73 F5
Ballogie **AB34** 90 D5
Balls Cross **GU28** 12 C4
Ballyaurgan **PA31** 73 F3
Ballygown **PA73** 79 F3
Ballygrant **PA45** 72 B4
Ballyhaugh **PA78** 78 C2
Ballymeanoch **PA31** 73 G1
Ballymichael **KA27** 73 H7
Balmacara **IV40** 86 E2
Balmaclellan **DG7** 65 G3
Balmacneil **PH9** 82 A2
Balmadies **DD8** 83 G3
Balmae **DG6** 65 G6
Balmaha **G63** 74 C1
Balmalcolm **KY15** 82 E7
Balmartin (Baile Mhartainn) **HS6** 92 C4
Balmeanach **PA68** 79 F4
Balmedie **AB23** 91 H3
Balmerino **DD6** 82 E5
Balmerlawn **SO42** 10 E4
Balminnoch **DG8** 64 C4
Balmore, *E.Dun.* **G64** 74 E3
Balmore, *High.* **IV12** 97 F7
Balmore, *High.* **IV55** 93 H7
Balmore, *High.* **IV4** 87 K1
Balmullo **KY16** 83 F5
Balmungie **IV10** 96 E6
Balmyle **PH10** 82 B2
Balnaboth **DD8** 82 E1
Balnabruaich **IV19** 96 E4
Balnacra **IV54** 95 F7
Balnafoich **IV2** 88 D1
Balnagall **IV20** 97 F3
Balnagown Castle **IV18** 96 E4
Balnaguard **PH9** 82 A2
Balnaguisich **IV18** 96 D4
Balnahard, *Arg. & B.* **PA68** 79 F4
Balnahard, *Arg. & B.* **PA61** 72 C1
Balnain **IV63** 88 B1
Balnakeil **IV27** 103 F2
Balnaknock **IV51** 93 K5
Balnamoon **DD9** 83 G1
Balnapaling **IV19** 96 E5
Balnespick **PH21** 89 F4
Balquhidder **FK19** 81 G5
Balsall **CV7** 30 D1
Balsall Common **CV7** 30 D1
Balscote **OX15** 30 E4
Balsham **CB1** 33 J3
Baltasound **ZE2** 108 F2
Balterley **CW2** 49 G7
Baltersan **DG8** 64 E4
Balthangie **AB53** 99 G5
Balthayock **PH2** 82 C5
Baltonsborough **BA6** 8 E1
Baluachraig **PA31** 73 G1
Balulive **PA45** 72 C4
Balure, *Arg. & B.* **PA37** 79 K4
Balure, *Arg. & B.* **PA35** 80 B4
Balvaird **IV6** 96 C6
Balvarran **PH10** 82 B1
Balvicar **PA34** 79 J6
Balvraid, *High.* **IV13** 89 F1
Balvraid, *High.* **IV40** 86 E3
Bamber Bridge **PR5** 55 J7
Bamber's Green **CM22** 33 J6
Bamburgh **NE69** 77 K7
Bamff **PH11** 82 D2
Bamford **S33** 50 E4
Bampton, *Cumb.* **CA10** 61 G5
Bampton, *Devon* **EX16** 7 H3
Bampton, *Oxon.* **OX18** 21 G1
Banavie **PH33** 87 H7
Banbury **OX16** 31 F4
Banc-y-ffordd **SA44** 17 H1
Bancffosfelen **SA15** 17 H3
Banchor **IV12** 97 G7
Banchory **AB31** 91 F5
Banchory-Devenick **AB12** 91 H4
Bancyfelin **SA33** 17 G3
Bandon **KY7** 82 D7
Banff **AB45** 98 E4
Bangor **LL57** 46 D5
Bangor Teifi **SA44** 26 C4
Bangor-is-y-coed **LL13** 38 C1
Banham **NR16** 44 E7
Bank **SO43** 10 D4
Bank End **LA20** 55 F1
Bank Newton **BD23** 56 E4
Bank Street **WR15** 29 F2
Bankend, *D. & G.* **DG1** 69 F7
Bankend, *S.Lan.* **ML11** 75 G7
Bankfoot **PH1** 82 B4
Bankhead, *Aber.* **AB33** 90 E3
Bankhead, *Aber.* **AB51** 90 E4
Bankhead, *Aberdeen* **AB21** 91 G4
Bankhead, *D. & G.* **DG6** 65 H6
Banknock **FK4** 75 F3
Banks, *Cumb.* **CA8** 70 A7
Banks, *Lancs.* **PR9** 55 G7
Bankshill **DG11** 69 G5
Banningham **NR11** 45 G3
Bannister Green **CM6** 33 K6
Bannockburn **FK7** 75 G1
Banstead **SM7** 23 F6
Bantham **TQ7** 5 G6
Banton **G65** 75 F3
Banwell **BS29** 19 G6
Bapchild **ME9** 25 F5
Baptiston **G63** 74 D2
Bar Hill **CB3** 33 G2
Barabhas (Barvas) **HS2** 101 F2
Barachander **PA35** 80 B5
Barassie **KA10** 74 B7
Barbaraville **IV18** 96 E4
Barber Booth **S33** 50 D4
Barbon **LA6** 56 B1
Barbrook **EX35** 7 F1
Barby **CV23** 31 G1
Barcaldine **PA37** 80 A3
Barcaple **DG7** 65 G5
Barcheston **CV36** 30 D4
Barcombe **BN8** 13 H5
Barcombe Cross **BN8** 13 H5
Barden **DL8** 62 C7
Bardennoch **DG7** 67 K4
Bardfield End Green **CM6** 33 K5
Bardfield Saling **CM7** 33 K6
Bardister **ZE2** 108 C5
Bardney **LN3** 52 E6
Bardon, *Leics.* **LE67** 41 G4
Bardon, *Moray* **IV30** 97 K6
Bardon Mill **NE47** 70 C7
Bardsea **LA12** 55 G2
Bardsey **LS17** 57 J5
Bardsley **OL8** 49 J2
Bardwell **IP31** 34 D1
Barewood **HR6** 28 C3
Barfad **PA29** 73 G4
Barford, *Norf.* **NR9** 45 F5
Barford, *Warks.* **CV35** 30 D2
Barford St. John **OX15** 31 F5
Barford St. Martin **SP3** 10 B1
Barford St. Michael **OX15** 31 F5
Barfreston **CT15** 15 H2
Bargaly **DG8** 64 E4
Bargany **KA26** 67 G3
Bargoed **CF81** 18 E2
Bargrennan **DG8** 64 D3
Barham, *Cambs.* **PE28** 32 E1
Barham, *Kent* **CT4** 15 G2
Barham, *Suff.* **IP6** 35 F3
Barharrow **DG7** 65 G5
Barholm, *D. & G.* **DG8** 64 E5
Barholm, *Lincs.* **PE9** 42 D4
Barkby **LE7** 41 J5
Barkby Thorpe **LE7** 41 J5
Barkestone-le-Vale **NG13** 42 A2
Barkham **RG41** 22 A5
Barking, *Gt.Lon.* **IG11** 23 H3
Barking, *Suff.* **IP6** 34 E3
Barking & Dagenham **RM** 23 H3
Barkingside **IG6** 23 H3
Barkisland **HX4** 50 C1
Barkston, *Lincs.* **NG32** 42 C1
Barkston, *N.Yorks.* **LS24** 57 K6
Barkway **SG8** 33 G5
Barlae **DG8** 64 C4
Barlaston **ST12** 40 A2
Barlavington **GU28** 12 C5
Barlay **DG7** 65 F5
Barlborough **S43** 51 G5
Barlby **YO8** 58 C6
Barlestone **CV13** 41 G5
Barley, *Herts.* **SG8** 33 G5
Barley, *Lancs.* **BB12** 56 D5
Barleycroft End **SG9** 33 H6
Barleyhill **NE44** 62 B1
Barleythorpe **LE15** 42 B5
Barling **SS3** 25 F3
Barlings **LN3** 52 D5
Barlow, *Derbys.* **S18** 51 F5
Barlow, *N.Yorks.* **YO8** 58 C7
Barlow, *T. & W.* **NE21** 71 G7
Barmby Moor **YO42** 58 D5
Barmby on the Marsh **DN14** 58 C7
Barmer **PE31** 44 C2
Barmolloch **PA31** 73 G1
Barmoor Lane End **TD15** 77 J6
Barmouth **LL42** 37 F4
Barmpton **DL1** 62 E5
Barmston **YO25** 59 H4
Barnacabber **PA23** 73 K2
Barnacarry **PA27** 73 J1
Barnack **PE9** 42 D5
Barnacle **CV7** 41 F7
Barnamuc **PA38** 80 B3
Barnard Castle **DL12** 62 B5
Barnard Gate **OX29** 31 F7
Barnardiston **CB9** 34 B4
Barnard's Green **WR14** 29 G4
Barnbarroch, *D. & G.* **DG5** 65 J5
Barnbarroch, *D. & G.* **DG8** 64 D5
Barnburgh **DN5** 51 G2
Barnby **NR34** 45 J6
Barnby Dun **DN3** 51 J2
Barnby in the Willows **NG24** 52 B7
Barnby Moor **DN22** 51 J4
Barndennoch **DG3** 68 D5
Barnes **SW13** 23 F4
Barnet **EN** 23 F2
Barnetby le Wold **DN38** 52 D2
Barney **NR21** 44 D2
Barnham, *Suff.* **IP24** 34 C1
Barnham, *W.Suss.* **PO22** 12 C6
Barnham Broom **NR9** 44 E5
Barnhead **DD10** 83 H2
Barnhill **IV30** 97 J6
Barnhills **DG9** 66 D6
Barningham, *Dur.* **DL11** 62 B5
Barningham, *Suff.* **IP31** 34 D1
Barnoldby le Beck **DN37** 53 F2
Barnoldswick **BB18** 56 D5
Barns Green **RH13** 12 E4
Barnsdale Bar **WF8** 51 H1
Barnsley, *Glos.* **GL7** 20 D1
Barnsley, *S.Yorks.* **S70** 51 F2
Barnstaple **EX31** 6 D2
Barnston, *Essex* **CM6** 33 K7
Barnston, *Mersey.* **CH61** 48 B4
Barnstone **NG13** 42 A2
Barnt Green **B45** 30 B1
Barnton **CW8** 49 F5
Barnwell All Saints **PE8** 42 D7
Barnwell St. Andrew **PE8** 42 D7
Barnwood **GL4** 29 H7
Barr, *Arg. & B.* **PA44** 72 B4
Barr, *High.* **PA34** 79 H2
Barr, *S.Ayr.* **KA26** 67 G4
Barr Hall **CO9** 34 B5
Barra Airport **HS9** 84 C4
Barrackan **PA31** 79 J7
Barraer **DG8** 64 D4
Barraglom **HS2** 100 D4
Barrahormid **PA31** 73 F2
Barran **PA33** 80 C5
Barrapoll **PA77** 78 A3
Barrasford **NE48** 70 E6
Barravullin **PA31** 79 K7
Barregarrow **IM6** 54 C5
Barrhead **G78** 74 D5
Barrhill **KA26** 67 G5
Barrington, *Cambs.* **CB2** 33 G4
Barrington, *Som.* **TA19** 8 C3
Barripper **TR14** 2 D5
Barrisdale **IV40** 86 E4
Barrmill **KA15** 74 B5
Barrnacarry **PA34** 79 K5
Barrock **KW14** 105 H1
Barrow, *Lancs.* **BB7** 56 C6
Barrow, *Rut.* **LE15** 42 B4
Barrow, *Shrop.* **TF12** 39 F5
Barrow, *Som.* **BA9** 9 G1
Barrow, *Suff.* **IP29** 34 B2
Barrow Gurney **BS48** 19 J5
Barrow Haven **DN19** 59 G7
Barrow Nook **L39** 48 D2
Barrow Street **BA12** 9 H1
Barrow upon Humber **DN19** 59 G7
Barrow upon Soar **LE12** 41 H4
Barrow upon Trent **DE73** 41 F3
Barrow-in-Furness **LA14** 55 F3
Barrowby **NG32** 42 B2
Barrowden **LE15** 42 C5
Barrowford **BB9** 56 D6
Barry, *Angus* **DD7** 83 G4
Barry, *V. of Glam.* **CF62** 18 E5
Barsby **LE7** 42 A4
Barsham **NR34** 45 H6
Barskimming **KA5** 67 J1
Barsloisnach **PA31** 73 G1
Barston **B93** 30 D1
Bartestree **HR1** 28 E4
Barthol Chapel **AB51** 91 G1
Barthomley **CW2** 49 G7
Bartley **SO40** 10 E3
Bartlow **CB1** 33 J4
Barton, *Cambs.* **CB3** 33 H3
Barton, *Ches.* **SY14** 48 D7
Barton, *Glos.* **GL54** 30 B6
Barton, *Lancs.* **PR3** 55 J6
Barton, *Lancs.* **L39** 48 C2
Barton, *N.Yorks.* **DL10** 62 D6
Barton, *Torbay* **TQ2** 5 K4
Barton, *Warks.* **B50** 30 C3
Barton Bendish **PE33** 44 B5
Barton Common **NR12** 45 H3
Barton End **GL6** 20 B2
Barton Hartshorn **MK18** 31 H5
Barton in Fabis **NG11** 41 H2
Barton in the Beans **CV13** 41 F5
Barton Mills **IP28** 34 B1
Barton on Sea **BH25** 10 D5
Barton St. David **TA11** 8 E1
Barton Seagrave **NN15** 32 B1
Barton Stacey **SO21** 21 H7
Barton Stacey Camp **SO21** 21 H7
Barton Turf **NR12** 45 H3
Barton-le-Clay **MK45** 32 D5
Barton-le-Street **YO17** 58 D2
Barton-le-Willows **YO60** 58 D3
Barton-on-the-Heath **GL56** 30 D5
Barton-under-Needwood **DE13** 40 D4
Barton-upon-Humber **DN18** 59 G7
Barvas (Barabhas) **HS2** 101 F2
Barway **CB7** 33 J1
Barwell **LE9** 41 G6
Barwhinnock **DG6** 65 G5
Barwick **BA22** 8 E3
Barwick in Elmet **LS15** 57 J6
Barwinnock **DG8** 64 D6
Baschurch **SY4** 38 D3
Bascote **CV47** 31 F2
Basford Green **ST13** 49 J7
Bashall Eaves **BB7** 56 B5
Bashall Town **BB7** 56 C5
Bashley **BH25** 10 D5
Basildon, *Essex* **SS14** 24 D3
Basildon, *W.Berks.* **RG8** 21 K4
Basingstoke **RG21** 21 K6
Baslow **DE45** 50 E5
Bason Bridge **TA9** 19 G7
Bassaleg **NP10** 19 F3
Bassenthwaite **CA12** 60 D3
Bassett **SO16** 11 F3
Bassett's Cross **EX20** 6 D5
Bassingbourn **SG8** 33 G4
Bassingfield **NG12** 41 J2
Bassingham **LN5** 52 C6
Bassingthorpe **NG33** 42 C3
Basta **ZE2** 108 E3
Baston **PE6** 42 E4
Bastwick **NR29** 45 J4
Batavaime **FK21** 81 F4
Batchworth **WD3** 22 D2
Batchworth Heath **WD3** 22 D2
Batcombe, *Dorset* **DT2** 9 F4
Batcombe, *Som.* **BA4** 9 F1
Bate Heath **CW9** 49 F5
BATH BA 20 A5
Bathampton **BA2** 20 A5
Bathealton **TA4** 7 J3
Batheaston **BA1** 20 A5
Bathford **BA1** 20 A5
Bathgate **EH48** 75 H4
Bathley **NG23** 51 K7
Bathpool, *Cornw.* **PL15** 4 C3
Bathpool, *Som.* **TA1** 8 B2
Batley **WF17** 57 H7
Batsford **GL56** 30 C5
Battersby **TS9** 63 G6
Battersea **SW11** 23 F4
Battisborough Cross **PL8** 5 G6
Battisford **IP14** 34 E3
Battisford Tye **IP14** 34 E3
Battle, *E.Suss.* **TN33** 14 C6
Battle, *Powys* **LD3** 27 K5
Battlefield **SY1** 38 E4
Battlesbridge **SS11** 24 D2
Battlesden **MK17** 32 C6
Battleton **TA22** 7 H3
Battramsley **SO41** 10 E5
Batt's Corner **GU10** 22 B7
Bauds of Cullen **AB56** 98 C4
Baugh **PA77** 78 B3
Baughton **WR8** 29 H4
Baughurst **RG26** 21 J6
Baulds **AB31** 90 E5
Baulking **SN7** 21 G2
Baumber **LN9** 53 F5
Baunton **GL7** 20 D1
Baveney Wood **DY14** 29 F1
Baverstock **SP3** 10 B1
Bawburgh **NR9** 45 F5
Bawdeswell **NR20** 44 E3
Bawdrip **TA7** 8 C1
Bawdsey **IP12** 35 H4
Bawtry **DN10** 51 J3
Baxenden **BB5** 56 C7
Baxterley **CV9** 40 E6
Baycliff **LA12** 55 F2
Baydon **SN8** 21 F4
Bayford, *Herts.* **SG13** 23 G1
Bayford, *Som.* **BA9** 9 G2
Bayfordbury **SG13** 33 G7
Bayham Abbey **TN3** 13 K3
Bayles **CA9** 61 J2
Baylham **IP6** 35 F3
Baynards Green **OX27** 31 G6
Baysham **HR9** 28 E6
Bayston Hill **SY3** 38 D5
Baythorn End **CO9** 34 B4

Bishopstone

Bayton **DY14** 29 F1
Beach **PA34** 79 J2
Beachampton **MK19** 31 J5
Beacharr **PA29** 72 E6
Beachborough **CT18** 15 G4
Beachley **NP16** 19 J2
Beacon **EX14** 7 K5
Beacon End **CO3** 34 D6
Beacon Hill **GU26** 12 B3
Beacon's Bottom **HP14** 22 A2
Beaconsfield **HP9** 22 C2
Beadlam **YO62** 58 C1
Beadnell **NE67** 71 H1
Beaford **EX19** 6 D4
Beal, *N.Yorks.* **DN14** 58 B7
Beal, *Northumb.* **TD15** 77 J6
Bealach **PA38** 80 A2
Beambridge **CW5** 49 F7
Beamhurst **ST14** 40 C2
Beaminster **DT8** 8 D4
Beamish **DH9** 62 D1
Beamsley **BD23** 57 F4
Bean **DA2** 23 J4
Beanacre **SN12** 20 B5
Beanley **NE66** 71 F2
Beaquoy **KW17** 106 C5
Beardon **EX20** 6 D7
Beare Green **RH5** 22 E7
Bearley **CV37** 30 C2
Bearnie **AB41** 91 H1
Bearnock **IV63** 88 B1
Bearnus **PA73** 79 F3
Bearpark **DH7** 62 D2
Bearsbridge **NE47** 61 J1
Bearsden **G61** 74 D3
Bearsted **ME14** 14 C2
Bearwood **BH11** 10 B5
Beattock **DG10** 69 F3
Beauchamp Roding **CM5** 23 J1
Beauchief **S8** 51 F4
Beaudesert **B95** 30 C2
Beaufort **NP23** 28 A7
Beaulieu **SO42** 10 E4
Beauly **IV4** 96 C7
Beaumaris (Biwmaris) **LL58** 46 E5
Beaumont, *Cumb.* **CA5** 60 E1
Beaumont, *Essex* **CO16** 35 F6
Beausale **CV35** 30 D1
Beauworth **SO24** 11 G2
Beaworthy **EX21** 6 C6
Beazley End **CM7** 34 B6
Bebington **CH63** 48 C4
Bebside **NE24** 71 H5
Beccles **NR34** 45 J6
Becconsall **PR4** 55 H7
Beck Foot **LA8** 61 H7
Beck Hole **YO22** 63 K6
Beck Row **IP28** 33 K1
Beck Side **LA17** 55 F1
Beckbury **TF11** 39 G5
Beckenham **BR3** 23 G5
Beckermet **CA21** 60 B6
Beckfoot, *Cumb.* **CA7** 60 B2
Beckfoot, *Cumb.* **CA19** 60 C6
Beckford **GL20** 29 J5
Beckhampton **SN8** 20 D5
Beckingham, *Lincs.* **LN5** 52 B7
Beckingham, *Notts.* **DN10** 51 K4
Beckington **BA11** 20 A6
Beckley, *E.Suss.* **TN31** 14 D5
Beckley, *Oxon.* **OX3** 31 G7
Beckton **E6** 23 H3
Beckwithshaw **HG3** 57 H4
Becontree **RM8** 23 H3
Bedale **DL8** 57 H1
Bedburn **DL13** 62 C3
Bedchester **SP7** 9 H3
Beddau **CF38** 18 D3
Beddgelert **LL55** 36 E1
Beddingham **BN8** 13 H6
Beddington **SM6** 23 G5
Beddington Corner **CR4** 23 F5
Bedfield **IP13** 35 G2
Bedford **MK40** 32 D4
Bedgebury Cross **TN17** 14 C4
Bedhampton **PO9** 11 J4
Bedingfield **IP23** 35 F2
Bedlington **NE22** 71 H5
Bedlinog **CF46** 18 D1
Bedmond **WD5** 22 E1
Bednall **ST17** 40 B4
Bedol **CH6** 48 B5
Bedrule **TD9** 70 A2
Bedstone **SY7** 28 C1
Bedwas **CF83** 18 E3
Bedwellty **NP12** 18 E1
Bedworth **CV12** 41 F7
Beeby **LE7** 41 J5
Beech, *Hants.* **GU34** 11 H1
Beech, *Staffs.* **ST4** 40 A2
Beech Hill **RG7** 21 K5
Beechamwell **PE37** 44 B5
Beechingstoke **SN9** 20 D6
Beedon **RG20** 21 H4
Beeford **YO25** 59 H4
Beeley **DE4** 50 E6
Beelsby **DN37** 53 F2
Beenham **RG7** 21 J5
Beer **EX12** 8 B6
Beer Hackett **DT9** 8 E3
Beercrocombe **TA3** 8 C2
Beesands **TQ7** 5 J6
Beesby **LN13** 53 H4
Beeson **TQ7** 5 J6
Beeston, *Beds.* **SG19** 32 E4
Beeston, *Ches.* **CW6** 48 E7
Beeston, *Norf.* **PE32** 44 D4
Beeston, *Notts.* **NG9** 41 H2
Beeston, *W.Yorks.* **LS11** 57 H6
Beeston Regis **NR26** 45 F1
Beeston St. Lawrence **NR12** 45 H3
Beeswing **DG2** 65 J4
Beetham **LA7** 55 H2
Beetley **NR20** 44 D4
Began **CF3** 19 F3
Begbroke **OX5** 31 F7
Begelly **SA68** 16 E4
Beggshill **AB54** 90 D1
Beguildy **LD7** 28 A1
Beighton, *Norf.* **NR13** 45 H5
Beighton, *S.Yorks.* **S20** 51 G4
Beith **KA15** 74 B5
Bekesbourne **CT4** 15 G2
Belaugh **NR12** 45 G4
Belbroughton **DY9** 29 J1
Belchamp Otten **CO10** 34 C4
Belchamp St. Paul **CO10** 34 B4
Belchamp Walter **CO10** 34 C4
Belchford **LN9** 53 F5
Belford **NE70** 77 K7
Belgrave **LE4** 41 H5
Belhaven **EH42** 76 E3
Belhelvie **AB23** 91 H3
Belhinnie **AB54** 90 C2
Bell Bar **AL9** 23 F1
Bell Busk **BD23** 56 E4
Bell End **DY9** 29 J1
Bellabeg **AB36** 90 B3
Belladrum **IV4** 96 C7
Bellanoch **PA31** 73 G1
Bellasize **DN14** 58 E7
Bellaty **PH11** 82 D2
Belleau **LN13** 53 H5
Bellehiglash **AB37** 89 J1
Bellerby **DL8** 62 C7
Bellever **PL20** 5 G3
Belliehill **DD9** 83 G1
Bellingdon **HP5** 22 C1
Bellingham **NE48** 70 D5
Belloch **PA29** 72 E7
Bellochantuy **PA28** 72 E7
Bells Yew Green **TN3** 13 K3
Bellsdyke **FK2** 75 H2
Bellshill, *N.Lan.* **ML4** 75 F5
Bellshill, *Northumb.* **NE70** 77 K7
Bellside **ML1** 75 G5
Bellsquarry **EH54** 75 J4
Belluton **BS39** 19 K5
Belmaduthy **IV8** 96 D6
Belmesthorpe **PE9** 42 D4
Belmont, *B'burn.* **BL7** 49 F1
Belmont, *Gt.Lon.* **SM2** 23 F5
Belmont, *Shet.* **ZE2** 108 E2
Belowda **PL26** 3 G2
Belper **DE56** 41 F1
Belper Lane End **DE56** 41 F1
Belsay **NE20** 71 G6
Belsford **TQ9** 5 H5
Belstead **IP8** 35 F4
Belston **KA6** 67 H1
Belstone **EX20** 6 E6
Belstone Corner **EX20** 6 E6
Belsyde **EH49** 75 H3
Belthorn **BB1** 56 C7
Beltinge **CT6** 25 H5
Beltoft **DN9** 52 B2
Belton, *Leics.* **LE12** 41 G3
Belton, *Lincs.* **NG32** 42 C2
Belton, *N.Lincs.* **DN9** 51 K2
Belton, *Norf.* **NR31** 45 J5
Belton, *Rut.* **LE15** 42 B5
Beltring **TN12** 23 K7
Belvedere **DA17** 23 H4
Belvoir **NG32** 42 B2
Bembridge **PO35** 11 H6
Bemersyde **TD6** 76 D7
Bempton **YO15** 59 H2
Ben Alder Cottage **PH17** 81 F1
Ben Alder Lodge **PH19** 88 C7
Benacre **NR34** 45 K7
Benbecula Aerodrome **HS7** 92 C6
Benbuie **DG3** 68 C4
Benderloch **PA37** 80 A4
Bendish **SG4** 32 E6
Benenden **TN17** 14 D4
Benfield **DG8** 64 D4
Bengate **NR28** 45 H3
Bengeo **SG14** 33 G7
Benholm **DD10** 83 K1
Beningbrough **YO30** 58 B4
Benington, *Herts.* **SG2** 33 F6
Benington, *Lincs.* **PE22** 43 G1
Benington Sea End **PE22** 43 H1
Benllech **LL74** 46 D4
Benmore, *Arg. & B.* **PA23** 73 K2
Benmore, *Stir.* **FK20** 81 F5
Bennacott **PL15** 4 C1
Bennan **DG7** 65 G3
Benniworth **LN8** 53 F4
Benover **ME18** 14 C3
Benson **OX10** 21 K2
Benthall, *Northumb.* **NE67** 71 H1
Benthall, *Shrop.* **TF12** 39 F5
Bentham **GL51** 29 J7
Benthoul **AB14** 91 G4
Bentley, *E.Riding* **HU17** 59 G6
Bentley, *Hants.* **GU10** 22 A7
Bentley, *S.Yorks.* **DN5** 51 H2
Bentley, *Suff.* **IP9** 35 F5
Bentley, *Warks.* **CV9** 40 E6
Bentley Heath **B93** 30 C1
Benton **EX32** 6 E2
Benton Square **NE12** 71 J6
Bentpath **DG13** 69 J4
Bentworth **GU34** 21 K7
Benvie **DD2** 82 E4
Benville Lane **DT2** 8 E4
Benwick **PE15** 43 G7
Beoley **B98** 30 B2
Bepton **GU29** 12 B5
Berden **CM23** 33 H6
Bere Alston **PL20** 4 E4
Bere Ferrers **PL20** 4 E4
Bere Regis **BH20** 9 H5
Berea **SA62** 16 A2
Berepper **TR12** 2 D6
Bergh Apton **NR15** 45 H5
Berinsfield **OX10** 21 J2
Berkeley **GL13** 19 K2
Berkhamsted **HP4** 22 C1
Berkley **BA11** 20 B7
Berkswell **CV7** 30 D1
Bermondsey **SE16** 23 G4
Bernera **IV40** 86 E2
Berners Roding **CM5** 24 C1
Bernice **PA23** 73 K1
Bernisdale **IV51** 93 K6
Berrick Salome **OX10** 21 K2
Berriedale **KW7** 105 G6
Berriew (Aberriw) **SY21** 38 A5
Berrington, *Northumb.* **TD15** 77 J6
Berrington, *Shrop.* **SY5** 38 E5
Berrow **TA8** 19 F6
Berrow Green **WR6** 29 G3
Berry Down Cross **EX34** 6 D1
Berry Hill, *Glos.* **GL16** 28 E7
Berry Hill, *Pembs.* **SA42** 26 A4
Berry Pomeroy **TQ9** 5 J4
Berryhillock **AB56** 98 D4
Berrynarbor **EX34** 6 D1
Bersham **LL14** 38 C1
Berstane **KW15** 107 D6
Berwick **BN26** 13 J6
Berwick Bassett **SN4** 20 D4
Berwick Hill **NE20** 71 G6
Berwick St. James **SP3** 10 B1
Berwick St. John **SP7** 9 J2
Berwick St. Leonard **SP3** 9 J1
Berwick-upon-Tweed **TD15** 77 H5
Bescar **L40** 48 C1
Besford, *Shrop.* **SY4** 38 E3
Besford, *Worcs.* **WR8** 29 J4
Bessacarr **DN4** 51 J2
Bessels Leigh **OX13** 21 H1
Bessingby **YO16** 59 H3
Bessingham **NR11** 45 F2
Best Beech Hill **TN5** 13 K3
Besthorpe, *Norf.* **NR17** 44 E6
Besthorpe, *Notts.* **NG23** 52 B6
Beswick **YO25** 59 G5
Betchworth **RH3** 23 F6
Bethania, *Cere.* **SY23** 26 E2
Bethania, *Gwyn.* **LL41** 37 G1
Bethel, *Gwyn.* **LL55** 46 D6
Bethel, *Gwyn.* **LL21** 37 J1
Bethel, *I.o.A.* **LL62** 46 B5
Bethersden **TN26** 14 E3
Bethesda, *Gwyn.* **LL57** 46 E6
Bethesda, *Pembs.* **SA67** 16 D3
Bethlehem **SA19** 17 K2
Bethnal Green **E2** 23 G3
Betley **CW3** 39 G1
Betsham **DA13** 24 C4
Betteshanger **CT14** 15 J2
Bettiscombe **DT6** 8 C5
Bettisfield **SY13** 38 D2
Betton, *Shrop.* **TF9** 39 F2
Betton, *Shrop.* **SY5** 38 C5
Bettws **NP20** 19 F2
Bettws Bledrws **SA48** 26 E3
Bettws Cedewain **SY16** 38 A6
Bettws Evan **SA38** 26 C4
Bettws Gwerfil Goch **LL21** 37 K1
Bettws Newydd **NP15** 19 G1
Bettws-y-crwyn **SY7** 38 B7
Bettyhill **KW14** 104 C2
Betws, *Bridgend* **CF32** 18 C3
Betws, *Carmar.* **SA18** 17 K3
Betws Disserth **LD1** 28 A3
Betws Garmon **LL54** 46 D7
Betws-y-coed **LL24** 47 F7
Betws-yn-Rhos **LL22** 47 H5
Beulah, *Cere.* **SA38** 26 B4
Beulah, *Powys* **LD5** 27 J3
Bevendean **BN2** 13 G6
Bevercotes **NG22** 51 K5
Beverley **HU17** 59 G6
Beverstone **GL8** 20 B2
Bevington **GL13** 19 K2
Bewaldeth **CA13** 60 D3
Bewcastle **CA6** 70 A6
Bewdley **DY12** 29 G1
Bewerley **HG3** 57 G3
Bewholme **YO25** 59 H5
Bewley Common **SN15** 20 C5
Bexhill **TN40** 14 C7
Bexley **DA** 23 H4
Bexleyheath **DA6** 23 H4
Bexwell **PE38** 44 A5
Beyton **IP30** 34 D2
Beyton Green **IP30** 34 D2
Bhalamus **HS2** 100 E7
Bhaltos **HS2** 100 C4
Bhatarsaigh (Vatersay) **HS9** 84 B5
Biallaid **PH20** 88 E5
Bibury **GL7** 20 E1
Bicester **OX26** 31 G6
Bickenhall **TA3** 8 B3
Bickenhill **B92** 40 D7
Bicker **PE20** 43 F2
Bickerstaffe **L39** 48 D2
Bickerton, *Ches.* **SY14** 48 E7
Bickerton, *N.Yorks.* **LS22** 57 K4
Bickford **ST19** 40 A4
Bickham Bridge **TQ9** 5 H5
Bickham House **EX6** 7 H7
Bickington, *Devon* **EX31** 6 D2
Bickington, *Devon* **TQ12** 5 H3
Bickleigh, *Devon* **EX16** 7 H5
Bickleigh, *Devon* **PL6** 5 F4
Bickleton **EX31** 6 D2
Bickley **BR1** 23 H5
Bickley Moss **SY14** 38 E1
Bickley Town **SY14** 38 E1
Bicknacre **CM3** 24 D1
Bicknoller **TA4** 7 K2
Bicknor **ME9** 14 D2
Bickton **SP6** 10 C3
Bicton, *Shrop.* **SY3** 38 D4
Bicton, *Shrop.* **SY7** 38 B7
Bicton Heath **SY3** 38 D4
Bidborough **TN4** 23 J7
Biddenden **TN27** 14 D4
Biddenham **MK40** 32 D4
Biddestone **SN14** 20 B4
Biddisham **BS26** 19 G6
Biddlesden **NN13** 31 H4
Biddlestone **NE65** 70 E3
Biddulph **ST8** 49 H7
Biddulph Moor **ST8** 49 J7
Bideford **EX39** 6 C3
Bidford-on-Avon **B50** 30 B3
Bidston **CH43** 48 B3
Bielby **YO42** 58 D5
Bieldside **AB15** 91 G4
Bierley, *I.o.W.* **PO38** 11 G7
Bierley, *W.Yorks.* **BD4** 57 G6
Bierton **HP22** 32 B7
Big Sand **IV21** 94 D4
Bigbury **TQ7** 5 G6
Bigbury-on-Sea **TQ7** 5 G6
Bigby **DN38** 52 D2
Bigert Mire **LA20** 60 C7
Biggar, *Cumb.* **LA14** 54 E3
Biggar, *S.Lan.* **ML12** 75 J7
Biggin, *Derbys.* **SK17** 50 D7
Biggin, *Derbys.* **DE6** 40 E1
Biggin, *N.Yorks.* **LS25** 58 B6
Biggin Hill **TN16** 23 H6
Biggings **ZE2** 109 A6
Biggleswade **SG18** 32 E4
Bigholms **DG13** 69 J5
Bighouse **KW14** 104 D2
Bighton **SO24** 11 H1
Biglands **CA7** 60 D1
Bignor **RH20** 12 C5
Bigrigg **CA24** 60 B5
Bigton **ZE2** 109 C10
Bilberry **PL26** 4 A4
Bilborough **NG8** 41 H1
Bilbrook, *Som.* **TA24** 7 J1
Bilbrook, *Staffs.* **WV8** 40 A5
Bilbrough **YO23** 58 B5
Bilbster **KW1** 105 H3
Bildershaw **DL14** 62 C4
Bildeston **IP7** 34 D4
Billericay **CM12** 24 C2
Billesdon **LE7** 42 A5
Billesley **B49** 30 C3
Billholm **DG13** 69 H4
Billingborough **NG34** 42 E2
Billinge **WN5** 48 E2
Billingford, *Norf.* **NR20** 44 E3
Billingford, *Norf.* **IP21** 35 F1
Billingham **TS23** 63 F4
Billinghay **LN4** 52 E7
Billingley **S72** 51 G2
Billingshurst **RH14** 12 D4
Billingsley **WV16** 39 G7
Billington, *Beds.* **LU7** 32 C6
Billington, *Lancs.* **BB7** 56 C6
Billockby **NR29** 45 J4
Billy Row **DL15** 62 C3
Bilsborrow **PR3** 55 J5
Bilsby **LN13** 53 H5
Bilsdean **TD13** 77 F3
Bilsham **BN18** 12 C6
Bilsington **TN25** 15 F4
Bilsthorpe **NG22** 51 J6
Bilston, *Midloth.* **EH25** 76 A4
Bilston, *W.Mid.* **WV14** 40 B6
Bilstone **CV13** 41 F5
Bilting **TN25** 15 F3
Bilton, *E.Riding* **HU11** 59 H6
Bilton, *N.Yorks.* **HG1** 57 J4
Bilton, *N.Yorks.* **YO26** 57 K4
Bilton, *Northumb.* **NE66** 71 H2
Bilton, *Warks.* **CV22** 31 F1
Bimbister **KW17** 107 C6
Binbrook **LN8** 53 F3
Bincombe **DT3** 9 F6
Bindal **IV20** 97 G3
Binegar **BA3** 19 K7
Bines Green **RH13** 12 E5
Binfield **RG42** 22 B4
Binfield Heath **RG9** 22 A4
Bingfield **NE19** 70 E6
Bingham **NG13** 42 A2
Bingham's Melcombe **DT2** 9 G4
Bingley **BD16** 57 G6
Binham **NR21** 44 D2
Binley, *Hants.* **SP11** 21 H6
Binley, *W.Mid.* **CV3** 30 E1
Binniehill **FK1** 75 G3
Binsoe **HG4** 57 H2
Binstead **PO33** 11 G5
Binsted, *Hants.* **GU34** 22 A7
Binsted, *W.Suss.* **BN18** 12 C6
Binton **CV37** 30 C3
Bintree **NR20** 44 E3
Binweston **SY5** 38 B5
Birch, *Essex* **CO2** 34 D7
Birch, *Gt.Man.* **M24** 49 H2
Birch Green **CO2** 34 D7
Birch Heath **CW6** 48 E6
Birch Vale **SK22** 50 C4
Bircham Newton **PE31** 44 B2
Bircham Tofts **PE31** 44 B2
Birchanger **CM23** 33 J6
Bircher **HR6** 28 D2
Birchfield **IV24** 96 B2
Birchgrove, *Cardiff* **CF14** 18 E3
Birchgrove, *Swan.* **SA7** 18 A2
Birchington **CT7** 25 J5
Birchover **DE4** 50 E6
Birchwood **WA3** 49 F3
Bircotes **DN11** 51 J3
Bird End **B71** 40 C6
Birdbrook **CO9** 34 B4
Birdfield **PA32** 73 H1
Birdham **PO20** 12 B7
Birdingbury **CV23** 31 F2
Birdlip **GL4** 29 J7
Birdsall **YO17** 58 E3
Birdsgreen **WV15** 39 G7
Birdsmoor Gate **DT6** 8 C4
Birdwell **S70** 51 F2
Birdwood **GL19** 29 G7
Birgham **TD12** 77 F7
Birichen **IV25** 96 E2
Birkby **DL7** 62 E6
Birkdale, *Mersey.* **PR8** 48 C1
Birkdale, *N.Yorks.* **DL11** 61 K6
Birkenhead **CH41** 48 C4
Birkenhills **AB53** 99 F6
Birkenshaw **BD11** 57 H7
Birkhall **AB35** 90 B5
Birkhill, *Angus* **DD2** 82 E4
Birkhill, *Sc.Bord.* **TD4** 76 D6
Birkhill, *Sc.Bord.* **TD7** 69 H2
Birkin **WF11** 58 B7
Birkwood **ML11** 75 G7
Birley **HR4** 28 D3
Birley Carr **S6** 51 F3
Birling, *Kent* **ME19** 24 C5
Birling, *Northumb.* **NE65** 71 H3
Birling Gap **BN20** 13 J7
Birlingham **WR10** 29 J4
BIRMINGHAM B 40 C7
Birmingham International Airport **B26** 40 D7
Birnam **PH8** 82 B3
Birsay **KW17** 106 B5
Birse **AB34** 90 D5
Birsemore **AB34** 90 D5
Birstall **LE4** 41 H5
Birstall Smithies **WF17** 57 H7
Birstwith **HG3** 57 H4
Birthorpe **NG34** 42 E2
Birtley, *Here.* **SY7** 28 C2
Birtley, *Northumb.* **NE48** 70 D6
Birtley, *T. & W.* **DH3** 62 D1
Birts Street **WR13** 29 G5
Bisbrooke **LE15** 42 B6
Bish Mill **EX36** 7 F3
Bisham **SL7** 22 B3
Bishampton **WR10** 29 J3
Bishop Auckland **DL14** 62 D3
Bishop Burton **HU17** 59 F6
Bishop Middleham **DL17** 62 E3
Bishop Monkton **HG3** 57 J3
Bishop Norton **LN8** 52 C3
Bishop Sutton **BS39** 19 J6
Bishop Thornton **HG3** 57 H3
Bishop Wilton **YO42** 58 D4
Bishopbridge **LN8** 52 D3
Bishopbriggs **G64** 74 E4
Bishopmill **IV30** 97 K5
Bishops Cannings **SN10** 20 D5
Bishop's Castle **SY9** 38 C7
Bishop's Caundle **DT9** 9 F3
Bishop's Cleeve **GL52** 29 J6
Bishop's Frome **WR6** 29 F4
Bishop's Green **CM6** 33 K7
Bishop's Hull **TA1** 8 B2
Bishop's Itchington **CV47** 30 E3
Bishop's Lydeard **TA4** 7 K3
Bishop's Nympton **EX36** 7 F3
Bishop's Offley **ST21** 39 G3
Bishop's Stortford **CM23** 33 H6
Bishop's Sutton **SO24** 11 H1
Bishop's Tachbrook **CV33** 30 E2
Bishop's Tawton **EX32** 6 D2
Bishop's Waltham **SO32** 11 G3
Bishop's Wood **ST19** 40 A5
Bishopsbourne **CT4** 15 G2
Bishopsteignton **TQ14** 5 K3
Bishopstoke **SO50** 11 F3
Bishopston **SA3** 17 J6
Bishopstone, *Bucks.* **HP17** 32 B7
Bishopstone, *E.Suss.* **BN25** 13 H6
Bishopstone, *Here.* **HR4** 28 D4
Bishopstone, *Swin.* **SN6** 21 F3

Bishopstone

Broadwell

Bow Brickhill **MK17** 32 C5
Bow of Fife **KY15** 82 E6
Bow Street **SY24** 37 F7
Bowbank **DL12** 62 A4
Bowburn **DH6** 62 E3
Bowcombe **PO30** 11 F6
Bowd **EX10** 7 K7
Bowden, *Devon* **TQ6** 5 J6
Bowden, *Sc.Bord.* **TD6** 76 D7
Bowden Hill **SN15** 20 C5
Bowdon **WA14** 49 G4
Bower **NE48** 70 C5
Bower Hinton **TA12** 8 D3
Bowerchalke **SP5** 10 B2
Bowermadden **KW1** 105 H2
Bowers Gifford **SS13** 24 D3
Bowershall **KY12** 75 J1
Bowertower **KW1** 105 H2
Bowes **DL12** 62 A5
Bowgreave **PR3** 55 H5
Bowland Bridge **LA11** 55 H1
Bowley **HR1** 28 E3
Bowlhead Green **GU8** 12 C3
Bowling **G60** 74 C3
Bowling Bank **LL13** 38 C1
Bowlish **BA4** 19 K7
Bowmanstead **LA21** 60 E7
Bowmore **PA43** 72 B5
Bowness-on-Solway **CA7** 69 H7
Bowness-on-Windermere **LA23** 60 F7
Bowsden **TD15** 77 H6
Bowside Lodge **KW14** 104 D2
Bowthorpe **NR5** 45 F5
Bowtrees **FK2** 75 H2
Box, *Glos.* **GL6** 20 B1
Box, *Wilts.* **SN14** 20 B5
Box End **MK43** 32 D4
Boxbush **GL14** 29 G7
Boxford, *Suff.* **CO10** 34 D4
Boxford, *W.Berks.* **RG20** 21 H4
Boxgrove **PO18** 12 C6
Boxley **ME14** 14 C2
Boxmoor **HP1** 22 D1
Boxted, *Essex* **CO4** 34 D5
Boxted, *Suff.* **IP29** 34 C3
Boxted Cross **CO4** 34 E5
Boxworth **CB3** 33 G2
Boxworth End **CB4** 33 G2
Boyden Gate **CT3** 25 J5
Boydston **KA1** 74 C7
Boylestone **DE6** 40 D2
Boyndie **AB45** 98 E4
Boynton **YO16** 59 H3
Boysack **DD11** 83 H3
Boyton, *Cornw.* **PL15** 6 B6
Boyton, *Suff.* **IP12** 35 H4
Boyton, *Wilts.* **BA12** 9 J1
Boyton Cross **CM1** 24 C1
Bozeat **NN29** 32 C3
Braaid **IM4** 54 C6
Braal Castle **KW12** 105 G2
Brabling Green **IP13** 35 G2
Brabourne **TN25** 15 F3
Brabourne Lees **TN25** 15 F3
Brabster **KW1** 105 J2
Bracadale **IV56** 85 J1
Braceborough **PE9** 42 D4
Bracebridge **LN5** 52 C6
Bracebridge Heath **LN4** 52 C6
Braceby **NG34** 42 D2
Bracewell **BD23** 56 D5
Brachla **IV3** 88 C1
Brackenber **CA16** 61 J4
Brackenfield **DE55** 51 F7
Brackens **AB53** 99 F5
Bracklach **AB54** 90 B2
Bracklamore **AB43** 99 G5
Brackletter **PH34** 87 H6
Brackley, *High.* **IV2** 97 F6
Brackley, *Northants.* **NN13** 31 G5
Brackly **PA31** 73 G2
Bracknell **RG12** 22 B5
Braco **FK15** 81 K7
Bracobrae **AB55** 98 D5
Bracon Ash **NR14** 45 F6
Bracora **PH40** 86 D5
Bracorina **PH40** 86 D5
Bradbourne **DE6** 50 E7
Bradbury **TS21** 62 E4
Bradda **IM9** 54 B6
Bradden **NN12** 31 H4
Bradenham **HP14** 22 B2
Bradenstoke **SN15** 20 D3
Bradfield, *Devon* **EX15** 7 J5
Bradfield, *Essex* **CO11** 35 F5
Bradfield, *Norf.* **NR28** 45 G2
Bradfield, *W.Berks.* **RG7** 21 K4
Bradfield Combust **IP30** 34 C3
Bradfield Green **CW1** 49 F7
Bradfield Heath **CO11** 35 F6
Bradfield St. Clare **IP30** 34 D3
Bradfield St. George **IP30** 34 D3
Bradford, *Devon* **EX22** 6 C5
Bradford, *Northumb.* **NE70** 77 K7
BRADFORD, *W.Yorks.* BD 57 G6
Bradford Abbas **DT9** 8 E3
Bradford Leigh **BA15** 20 B5
Bradford Peverell **DT2** 9 F5
Bradford-on-Avon **BA15** 20 B5
Bradford-on-Tone **TA4** 7 K3
Brading **PO36** 11 H6
Bradley, *Derbys.* **DE6** 40 E1
Bradley, *Hants.* **SO24** 21 K7
Bradley, *N.E.Lincs.* **DN37** 53 F2
Bradley, *N.Yorks.* **DL8** 57 F1
Bradley, *Staffs.* **ST18** 40 A4
Bradley, *W.Mid.* **WV14** 40 B6
Bradley Green **B96** 29 J2
Bradley in the Moors **ST10** 40 C1
Bradley Stoke **BS34** 19 K3
Bradmore, *Notts.* **NG11** 41 H2
Bradmore, *W.Mid.* **WV3** 40 A6
Bradninch **EX5** 7 J5
Bradnop **ST13** 50 C7
Bradpole **DT6** 8 D5
Bradshaw **BL2** 49 G1
Bradstone **PL19** 6 B7
Bradwall Green **CW11** 49 G6
Bradwell, *Derbys.* **S33** 50 D4
Bradwell, *Essex* **CM7** 34 C6
Bradwell, *M.K.* **MK13** 32 B5
Bradwell, *Norf.* **NR31** 45 K5
Bradwell Grove **OX18** 21 F1
Bradwell Waterside **CM0** 25 F1
Bradwell-on-Sea **CM0** 25 F1
Bradworthy **EX22** 6 B4
Brae, *D. & G.* **DG2** 65 J3
Brae, *High.* **IV24** 96 B1
Brae, *Shet.* **ZE2** 109 C6
Braeantra **IV17** 96 C4
Braedownie **DD8** 89 K7
Braefoot **AB53** 99 F6
Braegrum **PH1** 82 B5
Braehead, *Angus* **DD10** 83 H2
Braehead, *Moray* **AB55** 98 B6
Braehead, *Ork.* **KW17** 106 D3
Braehead, *Ork.* **KW17** 107 E7
Braehead, *S.Lan.* **ML11** 75 H5
Braehead, *S.Lan.* **ML11** 75 G7
Braehoulland **ZE2** 108 B5
Braeleny **FK17** 81 H6
Braemar **AB35** 89 J5
Braemore, *High.* **KW6** 105 F5
Braemore, *High.* **IV27** 96 C1
Braemore, *High.* **IV23** 95 H4
Braenaloin **AB35** 89 K5
Braes of Enzie **AB56** 98 B5
Braes of Foss **PH16** 81 J2
Braes of Ullapool **IV26** 95 H2
Braeswick **KW17** 106 F4
Braeval **FK8** 81 G7
Brafferton, *Darl.* **DL1** 62 D4
Brafferton, *N.Yorks.* **YO61** 57 K2
Brafield-on-the-Green **NN7** 32 B3
Bragar **HS2** 100 E3
Bragbury End **SG2** 33 F6
Bragleenbeg **PA34** 80 A5
Braichmelyn **LL57** 46 E6
Braides **LA2** 55 H4
Braidwood **ML8** 75 G6
Braigo **PA44** 72 A4
Brailsford **DE6** 40 E1
Braintree **CM7** 34 B6
Braiseworth **IP23** 35 F1
Braishfield **SO51** 10 E2
Braithwaite, *Cumb.* **CA12** 60 D4
Braithwaite, *S.Yorks.* **DN7** 51 J1
Braithwell **S66** 51 H3
Bramber **BN44** 12 E5
Brambletye **RH18** 13 H3
Bramcote **NG9** 41 H2
Bramdean **SO24** 11 H2
Bramerton **NR14** 45 G5
Bramfield, *Herts.* **SG14** 33 F7
Bramfield, *Suff.* **IP19** 35 H1
Bramford **IP8** 35 F4
Bramhall **SK7** 49 H4
Bramham **LS23** 57 K5
Bramhope **LS16** 57 H5
Bramley, *Hants.* **RG26** 21 K6
Bramley, *S.Yorks.* **S66** 51 G3
Bramley, *Surr.* **GU5** 22 D7
Bramling **CT3** 15 H2
Brampford Speke **EX5** 7 H6
Brampton, *Cambs.* **PE28** 33 F1
Brampton, *Cumb.* **CA8** 70 A7
Brampton, *Cumb.* **CA16** 61 H4
Brampton, *Derbys.* **S40** 51 F5
Brampton, *Lincs.* **LN1** 52 B5
Brampton, *Norf.* **NR10** 45 G3
Brampton, *S.Yorks.* **S73** 51 G2
Brampton, *Suff.* **NR34** 45 J7
Brampton Abbotts **HR9** 29 F6
Brampton Ash **LE16** 42 A7
Brampton Bryan **SY7** 28 C1
Brampton en le Morthen **S66** 51 G4
Bramshall **ST14** 40 C2
Bramshaw **SO43** 10 D3
Bramshill **RG27** 22 A5
Bramshott **GU30** 12 B3
Bramwell **TA10** 8 D2
Bran End **CM6** 33 K6
Branault **PH36** 79 G1
Brancaster **PE31** 44 B1
Brancepeth **DH7** 62 D3
Branchill **IV36** 97 H6
Brand Green **GL19** 29 G6
Branderburgh **IV31** 97 K4
Brandesburton **YO25** 59 H5
Brandeston **IP13** 35 G2
Brandis Corner **EX22** 6 C5
Brandiston **NR10** 45 F3
Brandon, *Dur.* **DH7** 62 D3
Brandon, *Lincs.* **NG32** 42 C1
Brandon, *Northumb.* **NE66** 71 F2
Brandon, *Suff.* **IP27** 44 B7
Brandon, *Warks.* **CV8** 31 F1
Brandon Bank **CB7** 44 A7
Brandon Creek **PE38** 44 A6
Brandon Parva **NR9** 44 E5
Brandsby **YO61** 58 B2
Brandy Wharf **DN21** 52 D3
Brane **TR19** 2 A6
Branksome **BH12** 10 B5
Branksome Park **BH13** 10 B5
Bransby **LN1** 52 B5
Branscombe **EX12** 7 K7
Bransford **WR6** 29 G3
Bransford Bridge **WR6** 29 H3
Bransgore **BH23** 10 C5
Branson's Cross **B98** 30 B1
Branston, *Leics.* **NG32** 42 B3
Branston, *Lincs.* **LN4** 52 D6
Branston, *Staffs.* **DE14** 40 E3
Branston Booths **LN4** 52 D6
Branstone **PO36** 11 G6
Brant Broughton **LN5** 52 C7
Brantham **CO11** 35 F5
Branthwaite, *Cumb.* **CA7** 60 D3
Branthwaite, *Cumb.* **CA14** 60 B4
Brantingham **HU15** 59 F7
Branton, *Northumb.* **NE66** 71 F2
Branton, *S.Yorks.* **DN3** 51 J2
Brantwood **LA21** 60 E7
Branxholm Bridgend **TD9** 69 K2
Branxholme **TD9** 69 K2
Branxton **TD12** 77 G7
Brassington **DE4** 50 E7
Brasted **TN16** 23 H6
Brasted Chart **TN16** 23 H6
Brathens **AB31** 90 E5
Bratoft **PE24** 53 H6
Brattleby **LN1** 52 C4
Bratton **BA13** 20 C6
Bratton Clovelly **EX20** 6 C6
Bratton Fleming **EX31** 6 E2
Bratton Seymour **BA9** 9 F2
Braughing **SG11** 33 G6
Braunston, *Northants.* **NN11** 31 G2
Braunston, *Rut.* **LE15** 42 B5
Braunstone **LE3** 41 H5
Braunton **EX33** 6 C2
Brawby **YO17** 58 D2
Brawdy **SA62** 16 B2
Brawl **KW14** 104 D2
Brawlbin **KW12** 105 F3
Bray **SL6** 22 C4
Bray Shop **PL17** 4 D3
Bray Wick **SL6** 22 B4
Braybrooke **LE16** 42 A7
Brayford **EX32** 6 E2
Brayshaw **BD23** 56 C4
Brayton **YO8** 58 C6
Brazacott **PL15** 4 C1
Breach **CT4** 15 G3
Breachwood Green **SG4** 32 E6
Breacleit **HS2** 100 D4
Breadsall **DE7** 41 F2
Breadstone **GL13** 20 A1
Breage **TR13** 2 D6
Breakish **IV42** 86 C2
Breakon **ZE2** 108 E2
Bream **GL15** 19 K1
Breamore **SP6** 10 C3
Brean **TA8** 19 F6
Breanais **HS2** 100 B5
Brearton **HG3** 57 J3
Breascleit **HS2** 100 E4
Breaston **DE72** 41 G2
Brechfa **SA32** 17 J1
Brechin **DD9** 83 H1
Brecklate **PA28** 66 A2
Breckles **NR17** 44 D6
Breckonside **DG3** 68 D3
Brecon (Aberhonddu) **LD3** 27 K6
Bredbury **SK6** 49 J3
Brede **TN31** 14 D6
Bredenbury **HR7** 29 F3
Bredfield **IP13** 35 G3
Bredgar **ME9** 24 E5
Bredhurst **ME7** 24 D5
Bredicot **WR7** 29 J3
Bredon **GL20** 29 J5
Bredon's Hardwick **GL20** 29 J5
Bredon's Norton **GL20** 29 J5
Bredwardine **HR3** 28 C4
Breedon on the Hill **DE73** 41 G3
Breibhig **HS2** 101 G4
Breich **EH55** 75 H4
Breighton **YO8** 58 D6
Breinton **HR4** 28 D4
Bremhill **SN11** 20 C4
Brenachoille **PA32** 80 B7
Brenchley **TN12** 23 K7
Brendon, *Devon* **EX35** 7 F1
Brendon, *Devon* **EX22** 6 B4
Brenkley **NE13** 71 H6
Brent **NW** 22 E3
Brent Eleigh **CO10** 34 D4
Brent Knoll **TA9** 19 G6
Brent Pelham **SG9** 33 H5
Brentford **TW8** 22 E4
Brentingby **LE14** 42 A4
Brentwood **CM14** 23 J2
Brenzett **TN29** 15 F5
Breoch **DG7** 65 H5
Brereton **WS15** 40 C4
Brereton Green **CW11** 49 G6
Brereton Heath **CW12** 49 H6
Bressingham **IP22** 44 E7
Bretabister **ZE2** 109 D7
Bretby **DE15** 40 E3
Bretford **CV23** 31 F1
Bretforton **WR11** 30 B4
Bretherdale Head **CA10** 61 G6
Bretherton **PR26** 55 H7
Brettenham, *Norf.* **IP24** 44 D7
Brettenham, *Suff.* **IP7** 34 D3
Bretton **CH4** 48 C6
Brewood **ST19** 40 A5
Briach **IV36** 97 H6
Briantspuddle **DT2** 9 H5
Bricket Wood **AL2** 22 E1
Bricklehampton **WR10** 29 J4
Bride **IM7** 54 D3
Bridekirk **CA13** 60 C3
Bridell **SA43** 26 A4
Bridestones **CW12** 49 J6
Bridestowe **EX20** 6 D7
Brideswell **AB54** 90 D1
Bridford **EX6** 7 G7
Bridge, *Cornw.* **TR16** 2 D4
Bridge, *Kent* **CT4** 15 G2
Bridge End, *Lincs.* **NG34** 42 E2
Bridge End, *Shet.* **ZE2** 109 C9
Bridge Hewick **HG4** 57 J2
Bridge of Alford **AB33** 90 D3
Bridge of Allan **FK9** 75 F1
Bridge of Avon **AB37** 89 J1
Bridge of Balgie **PH15** 81 G3
Bridge of Bogendreip **AB31** 90 E5
Bridge of Brewlands **PH11** 82 C1
Bridge of Brown **AB37** 89 J2
Bridge of Cally **PH10** 82 C2
Bridge of Canny **AB31** 90 E5
Bridge of Craigisla **PH11** 82 D2
Bridge of Dee, *Aber.* **AB31** 90 E5
Bridge of Dee, *Aber.* **AB35** 89 J5
Bridge of Dee, *D. & G.* **DG7** 65 H4
Bridge of Don **AB23** 91 H4
Bridge of Dun **DD10** 83 H2
Bridge of Dye **AB31** 90 E6
Bridge of Earn **PH2** 82 C6
Bridge of Ericht **PH17** 81 G2
Bridge of Ess **AB34** 90 D5
Bridge of Feugh **AB31** 90 E5
Bridge of Forss **KW14** 105 F2
Bridge of Gairn **AB35** 90 B5
Bridge of Gaur **PH17** 81 G2
Bridge of Muchalls **AB39** 91 G5
Bridge of Orchy **PA36** 80 E4
Bridge of Tilt **PH18** 81 K1
Bridge of Tynet **AB56** 98 B4
Bridge of Walls **ZE2** 109 B7
Bridge of Weir **PA11** 74 B4
Bridge Sollers **HR4** 28 D4
Bridge Street **CO10** 34 C4
Bridge Trafford **CH2** 48 D5
Bridgefoot, *Cambs.* **SG8** 33 H4
Bridgefoot, *Cumb.* **CA14** 60 B4
Bridgehampton **BA22** 8 E2
Bridgemary **PO13** 11 G4
Bridgemere **CW5** 39 G1
Bridgend, *Aber.* **AB54** 90 D1
Bridgend, *Aber.* **AB35** 90 B5
Bridgend, *Angus* **DD9** 83 G1
Bridgend, *Arg. & B.* **PA31** 73 G1
Bridgend, *Arg. & B.* **PA43** 72 B4
Bridgend (Pen-y-Bont ar Ogwr), *Bridgend* **CF31** 18 C4
Bridgend, *Cornw.* **PL22** 4 B4
Bridgend, *Cumb.* **CA11** 60 F5
Bridgend, *Fife* **KY15** 82 E6
Bridgend, *Moray* **AB54** 90 B1
Bridgend, *P. & K.* **PH2** 82 C5
Bridgend, *W.Loth.* **EH49** 75 J3
Bridgend of Lintrathen **DD8** 82 D2
Bridgerule **EX22** 6 A5
Bridges **SY5** 38 C6
Bridgeton **AB33** 90 D3
Bridgetown, *Cornw.* **PL15** 6 B7
Bridgetown, *Som.* **TA22** 7 H2
Bridgeyate **BS30** 19 K4
Bridgham **NR16** 44 D7
Bridgnorth **WV16** 39 G6
Bridgtown **WS11** 40 B5
Bridgwater **TA6** 8 B1
Bridlington **YO16** 59 H3
Bridport **DT6** 8 D5
Bridstow **HR9** 28 E6
Brierfield **BB10** 56 D6
Brierley, *Glos.* **GL17** 29 F7
Brierley, *Here.* **HR6** 28 D3
Brierley, *S.Yorks.* **S72** 51 G1
Brierley Hill **DY5** 40 B7
Brig o'Turk **FK17** 81 G7
Brigehaugh **AB55** 90 B1
Brigg **DN20** 52 D2
Brigham, *Cumb.* **CA13** 60 B3
Brigham, *E.Riding* **YO25** 59 G4
Brighouse **HD6** 57 G7
Brighstone **PO30** 11 F6
Brightgate **DE4** 50 E7
Brighthampton **OX29** 21 G1
Brightling **TN32** 13 K4
Brightlingsea **CO7** 34 E7
BRIGHTON, *B. & H.* BN 13 G6
Brighton, *Cornw.* **TR2** 3 G3
Brightons **FK2** 75 H3
Brightwalton **RG20** 21 H4
Brightwell, *Oxon.* **OX10** 21 J2
Brightwell, *Suff.* **IP10** 35 G4
Brightwell Baldwin **OX49** 21 K2
Brignall **DL12** 62 B5
Brigsley **DN37** 53 F2
Brigsteer **LA8** 55 H1
Brigstock **NN14** 42 C7
Brill, *Bucks.* **HP18** 31 H7
Brill, *Cornw.* **TR11** 2 E6
Brilley **HR3** 28 B4
Brilley Mountain **HR3** 28 B3
Brimfield **SY8** 28 E2
Brimington **S43** 51 G5
Brimington Common **S43** 51 G5
Brimley **TQ13** 5 J3
Brimpsfield **GL4** 29 J7
Brimpton **RG7** 21 J5
Brimscombe **GL5** 20 B1
Brimstage **CH63** 48 C4
Brind **DN14** 58 D6
Brindister, *Shet.* **ZE2** 109 B7
Brindister, *Shet.* **ZE2** 109 D9
Brindle **PR6** 55 J7
Brindley Ford **ST8** 49 H7
Brineton **TF11** 40 A4
Bringhurst **LE16** 42 B6
Brington **PE28** 32 D1
Briningham **NR24** 44 E2
Brinkhill **LN11** 53 G5
Brinkley **CB8** 33 K3
Brinklow **CV23** 31 F1
Brinkworth **SN15** 20 D3
Brinmore **IV2** 88 D2
Brinscall **PR6** 56 B7
Brinsley **NG16** 41 G1
Brinsop **HR4** 28 D4
Brinsworth **S60** 51 G4
Brinton **NR24** 44 E2
Brinyan **KW17** 106 D5
Brisco **CA4** 60 F1
Brisley **NR20** 44 D3
Brislington **BS4** 19 K4
BRISTOL BS 19 J4
Bristol International Airport **BS48** 19 H5
Briston **NR24** 44 E2
Britannia **OL13** 56 D7
Britford **SP5** 10 C2
Brithdir **LL40** 37 G4
Brithem Bottom **EX15** 7 J4
Briton Ferry (Llansawel) **SA11** 18 A2
Britwell Salome **OX49** 21 K2
Brixham **TQ5** 5 K5
Brixton **PL8** 5 F5
Brixton Deverill **BA12** 9 H1
Brixworth **NN6** 31 J1
Brize Norton **OX18** 21 F1
Broad Blunsdon **SN26** 20 E2
Broad Campden **GL55** 30 C5
Broad Chalke **SP5** 10 B2
Broad Green, *Beds.* **MK43** 32 C4
Broad Green, *Essex* **CO6** 34 C6
Broad Green, *Worcs.* **WR6** 29 G3
Broad Haven **SA62** 16 B3
Broad Heath **WR15** 29 F2
Broad Hill **CB7** 33 J1
Broad Hinton **SN4** 20 E4
Broad Laying **RG20** 21 H5
Broad Marston **CV37** 30 C4
Broad Oak, *Cumb.* **CA18** 60 C7
Broad Oak, *E.Suss.* **TN31** 14 D6
Broad Oak, *Here.* **HR2** 28 D6
Broad Street **ME17** 14 D2
Broad Street Green **CM9** 24 E1
Broad Town **SN4** 20 D4
Broadbottom **SK14** 49 J3
Broadbridge **PO18** 12 B6
Broadbridge Heath **RH12** 12 E3
Broadclyst **EX5** 7 H6
Broadford **IV49** 86 C2
Broadford Bridge **RH14** 12 D4
Broadgate **LA18** 54 E1
Broadgroves **CM6** 33 K7
Broadhaugh **TD9** 69 K3
Broadheath **WA14** 49 G4
Broadhembury **EX14** 7 K5
Broadhempston **TQ9** 5 J4
Broadholme **LN1** 52 B5
Broadland Row **TN31** 14 D6
Broadlay **SA17** 17 G4
Broadley, *Lancs.* **OL12** 49 H1
Broadley, *Moray* **AB56** 98 B4
Broadley Common **EN9** 23 H1
Broadmayne **DT2** 9 G6
Broadmeadows **TD7** 69 K1
Broadmere **RG25** 21 K7
Broadnymet **EX17** 7 F5
Broadoak, *Carmar.* **SA32** 17 J2
Broadoak, *Dorset* **DT6** 8 D5
Broadoak, *E.Suss.* **TN21** 13 K4
Broadoak, *Kent* **CT2** 25 H5
Broadrashes **AB55** 98 C5
Broadsea **AB43** 99 H4
Broadstairs **CT10** 25 K5
Broadstone, *Poole* **BH18** 10 B5
Broadstone, *Shrop.* **SY7** 38 E7
Broadstreet Common **NP18** 19 G3
Broadwas **WR6** 29 G3
Broadwater, *Herts.* **SG2** 33 F6
Broadwater, *W.Suss.* **BN14** 12 E6
Broadway, *Carmar.* **SA33** 17 F3
Broadway, *Carmar.* **SA17** 17 G4
Broadway, *Pembs.* **SA62** 16 B3
Broadway, *Som.* **TA19** 8 C3
Broadway, *Suff.* **IP19** 35 H1
Broadway, *Worcs.* **WR12** 30 B5
Broadwell, *Glos.* **GL56** 30 D6
Broadwell, *Glos.* **GL16** 28 E7

Castle Gresley

Butsfield **DL13** 62 C2
Butt Green **CW5** 49 F7
Butt Lane **ST7** 49 H7
Butterburn **CA8** 70 B6
Buttercrambe **YO41** 58 D4
Butterknowle **DL13** 62 C4
Butterleigh **EX15** 7 H5
Butterley **DE5** 51 G7
Buttermere, *Cumb.* **CA13** 60 C5
Buttermere, *Wilts.* **SN8** 21 G5
Butters Green **ST7** 49 H7
Buttershaw **BD6** 57 G7
Butterstone **PH8** 82 B3
Butterton **ST13** 50 C7
Butterwick, *Lincs.* **PE22** 43 G1
Butterwick, *N.Yorks.* **YO17** 58 D2
Butterwick, *N.Yorks.* **YO17** 59 F2
Buttington **SY21** 38 B5
Buttonoak **DY12** 29 G1
Buxhall **IP14** 34 E3
Buxted **TN22** 13 H4
Buxton, *Derbys.* **SK17** 50 C5
Buxton, *Norf.* **NR10** 45 G3
Buxton Heath **NR10** 45 F3
Buxworth **SK23** 50 C4
Bwcle (Buckley) **CH7** 48 B6
Bwlch **LD3** 28 A6
Bwlch Derwin **LL54** 36 D1
Bwlch-clawdd **SA44** 17 G1
Bwlch-llan **SA48** 26 E3
Bwlch-y-cibau **SY22** 38 A4
Bwlch-y-ddar **SY10** 38 A3
Bwlch-y-ffridd **SY16** 37 K6
Bwlch-y-groes **SA35** 17 F1
Bwlch-y-sarnau **LD6** 27 K1
Bwlchgwyn **LL11** 48 B7
Bwlchnewydd **SA33** 17 G2
Bwlchtocyn **LL53** 36 C3
Byers Green **DL16** 62 D3
Byfield **NN11** 31 G3
Byfleet **KT14** 22 D5
Byford **HR4** 28 C4
Bygrave **SG7** 33 F5
Byker **NE6** 71 H7
Bylane End **PL14** 4 C5
Bylchau **LL16** 47 H6
Byley **CW10** 49 G6
Bynea **SA14** 17 J5
Byrness **NE19** 70 C3
Bythorn **PE28** 32 D1
Byton **LD8** 28 C2
Byworth **GU28** 12 C4

C

Cabharstadh **HS2** 101 F5
Cabourne **LN7** 52 E2
Cabrach, *Arg. & B.* **PA60** 72 C4
Cabrach, *Moray* **AB54** 90 B2
Cackle Street **TN31** 14 D6
Cacrabank **TD7** 69 J2
Cadboll **IV20** 97 F4
Cadbury **EX5** 7 H5
Cadbury Barton **EX18** 6 E4
Cadbury Heath **BS30** 19 K4
Cadder **G64** 74 E3
Cadderlie **PA35** 80 B4
Caddington **LU1** 32 D7
Caddleton **PA34** 79 J6
Caddonfoot **TD1** 76 C7
Cade Street **TN21** 13 K4
Cadeby, *Leics.* **CV13** 41 G5
Cadeby, *S.Yorks.* **DN5** 51 H2
Cadeleigh **EX16** 7 H5
Cadgwith **TR12** 2 E7
Cadham **KY7** 82 D7
Cadishead **M44** 49 G3
Cadle **SA5** 17 K5
Cadley **SN8** 21 F5
Cadmore End **HP14** 22 A2
Cadnam **SO40** 10 E3
Cadney **DN20** 52 D2
Cadole **CH7** 48 B6
Cadover Bridge **PL7** 5 F4
Cadoxton, *N.P.T.* **SA10** 18 A2
Cadoxton, *V. of Glam.* **CF63** 18 E5
Cae Ddafydd **LL48** 37 F1
Caeathro **LL55** 46 D6
Caehopkin **SA9** 27 H7
Caen **KW8** 105 F7
Caenby **LN8** 52 D4
Caenby Corner **LN8** 52 C4
Caeo **SA19** 17 K1
Caer Farchell **SA62** 16 A2
Caer Llan **NP25** 19 H1
Caer-Lan **SA9** 27 H7
Caerau, *Bridgend* **CF34** 18 B2
Caerau, *Cardiff* **CF5** 18 E4
Caerdeon **LL42** 37 F4
CAERDYDD (CARDIFF) CF 18 E4
Caerfyrddin (Carmarthen) **SA31** 17 H3
Caergeiliog **LL65** 46 B5
Caergwrle **LL12** 48 C7
Caergybi (Holyhead) **LL65** 46 A4
Caerhun **LL32** 47 F5
Caerleon **NP18** 19 G2
Caernarfon **LL55** 46 C6
Caerphilly **CF83** 18 E3
Caersws **SY17** 37 K6
Caerwent **NP26** 19 H2
Caerwys **CH7** 47 K5
Caethle **LL36** 37 F6
Caggan **PH22** 89 F3
Cairinis **HS6** 92 D6
Cairisiadar **HS2** 100 C4
Cairminis **HS5** 93 F3
Cairnargat **AB54** 90 C1
Cairnbaan **PA31** 73 G1
Cairnbeathie **AB31** 90 D4
Cairnbrogie **AB51** 91 G2
Cairnbulg **AB43** 99 J4
Cairncross **TD14** 77 G4
Cairncurran **PA13** 74 B4
Cairndoon **DG8** 64 D7
Cairndow **PA26** 80 C6
Cairne **AB32** 91 G4
Cairness **AB43** 99 J4
Cairney Lodge **KY15** 82 E6
Cairneyhill **KY12** 75 J2
Cairnhill, *Aber.* **AB52** 90 E1
Cairnhill, *Aber.* **AB41** 91 H2
Cairnie **AB54** 98 C6
Cairnorrie **AB41** 99 G6
Cairnryan **DG9** 64 A4
Cairnsmore **DG8** 64 E4
Caister-on-Sea **NR30** 45 K4
Caistor **LN7** 52 E2
Caistor St. Edmund **NR14** 45 G5
Caistron **NE65** 70 E3
Cake Street **NR17** 44 E6
Calanais (Callanish) **HS2** 100 E4
Calbost **HS2** 101 G6
Calbourne **PO30** 11 F6
Calcot **RG31** 21 K4
Calcott **CT3** 25 H5
Caldarvan **G83** 74 C2
Caldback **ZE2** 108 F2
Caldbeck **CA7** 60 E3
Caldbergh **DL8** 57 F1
Caldecote, *Cambs.* **PE7** 42 E7
Caldecote, *Cambs.* **CB3** 33 G3
Caldecote, *Herts.* **SG7** 33 F5
Caldecote, *Warks.* **CV10** 41 F6
Caldecott, *Northants.* **NN9** 32 C2
Caldecott, *Rut.* **LE16** 42 B6
Calder Bridge **CA20** 60 B6
Calder Mains **KW12** 105 F3
Calder Vale **PR3** 55 J5
Calderbank **ML6** 75 F4
Calderbrook **OL15** 49 J1
Caldercruix **ML6** 75 G4
Calderglen **G72** 74 E5
Caldermill **ML10** 74 E6
Caldhame **DD8** 83 F3
Caldicot **NP26** 19 H3
Caldwell, *Derbys.* **DE12** 40 E4
Caldwell, *E.Renf.* **G78** 74 C5
Caldwell, *N.Yorks.* **DL11** 62 C5
Caldy **CH48** 48 B4
Caledrhydiau **SA48** 26 D3
Calfsound **KW17** 106 E4
Calgary **PA75** 78 E2
Califer **IV36** 97 H6
California, *Falk.* **FK1** 75 H3
California, *Norf.* **NR29** 45 K4
Calke **DE73** 41 F3
Callaly **NE65** 71 F3
Callander **FK17** 81 H7
Callanish (Calanais) **HS2** 100 E4
Callerton Lane End **NE5** 71 G7
Callestick **TR4** 2 E3
Calligarry **IV45** 86 C4
Callington **PL17** 4 D4
Callisterhall **DG11** 69 H5
Callow **HR2** 28 D5
Callow End **WR2** 29 H4
Callow Hill, *Wilts.* **SN15** 20 D3
Callow Hill, *Worcs.* **DY14** 29 G1
Callows Grave **WR15** 28 E2
Callyburn **PA28** 66 B1
Calmore **SO40** 10 E3
Calmsden **GL7** 20 D1
Calne **SN11** 20 C4
Calow **S44** 51 G5
Calrossie **IV19** 96 E4
Calshot **SO45** 11 F4
Calstock **PL18** 4 E4
Calstone Wellington **SN10** 20 D5
Calthorpe **NR11** 45 F2
Calthwaite **CA11** 61 F2
Calton, *N.Yorks.* **BD23** 56 E4
Calton, *Staffs.* **ST10** 50 D7
Calveley **CW6** 48 E7
Calver **S32** 50 E5
Calver Hill **HR4** 28 C4
Calverhall **SY13** 39 F2
Calverleigh **EX16** 7 H4
Calverley **LS28** 57 H6
Calvert **MK18** 31 H6
Calverton, *M.K.* **MK19** 31 J5
Calverton, *Notts.* **NG14** 41 J1
Calvine **PH18** 81 K1
Calvo **CA7** 60 C1
Cam **GL11** 20 A2
Camasnacroise **PH33** 79 K2
Camastianavaig **IV51** 86 B1
Camasunary **IV49** 86 B3
Camault Muir **IV4** 96 C7
Camb **ZE2** 108 E3
Camber **TN31** 14 E6
Camberley **GU15** 22 B5
Camberwell **SE15** 23 G4
Camblesforth **YO8** 58 C7
Cambo **NE61** 71 F5
Cambois **NE24** 71 J5
Camborne **TR14** 2 D4
CAMBRIDGE, *Cambs.* CB 33 H3
Cambridge, *Glos.* **GL2** 20 A1
Cambridge Airport **CB5** 33 H3
Cambus **FK10** 75 G1
Cambus o'May **AB34** 90 C5
Cambusbarron **FK7** 75 F1
Cambuskenneth **FK9** 75 G1
Cambuslang **G72** 74 E4
Cambusnethan **ML2** 75 G5
Camchuart **PA22** 73 H2
Camden **NW** 23 F3
Cameley **BS39** 19 K6
Camelford **PL32** 4 B2
Camelon **FK1** 75 G2
Camelsdale **GU27** 12 B3
Camer **DA13** 24 C5
Cameron **G83** 74 B2
Camerory **PH26** 89 H1
Camer's Green **WR13** 29 G5
Camerton, *B. & N.E.Som.* **BA2** 19 K6
Camerton, *Cumb.* **CA14** 60 B3
Camghouran **PH17** 81 G2
Camis Eskan **G84** 74 B2
Cammachmore **AB39** 91 H5
Cammeringham **LN1** 52 C4
Campbeltown **PA28** 66 B2
Campbeltown (Machrihanish) Airport **PA28** 66 A1
Camperdown **NE12** 71 H6
Camphouse **PH36** 79 G1
Campmuir **PH13** 82 D4
Camps End **CB1** 33 K4
Camps Heath **NR32** 45 K6
Campsall **DN6** 51 H1
Campsey Ash **IP13** 35 H3
Campton **SG17** 32 E5
Camptown **TD8** 70 B2
Camrose **SA62** 16 C3
Camsail **G84** 74 A2
Camserney **PH15** 81 K3
Camstraddan **G83** 74 B1
Camus Croise **IV43** 86 C3
Camus-luinie **IV40** 87 F2
Camusnagaul, *High.* **IV23** 95 G3
Camusnagaul, *High.* **PH33** 87 G7
Camusrory **PH41** 86 E5
Camusteel **IV54** 94 D7
Camusterrach **IV54** 94 D7
Camusurich **FK21** 81 H4
Camusvrachan **PH15** 81 H3
Canada **SO51** 10 D3
Candacraig **AB35** 90 B5
Candlesby **PE23** 53 H6
Candy Mill **ML12** 75 J6
Cane End **RG4** 21 K4
Canewdon **SS4** 24 E2
Canford Bottom **BH21** 10 B4
Canford Cliffs **BH13** 10 B6
Canford Magna **BH21** 10 B5
Canisbay **KW1** 105 J1
Cann **SP7** 9 H2
Cann Common **SP7** 9 H2
Cannard's Grave **BA4** 19 K7
Cannich **IV4** 87 K1
Cannington **TA5** 8 B1
Cannock **WS11** 40 B4
Cannock Wood **WS15** 40 C4
Cannop **GL16** 29 F7
Canon Bridge **HR2** 28 D4
Canon Frome **HR8** 29 F4
Canon Pyon **HR4** 28 D4
Canonbie **DG14** 69 J6
Canons Ashby **NN11** 31 G3
Canon's Town **TR27** 2 C5
Canterbury, *Aber.* **AB45** 98 D5
CANTERBURY, *Kent* CT 15 G2
Cantley, *Norf.* **NR13** 45 H5
Cantley, *S.Yorks.* **DN3** 51 J2
Cantlop **SY5** 38 E5
Canton **CF11** 18 E4
Cantray **IV2** 96 E7
Cantraydoune **IV12** 96 E7
Cantraywood **IV2** 96 E7
Cantsfield **LA6** 56 B2
Canvey Island **SS8** 24 D3
Canwell Hall **B75** 40 D5
Canwick **LN4** 52 C6
Canworthy Water **PL15** 4 C1
Caol **PH33** 87 H7
Caolas, *Arg. & B.* **PA77** 78 B3
Caolas, *W.Isles* **HS9** 84 B5
Caolas Scalpaigh (Kyles Scalpay) **HS3** 93 H2
Caolasnacon **PH50** 80 C1
Capel, *Kent* **TN12** 23 K7
Capel, *Surr.* **RH5** 22 E7
Capel Bangor **SY23** 37 F7
Capel Betws Lleucu **SY25** 27 F3
Capel Carmel **LL53** 36 A3
Capel Coch **LL77** 46 C4
Capel Curig **LL24** 47 F7
Capel Cynon **SA44** 26 C4
Capel Dewi, *Carmar.* **SA32** 17 H2
Capel Dewi, *Cere.* **SY23** 37 F7
Capel Dewi, *Cere.* **SA44** 26 D4
Capel Garmon **LL26** 47 G7
Capel Gwyn, *Carmar.* **SA32** 17 H2
Capel Gwyn, *I.o.A.* **LL65** 46 B5
Capel Gwynfe **SA19** 27 G6
Capel Hendre **SA18** 17 J3
Capel Isaac **SA19** 17 J2
Capel Iwan **SA38** 17 F1
Capel le Ferne **CT18** 15 H4
Capel Parc **LL68** 46 C4
Capel St. Andrew **IP12** 35 H4
Capel St. Mary **IP9** 34 E5
Capel St. Silin **SA48** 26 E3
Capel Seion **SY23** 27 F1
Capel Tygwydd **SA38** 26 B4
Capel-y-ffin **NP7** 28 B5
Capeluchaf **LL54** 36 D1
Capelulo **LL34** 47 F5
Capenhurst **CH1** 48 C5
Capernwray **LA6** 55 J2
Capheaton **NE19** 71 F5
Caplaw **G78** 74 C5
Cappercleuch **TD7** 69 H1
Capplegill **DG10** 69 G3
Capstone **ME7** 24 D5
Capton **TQ6** 5 J5
Caputh **PH1** 82 B3
Car Colston **NG13** 42 A1
Carbellow **KA18** 68 B1
Carbeth **G63** 74 D3
Carbis Bay **TR26** 2 C5
Carbost, *High.* **IV51** 93 K7
Carbost, *High.* **IV47** 85 J1
Carbrain **G67** 75 F3
Carbrooke **IP25** 44 D5
Carburton **S80** 51 J5
Carcary **DD9** 83 H2
Carclew **TR3** 2 E5
Carco **DG4** 68 C2
Carcroft **DN6** 51 H2
Cardenden **KY5** 76 A1
Cardeston **SY5** 38 C4
CARDIFF (CAERDYDD) CF 18 E4
Cardiff International Airport **CF62** 18 D5
Cardigan (Aberteifi) **SA43** 26 A4
Cardington, *Beds.* **MK44** 32 D4
Cardington, *Shrop.* **SY6** 38 E6
Cardinham **PL30** 4 B4
Cardno **AB43** 99 H4
Cardoness **DG7** 65 F5
Cardow **AB38** 97 J7
Cardrona **EH45** 76 A7
Cardross **G82** 74 B3
Cardurnock **CA7** 60 C1
Careby **PE9** 42 D4
Careston **DD9** 83 G1
Carew **SA70** 16 D4
Carew Cheriton **SA70** 16 D4
Carew Newton **SA68** 16 D4
Carey **HR2** 28 E5
Carfrae **EH41** 76 D4
Carfraemill **TD2** 76 D5
Cargen **DG2** 65 K3
Cargenbridge **DG2** 65 K3
Cargill **PH2** 82 C4
Cargo **CA6** 60 E1
Cargo Fleet **TS3** 63 G4
Cargreen **PL12** 4 E4
Carham **TD12** 77 F7
Carhampton **TA24** 7 J1
Carharrack **TR16** 2 E4
Carie, *P. & K.* **PH17** 81 H2
Carie, *P. & K.* **PH15** 81 H4
Carines **TR8** 2 E3
Carisbrooke **PO30** 11 F6
Cark **LA11** 55 G2
Carkeel **PL12** 4 E4
Carlabhagh (Carloway) **HS2** 100 E3
Carland Cross **TR8** 3 F3
Carlby **PE9** 42 D4
Carlecotes **S36** 50 D2
Carleton, *Cumb.* **CA1** 60 F1
Carleton, *Lancs.* **FY6** 55 G5
Carleton, *N.Yorks.* **BD23** 56 E5
Carleton, *W.Yorks.* **WF8** 57 K7
Carleton Fishery **KA26** 67 F5
Carleton Forehoe **NR9** 44 E5
Carleton Rode **NR16** 45 F6
Carlin How **TS13** 63 J5
Carlingcott **BA2** 19 K6
CARLISLE CA 60 F1
Carlops **EH26** 75 K5
Carloway (Carlabhagh) **HS2** 100 E3
Carlton, *Beds.* **MK43** 32 C3
Carlton, *Cambs.* **CB8** 33 K3
Carlton, *Leics.* **CV13** 41 F5
Carlton, *N.Yorks.* **YO62** 58 C1
Carlton, *N.Yorks.* **DL8** 57 F1
Carlton, *N.Yorks.* **DN14** 58 C7
Carlton, *Notts.* **NG4** 41 J1
Carlton, *S.Yorks.* **S71** 51 F2
Carlton, *Stock.* **TS21** 62 E4
Carlton, *Suff.* **IP17** 35 H2
Carlton, *W.Yorks.* **WF3** 57 J7
Carlton Colville **NR33** 45 K6
Carlton Curlieu **LE8** 41 J6
Carlton Husthwaite **YO7** 57 K2
Carlton in Cleveland **TS9** 63 G6
Carlton in Lindrick **S81** 51 H4
Carlton Miniott **YO7** 57 J1
Carlton Scroop **NG32** 42 C1
Carlton-le-Moorland **LN5** 52 C7
Carlton-on-Trent **NG23** 52 B6
Carluke **ML8** 75 G5
Carlyon Bay **PL25** 4 A5
Carmacoup **ML11** 68 C1
Carmarthen (Caerfyrddin) **SA31** 17 H3
Carmel, *Carmar.* **SA14** 17 J3
Carmel, *Flints.* **CH8** 47 K5
Carmel, *Gwyn.* **LL54** 46 C7
Carmel, *I.o.A.* **LL77** 46 B4
Carmont **AB39** 91 G6
Carmore **IV25** 96 E2
Carmunnock **G76** 74 E5
Carmyle **G32** 74 E4
Carmyllie **DD11** 83 G3
Carn **PA48** 72 A5
Carn Brea **TR15** 2 D4
Carn Dearg **IV21** 94 D4
Carnaby **YO16** 59 H3
Carnach, *High.* **IV23** 95 G2
Carnach, *High.* **IV40** 87 G2
Carnassarie **PA31** 79 K7
Carnbee **KY10** 83 G7
Carnbo **KY13** 82 B7
Carnduncan **PA44** 72 A4
Carne **TR2** 3 G5
Carnforth **LA5** 55 H2
Carnhell Green **TR14** 2 D5
Carnichal **AB43** 99 H5
Carnmore **PA42** 72 B6
Carno **SY17** 37 J6
Carnoch, *High.* **IV6** 95 J6
Carnoch, *High.* **IV12** 97 F7
Carnoch, *High.* **IV4** 87 K1
Carnock **KY12** 75 J2
Carnon Downs **TR3** 2 E4
Carnousie **AB53** 98 E5
Carnoustie **DD7** 83 G4
Carnwath **ML11** 75 H6
Carnyorth **TR19** 2 A5
Carperby **DL8** 62 B7
Carr Shield **NE47** 61 K2
Carr Vale **S44** 51 G5
Carradale **PA28** 73 G7
Carragrich **HS3** 93 G2
Carrbridge **PH23** 89 G2
Carreglefn **LL68** 46 B4
Carrick, *Arg. & B.* **PA24** 73 K1
Carrick, *Arg. & B.* **PA31** 73 H2
Carrick, *Fife* **KY16** 83 F5
Carriden **EH51** 75 J2
Carrine **PA28** 66 A3
Carrington, *Gt.Man.* **M31** 49 G3
Carrington, *Lincs.* **PE22** 53 G7
Carrington, *Midloth.* **EH23** 76 B4
Carroch **DG7** 68 B4
Carrog **LL21** 38 A1
Carroglen **PH6** 81 J5
Carrol **KW9** 97 F1
Carron, *Arg. & B.* **PA31** 73 H1
Carron, *Falk.* **FK2** 75 G2
Carron, *Moray* **AB38** 97 K7
Carron Bridge **FK6** 75 F2
Carronbridge **DG3** 68 D4
Carronshore **FK2** 75 G2
Carrot **DD8** 83 F3
Carrutherstown **DG1** 69 G6
Carruthmuir **PA10** 74 B4
Carrville **DH1** 62 E2
Carry **PA21** 73 H4
Carsaig **PA70** 79 G5
Carscreugh **DG8** 64 C4
Carse **PA29** 73 F4
Carse of Ardesier **IV2** 97 F6
Carsegowan **DG8** 64 E5
Carseriggan **DG8** 64 D4
Carsethorn **DG2** 65 K5
Carsgoe **KW12** 105 G2
Carshalton **SM5** 23 F5
Carsington **DE4** 50 E7
Carsluith **DG8** 64 E5
Carsphairn **DG7** 67 K4
Carstairs **ML11** 75 H6
Carstairs Junction **ML11** 75 H6
Carswell Marsh **SN7** 21 G2
Carter's Clay **SO51** 10 E2
Carterton **OX18** 21 F1
Carterway Heads **DH8** 62 B1
Carthew **PL26** 4 A5
Carthorpe **DL8** 57 J1
Cartington **NE65** 71 F3
Cartmel **LA11** 55 G2
Cartmel Fell **LA11** 55 H1
Carway **SA17** 17 H4
Cascob **LD8** 28 B2
Cashel **G63** 74 C1
Cashlie **PH15** 81 F3
Cashmoor **DT11** 9 J3
CASNEWYDD (NEWPORT), *Newport* NP 19 G3
Cassencarie **DG8** 64 E5
Cassington **OX29** 31 F7
Cassop **DH6** 62 E3
Castell Gorfod **SA33** 17 F2
Castell Howell **SA44** 26 D4
Castell Newydd Emlyn (Newcastle Emlyn) **SA38** 26 C4
Castell-Nedd (Neath) **SA11** 18 A2
Castell-y-bwch **NP44** 19 F2
Castellau **CF38** 18 D3
Casterton **LA6** 56 B2
Castle Acre **PE32** 44 C4
Castle Ashby **NN7** 32 B3
Castle Bank **ST16** 40 B3
Castle Bolton **DL8** 62 B7
Castle Bromwich **B36** 40 D7
Castle Bytham **NG33** 42 C4
Castle Caereinion **SY21** 38 A5
Castle Camps **CB1** 33 K4
Castle Carrock **CA8** 61 G1
Castle Cary **BA7** 9 F1
Castle Combe **SN14** 20 B4
Castle Donington **DE74** 41 G3
Castle Douglas **DG7** 65 H4
Castle Eaton **SN6** 20 E2
Castle Eden **TS27** 63 F3
Castle End **CV8** 30 D1
Castle Frome **HR8** 29 F4
Castle Gresley **DE11** 40 E4

Castle Heaton

Castle Heaton **TD12** 77 H6
Castle Hedingham **CO9** 34 B5
Castle Hill **IP1** 35 F4
Castle Kennedy **DG9** 64 B5
Castle Leod **IV14** 96 B6
Castle Levan **PA19** 74 A3
Castle Madoc **LD3** 27 K5
Castle Morris **SA62** 16 C1
Castle O'er **DG13** 69 H4
Castle Rising **PE31** 44 A3
Castle Stuart **IV2** 96 E6
Castlebay (Bagh a' Chaisteil) **HS9** 84 B5
Castlebythe **SA62** 16 D2
Castlecary **G68** 75 F3
Castlecraig, *High.* **IV19** 97 F5
Castlecraig, *Sc.Bord.* **EH46** 75 K6
Castlefairn **DG3** 68 C5
Castleford **WF10** 57 K7
Castlemartin **SA71** 16 C5
Castlemilk, *D. & G.* **DG11** 69 G6
Castlemilk, *Glas.* **G45** 74 E5
Castlemorton **WR13** 29 G5
Castleside **DH8** 62 B2
Castlethorpe **MK19** 32 B4
Castleton, *Aber.* **AB45** 99 F5
Castleton, *Angus* **DD8** 82 E3
Castleton, *Arg. & B.* **PA31** 73 G2
Castleton, *Derbys.* **S33** 50 D4
Castleton, *Gt.Man.* **OL11** 49 H1
Castleton, *N.Yorks.* **YO21** 63 H6
Castleton, *Newport* **CF3** 19 F3
Castleton, *Sc.Bord.* **TD9** 70 A4
Castletown, *High.* **KW14** 105 G2
Castletown, *High.* **IV2** 96 E7
Castletown, *I.o.M.* **IM9** 54 B7
Castletown, *T. & W.* **SR5** 62 E1
Castleweary **TD9** 69 K3
Castlewigg **DG8** 64 E6
Caston **NR17** 44 D6
Castor **PE5** 42 E6
Castramont **DG7** 65 F4
Cat and Fiddle Inn **SK11** 50 C5
Catbrain **BS10** 19 J3
Catchall **TR20** 2 B6
Catcleugh **NE19** 70 C3
Catcliffe **S60** 51 G4
Catcott **TA7** 8 C1
Caterham **CR3** 23 G6
Catesby **NN11** 31 G3
Catfield **NR29** 45 H3
Catfirth **ZE2** 109 D7
Catford **SE6** 23 G4
Catforth **PR4** 55 H6
Cathedine **LD3** 28 A6
Catherington **PO8** 11 H3
Catherton **DY14** 29 F1
Catlow **BB10** 56 D6
Catlowdy **CA6** 69 K6
Catmore **RG20** 21 H4
Caton, *Devon* **TQ13** 5 H3
Caton, *Lancs.* **LA2** 55 J3
Cator Court **TQ13** 5 G3
Catrine **KA5** 67 K1
Catsfield **TN33** 14 C6
Catshill **B61** 29 J1
Cattadale **PA44** 72 B5
Cattal **YO26** 57 K4
Cattawade **CO11** 35 F5
Catterall **PR3** 55 J5
Catterick **DL10** 62 D7
Catterick Camp **DL9** 62 C7
Catterlen **CA11** 61 F3
Catterline **AB39** 91 G7
Catterton **LS24** 58 B5
Catthorpe **LE17** 31 G1
Cattistock **DT2** 8 E4
Catton, *N.Yorks.* **YO7** 57 J2
Catton, *Norf.* **NR6** 45 G4
Catton, *Northumb.* **NE47** 61 K1
Catton Hall **DE12** 40 E4
Catwick **HU17** 59 H5
Catworth **PE28** 32 D1
Caudworthy **PL15** 4 C1
Caulcott **OX25** 31 G6
Cauldcots **DD11** 83 H3
Cauldhame, *Stir.* **FK15** 81 K7
Cauldhame, *Stir.* **FK8** 74 E1
Cauldon **ST10** 40 C1
Cauldside **DG14** 69 K5
Caulkerbush **DG2** 65 K5
Caundle Marsh **DT9** 9 F3
Caunsall **DY11** 40 A7
Caunton **NG23** 51 K6
Causeway End, *D. & G.* **DG8** 64 E4
Causeway End, *Essex* **CM6** 33 K7
Causewayhead, *Cumb.* **CA7** 60 C1
Causewayhead, *Stir.* **FK9** 75 G1
Causey Park **NE61** 71 G4
Causeyend **AB23** 91 H3
Cautley **LA10** 61 H7
Cavendish **CO10** 34 C4
Cavenham **IP28** 34 B2
Cavens **DG2** 65 K5
Caversfield **OX27** 31 G6
Caversham **RG4** 22 A4
Caverswall **ST11** 40 B1
Cawdor **IV12** 97 F6
Cawkwell **LN11** 53 F5
Cawood **YO8** 58 B6
Cawsand **PL10** 4 E5
Cawston **NR10** 45 F3
Cawthorne **S75** 50 E2
Cawthorpe **PE10** 42 D3
Cawton **YO62** 58 C2
Caxton **CB3** 33 G3
Caxton Gibbet **CB3** 33 F3
Caynham **SY8** 28 E1
Caythorpe, *Lincs.* **NG32** 42 C1
Caythorpe, *Notts.* **NG14** 41 J1
Cayton **YO11** 59 G1
Ceallan **HS6** 92 D6
Ceann a' Bhàigh, *W.Isles* **HS3** 93 F3
Ceann a' Bhàigh, *W.Isles* **HS6** 92 C5
Ceann Loch Shiphoirt **HS2** 100 E6
Cearsiadar **HS2** 101 F5
Ceathramh Meadhanach **HS6** 92 C4
Cedig **SY10** 37 J3
Cefn Bycharn (Newbridge) **NP11** 19 F2
Cefn Cantref **LD3** 27 K6
Cefn Coch **LL15** 47 K7
Cefn Cribwr **CF32** 18 B3
Cefn Cross **CF32** 18 B3
Cefn Einion **SY9** 38 B7
Cefn Hengoed **CF82** 18 E2
Cefn-brith **LL21** 47 H7
Cefn-caer-Ferch **LL53** 36 D1
Cefn-coch **SY10** 38 A3
Cefn-coed-y-cymmer **CF48** 18 D1
Cefn-ddwysarn **LL23** 37 J2
Cefn-gorwydd **LD4** 27 J4
Cefn-gwyn **SY16** 38 A7
Cefn-mawr **LL14** 38 B1
Cefn-y-bedd **LL12** 48 C7
Cefn-y-pant **SA34** 16 E2
Cefndeuddwr **LL41** 37 G3
Cefneithin **SA14** 17 J3
Ceidio **LL71** 46 C4
Ceidio Fawr **LL53** 36 B2
Ceinewydd (New Quay) **SA45** 26 C3
Ceint **LL61** 46 C5
Cellan **SA48** 27 F4
Cellardyke **KY10** 83 G7
Cellarhead **ST9** 40 B1
Cemaes **LL67** 46 B3
Cemmaes **SY20** 37 H5
Cemmaes Road **SY20** (Glantwymyn) 37 H5
Cenarth **SA38** 26 B4
Cennin **LL54** 36 D1
Ceos **HS2** 101 F5
Ceres **KY15** 82 E6
Cerne Abbas **DT2** 9 F4
Cerney Wick **GL7** 20 D2
Cerrigceinwen **LL62** 46 C5
Cerrigydrudion **LL21** 37 J1
Cessford **TD5** 70 C1
Chaceley **GL19** 29 H5
Chacewater **TR4** 2 E4
Chackmore **MK18** 31 H5
Chacombe **OX17** 31 F4
Chad Valley **B15** 40 C7
Chadderton **OL9** 49 J2
Chaddesden **DE21** 41 F2
Chaddesley Corbett **DY10** 29 H1
Chaddleworth **RG20** 21 H4
Chadlington **OX7** 30 E6
Chadshunt **CV35** 30 E3
Chadwell **LE14** 42 A3
Chadwell St. Mary **RM16** 24 C4
Chadwick End **B93** 30 D1
Chaffcombe **TA20** 8 C3
Chagford **TQ13** 7 F7
Chailey **BN8** 13 G5
Chainhurst **TN12** 14 C3
Chalbury Common **BH21** 10 B4
Chaldon **CR3** 23 G6
Chaldon Herring or East Chaldon **DT2** 9 G6
Chale **PO38** 11 F7
Chale Green **PO38** 11 F7
Chalfont Common **SL9** 22 D2
Chalfont St. Giles **HP8** 22 C2
Chalfont St. Peter **SL9** 22 D2
Chalford **GL6** 20 B1
Chalgrove **OX44** 21 K2
Chalk **DA12** 24 C4
Challacombe **EX31** 6 E1
Challoch **DG8** 64 D4
Challock **TN25** 15 F2
Chalmington **DT2** 8 E4
Chalton, *Beds.* **LU4** 32 D6
Chalton, *Hants.* **PO8** 11 J3
Chalvington **BN27** 13 J6
Champany **EH49** 75 J3
Chandler's Cross **WD3** 22 D2
Chandler's Ford **SO53** 11 F2
Channerwick **ZE2** 109 D10
Chantry, *Som.* **BA11** 20 A7
Chantry, *Suff.* **IP2** 35 F4
Chapel **KY2** 76 A1
Chapel Allerton, *Som.* **BS26** 19 H6
Chapel Allerton, *W.Yorks.* **LS7** 57 J6
Chapel Amble **PL27** 3 G1
Chapel Brampton **NN6** 31 J2
Chapel Chorlton **ST5** 40 A2
Chapel Cross **TN21** 13 K4
Chapel End **CV10** 41 F6
Chapel Fields **CV5** 30 E1
Chapel Haddlesey **YO8** 58 B7
Chapel Hill, *Aber.* **AB42** 91 J1
Chapel Hill, *Lincs.* **LN4** 53 F7
Chapel Hill, *Mon.* **NP16** 19 J1
Chapel Lawn **SY7** 28 C1
Chapel of Garioch **AB51** 91 F2
Chapel Rossan **DG9** 64 B6
Chapel Row **RG7** 21 J5
Chapel St. Leonards **PE24** 53 J5
Chapel Stile **LA22** 60 E6
Chapel Town **TR8** 3 F3
Chapel-en-le-Frith **SK23** 50 C4
Chapel-le-Dale **LA6** 56 C2
Chapelbank **PH3** 82 B6
Chapeldonan **KA26** 67 F3
Chapelgate **PE12** 43 H3
Chapelhall **ML6** 75 F4
Chapelhill, *High.* **IV19** 97 F4
Chapelhill, *P. & K.* **PH1** 82 B4
Chapelhill, *P. & K.* **PH2** 82 D5
Chapelknowe **DG14** 69 J6
Chapelton, *Aber.* **AB39** 91 G6
Chapelton, *Angus* **DD11** 83 H3
Chapelton, *S.Lan.* **ML10** 74 E6
Chapeltown, *B'burn.* **BL7** 49 G1
Chapeltown, *Cumb.* **CA6** 69 K6
Chapeltown, *Moray* **AB37** 89 K2
Chapeltown, *S.Yorks.* **S35** 51 F3
Chapman's Well **PL15** 6 B6
Chapmanslade **BA13** 20 B7
Chapmore End **SG12** 33 G7
Chappel **CO6** 34 C6
Chard **TA20** 8 C4
Chard Junction **TA20** 8 C4
Chardstock **EX13** 8 C4
Charfield **GL12** 20 A2
Charing **TN27** 14 E3
Charing Heath **TN27** 14 E3
Charingworth **GL55** 30 C4
Charlbury **OX7** 30 E7
Charlcombe **BA1** 20 A5
Charlcutt **SN11** 20 C4
Charlecote **CV35** 30 D3
Charles **EX32** 6 E2
Charles Tye **IP14** 34 E3
Charlesfield **TD6** 70 A1
Charleshill **GU10** 22 B7
Charleston **DD8** 82 E3
Charlestown, *Aber.* **AB43** 99 J4
Charlestown, *Aberdeen* **AB12** 91 H4
Charlestown, *Cornw.* **PL25** 4 A5
Charlestown, *Dorset* **DT3** 9 F7
Charlestown, *Fife* **KY11** 75 J2
Charlestown, *High.* **IV21** 94 E4
Charlestown, *High.* **IV1** 96 D7
Charlestown of Aberlour **AB38** 97 K7
Charlesworth **SK13** 50 C3
Charlinch **TA5** 8 B1
Charlton, *Gt.Lon.* **SE7** 23 H4
Charlton, *Hants.* **SP10** 21 G7
Charlton, *Herts.* **SG5** 32 E6
Charlton, *Northants.* **OX17** 31 G5
Charlton, *Northumb.* **NE48** 70 D5
Charlton, *Oxon.* **OX12** 21 H3
Charlton, *Som.* **BA3** 19 K6
Charlton, *W.Suss.* **PO18** 12 B5
Charlton, *Wilts.* **SN16** 20 C3
Charlton, *Wilts.* **SN9** 20 E6
Charlton, *Wilts.* **SP7** 9 J2
Charlton, *Worcs.* **WR10** 30 B4
Charlton Abbots **GL54** 30 B6
Charlton Adam **TA11** 8 E2
Charlton Horethorne **DT9** 9 F2
Charlton Kings **GL52** 29 J6
Charlton Mackrell **TA11** 8 E2
Charlton Marshall **DT11** 9 H4
Charlton Musgrove **BA9** 9 G2
Charlton-All-Saints **SP5** 10 C2
Charlton-on-Otmoor **OX5** 31 G7
Charlwood **RH6** 23 F7
Charminster **DT2** 9 F5
Charmouth **DT6** 8 C5
Charndon **OX27** 31 H6
Charney Bassett **OX12** 21 G2
Charnock Richard **PR7** 48 E1
Charsfield **IP13** 35 G3
Chart Corner **ME17** 14 C3
Chart Sutton **ME17** 14 D3
Charter Alley **RG26** 21 K6
Charterhouse **BS40** 19 H6
Charterville Allotments **OX29** 30 E7
Chartham **CT4** 15 G2
Chartham Hatch **CT4** 15 F2
Chartridge **HP5** 22 C1
Charwelton **NN11** 31 G3
Chase End Street **HR8** 29 G5
Chase Terrace **WS7** 40 C4
Chasetown **WS7** 40 C5
Chastleton **GL56** 30 D6
Chasty **EX22** 6 B5
Chatburn **BB7** 56 C5
Chatcull **ST21** 39 G2
Chatham **ME4** 24 D5
Chathill **NE67** 71 G1
Chattenden **ME3** 24 D4
Chatteris **PE16** 43 G7
Chattisham **IP8** 34 E4
Chatto **TD5** 70 C2
Chatton **NE66** 71 F1
Chawleigh **EX18** 7 F4
Chawley **OX2** 21 H1
Chawston **MK44** 32 E3
Chawton **GU34** 11 J1
Cheadle, *Gt.Man.* **SK8** 49 H4
Cheadle, *Staffs.* **ST10** 40 C1
Cheadle Hulme **SK8** 49 H4
Cheam **SM3** 23 F5
Cheapside **SL5** 22 C5
Chearsley **HP18** 22 A1
Chebsey **ST21** 40 A3
Checkendon **RG8** 21 K3
Checkley, *Ches.* **CW5** 39 G1
Checkley, *Here.* **HR1** 28 E5
Checkley, *Staffs.* **ST10** 40 C2
Chedburgh **IP29** 34 B3
Cheddar **BS27** 19 H6
Cheddington **LU7** 32 C7
Cheddleton **ST13** 49 J7
Cheddon Fitzpaine **TA2** 8 B2
Chedglow **SN16** 20 C2
Chedgrave **NR14** 45 H6
Chedington **DT8** 8 D4
Chediston **IP19** 35 H1
Chedworth **GL54** 30 B7
Chedzoy **TA7** 8 C1
Cheeklaw **TD11** 77 F5
Cheesden **OL12** 49 H1
Cheeseman's Green **TN24** 15 F4
Cheetham Hill **M8** 49 H2
Cheldon **EX18** 7 F4
Chelford **SK11** 49 H5
Chellaston **DE73** 41 F2
Chelmarsh **WV16** 39 G7
Chelmondiston **IP9** 35 G5
Chelmorton **SK17** 50 D6
CHELMSFORD CM 24 **D1**
Chelsfield **BR6** 23 H5
Chelsham **CR6** 23 G6
Chelsworth **IP7** 34 D4
Cheltenham **GL52** 29 J6
Chelveston **NN9** 32 C2
Chelvey **BS48** 19 H5
Chelwood **BS39** 19 K5
Chelwood Gate **RH17** 13 H4
Chelworth **SN16** 20 C2
Cheney Longville **SY7** 38 D7
Chenies **WD3** 22 D2
Chepstow **NP16** 19 J2
Cherhill **SN11** 20 D4
Cherington, *Glos.* **GL8** 20 C2
Cherington, *Warks.* **CV36** 30 D5
Cheriton, *Devon* **EX35** 7 F1
Cheriton, *Hants.* **SO24** 11 G2
Cheriton, *Kent* **CT19** 15 H4
Cheriton, *Pembs.* **SA71** 16 C5
Cheriton, *Swan.* **SA3** 17 H5
Cheriton Bishop **EX6** 7 F6
Cheriton Cross **EX6** 7 F6
Cheriton Fitzpaine **EX17** 7 G5
Cherrington **TF6** 39 F4
Cherry Burton **HU17** 59 F5
Cherry Hinton **CB1** 33 H3
Cherry Willingham **LN3** 52 D5
Chertsey **KT16** 22 D5
Cheselbourne **DT2** 9 G5
Chesham **HP5** 22 C1
Chesham Bois **HP6** 22 C2
Cheshunt **EN8** 23 G1
Cheslyn Hay **WS6** 40 B5
Chessington **KT9** 22 E5
CHESTER CH 48 **D6**
Chester-le-Street **DH3** 62 D1
Chesterblade **BA4** 19 K7
Chesterfield, *Derbys.* **S40** 51 F5
Chesterfield, *Staffs.* **WS14** 40 D5
Chesters, *Sc.Bord.* **TD8** 70 B1
Chesters, *Sc.Bord.* **TD9** 70 B2
Chesterton, *Cambs.* **PE7** 42 E6
Chesterton, *Cambs.* **CB4** 33 H3
Chesterton, *Oxon.* **OX26** 31 G6
Chesterton, *Shrop.* **WV15** 39 G6
Chesterton, *Staffs.* **ST5** 40 A1
Chesterton Green **CV33** 30 E3
Chestfield **CT5** 25 H5
Cheswardine **TF9** 39 G3
Cheswick **TD15** 77 J6
Chetnole **DT9** 9 F4
Chettiscombe **EX16** 7 H4
Chettisham **CB6** 43 J7
Chettle **DT11** 9 J3
Chetton **WV16** 39 F6
Chetwode **MK18** 31 H6
Chetwynd Aston **TF10** 39 G4
Cheveley **CB8** 33 K2
Chevening **TN14** 23 H6
Cheverell's Green **AL3** 32 D7
Chevington **IP29** 34 B3
Chevington Drift **NE61** 71 H4
Chevithorne **EX16** 7 H4
Chew Magna **BS40** 19 J5
Chew Stoke **BS40** 19 J5
Chewton Keynsham **BS31** 19 K5
Chewton Mendip **BA3** 19 J6
Chicheley **MK16** 32 C4
Chichester **PO19** 12 B6
Chickerell **DT3** 9 F6
Chickering **IP21** 35 G1
Chicklade **SP3** 9 J1
Chickney **CM6** 33 J6
Chicksands **SG17** 32 E5
Chidden **PO7** 11 H3
Chiddingfold **GU8** 12 C3
Chiddingly **BN8** 13 J5
Chiddingstone **TN8** 23 H7
Chiddingstone Causeway **TN11** 23 J7
Chiddingstone Hoath **TN8** 23 H7
Chideock **DT6** 8 D5
Chidham **PO18** 11 J4
Chieveley **RG20** 21 H4
Chignall St. James **CM1** 24 C1
Chignall Smealy **CM1** 33 K7
Chigwell **IG7** 23 H2
Chigwell Row **IG7** 23 H2
Chilbolton **SO20** 21 G7
Chilcomb **SO21** 11 G2
Chilcombe **DT6** 8 E5
Chilcompton **BA3** 19 K6
Chilcote **DE12** 40 E4
Child Okeford **DT11** 9 H3
Childer Thornton **CH66** 48 C5
Childerditch **CM13** 24 C3
Childrey **OX12** 21 G3
Child's Ercall **TF9** 39 F3
Childswickham **WR12** 30 B5
Childwall **L16** 48 D4
Childwick Green **AL3** 32 E7
Chilfrome **DT2** 8 E5
Chilgrove **PO18** 12 B5
Chilham **CT4** 15 F2
Chillaton **PL16** 6 C7
Chillenden **CT3** 15 H2
Chillerton **PO30** 11 F6
Chillesford **IP12** 35 H3
Chillingham **NE66** 71 F1
Chillington, *Devon* **TQ7** 5 H6
Chillington, *Som.* **TA19** 8 C3
Chilmark **SP3** 9 J1
Chilson **OX7** 30 E7
Chilsworthy, *Cornw.* **PL18** 4 E3
Chilsworthy, *Devon* **EX22** 6 B5
Chilthorne Domer **BA22** 8 E3
Chilton, *Bucks.* **HP18** 31 H7
Chilton, *Dur.* **DL17** 62 D3
Chilton, *Oxon.* **OX11** 21 H3
Chilton Candover **SO24** 11 G1
Chilton Cantelo **BA22** 8 E2
Chilton Foliat **RG17** 21 G4
Chilton Polden **TA7** 8 C1
Chilton Street **CO10** 34 B4
Chilton Trinity **TA5** 8 B1
Chilvers Coton **CV10** 41 F6
Chilworth, *Hants.* **SO16** 11 F3
Chilworth, *Surr.* **GU4** 22 D7
Chimney **OX18** 21 G1
Chineham **RG24** 21 K6
Chingford **E4** 23 G2
Chinley **SK23** 50 C4
Chinley Head **SK23** 50 C4
Chinnor **OX39** 22 A1
Chipchase Castle **NE48** 70 D6
Chipley Park **TA21** 7 K3
Chipnall **TF9** 39 G2
Chippenham, *Cambs.* **CB7** 33 K2
Chippenham, *Wilts.* **SN15** 20 C4
Chipperfield **WD4** 22 D1
Chipping, *Herts.* **SG9** 33 G5
Chipping, *Lancs.* **PR3** 56 B5
Chipping Campden **GL55** 30 C5
Chipping Hill **CM8** 34 C7
Chipping Norton **OX7** 30 E6
Chipping Ongar **CM5** 23 J1
Chipping Sodbury **BS37** 20 A3
Chipping Warden **OX17** 31 F4
Chipstable **TA4** 7 J3
Chipstead, *Kent* **TN13** 23 H6
Chipstead, *Surr.* **CR5** 23 F6
Chirbury **SY15** 38 B6
Chirk **LL14** 38 B2
Chirmorrie **KA26** 64 C3
Chirnside **TD11** 77 G5
Chirnsidebridge **TD11** 77 G5
Chirton **SN10** 20 D6
Chisbury **SN8** 21 F5
Chiscan **PA28** 66 A2
Chiselborough **TA14** 8 D3
Chiseldon **SN4** 20 E3
Chislehampton **OX44** 21 J2
Chislehurst **BR7** 23 H4
Chislet **CT3** 25 J5
Chiswell Green **AL2** 22 E1
Chiswick **W4** 23 F4
Chisworth **SK13** 49 J3
Chithurst **GU31** 12 B4
Chittering **CB5** 33 H2
Chitterne **BA12** 20 C7
Chittlehamholt **EX37** 6 E3
Chittlehampton **EX37** 6 E3
Chittoe **SN15** 20 C5
Chivelstone **TQ7** 5 H7
Chobham **GU24** 22 C5
Choicelee **TD11** 77 F5
Cholderton **SP4** 21 F7
Cholesbury **HP23** 22 C1
Chollerton **NE46** 70 E6
Cholsey **OX10** 21 J3
Cholstrey **HR6** 28 D3
Cholwell, *B. & N.E.Som.* **BS39** 19 K6
Cholwell, *Devon* **PL19** 4 E3
Chop Gate **TS9** 63 G6
Chopwell **NE17** 62 C1
Chorley, *Ches.* **CW5** 48 E7
Chorley, *Lancs.* **PR7** 48 E1
Chorley, *Shrop.* **WV16** 39 F7
Chorley, *Staffs.* **WS13** 40 C4
Chorleywood **WD3** 22 D2
Chorlton **CW2** 49 G7
Chorlton Lane **SY14** 38 D1
Chorlton-cum-Hardy **M21** 49 H3
Chowley **CH3** 48 D7
Chrishall **SG8** 33 H5
Chrishall Grange **SG8** 33 H4
Chrisswell **PA16** 74 A3
Christchurch, *Cambs.* **PE14** 43 H6
Christchurch, *Dorset* **BH23** 10 C5

Dalballoch

Dalballoch **PH20** 88 D5
Dalbeattie **DG5** 65 J4
Dalblair **KA18** 68 B2
Dalbog **DD9** 90 D7
Dalbreck **IV28** 104 C7
Dalbury **DE65** 40 E2
Dalby **IM5** 54 B6
Dalcairnie **KA6** 67 J3
Dalchalloch **PH18** 81 J1
Dalchalm **KW9** 97 G1
Dalchenna **PA32** 80 B7
Dalchirach **AB37** 89 J1
Dalchork **IV27** 103 H7
Dalchreichart **IV63** 87 J3
Dalchruin **PH6** 81 J6
Dalcross **IV2** 96 E7
Dalderby **LN9** 53 F6
Daldownie **AB35** 89 K4
Dale, *Derbys.* **DE7** 41 G2
Dale, *Pembs.* **SA62** 16 B4
Dale Head **CA10** 60 F5
Dale of Walls **ZE2** 109 A7
Dale Park **BN18** 12 C6
Dalehouse **TS13** 63 J5
Dalelia **PH36** 79 J1
Daless **IV12** 89 F1
Dalestie **AB37** 89 J3
Dalfad **AB35** 90 B4
Dalganachan **KW12** 105 F4
Dalgarven **KA13** 74 A6
Dalgety Bay **KY11** 75 K2
Dalgig **KA18** 67 K2
Dalginross **PH6** 81 J5
Dalgonar **DG3** 68 C3
Dalguise **PH8** 82 A3
Dalhalvaig **KW13** 104 D3
Dalham **CB8** 34 B2
Daligan **G84** 74 B2
Dalivaddy **PA28** 66 A2
Daljarrock **KA26** 67 F5
Dalkeith **EH22** 76 B4
Dallas **IV36** 97 J6
Dallaschyle **IV12** 97 F7
Dallash **DG8** 64 E4
Dallinghoo **IP13** 35 G3
Dallington, *E.Suss.* **TN21** 13 K5
Dallington, *Northants.* **NN5** 31 J2
Dalmadilly **AB51** 91 F3
Dalmally **PA33** 80 C5
Dalmarnock **PH8** 82 A3
Dalmary **FK8** 74 D1
Dalmellington **KA6** 67 J3
Dalmeny **EH30** 75 K3
Dalmichy **IV27** 103 H7
Dalmigavie **IV13** 88 E3
Dalmore **IV17** 96 D5
Dalmunzie Hotel **PH10** 89 H7
Dalnabreck **PH36** 79 J1
Dalnacarn **PH10** 82 B1
Dalnaglar Castle **PH10** 82 C1
Dalnaha **PA63** 79 H5
Dalnahaitnach **PH23** 89 F3
Dalnamain **IV25** 96 E2
Dalnatrat **PA38** 80 A2
Dalnavie **IV17** 96 D4
Dalness **PH49** 80 C2
Dalnessie **IV27** 103 J7
Dalnigap **DG8** 64 B3
Dalqueich **KY13** 82 B7
Dalreoch **KA26** 67 F5
Dalriech **PH8** 81 J4
Dalroy **IV2** 96 E7
Dalrulzian **PH10** 82 C2
Dalry **KA24** 74 A6
Dalrymple **KA6** 67 H2
Dalserf **ML8** 75 F5
Dalshangan **DG7** 67 K5
Dalskairth **DG2** 65 K3
Dalston **CA5** 60 E1
Dalswinton **DG2** 68 E5
Daltomach **IV13** 88 E2
Dalton, *D. & G.* **DG11** 69 G6
Dalton, *Lancs.* **WN8** 48 D2
Dalton, *N.Yorks.* **DL11** 62 C6
Dalton, *N.Yorks.* **YO7** 57 K2
Dalton, *Northumb.* **NE20** 71 G6
Dalton, *Northumb.* **NE46** 62 A1
Dalton, *S.Yorks.* **S65** 51 G3
Dalton Piercy **TS27** 63 F3
Dalton-in-Furness **LA15** 55 F2
Dalton-le-Dale **SR7** 63 F2
Dalton-on-Tees **DL2** 62 D6
Daltot **PA31** 73 F2
Daltra **IV12** 97 G7
Dalveich **FK19** 81 H5
Dalvennan **KA19** 67 H2
Dalvourn **IV2** 88 D1
Dalwhinnie **PH19** 88 D6
Dalwood **EX13** 8 B4
Damerham **SP6** 10 C3
Damgate **NR13** 45 J5
Damnaglaur **DG9** 64 B7
Damside **PH3** 82 A6
Danbury **CM3** 24 D1
Danby **YO21** 63 J6
Danby Wiske **DL7** 62 E7
Dandaleith **AB38** 97 K7
Danderhall **EH22** 76 B4
Dane End **SG12** 33 G6
Dane Hills **LE3** 41 H5
Danebridge **SK11** 49 J6
Danehill **RH17** 13 H4
Danesmoor **S45** 51 G6
Danestone **AB22** 91 H3
Danskine **EH41** 76 D4
Darby Green **GU46** 22 B5
Darenth **DA2** 23 J4
Daresbury **WA4** 48 E4
Darfield **S73** 51 G2
Dargate **ME13** 25 G5
Dargues **NE19** 70 D4
Darite **PL14** 4 C4
Darlaston **WS10** 40 B6
Darley **HG3** 57 H4
Darley Dale **DE4** 50 E6
Darlingscott **CV36** 30 D4
DARLINGTON DL 62 D5
Darliston **SY13** 38 E2
Darlton **NG22** 51 K5
Darnabo **AB53** 99 F6
Darnall **S9** 51 F4
Darnconner **KA18** 67 K1
Darnford **AB31** 91 F5
Darngarroch **DG7** 65 G4
Darnick **TD6** 76 D7
Darowen **SY20** 37 H5
Darra **AB53** 99 F6
Darras Hall **NE20** 71 G6
Darrington **WF8** 51 G1
Darsham **IP17** 35 J2
Dartfield **AB43** 99 J5
DARTFORD DA 23 J4
Dartington **TQ9** 5 H4
Dartmeet **TQ13** 5 G3
Dartmouth **TQ6** 5 J5
Darton **S75** 51 F2
Darvel **KA17** 74 D7
Darwell **TN32** 14 C5
Darwen **BB3** 56 B7
Datchet **SL3** 22 C4
Datchworth **SG3** 33 F7
Datchworth Green **SG3** 33 F7
Daubhill **BL3** 49 G2
Daugh of Kinermony **AB38** 97 K7
Dauntsey **SN15** 20 C3
Dava **PH26** 89 H1
Davaar **PA28** 66 B2
Davan **AB34** 90 C4
Davenham **CW9** 49 F5
Daventry **NN11** 31 G2
Davidstow **PL32** 4 B2
Davington **DG13** 69 H3
Daviot, *Aber.* **AB51** 91 F2
Daviot, *High.* **IV2** 88 E1
Davoch of Grange **AB55** 98 C5
Dawley **TF4** 39 F5
Dawlish **EX7** 5 K3
Dawn **LL22** 47 G5
Daws Heath **SS7** 24 E3
Dawsmere **PE12** 43 H2
Daylesford **GL56** 30 D6
Ddol **CH7** 47 K5
Deadwaters **ML11** 75 F6
Deal **CT14** 15 J2
Deal Hall **CM0** 25 G2
Dean, *Cumb.* **CA14** 60 B4
Dean, *Devon* **TQ11** 5 H4
Dean, *Dorset* **SP5** 9 J3
Dean, *Hants.* **SO32** 11 G3
Dean, *Oxon.* **OX7** 30 E6
Dean, *Som.* **BA4** 19 K7
Dean Bank **DL17** 62 D3
Dean Prior **TQ11** 5 H4
Dean Row **SK9** 49 H4
Dean Street **ME15** 14 C2
Deanburnhaugh **TD9** 69 J2
Deane **RG25** 21 J7
Deanland **SP5** 9 J3
Deanscales **CA13** 60 B4
Deanshanger **MK19** 31 J4
Deanston **FK16** 81 J7
Dearham **CA15** 60 B3
Debach **IP13** 35 G3
Debate **DG11** 69 H5
Debden **CB11** 33 J5
Debden Green **CB11** 33 J5
Debenham **IP14** 35 F2
Dechmont **EH52** 75 J3
Deddington **OX15** 31 F5
Dedham **CO7** 34 E5
Deecastle **AB34** 90 C5
Deene **NN17** 42 C6
Deenethorpe **NN17** 42 C6
Deepcar **S36** 50 E3
Deepcut **GU16** 22 C6
Deepdale, *Cumb.* **LA10** 56 C1
Deepdale, *N.Yorks.* **BD23** 56 D2
Deeping Gate **PE6** 42 E5
Deeping St. James **PE6** 42 E5
Deeping St. Nicholas **PE11** 43 F4
Deerhill **AB55** 98 C5
Deerhurst **GL19** 29 H6
Defford **WR8** 29 J4
Defynnog **LD3** 27 J6
Deganwy **LL31** 47 F5
Degnish **PA34** 79 J6
Deighton, *N.Yorks.* **DL6** 62 E6
Deighton, *York* **YO19** 58 C5
Deiniolen **LL55** 46 D6
Delabole **PL33** 4 A2
Delamere **CW8** 48 E6
Delavorar **AB37** 89 J3
Delfrigs **AB41** 91 H2
Dell Lodge **PH25** 89 H3
Delliefure **PH26** 89 H1
Delnabo **AB37** 89 J3
Delny **IV18** 96 E4
Delph **OL3** 49 J2
Delphorie **AB33** 90 C3
Delves **DH8** 62 C2
Delvine **PH1** 82 C3
Dembleby **NG34** 42 D2
Denaby **DN12** 51 G3
Denaby Main **DN12** 51 G3
Denbigh (Dinbych) **LL16** 47 J6
Denbury **TQ12** 5 J4
Denby **DE5** 41 F1
Denby Dale **HD8** 50 E2
Denchworth **OX12** 21 G2
Dendron **LA13** 55 F2
Denend **AB54** 90 D1
Denford **NN14** 32 C1
Dengie **CM0** 25 F1
Denham, *Bucks.* **UB9** 22 D3
Denham, *Suff.* **IP21** 35 F1
Denham, *Suff.* **IP29** 34 B2
Denham Green **UB9** 22 D3
Denhead, *Aber.* **AB42** 99 H5
Denhead, *Aber.* **AB51** 91 F3
Denhead, *Angus* **DD11** 83 G3
Denhead, *Dundee* **DD2** 82 E4
Denhead, *Fife* **KY16** 83 F6
Denholm **TD9** 70 A2
Denholme **BD13** 57 F6
Denholme Clough **BD13** 57 F6
Denio **LL53** 36 C2
Denmead **PO7** 11 H3
Denmill **AB51** 91 G3
Denmoss **AB54** 98 E6
Dennington **IP13** 35 G2
Denny **FK6** 75 G2
Dennyloanhead **FK4** 75 G2
Denshaw **OL3** 49 J1
Denside **AB31** 91 G5
Densole **CT18** 15 H3
Denston **CB8** 34 B3
Denstone **ST14** 40 C1
Dent **LA10** 56 C1
Denton, *Cambs.* **PE7** 42 E7
Denton, *Darl.* **DL2** 62 D5
Denton, *E.Suss.* **BN9** 13 H6
Denton, *Gt.Man.* **M34** 49 J3
Denton, *Kent* **CT4** 15 H3
Denton, *Lincs.* **NG32** 42 B2
Denton, *N.Yorks.* **LS29** 57 G5
Denton, *Norf.* **IP20** 45 G7
Denton, *Northants.* **NN7** 32 B3
Denton, *Oxon.* **OX44** 21 J1
Denver **PE38** 44 A5
Denvilles **PO9** 11 J4
Denwick **NE66** 71 H2
Deopham **NR18** 44 E5
Deopham Green **NR18** 44 E6
Depden **IP29** 34 B3
Deptford, *Gt.Lon.* **SE8** 23 G4
Deptford, *Wilts.* **BA12** 10 B1
DERBY DE 41 F2
Derbyhaven **IM9** 54 B7
Dererach **PA70** 79 G5
Deri **CF81** 18 E1
Derringstone **CT4** 15 G3
Derrington **ST18** 40 A3
Derry **FK19** 81 H5
Derry Hill **SN11** 20 C4
Derrythorpe **DN17** 52 B2
Dersingham **PE31** 44 A2
Dervaig **PA75** 79 F2
Derwen **LL21** 47 J7
Derwenlas **SY20** 37 G6
Derwydd **SA18** 17 K3
Derybruich **PA21** 73 H3
Desborough **NN14** 42 B7
Desford **LE9** 41 G5
Detchant **NE70** 77 J7
Detling **ME14** 14 C2
Deuddwr **SY22** 38 B4
Deunant **LL16** 47 H6
Deuxhill **WV16** 39 F7
Devauden **NP16** 19 H2
Devil's Bridge (Pontarfynach) **SY23** 27 G1
Devizes **SN10** 20 D5
Devonport **PL1** 4 E5
Devonside **FK13** 75 H1
Devoran **TR3** 2 E5
Dewar **EH38** 76 B6
Dewlish **DT2** 9 G5
Dewsall Court **HR2** 28 D5
Dewsbury **WF12** 57 H7
Dhoon **IM7** 54 D5
Dhoor **IM7** 54 D4
Dhowin **IM7** 54 D3
Dhuhallow **IV2** 88 C2
Dial Post **RH13** 12 E5
Dibden **SO45** 11 F4
Dibden Purlieu **SO45** 11 F4
Dickleburgh **IP21** 45 F7
Didbrook **GL54** 30 B5
Didcot **OX11** 21 J3
Diddington **PE19** 32 E2
Diddlebury **SY7** 38 E7
Didley **HR2** 28 D5
Didling **GU29** 12 B5
Didmarton **GL9** 20 B3
Didsbury **M20** 49 H3
Didworthy **TQ10** 5 G4
Digby **LN4** 52 D7
Digg **IV51** 93 K5
Diggle **OL3** 50 C2
Digmoor **WN8** 48 D2
Digswell **AL8** 33 F7
Dihewyd **SA48** 26 D3
Dildawn **DG7** 65 H5
Dilham **NR28** 45 H3
Dilhorne **ST10** 40 B1
Dilston **NE45** 70 E7
Dilton Marsh **BA13** 20 B6
Dilwyn **HR4** 28 D3
Dilwyn Common **HR4** 28 D3
Dinas, *Carmar.* **SA33** 17 F1
Dinas, *Gwyn.* **LL54** 46 C7
Dinas, *Gwyn.* **LL53** 36 B2
Dinas, *Pembs.* **SA42** 16 D1
Dinas Dinlle **LL54** 46 C7
Dinas Powys **CF64** 18 E4
Dinas-Mawddwy **SY20** 37 H4
Dinbych (Denbigh) **LL16** 47 J6
Dinbych-y-Pysgod (Tenby) **SA70** 16 E4
Dinder **BA5** 19 J7
Dinedor **HR2** 28 E5
Dingestow **NP25** 28 D7
Dingley **LE16** 42 A7
Dingwall **IV15** 96 C6
Dinlabyre **TD9** 70 A4
Dinnet **AB34** 90 C5
Dinnington, *S.Yorks.* **S25** 51 H4
Dinnington, *Som.* **TA17** 8 D3
Dinnington, *T. & W.* **NE13** 71 H6
Dinorwic **LL55** 46 D6
Dinton, *Bucks.* **HP17** 31 J7
Dinton, *Wilts.* **SP3** 10 B1
Dinvin **DG9** 64 A5
Dinwoodie Mains **DG11** 69 G4
Dinworthy **EX22** 6 B4
Dippen **PA28** 73 F7
Dippenhall **GU10** 22 B7
Dippin **KA27** 66 E1
Dipple, *Moray* **IV32** 98 B5
Dipple, *S.Ayr.* **KA26** 67 G3
Diptford **TQ9** 5 H5
Dipton **DH9** 62 C1
Dirdhu **PH26** 89 H2
Dirleton **EH39** 76 D2
Discoed **LD8** 28 B2
Diseworth **DE74** 41 G3
Dishes **KW17** 106 F5
Dishforth **YO7** 57 J2
Dishig **PA68** 79 F4
Disley **SK12** 49 J4
Diss **IP22** 45 F7
Disserth **LD1** 27 K3
Distington **CA14** 60 B4
Ditcheat **BA4** 9 F1
Ditchingham **NR35** 45 H6
Ditchley **OX29** 30 E6
Ditchling **BN6** 13 G5
Ditteridge **SN14** 20 B5
Dittisham **TQ6** 5 J5
Ditton, *Halton* **WA8** 48 D4
Ditton, *Kent* **ME20** 14 C2
Ditton Green **CB8** 33 K3
Ditton Priors **WV16** 39 F7
Dixton, *Glos.* **GL20** 29 J5
Dixton, *Mon.* **NP25** 28 E7
Dobwalls **PL14** 4 C4
Doc Penfro (Pembroke Dock) **SA72** 16 C4
Doccombe **TQ13** 7 F7
Dochgarroch **IV3** 96 D7
Docking **PE31** 44 B2
Docklow **HR6** 28 E3
Dockray **CA11** 60 E4
Doddinghurst **CM15** 23 J2
Doddington, *Cambs.* **PE15** 43 G6
Doddington, *Kent* **ME9** 14 E2
Doddington, *Lincs.* **LN6** 52 C5
Doddington, *Northumb.* **NE71** 77 H7
Doddington, *Shrop.* **DY14** 29 F1
Doddiscombsleigh **EX6** 7 G7
Dodford, *Northants.* **NN7** 31 H2
Dodford, *Worcs.* **B61** 29 J1
Dodington, *S.Glos.* **BS37** 20 A3
Dodington, *Som.* **TA5** 7 K1
Dodington Ash **BS37** 20 A4
Dodleston **CH4** 48 C6
Dodworth **S75** 51 F2
Doe Lea **S44** 51 G6
Dog Village **EX5** 7 H6
Dogdyke **LN4** 53 F7
Dogmersfield **RG27** 22 A6
Dol Fawr **SY19** 37 H5
Dol-gran **SA39** 17 H1
Dolanog **SY21** 37 K4
Dolau **LD1** 28 A2
Dolbenmaen **LL49** 36 E1
Dolfach **SY18** 27 J1
Dolfor **SY16** 38 A7
Dolgarreg **SA20** 27 G5
Dolgarrog **LL32** 47 F6
Dolgellau **LL40** 37 G4
Dolgoch **LL36** 37 F5
Doll **KW9** 97 F1
Dollar **FK14** 75 H1
Dollarbeg **FK14** 75 H1
Dolleycanney **HR5** 28 A4
Dolphinholme **LA2** 55 J4
Dolphinton **EH46** 75 K6
Dolton **EX19** 6 D4
Dolwen, *Conwy* **LL22** 47 G5
Dolwen, *Powys* **SY21** 37 J5
Dolwyddelan **LL25** 47 F7
Dolybont **SY24** 37 F7
Dolyhir **LD8** 28 B3
Dolywern **LL20** 38 B2
Domgay **SY22** 38 B4
DONCASTER DN 51 H2
Donhead St. Andrew **SP7** 9 J2
Donhead St. Mary **SP7** 9 J2
Donibristle **KY4** 75 K2
Doniford **TA23** 7 J1
Donington **PE11** 43 F2
Donington le Heath **LE67** 41 G4
Donington on Bain **LN11** 53 F4
Donisthorpe **DE12** 41 F4
Donkey Town **GU24** 22 C5
Donnington, *Glos.* **GL56** 30 C6
Donnington, *Here.* **HR8** 29 G5
Donnington, *Shrop.* **SY5** 38 E5
Donnington, *Tel. & W.* **TF2** 39 G4
Donnington, *W.Berks.* **RG14** 21 H5
Donnington, *W.Suss.* **PO20** 12 B6
Donyatt **TA19** 8 C3
DORCHESTER, *Dorset* DT 9 F5
Dorchester, *Oxon.* **OX10** 21 J2
Dordon **B78** 40 E5
Dore **S17** 51 F4
Dores **IV2** 88 C1
Dorket Head **NG5** 41 H1
Dorking **RH4** 22 E7
Dormans Park **RH19** 23 G7
Dormansland **RH7** 23 H7
Dormanstown **TS10** 63 G4
Dormington **HR1** 28 E4
Dorney **SL4** 22 C4
Dornie **IV40** 86 E2
Dornoch **IV25** 96 E3
Dornock **DG12** 69 H7
Dorrery **KW12** 105 F3
Dorridge **B93** 30 C1
Dorrington, *Lincs.* **LN4** 52 D7
Dorrington, *Shrop.* **SY5** 38 D5
Dorsell **AB33** 90 D3
Dorsington **CV37** 30 C3
Dorstone **HR3** 28 C4
Dorton **HP18** 31 H7
Dorusduain **IV40** 87 F2
Dosthill **B77** 40 E5
Dotland **NE46** 62 A1
Dottery **DT6** 8 D5
Doublebois **PL14** 4 B4
Dougalston **G62** 74 D3
Dougarie **KA27** 73 G7
Doughton **GL8** 20 B2
Douglas, *I.o.M.* **IM1** 54 C6
Douglas, *S.Lan.* **ML11** 75 G7
Douglas and Angus **DD5** 83 F4
Douglas Hall **DG5** 65 J5
Douglas Hill **LL57** 46 E6
Douglas Water **ML11** 75 G7
Douglastown **DD8** 83 F3
Doulting **BA4** 19 K7
Dounby **KW17** 106 B5
Doune, *Arg. & B.* **FK17** 80 E6
Doune, *Arg. & B.* **G83** 74 B1
Doune, *High.* **IV24** 96 B1
Doune, *High.* **PH22** 89 F3
Doune, *Stir.* **FK16** 81 J7
Doune Park **AB45** 99 F4
Douneside **AB34** 90 C4
Dounie, *High.* **IV24** 96 C2
Dounie, *High.* **IV19** 96 D3
Dounreay **KW14** 104 E2
Dousland **PL20** 5 F4
Dovaston **SY10** 38 C3
Dove Holes **SK17** 50 C5
Dovenby **CA13** 60 B3
Dover **CT16** 15 J3
Dovercourt **CO12** 35 G6
Doverdale **WR9** 29 H2
Doveridge **DE6** 40 D2
Doversgreen **RH2** 23 F7
Dowally **PH9** 82 B3
Dowdeswell **GL54** 30 B6
Dowhill **KA26** 67 G3
Dowland **EX19** 6 D4
Dowlands **DT7** 8 B5
Dowlish Wake **TA19** 8 C3
Down Ampney **GL7** 20 E2
Down End **TA6** 19 G7
Down Field **CB7** 33 J1
Down Hatherley **GL2** 29 H6
Down St. Mary **EX17** 7 F5
Down Thomas **PL9** 5 F6
Downderry **PL11** 4 D5
Downe **BR6** 23 H5
Downend, *I.o.W.* **PO30** 11 G6
Downend, *S.Glos.* **BS16** 19 K4
Downend, *W.Berks.* **RG20** 21 H4
Downfield **DD3** 82 E4
Downgate **PL17** 4 D3
Downham, *Essex* **CM11** 24 D2
Downham, *Lancs.* **BB7** 56 C5
Downham, *Northumb.* **TD12** 77 G7
Downham Market **PE38** 44 A5
Downhead, *Cornw.* **PL15** 4 C2
Downhead, *Som.* **BA4** 19 K7
Downholland Cross **L39** 48 C2
Downholme **DL11** 62 C7
Downies **AB12** 91 H5
Downing **CH8** 47 K5
Downley **HP13** 22 B2
Downside, *N.Som.* **BS48** 19 H5
Downside, *Som.* **BA4** 19 K7
Downside, *Surr.* **KT11** 22 E6
Downton, *Devon* **EX20** 6 D7
Downton, *Devon* **TQ6** 5 J5
Downton, *Hants.* **SO41** 10 D5
Downton, *Wilts.* **SP5** 10 C2
Downton on the Rock **SY8** 28 D1
Dowsby **PE10** 42 E2
Dowthwaitehead **CA11** 60 E4

East Learney

Doynton BS30 20 A4
Draethen NP10 19 F3
Draffan ML11 75 F6
Drakeland Corner PL7 5 F5
Drakes Broughton WR10 29 J4
Drakes Cross B47 30 B1
Drambuie DG4 68 C2
Draughton, N.Yorks. BD23 57 F4
Draughton, Northants. NN6 31 J1
Drax YO8 58 C7
Draycote CV23 31 F1
Draycott, Derbys. DE72 41 G2
Draycott, Glos. GL56 30 C5
Draycott, Som. BS27 19 H6
Draycott, Worcs. WR5 29 H4
Draycott in the Clay DE6 40 D3
Draycott in the Moors ST10 40 B2
Drayton, Leics. LE16 42 B6
Drayton, Lincs. PE20 43 F2
Drayton, Norf. NR8 45 F4
Drayton, Oxon. OX15 31 F4
Drayton, Oxon. OX14 21 H2
Drayton, Ports. PO6 11 H4
Drayton, Som. TA10 8 D2
Drayton, Worcs. DY9 29 J1
Drayton Bassett B78 40 D5
Drayton Beauchamp HP22 32 C7
Drayton Parslow MK17 32 B6
Drayton St. Leonard OX10 21 J2
Dre-fach SA40 26 E4
Drebley BD23 57 F4
Dreemskerry IM7 54 D4
Dreenhill SA62 16 C3
Drefach, Carmar. SA44 17 G1
Drefach, Carmar. SA14 17 J3
Dreghorn KA11 74 B7
Drellingore CT18 15 H3
Drem EH39 76 D3
Drewsteignton EX6 7 F6
Driby LN13 53 G5
Driffield GL7 20 D2
Drigg CA19 60 B7
Drighlington BD11 57 H7
Drimfern PA32 80 B6
Drimlee PA32 80 C6
Drimnin PA34 79 G2
Drimore HS8 84 C1
Drimpton DT8 8 D4
Drimsynie PA24 80 C7
Drimvore PA31 73 G1
Drinan IV49 86 B3
Drinkstone IP30 34 D2
Drinkstone Green IP30 34 D3
Drishaig PA32 80 C6
Drissaig PA35 80 A6
Drointon ST18 40 C3
Droitwich WR9 29 H2
Dron PH2 82 C6
Dronfield S18 51 F5
Dronfield Woodhouse S18 51 F5
Drongan KA6 67 J2
Dronley DD2 82 E4
Dropmore SL1 22 C3
Droxford SO32 11 H3
Droylsden M43 49 J3
Druid LL21 37 K1
Druidston SA62 16 B3
Druimarbin PH33 80 B1
Druimavuic PA38 80 B3
Druimdrishaig PA31 73 F3
Druimindarroch PH39 86 C6
Druimkinnerras IV4 96 B7
Drum, Arg. & B. PA21 73 H3
Drum, P. & K. KY13 82 B7
Drumachloy PA20 73 J4
Drumbeg IV27 102 D5
Drumblade AB54 98 D6
Drumblair AB54 98 E6
Drumbuie IV40 86 D1
Drumburgh CA7 60 D1
Drumchapel G15 74 D3
Drumchardine IV5 96 C7
Drumchork IV22 94 E3
Drumclog ML10 74 E7
Drumdelgie AB54 98 C6
Drumderfit IV1 96 D6
Drumeldrie KY8 83 F7
Drumelzier ML12 75 K7
Drumfearn IV43 86 C3
Drumfern PH33 87 F7
Drumgarve PA28 66 B1
Drumgley DD8 83 F3
Drumguish PH21 88 E5
Drumhead AB31 90 E5
Drumin AB37 89 J1
Drumine IV2 96 E6
Drumjohn DG7 67 K4
Drumlamford Ho. KA26 64 C3
Drumlasie AB31 90 E4
Drumlemble PA28 66 A2
Drumlithie AB39 91 F6
Drummond, High. IV16 96 D5
Drummond, Stir. FK17 81 H7
Drummore DG9 64 B7
Drummuir Castle AB55 98 B6
Drumnadrochit IV63 88 C1
Drumnagorrach AB55 98 D5
Drumnatorran PH36 79 K1
Drumoak AB31 91 F5
Drumore PA28 66 B1
Drumour PH8 82 A3
Drumrash DG7 65 G3
Drumrunie IV26 95 H1
Drums AB41 91 H2
Drumsturdy DD5 83 F4
Drumuie IV51 93 K7
Drumuillie PH24 89 G2
Drumvaich FK17 81 H7
Drumwhindle AB41 91 H1
Drumwhirn DG7 68 C5
Drunkendub DD11 83 H3
Drury CH7 48 B6
Dry Doddington NG23 42 B1
Dry Drayton CB3 33 G2
Dry Harbour IV40 94 C6
Dry Sandford OX13 21 H2
Dry Street SS16 24 C3
Drybeck CA16 61 H5
Drybridge, Moray AB56 98 C4
Drybridge, N.Ayr. KA11 74 B7
Drybrook GL17 29 F7
Drygrange TD6 76 D7
Dryhope TD7 69 H1
Drymen G63 74 C2
Drymuir AB42 99 H6
Drynoch IV47 85 K1
Dryslwyn SA32 17 J2
Dryton SY5 38 E5
Duachy PA34 79 K5
Dubford AB45 99 F4
Dubhchladach PA29 73 G4
Dubheads PH7 82 A5
Dubton DD8 83 G2
Duchal PA13 74 B4
Duchally IV27 103 F7
Duchray FK8 74 C1
Duck End CM6 33 K6
Duckington SY14 48 D7
Ducklington OX29 21 G1
Duck's Cross MK44 32 E3
Duddenhoe End CB11 33 H5
Duddingston EH15 76 A3
Duddington PE9 42 C5
Duddleswell TN22 13 H4
Duddo TD15 77 H6
Duddon CW6 48 E6
Duddon Bridge LA18 54 E1
Dudleston Heath SY12 38 C2
Dudley, T. & W. NE23 71 H6
DUDLEY, W.Mid. DY 40 B6
Dudley Hill BD4 57 G6
Dudley Port DY4 40 B6
Dudsbury BH22 10 B5
Duffield DE56 41 F1
Duffryn SA13 18 B2
Dufftown AB55 98 B6
Duffus IV30 97 J5
Dufton CA16 61 H4
Duggleby YO17 58 E3
Duiar PH26 89 J1
Duible KW8 104 E6
Duiletter PA33 80 C5
Duinish PH18 81 H1
Duirinish IV40 86 D1
Duisdealmor IV43 86 D3
Duisky PH33 87 G7
Dukestown NP22 28 A7
Dukinfield SK16 49 J3
Dulas LL70 46 C4
Dulax AB36 90 B3
Dulcote BA5 19 J7
Dulford EX15 7 J5
Dull PH15 81 K3
Dullatur G68 75 F3
Dullingham CB8 33 K3
Dulnain Bridge PH26 89 G2
Duloe, Beds. PE19 32 E2
Duloe, Cornw. PL14 4 C5
Dulsie IV12 97 G7
Dulverton TA22 7 H3
Dulwich SE21 23 G4
Dumbarton G82 74 C3
Dumbleton WR11 30 B5
Dumcrieff DG10 69 G3
Dumeath AB54 90 C1
Dumfin G84 74 B2
DUMFRIES DG 65 K3
Dumgoyne G63 74 D2
Dummer RG25 21 J7
Dun DD10 83 H2
Dunach PA34 79 K5
Dunalastair PH16 81 J2
Dunan, Arg. & B. PA23 73 K3
Dunan, High. IV49 86 B2
Dunans PA22 73 J1
Dunball TA6 19 G7
Dunbar EH42 76 E3
Dunbeath KW6 105 G6
Dunbeg PA37 79 K4
Dunblane FK15 81 J7
Dunbog KY14 82 D6
Duncanston, Aber. AB52 90 D2
Duncanston, High. IV7 96 C6
Dunchideock EX6 7 G7
Dunchurch CV22 31 F1
Duncote NN12 31 H3
Duncow DG1 68 E5
Duncraggan FK17 81 G7
Duncrievie PH2 82 C7
Duncroist FK21 81 G4
Duncrub PH2 82 B6
Duncryne G83 74 C2
Duncton GU28 12 C5
DUNDEE DD 83 F4
Dundee Airport DD2 82 E5
Dundon TA11 8 D1
Dundonald KA2 74 B7
Dundonnell IV23 95 G3
Dundraw CA7 60 D2
Dundreggan IV63 87 K3
Dundrennan DG6 65 H6
Dundry BS41 19 J5
Dunearn KY3 76 A2
Dunecht AB32 91 F4
Dunfermline KY12 75 J2
Dunfield GL7 20 E2
Dunford Bridge S36 50 D2
Dungavel ML10 74 E7
Dunham NG22 52 B5
Dunham Town WA14 49 G4
Dunham-on-the-Hill WA6 48 D5
Dunhampton DY13 29 H2
Dunholme LN2 52 D5
Dunino KY16 83 G6
Dunipace FK6 75 G2
Dunira PH6 81 J5
Dunkeld PH8 82 B3
Dunkerton BA2 20 A6
Dunkeswell EX14 7 K5
Dunkeswick LS17 57 J5
Dunkirk ME13 15 F2
Dunk's Green TN11 23 K6
Dunlappie DD9 83 G1
Dunley DY13 29 G2
Dunlop KA3 74 C6
Dunloskin PA23 73 K3
Dunmere PL31 4 A4
Dunmore, Arg. & B. PA29 73 F4
Dunmore, Falk. FK2 75 G2
Dunn KW1 105 G3
Dunnabie DG11 69 H5
Dunnet KW14 105 H1
Dunnichen DD8 83 G3
Dunning PH2 82 B6
Dunnington, E.Riding YO25 59 H4
Dunnington, Warks. B49 30 B3
Dunnington, York YO19 58 C4
Dunnockshaw BB4 56 D7
Dunoon PA23 73 K3
Dunragit DG9 64 B5
Dunrostan PA31 73 F2
Duns TD11 77 F5
Duns Tew OX25 31 F6
Dunsby PE10 42 E3
Dunscore DG2 68 D5
Dunscroft DN7 51 J2
Dunsdale TS14 63 H5
Dunsden Green RG4 22 A4
Dunsfold GU8 12 D3
Dunsford EX6 7 G7
Dunshelt KY14 82 D6
Dunsinnan PH2 82 C4
Dunsland Cross EX22 6 C5
Dunsley YO21 63 K5
Dunsmore HP22 22 B1
Dunsop Bridge BB7 56 B4
Dunstable LU6 32 D6
Dunstall DE13 40 D3
Dunstall Green CB8 34 B2
Dunstan NE66 71 H1
Dunster TA24 7 H1
Dunston, Lincs. LN4 52 D6
Dunston, Norf. NR14 45 G5
Dunston, Staffs. ST18 40 B4
Dunston, T. & W. NE11 71 H7
Dunstone, Devon TQ13 5 H3
Dunstone, Devon PL8 5 F5
Dunstone, Devon TQ7 5 H6
Dunsville DN7 51 J2
Dunswell HU6 59 G6
Dunsyre ML11 75 J6
Dunterton PL19 4 D3
Duntisbourne Abbots GL7 20 C1
Duntisbourne Leer GL7 20 C1
Duntisbourne Rouse GL7 20 C1
Duntish DT2 9 F4
Duntocher G81 74 C3
Dunton, Beds. SG18 33 F4
Dunton, Bucks. MK18 32 B6
Dunton, Norf. NR21 44 C2
Dunton Bassett LE17 41 H6
Dunton Green TN13 23 J6
Dunton Wayletts CM13 24 C3
Duntulm IV51 93 K4
Dunure KA7 67 G2
Dunure Mains KA7 67 G2
Dunvant SA2 17 J5
Dunvegan IV55 93 H7
Dunwich IP17 35 J1
Dura KY15 83 F6
Durdar CA2 60 F1
Durgates TN5 13 K3
DURHAM DH 62 D2
Durinemast PA34 79 H2
Durisdeer DG3 68 D3
Durleigh TA5 8 B1
Durley, Hants. SO32 11 G3
Durley, Wilts. SN8 21 F5
Durnamuck IV23 95 G2
Durness IV27 103 F2
Durno AB51 91 F2
Duror PA38 80 A2
Durran, Arg. & B. PA33 80 A7
Durran, High. KW14 105 G2
Durrington, W.Suss. BN13 12 E6
Durrington, Wilts. SP4 20 E7
Dursley GL11 20 A2
Durston TA3 8 B2
Durweston DT11 9 H4
Dury ZE2 109 D6
Duston NN5 31 J2
Duthil PH23 89 G2
Dutlas LD7 28 B1
Duton Hill CM6 33 K6
Dutton WA4 48 E5
Duxford CB2 33 H4
Dwygyfylchi LL34 47 F5
Dwyran LL61 46 C6
Dyce AB21 91 G3
Dyfatty SA16 17 H4
Dyffryn, Bridgend CF34 18 B2
Dyffryn (Valley), I.o.A. LL65 46 A5
Dyffryn, Pembs. SA64 16 C1
Dyffryn Ardudwy LL44 36 E3
Dyffryn Castell SY23 37 G7
Dyffryn Ceidrych SA19 27 G6
Dyffryn Cellwen SA10 27 H7
Dyke, Devon EX39 6 B3
Dyke, Lincs. PE10 42 E3
Dyke, Moray IV36 97 G6
Dykehead, Angus DD8 82 E1
Dykehead, N.Lan. ML7 75 G5
Dykehead, Stir. FK8 74 D1
Dykelands AB30 83 J1
Dykends PH11 82 D2
Dykeside AB53 99 F6
Dylife SY19 37 H6
Dymchurch TN29 15 F5
Dymock GL18 29 G5
Dyrham BS30 20 A4
Dysart KY1 76 B1
Dyserth LL18 47 J5

E

Eadar dha Fhadhail HS2 100 C4
Eagland Hill PR3 55 H5
Eagle LN6 52 B6
Eaglescliffe TS16 63 F5
Eaglesfield, Cumb. CA13 60 B4
Eaglesfield, D. & G. DG11 69 H6
Eaglesham G76 74 D5
Eaglethorpe PE8 42 D6
Eagley BL1 49 G1
Eairy IM4 54 C6
Eakley MK16 32 B3
Eakring NG22 51 J6
Ealand DN17 51 K1
Ealing W 22 E3
Eamont Bridge CA10 61 G4
Earby BB18 56 E5
Earcroft BB2 56 B7
Eardington WV16 39 G6
Eardisland HR6 28 D3
Eardisley HR3 28 C4
Eardiston, Shrop. SY11 38 C3
Eardiston, Worcs. WR15 29 F2
Earith PE28 33 G1
Earl Shilton LE9 41 G6
Earl Soham IP13 35 G2
Earl Sterndale SK17 50 C6
Earl Stonham IP14 35 F3
Earle NE71 70 E1
Earlestown WA12 48 E3
Earlham NR4 45 F5
Earlish IV51 93 J5
Earls Barton NN6 32 B2
Earls Colne CO6 34 C6
Earl's Common WR9 29 J3
Earl's Croome WR8 29 H4
Earl's Green IP14 34 E2
Earlsdon CV5 30 E1
Earlsferry KY9 83 F7
Earlsford AB51 91 G1
Earlston TD4 76 D7
Earlswood, Mon. NP16 19 H2
Earlswood, Warks. B94 30 C1
Earnley PO20 12 B7
Earsairidh HS9 84 C5
Earsdon NE25 71 J6
Earsdon Moor NE61 71 G4
Earsham NR35 45 H7
Earswick YO32 58 C4
Eartham PO18 12 C6
Earthcote Green BS32 19 K3
Easby TS9 63 G6
Eascairt PA29 73 G5
Easdale PA34 79 J6
Easebourne GU29 12 B4
Easenhall CV23 31 F1
Eashing GU7 22 C7
Easington, Bucks. HP18 21 K1
Easington, Dur. SR8 63 F2
Easington, E.Riding HU12 53 H1
Easington, Northumb. NE70 77 K7
Easington, Oxon. OX49 21 K2
Easington, R. & C. TS13 63 J5
Easington Colliery SR8 63 F2
Easington Lane DH5 62 E2
Easingwold YO61 58 B3
Easole Street CT15 15 H2
Eassie and Nevay DD8 82 E3
East Aberthaw CF62 18 D5
East Allington TQ9 5 H6
East Anstey EX16 7 G3
East Appleton DL10 62 D7
East Ardsley WF3 57 J7
East Ashey PO33 11 G6
East Ashling PO18 12 B6
East Auchronie AB32 91 G4
East Ayton YO12 59 F1
East Barkwith LN8 52 E4
East Barming ME16 14 C2
East Barnby YO21 63 K5
East Barnet EN4 23 F2
East Barsham NR22 44 D2
East Beckham NR11 45 F2
East Bedfont TW14 22 D4
East Bergholt CO7 34 E5
East Bilney NR20 44 D4
East Blatchington BN25 13 H7
East Boldon NE36 71 J7
East Boldre SO42 10 E4
East Bolton NE66 71 G2
East Bradenham IP25 44 D5
East Brent TA9 19 G6
East Bridge IP16 35 J2
East Bridgford NG13 41 J1
East Brora KW9 97 F1
East Buckland EX32 6 E2
East Budleigh EX9 7 J7
East Burrafirth ZE2 109 C7
East Burton BH20 9 H6
East Cairnbeg AB30 91 F7
East Calder EH53 75 J4
East Carleton NR14 45 F5
East Carlton LE16 42 B7
East Chaldon or Chaldon Herring DT2 9 G6
East Challow OX12 21 G3
East Charleton TQ7 5 H6
East Chelborough DT2 8 E4
East Chiltington BN7 13 G5
East Chinnock BA22 8 D3
East Chisenbury SN9 20 E6
East Clandon GU4 22 D6
East Claydon MK18 31 J6
East Clyth KW3 105 H5
East Coker BA22 8 E3
East Combe TA4 7 K2
East Cornworthy TQ9 5 J5
East Cottingwith YO42 58 D5
East Cowes PO32 11 G5
East Cowick DN14 58 C7
East Cowton DL7 62 E6
East Cranmore BA4 19 K7
East Creech BH20 9 J6
East Croachy IV2 88 D2
East Darlochan PA28 66 A1
East Davoch AB34 90 C4
East Dean, E.Suss. BN20 13 J7
East Dean, Hants. SP5 10 D2
East Dean, W.Suss. PO18 12 C5
East Dereham NR19 44 D4
East Down EX31 6 E1
East Drayton DN22 51 K5
East End, Hants. RG20 21 H5
East End, Hants. SO41 10 E5
East End, Herts. SG9 33 H6
East End, Kent TN17 14 D4
East End, N.Som. BS48 19 H4
East End, Oxon. OX29 30 E7
East End, Poole BH21 9 J5
East End, Suff. CO7 35 F5
East Farleigh ME15 14 C2
East Farndon LE16 42 A7
East Ferry DN21 52 B3
East Fortune EH39 76 D3
East Garston RG17 21 G4
East Ginge OX12 21 H3
East Goscote LE7 41 J4
East Grafton SN8 21 F5
East Grimstead SP5 10 D2
East Grinstead RH19 13 G3
East Guldeford TN31 14 E5
East Haddon NN6 31 H2
East Hagbourne OX11 21 J3
East Halton DN40 52 E1
East Ham E6 23 H3
East Hanney OX12 21 H2
East Hanningfield CM3 24 D1
East Hardwick WF8 51 G1
East Harling NR16 44 D7
East Harlsey DL6 63 F7
East Harptree BS40 19 J6
East Hartford NE23 71 H6
East Harting GU31 11 J3
East Hatch SP3 9 J2
East Hatley SG19 33 F3
East Hauxwell DL8 62 C7
East Haven DD7 83 G4
East Heckington PE20 42 E1
East Hedleyhope DL13 62 C2
East Helmsdale KW8 105 F7
East Hendred OX12 21 H3
East Heslerton YO17 59 F2
East Hoathly BN8 13 J5
East Horndon CM13 24 C3
East Horrington BA5 19 J7
East Horsley KT24 22 D6
East Horton NE71 77 J7
East Huntspill TA9 19 G7
East Hyde LU1 32 E7
East Ilsley RG20 21 H3
East Keal PE23 53 G6
East Kennett SN8 20 E5
East Keswick LS17 57 J5
East Kilbride G74 74 E5
East Kirkby PE23 53 G6
East Knapton YO17 58 E2
East Knighton DT2 9 H6
East Knoyle SP3 9 H1
East Lambrook TA13 8 D3
East Langdon CT15 15 J3
East Langton LE16 42 A6
East Langwell IV28 96 E1
East Lavant PO18 12 B6
East Lavington GU28 12 C5
East Layton DL11 62 C5
East Leake LE12 41 H3
East Learmouth TD12 77 G7
East Learney AB31 90 E4

East Leigh

East Leigh **EX17** 7 F5
East Lexham **PE32** 44 C4
East Lilburn **NE66** 71 F1
East Linton **EH40** 76 D3
East Liss **GU33** 11 J2
East Looe **PL13** 4 C5
East Lound **DN9** 51 K3
East Lulworth **BH20** 9 H6
East Lutton **YO17** 59 F3
East Lydford **TA11** 8 E1
East Mains **AB31** 90 E5
East Malling **ME19** 14 C2
East March **DD4** 83 F4
East Marden **PO18** 12 B5
East Markham **NG22** 51 K5
East Marton **BD23** 56 E4
East Meon **GU32** 11 H2
East Mere **EX16** 7 H4
East Mersea **CO5** 34 E7
East Mey **KW14** 105 J1
East Midlands International Airport **DE74** 41 G3
East Molesey **KT8** 22 E5
East Morden **BH20** 9 J5
East Morton **BD20** 57 F5
East Ness **YO62** 58 C2
East Norton **LE7** 42 A5
East Oakley **RG23** 21 J7
East Ogwell **TQ12** 5 J3
East Orchard **SP7** 9 H3
East Ord **TD15** 77 H5
East Panson **PL15** 6 B6
East Peckham **TN12** 23 K7
East Pennard **BA4** 8 E1
East Portlemouth **TQ8** 5 H7
East Prawle **TQ7** 5 H7
East Preston **BN16** 12 D6
East Putford **EX22** 6 B4
East Quantoxhead **TA5** 7 K1
East Rainton **DH5** 62 E2
East Ravendale **DN37** 53 F3
East Raynham **NR21** 44 C3
East Rigton **LS17** 57 J5
East Rolstone **BS24** 19 G5
East Rounton **DL6** 63 F6
East Rudham **PE31** 44 C3
East Runton **NR27** 45 F1
East Ruston **NR12** 45 H3
East Saltoun **EH34** 76 C4
East Shefford **RG17** 21 G4
East Sleekburn **NE22** 71 H5
East Somerton **NR29** 45 J4
East Stockwith **DN21** 51 K3
East Stoke, *Dorset* **BH20** 9 H6
East Stoke, *Notts.* **NG23** 42 A1
East Stour **SP8** 9 G2
East Stourmouth **CT3** 25 J5
East Stratton **SO21** 11 G1
East Studdal **CT15** 15 J3
East Suisnish **IV40** 86 B1
East Taphouse **PL14** 4 B4
East Thirston **NE65** 71 G4
East Tilbury **RM18** 24 C4
East Tisted **GU34** 11 J1
East Torrington **LN8** 52 E4
East Tuddenham **NR20** 44 E4
East Tytherley **SP5** 10 D2
East Tytherton **SN15** 20 C4
East Village **EX17** 7 G5
East Wall **TF13** 38 E6
East Walton **PE32** 44 B4
East Wellow **SO51** 10 E2
East Wemyss **KY1** 76 B1
East Whitburn **EH47** 75 H4
East Wickham **DA16** 23 H4
East Williamston **SA68** 16 D4
East Winch **PE32** 44 A4
East Wittering **PO20** 12 B7
East Witton **DL8** 57 G1
East Woodhay **RG20** 21 H5
East Worldham **GU34** 11 J1
East Worlington **EX17** 7 F4
East-the-Water **EX39** 6 C3
Eastbourne, *Darl.* **DL1** 62 E5
Eastbourne, *E.Suss.* **BN21** 13 K7
Eastburn **YO25** 59 F4
Eastbury, *Herts.* **HA6** 22 E2
Eastbury, *W.Berks.* **RG17** 21 G4
Eastby **BD23** 57 F4
Eastchurch **ME12** 25 F4
Eastcombe **GL6** 20 B1
Eastcote, *Gt.Lon.* **HA5** 22 E3
Eastcote, *Northants.* **NN12** 31 H3
Eastcote, *W.Mid.* **B92** 30 C1
Eastcott, *Cornw.* **EX23** 6 A4
Eastcott, *Wilts.* **SN10** 20 D6
Eastcourt **SN16** 20 C2
Eastend **OX7** 30 E6
Easter Ardross **IV17** 96 D4
Easter Balmoral **AB35** 89 K5
Easter Boleskine **IV2** 88 C2
Easter Borland **FK8** 81 H7
Easter Brae **IV7** 96 D5
Easter Buckieburn **FK6** 75 F2
Easter Compton **BS35** 19 J3
Easter Drummond **IV2** 88 B3
Easter Dullater **FK17** 81 G7
Easter Ellister **PA48** 72 A5
Easter Fearn **IV24** 96 D3
Easter Galcantray **IV12** 97 F7
Easter Howlaws **TD10** 77 F6
Easter Kinkell **IV6** 96 C6
Easter Knox **DD11** 83 G3
Easter Lednathie **DD8** 82 E1
Easter Moniack **IV5** 96 C7
Easter Ord **AB32** 91 G4
Easter Poldar **FK8** 74 E1
Easter Quarff **ZE2** 109 D9
Easter Skeld **ZE2** 109 C8
Easter Suddie **IV8** 96 D6
Easter Tulloch **AB30** 91 F7
Easter Whyntie **AB45** 98 E4
Eastergate **PO20** 12 C6
Easterton **SN10** 20 D6
Eastertown **BS24** 19 G6
Eastfield, *N.Lan.* **ML7** 75 G4
Eastfield, *N.Yorks.* **YO11** 59 G1
Eastfield Hall **NE65** 71 H3
Eastgate, *Dur.* **DL13** 62 A3
Eastgate, *Lincs.* **PE10** 42 E4
Eastgate, *Norf.* **NR10** 45 F3
Eastham **CH62** 48 C4
Easthampstead **RG12** 22 B5
Eastheath **RG41** 22 B5
Easthope **TF13** 38 E6
Easthorpe, *Essex* **CO6** 34 D6
Easthorpe, *Leics.* **NG13** 42 B2
Easthorpe, *Notts.* **NG25** 51 K7
Easthouses **EH22** 76 B4
Eastington, *Devon* **EX17** 7 F5
Eastington, *Glos.* **GL54** 30 C7
Eastington, *Glos.* **GL10** 20 A1
Eastleach Martin **GL7** 21 F1
Eastleach Turville **GL7** 21 F1
Eastleigh, *Devon* **EX39** 6 C3
Eastleigh, *Hants.* **SO50** 11 F3
Eastling **ME13** 14 E2
Eastney **PO4** 11 H5
Eastnor **HR8** 29 G5
Eastoft **DN17** 52 B1
Eastoke **PO11** 11 J5
Easton, *Cambs.* **PE28** 32 E1
Easton, *Cumb.* **CA6** 69 K6
Easton, *Cumb.* **CA7** 60 D1
Easton, *Devon* **TQ13** 7 F7
Easton, *Dorset* **DT5** 9 F7
Easton, *Hants.* **SO21** 11 G1
Easton, *I.o.W.* **PO40** 10 E6
Easton, *Lincs.* **NG33** 42 C3
Easton, *Norf.* **NR9** 45 F4
Easton, *Som.* **BA5** 19 J7
Easton, *Suff.* **IP13** 35 G3
Easton, *Wilts.* **SN13** 20 B4
Easton Grey **SN16** 20 B3
Easton Maudit **NN29** 32 B3
Easton on the Hill **PE9** 42 D5
Easton Royal **SN9** 21 F5
Easton-in-Gordano **BS20** 19 J4
Eastrea **PE7** 43 F6
Eastriggs **DG12** 69 H7
Eastrington **DN14** 58 D6
Eastry **CT13** 15 H2
Eastside **KW17** 107 D8
Eastville **PE22** 53 H7
Eastwell **LE14** 42 A3
Eastwick **CM20** 33 H7
Eastwood, *Notts.* **NG16** 41 G1
Eastwood, *S'end* **SS9** 24 E3
Eastwood, *W.Yorks.* **HX7** 56 E7
Eathorpe **CV33** 30 E2
Eaton, *Ches.* **CW12** 49 H6
Eaton, *Ches.* **CW6** 48 E6
Eaton, *Leics.* **NG32** 42 A3
Eaton, *Norf.* **NR2** 45 G5
Eaton, *Notts.* **DN22** 51 K5
Eaton, *Oxon.* **OX13** 21 H1
Eaton, *Shrop.* **SY6** 38 E6
Eaton, *Shrop.* **SY9** 38 C7
Eaton Bishop **HR2** 28 D5
Eaton Bray **LU6** 32 C6
Eaton Constantine **SY5** 38 E5
Eaton Ford **PE19** 32 E3
Eaton Green **LU6** 32 C6
Eaton Hall **CH4** 48 D6
Eaton Hastings **SN7** 21 F2
Eaton Socon **PE19** 32 E3
Eaton upon Tern **TF9** 39 F3
Eavestone **HG4** 57 H3
Ebberston **YO13** 59 F1
Ebbesborne Wake **SP5** 9 J2
Ebbw Vale **NP23** 18 E1
Ebchester **DH8** 62 C1
Ebford **EX3** 7 H7
Ebrington **GL55** 30 C4
Ecchinswell **RG20** 21 J6
Ecclaw **TD13** 77 F4
Ecclefechan **DG11** 69 G6
Eccles, *Gt.Man.* **M30** 49 G3
Eccles, *Kent* **ME20** 24 D5
Eccles, *Sc.Bord.* **TD5** 77 F6
Eccles Road **NR16** 44 E6
Ecclesfield **S35** 51 F3
Ecclesgreig **DD10** 83 J1
Eccleshall **ST21** 40 A3
Ecclesmachan **EH52** 75 J3
Eccleston, *Ches.* **CH4** 48 D6
Eccleston, *Lancs.* **PR7** 48 E1
Eccleston, *Mersey.* **WA10** 48 D3
Eccup **LS16** 57 H5
Echt **AB32** 91 F4
Eckford **TD5** 70 C1
Eckington, *Derbys.* **S21** 51 G5
Eckington, *Worcs.* **WR10** 29 J4
Ecton, *Northants.* **NN6** 32 B2
Ecton, *Staffs.* **SK17** 50 C7
Edale **S33** 50 D4
Edburton **BN5** 13 F5
Edderside **CA15** 60 C2
Edderton **IV19** 96 E3
Eddington **RG17** 21 G5
Eddleston **EH45** 76 A6
Eddlewood **ML3** 75 F5
Eden Park **BR3** 23 G5
Edenbridge **TN8** 23 H7
Edendonich **PA33** 80 C5
Edenfield **BL0** 49 H1
Edenhall **CA11** 61 G3
Edenham **PE10** 42 D3
Edensor **DE45** 50 E6
Edentaggart **G83** 74 B1
Edenthorpe **DN3** 51 J2
Edern **LL53** 36 B2
Edgarley **BA6** 8 E1
Edgbaston **B15** 40 C7
Edgcott **HP18** 31 H6
Edgcumbe **TR10** 2 E5
Edge, *Glos.* **GL6** 20 B1
Edge, *Shrop.* **SY5** 38 C5
Edge End **GL16** 28 E7
Edgebolton **SY4** 38 E3
Edgefield **NR24** 45 F2
Edgeley **SY13** 38 E1
Edgerley **SY10** 38 C4
Edgeworth **GL6** 20 C1
Edginswell **TQ2** 5 J4
Edgmond **TF10** 39 G4
Edgmond Marsh **TF10** 39 G3
Edgton **SY7** 38 C7
Edgware **HA8** 23 F2
Edgworth **BL7** 49 G1
Edial **WS7** 40 C5
Edinample **FK19** 81 H5
Edinbain **IV51** 93 J6
Edinbanchory **AB33** 90 C3
Edinbarnet **G81** 74 D3
EDINBURGH EH 76 **A3**
Edinburgh Airport **EH12** 75 K3
Edinchip **FK19** 81 G5
Edingale **B79** 40 E4
Edingley **NG22** 51 J7
Edingthorpe **NR28** 45 H2
Edington, *Som.* **TA7** 8 C1
Edington, *Wilts.* **BA13** 20 C6
Edintore **AB55** 98 C6
Edinvale **IV36** 97 J6
Edistone **EX39** 6 A3
Edith Weston **LE15** 42 C5
Edithmead **TA9** 19 G7
Edlaston **DE6** 40 D1
Edlesborough **LU6** 32 C7
Edlingham **NE66** 71 G3
Edlington **LN9** 53 F5
Edmondsham **BH21** 10 B3
Edmondsley **DH2** 62 D2
Edmondthorpe **LE14** 42 B4
Edmonstone **KW17** 106 E5
Edmonton **N18** 23 G2
Edmundbyres **DH8** 62 B1
Ednam **TD5** 77 F7
Ednaston **DE6** 40 E1
Edney Common **CM1** 24 C1
Edra **FK17** 81 F6
Edradynate **PH9** 81 K2
Edrom **TD11** 77 G5
Edstaston **SY4** 38 E2
Edstone **B95** 30 C2
Edvin Loach **HR7** 29 F3
Edwalton **NG12** 41 H2
Edwardstone **CO10** 34 D4
Edwinsford **SA19** 17 K1
Edwinstowe **NG21** 51 J6
Edworth **SG18** 33 F4
Edwyn Ralph **HR7** 29 F3
Edzell **DD9** 83 G1
Efail Isaf **CF38** 18 D3
Efailnewydd **LL53** 36 C2
Efailwen **SA66** 16 E2
Efenechtyd **LL15** 47 K7
Effingham **KT24** 22 E6
Effirth **ZE2** 109 C7
Efford **EX17** 7 G5
Egbury **SP11** 21 H6
Egdean **RH20** 12 C4
Egerton, *Gt.Man.* **BL7** 49 G1
Egerton, *Kent* **TN27** 14 E3
Egerton Forstal **TN27** 14 D3
Egerton Green **SY14** 48 E7
Egg Buckland **PL6** 5 F5
Eggerness **DG8** 64 E6
Eggesford Barton **EX18** 6 E4
Eggington **LU7** 32 C6
Egginton **DE65** 40 E3
Egglescliffe **TS16** 63 F5
Eggleston **DL12** 62 B4
Egham **TW20** 22 D4
Egleton **LE15** 42 B5
Eglingham **NE66** 71 G2
Egloshayle **PL27** 4 A3
Egloskerry **PL15** 4 C2
Eglwys Cross **SY13** 38 D1
Eglwys Fach **SY20** 37 F6
Eglwys-Brewis **CF62** 18 D5
Eglwysbach **LL28** 47 G5
Eglwyswrw **SA41** 16 E1
Egmanton **NG22** 51 K6
Egmere **NR22** 44 D2
Egremont **CA22** 60 B5
Egton **YO21** 63 K6
Egton Bridge **YO21** 63 K6
Egypt **SO21** 21 H7
Eight Ash Green **CO6** 34 D6
Eignaig **PA34** 79 J3
Eil **PH22** 89 F3
Eilanreach **IV40** 86 E3
Eilean Darach **IV23** 95 H3
Eilean Iarmain (Isleornsay) **IV43** 86 C3
Einacleit **HS2** 100 D5
Eisgean **HS2** 101 F6
Eisingrug **LL46** 37 F2
Eisteddfa Gurig **SY23** 37 G7
Elan Village **LD1** 27 J2
Elberton **BS35** 19 J3
Elburton **PL9** 5 F5
Elcho **PH2** 82 C5
Elcombe **SN4** 20 E3
Eldernell **PE7** 43 G6
Eldersfield **GL19** 29 G5
Elderslie **PA5** 74 C4
Eldrick **KA26** 67 G5
Eldroth **LA2** 56 C3
Eldwick **BD16** 57 G5
Elerch (Bont-goch) **SY24** 37 F7
Elford, *Northumb.* **NE68** 77 K7
Elford, *Staffs.* **B79** 40 D4
Elgin **IV30** 97 K5
Elgol **IV49** 86 B3
Elham **CT4** 15 G3
Elie **KY9** 83 F7
Elilaw **NE65** 70 E3
Elim **LL65** 46 B4
Eling **SO40** 10 E3
Eliock **DG4** 68 D3
Elishader **IV51** 94 B5
Elishaw **NE19** 70 D4
Elkesley **DN22** 51 J5
Elkstone **GL53** 29 J7
Elland **HX5** 57 G7
Ellary **PA31** 73 F3
Ellastone **DE6** 40 D1
Ellemford **TD11** 77 F4
Ellenborough **CA15** 60 B3
Ellenhall **ST21** 40 A3
Ellen's Green **RH12** 12 D3
Ellerbeck **DL6** 63 F7
Ellerby **TS13** 63 J5
Ellerdine Heath **TF6** 39 F3
Elleric **PA38** 80 B3
Ellerker **HU15** 59 F7
Ellerton, *E.Riding* **YO42** 58 D5
Ellerton, *N.Yorks.* **DL10** 62 D7
Ellerton, *Shrop.* **TF9** 39 G3
Ellesborough **HP17** 22 B1
Ellesmere **SY12** 38 C2
Ellesmere Port **CH65** 48 C5
Ellingham, *Hants.* **BH24** 10 C4
Ellingham, *Norf.* **NR35** 45 H6
Ellingham, *Northumb.* **NE67** 71 G1
Ellingstring **HG4** 57 G1
Ellington, *Cambs.* **PE28** 32 E1
Ellington, *Northumb.* **NE61** 71 H4
Ellisfield **RG25** 21 K7
Ellistown **LE67** 41 G4
Ellon **AB41** 91 H1
Ellonby **CA11** 60 F3
Ellough **NR34** 45 J7
Elloughton **HU15** 59 F7
Ellwood **GL16** 19 J1
Elm **PE14** 43 H5
Elm Park **RM12** 23 J3
Elmbridge **WR9** 29 J2
Elmdon, *Essex* **CB11** 33 H5
Elmdon, *W.Mid.* **B26** 40 D7
Elmdon Heath **B92** 40 D7
Elmesthorpe **LE9** 41 G6
Elmhurst **WS13** 40 D4
Elmley Castle **WR10** 29 J4
Elmley Lovett **WR9** 29 H2
Elmore **GL2** 29 G7
Elmore Back **GL2** 29 G7
Elmscott **EX39** 6 A3
Elmsett **IP7** 34 E4
Elmstead Market **CO7** 34 E6
Elmstone **CT3** 25 J5
Elmstone Hardwicke **GL51** 29 J6
Elmswell, *E.Riding* **YO25** 59 F4
Elmswell, *Suff.* **IP30** 34 D2
Elmton **S80** 51 H5
Elphin **IV27** 102 E7
Elphinstone **EH33** 76 B3
Elrick, *Aber.* **AB32** 91 G4
Elrick, *Moray* **AB54** 90 C2
Elrig **DG8** 64 D6
Elrigbeag **PA32** 80 C6
Elsdon **NE19** 70 E4
Elsecar **S74** 51 F2
Elsenham **CM22** 33 J6
Elsfield **OX3** 21 J1
Elsham **DN20** 52 D1
Elsing **NR20** 44 E4
Elslack **BD23** 56 E5
Elson **SY12** 38 C2
Elsrickle **ML12** 75 J6
Elstead **GU8** 22 C7
Elsted **GU31** 12 B5
Elsthorpe **PE10** 42 D3
Elstob **TS21** 62 E4
Elston, *Lancs.* **PR2** 55 J6
Elston, *Notts.* **NG23** 42 A1
Elstone **EX37** 6 E4
Elstow **MK42** 32 D4
Elstree **WD6** 22 E2
Elstronwick **HU12** 59 J6
Elswick **PR4** 55 H6
Elsworth **CB3** 33 G2
Elterwater **LA22** 60 E6
Eltham **SE9** 23 H4
Eltisley **PE19** 33 F3
Elton, *Cambs.* **PE8** 42 D6
Elton, *Ches.* **CH2** 48 D5
Elton, *Derbys.* **DE4** 50 E6
Elton, *Glos.* **GL14** 29 G7
Elton, *Here.* **SY8** 28 D1
Elton, *Notts.* **NG13** 42 A2
Elton, *Stock.* **TS21** 63 F5
Elvanfoot **ML12** 68 E2
Elvaston **DE72** 41 G2
Elveden **IP24** 34 C1
Elvingston **EH33** 76 C3
Elvington, *Kent* **CT15** 15 H2
Elvington, *York* **YO41** 58 D5
Elwick, *Hart.* **TS27** 63 F3
Elwick, *Northumb.* **NE70** 77 K7
Elworth **CW11** 49 G6
Elworthy **TA4** 7 J2
Ely, *Cambs.* **CB7** 33 J1
Ely, *Cardiff* **CF5** 18 E4
Emberton **MK46** 32 B4
Embleton, *Cumb.* **CA13** 60 C3
Embleton, *Northumb.* **NE66** 71 H1
Embo **IV25** 97 F2
Embo Street **IV25** 97 F2
Emborough **BA3** 19 K6
Embsay **BD23** 57 F4
Emery Down **SO43** 10 D4
Emley **HD8** 50 E1
Emmer Green **RG4** 22 A4
Emmington **OX39** 22 A1
Emneth **PE14** 43 H5
Emneth Hungate **PE14** 43 J5
Empingham **LE15** 42 C5
Empshott **GU33** 11 J1
Emsworth **PO10** 11 J4
Enborne **RG20** 21 H5
Enchmarsh **SY6** 38 E6
Enderby **LE9** 41 H6
Endmoor **LA8** 55 J1
Endon **ST9** 49 J7
ENFIELD EN 23 **G2**
Enford **SN9** 20 E6
Engine Common **BS37** 19 K3
Englefield **RG7** 21 K4
Englefield Green **TW20** 22 C4
Englesea-brook **CW2** 49 G7
English Bicknor **GL16** 28 E7
English Frankton **SY12** 38 D3
Englishcombe **BA2** 20 A5
Enham Alamein **SP11** 21 G7
Enmore **TA5** 8 B1
Ennerdale Bridge **CA23** 60 B5
Enochdu **PH10** 82 B1
Ensay **PA75** 78 E3
Ensdon **SY4** 38 D4
Ensis **EX31** 6 D3
Enstone **OX7** 30 E6
Enterkinfoot **DG3** 68 D3
Enterpen **TS15** 63 F6
Enville **DY7** 40 A7
Eolaigearraidh **HS9** 84 C4
Eorabus **PA67** 78 E5
Eorodal **HS2** 101 H1
Eoropaidh **HS2** 101 H1
Epperstone **NG14** 41 J1
Epping **CM16** 23 H1
Epping Green, *Essex* **CM16** 23 H1
Epping Green, *Herts.* **SG13** 23 F1
Epping Upland **CM16** 23 H1
Eppleby **DL11** 62 C5
Eppleworth **HU16** 59 G6
Epsom **KT17** 23 F5
Epwell **OX15** 30 E4
Epworth **DN9** 51 K2
Erbistock **LL13** 38 C1
Erbusaig **IV40** 86 D2
Erchless Castle **IV4** 96 B7
Erdington **B24** 40 D6
Eredine **PA33** 80 A7
Eriboll **IV27** 103 G3
Ericstane **DG10** 69 F2
Eridge Green **TN3** 13 J3
Eriff **DG7** 67 K3
Erines **PA29** 73 G3
Eriswell **IP28** 34 B1
Erith **DA8** 23 J4
Erlestoke **SN10** 20 C6
Ermington **PL21** 5 G5
Erpingham **NR11** 45 F2
Errogie **IV2** 88 C2
Errol **PH2** 82 D5
Errollston **AB42** 91 J1
Erskine **PA8** 74 C3
Ervie **DG9** 64 A4
Erwarton **IP9** 35 G5
Erwood **LD2** 27 K4
Eryholme **DL2** 62 E6
Eryrys **CH7** 48 B7
Escart **PA29** 73 G4
Escrick **YO19** 58 C5
Esgair **SA33** 17 G2
Esgairgeiliog **SY20** 37 G5
Esh **DH7** 62 C2
Esh Winning **DH7** 62 C2
Esher **KT10** 22 E5
Eshott **NE61** 71 H4
Eshton **BD23** 56 E4
Eskadale **IV4** 88 B1
Eskbank **EH22** 76 B4
Eskdale Green **CA19** 60 C6
Eskdalemuir **DG13** 69 H4
Eskham **DN36** 53 G3
Esknish **PA44** 72 B4
Espley Hall **NE61** 71 G4
Esprick **PR4** 55 H6
Essendine **PE9** 42 D4
Essendon **AL9** 23 F1
Essich **IV2** 88 D1

Flodigarry

Essington **WV11** 40 B5
Esslemont **AB41** 91 H2
Eston **TS6** 63 G5
Etal **TD12** 77 H7
Etchilhampton **SN10** 20 D5
Etchingham **TN19** 14 C5
Etchinghill, *Kent* **CT18** 15 G4
Etchinghill, *Staffs.* **WS15** 40 C4
Ethie Mains **DD11** 83 H3
Eton **SL4** 22 C4
Eton Wick **SL4** 22 C4
Etteridge **PH20** 88 D5
Ettingshall **WV4** 40 B6
Ettington **CV37** 30 D4
Etton, *E.Riding* **HU17** 59 F5
Etton, *Peter.* **PE6** 42 E5
Ettrick **TD7** 69 H2
Ettrickbridge **TD7** 69 J1
Ettrickhill **TD7** 69 H2
Etwall **DE65** 40 E2
Eurach **PA31** 79 K7
Euston **IP24** 34 C1
Euxton **PR7** 48 E1
Evanton **IV16** 96 D5
Evedon **NG34** 42 D1
Evelix **IV25** 96 E2
Evenjobb **LD8** 28 B2
Evenley **NN13** 31 G5
Evenlode **GL56** 30 D6
Evenwood **DL14** 62 C4
Everbay **KW17** 106 F5
Evercreech **BA4** 9 F1
Everdon **NN11** 31 G3
Everingham **YO42** 58 E5
Everleigh **SN8** 21 F6
Everley, *High.* **KW1** 105 J2
Everley, *N.Yorks.* **YO13** 59 F1
Eversholt **MK17** 32 C5
Evershot **DT2** 8 E4
Eversley **RG27** 22 A5
Eversley Cross **RG27** 22 A5
Everthorpe **HU15** 59 F6
Everton, *Beds.* **SG19** 33 F3
Everton, *Hants.* **SO41** 10 D5
Everton, *Notts.* **DN10** 51 J3
Evertown **DG14** 69 J6
Evesbatch **WR6** 29 F4
Evesham **WR11** 30 B4
Evie **KW17** 106 C5
Evington **LE2** 41 J5
Ewart Newtown **NE71** 77 H7
Ewden Village **S36** 50 E3
Ewell **KT17** 23 F5
Ewell Minnis **CT15** 15 H3
Ewelme **OX10** 21 K2
Ewen **GL7** 20 D2
Ewenny **CF35** 18 C4
Ewerby **NG34** 42 E1
Ewerby Thorpe **NG34** 42 E1
Ewhurst, *E.Suss.* **TN32** 14 C5
Ewhurst, *Surr.* **GU6** 22 D7
Ewhurst Green **GU6** 12 D3
Ewloe **CH5** 48 B6
Ewood **BB2** 56 B7
Eworthy **EX21** 6 C6
Ewshot **GU10** 22 B7
Ewyas Harold **HR2** 28 C6
Exbourne **EX20** 6 E5
Exbury **SO45** 11 F4
Exebridge **TA22** 7 H3
Exelby **DL8** 57 H1
EXETER EX 7 **H6**
Exeter Airport **EX5** 7 H6
Exford **TA24** 7 G2
Exfords Green **SY5** 38 D5
Exhall, *Warks.* **CV7** 41 F7
Exhall, *Warks.* **B49** 30 C3
Exlade Street **RG8** 21 K3
Exminster **EX6** 7 H7
Exmouth **EX8** 7 J7
Exnaboe **ZE3** 109 G10
Exning **CB8** 33 K2
Exton, *Devon* **EX3** 7 H7
Exton, *Hants.* **SO32** 11 H2
Exton, *Rut.* **LE15** 42 C4
Exton, *Som.* **TA22** 7 H2
Exwick **EX4** 7 H6
Eyam **S32** 50 E5
Eydon **NN11** 31 G3
Eye, *Here.* **HR6** 28 D2
Eye, *Peter.* **PE6** 43 F5
Eye, *Suff.* **IP23** 35 F1
Eye Green **PE6** 43 F5
Eyemouth **TD14** 77 H4
Eyeworth **SG19** 33 F4
Eyhorne Street **ME17** 14 D2
Eyke **IP12** 35 H3
Eynesbury **PE19** 32 E3
Eynort **IV47** 85 J2
Eynsford **DA4** 23 J5
Eynsham **OX29** 21 H1
Eype **DT6** 8 D5
Eyre **IV51** 93 K6
Eythorne **CT15** 15 H3
Eyton, *Here.* **HR6** 28 D2
Eyton, *Shrop.* **SY7** 38 C7
Eyton, *Wrex.* **LL13** 38 C1
Eyton upon the Weald Moors **TF6** 39 F4
Eywood **HR5** 28 C3

F

Faccombe **SP11** 21 G6
Faceby **TS9** 63 F6
Fachwen **LL55** 46 D6
Faddiley **CW5** 48 E7
Fadmoor **YO62** 58 C1
Faebait **IV6** 96 B6
Faifley **G81** 74 D3
Fail **KA5** 67 J1
Failand **BS8** 19 J4
Failford **KA5** 67 J1
Failsworth **M35** 49 H2
Fain **IV23** 95 H4
Fair Oak, *Hants.* **RG19** 21 J5
Fair Oak, *Hants.* **SO50** 11 F3
Fairbourne **LL38** 37 F4
Fairburn **WF11** 57 K7
Fairfield, *Derbys.* **SK17** 50 C5
Fairfield, *Worcs.* **B61** 29 J1
Fairford **GL7** 20 E1
Fairgirth **DG5** 65 J5
Fairholm **ML9** 75 F5
Fairley **AB15** 91 G4
Fairlie **KA29** 74 A5
Fairlight **TN35** 14 D6
Fairlight Cove **TN35** 14 D6
Fairmile **EX11** 7 J6
Fairmilehead **EH10** 76 A4
Fairnington **TD5** 70 B1
Fairoak **ST21** 39 G2
Fairseat **TN15** 24 C5
Fairstead, *Essex* **CM3** 34 B7
Fairstead, *Norf.* **NR10** 45 G3
Fairwarp **TN22** 13 H4
Fairy Cross **EX39** 6 C3
Fairyhill **SA3** 17 H5
Fakenham **NR21** 44 D3
Fala **EH37** 76 C4
Fala Dam **EH37** 76 C4
Falahill **EH38** 76 B5
Faldingworth **LN8** 52 D4
Falfield, *Fife* **KY15** 83 F7
Falfield, *S.Glos.* **GL12** 19 K2
Falkenham **IP11** 35 G5
FALKIRK FK 75 **G3**
Falkland **KY15** 82 D7
Falla **TD8** 70 C2
Fallgate **S45** 51 F6
Fallin **FK7** 75 G1
Falmer **BN1** 13 G6
Falmouth **TR11** 3 F5
Falsgrave **YO12** 59 G1
Falstone **NE48** 70 C5
Fanagmore **IV27** 102 D3
Fanans **PA35** 80 B5
Fancott **LU5** 32 D6
Fangdale Beck **TS9** 63 G7
Fangfoss **YO41** 58 D4
Fanmore **PA73** 79 F3
Fans **TD4** 76 E6
Far Cotton **NN4** 31 J3
Far Forest **DY14** 29 G1
Far Gearstones **LA6** 56 C1
Farcet **PE7** 43 F6
Farden **SY8** 28 E1
Fareham **PO16** 11 G4
Farewell **WS13** 40 C4
Farforth **LN11** 53 G5
Faringdon **SN7** 21 F2
Farington **PR25** 55 J7
Farlam **CA8** 61 G1
Farlary **IV28** 96 E1
Farleigh, *N.Som.* **BS48** 19 H5
Farleigh, *Surr.* **CR6** 23 G5
Farleigh Hungerford **BA2** 20 A6
Farleigh Wallop **RG25** 21 K7
Farlesthorpe **LN13** 53 H5
Farleton **LA6** 55 J1
Farley, *Shrop.* **SY5** 38 C5
Farley, *Staffs.* **ST10** 40 C1
Farley, *Wilts.* **SP5** 10 D2
Farley Green **GU5** 22 D7
Farley Hill **RG7** 22 A5
Farleys End **GL2** 29 G7
Farlington **YO61** 58 C3
Farlow **DY14** 39 F7
Farmborough **BA2** 19 K5
Farmcote **GL54** 30 B6
Farmington **GL54** 30 C7
Farmoor **OX2** 21 H1
Farmtown **AB55** 98 D5
Farnborough, *Gt.Lon.* **BR6** 23 H5
Farnborough, *Hants.* **GU14** 22 B6
Farnborough, *W.Berks.* **OX12** 21 H3
Farnborough, *Warks.* **OX17** 31 F3
Farnborough Green **GU14** 22 B6
Farncombe **GU7** 22 C7
Farndish **NN29** 32 C2
Farndon, *Ches.* **CH3** 48 D7
Farndon, *Notts.* **NG24** 51 K7
Farnell **DD9** 83 H2
Farnham, *Dorset* **DT11** 9 J3
Farnham, *Essex* **CM23** 33 H6
Farnham, *N.Yorks.* **HG5** 57 J3
Farnham, *Suff.* **IP17** 35 H3
Farnham, *Surr.* **GU9** 22 B7
Farnham Common **SL2** 22 C3
Farnham Green **CM23** 33 H6
Farnham Royal **SL2** 22 C3
Farningham **DA4** 23 J5
Farnley **LS21** 57 H5
Farnley Tyas **HD4** 50 D1
Farnsfield **NG22** 51 J7
Farnworth, *Gt.Man.* **BL4** 49 G2
Farnworth, *Halton* **WA8** 48 E4
Farr, *High.* **KW14** 104 C2
Farr, *High.* **IV2** 88 D1
Farr, *High.* **PH21** 89 F4
Farr Ho. **IV2** 88 D1
Farraline **IV2** 88 C2
Farringdon **EX5** 7 J6
Farrington Gurney **BS39** 19 K6
Farsley **LS28** 57 H6
Farthinghoe **NN13** 31 G5
Farthingloe **CT15** 15 H3
Farthingstone **NN12** 31 H3
Farway **EX24** 7 K6
Fasag **IV22** 94 E6
Fasagrianach **IV23** 95 H3
Fascadale **PH36** 86 B7
Faslane **G84** 74 A2
Fasnacloich **PA38** 80 B3
Fasnakyle **IV4** 87 K2
Fassfern **PH33** 87 G7
Fatfield **NE38** 62 E1
Fattahead **AB45** 98 E5
Faugh **CA8** 61 G1
Fauldhouse **EH47** 75 H4
Faulkbourne **CM8** 34 B7
Faulkland **BA3** 20 A6
Fauls **SY13** 38 E2
Faversham **ME13** 25 G5
Favillar **AB55** 89 K1
Fawdington **YO61** 57 K2
Fawdon **NE3** 71 H7
Fawfieldhead **SK17** 50 C6
Fawkham Green **DA3** 23 J5
Fawler **OX7** 30 E7
Fawley, *Bucks.* **RG9** 22 A3
Fawley, *Hants.* **SO45** 11 F4
Fawley, *W.Berks.* **OX12** 21 G3
Fawley Chapel **HR1** 28 E6
Fawsyde **DD10** 91 G7
Faxfleet **DN14** 58 E7
Faxton **NN6** 31 J1
Faygate **RH12** 13 F3
Fazeley **B78** 40 E5
Fearby **HG4** 57 G1
Fearn **IV20** 97 F4
Fearnach **PA22** 73 J3
Fearnan **PH15** 81 J3
Fearnbeg **IV54** 94 D6
Fearnhead **WA2** 49 F3
Fearnmore **IV54** 94 D5
Fearnoch **PA21** 73 H3
Featherstone, *Staffs.* **WV10** 40 B5
Featherstone, *W.Yorks.* **WF7** 51 G1
Featherstone Castle **NE49** 70 B7
Feckenham **B96** 30 B2
Feering **CO5** 34 C6
Feetham **DL11** 62 A7
Feith-hill **AB53** 98 E6
Feizor **LA2** 56 C3
Felbridge **RH19** 13 G3
Felbrigg **NR11** 45 G2
Felcourt **RH19** 23 G7
Felden **HP3** 22 D1
Felindre, *Carmar.* **SA44** 17 G1
Felindre, *Carmar.* **SA19** 27 G6
Felindre, *Carmar.* **SA32** 17 J2
Felindre, *Powys* **LD7** 38 A7
Felindre, *Swan.* **SA5** 17 K4
Felinfach **LD3** 27 K5
Felinfoel **SA14** 17 J4
Felingwmuchaf **SA32** 17 J2
Felixkirk **YO7** 57 K1
Felixstowe **IP11** 35 G5
Felixstowe Ferry **IP11** 35 H5
Felkington **TD15** 77 H6
Felldownhead **PL19** 6 B7
Felling **NE10** 71 H7
Fellonmore **PA65** 79 H5
Felmersham **MK43** 32 C3
Felmingham **NR28** 45 G3
Felpham **PO22** 12 C7
Felsham **IP30** 34 D3
Felsted **CM6** 33 K6
Feltham **TW13** 22 E4
Felthorpe **NR10** 45 F4
Felton, *Here.* **HR1** 28 E4
Felton, *N.Som.* **BS40** 19 J5
Felton, *Northumb.* **NE65** 71 G3
Felton Butler **SY4** 38 C4
Feltwell **IP26** 44 B7
Fen Ditton **CB5** 33 H3
Fen Drayton **CB4** 33 G2
Fen End **CV8** 30 D1
Fen Street **IP22** 34 D1
Fence **BB12** 56 D6
Fence Houses **DH4** 62 E1
Fencott **OX5** 31 G7
Fendike Corner **PE24** 53 H6
Fenhouses **PE20** 43 F1
Feniscowles **BB2** 56 B7
Feniton **EX14** 7 K6
Fenny Bentley **DE6** 50 D7
Fenny Bridges **EX14** 7 K6
Fenny Compton **CV47** 31 F3
Fenny Drayton **CV13** 41 F6
Fenny Stratford **MK2** 32 B5
Fenrother **NE61** 71 G4
Fenstanton **PE28** 33 G2
Fenton, *Cambs.* **PE28** 33 G1
Fenton, *Lincs.* **LN1** 52 B5
Fenton, *Lincs.* **NG23** 52 B7
Fenton, *Northumb.* **NE71** 77 H7
Fenton, *Stoke* **ST4** 40 A1
Fenwick, *E.Ayr.* **KA3** 74 C6
Fenwick, *Northumb.* **TD15** 77 J6
Fenwick, *Northumb.* **NE20** 71 F6
Fenwick, *S.Yorks.* **DN6** 51 H1
Feochaig **PA28** 66 B2
Feock **TR3** 3 F5
Feolin **PA60** 72 D4
Feolin Ferry **PA60** 72 C4
Feorlan **PA28** 66 A3
Feorlin **PA32** 73 H1
Feriniquarrie **IV55** 93 G6
Fern **DD8** 83 F1
Ferndale **CF43** 18 C2
Ferndown **BH22** 10 B4
Ferness **IV12** 97 G7
Fernham **SN7** 21 F2
Fernhill Heath **WR3** 29 H3
Fernhurst **GU27** 12 B4
Fernie **KY15** 82 E6
Fernilea **IV47** 85 J1
Fernilee **SK23** 50 C5
Fernybank **DD9** 90 D7
Ferrensby **HG5** 57 J3
Ferring **BN12** 12 D6
Ferrybridge **WF11** 57 K7
Ferryden **DD10** 83 J2
Ferryhill **DL17** 62 D3
Ferryside **SA17** 17 G3
Fersfield **IP22** 44 E7
Fersit **PH31** 87 K7
Feshiebridge **PH21** 89 F4
Fetcham **KT23** 22 E6
Fetterangus **AB42** 99 H5
Fettercairn **AB30** 90 E7
Fetternear Ho. **AB51** 91 F3
Feus of Caldhame **AB30** 83 H1
Fewcott **OX27** 31 G6
Fewston **HG3** 57 G4
Ffair-Rhos **SY25** 27 G2
Ffairfach **SA19** 17 K2
Ffarmers **SA19** 27 F4
Ffawyddog **NP8** 28 B7
Ffestiniog **LL41** 37 G1
Ffordd-las **LL16** 47 K6
Fforest **SA4** 17 J4
Fforest-fach **SA5** 17 K5
Ffos-y-ffin **SA46** 26 D2
Ffostrasol **SA44** 26 C4
Ffridd Uchaf **LL54** 46 D7
Ffrith **LL11** 48 B7
Ffrwdgrech **LD3** 27 K6
Ffynnon-ddrain **SA31** 17 H2
Ffynnongroyw **CH8** 47 K4
Fibhig **HS2** 100 E3
Fichlie **AB33** 90 C3
Fidden **PA66** 78 E5
Fiddington, *Glos.* **GL20** 29 J5
Fiddington, *Som.* **TA5** 19 F7
Fiddler's Green **HR1** 28 E5
Fiddlers Hamlet **CM16** 23 H1
Field **ST14** 40 C2
Field Broughton **LA11** 55 G1
Field Dalling **NR25** 44 E2
Field Head **LE67** 41 G5
Fife Keith **AB55** 98 C5
Fifehead Magdalen **SP8** 9 G2
Fifehead Neville **DT10** 9 G3
Fifield, *Oxon.* **OX7** 30 D7
Fifield, *W. & M.* **SL4** 22 C4
Fifield Bavant **SP5** 10 B2
Figheldean **SP4** 20 E7
Filby **NR29** 45 J4
Filey **YO14** 59 H2
Filgrave **MK16** 32 B4
Filkins **GL7** 21 F1
Filleigh, *Devon* **EX32** 6 E3
Filleigh, *Devon* **EX17** 7 F4
Fillingham **DN21** 52 C4
Fillongley **CV7** 40 E7
Filmore Hill **GU34** 11 H2
Filton **BS10** 19 J4
Fimber **YO25** 59 F3
Finavon **DD8** 83 F2
Fincham **PE33** 44 A5
Finchampstead **RG40** 22 A5
Finchdean **PO8** 11 J3
Finchingfield **CM7** 33 K5
Finchley **N3** 23 F2
Findern **DE65** 41 F2
Findhorn **IV36** 97 H5
Findhorn Bridge **IV13** 89 F2
Findhuglen **PH6** 81 J6
Findo Gask **PH7** 82 B5
Findochty **AB56** 98 C4
Findon, *Aber.* **AB12** 91 H5
Findon, *W.Suss.* **BN14** 12 E6
Findon Mains **IV7** 96 D5
Findrassie **IV30** 97 J5
Findron **AB37** 89 J3
Finedon **NN9** 32 C1
Finegand **PH10** 82 C1
Fingal Street **IP13** 35 G2
Fingask **AB51** 91 F2
Fingerpost **DY14** 29 G1
Fingest **RG9** 22 A2
Finghall **DL8** 62 C7
Fingland, *Cumb.* **CA7** 60 D1
Fingland, *D. & G.* **DG4** 68 C2
Fingland, *D. & G.* **DG13** 69 H3
Finglesham **CT14** 15 J2
Fingringhoe **CO5** 34 E7
Finlarig **FK21** 81 G4
Finmere **MK18** 31 H5
Finnart, *Arg. & B.* **G84** 74 A1
Finnart, *P. & K.* **PH17** 81 G2
Finningham **IP14** 34 E2
Finningley **DN9** 51 J3
Finnygaud **AB54** 98 E5
Finsbury **EC1R** 23 G3
Finstall **B60** 29 J1
Finsthwaite **LA12** 55 G1
Finstock **OX7** 30 E7
Finstown **KW17** 107 C6
Fintry, *Aber.* **AB53** 99 F5
Fintry, *Stir.* **G63** 74 E2
Finzean **AB31** 90 D5
Fionnphort **PA66** 78 E5
Fir Tree **DL15** 62 C3
Fir Vale **S5** 51 F4
Firbank **LA10** 61 H7
Firbeck **S81** 51 H4
Firgrove **OL16** 49 J1
Firs Road **SP5** 10 D1
Firsby **PE23** 53 H6
First Coast **IV22** 95 F2
Firth **ZE2** 108 D5
Fishbourne, *I.o.W.* **PO33** 11 G5
Fishbourne, *W.Suss.* **PO18** 12 B6
Fishburn **TS21** 62 E3
Fisherford **AB51** 90 E1
Fisher's Pond **SO50** 11 F2
Fisher's Row **PR3** 55 H5
Fisherstreet **GU8** 12 C3
Fisherton, *High.* **IV2** 96 E6
Fisherton, *S.Ayr.* **KA7** 67 G2
Fisherton de la Mere **BA12** 10 B1
Fishguard (Abergwaun) **SA65** 16 C1
Fishlake **DN7** 51 J1
Fishley Barton **EX37** 6 D3
Fishnish **PA65** 79 H3
Fishpond Bottom **DT6** 8 C5
Fishponds **BS16** 19 K4
Fishpool **BL9** 49 H1
Fishtoft **PE21** 43 G1
Fishtoft Drove **PE22** 43 G1
Fishtown of Usan **DD10** 83 J2
Fishwick, *Lancs.* **PR1** 55 J6
Fishwick, *Sc.Bord.* **TD15** 77 H5
Fiskerton, *Lincs.* **LN3** 52 D5
Fiskerton, *Notts.* **NG25** 51 K7
Fittleton **SP4** 20 E6
Fittleworth **RH20** 12 D5
Fitton End **PE13** 43 H4
Fitz **SY4** 38 D4
Fitzhead **TA4** 7 K3
Fitzwilliam **WF9** 51 G1
Fiunary **PA34** 79 H3
Five Ash Down **TN22** 13 H4
Five Ashes **TN20** 13 J4
Five Bridges **WR6** 29 F4
Five Oak Green **TN12** 23 K7
Five Oaks, *W.Suss.* **RH14** 12 D4
Five Roads **SA15** 17 H4
Five Turnings **LD7** 28 B1
Five Wents **ME17** 14 D2
Fivehead **TA3** 8 C2
Fivelanes **PL15** 4 C2
Flackwell Heath **HP10** 22 B3
Fladbury **WR10** 29 J4
Fladdabister **ZE2** 109 D9
Flagg **SK17** 50 D6
Flamborough **YO15** 59 J2
Flamstead **AL3** 32 D7
Flamstead End **EN7** 23 G1
Flansham **PO22** 12 C6
Flasby **BD23** 56 E4
Flash **SK17** 50 C6
Flashader **IV51** 93 J6
Flask Inn **YO22** 63 J2
Flaunden **HP3** 22 D1
Flawborough **NG13** 42 A1
Flawith **YO61** 57 K3
Flax Bourton **BS48** 19 J5
Flaxby **HG5** 57 J4
Flaxley **GL14** 29 F7
Flaxpool **TA4** 7 K2
Flaxton **YO60** 58 C3
Fleckney **LE8** 41 J6
Flecknoe **CV23** 31 G2
Fleet, *Hants.* **GU51** 22 B6
Fleet, *Lincs.* **PE12** 43 G3
Fleet Hargate **PE12** 43 G3
Fleetwood **FY7** 55 G5
Flemingston **CF62** 18 D5
Flemington **G72** 74 E5
Flempton **IP28** 34 C2
Fleoideabhagh **HS3** 93 F3
Fletchertown **CA7** 60 D2
Fletching **TN22** 13 H4
Flete **PL21** 5 G5
Fleuchats **AB36** 90 B4
Fleur-de-lis **NP12** 18 E2
Flexbury **EX23** 6 A5
Flexford **GU3** 22 C6
Flimby **CA15** 60 B3
Flimwell **TN5** 14 C4
Flint (Y Fflint) **CH6** 48 B5
Flint Cross **SG8** 33 H4
Flint Mountain **CH6** 48 B5
Flintham **NG23** 42 A1
Flinton **HU11** 59 J6
Flishinghurst **TN17** 14 C4
Flitcham **PE31** 44 B3
Flitton **MK45** 32 D5
Flitwick **MK45** 32 D5
Flixborough **DN15** 52 B1
Flixton, *Gt.Man.* **M31** 49 G3
Flixton, *N.Yorks.* **YO11** 59 G2
Flixton, *Suff.* **NR35** 45 H7
Flockton **WF4** 50 E1
Flockton Green **WF4** 50 E1
Flodden **NE71** 77 H7
Flodigarry **IV51** 93 K4

Flookburgh

Flookburgh **LA11** 55 G2
Floors **AB55** 98 C5
Flordon **NR15** 45 F6
Flore **NN7** 31 H2
Flotterton **NE65** 71 F3
Flowton **IP8** 34 E4
Flushing, *Aber.* **AB42** 99 J6
Flushing, *Cornw.* **TR11** 3 F5
Flyford Flavell **WR7** 29 J3
Fobbing **SS17** 24 D3
Fochabers **IV32** 98 B5
Fochriw **CF81** 18 E1
Fockerby **DN17** 52 B1
Fodderletter **AB37** 89 J2
Fodderty **IV15** 96 C6
Foel **SY21** 37 J4
Foffarty **DD8** 83 F3
Foggathorpe **YO8** 58 D6
Fogo **TD11** 77 F6
Fogorig **TD11** 77 F6
Foindle **IV27** 102 D4
Folda **PH11** 82 C1
Fole **ST14** 40 C2
Foleshill **CV6** 41 F7
Folke **DT9** 9 F3
Folkestone **CT19** 15 H4
Folkingham **NG34** 42 D2
Folkington **BN26** 13 J6
Folksworth **PE7** 42 E7
Folkton **YO11** 59 G2
Folla Rule **AB51** 91 F1
Follifoot **HG3** 57 J4
Folly, *Dorset* **DT2** 9 G4
Folly, *Pembs.* **SA62** 16 C2
Folly Gate **EX20** 6 D6
Fonthill Bishop **SP3** 9 J1
Fonthill Gifford **SP3** 9 J1
Fontmell Magna **SP7** 9 H3
Fontwell **BN18** 12 C6
Foolow **S32** 50 D5
Foots Cray **DA14** 23 H4
Forbestown **AB36** 90 B3
Force Forge **LA12** 60 E7
Forcett **DL11** 62 C5
Forches Cross **EX17** 7 F5
Ford, *Arg. & B.* **PA31** 79 K7
Ford, *Bucks.* **HP17** 22 A1
Ford, *Devon* **EX39** 6 C3
Ford, *Devon* **PL8** 5 G5
Ford, *Devon* **TQ7** 5 H6
Ford, *Glos.* **GL54** 30 B6
Ford, *Mersey.* **L30** 48 C2
Ford, *Midloth.* **EH37** 76 B4
Ford, *Northumb.* **TD15** 77 H7
Ford, *Pembs.* **SA62** 16 C2
Ford, *Shrop.* **SY5** 38 D4
Ford, *Som.* **TA4** 7 J3
Ford, *W.Suss.* **BN18** 12 C6
Ford, *Wilts.* **SN14** 20 B4
Ford End **CM3** 33 K7
Ford Street **TA21** 7 K4
Fordcombe **TN3** 23 J7
Fordell **KY4** 75 K2
Forden **SY21** 38 B5
Forder Green **TQ13** 5 H4
Fordham, *Cambs.* **CB7** 33 K1
Fordham, *Essex* **CO6** 34 D6
Fordham, *Norf.* **PE38** 44 A6
Fordham Abbey **CB7** 33 K2
Fordingbridge **SP6** 10 C3
Fordon **YO25** 59 G2
Fordoun **AB30** 91 F7
Fordstreet **CO6** 34 D6
Fordwells **OX29** 30 E7
Fordwich **CT2** 15 G2
Fordyce **AB45** 98 D4
Forebrae **PH1** 82 A5
Foreland **PA49** 72 A4
Forest Gate **E7** 23 H3
Forest Green **RH5** 22 E7
Forest Hall, *Cumb.* **LA8** 61 G6
Forest Hall, *T. & W.* **NE12** 71 H7
Forest Head **CA8** 61 G1
Forest Hill **OX33** 21 J1
Forest Lodge, *Arg. & B.* **PA36** 80 D3
Forest Lodge, *P. & K.* **PH18** 89 G7
Forest Mill **FK10** 75 H1
Forest Row **RH18** 13 H3
Forest Town **NG19** 51 H6
Forest-in-Teesdale **DL12** 61 K3
Forestburn Gate **NE61** 71 F4
Forestside **PO9** 11 J3
Forfar **DD8** 83 F2
Forgandenny **PH2** 82 B6
Forgie **AB55** 98 B5
Formby **L37** 48 B2
Forncett End **NR16** 45 F6
Forncett St. Mary **NR16** 45 F6
Forncett St. Peter **NR16** 45 F6
Forneth **PH10** 82 B3
Fornham All Saints **IP28** 34 C2
Fornham St. Martin **IP31** 34 C2
Fornighty **IV12** 97 G6
Forres **IV36** 97 H6
Forrest **ML6** 75 G4
Forrest Lodge **DG7** 67 K5
Forsbrook **ST11** 40 B1
Forse **KW5** 105 H5
Forsie **KW14** 105 F2
Forsinain **KW13** 104 E4
Forsinard **KW13** 104 D4
Forston **DT2** 9 F5
Fort Augustus **PH32** 87 K4
Fort George **IV2** 96 E6
Fort William **PH33** 87 H7
Forter **PH11** 82 C1
Forteviot **PH2** 82 B6
Forth **ML11** 75 H5
Forthampton **GL19** 29 H5
Fortingall **PH15** 81 J3
Forton, *Hants.* **SP11** 21 H7
Forton, *Lancs.* **PR3** 55 H4
Forton, *Shrop.* **SY4** 38 D4
Forton, *Som.* **TA20** 8 C4
Forton, *Staffs.* **TF10** 39 G3
Fortrie **AB53** 98 E6
Fortrose **IV10** 96 E6
Fortuneswell **DT5** 9 F7
Forty Green **HP9** 22 C2
Forty Hill **EN2** 23 G2
Forward Green **IP14** 34 E3
Fosbury **SN8** 21 G6
Foscot **OX7** 30 D6
Fosdyke **PE20** 43 G2
Foss **PH16** 81 J2
Foss Cross **GL54** 20 D1
Fossdale **DL8** 61 K7
Fossebridge **GL54** 30 B7
Foster Street **CM17** 23 H1
Foster's Booth **NN12** 31 H3
Foston, *Derbys.* **DE65** 40 D2
Foston, *Lincs.* **NG32** 42 B1
Foston, *N.Yorks.* **YO60** 58 C3
Foston on the Wolds **YO25** 59 H4
Fotherby **LN11** 53 G3
Fotheringhay **PE8** 42 D6
Foubister **KW17** 107 E7
Foul Mile **BN27** 13 K5
Foulbog **DG13** 69 H3
Foulden, *Norf.* **IP26** 44 B6
Foulden, *Sc.Bord.* **TD15** 77 H5
Foulridge **BB8** 56 D5
Foulsham **NR20** 44 E3
Foulzie **AB45** 99 F4
Fountainhall **TD1** 76 C6
Four Ashes, *Staffs.* **WV10** 40 B5
Four Ashes, *Suff.* **IP31** 34 D1
Four Crosses, *Denb.* **LL21** 37 K1
Four Crosses, *Powys* **SY22** 38 B4
Four Crosses, *Powys* **SY21** 37 K5
Four Crosses, *Staffs.* **WS11** 40 B5
Four Elms **TN8** 23 H7
Four Forks **TA5** 8 B1
Four Gotes **PE13** 43 H4
Four Lanes **TR16** 2 D5
Four Marks **GU34** 11 H1
Four Mile Bridge **LL65** 46 A5
Four Oaks, *E.Suss.* **TN31** 14 D5
Four Oaks, *W.Mid.* **B74** 40 D6
Four Oaks, *W.Mid.* **CV7** 40 E7
Four Roads **SA17** 17 H4
Four Throws **TN18** 14 C5
Fourlane Ends **DE55** 51 F7
Fourlanes End **CW11** 49 H7
Fourpenny **IV25** 96 E2
Fourstones **NE47** 70 D7
Fovant **SP3** 10 B2
Foveran **AB41** 91 H2
Fowey **PL23** 4 B5
Fowlis **DD2** 82 E4
Fowlis Wester **PH7** 82 A5
Fowlmere **SG8** 33 H4
Fownhope **HR1** 28 E5
Fox Lane **GU14** 22 B6
Fox Street **CO7** 34 E6
Foxcote **GL54** 30 B7
Foxdale **IM4** 54 B6
Foxearth **CO10** 34 C4
Foxfield **LA20** 55 F1
Foxham **SN15** 20 C4
Foxhole, *Cornw.* **PL26** 3 G3
Foxhole, *High.* **IV4** 88 C1
Foxholes **YO25** 59 G2
Foxhunt Green **TN21** 13 J5
Foxley, *Here.* **HR4** 28 D4
Foxley, *Norf.* **NR20** 44 E3
Foxley, *Northants.* **NN12** 31 H3
Foxley, *Wilts.* **SN16** 20 B3
Foxt **ST10** 40 C1
Foxton, *Cambs.* **CB2** 33 H4
Foxton, *Dur.* **TS21** 62 E4
Foxton, *Leics.* **LE16** 42 A6
Foxup **BD23** 56 D2
Foxwist Green **CW7** 49 F6
Foy **HR9** 28 E6
Foyers **IV2** 88 B2
Frachadil **PA75** 78 E2
Fraddam **TR27** 2 C5
Fraddon **TR9** 3 G3
Fradley **WS13** 40 D4
Fradswell **ST18** 40 B2
Fraisthorpe **YO15** 59 H3
Framfield **TN22** 13 H4
Framingham Earl **NR14** 45 G5
Framingham Pigot **NR14** 45 G5
Framlingham **IP13** 35 G2
Frampton, *Dorset* **DT2** 9 F5
Frampton, *Lincs.* **PE20** 43 G2
Frampton Cotterell **BS36** 19 K3
Frampton Mansell **GL6** 20 C1
Frampton on Severn **GL2** 20 A1
Frampton West End **PE20** 43 G1
Framsden **IP14** 35 G3
Framwellgate Moor **DH1** 62 D2
Franche **DY11** 29 H1
Frankby **CH48** 48 B4
Frankley **B32** 40 B7
Frankton **CV23** 31 F1
Frant **TN3** 13 J3
Fraserburgh **AB43** 99 H4
Frating Green **CO7** 34 E6
Fratton **PO1** 11 H4
Freathy **PL10** 4 D5
Freckenham **IP28** 33 K1
Freckleton **PR4** 55 H7
Freeby **LE14** 42 B3
Freefolk **RG28** 21 H7
Freeland **OX29** 31 F7
Freemantle **SO15** 11 F3
Freester **ZE2** 109 D7
Freethorpe **NR13** 45 J5
Freethorpe Common **NR13** 45 J5
Freiston **PE22** 43 G1
Freiston Shore **PE22** 43 G1
Fremington, *Devon* **EX31** 6 D2
Fremington, *N.Yorks.* **DL11** 62 B7
Frenchay **BS16** 19 K4
Frenchbeer **TQ13** 6 E7
Frendraught **AB54** 98 E6
Frenich **FK8** 81 F7
Frensham **GU10** 22 B7
Fresgoe **KW14** 104 E2
Freshfield **L37** 48 B2
Freshford **BA2** 20 A5
Freshwater **PO40** 10 E6
Freshwater East **SA71** 16 D5
Fressingfield **IP21** 35 G1
Freston **IP9** 35 F5
Freswick **KW1** 105 J2
Frettenham **NR12** 45 G4
Freuchie **KY15** 82 D7
Freystrop Cross **SA62** 16 C3
Friars Carse **DG2** 68 E5
Friar's Gate **TN6** 13 H3
Friarton **PH2** 82 C5
Friday Bridge **PE14** 43 H5
Friday Street, *E.Suss.* **BN23** 13 K6
Friday Street, *Surr.* **RH5** 22 E7
Fridaythorpe **YO25** 58 E4
Friern Barnet **N11** 23 F2
Friesthorpe **LN3** 52 D4
Frieston **NG32** 42 C1
Frieth **RG9** 22 A2
Frilford **OX13** 21 H2
Frilsham **RG18** 21 J4
Frimley **GU16** 22 B6
Frimley Green **GU16** 22 B6
Frindsbury **ME2** 24 D5
Fring **PE31** 44 B2
Fringford **OX27** 31 H6
Frinsted **ME9** 14 D2
Frinton-on-Sea **CO13** 35 G7
Friockheim **DD11** 83 G3
Friog **LL38** 37 F4
Frisby on the Wreake **LE14** 41 J4
Friskney **PE22** 53 H7
Friskney Eaudike **PE22** 53 H7
Friston, *E.Suss.* **BN20** 13 J7
Friston, *Suff.* **IP17** 35 J3
Fritchley **DE56** 51 F7
Frith **ME13** 14 E2
Frith Bank **PE22** 43 G1
Frith Common **WR15** 29 F2
Fritham **SO43** 10 D3
Frithelstock **EX38** 6 C4
Frithelstock Stone **EX38** 6 C4
Frithville **PE22** 53 G7
Frittenden **TN17** 14 D3
Fritton, *Norf.* **NR31** 45 J5
Fritton, *Norf.* **NR15** 45 G6
Fritwell **OX27** 31 G6
Frizington **CA26** 60 B5
Frocester **GL10** 20 A1
Frochas **SY21** 38 B4
Frodesley **SY5** 38 E5
Frodingham **DN15** 52 B1
Frodsham **WA6** 48 E5
Frog End **CB3** 33 H3
Frog Pool **WR6** 29 G2
Frogden **TD5** 70 C1
Froggatt **S32** 50 E5
Froghall **ST10** 40 C1
Frogham **SP6** 10 C3
Frogmore, *Devon* **TQ7** 5 H6
Frogmore, *Hants.* **GU17** 22 B6
Frogmore, *Herts.* **AL2** 22 E1
Frolesworth **LE17** 41 H6
Frome **BA11** 20 A7
Frome St. Quentin **DT2** 8 E4
Fromes Hill **HR8** 29 F4
Fron, *Gwyn.* **LL53** 36 C2
Fron, *Powys* **SY21** 38 B5
Fron, *Powys* **LD1** 27 K2
Fron-goch **LL23** 37 J2
Froncysyllte **LL20** 38 B1
Frostenden **NR34** 45 J7
Frosterley **DL13** 62 B3
Froxfield **SN8** 21 F5
Froxfield Green **GU32** 11 J2
Fryerning **CM4** 24 C1
Fryton **YO62** 58 C2
Fugglestone St. Peter **SP2** 10 C1
Fulbeck **NG32** 52 C7
Fulbourn **CB1** 33 J3
Fulbrook **OX18** 30 D7
Fulford, *Som.* **TA2** 8 B2
Fulford, *Staffs.* **ST15** 40 B2
Fulford, *York* **YO10** 58 C5
Fulham **SW6** 23 F4
Fulking **BN5** 13 F5
Full Sutton **YO41** 58 D4
Fuller Street **CM3** 34 B7
Fuller's Moor **CH3** 48 D7
Fullerton **SP11** 10 E1
Fulletby **LN9** 53 F5
Fullwood **KA3** 74 C6
Fulmer **SL3** 22 C3
Fulmodeston **NR21** 44 D2
Fulnetby **LN8** 52 E5
Fulready **CV37** 30 D4
Fulstow **LN11** 53 G3
Fulwell, *Oxon.* **OX7** 30 E6
Fulwell, *T. & W.* **SR5** 62 E1
Fulwood, *Lancs.* **PR2** 55 J6
Fulwood, *S.Yorks.* **S10** 51 F4
Fundenhall **NR16** 45 F6
Funtington **PO18** 12 B6
Funtley **PO16** 11 G4
Funzie **ZE2** 108 F4
Furley **EX13** 8 B4
Furnace, *Arg. & B.* **PA32** 80 B7
Furnace, *Cere.* **SY20** 37 F6
Furnace, *High.* **IV22** 95 F4
Furness Vale **SK23** 50 C4
Furneux Pelham **SG9** 33 H6
Furze Platt **SL6** 22 B3
Furzehill **EX35** 7 F1
Fyfett **TA20** 8 B3
Fyfield, *Essex* **CM5** 23 J1
Fyfield, *Glos.* **GL7** 21 F1
Fyfield, *Hants.* **SP11** 21 F7
Fyfield, *Oxon.* **OX13** 21 H2
Fyfield, *Wilts.* **SN8** 20 E5
Fylingthorpe **YO22** 63 J2
Fyvie **AB53** 91 F1

G

Gabhsunn Bho Dheas **HS2** 101 G2
Gabhsunn Bho Thuath **HS2** 101 G2
Gablon **IV25** 96 E2
Gabroc Hill **KA3** 74 C5
Gaddesby **LE7** 41 J4
Gaddesden Row **HP2** 32 D7
Gaer **NP8** 28 A6
Gaerllwyd **NP16** 19 H2
Gaerwen **LL60** 46 C5
Gagingwell **OX7** 31 F6
Gaich **PH26** 89 H2
Gaick **IV2** 88 D1
Gaick Lodge **PH21** 88 E6
Gailey **ST19** 40 B4
Gainford **DL2** 62 C5
Gainsborough **DN21** 52 B3
Gairloch **IV21** 94 E4
Gairlochy **PH34** 87 H6
Gairney Bank **KY13** 75 K1
Gairnshiel Lodge **AB35** 89 K4
Gaitsgill **CA5** 60 E2
Galabank **TD1** 76 C6
GALASHIELS TD 76 C7
Galdenoch **DG8** 64 B4
Galgate **LA2** 55 H4
Galhampton **BA22** 9 F2
Gallanach **PA34** 79 K5
Gallantry Bank **SY14** 48 E7
Gallatown **KY1** 76 A1
Gallchoille **PA31** 73 F2
Gallery **AB30** 83 H1
Galley Common **CV10** 41 F6
Galleyend **CM2** 24 D1
Galleywood **CM2** 24 D1
Gallowfauld **DD8** 83 F3
Gallowstree Common **RG4** 21 K4
Gallowstree Elm **DY7** 40 A7
Gallt Melyd (Meliden) **LL19** 47 J4
Galltair **IV40** 86 E3
Galmisdale **PH42** 85 K6
Galmpton, *Devon* **TQ7** 5 G6
Galmpton, *Torbay* **TQ5** 5 J5
Galphay **HG4** 57 H2
Galston **KA4** 74 D7
Galtrigill **IV55** 93 G6
Gamble's Green **CM3** 34 B7
Gamblesby **CA10** 61 H3
Gamelsby **CA7** 60 D1
Gamlingay **SG19** 33 F3
Gammaton Moor **EX39** 6 C3
Gammersgill **DL8** 57 F1
Gamrie **AB45** 99 F4
Gamston, *Notts.* **DN22** 51 K5
Gamston, *Notts.* **NG2** 41 J2
Ganarew **NP25** 28 E7
Ganllwyd **LL40** 37 G3
Gannochy **DD9** 90 E7
Ganstead **HU11** 59 H6
Ganthorpe **YO60** 58 C2
Ganton **YO12** 59 F2
Gaodhail **PA72** 79 H4
Gara Bridge **TQ9** 5 H5
Garabal **G83** 80 E6
Garadheancal **IV26** 95 F1
Garbat **IV23** 96 B5
Garbhallt **PA27** 73 J1
Garboldisham **IP22** 44 E7
Garden **FK8** 74 D1
Garden City **CH5** 48 C6
Gardenstown **AB45** 99 F4
Garderhouse **ZE2** 109 C8
Gardham **HU17** 59 F5
Gare Hill **BA11** 20 A7
Garelochhead **G84** 74 A1
Garford **OX13** 21 H2
Garforth **LS25** 57 K6
Gargrave **BD23** 56 E4
Gargunnock **FK8** 75 F1
Gariob **PA31** 73 F2
Garlies Castle **DG8** 64 E4
Garlieston **DG8** 64 E6
Garlogie **AB32** 91 F4
Garmond **AB53** 99 G5
Garmony **PA65** 79 H3
Garmouth **IV32** 98 B4
Garn **LL53** 36 B2
Garn-Dolbenmaen **LL51** 36 D1
Garnant **SA18** 17 K3
Garneddwen **SY20** 37 G5
Garnett Bridge **LA8** 61 G7
Garnswllt **SA18** 17 K4
Garrabost **HS2** 101 H4
Garrachra **PA23** 73 J2
Garralburn **AB55** 98 C5
Garras **TR12** 2 D6
Garreg **LL48** 37 F1
Garreg Bank **SY21** 38 B4
Garrick **FK15** 81 K6
Garrigill **CA9** 61 J2
Garroch **DG7** 67 K5
Garrochty **PA20** 73 J5
Garros **IV51** 94 B5
Garrow **PH8** 81 K4
Garryhorn **DG7** 67 K4
Garrynahine (Gearraidh na h-Aibhne) **HS2** 100 E4
Garsdale Head **LA10** 61 J7
Garsdon **SN16** 20 C3
Garshall Green **ST18** 40 B2
Garsington **OX44** 21 J1
Garstang **PR3** 55 H5
Garston **L19** 48 D4
Garswood **WN4** 48 E3
Gartachoil **G63** 74 D1
Gartally **IV63** 88 B1
Gartavaich **PA29** 73 G5
Gartbreck **PA43** 72 A5
Gartcosh **G69** 74 E4
Garth, *Bridgend* **CF34** 18 B2
Garth, *Gwyn.* **LL57** 46 D5
Garth, *I.o.M.* **IM4** 54 C6
Garth, *Powys* **LD4** 27 J4
Garth, *Shet.* **ZE2** 109 B7
Garth, *Wrex.* **LL20** 38 B1
Garthbrengy **LD3** 27 K5
Gartheli **SA48** 26 E3
Garthmyl **SY21** 38 A6
Garthorpe, *Leics.* **LE14** 42 B3
Garthorpe, *N.Lincs.* **DN17** 52 B1
Garths **LA8** 61 G7
Garthynty **SA20** 27 G4
Gartincaper **FK16** 81 H7
Gartly **AB54** 90 D1
Gartmore **FK8** 74 D1
Gartnagrenach **PA29** 73 F5
Gartnatra **PA43** 72 B5
Gartness **G63** 74 D2
Gartocharn **G83** 74 C2
Garton **HU11** 59 J6
Garton-on-the-Wolds **YO25** 59 F3
Gartymore **KW8** 105 F7
Garvald **EH41** 76 D3
Garvamore **PH20** 88 C5
Garvan **PH33** 87 F7
Garvard **PA61** 72 B1
Garve **IV23** 95 K5
Garveld **PA28** 66 A3
Garvestone **NR9** 44 E5
Garvie **PA22** 73 J2
Garvock, *Aber.* **AB30** 91 F7
Garvock, *Inclyde* **PA16** 74 A3
Garvock, *P. & K.* **PH2** 82 B6
Garwald **DG13** 69 H3
Garwaldwaterfoot **DG13** 69 H3
Garway **HR2** 28 D6
Garway Hill **HR2** 28 D6
Gask, *Aber.* **AB53** 99 F6
Gask, *Aber.* **AB42** 99 J6
Gask, *P. & K.* **PH3** 82 A6
Gaskan **PH37** 86 E7
Gass **KA19** 67 J3
Gastard **SN13** 20 B5
Gasthorpe **IP22** 44 D7
Gatcombe **PO30** 11 F6
Gate Burton **DN21** 52 B4
Gate Helmsley **YO41** 58 C4
Gateacre **L25** 48 D4
Gatebeck **LA8** 55 J1
Gateford **S81** 51 H4
Gateforth **YO8** 58 B7
Gatehead **KA2** 74 B7
Gatehouse, *Arg. & B.* **PA60** 72 D3
Gatehouse, *P. & K.* **PH15** 81 K3
Gatehouse of Fleet **DG7** 65 G5
Gatelawbridge **DG3** 68 E4
Gateley **NR20** 44 D3
Gatenby **DL7** 57 J1
Gateshaw **TD5** 70 C1
Gateshead **NE8** 71 H7
Gatesheath **CH3** 48 D6
Gateside, *Aber.* **AB33** 90 E3
Gateside, *Angus* **DD8** 83 F3
Gateside, *Fife* **KY14** 82 C7
Gateside, *N.Ayr.* **KA15** 74 B5
Gateslack **DG3** 68 D3
Gathurst **WN5** 48 E2
Gatley **SK8** 49 H4
Gattonside **TD6** 76 D7
Gatwick (London) Airport **RH6** 23 F7

Grasby

Gaufron **LD6** 27 J2
Gaulby **LE7** 41 J5
Gauldry **DD6** 82 E5
Gaunt's Common **BH21** 10 B4
Gautby **LN8** 52 E5
Gavinton **TD11** 77 F5
Gawber **S75** 51 F2
Gawcott **MK18** 31 H5
Gawsworth **SK11** 49 H6
Gawthrop **LA10** 56 B1
Gawthwaite **LA12** 55 F1
Gay Street **RH20** 12 D4
Gaydon **CV35** 30 E3
Gayhurst **MK16** 32 B4
Gayles **DL11** 62 C6
Gayton, *Mersey.* **CH60** 48 B4
Gayton, *Norf.* **PE32** 44 B4
Gayton, *Northants.* **NN7** 31 J3
Gayton, *Staffs.* **ST18** 40 B3
Gayton le Marsh **LN13** 53 H4
Gayton le Wold **LN11** 53 F4
Gayton Thorpe **PE32** 44 B4
Gaywood **PE30** 44 A3
Gazeley **CB8** 34 B2
Geanies Ho. **IV20** 97 F4
Gearach **PA48** 72 A5
Gearnsary **KW11** 104 C5
Gearradh **PH33** 80 A1
Gearraidh Bhailteas **HS8** 84 C2
Gearraidh Bhaird **HS2** 101 F5
Gearraidh na h-Aibhne (Garrynahine) **HS2** 100 E4
Gearraidh na Monadh **HS8** 84 C3
Gearrannan **HS2** 100 D3
Geary **IV55** 93 H5
Gedding **IP30** 34 D3
Geddington **NN14** 42 B7
Gedgrave Hall **IP12** 35 J4
Gedling **NG4** 41 J1
Gedney **PE12** 43 H3
Gedney Broadgate **PE12** 43 H3
Gedney Drove End **PE12** 43 H3
Gedney Dyke **PE12** 43 H3
Gedney Hill **PE12** 43 G4
Gee Cross **SK14** 49 J3
Geirninis **HS8** 92 C7
Geisiadar **HS2** 100 D4
Geldeston **NR34** 45 H6
Gell, *Conwy* **LL22** 47 G6
Gell, *Gwyn.* **LL52** 36 D2
Gelli Gynan **CH7** 47 K7
Gelligaer **CF82** 18 E2
Gellilydan **LL41** 37 F2
Gellioedd **LL21** 37 J1
Gelly **SA66** 16 D3
Gellyburn **PH1** 82 B4
Gellywen **SA33** 17 F2
Gelston **DG7** 65 H5
Gembling **YO25** 59 H4
Gemmil **PA31** 79 J7
Genoch **DG9** 64 B5
Genoch Square **DG9** 64 B5
Gentleshaw **WS15** 40 C4
George Green **SL3** 22 D3
George Nympton **EX36** 7 F3
Georgeham **EX33** 6 C2
Georgetown **PA6** 74 C4
Gerlan **LL57** 46 E6
Germansweek **EX21** 6 C6
Germoe **TR20** 2 C6
Gerrans **TR2** 3 F5
Gerrards Cross **SL9** 22 C3
Gerston **KW12** 105 G3
Gestingthorpe **CO9** 34 C5
Geuffordd **SY22** 38 B4
Geufron **SY18** 37 H7
Gibbshill **DG7** 65 H3
Gibraltar **PE24** 53 J7
Gidea Park **RM2** 23 J3
Gidleigh **TQ13** 6 E7
Giffnock **G46** 74 D5
Gifford **EH41** 76 D4
Giffordland **KA24** 74 A6
Giggleswick **BD24** 56 D3
Gilberdyke **HU15** 58 E7
Gilchriston **EH36** 76 C4
Gilcrux **CA7** 60 C3
Gildersome **LS27** 57 H7
Gildingwells **S81** 51 H4
Gileston **CF62** 18 D5
Gilfach **CF81** 18 E2
Gilfach Goch **CF39** 18 C3
Gilfachrheda **SA45** 26 D3
Gilgarran **CA14** 60 B4
Gillamoor **YO62** 63 H7
Gillen **IV55** 93 H5
Gillenbie **DG11** 69 G5
Gillfoot **DG2** 65 K3
Gilling East **YO62** 58 C2
Gilling West **DL10** 62 C6
Gillingham, *Dorset* **SP8** 9 H2
Gillingham, *Med.* **ME7** 24 D5
Gillingham, *Norf.* **NR34** 45 J6
Gillivoan **KW5** 105 G5
Gillock **KW1** 105 H3
Gillow Heath **ST8** 49 H7
Gills **KW1** 105 J1
Gill's Green **TN18** 14 C4
Gilmanscleuch **TD7** 69 J1
Gilmerton, *Edin.* **EH17** 76 A4
Gilmerton, *P. & K.* **PH7** 81 K5
Gilmilnscroft **KA5** 67 K1
Gilmonby **DL12** 62 A5
Gilmorton **LE17** 41 H7
Gilsland **CA8** 70 B7
Gilsland Spa **CA8** 70 B7
Gilston **EH38** 76 C5
Gilston Park **CM20** 33 H7
Gilwern **NP7** 28 B7
Gimingham **NR11** 45 G2
Giosla **HS2** 100 D5
Gipping **IP14** 34 E2
Gipsey Bridge **PE22** 43 F1
Girlsta **ZE2** 109 D7
Girsby **DL2** 62 E6
Girtford **SG19** 32 E4
Girthon **DG7** 65 G5
Girton, *Cambs.* **CB3** 33 H2
Girton, *Notts.* **NG23** 52 B6
Girvan **KA26** 67 F4
Gisburn **BB7** 56 D5
Gisleham **NR33** 45 K7
Gislingham **IP23** 34 E1
Gissing **IP22** 45 F7
Gittisham **EX14** 7 K6
Givons Grove **KT22** 22 E6
Glack **AB51** 91 F2
Glackour **IV23** 95 H3
Gladestry **HR5** 28 B3
Gladsmuir **EH33** 76 C3
Glaic **PA22** 73 J3
Glais **SA7** 18 A1
Glaisdale **YO21** 63 J6
Glaister **KA27** 73 H7
Glame **IV40** 94 B7
Glamis **DD8** 82 E3
Glan Adda **LL57** 46 D5
Glan Honddu **LD3** 27 K5
Glan-Conwy **LL24** 47 G7
Glan-Dwyfach **LL51** 36 D1
Glan-llynfi **CF34** 18 B2
Glan-y-don **CH8** 47 K5
Glan-y-llyn **CF15** 18 E3
Glan-yr-afon, *Gwyn.* **LL21** 37 K1
Glan-yr-afon, *Gwyn.* **LL23** 37 J1
Glanaber Terrace **LL24** 37 G1
Glanaman **SA18** 17 K3
Glanbran **SA20** 27 G5
Glanderston **AB52** 90 D2
Glandford **NR25** 44 E1
Glandwr, *B.Gwent* **NP13** 19 F1
Glandwr, *Pembs.* **SA34** 16 E2
Glangrwyne **NP8** 28 B7
Glanmule **SY16** 38 A6
Glanrhyd **SA43** 26 A4
Glanton **NE66** 71 F2
Glantwymyn (Cemmaes Road) **SY20** 37 H5
Glanvilles Wootton **DT9** 9 F4
Glapthorn **PE8** 42 D7
Glapwell **S44** 51 G6
Glasahoile **FK8** 81 F7
Glasbury **HR3** 28 A5
Glaschoil **PH26** 89 H1
Glascoed **NP4** 19 G1
Glascorrie **AB35** 90 B5
Glascote **B77** 40 E5
Glascwm **LD1** 28 A3
Glasdrum **PA38** 80 B3
Glasfryn **LL21** 47 H7
GLASGOW G 74 D4
Glasgow Airport **PA3** 74 C4
Glashmore **AB31** 91 F4
Glasinfryn **LL57** 46 D6
Glasnacardoch **PH41** 86 C5
Glasnakille **IV49** 86 B3
Glaspant **SA38** 17 F1
Glaspwll **SY20** 37 G6
Glassaugh **AB45** 98 D4
Glassburn **IV4** 87 K1
Glassel **AB31** 90 E5
Glassenbury **TN17** 14 C4
Glasserton **DG8** 64 E7
Glassford **ML10** 75 F6
Glasshouse Hill **GL17** 29 G6
Glasshouses **HG3** 57 G3
Glassingall **FK15** 81 J7
Glasslie **KY6** 82 D7
Glasson, *Cumb.* **CA7** 69 H7
Glasson, *Lancs.* **LA2** 55 H4
Glassonby **CA10** 61 G3
Glasterlaw **DD11** 83 G2
Glaston **LE15** 42 B5
Glastonbury **BA6** 8 D1
Glatton **PE28** 42 E7
Glazebury **WA3** 49 F3
Glazeley **WV16** 39 G7
Gleadless **S12** 51 F4
Gleadsmoss **SK11** 49 H6
Gleann Ghrabhair **HS2** 101 F5
Gleann Tholastaidh **HS2** 101 H3
Gleaston **LA12** 55 F2
Glecknabae **PA20** 73 J4
Gledhow **LS8** 57 J6
Gledrid **LL14** 38 B2
Glemsford **CO10** 34 C4
Glen, *D. & G.* **DG2** 65 J3
Glen, *D. & G.* **DG7** 65 F5
Glen Auldyn **IM7** 54 D4
Glen Parva **LE2** 41 H6
Glen Trool Lodge **DG8** 67 J5
Glen Vine **IM4** 54 C6
Glenae **DG1** 68 E5
Glenaladale **PH37** 86 E7
Glenald **G84** 74 A1
Glenamachrie **PA34** 80 A5
Glenapp Castle **KA26** 66 E5
Glenarm **DD8** 82 E1
Glenbarr **PA29** 72 E7
Glenbatrick **PA60** 72 D3
Glenbeg, *High.* **IV23** 95 K3
Glenbeg, *High.* **PH26** 89 H2
Glenbeg, *High.* **PH36** 79 G1
Glenbeich **FK19** 81 H5
Glenbervie, *Aber.* **AB39** 91 F6
Glenbervie, *Falk.* **FK5** 75 G2
Glenboig **ML5** 75 F4
Glenborrodale **PH36** 79 H1
Glenbranter **PA27** 73 K1
Glenbreck **ML12** 69 F1
Glenbrittle **IV47** 85 K2
Glenbuck **KA18** 68 C1
Glenbyre **PA62** 79 G5
Glencaple **DG1** 65 K4
Glencarse **PH2** 82 C5
Glencat **AB34** 90 D5
Glenceitlein **PH49** 80 C3
Glencloy **KA27** 73 J7
Glencoe **PH49** 80 C2
Glenconglass **AB37** 89 J2
Glencraig **KY5** 75 K1
Glencripesdale **PH36** 79 H2
Glencrosh **DG3** 68 C5
Glencruittein **PA34** 79 K5
Glencuie **AB33** 90 C3
Glendearg, *D. & G.* **DG13** 69 H3
Glendearg, *Sc.Bord.* **TD1** 76 D7
Glendessary **PH34** 87 F5
Glendevon **FK14** 82 A7
Glendoebeg **PH32** 88 B4
Glendoick **PH2** 82 D5
Glendoll Lodge **DD8** 89 K7
Glendoune **KA26** 67 F4
Glendrissaig **KA26** 67 F4
Glenduckie **KY14** 82 D6
Glenduisk **KA26** 67 G5
Glendye Lodge **AB31** 90 E6
Gleneagles **PH3** 82 A7
Gleneagles Hotel **PH3** 82 A6
Glenearn **PH2** 82 C6
Glenegedale **PA42** 72 B5
Glenelg **IV40** 86 E3
Glenfarg **PH2** 82 C6
Glenfeochan **PA34** 79 K5
Glenfield **LE3** 41 H5
Glenfinnan **PH37** 87 F6
Glenfoot **PH2** 82 C6
Glengalmadale **PH33** 79 K2
Glengap **DG6** 65 G5
Glengarnock **KA14** 74 B5
Glengarrisdale **PA60** 72 E1
Glengennet **KA26** 67 G4
Glengolly **KW14** 105 G2
Glengrasco **IV51** 93 K7
Glengyle **FK17** 80 E6
Glenhead **DG2** 68 D5
Glenhead Farm **PH11** 82 D1
Glenhurich **PH37** 79 K1
Glenkerry **TD7** 69 H2
Glenkiln **KA27** 73 J7
Glenkin **PA23** 73 K3
Glenkindie **AB33** 90 C3
Glenlair **DG7** 65 H3
Glenlatterach **IV30** 97 K6
Glenlean **PA23** 73 J2
Glenlee, *Angus* **DD9** 90 C6
Glenlee, *D. & G.* **DG7** 68 B5
Glenlichorn **FK15** 81 J6
Glenlivet **AB37** 89 J2
Glenlochar **DG7** 65 H4
Glenluce **DG8** 64 B5
Glenmallan **G84** 74 A1
Glenmanna **DG3** 68 C3
Glenmavis **ML6** 75 F4
Glenmaye **IM5** 54 B5
Glenmeanie **IV6** 95 J6
Glenmore, *Arg. & B.* **PA20** 73 J4
Glenmore, *High.* **IV51** 93 K7
Glenmore Lodge **PH22** 89 G4
Glenmoy **DD8** 83 F1
Glenmuick **IV27** 103 F7
Glennoe **PA35** 80 B4
Glenochar **ML12** 68 E2
Glenogil **DD8** 83 F1
Glenprosen **DD8** 82 E1
Glenquiech **DD8** 83 F1
Glenramskill **PA28** 66 B2
Glenrazie **DG8** 64 D4
Glenridding **CA11** 60 E5
Glenrisdell **PA29** 73 G5
Glenrossal **IV27** 96 B1
Glenrothes **KY7** 82 D7
Glensanda **PA34** 79 K3
Glensaugh **AB30** 90 E7
Glensgaich **IV14** 96 B5
Glenshalg **AB31** 90 D4
Glenshee **PH1** 82 A4
Glenshellish **PA27** 73 K1
Glensluan **PA27** 73 J1
Glentaggart **ML11** 68 D1
Glentham **LN8** 52 D3
Glenton **AB51** 90 E2
Glentress **EH45** 76 A7
Glentrool **DG8** 64 D3
Glentruan **IM7** 54 D3
Glentworth **DN21** 52 C4
Glenuachdarach **IV51** 93 K6
Glenure **PA38** 80 B3
Glenurquhart **IV11** 96 E5
Glenwhilly **DG8** 64 B3
Glespin **ML11** 68 D1
Gletness **ZE2** 109 D7
Glewstone **HR9** 28 E6
Glinton **PE6** 42 E5
Glooston **LE16** 42 A6
Glororum **NE69** 77 K7
Glossop **SK13** 50 C3
Gloster Hill **NE65** 71 H3
GLOUCESTER GL 29 H7
Gloup **ZE2** 108 E2
Gloweth **TR1** 2 E4
Glusburn **BD20** 57 F5
Gluss **ZE2** 108 C5
Glympton **OX20** 31 F6
Glyn **LL24** 47 F7
Glyn Ceiriog **LL20** 38 B2
Glyn-Cywarch **LL46** 37 F2
Glyn-Neath **SA11** 18 B1
Glynarthen **SA44** 26 C4
Glyncoch **CF37** 18 D2
Glyncorrwg **SA13** 18 B2
Glynde **BN8** 13 H6
Glyndebourne **BN8** 13 H5
Glyndyfrdwy **LL21** 38 A1
Glynogwr **CF35** 18 C3
Glyntaff **CF37** 18 D3
Glynteg **SA44** 17 G1
Gnosall **ST20** 40 A3
Gnosall Heath **ST20** 40 A4
Goadby **LE7** 42 A6
Goadby Marwood **LE14** 42 A3
Goatacre **SN11** 20 D4
Goatfield **PA32** 80 B7
Goathill **DT9** 9 F3
Goathland **YO22** 63 K6
Goathurst **TA5** 8 B1
Gobernuisgeach **KW12** 104 E5
Gobhaig **HS3** 100 C7
Gobowen **SY10** 38 B2
Godalming **GU7** 22 C7
Godford Cross **EX14** 7 K5
Godmanchester **PE29** 33 F2
Godmanstone **DT2** 9 F5
Godmersham **CT4** 15 F2
Godolphin Cross **TR13** 2 D5
Godor **SY22** 38 B4
Godre'r-graig **SA9** 18 A1
Godshill, *Hants.* **SP6** 10 C3
Godshill, *I.o.W.* **PO38** 11 G6
Godstone **RH9** 23 G6
Goetre **NP4** 19 G1
Goff's Oak **EN7** 23 G1
Gogar **EH12** 75 K3
Gogarth **LL30** 47 F4
Goginan **SY23** 37 F7
Goirtean a' Chladaich **PH33** 87 G7
Goirtein **PA27** 73 H2
Golan **LL49** 36 E1
Golant **PL23** 4 B5
Golberdon **PL17** 4 D3
Golborne **WA3** 49 F3
Golcar **HD7** 50 D1
Gold Hill **PE14** 43 J6
Goldcliff **NP18** 19 G3
Golden Cross **BN27** 13 J5
Golden Green **TN11** 23 K7
Golden Grove **SA32** 17 J3
Golden Pot **GU34** 22 A7
Golden Valley **GL51** 29 J6
Goldenhill **ST6** 49 H7
Golders Green **NW11** 23 F3
Goldhanger **CM9** 24 E1
Goldielea **DG2** 65 K3
Golding **SY5** 38 E5
Goldington **MK41** 32 D3
Goldsborough, *N.Yorks.* **YO21** 63 K5
Goldsborough, *N.Yorks.* **HG5** 57 J4
Goldsithney **TR20** 2 C5
Goldthorpe **S63** 51 G2
Goldworthy **EX39** 6 B3
Gollanfield **IV2** 97 F6
Golspie **KW10** 97 F2
Golval **KW13** 104 D2
Gomeldon **SP4** 10 C1
Gomersal **BD19** 57 H7
Gometra Ho. **PA73** 78 E3
Gomshall **GU5** 22 D7
Gonachan **G63** 74 E2
Gonalston **NG14** 41 J1
Gonfirth **ZE2** 109 C6
Good Easter **CM1** 33 K7
Gooderstone **PE33** 44 B5
Goodleigh **EX32** 6 E2
Goodmanham **YO43** 58 E5
Goodnestone, *Kent* **ME13** 25 G5
Goodnestone, *Kent* **CT3** 15 H2
Goodrich **HR9** 28 E7
Goodrington **TQ4** 5 J5
Goodwick (Wdig) **SA64** 16 C1
Goodworth Clatford **SP11** 21 G7
Goodyers End **CV12** 41 F7
Goole **DN14** 58 D7
Goonbell **TR5** 2 E4
Goonhavern **TR4** 2 E3
Goose Green **TN11** 23 K6
Gooseham **EX23** 6 A4
Goosewell **PL9** 5 F5
Goosey **SN7** 21 G2
Goosnargh **PR3** 55 J6
Goostrey **CW4** 49 G5
Gorcott Hill **B80** 30 B2
Gorddinog **LL33** 46 E5
Gordon **TD3** 76 E6
Gordonbush **KW9** 97 F1
Gordonstoun **IV30** 97 J5
Gordonstown, *Aber.* **AB45** 98 D5
Gordonstown, *Aber.* **AB51** 91 F1
Gore Cross **SN10** 20 D6
Gore Street **CT12** 25 J5
Gorebridge **EH23** 76 B4
Gorefield **PE13** 43 H4
Goring **RG8** 21 K3
Goring-by-Sea **BN12** 12 E6
Gorleston on Sea **NR31** 45 K5
Gorllwyn **SA33** 17 G1
Gornalwood **DY3** 40 B6
Gorrachie **AB45** 99 F5
Gorran Churchtown **PL26** 3 G4
Gorran Haven **PL26** 4 A6
Gors **SY23** 27 F1
Gorsedd **CH8** 47 K5
Gorseinon **SA4** 17 J5
Gorseness **KW17** 107 D6
Gorsgoch **SA40** 26 D3
Gorslas **SA14** 17 J3
Gorsley **HR9** 29 F6
Gorsley Common **HR9** 29 F6
Gorstan **IV23** 95 K5
Gorstanvorran **PH37** 86 E7
Gorten **PA64** 79 J4
Gortenbuie **PA70** 79 G4
Gorteneorn **PH36** 79 H1
Gorton, *Arg. & B.* **PA78** 78 C2
Gorton, *Gt.Man.* **M18** 49 H3
Gosbeck **IP6** 35 F3
Gosberton **PE11** 43 F2
Goseley Dale **DE11** 41 F3
Gosfield **CO9** 34 B6
Gosforth, *Cumb.* **CA20** 60 B6
Gosforth, *T. & W.* **NE3** 71 H7
Gosmore **SG4** 32 E6
Gospel End **DY3** 40 B6
Gosport **PO12** 11 H5
Gossabrough **ZE2** 108 E4
Gossops Green **RH11** 13 F3
Goswick **TD15** 77 J6
Gotham **NG11** 41 H2
Gotherington **GL52** 29 J6
Gott **ZE2** 109 D8
Goudhurst **TN17** 14 C4
Goulceby **LN11** 53 F5
Gourdas **AB53** 99 F6
Gourdon **DD10** 91 G7
Gourock **PA19** 74 A3
Govan **G51** 74 D4
Goveton **TQ7** 5 H6
Govilon **NP7** 28 B7
Gowanhill **AB43** 99 J4
Gowdall **DN14** 58 C7
Gowerton **SA4** 17 J5
Gowkhall **KY12** 75 J2
Gowthorpe **YO41** 58 D4
Goxhill, *E.Riding* **HU11** 59 H5
Goxhill, *N.Lincs.* **DN19** 59 H7
Goytre **SA13** 18 A3
Grabhair **HS2** 101 F6
Gradbach **SK17** 49 J6
Grade **TR12** 2 E7
Graffham **GU28** 12 C5
Grafham, *Cambs.* **PE28** 32 E2
Grafham, *Surr.* **GU5** 22 D7
Grafton, *Here.* **HR2** 28 D5
Grafton, *N.Yorks.* **YO51** 57 K3
Grafton, *Oxon.* **OX18** 21 F1
Grafton, *Shrop.* **SY4** 38 D4
Grafton, *Worcs.* **HR6** 28 E2
Grafton Flyford **WR7** 29 J3
Grafton Regis **NN12** 31 J4
Grafton Underwood **NN14** 32 C1
Grafty Green **ME17** 14 D3
Graianrhyd **CH7** 48 B7
Graig, *Conwy* **LL28** 47 G5
Graig, *Denb.* **LL17** 47 J5
Graig-fechan **LL15** 47 K7
Grain **ME3** 24 E4
Grainel **PA44** 72 A4
Grainhow **AB53** 99 G6
Grainsby **DN36** 53 F3
Grainthorpe **LN11** 53 G3
Grampound **TR2** 3 G4
Grampound Road **TR2** 3 G3
Gramsdal **HS7** 92 D6
Granborough **MK18** 31 J6
Granby **NG13** 42 A2
Grandborough **CV23** 31 F2
Grandtully **PH9** 82 A2
Grange, *Cumb.* **CA12** 60 D5
Grange, *High.* **IV63** 87 K1
Grange, *Med.* **ME7** 24 D5
Grange, *N.Yorks.* **TS9** 63 G7
Grange, *P. & K.* **PH2** 82 D5
Grange Crossroads **AB55** 98 C5
Grange Hall **IV36** 97 H5
Grange Hill **IG7** 23 H2
Grange Moor **WF4** 50 E1
Grange of Lindores **KY14** 82 D6
Grange Villa **DH2** 62 D1
Grange-over-Sands **LA11** 55 H2
Grangemill **DE4** 50 E7
Grangemouth **FK3** 75 H2
Grangemuir **KY10** 83 G7
Grangeston **KA26** 67 G4
Grangetown, *Cardiff* **CF11** 18 E4
Grangetown, *R. & C.* **TS6** 63 G4
Granish **PH22** 89 G3
Gransmoor **YO25** 59 H4
Granston **SA62** 16 B1
Grantchester **CB3** 33 H3
Grantham **NG31** 42 C2
Grantley **HG4** 57 H2
Grantlodge **AB51** 91 F3
Granton House **DG10** 69 F3
Grantown-on-Spey **PH26** 89 H2
Grantshouse **TD11** 77 G4
Grappenhall **WA4** 49 F4
Grasby **DN38** 52 D2

Grasmere

Grasmere **LA22** 60 E6
Grasscroft **OL4** 49 J2
Grassendale **L19** 48 C4
Grassholme **DL12** 62 A4
Grassington **BD23** 57 F3
Grassmoor **S42** 51 G6
Grassthorpe **NG23** 51 K6
Grateley **SP11** 21 F7
Gratwich **ST14** 40 C2
Graveley, *Cambs.* **PE19** 33 F2
Graveley, *Herts.* **SG4** 33 F6
Gravelly Hill **B23** 40 D6
Gravels **SY5** 38 C5
Graven **ZE2** 108 D5
Graveney **ME13** 25 G5
Gravesend **DA11** 24 C4
Grayingham **DN21** 52 C3
Grayrigg **LA8** 61 G7
Grays **RM17** 24 C4
Grayshott **GU26** 12 B3
Grayswood **GU27** 12 C3
Grazeley **RG7** 22 A5
Greasbrough **S61** 51 G3
Greasby **CH49** 48 B4
Great Abington **CB1** 33 J4
Great Addington **NN14** 32 C1
Great Alne **B49** 30 C3
Great Altcar **L37** 48 C2
Great Amwell **SG12** 33 G7
Great Asby **CA16** 61 H5
Great Ashfield **IP31** 34 D2
Great Ayton **TS9** 63 G5
Great Baddow **CM2** 24 D1
Great Bardfield **CM7** 33 K5
Great Barford **MK44** 32 E3
Great Barr **B43** 40 C6
Great Barrington **OX18** 30 D7
Great Barrow **CH3** 48 D6
Great Barton **IP31** 34 C2
Great Barugh **YO17** 58 D2
Great Bavington **NE19** 70 E5
Great Bealings **IP13** 35 G4
Great Bedwyn **SN8** 21 F5
Great Bentley **CO7** 35 F6
Great Billing **NN3** 32 B2
Great Bircham **PE31** 44 B2
Great Blakenham **IP6** 35 F3
Great Bolas **TF6** 39 F3
Great Bookham **KT23** 22 E6
Great Bourton **OX17** 31 F4
Great Bowden **LE16** 42 A7
Great Bradley **CB8** 33 K3
Great Braxted **CM8** 34 C7
Great Bricett **IP7** 34 E3
Great Brickhill **MK17** 32 C5
Great Bridgeford **ST18** 40 A3
Great Brington **NN7** 31 H2
Great Bromley **CO7** 34 E6
Great Broughton, *Cumb.* **CA13** 60 B3
Great Broughton, *N.Yorks.* **TS9** 63 G6
Great Budworth **CW9** 49 F5
Great Burdon **DL1** 62 E5
Great Burstead **CM12** 24 C2
Great Busby **TS9** 63 G6
Great Canfield **CM6** 33 J7
Great Canney **CM3** 24 E1
Great Carlton **LN11** 53 H4
Great Casterton **PE9** 42 D5
Great Chart **TN23** 14 E3
Great Chatwell **TF10** 39 G4
Great Chesterford **CB10** 33 J4
Great Cheverell **SN10** 20 C6
Great Chishill **SG8** 33 H5
Great Clacton **CO15** 35 F7
Great Clifton **CA14** 60 B4
Great Coates **DN37** 53 F2
Great Comberton **WR10** 29 J4
Great Corby **CA4** 61 F1
Great Cornard **CO10** 34 C4
Great Cowden **HU11** 59 J5
Great Coxwell **SN7** 21 F2
Great Crakehall **DL8** 62 D7
Great Cransley **NN14** 32 B1
Great Cressingham **IP25** 44 C5
Great Crosby **L23** 48 C2
Great Cubley **DE6** 40 D2
Great Dalby **LE14** 42 A4
Great Doddington **NN29** 32 B2
Great Driffield **YO25** 59 G4
Great Dunham **PE32** 44 C4
Great Dunmow **CM6** 33 K6
Great Durnford **SP4** 10 C1
Great Easton, *Essex* **CM6** 33 K6
Great Easton, *Leics.* **LE16** 42 B6
Great Eccleston **PR3** 55 H5
Great Edstone **YO62** 58 D1
Great Ellingham **NR17** 44 E6
Great Elm **BA11** 20 A7
Great Eversden **CB3** 33 G3
Great Fencote **DL7** 62 D7
Great Finborough **IP14** 34 E3
Great Fransham **NR19** 44 C4
Great Gaddesden **HP1** 32 D7
Great Gidding **PE28** 42 E7
Great Givendale **YO42** 58 E4
Great Glemham **IP17** 35 H2
Great Glen **LE8** 41 J6
Great Gonerby **NG31** 42 B2
Great Gransden **SG19** 33 F3
Great Green, *Norf.* **IP20** 45 G6
Great Green, *Suff.* **IP30** 34 D3
Great Habton **YO17** 58 D2
Great Hale **NG34** 42 E1
Great Hallingbury **CM22** 33 J7
Great Hanwood **SY5** 38 D5
Great Harrowden **NN9** 32 B1
Great Harwood **BB6** 56 C6
Great Haseley **OX44** 21 K1
Great Hatfield **HU11** 59 H5
Great Haywood **ST18** 40 C3
Great Heath **CV6** 41 F7
Great Heck **DN14** 58 B7
Great Henny **CO10** 34 C5
Great Hinton **BA14** 20 C6
Great Hockham **IP24** 44 D6
Great Holland **CO13** 35 G7
Great Horkesley **CO6** 34 D5
Great Hormead **SG9** 33 H5
Great Horwood **MK17** 31 J5
Great Houghton, *Northants.* **NN4** 31 J3
Great Houghton, *S.Yorks.* **S72** 51 G2
Great Hucklow **SK17** 50 D5
Great Kelk **YO25** 59 H4
Great Kimble **HP17** 22 B1
Great Kingshill **HP15** 22 B2
Great Langton **DL7** 62 D7
Great Leighs **CM3** 34 B7
Great Limber **DN37** 52 E2
Great Linford **MK14** 32 B4
Great Livermere **IP31** 34 C1
Great Longstone **DE45** 50 E5
Great Lumley **DH3** 62 D2
Great Lyth **SY3** 38 D5
Great Malvern **WR14** 29 G4
Great Maplestead **CO9** 34 C5
Great Marton **FY4** 55 G6
Great Massingham **PE32** 44 B3
Great Melton **NR9** 45 F5
Great Milton **OX44** 21 K1
Great Missenden **HP16** 22 B1
Great Mitton **BB7** 56 C6
Great Mongeham **CT14** 15 J2
Great Moulton **NR15** 45 F6
Great Munden **SG11** 33 G6
Great Musgrave **CA17** 61 J5
Great Ness **SY4** 38 C4
Great Oak **NP15** 28 C7
Great Oakley, *Essex* **CO12** 35 F6
Great Oakley, *Northants.* **NN14** 42 B7
Great Offley **SG5** 32 E6
Great Ormside **CA16** 61 J5
Great Orton **CA5** 60 E1
Great Ouseburn **YO26** 57 K3
Great Oxendon **LE16** 42 A7
Great Oxney Green **CM1** 24 C1
Great Palgrave **PE32** 44 C4
Great Parndon **CM19** 23 H1
Great Paxton **PE19** 33 F2
Great Plumpton **PR4** 55 G6
Great Plumstead **NR13** 45 G5
Great Ponton **NG33** 42 C2
Great Preston **LS26** 57 J7
Great Raveley **PE28** 43 F7
Great Rissington **GL54** 30 C7
Great Rollright **OX7** 30 E5
Great Ryburgh **NR21** 44 D3
Great Ryle **NE66** 71 F2
Great Ryton **SY5** 38 D5
Great Saling **CM7** 33 K6
Great Salkeld **CA11** 61 G3
Great Sampford **CB10** 33 K5
Great Sankey **WA5** 48 E4
Great Saxham **IP29** 34 B2
Great Shefford **RG17** 21 G4
Great Shelford **CB2** 33 H3
Great Smeaton **DL6** 62 E6
Great Snoring **NR21** 44 D2
Great Somerford **SN15** 20 C3
Great Stainton **TS21** 62 E4
Great Stambridge **SS4** 24 E2
Great Staughton **PE19** 32 E2
Great Steeping **PE23** 53 H6
Great Stonar **CT13** 15 J2
Great Strickland **CA10** 61 G4
Great Stukeley **PE28** 33 F1
Great Sturton **LN9** 53 F5
Great Sutton, *Ches.* **CH66** 48 C5
Great Sutton, *Shrop.* **SY8** 38 E7
Great Swinburne **NE48** 70 E6
Great Tew **OX7** 30 E6
Great Tey **CO6** 34 C6
Great Thurlow **CB9** 33 K4
Great Torrington **EX38** 6 D4
Great Tosson **NE65** 71 F3
Great Totham, *Essex* **CM9** 34 C7
Great Totham, *Essex* **CM9** 34 C7
Great Urswick **LA12** 55 F2
Great Wakering **SS3** 25 F3
Great Waldingfield **CO10** 34 D4
Great Walsingham **NR22** 44 D2
Great Waltham **CM3** 33 K7
Great Warley **CM14** 23 J2
Great Washbourne **GL20** 29 J5
Great Welnetham **IP30** 34 C3
Great Wenham **CO7** 34 E5
Great Whittington **NE19** 71 F6
Great Wigborough **CO5** 34 D7
Great Wilbraham **CB1** 33 J3
Great Wishford **SP2** 10 B1
Great Witcombe **GL3** 29 J7
Great Witley **WR6** 29 G2
Great Wolford **CV36** 30 D5
Great Woolstone **MK6** 32 B5
Great Wratting **CB9** 33 K4
Great Wymondley **SG4** 33 F6
Great Wyrley **WS6** 40 B5
Great Wytheford **SY4** 38 E4
Great Yarmouth **NR30** 45 K5
Great Yeldham **CO9** 34 B5
Greatford **PE9** 42 D4
Greatgate **ST10** 40 C1
Greatham, *Hants.* **GU33** 11 J1
Greatham, *Hart.* **TS25** 63 F4
Greatham, *W.Suss.* **RH20** 12 D5
Greatstone-on-Sea **TN28** 15 F5
Greatworth **OX17** 31 G4
Green End, *Beds.* **MK44** 32 E3
Green End, *Herts.* **SG12** 33 G6
Green Hammerton **YO26** 57 K4
Green Ore **BA5** 19 J6
Green Street **WD6** 22 E2
Green Street Green, *Gt.Lon.* **BR6** 23 H5
Green Street Green, *Kent* **DA2** 23 J4
Green Tye **SG10** 33 H7
Greenburn **DD5** 83 F4
Greencroft Hall **DH7** 62 C2
Greendams **AB31** 90 E5
Greendykes **NE66** 71 F1
Greenfield, *Beds.* **MK45** 32 D5
Greenfield (Maes-Glas), *Flints.* **CH8** 47 K5
Greenfield, *Gt.Man.* **OL3** 50 C2
Greenfield, *High.* **PH35** 87 J4
Greenfield, *Oxon.* **RG9** 22 A2
Greenford **UB6** 22 E3
Greengairs **ML6** 75 F3
Greenhalgh **PR4** 55 H6
Greenhall **AB52** 90 E2
Greenham, *Som.* **TA21** 7 J3
Greenham, *W.Berks.* **RG14** 21 H5
Greenhaugh **NE48** 70 C5
Greenhead **CA8** 70 B7
Greenheads **AB42** 91 J1
Greenhill, *Gt.Lon.* **HA1** 22 E3
Greenhill, *High.* **KW9** 97 G1
Greenhill, *S.Yorks.* **S8** 51 F4
Greenhithe **DA9** 23 J4
Greenholm **KA16** 74 D7
Greenholme **CA10** 61 G6
Greenhow Hill **HG3** 57 G3
Greenigo **KW15** 107 D7
Greenland **KW14** 105 H2
Greenlands **RG9** 22 A3
Greenlaw, *Aber.* **AB45** 98 E5
Greenlaw, *Sc.Bord.* **TD10** 77 F6
Greenloaning **FK15** 81 K7
Greenmount **BL8** 49 G1
Greenmyre **AB53** 91 G1
Greenock **PA16** 74 A3
Greenodd **LA12** 55 G1
Greens Norton **NN12** 31 H3
Greenscares **FK15** 81 J6
Greenside **NE40** 71 G7
Greenskares **AB45** 99 F4
Greenstead Green **CO9** 34 C6
Greensted **CM5** 23 J1
Greenway, *Pembs.* **SA62** 16 D1
Greenway, *Som.* **TA3** 8 C2
Greenwich, *Gt.Lon.* **SE10** 23 G4
Greenwich, *Gt.Lon.* **SE** 23 G4
Greet **GL54** 30 B5
Greete **SY8** 28 E1
Greetham, *Lincs.* **LN9** 53 G5
Greetham, *Rut.* **LE15** 42 C4
Greetland **HX4** 57 F7
Greinetobht **HS6** 92 D4
Greinton **TA7** 8 D1
Grenaby **IM9** 54 B6
Grendon, *Northants.* **NN7** 32 B2
Grendon, *Warks.* **CV9** 40 E6
Grendon Common **CV9** 40 E6
Grendon Green **HR6** 28 E3
Grendon Underwood **HP18** 31 H6
Grenoside **S35** 51 F3
Greosabhagh **HS3** 93 G2
Gresford **LL12** 48 C7
Gresham **NR11** 45 F2
Greshornish **IV51** 93 J6
Gressenhall **NR20** 44 D4
Gressingham **LA2** 55 J2
Greta Bridge **DL12** 62 B5
Gretna **DG16** 69 J7
Gretna Green **DG16** 69 J7
Gretton, *Glos.* **GL54** 30 B5
Gretton, *Northants.* **NN17** 42 C6
Gretton, *Shrop.* **SY6** 38 E6
Grewelthorpe **HG4** 57 H2
Greygarth **HG4** 57 G2
Greylake **TA7** 8 C1
Greys Green **RG9** 22 A3
Greysouthen **CA13** 60 B4
Greystoke **CA11** 60 F3
Greystone, *Aber.* **AB35** 89 K5
Greystone, *Angus* **DD11** 83 G3
Greystone, *Lancs.* **BB9** 56 D5
Greywell **RG29** 22 A6
Griais **HS2** 101 G3
Gribthorpe **DN14** 58 D6
Gribton **DG2** 68 E5
Gridley Corner **PL15** 6 B6
Griff **CV10** 41 F7
Griffithstown **NP4** 19 F2
Grigadale **PH36** 79 F1
Grigghall **LA8** 61 F7
Grimeford Village **PR6** 49 F1
Grimethorpe **S72** 51 G2
Griminis **HS7** 92 C6
Grimister **ZE2** 108 D3
Grimley **WR2** 29 H2
Grimmet **KA19** 67 H2
Grimness **KW17** 107 D8
Grimoldby **LN11** 53 G4
Grimpo **SY11** 38 C3
Grimsargh **PR2** 55 J6
Grimsbury **OX16** 31 F4
Grimsby **DN32** 53 F2
Grimscote **NN12** 31 H3
Grimscott **EX23** 6 A5
Grimsiadar **HS2** 101 G5
Grimsthorpe **PE10** 42 D3
Grimston, *Leics.* **LE14** 41 J3
Grimston, *Norf.* **PE32** 44 B3
Grimstone **DT2** 9 F5
Grindale **YO16** 59 H2
Grindiscol **ZE2** 109 D9
Grindle **TF11** 39 G5
Grindleford **S32** 50 E5
Grindleton **BB7** 56 C5
Grindley **ST14** 40 C3
Grindlow **SK17** 50 D5
Grindon, *Northumb.* **TD15** 77 H6
Grindon, *Staffs.* **ST13** 50 C7
Gringley on the Hill **DN10** 51 K3
Grinsdale **CA5** 60 E1
Grinshill **SY4** 38 E3
Grinton **DL11** 62 B7
Griomarstaidh **HS2** 100 E4
Grishipoll **PA78** 78 C2
Gristhorpe **YO14** 59 G1
Griston **IP25** 44 D6
Gritley **KW17** 107 E7
Grittenham **SN15** 20 D3
Grittleton **SN14** 20 B3
Grizebeck **LA17** 55 F1
Grizedale **LA22** 60 E7
Grobister **KW17** 106 F5
Groby **LE6** 41 H5
Groes **LL16** 47 J6
Groes-faen **CF72** 18 D3
Groes-lwyd **SY21** 38 B4
Groesffordd **LL53** 36 B2
Groesffordd Marli **LL22** 47 J5
Groeslon **LL54** 46 C7
Grogport **PA28** 73 G6
Groigearraidh **HS8** 84 C1
Gromford **IP17** 35 H3
Gronant **LL19** 47 J4
Groombridge **TN3** 13 J3
Grosmont, *Mon.* **NP7** 28 D6
Grosmont, *N.Yorks.* **YO22** 63 K6
Grotaig **IV63** 88 B2
Groton **CO10** 34 D4
Groundistone Heights **TD9** 69 K2
Grove, *Dorset* **DT5** 9 F7
Grove, *Kent* **CT3** 25 J5
Grove, *Notts.* **DN22** 51 K5
Grove, *Oxon.* **OX12** 21 H2
Grove Park **SE12** 23 H4
Grovesend **SA4** 17 J4
Gruids **IV27** 96 C1
Gruinart Flats **PA44** 72 A4
Gruline **PA71** 79 G4
Grundcruie **PH1** 82 B5
Grundisburgh **IP13** 35 G3
Gruting **ZE2** 109 B8
Grutness **ZE3** 109 G10
Gualachulain **PH49** 80 C3
Guardbridge **KY16** 83 F6
Guarlford **WR13** 29 H4
Guay **PH9** 82 B3
Gubbergill **CA19** 60 B7
Guestling Green **TN35** 14 D6
Guestling Thorn **TN35** 14 D6
Guestwick **NR20** 44 E3
Guide Post **NE62** 71 H5
Guilden Morden **SG8** 33 F4
Guilden Sutton **CH3** 48 D6
GUILDFORD GU 22 C7
Guildtown **PH2** 82 C4
Guilsborough **NN6** 31 H1
Guilsfield **SY21** 38 B4
Guisborough **TS14** 63 H5
Guiseley **LS20** 57 G5
Guist **NR20** 44 D3
Guith **KW17** 106 E4
Guiting Power **GL54** 30 B6
Gulberwick **ZE2** 109 D9
Gullane **EH31** 76 C2
Gulval **TR18** 2 B5
Gulworthy **PL19** 4 E3
Gumfreston **SA70** 16 E4
Gumley **LE16** 41 J7
Gunby, *E.Riding* **YO8** 58 D6
Gunby, *Lincs.* **NG33** 42 C3
Gundleton **SO24** 11 H1
Gunn **EX32** 6 E2
Gunnerside **DL11** 62 A7
Gunnerton **NE48** 70 E6
Gunness **DN15** 52 B1
Gunnislake **PL18** 4 E3
Gunnista **ZE2** 109 D8
Gunter's Bridge **GU28** 12 C4
Gunthorpe, *Norf.* **NR24** 44 E2
Gunthorpe, *Notts.* **NG14** 41 J1
Gunville **PO30** 11 F6
Gunwalloe **TR12** 2 D6
Gurnard **PO31** 11 F5
Gurney Slade **BA3** 19 K7
Gurnos **SA9** 18 A1
Gussage All Saints **BH21** 10 B3
Gussage St. Michael **BH21** 9 J3
Guston **CT15** 15 J3
Gutcher **ZE2** 108 E3
Guthrie **DD8** 83 G2
Guyhirn **PE13** 43 G5
Guynd **DD11** 83 G3
Guy's Head **PE12** 43 H3
Guy's Marsh **SP7** 9 H2
Guyzance **NE65** 71 H3
Gwaelod-y-garth **CF15** 18 E3
Gwaenysgor **LL18** 47 J4
Gwaithla **HR5** 28 B3
Gwalchmai **LL65** 46 B5
Gwaun-Cae-Gurwen **SA18** 27 G7
Gwaun-leision **SA18** 27 G7
Gwaynynog **LL16** 47 J6
Gwbert **SA43** 26 A4
Gweek **TR11** 2 E6
Gwehelog **NP15** 19 G1
Gwenddwr **LD2** 27 K4
Gwennap **TR16** 2 E4
Gwenter **TR12** 2 E7
Gwernaffield **CH7** 48 B6
Gwernesney **NP15** 19 H1
Gwernogle **SA32** 17 J1
Gwernymynydd **CH7** 48 B6
Gwersyllt **LL11** 48 C7
Gwespyr **CH8** 47 K4
Gwinear **TR27** 2 C5
Gwithian **TR27** 2 C4
Gwyddelwern **LL21** 37 K1
Gwyddgrug **SA39** 17 H1
Gwystre **LD1** 27 K2
Gwytherin **LL22** 47 G6
Gyfelia **LL13** 38 C1
Gyffin **LL32** 47 F5
Gyre **KW17** 107 C7
Gyrn Goch **LL54** 36 D1

H

Habberley **SY5** 38 C5
Habrough **DN40** 52 E1
Haccombe **TQ12** 5 J3
Hacconby **PE10** 42 E3
Haceby **NG34** 42 D2
Hacheston **IP13** 35 H3
Hackenthorpe **S12** 51 G4
Hackford **NR18** 44 E5
Hackforth **DL8** 62 D7
Hackland **KW17** 106 C5
Hackleton **NN7** 32 B3
Hacklinge **CT14** 15 J2
Hackness, *N.Yorks.* **YO13** 63 J3
Hackness, *Ork.* **KW16** 107 C8
Hackney **E** 23 G3
Hackthorn **LN2** 52 C4
Hackthorpe **CA10** 61 G4
Hadden **TD5** 77 F7
Haddenham, *Bucks.* **HP17** 22 A1
Haddenham, *Cambs.* **CB6** 33 H1
Haddington, *E.Loth.* **EH41** 76 D3
Haddington, *Lincs.* **LN5** 52 C6
Haddiscoe **NR14** 45 J6
Haddon **PE7** 42 E6
Hademore **WS14** 40 D5
Hadfield **SK13** 50 C3
Hadham Cross **SG10** 33 H7
Hadham Ford **SG11** 33 H6
Hadleigh, *Essex* **SS7** 24 E3
Hadleigh, *Suff.* **IP7** 34 E4
Hadley **TF1** 39 F4
Hadley End **DE13** 40 D3
Hadley Wood **EN4** 23 F2
Hadlow **TN11** 23 K7
Hadlow Down **TN22** 13 J4
Hadnall **SY4** 38 E3
Hadstock **CB1** 33 J4
Hadzor **WR9** 29 J2
Haffenden Quarter **TN27** 14 D3
Hafod-Dinbych **LL24** 47 G7
Hafodunos **LL22** 47 G6
Haggate **BB10** 56 D6
Haggbeck **CA6** 69 K6
Haggs **FK4** 75 F3
Hagley, *Here.* **HR1** 28 E4
Hagley, *Worcs.* **DY9** 40 B7
Hagnaby **PE23** 53 G6
Hagworthingham **PE23** 53 G6
Haigh **WN2** 49 F2
Haighton Green **PR2** 55 J6
Hail Weston **PE19** 32 E2
Haile **CA22** 60 B6
Hailes **GL54** 30 B5
Hailey, *Herts.* **EN11** 33 G7
Hailey, *Oxon.* **OX29** 30 E7
Hailey, *Oxon.* **OX10** 21 K3
Hailsham **BN27** 13 J6
Haimer **KW14** 105 G2
Hainault **IG6** 23 H2
Hainford **NR10** 45 G4
Hainton **LN8** 52 E4
Haisthorpe **YO25** 59 H3
Halam **NG22** 51 J7
Halbeath **KY11** 75 K2
Halberton **EX16** 7 J4
Halcro **KW1** 105 H2
Hale, *Gt.Man.* **WA15** 49 G4
Hale, *Hants.* **SP6** 10 C3
Hale, *Surr.* **GU9** 22 B7
Hale Bank **WA8** 48 D4
Hale Street **TN12** 23 K7
Halebarns **WA15** 49 G4
Hales, *Norf.* **NR14** 45 H6
Hales, *Staffs.* **TF9** 39 G2
Hales Place **CT2** 15 G2
Halesowen **B63** 40 B7
Halesworth **IP19** 35 H1
Halewood **L26** 48 D4
Half Way Inn **EX5** 7 J6
Halford, *Shrop.* **SY7** 38 D7

Heath Hayes

Halford, Warks. CV36 30 D4
Halfpenny Green DY7 40 A6
Halfway, Carmar. SA19 17 K1
Halfway, Powys LD3 27 H5
Halfway, S.Yorks. S20 51 G4
Halfway, W.Berks. RG20 21 H5
Halfway House SY5 38 C4
Halfway Houses ME12 25 F4
Halghton Mill LL13 38 D1
HALIFAX HX 57 F7
Halistra IV55 93 H6
Halkirk KW12 105 G3
Halkyn CH8 48 B5
Hall G78 74 C5
Hall Dunnerdale LA20 60 D7
Hall Green B28 40 D7
Hall of the Forest SY7 38 B7
Halland BN8 13 J5
Hallaton LE16 42 A6
Hallatrow BS39 19 K6
Hallbankgate CA8 61 G1
Hallen BS10 19 J4
Hallin IV55 93 H6
Halling ME2 24 D5
Hallington, Lincs. LN11 53 G4
Hallington, Northumb. NE19 70 E6
Halloughton NG25 51 J7
Hallow WR2 29 H3
Hallow Heath WR2 29 H3
Hallrule TD9 70 A2
Halls EH42 76 E3
Hall's Green SG4 33 F6
Hall's Tenement CA8 61 G1
Hallsands TQ7 5 J7
Halltoft End PE22 43 G1
Hallworthy PL32 4 B2
Halmer End ST7 39 G1
Halmore GL13 19 K1
Halmyre Mains EH46 75 K6
Halnaker PO18 12 C6
Halsall L39 48 C1
Halse, Northants. NN13 31 G4
Halse, Som. TA4 7 K3
Halsetown TR26 2 C5
Halsham HU12 59 J7
Halsinger EX33 6 D2
Halstead, Essex CO9 34 C5
Halstead, Kent TN14 23 H5
Halstead, Leics. LE7 42 A5
Halstock BA22 8 E4
Haltham LN9 53 F6
Halton, Bucks. HP22 32 B7
Halton, Halton WA7 48 E4
Halton, Lancs. LA2 55 J3
Halton, Northumb. NE45 71 F7
Halton, Wrex. LL14 38 C2
Halton East BD23 57 F4
Halton Gill BD23 56 D2
Halton Holegate PE23 53 H6
Halton Lea Gate CA8 61 H1
Halton West BD23 56 D4
Haltwhistle NE49 70 C7
Halvergate NR13 45 J5
Halwell TQ9 5 H5
Halwill EX21 6 C6
Halwill Junction EX21 6 C6
Ham, Glos. GL13 19 K2
Ham, Gt.Lon. TW10 22 E4
Ham, High. KW14 105 H1
Ham, Kent CT14 15 J2
Ham, Shet. ZE2 108 B1
Ham, Som. TA3 8 B2
Ham, Wilts. SN8 21 G5
Ham Green, N.Som. BS20 19 J4
Ham Green, Worcs. B97 30 B2
Ham Hill ME6 24 C5
Ham Street BA6 8 E1
Hamble-le-Rice SO31 11 F4
Hambleden RG9 22 A3
Hambledon, Hants. PO7 11 H3
Hambledon, Surr. GU8 12 C3
Hambleton, Lancs. FY6 55 G5
Hambleton, N.Yorks. YO8 58 B6
Hambleton Moss Side FY6 55 G5
Hambridge TA10 8 C2
Hambrook, S.Glos. BS16 19 K4
Hambrook, W.Suss. PO18 11 J4
Hameringham LN9 53 G6
Hamerton PE28 32 E1
Hamilton ML3 75 F5
Hamlet EX14 7 K6
Hammer GU27 12 B3
Hammerpot BN16 12 D6
Hammersmith & Fulham W22 E4
Hammerwich WS7 40 C5
Hammerwood RH19 13 H3
Hammond Street EN7 23 G1
Hammoon DT10 9 H3
Hamnavoe, Shet. ZE2 108 D4
Hamnavoe, Shet. ZE2 108 B4
Hamnavoe, Shet. ZE2 108 D5
Hamnavoe, Shet. ZE2 109 C9
Hampden Park BN22 13 K6
Hampnett GL54 30 C7
Hampole DN6 51 H2
Hampreston BH21 10 B5
Hampstead NW3 23 F3
Hampstead Norreys RG18 21 J4
Hampsthwaite HG3 57 H4
Hampton, Gt.Lon. TW12 22 E5
Hampton, Shrop. WV16 39 G7
Hampton, Worcs. WR11 30 B4
Hampton Bishop HR1 28 E5
Hampton Heath SY14 38 D1
Hampton in Arden B92 40 E7
Hampton Lovett WR9 29 H2
Hampton Lucy CV35 30 D3
Hampton on the Hill CV35 30 D2
Hampton Poyle OX5 31 G7
Hamptworth SP5 10 D2
Hamsey BN8 13 H5
Hamstall Ridware WS15 40 D4
Hamstead, I.o.W. PO41 11 F5
Hamstead, W.Mid. B43 40 C6
Hamstead Marshall RG20 21 H5
Hamsterley, Dur. NE17 62 C1
Hamsterley, Dur. DL13 62 C3
Hamstreet TN26 15 F4
Hamworthy BH15 9 J5
Hanbury, Staffs. DE13 40 D3
Hanbury, Worcs. B60 29 J2
Hanbury Woodend DE13 40 D3
Hanchurch ST4 40 A1
Handbridge CH4 48 D6
Handcross RH17 13 F4
Handforth SK9 49 H4
Handley CH3 48 D7
Handsacre WS15 40 C4
Handsworth, S.Yorks. S13 51 G4
Handsworth, W.Mid. B21 40 C6
Handy Cross SL7 22 B2
Hanford ST4 40 A1
Hanging Bridge DE6 40 D1
Hanging Langford SP3 10 B1
Hangingshaw DG11 69 G5
Hangleton BN3 13 F6
Hanham BS15 19 K4
Hankelow CW3 39 F1
Hankerton SN16 20 C2
Hankham BN24 13 K6
Hanley ST1 40 A1
Hanley Castle WR8 29 H4
Hanley Child WR15 29 F2
Hanley Swan WR8 29 H4
Hanley William WR15 29 F2
Hanlith BD23 56 E3
Hanmer SY13 38 D2
Hannah LN13 53 H5
Hannington, Hants. RG26 21 J6
Hannington, Northants. NN6 32 B1
Hannington, Swin. SN6 20 E2
Hannington Wick SN6 20 E2
Hanslope MK19 32 B4
Hanthorpe PE10 42 D3
Hanwell, Gt.Lon. W7 22 E4
Hanwell, Oxon. OX17 31 F4
Hanworth, Gt.Lon. TW13 22 E4
Hanworth, Norf. NR11 45 F2
Happisburgh NR12 45 H2
Happisburgh Common NR12 45 H3
Hapsford WA6 48 D5
Hapton, Lancs. BB11 56 C6
Hapton, Norf. NR15 45 F6
Harberton TQ9 5 H5
Harbertonford TQ9 5 H5
Harbledown CT2 15 G2
Harborne B17 40 C7
Harborough Magna CV23 31 F1
Harbottle NE65 70 E3
Harbourneford TQ10 5 H4
Harbridge BH24 10 C3
Harburn EH55 75 J4
Harbury CV33 30 E3
Harby, Leics. LE14 42 A2
Harby, Notts. NG23 52 B5
Harcombe EX10 7 K6
Harden BD16 57 F6
Hardenhuish SN14 20 C4
Hardgate AB31 91 F4
Hardham RH20 12 D5
Hardingham NR9 44 E5
Hardings Wood ST7 49 H7
Hardingstone NN4 31 J3
Hardington BA11 20 A6
Hardington Mandeville BA22 8 E3
Hardington Marsh BA22 8 E4
Hardley SO45 11 F4
Hardley Street NR14 45 H5
Hardmead MK16 32 C4
Hardraw DL8 61 K7
Hardstoft S45 51 G6
Hardway, Hants. PO12 11 H4
Hardway, Som. BA10 9 G1
Hardwick, Bucks. HP22 32 B7
Hardwick, Cambs. CB3 33 G3
Hardwick, Norf. NR15 45 G6
Hardwick, Northants. NN9 32 B2
Hardwick, Oxon. OX27 31 G6
Hardwick, Oxon. OX29 21 G1
Hardwick Village S80 51 J5
Hardwicke, Glos. GL51 29 J6
Hardwicke, Glos. GL2 29 G7
Hardwicke, Here. HR3 28 B4
Hardy's Green CO2 34 D7
Hare Green CO7 34 E6
Hare Hatch RG10 22 B4
Hare Street, Herts. SG9 33 G6
Hare Street, Herts. SG2 33 G6
Hareby PE23 53 G6
Hareden BB7 56 B4
Harefield UB9 22 D2
Harehills LS9 57 J6
Harelaw ML11 75 H6
Harescegh CA10 61 H2
Harescombe GL4 29 H7
Haresfield GL10 29 H7
Hareshaw ML10 74 E6
Harewood LS17 57 J5
Harewood End HR2 28 E6
Harford PL21 5 G5
Hargate NR16 45 F6
Hargrave, Ches. CH3 48 D6
Hargrave, Northants. NN9 32 D1
Hargrave, Suff. IP29 34 B3
Haringey N 23 G3
Harker CA6 69 J7
Harkstead IP9 35 F5
Harlaston B79 40 E4
Harlaxton NG32 42 B2
Harle Syke BB10 56 D6
Harlech LL46 36 E2
Harlesden NW10 23 F3
Harleston, Norf. IP20 45 G7
Harleston, Suff. IP14 34 E3
Harlestone NN7 31 J2
Harley SY5 38 E5
Harleyholm ML12 75 H7
Harlington LU5 32 D5
Harlosh IV55 93 H7
Harlow CM17 33 H7
Harlow Hill NE15 71 F7
Harlthorpe YO8 58 D6
Harlton CB3 33 G3
Harman's Cross BH19 9 J6
Harmby DL8 62 C7
Harmer Green AL6 33 F7
Harmer Hill SY4 38 D3
Harmondsworth UB7 22 D4
Harmston LN5 52 C6
Harnham SP2 10 C2
Harnhill GL7 20 D1
Harold Hill RM3 23 J2
Harold Wood RM3 23 J2
Haroldston West SA62 16 B3
Haroldswick ZE2 108 F1
Harome YO62 58 C1
Harpenden AL5 32 E7
Harpford EX10 7 J6
Harpham YO25 59 G3
Harpley, Norf. PE31 44 B3
Harpley, Worcs. WR6 29 F2
Harpole NN7 31 H2
Harprigg LA6 56 B1
Harpsdale KW12 105 G3
Harpsden RG9 22 A3
Harpswell DN21 52 C3
Harpur Hill SK17 50 C5
Harpurhey M9 49 H2
Harrapool IV49 86 C2
Harrietfield PH1 82 A4
Harrietsham ME17 14 D2
Harrington, Lincs. PE23 53 G5
Harrington, Northants. NN6 31 J1
Harringworth NN17 42 C6
Harris PH43 85 J5
Harriseahead ST7 49 H7
HARROGATE HG 57 J4
Harrold MK43 32 C3
HARROW, Gt.Lon. HA 22 E3
Harrow, High. KW14 105 H1
Harrow on the Hill HA1 22 E3
Harrow Weald HA3 22 E2
Harrowbarrow PL17 4 E3
Harrowden MK42 32 D4
Harston, Cambs. CB2 33 H3
Harston, Leics. NG32 42 B2
Hart TS27 63 F3
Hartburn, Northumb. NE61 71 F5
Hartburn, Stock. TS18 63 F5
Hartest IP29 34 C3
Hartfield, E.Suss. TN7 13 H3
Hartfield, High. IV54 94 D7
Hartford, Cambs. PE29 33 F1
Hartford, Ches. CW8 49 F5
Hartford End CM6 33 K7
Hartfordbridge RG27 22 A6
Harthill, Ches. CH3 48 D7
Harthill, N.Lan. ML7 75 H4
Harthill, S.Yorks. S26 51 G4
Hartington SK17 50 D6
Hartland EX39 6 A3
Hartlebury DY11 29 H1
Hartlepool TS24 63 G3
Hartley, Cumb. CA17 61 J6
Hartley, Kent DA3 24 C5
Hartley, Kent TN17 14 C4
Hartley, Northumb. NE26 71 J6
Hartley Wespall RG27 22 A6
Hartley Wintney RG27 22 A6
Hartlip ME9 24 E5
Harton, N.Yorks. YO60 58 D3
Harton, Shrop. SY6 38 D7
Harton, T. & W. NE34 71 J7
Hartpury GL19 29 G6
Hartrigge TD8 70 B1
Hartshill CV10 41 F6
Hartshorne DE11 41 F3
Hartsop CA10 60 F5
Hartwell, Bucks. HP17 31 J7
Hartwell, E.Suss. TN7 13 H3
Hartwell, Northants. NN7 31 J3
Hartwood ML7 75 G5
Harvel DA13 24 C5
Harvington, Worcs. DY10 29 H1
Harvington, Worcs. WR11 30 B4
Harwell, Notts. DN10 51 J3
Harwell, Oxon. OX11 21 H3
Harwich CO12 35 G5
Harwood, Dur. DL12 61 K3
Harwood, Gt.Man. BL2 49 G1
Harwood Dale YO13 63 J3
Harwood on Teviot TD9 69 K3
Harworth DN11 51 J3
Hasbury B63 40 B7
Hascombe GU8 12 C3
Haselbech NN6 31 J1
Haselbury Plucknett TA18 8 D3
Haseley CV35 30 D2
Haselor B49 30 C3
Hasfield GL19 29 H6
Hasguard SA62 16 B4
Haskayne L39 48 C2
Hasketon IP13 35 G3
Hasland S41 51 F6
Haslemere GU27 12 C3
Haslingden BB4 56 C7
Haslingden Grane BB4 56 C7
Haslingfield CB3 33 H3
Haslington CW1 49 G7
Hassall CW11 49 G7
Hassall Green CW11 49 G7
Hassell Street TN25 15 F3
Hassendean TD9 70 A1
Hassingham NR13 45 H5
Hassocks BN6 13 F5
Hassop DE45 50 E5
Haster KW1 105 J3
Hastigrow KW1 105 H2
Hastingleigh TN25 15 F3
Hastings TN34 14 D7
Hastingwood CM17 23 H1
Hastoe HP23 22 C1
Haswell DH6 62 E2
Hatch, Beds. SG19 32 E4
Hatch, Hants. RG24 21 K6
Hatch Beauchamp TA3 8 B2
Hatch End HA5 22 E2
Hatch Green TA3 8 B3
Hatching Green AL5 32 E7
Hatchmere WA6 48 E5
Hatcliffe DN37 53 F2
Hatfield, Here. HR6 28 E3
Hatfield, Herts. AL10 23 F1
Hatfield, S.Yorks. DN7 51 J2
Hatfield Broad Oak CM22 33 J7
Hatfield Heath CM22 33 J7
Hatfield Hyde AL7 33 F7
Hatfield Peverel CM3 34 B7
Hatfield Woodhouse DN7 51 J2
Hatford SN7 21 G2
Hatherden SP11 21 G6
Hatherleigh EX20 6 D5
Hathern LE12 41 G3
Hatherop GL7 20 E1
Hathersage S32 50 E4
Hatherton, Ches. CW5 39 F1
Hatherton, Staffs. WS11 40 B4
Hatley St. George SG19 33 F3
Hatt PL12 4 D4
Hattingley GU34 11 H1
Hatton, Aber. AB42 91 J1
Hatton, Derbys. DE65 40 E3
Hatton, Gt.Lon. TW14 22 D4
Hatton, Lincs. LN8 52 E5
Hatton, Shrop. SY6 38 D6
Hatton, Warks. CV35 30 D2
Hatton, Warr. WA4 48 E4
Hatton Castle AB53 99 F6
Hatton Heath CH3 48 D6
Hatton of Fintray AB21 91 G3
Hattoncrook AB21 91 G2
Haugh Head NE71 71 F1
Haugh of Glass AB54 90 C1
Haugh of Urr DG7 65 J4
Haugham LN11 53 G4
Haughhead G66 74 E3
Haughley IP14 34 E2
Haughley Green IP14 34 E2
Haughley New Street IP14 34 E2
Haughs AB54 98 D6
Haughton, Notts. DN22 51 J5
Haughton, Shrop. SY11 38 C3
Haughton, Shrop. SY4 38 E4
Haughton, Shrop. WV16 39 F6
Haughton, Staffs. ST18 40 A3
Haughton Green M34 49 J3
Haughton Le Skerne DL1 62 E5
Haughton Moss CW6 48 E7
Haultwick SG11 33 G6
Haunn HS8 84 C3
Haunton B79 40 E4
Hauxley NE65 71 H3
Hauxton CB2 33 H3
Havant PO9 11 J4
Haven HR4 28 D3
Haven Side HU12 59 K7
Havenstreet PO33 11 G5
Haverfordwest (Hwllfforddd) SA61 16 C3
Haverhill CB9 33 K4
Haverigg LA18 54 E2
Havering RM 23 J3
Havering-atte-Bower RM4 23 J2
Haversham MK19 32 B4
Haverthwaite LA12 55 G1
Haverton Hill TS23 63 F4
Hawarden CH5 48 C6
Hawbridge WR8 29 J4
Hawbush Green CM7 34 B7
Hawcoat LA14 55 F2
Hawen SA44 26 C4
Hawes DL8 56 D1
Hawford WR9 29 H2
Hawick TD9 70 A2
Hawkchurch EX13 8 C4
Hawkedon IP29 34 B3
Hawkenbury TN2 13 J3
Hawkeridge BA13 20 B6
Hawkerland EX10 7 J7
Hawkes End CV5 41 F7
Hawkesbury GL9 20 A3
Hawkesbury Upton GL9 20 A3
Hawkhill NE66 71 H2
Hawkhurst TN18 14 C4
Hawkinge CT18 15 H3
Hawkley GU33 11 J2
Hawkridge TA22 7 G2
Hawkshead LA22 60 E7
Hawksland ML11 75 G7
Hawkswick BD23 56 E2
Hawksworth, Notts. NG13 42 A1
Hawksworth, W.Yorks. LS20 57 G5
Hawkwell, Essex SS5 24 E2
Hawkwell, Northumb. NE18 71 F6
Hawley, Hants. GU17 22 B6
Hawley, Kent DA2 23 J4
Hawling GL54 30 B6
Hawnby YO62 63 G7
Haworth BD22 57 F6
Hawstead IP29 34 C3
Hawthorn, Dur. SR7 63 F2
Hawthorn, Wilts. SN13 20 B5
Hawthorn Hill, Brack.F. RG42 22 B4
Hawthorn Hill, Lincs. LN4 53 F7
Hawthorpe PE10 42 D3
Hawton NG24 51 K7
Haxby YO32 58 C4
Haxey DN9 51 K3
Haxted TN8 23 H7
Hay Mills B25 40 D7
Hay Street SG11 33 G6
Hay-on-Wye HR3 28 B4
Haydock WA11 48 E3
Haydon DT9 9 F3
Haydon Bridge NE47 70 D7
Haydon Wick SN25 20 E3
Haye PL17 4 D4
Hayes, Gt.Lon. UB3 22 D3
Hayes, Gt.Lon. BR2 23 H5
Hayfield, Arg. & B. PA35 80 B5
Hayfield, Derbys. SK22 50 C4
Hayfield, High. KW14 105 G2
Hayhillock DD8 83 G3
Haylands PO33 11 G5
Hayle TR27 2 C5
Haynes MK45 32 E4
Haynes Church End MK45 32 D4
Hayscastle SA62 16 B2
Hayscastle Cross SA62 16 C2
Hayton, Cumb. CA8 61 G1
Hayton, Cumb. CA7 60 C2
Hayton, E.Riding YO42 58 E5
Hayton, Notts. DN22 51 K4
Hayton's Bent SY8 38 E7
Haytor Vale TQ13 5 H3
Haywards Heath RH16 13 G4
Haywood Oaks NG21 51 J7
Hazel End CM23 33 H6
Hazel Grove SK7 49 J4
Hazelbank, Arg. & B. PA25 80 B7
Hazelbank, S.Lan. ML11 75 G6
Hazelbury Bryan DT10 9 G4
Hazeleigh CM3 24 E1
Hazeley RG27 22 A6
Hazelhead AB15 91 G4
Hazelside ML11 68 D1
Hazelslade WS12 40 C4
Hazelton Walls KY15 82 E5
Hazelwood, Derbys. DE56 41 F1
Hazelwood, Gt.Lon. TN14 23 H5
Hazlefield DG7 65 H6
Hazlemere HP15 22 B2
Hazlerigg NE13 71 H6
Hazleton GL54 30 B7
Heacham PE31 44 A2
Head Bridge EX37 6 E4
Headbourne Worthy SO23 11 F1
Headcorn TN27 14 D3
Headington OX3 21 J1
Headlam DL2 62 C5
Headless Cross B97 30 B2
Headley, Hants. RG19 21 J5
Headley, Hants. GU35 12 B3
Headley, Surr. KT18 23 F6
Headley Down GU35 12 B3
Headon DN22 51 K5
Heads Nook CA8 61 F1
Heage DE56 51 F7
Healaugh, N.Yorks. DL11 62 B7
Healaugh, N.Yorks. LS24 58 B5
Heald Green SK8 49 H4
Heale EX31 6 E1
Healey, Lancs. OL12 49 H1
Healey, N.Yorks. HG4 57 G1
Healey, Northumb. NE44 62 B1
Healeyfield DH8 62 B2
Healing DN41 53 F1
Heamoor TR18 2 B5
Heanish PA77 78 B3
Heanor DE75 41 G1
Heanton Punchardon EX31 6 D2
Heanton Satchville EX20 6 D4
Heapey PR6 56 B7
Heapham DN21 52 B4
Hearthstane ML12 69 G1
Heasley Mill EX36 7 F2
Heast IV49 86 C3
Heath S44 51 G6
Heath and Reach LU7 32 C6
Heath End, Hants. RG26 21 J5
Heath End, Surr. GU9 22 B7
Heath Hayes WS12 40 C4

Heath Hill

Heath Hill **TF11** 39 G4
Heath House **BS28** 19 H7
Heath Town **WV10** 40 B6
Heathcot **AB12** 91 G4
Heathcote, *Derbys.* **SK17** 50 D6
Heathcote, *Shrop.* **TF9** 39 F3
Heather **LE67** 41 F4
Heathfield, *Devon* **TQ12** 5 J3
Heathfield, *E.Suss.* **TN21** 13 J4
Heathfield, *Som.* **TA4** 7 K3
Heathton **WV5** 40 A6
Heatley **WA13** 49 G4
Heaton, *Lancs.* **LA3** 55 H3
Heaton, *Staffs.* **SK11** 49 J6
Heaton, *T. & W.* **NE2** 71 H7
Heaton Moor **SK4** 49 H3
Heaverham **TN15** 23 J6
Heaviley **SK2** 49 J4
Hebburn **NE31** 71 J7
Hebden **BD23** 57 F3
Hebden Bridge **HX7** 56 E7
Hebden Green **CW7** 49 F6
Hebing End **SG2** 33 G6
Hebron, *Carmar.* **SA34** 16 E2
Hebron, *Northumb.* **NE61** 71 G5
Heck **DG11** 69 F5
Heckfield **RG27** 22 A5
Heckfield Green **IP21** 35 F1
Heckfordbridge **CO3** 34 D6
Heckingham **NR14** 45 H6
Heckington **NG34** 42 E1
Heckmondwike **WF16** 57 H7
Heddington **SN11** 20 C5
Heddle **KW17** 107 C6
Heddon-on-the-Wall **NE15** 71 G7
Hedenham **NR35** 45 H6
Hedge End **SO30** 11 F3
Hedgerley **SL2** 22 C3
Hedging **TA7** 8 B2
Hedley on the Hill **NE43** 62 B1
Hednesford **WS12** 40 C4
Hedon **HU12** 59 H7
Hedsor **HP10** 22 C3
Heeley **S8** 51 F4
Heglibister **ZE2** 109 C7
Heighington, *Darl.* **DL5** 62 D4
Heighington, *Lincs.* **LN4** 52 D6
Heights of Brae **IV14** 96 C5
Heilam **IV27** 103 G2
Heithat **DG11** 69 G5
Heiton **TD5** 77 F7
Hele, *Devon* **EX34** 6 D1
Hele, *Devon* **EX5** 7 H5
Hele Bridge **EX20** 6 D5
Hele Lane **EX17** 7 F4
Helebridge **EX23** 6 A5
Helensburgh **G84** 74 A2
Helford **TR12** 2 E6
Helhoughton **NR21** 44 C3
Helions Bumpstead **CB9** 33 K4
Helland **PL30** 4 A3
Hellandbridge **PL30** 4 A3
Hellesdon **NR6** 45 F4
Hellidon **NN11** 31 G3
Hellifield **BD23** 56 D4
Hellingly **BN27** 13 J5
Hellington **NR14** 45 H5
Hellister **ZE2** 109 C8
Helmdon **NN13** 31 G4
Helmingham **IP14** 35 F3
Helmsdale **KW8** 105 F7
Helmshore **BB4** 56 C7
Helmsley **YO62** 58 C1
Helperby **YO61** 57 K2
Helperthorpe **YO17** 59 F2
Helpringham **NG34** 42 E1
Helpston **PE6** 42 E5
Helsby **WA6** 48 D5
Helston **TR13** 2 D6
Helstone **PL32** 4 A2
Helton **CA10** 61 G4
Helwith Bridge **BD24** 56 D3
Hemblington **NR13** 45 H4
Hemborough Post **TQ9** 5 J5
HEMEL HEMPSTEAD HP 22 D1
Hemingbrough **YO8** 58 C6
Hemingby **LN9** 53 F5
Hemingford Abbots **PE28** 33 F1
Hemingford Grey **PE28** 33 F1
Hemingstone **IP6** 35 F3
Hemington, *Leics.* **DE74** 41 G3
Hemington, *Northants.* **PE8** 42 D7
Hemington, *Som.* **BA3** 20 A6
Hemley **IP12** 35 G4
Hemlington **TS8** 63 F5
Hempholme **YO25** 59 G5
Hempnall **NR15** 45 G6
Hempnall Green **NR15** 45 G6
Hempriggs **IV36** 97 J5
Hempriggs House **KW1** 105 J4
Hempstead, *Essex* **CB10** 33 K5
Hempstead, *Norf.* **NR25** 45 F2
Hempstead, *Norf.* **NR12** 45 J3
Hempsted **GL2** 29 H7
Hempton, *Norf.* **NR21** 44 D3
Hempton, *Oxon.* **OX15** 31 F5
Hemsby **NR29** 45 J4
Hemswell **DN21** 52 C3
Hemsworth **WF9** 51 G1
Hemyock **EX15** 7 K4
Henbury, *Bristol* **BS10** 19 J4
Henbury, *Ches.* **SK10** 49 H5
Henderland **DG2** 65 J3
Hendersyde Park **TD5** 77 F7
Hendon, *Gt.Lon.* **NW4** 23 F3
Hendon, *T. & W.* **SR2** 62 E1
Hendy **SA4** 17 J4
Heneglwys **LL77** 46 C5
Henfield **BN5** 13 F5
Henford **EX21** 6 B6
Henghurst **TN26** 14 E4
Hengoed, *Caerp.* **CF82** 18 E2
Hengoed, *Powys* **HR5** 28 B3
Hengoed, *Shrop.* **SY10** 38 B2
Hengrave **IP28** 34 C2
Henham **CM22** 33 J6
Heniarth **SY21** 38 A5
Henlade **TA3** 8 B2
Henley, *Shrop.* **SY8** 28 E1
Henley, *Som.* **TA10** 8 D1
Henley, *Suff.* **IP6** 35 F3
Henley, *W.Suss.* **GU27** 12 B4
Henley Corner **TA10** 8 D1
Henley Park **GU3** 22 C6
Henley-in-Arden **B95** 30 C2
Henley-on-Thames **RG9** 22 A3
Henley's Down **TN33** 14 C6
Henllan, *Carmar.* **SA44** 17 G1
Henllan, *Denb.* **LL16** 47 J6
Henllan Amgoed **SA34** 16 E2
Henllys **NP44** 19 F2
Henlow **SG16** 32 E5
Hennock **TQ13** 7 G7
Henny Street **CO10** 34 C5
Henryd **LL32** 47 F5
Henry's Moat **SA63** 16 D2
Hensall **DN14** 58 B7
Henshaw **NE47** 70 C7
Hensingham **CA28** 60 A5
Henstead **NR34** 45 J7
Hensting **SO21** 11 F2
Henstridge **BA8** 9 G3
Henstridge Ash **BA8** 9 G2
Henstridge Marsh **BA8** 9 G2
Henton, *Oxon.* **OX39** 22 A1
Henton, *Som.* **BA5** 19 H7
Henwick **WR2** 29 H3
Henwood **PL14** 4 C3
Heogan **ZE2** 109 D8
Heol Lly Goden **LD3** 28 A6
Heol Senni **LD3** 27 J6
Heol-ddu **SA14** 17 J3
Heol-y-Cyw **CF35** 18 C3
Hepburn **NE66** 71 F1
Hepple **NE65** 70 E3
Hepscott **NE61** 71 H5
Heptonstall **HX7** 56 E7
Hepworth, *Suff.* **IP22** 34 D1
Hepworth, *W.Yorks.* **HD9** 50 D2
Herbrandston **SA73** 16 B4
Herdicott **EX22** 6 B6
HEREFORD HR 28 **E4**
Heriot **EH38** 76 B5
Hermiston **EH14** 75 K3
Hermitage, *D. & G.* **DG7** 65 J4
Hermitage, *Dorset* **DT2** 9 F4
Hermitage, *Sc.Bord.* **TD9** 70 A4
Hermitage, *W.Berks.* **RG18** 21 J4
Hermitage, *W.Suss.* **PO10** 11 J4
Hermon, *Carmar.* **SA33** 17 G1
Hermon, *I.o.A.* **LL62** 46 B6
Hermon, *Pembs.* **SA36** 17 F1
Herne **CT6** 25 H5
Herne Bay **CT6** 25 H5
Herne Common **CT6** 25 H5
Herner **EX32** 6 D3
Hernhill **ME13** 25 G5
Herodsfoot **PL14** 4 C4
Herongate **CM13** 24 C2
Heron's Ghyll **TN22** 13 H4
Heronsgate **WD3** 22 D2
Herriard **RG25** 21 K7
Herringfleet **NR32** 45 J6
Herring's Green **MK45** 32 D4
Herringswell **IP28** 34 B2
Herrington **SR3** 62 E1
Hersden **CT3** 25 H5
Hersham, *Cornw.* **EX23** 6 A5
Hersham, *Surr.* **KT12** 22 E5
Herstmonceux **BN27** 13 K5
Herston, *Dorset* **BH19** 10 B7
Herston, *Ork.* **KW17** 107 D8
Hertford **SG13** 33 G7
Hertford Heath **SG13** 33 G7
Hertingfordbury **SG14** 33 G7
Hesket Newmarket **CA7** 60 E3
Hesketh Bank **PR4** 55 H7
Hesketh Lane **PR3** 56 B5
Heskin Green **PR7** 48 E1
Hesleden **TS27** 63 F3
Hesleyside **NE48** 70 D5
Heslington **YO10** 58 C4
Hessay **YO26** 58 B4
Hessenford **PL11** 4 D5
Hessett **IP30** 34 D2
Hessle **HU13** 59 G7
Hest Bank **LA2** 55 H3
Heston **TW5** 22 E4
Heswall **CH60** 48 B4
Hethe **OX27** 31 G6
Hetherington **NE48** 70 D6
Hethersett **NR9** 45 F5
Hethersgill **CA6** 69 K7
Hethpool **NE71** 70 D1
Hett **DH6** 62 D3
Hetton **BD23** 56 E4
Hetton-le-Hole **DH5** 62 E2
Heugh **NE18** 71 F6
Heugh-head, *Aber.* **AB36** 90 B3
Heugh-head, *Aber.* **AB34** 90 D5
Heveningham **IP19** 35 H1
Hever **TN8** 23 H7
Heversham **LA7** 55 H1
Hevingham **NR10** 45 F3
Hewas Water **PL26** 3 G4
Hewell Grange **B97** 30 B2
Hewell Lane **B60** 30 B2
Hewelsfield **GL15** 19 J1
Hewelsfield Common **GL15** 19 J1
Hewish, *N.Som.* **BS24** 19 G5
Hewish, *Som.* **TA18** 8 D4
Hewton **EX20** 6 D6
Hexham **NE46** 70 E7
Hextable **BR8** 23 J4
Hexton **SG5** 32 E5
Hexworthy **PL20** 5 G3
Heybridge, *Essex* **CM9** 24 E1
Heybridge, *Essex* **CM4** 24 C2
Heybridge Basin **CM9** 24 E1
Heybrook Bay **PL9** 5 F6
Heydon, *Cambs.* **SG8** 33 H4
Heydon, *Norf.* **NR11** 45 F3
Heydour **NG32** 42 D2
Heylipoll **PA77** 78 A3
Heylor **ZE2** 108 B4
Heysham **LA3** 55 H3
Heyshaw **HG3** 57 G3
Heyshott **GU29** 12 B5
Heyside **OL2** 49 J2
Heytesbury **BA12** 20 C7
Heythrop **OX7** 30 E6
Heywood, *Gt.Man.* **OL10** 49 H1
Heywood, *Wilts.* **BA13** 20 B6
Hibaldstow **DN20** 52 C2
Hickleton **DN5** 51 G2
Hickling, *Norf.* **NR12** 45 J3
Hickling, *Notts.* **LE14** 41 J3
Hickling Green **NR12** 45 J3
Hickling Heath **NR12** 45 J3
Hickstead **RH17** 13 F4
Hidcote Boyce **GL55** 30 C4
High Ackworth **WF7** 51 G1
High Balantyre **PA32** 80 B6
High Beach **IG10** 23 H2
High Bentham **LA2** 56 B3
High Bickington **EX37** 6 D3
High Birkwith **BD24** 56 D2
High Blantyre **G72** 74 E5
High Bonnybridge **FK4** 75 G3
High Borgue **DG6** 65 G5
High Bradfield **S6** 50 E3
High Bray **EX32** 6 E2
High Brooms **TN4** 23 J7
High Bullen **EX38** 6 D3
High Burton **HG4** 57 H1
High Buston **NE66** 71 H3
High Callerton **NE20** 71 G6
High Catton **YO41** 58 D4
High Cogges **OX29** 21 G1
High Coniscliffe **DL2** 62 D5
High Cross, *Hants.* **GU32** 11 J2
High Cross, *Herts.* **SG11** 33 G7
High Cross Bank **DE11** 40 E4
High Easter **CM1** 33 K7
High Ellington **HG4** 57 G1
High Entercommon **DL6** 62 E6
High Ercall **TF6** 38 E4
High Etherley **DL14** 62 C4
High Garrett **CM7** 34 B6
High Gate **HX7** 56 E7
High Grange **DL15** 62 C3
High Green, *Norf.* **NR9** 45 F5
High Green, *S.Yorks.* **S35** 51 F3
High Green, *Worcs.* **WR8** 29 H4
High Halden **TN26** 14 D4
High Halstow **ME3** 24 D4
High Ham **TA10** 8 D1
High Harrington **CA14** 60 B4
High Harrogate **HG1** 57 J4
High Hatton **SY4** 39 F3
High Hawsker **YO22** 63 J2
High Heath **TF9** 39 F3
High Hesket **CA4** 61 F2
High Hoyland **S75** 50 E2
High Hunsley **YO43** 59 F6
High Hurstwood **TN22** 13 H4
High Hutton **YO60** 58 D3
High Ireby **CA7** 60 D3
High Kilburn **YO61** 58 B1
High Lane, *Derbys.* **DE7** 41 G1
High Lane, *Worcs.* **WR6** 29 F2
High Laver **CM5** 23 J1
High Legh **WA16** 49 G4
High Leven **TS17** 63 F5
High Littleton **BS39** 19 K6
High Lorton **CA13** 60 C4
High Melton **DN5** 51 H2
High Newton **LA11** 55 H1
High Newton by-the-Sea **NE66** 71 H1
High Nibthwaite **LA12** 60 D7
High Offley **ST20** 39 G3
High Ongar **CM5** 23 J1
High Onn **ST20** 40 A4
High Risby **DN15** 52 C1
High Roding **CM6** 33 K7
High Salvington **BN14** 12 E6
High Shaw **DL8** 61 K7
High Spen **NE39** 71 G7
High Street, *Cornw.* **PL26** 3 G3
High Street, *Kent* **TN18** 14 C4
High Street, *Suff.* **IP12** 35 J3
High Street Green **IP14** 34 E3
High Toynton **LN9** 53 F6
High Trewhitt **NE65** 71 F3
High Wollaston **GL15** 19 J2
High Wray **LA22** 60 E7
High Wych **CM21** 33 H7
High Wycombe **HP11** 22 B2
Higham, *Derbys.* **DE55** 51 F7
Higham, *Kent* **ME3** 24 D4
Higham, *Lancs.* **BB12** 56 D6
Higham, *Suff.* **IP28** 34 B2
Higham, *Suff.* **CO7** 34 E5
Higham Dykes **NE20** 71 G6
Higham Ferrers **NN10** 32 C2
Higham Gobion **SG5** 32 E5
Higham on the Hill **CV13** 41 F6
Higham Wood **TN10** 23 K7
Highampton **EX21** 6 C5
Highbridge **TA9** 19 G7
Highbrook **RH17** 13 G3
Highburton **HD8** 50 D1
Highbury **BA3** 19 K7
Highbury Vale **NG6** 41 H1
Highclere **RG20** 21 H5
Highcliffe **BH23** 10 D5
Higher Ansty **DT2** 9 G4
Higher Ashton **EX6** 7 G7
Higher Ballam **FY8** 55 G6
Higher Blackley **M9** 49 H2
Higher Brixham **TQ5** 5 K5
Higher Cheriton **EX14** 7 J5
Higher Gabwell **TQ1** 5 K4
Higher Green **M29** 49 G3
Higher Kingcombe **DT2** 8 E5
Higher Tale **EX14** 7 J5
Higher Thrushgill **LA2** 56 B3
Higher Town **TR25** 2 C1
Higher Walreddon **PL19** 4 E3
Higher Walton, *Lancs.* **PR5** 55 J7
Higher Walton, *Warr.* **WA4** 48 E4
Higher Whatcombe **DT11** 9 H4
Higher Whitley **WA4** 49 F4
Higher Wych **SY14** 38 D1
Highfield, *E.Riding* **YO8** 58 D6
Highfield, *N.Ayr.* **KA24** 74 B5
Highfield, *T. & W.* **NE39** 62 C1
Highfields **CB3** 33 G3
Highgreen Manor **NE48** 70 D4
Highlane, *Ches.* **SK11** 49 H6
Highlane, *Derbys.* **S12** 51 G4
Highlaws **CA7** 60 C2
Highleadon **GL18** 29 G6
Highleigh **PO20** 12 B7
Highley **WV16** 39 G7
Highmead **SA40** 26 E4
Highmoor Cross **RG9** 21 K3
Highmoor Hill **NP26** 19 H3
Highnam **GL2** 29 G7
Highstead **CT3** 25 J5
Highsted **ME9** 25 F5
Highstreet Green **CO9** 34 B5
Hightae **DG11** 69 F6
Hightown, *Ches.* **CW12** 49 H6
Hightown, *Mersey.* **L38** 48 B2
Highway **SN11** 20 D4
Highweek **TQ12** 5 J3
Highworth **SN6** 21 F2
Hilborough **IP26** 44 C5
Hilcott **SN9** 20 E6
Hilden Park **TN11** 23 J7
Hildenborough **TN11** 23 J7
Hildersham **CB1** 33 J4
Hilderstone **ST15** 40 B2
Hilderthorpe **YO15** 59 H3
Hilfield **DT2** 9 F4
Hilgay **PE38** 44 A6
Hill **GL13** 19 K2
Hill Brow **GU33** 11 J2
Hill Chorlton **ST5** 39 G2
Hill Dyke **PE22** 43 G1
Hill End, *Dur.* **DL13** 62 B3
Hill End, *Fife* **KY12** 75 J1
Hill End, *N.Yorks.* **BD23** 57 F4
Hill Head **PO14** 11 G4
Hill of Beath **KY4** 75 K1
Hill of Fearn **IV20** 97 F4
Hill Ridware **WS15** 40 C4
Hill Top, *Hants.* **SO42** 11 F4
Hill Top, *W.Yorks.* **WF2** 51 F1
Hill View **BH21** 9 J5
Hillam **LS25** 58 B7
Hillbeck **CA17** 61 J5
Hillberry **IM4** 54 C5
Hillborough **CT6** 25 J5
Hillbrae, *Aber.* **AB54** 98 E6
Hillbrae, *Aber.* **AB51** 91 G1
Hillbrae, *Aber.* **AB51** 91 F2
Hillend, *Aber.* **AB55** 98 C6
Hillend, *Fife* **KY11** 75 K2
Hillend, *Midloth.* **EH10** 76 A4
Hillesden **MK18** 31 H6
Hillesley **GL12** 20 A3
Hillfarrance **TA4** 7 K3
Hillhead **TQ5** 5 K5
Hillhead of Auchentumb **AB43** 99 H5
Hillhead of Cocklaw **AB42** 99 J6
Hilliard's Cross **WS13** 40 D4
Hilliclay **KW14** 105 G2
Hillingdon **UB** 22 D3
Hillington **PE31** 44 B3
Hillmorton **CV22** 31 G1
Hillockhead, *Aber.* **AB33** 90 C3
Hillockhead, *Aber.* **AB36** 90 B4
Hillowton **DG7** 65 H4
Hillpound **SO32** 11 G3
Hills Town **S44** 51 G6
Hillsford Bridge **EX35** 7 F1
Hillside, *Aber.* **AB12** 91 H5
Hillside, *Angus* **DD10** 83 J1
Hillside, *Moray* **IV30** 97 J5
Hillside, *Shet.* **ZE2** 109 D6
Hillswick **ZE2** 108 B5
Hillway **PO35** 11 H6
Hillwell **ZE2** 109 F9
Hilmarton **SN11** 20 D4
Hilperton **BA14** 20 B6
Hilsea **PO2** 11 H4
Hilton, *Aber.* **AB41** 91 H1
Hilton, *Cambs.* **PE28** 33 F2
Hilton, *Cumb.* **CA16** 61 J4
Hilton, *Derbys.* **DE65** 40 E2
Hilton, *Dorset* **DT11** 9 G4
Hilton, *Dur.* **DL2** 62 C4
Hilton, *High.* **IV20** 97 G3
Hilton, *Shrop.* **WV15** 39 G6
Hilton, *Stock.* **TS15** 63 F5
Hilton of Cadboll **IV20** 97 F4
Hilton of Delnies **IV12** 97 F6
Himbleton **WR9** 29 J3
Himley **DY3** 40 A6
Hincaster **LA7** 55 J1
Hinckley **LE10** 41 G6
Hinderclay **IP22** 34 E1
Hinderwell **TS13** 63 J5
Hindford **SY11** 38 C2
Hindhead **GU26** 12 B3
Hindley **WN2** 49 F2
Hindley Green **WN2** 49 F2
Hindlip **WR3** 29 H3
Hindolveston **NR20** 44 E3
Hindon **SP3** 9 J1
Hindringham **NR21** 44 D2
Hingham **NR9** 44 E5
Hinstock **TF9** 39 F3
Hintlesham **IP8** 34 E4
Hinton, *Hants.* **BH23** 10 D5
Hinton, *Here.* **HR2** 28 C5
Hinton, *Northants.* **NN11** 31 G3
Hinton, *S.Glos.* **SN14** 20 A4
Hinton, *Shrop.* **SY5** 38 D5
Hinton Admiral **BH23** 10 D5
Hinton Ampner **SO24** 11 G2
Hinton Blewett **BS39** 19 J6
Hinton Charterhouse **BA2** 20 A6
Hinton Martell **BH21** 10 B4
Hinton on the Green **WR11** 30 B4
Hinton Parva **SN4** 21 F3
Hinton St. George **TA17** 8 D3
Hinton St. Mary **DT10** 9 G3
Hinton Waldrist **SN7** 21 G2
Hinton-in-the-Hedges **NN13** 31 G5
Hints, *Shrop.* **SY8** 29 F1
Hints, *Staffs.* **B78** 40 D5
Hinwick **NN29** 32 C2
Hinxhill **TN24** 15 F3
Hinxton **CB10** 33 H4
Hinxworth **SG7** 33 F4
Hipperholme **HX3** 57 G7
Hirn **AB31** 91 F4
Hirnant **SY10** 37 K3
Hirst **NE63** 71 H5
Hirst Courtney **YO8** 58 C7
Hirwaen **LL15** 47 K6
Hirwaun **CF44** 18 C1
Hiscott **EX31** 6 D3
Histon **CB4** 33 H2
Hitcham, *Bucks.* **SL6** 22 C3
Hitcham, *Suff.* **IP7** 34 D3
Hitchin **SG5** 32 E6
Hither Green **SE13** 23 G4
Hittisleigh **EX6** 7 F6
Hixon **ST18** 40 C3
Hoaden **CT3** 25 J5
Hoaldalbert **NP7** 28 C6
Hoar Cross **DE13** 40 D3
Hoarwithy **HR2** 28 E6
Hoath **CT3** 25 H5
Hobarris **SY7** 28 C1
Hobbister **KW17** 107 C7
Hobbs Lots Bridge **PE15** 43 G5
Hobkirk **TD9** 70 A2
Hobland Hall **NR31** 45 K5
Hobson **NE16** 62 C1
Hoby **LE14** 41 J4
Hockering **NR20** 44 E4
Hockerton **NG25** 51 K7
Hockley **SS5** 24 E2
Hockley Heath **B94** 30 C1
Hockliffe **LU7** 32 C6
Hockwold cum Wilton **IP26** 44 B7
Hockworthy **TA21** 7 J4
Hoddesdon **EN11** 23 G1
Hoddlesden **BB3** 56 C7
Hodgeston **SA71** 16 D5
Hodnet **TF9** 39 F3
Hodthorpe **S80** 51 H5
Hoe **NR20** 44 D4
Hoe Gate **PO7** 11 H3
Hoff **CA16** 61 H5
Hoffleet Stow **PE20** 43 F2
Hoggeston **MK18** 32 B6
Hoggie **AB56** 98 D4
Hogha Gearraidh **HS6** 92 C4
Hoghton **PR5** 56 B7
Hognaston **DE6** 50 E7
Hogsthorpe **PE24** 53 J5
Holbeach **PE12** 43 G3
Holbeach Bank **PE12** 43 G3
Holbeach Clough **PE12** 43 G3
Holbeach Drove **PE12** 43 G4
Holbeach Hurn **PE12** 43 G3
Holbeach St. Johns **PE12** 43 G4

Idbury

Holbeach St. Marks PE12 43 G2
Holbeach St. Matthew PE12 43 H2
Holbeck S80 51 H5
Holberrow Green B96 30 B3
Holbeton PL8 5 G5
Holborough ME2 24 D5
Holbrook, Derbys. DE56 41 F1
Holbrook, Suff. IP9 35 F5
Holburn TD15 77 J7
Holbury SO45 11 F4
Holcombe, Devon EX7 5 K3
Holcombe, Som. BA3 19 K7
Holcombe Rogus TA21 7 J4
Holcot NN6 31 J2
Holden BB7 56 C5
Holdenby NN6 31 H2
Holdenhurst BH8 10 C5
Holdgate TF13 38 E7
Holdingham NG34 42 D1
Holditch TA20 8 C4
Hole Park TN17 14 D4
Hole Street BN44 12 E5
Hole-in-the-Wall HR9 29 F6
Holford TA5 7 K1
Holker LA11 55 G2
Holkham NR23 44 C1
Hollacombe EX22 6 B5
Holland, Ork. KW17 106 D2
Holland, Ork. KW17 106 F5
Holland, Surr. RH8 23 H6
Holland-on-Sea CO15 35 F7
Hollandstoun KW17 106 G2
Hollee DG11 69 H7
Hollesley IP12 35 H4
Hollingbourne ME17 14 D2
Hollingbury BN1 13 G6
Hollington, Derbys. DE6 40 E2
Hollington, E.Suss. TN38 14 C6
Hollington, Staffs. ST10 40 C2
Hollingworth SK14 50 C3
Hollins BL9 49 H2
Hollins Green WA3 49 F3
Hollinsclough SK17 50 C6
Hollinswood TF3 39 G5
Hollinwood SY13 38 E2
Hollocombe EX18 6 E4
Holloway DE4 51 F7
Hollowell NN6 31 H1
Holly End PE14 43 J5
Holly Green WR8 29 H4
Hollybush, Caerp. NP12 18 E1
Hollybush, E.Ayr. KA6 67 H2
Hollybush, Worcs. HR8 29 G5
Hollym HU19 59 K7
Holm DG13 69 H4
Holm of Drumlanrig DG3 68 D4
Holmbury St. Mary RH5 22 E7
Holmbush, Cornw. PL25 4 A5
Holmbush, W.Suss. RH12 13 F3
Holme, Cambs. PE7 42 E7
Holme, Cumb. LA6 55 J2
Holme, Notts. NG23 52 B7
Holme, W.Yorks. HD9 50 D2
Holme Chapel BB10 56 D7
Holme Hale IP25 44 C5
Holme Lacy HR2 28 E5
Holme Marsh HR5 28 C3
Holme next the Sea PE36 44 B1
Holme on the Wolds HU17 59 F5
Holme Pierrepont NG12 41 J2
Holme-on-Spalding-Moor YO43 58 E6
Holmebridge BH20 9 H6
Holmer HR1 28 E4
Holmer Green HP15 22 C2
Holmes Chapel CW4 49 G6
Holme's Hill BN8 13 J5
Holmesfield S18 51 F5
Holmeswood L40 48 D1
Holmewood S42 51 G6
Holmfield HX2 57 F7
Holmfirth HD9 50 D2
Holmhead, D. & G. DG7 68 C5
Holmhead, E.Ayr. KA18 67 K1
Holmpton HU19 59 K7
Holmrook CA19 60 B6
Holmsgarth ZE1 109 D8
Holmside DH7 62 D2
Holmston KA7 67 H1
Holmwrangle CA4 61 G2
Holne TQ13 5 H4
Holnest DT9 9 F4
Holsworthy EX22 6 B5
Holsworthy Beacon EX22 6 B5
Holt, Dorset BH21 10 B4
Holt, Norf. NR25 44 E2
Holt, Wilts. BA14 20 B5
Holt, Worcs. WR6 29 H2
Holt, Wrex. LL13 48 D7
Holt End, Hants. GU34 11 H1
Holt End, Worcs. B98 30 B2
Holt Fleet WR9 29 H2
Holt Heath, Dorset BH21 10 B4
Holt Heath, Worcs. WR6 29 H2
Holtby YO19 58 C4
Holton, Oxon. OX33 21 K1
Holton, Som. BA9 9 F2
Holton, Suff. IP19 35 H1
Holton cum Beckering LN8 52 E4
Holton Heath BH16 9 J5
Holton le Clay DN36 53 F2
Holton le Moor LN7 52 D3
Holton St. Mary CO7 34 E5
Holtspur HP9 22 C2
Holtye Common TN8 13 H3
Holwell, Dorset DT10 9 G3
Holwell, Herts. SG5 32 E5
Holwell, Leics. LE14 42 A3
Holwell, Oxon. OX18 21 F1
Holwell, Som. BA11 20 A7
Holwick DL12 62 A4
Holworth DT2 9 G6
Holy Cross DY9 29 J1
Holy Island TD15 77 K6
Holybourne GU34 22 A7
Holyhead (Caergybi) LL65 46 A4
Holymoorside S42 51 F6
Holyport SL6 22 B4
Holystone NE65 70 E3
Holytown ML1 75 F4
Holywell, Cambs. PE27 33 G1
Holywell, Cornw. TR8 2 E3
Holywell, Dorset DT2 8 E4
Holywell, E.Suss. BN20 13 J7
Holywell (Treffynnon), Flints. CH8 47 K5
Holywell Green HX4 50 C1
Holywell Lake TA21 7 K3
Holywell Row IP28 34 B1
Holywood DG2 68 E5
Hom Green HR9 28 E6
Homer TF13 39 F5
Homersfield IP20 45 G7
Homington SP5 10 C2
Honey Hill CT2 25 H5
Honey Tye CO6 34 D5
Honeyborough SA73 16 C4
Honeybourne WR11 30 C4
Honeychurch EX20 6 E5
Honiley CV35 30 D1
Honing NR28 45 H3
Honingham NR9 45 F4
Honington, Lincs. NG32 42 C1
Honington, Suff. IP31 34 D1
Honington, Warks. CV36 30 D4
Honiton EX14 7 K5
Honley HD9 50 D1
Hoo, Med. ME3 24 D4
Hoo, Suff. IP13 35 G3
Hooe, E.Suss. TN33 13 K6
Hooe, Plym. PL9 5 F5
Hooe Common TN33 13 K5
Hook, E.Riding DN14 58 D7
Hook, Gt.Lon. KT9 22 E5
Hook, Hants. RG27 22 A6
Hook, Pembs. SA62 16 C3
Hook, Wilts. SN4 20 D3
Hook Green, Kent DA13 24 C4
Hook Green, Kent DA13 24 C5
Hook Green, Kent TN3 13 K3
Hook Norton OX15 30 E5
Hook-a-Gate SY5 38 D5
Hooke DT8 8 E4
Hookgate TF9 39 G2
Hookway EX17 7 G6
Hookwood RH6 23 F7
Hoole CH3 48 D6
Hooley CR5 23 F6
Hooton CH66 48 C5
Hooton Levitt S66 51 H3
Hooton Pagnell DN5 51 G2
Hooton Roberts S65 51 G3
Hopcrofts Holt OX25 31 F6
Hope, Derbys. S33 50 D4
Hope, Devon TQ7 5 G7
Hope, Flints. LL12 48 C7
Hope, Powys SY21 38 B5
Hope, Shrop. SY5 38 C5
Hope Bagot SY8 28 E1
Hope Bowdler SY6 38 D6
Hope End Green CM22 33 J7
Hope Mansell HR9 29 F7
Hope under Dinmore HR6 28 E3
Hopehouse TD7 69 H2
Hopeman IV30 97 J5
Hope's Green SS7 24 D3
Hopesay SY7 38 C7
Hopkinstown CF37 18 D2
Hopton, Derbys. DE4 50 E7
Hopton, Norf. NR31 45 K5
Hopton, Shrop. TF9 38 E3
Hopton, Staffs. ST18 40 B3
Hopton, Suff. IP22 34 D1
Hopton Cangeford SY8 38 E7
Hopton Castle SY7 28 C1
Hopton Wafers DY14 29 F1
Hoptonheath SY7 28 C1
Hopwas B78 40 D5
Hopwood B48 30 B1
Horam TN21 13 J5
Horbling NG34 42 E2
Horbury WF4 50 E1
Horden SR8 63 F2
Horderley SY7 38 D7
Hordle SO41 10 D5
Hordley SY12 38 C2
Horeb, Carmar. SA15 17 H4
Horeb, Cere. SA44 26 C4
Horfield BS7 19 J4
Horham IP21 35 G1
Horkesley Heath CO6 34 D6
Horkstow DN18 52 C1
Horley, Oxon. OX15 31 F4
Horley, Surr. RH6 23 F7
Horn Hill SL9 22 D2
Hornblotton Green BA4 8 E1
Hornby, Lancs. LA2 55 J3
Hornby, N.Yorks. DL6 62 E6
Hornby, N.Yorks. DL8 62 D7
Horncastle LN9 53 F6
Hornchurch RM12 23 J3
Horncliffe TD15 77 H5
Horndean, Hants. PO8 11 J3
Horndean, Sc.Bord. TD15 77 G6
Horndon PL19 6 D7
Horndon on the Hill SS17 24 C3
Horne RH6 23 G7
Horniehaugh DD8 83 F1
Horning NR12 45 H4
Horninghold LE16 42 B6
Horninglow DE13 40 E3
Horningsea CB5 33 H2
Horningsham BA12 20 B7
Horningtoft NR20 44 D3
Horningtops PL14 4 C4
Horns Cross, Devon EX39 6 B3
Horns Cross, E.Suss. TN31 14 D5
Hornsby CA8 61 G2
Hornsby Gate CA8 61 G1
Hornsea HU18 59 J5
Hornsey N8 23 G3
Hornton OX15 30 E4
Horrabridge PL20 5 F4
Horridge TQ13 5 H3
Horringer IP29 34 C2
Horse Bridge ST9 49 J7
Horsebridge, Devon PL19 4 E3
Horsebridge, Hants. SO20 10 E1
Horsebrook ST19 40 A4
Horsehay TF4 39 F5
Horseheath CB1 33 K4
Horsehouse DL8 57 F1
Horsell GU21 22 C6
Horseman's Green SY13 38 D1
Horseway PE16 43 H7
Horsey NR29 45 J3
Horsford NR10 45 F4
Horsforth LS18 57 H6
Horsham, W.Suss. RH12 12 E3
Horsham, Worcs. WR6 29 G3
Horsham St. Faith NR10 45 G4
Horsington, Lincs. LN10 52 E6
Horsington, Som. BA8 9 F2
Horsley, Derbys. DE21 41 F1
Horsley, Glos. GL6 20 B2
Horsley, Northumb. NE19 70 D4
Horsley, Northumb. NE15 71 F7
Horsley Cross CO11 35 F6
Horsley Woodhouse DE7 41 F1
Horsleycross Street CO11 35 F6
Horsmonden TN12 14 C3
Horspath OX33 21 J1
Horstead NR12 45 G4
Horsted Keynes RH17 13 G4
Horton, Bucks. LU7 32 C7
Horton, Dorset BH21 10 B4
Horton, Lancs. BD23 56 D4
Horton, Northants. NN7 32 B3
Horton, S.Glos. BS37 20 A3
Horton, Som. TA19 8 C3
Horton, Staffs. ST13 49 J7
Horton, Swan. SA3 17 H6
Horton, W. & M. SL3 22 D4
Horton, Wilts. SN10 20 D5
Horton Cross TA19 8 C3
Horton Green SY14 38 D1
Horton Heath SO50 11 F3
Horton in Ribblesdale BD24 56 D2
Horton Inn BH21 10 B4
Horton Kirby DA4 23 J5
Horton-cum-Studley OX33 31 G7
Horwich BL6 49 F1
Horwich End SK23 50 C4
Horwood EX39 6 D3
Hose LE14 42 A3
Hoses LA20 60 D7
Hosh PH7 81 K5
Hosta HS6 92 C4
Hoswick ZE2 109 D10
Hotham YO43 58 E6
Hothfield TN26 14 E3
Hoton LE12 41 H3
Houbie ZE2 108 F3
Hough CW2 49 G7
Hough Green WA8 48 D4
Hough-on-the-Hill NG32 42 C1
Hougham NG32 42 B1
Houghton, Cambs. PE28 33 F1
Houghton, Cumb. CA3 60 F1
Houghton, Devon TQ7 5 G6
Houghton, Hants. SO20 10 E1
Houghton, Pembs. SA73 16 C4
Houghton, W.Suss. BN18 12 D5
Houghton Bank DL2 62 D4
Houghton Conquest MK45 32 D4
Houghton le Spring DH4 62 E2
Houghton on the Hill LE7 41 J5
Houghton Regis LU5 32 D6
Houghton St. Giles NR22 44 D2
Houghton-le-Side DL2 62 D4
Houlsyke YO21 63 J6
Hound SO31 11 F4
Hound Green RG27 22 A6
Houndslow TD3 76 E6
Houndwood TD14 77 G4
Hounsdown SO40 10 E3
Hounslow TW 22 E4
Hounslow Green CM6 33 K7
Househill IV12 97 F6
Housetter ZE2 108 C4
Houston PA6 74 C4
Houstry KW6 105 G5
Houstry of Dunn KW1 105 H3
Houton KW17 107 C7
Hove BN3 13 F6
Hoveringham NG14 41 J1
Hoveton NR12 45 H4
Hovingham YO62 58 C2
How CA8 61 G1
How Caple HR1 29 F5
How End MK45 32 D4
How Man CA22 60 A5
Howden DN14 58 D7
Howden-le-Wear DL15 62 C3
Howe, Cumb. LA8 55 H1
Howe, High. KW1 105 J2
Howe, N.Yorks. YO7 57 J1
Howe, Norf. NR15 45 G5
Howe Green CM2 24 D1
Howe of Teuchar AB53 99 F6
Howe Street, Essex CM7 33 K5
Howe Street, Essex CM3 33 K7
Howell NG34 42 E1
Howey LD1 27 K3
Howgate EH26 76 A5
Howgill BD23 57 F4
Howick NE66 71 H2
Howle TF10 39 F3
Howlett End CB10 33 J5
Howley TA20 8 B4
Hownam TD5 70 C2
Hownam Mains TD5 70 C1
Howpasley TD9 69 J3
Howsham, N.Lincs. LN7 52 D2
Howsham, N.Yorks. YO60 58 D3
Howtel TD12 77 G7
Howton HR2 28 D6
Howwood PA9 74 C4
Hoxa KW17 107 D8
Hoxne IP21 35 F1
Hoy KW14 105 H2
Hoylake CH47 48 B4
Hoyland S74 51 F2
Hoyland Swaine S36 50 E2
Hubberholme BD23 56 E2
Hubbert's Bridge PE20 43 F1
Huby, N.Yorks. YO61 58 B3
Huby, N.Yorks. LS17 57 H5
Hucclecote GL3 29 H7
Hucking ME17 14 D2
Hucknall NG15 41 H1
HUDDERSFIELD HD 50 D1
Huddington WR9 29 J3
Hudscott EX37 6 E3
Hudswell DL11 62 C6
Huggate YO42 58 E4
Hugglescote LE67 41 G4
Hugh Town TR21 2 C1
Hughenden Valley HP15 22 B2
Hughley SY5 38 E6
Hugmore LL13 48 C7
Huish, Devon EX20 6 D4
Huish, Wilts. SN8 20 E5
Huish Champflower TA4 7 J3
Huish Episcopi TA10 8 D2
Huisinis HS3 100 B6
Hulcott HP22 32 B7
Hulland DE6 40 E1
Hullavington SN14 20 B3
Hullbridge SS5 24 E2
Hulme End SK17 50 D7
Hulme Walfield CW12 49 H6
Hulver Street NR34 45 J7
Humber Court HR6 28 E3
Humberside International Airport DN39 52 E2
Humberston DN36 53 G2
Humberstone LE5 41 J5
Humbie EH36 76 C4
Humbleton, E.Riding HU11 59 J6
Humbleton, Northumb. NE71 70 E1
Humby NG33 42 D2
Hume TD5 77 F6
Humehall TD5 77 F6
Humshaugh NE46 70 E6
Huna KW1 105 J1
Huncoat BB5 56 C6
Huncote LE9 41 H6
Hundalee TD8 70 B2
Hunderthwaite DL12 62 A4
Hundleby PE23 53 G6
Hundleton SA71 16 C4
Hundon CO10 34 B4
Hundred Acres PO17 11 G3
Hundred End PR9 55 H7
Hundred House LD1 28 A3
Hungarton LE7 41 J5
Hungerford, Hants. SP6 10 C3
Hungerford, W.Berks. RG17 21 G5
Hungerford Newtown RG17 21 G4
Hunglader IV51 93 J4
Hunmanby YO14 59 H2
Hunningham CV33 30 E2
Hunny Hill PO30 11 F6
Hunsdon SG12 33 H7
Hunsingore LS22 57 K4
Hunsonby CA10 61 G3
Hunspow KW14 105 H1
Hunstanton PE36 44 A1
Hunstanworth DH8 62 A2
Hunston, Suff. IP31 34 D2
Hunston, W.Suss. PO20 12 B6
Hunstrete BS39 19 K5
Hunt End B97 30 B2
Hunt House YO22 63 K7
Huntercombe End RG9 21 K3
Hunters Forstal CT6 25 H5
Hunter's Quay PA23 73 K3
Hunterston KA23 73 K5
Huntford TD8 70 B3
Huntingdon PE29 33 F1
Huntingfield IP19 35 H1
Huntingford SP8 9 H1
Huntington, Here. HR5 28 B3
Huntington, Staffs. WS12 40 B4
Huntington, York YO32 58 C4
Huntingtower PH1 82 B5
Huntley GL19 29 G7
Huntly AB54 98 D6
Huntlywood TD4 76 E6
Hunton, Hants. SO21 11 F1
Hunton, Kent ME15 14 C3
Hunton, N.Yorks. DL8 62 C7
Huntonbridge WD4 22 D1
Hunt's Cross L25 48 D4
Huntsham EX16 7 J3
Huntshaw Cross EX31 6 D3
Huntspill TA9 19 G7
Huntworth TA7 8 C1
Hunwick DL15 62 C3
Hunworth NR24 44 E2
Hurdsfield SK10 49 J5
Hurley, W. & M. SL6 22 B3
Hurley, Warks. CV9 40 E6
Hurley Bottom SL6 22 B3
Hurlford KA1 74 C7
Hurliness KW16 107 B9
Hurn BH23 10 C5
Hursley SO21 11 F2
Hurst, Gt.Man. OL6 49 J2
Hurst, N.Yorks. DL11 62 B6
Hurst, W'ham RG10 22 A4
Hurst Green, E.Suss. TN19 14 C5
Hurst Green, Lancs. BB7 56 B6
Hurst Green, Surr. RH8 23 G6
Hurstbourne Priors RG28 21 H7
Hurstbourne Tarrant SP11 21 G6
Hurstpierpoint BN6 13 F5
Hurstway Common HR3 28 B4
Hurstwood BB10 56 D6
Hurtmore GU7 22 C7
Hurworth-on-Tees DL2 62 E5
Hury DL12 62 A4
Husabost IV55 93 H6
Husbands Bosworth LE17 41 J7
Husborne Crawley MK43 32 C5
Husthwaite YO61 58 B2
Huthwaite NG17 51 G7
Huttoft LN13 53 J5
Hutton, Cumb. CA11 60 F4
Hutton, Essex CM13 24 C2
Hutton, Lancs. PR4 55 H7
Hutton, N.Som. BS24 19 G6
Hutton, Sc.Bord. TD15 77 H5
Hutton Bonville DL7 62 E6
Hutton Buscel YO13 59 F1
Hutton Conyers HG4 57 J2
Hutton Cranswick YO25 59 G4
Hutton End CA11 60 F3
Hutton Henry TS27 63 F3
Hutton Magna DL11 62 C5
Hutton Roof, Cumb. CA11 60 E3
Hutton Roof, Cumb. LA6 55 J2
Hutton Rudby TS15 63 F6
Hutton Sessay YO7 57 K2
Hutton Wandesley YO26 58 B4
Hutton-le-Hole YO62 63 J7
Huxley CH3 48 E6
Huxter, Shet. ZE2 109 E6
Huxter, Shet. ZE2 109 C7
Huyton L36 48 D3
Hwllffordd (Haverfordwest) SA61 16 C3
Hycemoor LA19 54 D1
Hyde, Glos. GL6 20 B1
Hyde, Gt.Man. SK14 49 J3
Hyde Heath HP6 22 C1
Hyde Lea ST18 40 B4
Hydestile GU8 22 C7
Hyndford Bridge ML11 75 H6
Hyndlee TD9 70 A3
Hynish PA77 78 A4
Hyssington SY15 38 C6
Hythe, Hants. SO45 11 F4
Hythe, Kent CT21 15 G4
Hythe End TW19 22 D4
Hythie AB42 99 J5
Hyton LA19 54 D1

I

Ianstown AB56 98 C4
Ibberton DT11 9 G4
Ible DE4 50 E7
Ibsley BH24 10 C4
Ibstock LE67 41 G4
Ibstone HP14 22 A2
Ibthorpe SP11 21 G6
Ibworth RG26 21 J6
Icelton BS22 19 G5
Ickburgh IP26 44 C6
Ickenham UB10 22 D3
Ickford HP18 21 K1
Ickham CT3 15 H2
Ickleford SG5 32 E5
Icklesham TN36 14 D6
Ickleton CB10 33 H4
Icklingham IP28 34 B1
Ickwell Green SG18 32 E4
Icomb GL54 30 D6
Idbury OX7 30 D6

Iddesleigh

Iddesleigh **EX19** 6 D5
Ide **EX2** 7 H6
Ide Hill **TN14** 23 H6
Ideford **TQ13** 5 J3
Iden **TN31** 14 E5
Iden Green, *Kent* **TN17** 14 C4
Iden Green, *Kent* **TN17** 14 D4
Idlicote **CV36** 30 D4
Idmiston **SP4** 10 C1
Idridgehay **DE56** 40 E1
Idrigil **IV51** 93 J5
Idstone **SN6** 21 F3
Idvies **DD8** 83 G3
Iffley **OX4** 21 J1
Ifield **RH11** 13 F3
Ifield or Singlewell **DA12** 24 C4
Ifieldwood **RH11** 13 F3
Ifold **RH14** 12 D3
Iford **BN7** 13 H6
Ifton Heath **SY11** 38 C2
Ightfield **SY13** 38 E2
Ightham **TN15** 23 J6
Iken **IP12** 35 J3
Ilam **DE6** 50 D7
Ilchester **BA22** 8 E2
Ilderton **NE66** 71 F1
ILFORD IG 23 **H3**
Ilfracombe **EX34** 6 D1
Ilkeston **DE7** 41 G1
Ilketshall St. Andrew **NR34** 45 H7
Ilketshall St. Lawrence **NR34** 45 H7
Ilketshall St. Margaret **NR35** 45 H7
Ilkley **LS29** 57 G5
Illey **B62** 40 B7
Illington **IP24** 44 D7
Illingworth **HX2** 57 F7
Illogan **TR16** 2 D4
Illston on the Hill **LE7** 42 A6
Ilmer **HP27** 22 A1
Ilmington **CV36** 30 D4
Ilminster **TA19** 8 C3
Ilsington **TQ13** 5 H3
Ilston **SA2** 17 J5
Ilton, *N.Yorks.* **HG4** 57 G2
Ilton, *Som.* **TA19** 8 C3
Imachar **KA27** 73 G6
Immeroin **FK19** 81 G6
Immingham **DN40** 52 E1
Immingham Dock **DN40** 53 F1
Impington **CB4** 33 H2
Ince **CH2** 48 D5
Ince Blundell **L38** 48 C2
Ince-in-Makerfield **WN3** 48 E2
Inch **DD9** 90 E7
Inchbare **DD9** 83 H1
Inchberry **IV32** 98 B5
Inchbraoch **DD10** 83 J2
Inchgrundle **DD9** 90 C7
Inchindown **IV18** 96 D4
Inchinnan **PA4** 74 C4
Inchkinloch **IV27** 103 J4
Inchlaggan **PH35** 87 H4
Inchlumpie **IV17** 96 C4
Inchmarlo **AB31** 90 E5
Inchnabobart **AB35** 90 B6
Inchnacardoch Hotel **PH32** 87 K3
Inchnadamph **IV27** 102 E6
Inchock **DD11** 83 H3
Inchrory **AB37** 89 J4
Inchture **PH14** 82 D5
Inchvuilt **IV4** 87 J1
Inchyra **PH2** 82 C6
Indian Queens **TR9** 3 G3
Inerval **PA42** 72 B6
Ingatestone **CM4** 24 C1
Ingbirchworth **S36** 50 E2
Ingerthorpe **HG3** 57 H3
Ingestre **ST18** 40 B3
Ingham, *Lincs.* **LN1** 52 C4
Ingham, *Norf.* **NR12** 45 H3
Ingham, *Suff.* **IP31** 34 C1
Ingleby, *Derbys.* **DE73** 41 F3
Ingleby, *Lincs.* **LN1** 52 B5
Ingleby Arncliffe **DL6** 63 F6
Ingleby Barwick **TS17** 63 F5
Ingleby Cross **DL6** 63 F6
Ingleby Greenhow **TS9** 63 G6
Inglesbatch **BA2** 19 K5
Inglesham **SN6** 21 F2
Ingleton, *Dur.* **DL2** 62 C4
Ingleton, *N.Yorks.* **LA6** 56 B2
Inglewhite **PR3** 55 J5
Ingmire Hall **LA10** 61 H7
Ingoe **NE20** 71 F6
Ingoldisthorpe **PE31** 44 A2
Ingoldmells **PE25** 53 J6
Ingoldsby **NG33** 42 D2
Ingon **CV37** 30 D3
Ingram **NE66** 71 F2
Ingrave **CM13** 24 C2
Ingrow **BD21** 57 F6
Ings **LA8** 60 F7
Ingst **BS35** 19 J3
Ingworth **NR11** 45 F3
Inistrynich **PA33** 80 C5
Injebreck **IM4** 54 C5
Inkberrow **WR7** 30 B3
Inkhorn **AB41** 91 H1
Inkpen **RG17** 21 G5
Inkstack **KW14** 105 H1
Innellan **PA23** 73 K4
Innergellie **KY10** 83 G7
Innerleithen **EH44** 76 B7
Innerleven **KY8** 82 E7
Innermessan **DG9** 64 A4
Innerwick, *E.Loth.* **EH42** 77 F3
Innerwick, *P. & K.* **PH15** 81 G3
Inninbeg **PA34** 79 J3
Innsworth **GL2** 29 H6
Insch **AB52** 90 E2
Insh **PH21** 89 F4
Inshore **IV27** 103 F2
Inskip **PR4** 55 H6
Instow **EX39** 6 C2
Intake **S12** 51 F4
Intwood **NR4** 45 F5
Inver, *Aber.* **AB35** 89 K5
Inver, *Arg. & B.* **PA38** 80 A3
Inver, *High.* **KW6** 105 G5
Inver, *High.* **IV20** 97 F3
Inver, *P. & K.* **PH8** 82 B3
Inver Mallie **PH34** 87 H6
Inverailort **PH38** 86 D6
Inveralligin **IV22** 94 E6
Inverallochy **AB43** 99 J4
Inveran **IV27** 96 C2
Inveraray **PA32** 80 B7
Inverardoch Mains **FK15** 81 J7
Inverardran **FK20** 80 E5
Inverarish **IV40** 86 B1
Inverarity **DD8** 83 F3
Inverarnan **G83** 80 E6
Inverasdale **IV22** 94 E3
Inverbain **IV54** 94 D6
Inverbeg **G83** 74 B1
Inverbervie **DD10** 91 G7
Inverbroom **IV23** 95 H3
Inverbrough **IV13** 89 F2
Invercassley **IV27** 96 B1
Inverchaolain **PA23** 73 J3
Invercharnan **PH49** 80 C3
Inverchorachan **PA26** 80 D6
Inverchoran **IV6** 95 J6
Invercreran **PA38** 80 B3
Inverdruie **PH22** 89 G3
Inverebrie **AB41** 91 H1
Invereen **IV13** 89 F1
Inverernie **IV36** 97 H5
Inveresk **EH21** 76 B3
Inverey **AB35** 89 H6
Inverfarigaig **IV2** 88 C2
Invergarry **PH35** 87 K4
Invergelder **AB35** 89 K5
Invergeldie **PH6** 81 J5
Invergloy **PH34** 87 J6
Invergordon **IV18** 96 E5
Invergowrie **DD2** 82 E4
Inverguseran **PH41** 86 D4
Inverhadden **PH16** 81 H2
Inverharroch **AB54** 90 B1
Inverherive **FK20** 80 E5
Inverhope **IV27** 103 G2
Inverie **PH41** 86 D4
Inverinan **PA35** 80 A6
Inverinate **IV40** 87 F2
Inverkeilor **DD11** 83 H3
Inverkeithing **KY11** 75 K2
Inverkeithny **AB54** 98 E6
Inverkip **PA16** 74 A3
Inverkirkaig **IV27** 102 C7
Inverlael **IV23** 95 H3
Inverlauren **G84** 74 B2
Inverliever **PA31** 79 K7
Inverliver **PA35** 80 B4
Inverlochlarig **FK19** 81 F6
Inverlochy **PA33** 80 C5
Inverlussa **PA60** 72 E2
Invermay **PH2** 82 B6
Invermoriston **IV63** 88 B3
Invernaver **KW14** 104 C2
Inverneil **PA30** 73 G2
INVERNESS IV 96 **D7**
Inverness Airport **IV2** 96 E6
Invernettie **AB42** 99 K6
Invernoaden **PA27** 73 K1
Inveroran Hotel **PA36** 80 D3
Inverquharity **DD8** 83 F2
Inverquhomery **AB42** 99 J6
Inverroy **PH31** 87 J6
Inversanda **PH33** 80 A2
Invershiel **IV40** 87 F3
Inversnaid Hotel **FK8** 80 E7
Invertrossachs **FK17** 81 G7
Inverugie **AB42** 99 K6
Inveruglas **G83** 80 E7
Inveruglass **PH21** 89 F4
Inverurie **AB51** 91 F2
Invervar **PH15** 81 H3
Invervegain **PA23** 73 J3
Invery Ho. **AB31** 90 E5
Inverythan **AB53** 99 F6
Inwardleigh **EX20** 6 D6
Inworth **CO5** 34 C7
Iochdar **HS8** 92 C7
Iping **GU29** 12 B4
Ipplepen **TQ12** 5 J4
Ipsden **OX10** 21 K3
Ipstones **ST10** 50 C7
IPSWICH IP 35 **F4**
Irby **CH61** 48 B4
Irby in the Marsh **PE24** 53 H6
Irby upon Humber **DN37** 52 E2
Irchester **NN29** 32 C2
Ireby, *Cumb.* **CA7** 60 D3
Ireby, *Lancs.* **LA6** 56 B2
Ireland, *Ork.* **KW16** 107 C7
Ireland, *Shet.* **ZE2** 109 C10
Ireleth **LA16** 55 F2
Ireshopeburn **DL13** 61 K3
Irlam **M44** 49 G3
Irnham **NG33** 42 D3
Iron Acton **BS36** 19 K3
Iron Cross **WR11** 30 B3
Ironbridge **TF8** 39 F5
Ironside **AB53** 99 G5
Ironville **NG16** 51 G7
Irstead **NR12** 45 H3
Irthington **CA6** 69 K7
Irthlingborough **NN9** 32 C1
Irton **YO12** 59 G1
Irvine **KA12** 74 B7
Isauld **KW14** 104 E2
Isbister, *Ork.* **KW17** 106 B5
Isbister, *Ork.* **KW17** 107 C6
Isbister, *Shet.* **ZE2** 108 C3
Isbister, *Shet.* **ZE2** 109 E6
Isfield **TN22** 13 H5
Isham **NN14** 32 B1
Ishriff **PA65** 79 H4
Islay Airport **PA42** 72 B5
Islay Ho. **PA44** 72 B4
Isle Abbotts **TA3** 8 C2
Isle Brewers **TA3** 8 C2
Isle of Man Airport **IM9** 54 B7
Isle of Whithorn **DG8** 64 E7
Isleham **CB7** 33 K1
Isleornsay (Eilean Iarmain) **IV43** 86 C3
Islesburgh **ZE2** 109 C6
Isleworth **TW7** 22 E4
Isley Walton **DE74** 41 G3
Islibhig **HS2** 100 B5
Islington **N** 23 G3
Islip, *Northants.* **NN14** 32 C1
Islip, *Oxon.* **OX5** 31 G7
Isombridge **TF6** 39 F4
Istead Rise **DA13** 24 C5
Itchen **SO19** 11 F3
Itchen Abbas **SO21** 11 G1
Itchen Stoke **SO24** 11 G1
Itchingfield **RH13** 12 E4
Itchington **BS35** 19 K3
Itteringham **NR11** 45 F2
Itton **EX20** 6 E6
Itton Common **NP16** 19 H2
Ivegill **CA4** 60 F2
Ivelet **DL11** 62 A7
Iver **SL0** 22 D3
Iver Heath **SL0** 22 D3
Iveston **DH8** 62 C1
Ivinghoe **LU7** 32 C7
Ivinghoe Aston **LU7** 32 C7
Ivington **HR6** 28 D3
Ivington Green **HR6** 28 D3
Ivy Hatch **TN15** 23 J6
Ivy Todd **PE37** 44 C5
Ivybridge **PL21** 5 G5
Ivychurch **TN29** 15 F5
Iwade **ME9** 25 F5
Iwerne Courtney or Shroton **DT11** 9 H3
Iwerne Minster **DT11** 9 H3
Ixworth **IP31** 34 D1
Ixworth Thorpe **IP31** 34 D1

J

Jack Hill **LS21** 57 G4
Jackstown **AB51** 91 F1
Jackton **G75** 74 D5
Jacobstow **EX23** 4 B1
Jacobstowe **EX20** 6 D5
Jameston **SA70** 16 D5
Jamestown, *D. & G.* **DG13** 69 J4
Jamestown, *High.* **IV14** 96 B6
Jamestown, *W.Dun.* **G83** 74 B2
Janefield **IV10** 96 E6
Janetstown **KW14** 105 F2
Jarrow **NE32** 71 J7
Jarvis Brook **TN6** 13 J4
Jasper's Green **CM7** 34 B6
Jawcraig **FK1** 75 G3
Jayes Park **RH5** 22 E7
Jaywick **CO15** 35 F7
Jedburgh **TD8** 70 B1
Jeffreyston **SA68** 16 D4
Jemimaville **IV7** 96 E5
Jersay **ML7** 75 G4
Jerviswood **ML11** 75 G6
Jesmond **NE2** 71 H7
Jevington **BN26** 13 J6
Jodrell Bank **SK11** 49 G5
John o' Groats **KW1** 105 J1
Johnby **CA11** 60 F3
John's Cross **TN32** 14 C5
Johnshaven **DD10** 83 J1
Johnston **SA62** 16 C3
Johnston Mains **AB30** 83 J1
Johnstone **PA5** 74 C4
Johnstone Castle **PA5** 74 C4
Johnstonebridge **DG11** 69 F4
Johnstown, *Carmar.* **SA31** 17 G3
Johnstown, *Wrex.* **LL14** 38 C1
Joppa, *Edin.* **EH15** 76 B3
Joppa, *S.Ayr.* **KA6** 67 J2
Jordans **HP9** 22 C2
Jordanston **SA62** 16 C1
Jordanstone **PH11** 82 D3
Jump **S74** 51 F2
Juniper Green **EH14** 75 K4
Jura Ho. **PA60** 72 C4
Jurby East **IM7** 54 C4
Jurby West **IM7** 54 C4

K

Kaber **CA17** 61 J5
Kaimes **EH17** 76 A4
Kalnakill **IV54** 94 C6
Kames, *Arg. & B.* **PA34** 79 K6
Kames, *Arg. & B.* **PA21** 73 H3
Kames, *E.Ayr.* **KA18** 68 B1
Kea **TR3** 3 F4
Keadby **DN17** 52 B1
Keal Cotes **PE23** 53 G6
Kearsley **BL4** 49 G2
Kearstwick **LA6** 56 B1
Kearton **DL11** 62 B7
Kearvaig **IV27** 102 E1
Keasden **LA2** 56 C3
Kebholes **AB45** 98 E5
Keckwick **WA4** 48 E4
Keddington **LN11** 53 G4
Kedington **CB9** 34 B4
Kedleston **DE22** 41 F1
Keelby **DN41** 52 E2
Keele **ST5** 40 A1
Keeley Green **MK43** 32 D4
Keeres Green **CM6** 33 J7
Keeston **SA62** 16 C3
Keevil **BA14** 20 C6
Kegworth **DE74** 41 G3
Kehelland **TR14** 2 D4
Keig **AB33** 90 E3
Keighley **BD21** 57 F5
Keil, *Arg. & B.* **PA28** 66 A3
Keil, *High.* **PA38** 80 A2
Keilhill **AB45** 99 F5
Keillmore **PA31** 72 E2
Keillor **PH13** 82 D3
Keillour **PH1** 82 A5
Keills **PA46** 72 C4
Keils **PA60** 72 D4
Keinton Mandeville **TA11** 8 E1
Keir **FK15** 75 F1
Keir Mill **DG3** 68 D4
Keisby **PE10** 42 D3
Keisley **CA16** 61 J4
Keiss **KW1** 105 J2
Keith **AB55** 98 C5
Keithick **PH13** 82 D4
Keithmore **AB55** 90 B1
Keithock **DD9** 83 H1
Kelbrook **BB18** 56 E5
Kelby **NG32** 42 D1
Keld, *Cumb.* **CA10** 61 G5
Keld, *N.Yorks.* **DL11** 61 K6
Keldholme **YO62** 58 D1
Keldy Castle **YO18** 63 J7
Kelfield, *N.Lincs.* **DN9** 52 B2
Kelfield, *N.Yorks.* **YO19** 58 B6
Kelham **NG23** 51 K7
Kellan **PA72** 79 G3
Kellas, *Angus* **DD5** 83 F4
Kellas, *Moray* **IV30** 97 J6
Kellaton **TQ7** 5 J7
Kelleth **CA10** 61 H6
Kelleythorpe **YO25** 59 G4
Kelling **NR25** 44 E1
Kellington **DN14** 58 B7
Kelloe **DH6** 62 E3
Kelloholm **DG4** 68 C2
Kelly, *Cornw.* **PL27** 4 A3
Kelly, *Devon* **PL16** 6 B7
Kelly Bray **PL17** 4 D3
Kelmarsh **NN6** 31 J1
Kelmscott **GL7** 21 F2
Kelsale **IP17** 35 H2
Kelsall **CW6** 48 E6
Kelsay **PA47** 72 A5
Kelshall **SG8** 33 G5
Kelsick **CA7** 60 C1
Kelso **TD5** 77 F7
Kelstedge **S45** 51 F6
Kelstern **LN11** 53 F3
Kelston **BA1** 19 K5
Keltneyburn **PH15** 81 J3
Kelton **DG1** 65 K3
Kelton Hill or Rhonehouse **DG7** 65 H5
Kelty **KY4** 75 K1
Kelvedon **CO5** 34 C7
Kelvedon Hatch **CM15** 23 J2
Kelynack **TR19** 2 A5
Kemback **KY15** 83 F6
Kemberton **TF11** 39 G5
Kemble **GL7** 20 C2
Kemerton **GL20** 29 J5
Kemeys Commander **NP15** 19 G1
Kemeys Inferior **NP18** 19 G2
Kemnay **AB51** 91 F3
Kemp Town **BN2** 13 G6
Kempley **GL18** 29 F6
Kempley Green **GL18** 29 F6
Kempsey **WR5** 29 H4
Kempsford **GL7** 20 E2
Kempshott **RG22** 21 K7
Kempston **MK42** 32 D4
Kempston Church End **MK43** 32 D4
Kempston Hardwick **MK45** 32 D4
Kempton **SY7** 38 C7
Kemsing **TN15** 23 J6
Kemsley **ME10** 25 F5
Kenardington **TN26** 14 E4
Kenchester **HR4** 28 D4
Kencott **GL7** 21 F1
Kendal **LA9** 61 G7
Kenderchurch **HR2** 28 D6
Kenfig **CF33** 18 B3
Kenfig Hill **CF33** 18 B3
Kenilworth **CV8** 30 D1
Kenknock, *P. & K.* **PH15** 81 G3
Kenknock, *Stir.* **FK21** 81 F4
Kenley, *Gt.Lon.* **CR8** 23 G6
Kenley, *Shrop.* **SY5** 38 E5
Kenmore, *Arg. & B.* **PA32** 80 B7
Kenmore, *High.* **IV54** 94 D6
Kenmore, *P. & K.* **PH15** 81 J3
Kenmore, *W.Isles* **HS2** 100 E7
Kenn, *Devon* **EX6** 7 H7
Kenn, *N.Som.* **BS21** 19 H5
Kennacraig **PA29** 73 G4
Kennards House **PL15** 4 C2
Kennavay **HS4** 93 H2
Kennerleigh **EX17** 7 G5
Kennerty **AB31** 90 E5
Kennet **FK10** 75 H1
Kennethmont **AB54** 90 D2
Kennett **CB8** 33 K2
Kennford **EX6** 7 H7
Kenninghall **NR16** 44 E7
Kennington, *Kent* **TN24** 15 F3
Kennington, *Oxon.* **OX1** 21 J1
Kennoway **KY8** 82 E7
Kennyhill **IP28** 33 K1
Kennythorpe **YO17** 58 D3
Kensaleyre **IV51** 93 K6
Kensington & Chelsea **SW** 23 F4
Kensworth **LU6** 32 D7
Kensworth Common **LU6** 32 D7
Kent Street, *E.Suss.* **TN33** 14 C6
Kent Street, *Kent* **ME18** 23 K6
Kentallen **PA38** 80 B2
Kentchurch **HR2** 28 D6
Kentford **CB8** 34 B2
Kentisbeare **EX15** 7 J5
Kentisbury **EX31** 6 E1
Kentisbury Ford **EX31** 6 E1
Kentmere **LA8** 61 F6
Kenton, *Devon* **EX6** 7 H7
Kenton, *Suff.* **IP14** 35 F2
Kenton, *T. & W.* **NE3** 71 H7
Kentra **PH36** 79 H1
Kents Bank **LA11** 55 H2
Kent's Green **GL18** 29 G6
Kent's Oak **SO51** 10 E2
Kenwick **SY12** 38 D2
Kenwyn **TR1** 3 F4
Kenyon **WA3** 49 F3
Keoldale **IV27** 103 F2
Keppanach **PH33** 80 B1
Keppoch, *Arg. & B.* **G82** 74 B3
Keppoch, *High.* **IV40** 86 E2
Keprigan **PA28** 66 A2
Kepwick **YO7** 63 F7
Keresley **CV6** 41 F7
Kerne Bridge **HR9** 28 E7
Kerridge **SK10** 49 J5
Kerris **TR19** 2 B6
Kerry **SY16** 38 A7
Kerrycroy **PA20** 73 K4
Kerry's Gate **HR2** 28 C5
Kerrysdale **IV21** 94 E4
Kersall **NG22** 51 K6
Kersey **IP7** 34 E4
Kershopefoot **CA6** 69 K5
Kerswell **EX15** 7 J5
Kerswell Green **WR5** 29 H4
Kesgrave **IP5** 35 G4
Kessingland **NR33** 45 K7
Kessingland Beach **NR33** 45 K7
Kestle Mill **TR8** 3 F3
Keston **BR2** 23 H5
Keswick, *Cumb.* **CA12** 60 D4
Keswick, *Norf.* **NR12** 45 H2
Keswick, *Norf.* **NR4** 45 G5
Ketsby **LN11** 53 G5
Kettering **NN15** 32 B1
Ketteringham **NR18** 45 F5
Kettins **PH13** 82 D4
Kettlebaston **IP7** 34 D4
Kettlebridge **KY15** 82 E7
Kettlebrook **B77** 40 E5
Kettleburgh **IP13** 35 G3
Kettleholm **DG11** 69 G6
Kettleness **YO21** 63 K5
Kettleshulme **SK23** 49 J5
Kettlesing **HG3** 57 H4
Kettlesing Bottom **HG3** 57 H4
Kettlestone **NR21** 44 D2
Kettlethorpe **LN1** 52 B5
Kettletoft **KW17** 106 F4
Kettlewell **BD23** 56 E2
Ketton **PE9** 42 C5
Kew **TW9** 22 E4
Kewstoke **BS22** 19 G5
Kexbrough **S75** 51 F2
Kexby, *Lincs.* **DN21** 52 B4
Kexby, *York* **YO41** 58 D4
Key Green **CW12** 49 H6
Keyham **LE7** 41 J5
Keyhaven **SO41** 10 E5
Keyingham **HU12** 59 J7
Keymer **BN6** 13 G5
Keynsham **BS31** 19 K5
Key's Toft **PE24** 53 H7
Keysoe **MK44** 32 D2
Keysoe Row **MK44** 32 D2
Keyston **PE28** 32 D1
Keyworth **NG12** 41 J2

Kirkwhelpington

Kibblesworth **NE11** 62 D1
Kibworth Beauchamp **LE8** 41 J6
Kibworth Harcourt **LE8** 41 J6
Kidbrooke **SE3** 23 H4
Kiddal Lane End **LS15** 57 J6
Kiddemore Green **ST19** 40 A5
Kidderminster **DY10** 29 H1
Kiddington **OX20** 31 F6
Kidlington **OX5** 31 F7
Kidmore End **RG4** 21 K4
Kidsdale **DG8** 64 E7
Kidsgrove **ST7** 49 H7
Kidstones **DL8** 56 E1
Kidwelly (Cydweli) **SA17** 17 H4
Kiel Crofts **PA37** 80 A4
Kielder **NE48** 70 B4
Kilbarchan **PA10** 74 C4
Kilbeg **IV44** 86 C4
Kilberry **PA29** 73 F4
Kilbirnie **KA25** 74 B5
Kilblaan **PA32** 80 C6
Kilbraur **KW9** 104 D7
Kilbrenan **PA73** 79 F3
Kilbride, *Arg. & B.* **PA34** 79 K5
Kilbride, *Arg. & B.* **PA20** 73 J4
Kilbride, *High.* **IV49** 86 B2
Kilbride Farm **PA21** 73 H4
Kilbridemore **PA22** 73 J1
Kilburn, *Derbys.* **DE56** 41 F1
Kilburn, *N.Yorks.* **YO61** 58 B2
Kilby **LE18** 41 J6
Kilcadzow **ML8** 75 G6
Kilchattan, *Arg. & B.* **PA20** 73 K5
Kilchenzie **PA28** 66 A1
Kilcheran **PA34** 79 K4
Kilchiaran **PA48** 72 A5
Kilchoan, *Arg. & B.* **PA34** 79 J6
Kilchoan, *High.* **PH36** 79 F1
Kilchoman **PA49** 72 A4
Kilchrenan **PA35** 80 B5
Kilchrist **PA28** 66 A2
Kilconquhar **KY9** 83 F7
Kilcot **GL18** 29 F6
Kilcoy **IV6** 96 C6
Kilcreggan **G84** 74 A2
Kildale **YO21** 63 H6
Kildary **IV18** 96 E4
Kildavie **PA28** 66 B2
Kildermorie Lodge **IV17** 96 C4
Kildonan **KA27** 66 E1
Kildonan Lodge **KW8** 104 E6
Kildonnan **PH42** 85 K6
Kildrochet **DG9** 64 A5
Kildrummy **AB33** 90 C3
Kildwick **BD20** 57 F5
Kilfinan **PA21** 73 H3
Kilfinnan **PH34** 87 J5
Kilgetty **SA68** 16 E4
Kilgwrrwg Common **NP16** 19 H2
Kilham, *E.Riding* **YO25** 59 G3
Kilham, *Northumb.* **TD12** 77 G7
Kilkenneth **PA77** 78 A3
Kilkenny **GL54** 30 B7
Kilkerran, *Arg. & B.* **PA28** 66 B2
Kilkerran, *S.Ayr.* **KA19** 67 H3
Kilkhampton **EX23** 6 A4
Killamarsh **S21** 51 G4
Killay **SA2** 17 K5
Killbeg **PA72** 79 H3
Killean, *Arg. & B.* **PA32** 80 B7
Killean, *Arg. & B.* **PA29** 72 E6
Killearn **G63** 74 D2
Killellan **PA28** 66 A2
Killen **IV9** 96 D6
Killerby **DL2** 62 C4
Killichonan **PH17** 81 G2
Killichronan **PA72** 79 G3
Killiechanate **PH34** 87 J6
Killiecrankie **PH16** 82 A1
Killiehuntly **PH21** 88 E5
Killiemor **PA72** 79 F4
Killilan **IV40** 87 F1
Killimster **KW1** 105 J3
Killin, *High.* **KW9** 97 F1
Killin, *Stir.* **FK21** 81 G4
Killinallan **PA44** 72 B3
Killinghall **HG3** 57 H4
Killington **LA6** 56 B1
Killingworth **NE12** 71 H6
Killochyett **TD1** 76 C6
Killocraw **PA28** 66 A1
Killunaig **PA70** 79 F5
Killundine **PA34** 79 G3
Kilmacolm **PA13** 74 B4
Kilmaha **PA35** 80 A7
Kilmahog **FK17** 81 H7
Kilmalieu **PH33** 79 K2
Kilmaluag **IV51** 93 K4
Kilmany **KY15** 82 E5
Kilmarie **IV49** 86 B3
KILMARNOCK KA 74 C7
Kilmartin **PA31** 73 G1
Kilmaurs **KA3** 74 C6
Kilmelford **PA34** 79 K6
Kilmersdon **BA3** 19 K6
Kilmeston **SO24** 11 G2
Kilmichael **PA28** 66 A1
Kilmichael Glassary **PA31** 73 G1
Kilmichael of Inverlussa **PA31** 73 F2
Kilmington, *Devon* **EX13** 8 B5
Kilmington, *Wilts.* **BA12** 9 G1
Kilmington Street **BA12** 9 G1
Kilmorack **IV4** 96 B7
Kilmore, *Arg. & B.* **PA34** 79 K5
Kilmore, *High.* **IV44** 86 C4
Kilmory, *Arg. & B.* **PA31** 73 F2
Kilmory, *Arg. & B.* **PA31** 73 F3
Kilmory, *High.* **PH43** 85 J4
Kilmory, *High.* **PH36** 79 G1
Kilmote **KW8** 104 E7
Kilmuir, *High.* **IV18** 96 E4
Kilmuir, *High.* **IV51** 93 J4
Kilmuir, *High.* **IV1** 96 D7
Kilmuir, *High.* **IV55** 93 H7
Kilmun **PA23** 73 K2
Kilmux **KY8** 82 E7
Kiln Green **RG10** 22 B4
Kiln Pit Hill **DH8** 62 B1
Kilnave **PA44** 72 A3
Kilndown **TN17** 14 C4
Kilnhurst **S64** 51 G3
Kilninian **PA74** 79 F3
Kilninver **PA34** 79 K5
Kilnsea **HU12** 53 H1
Kilnsey **BD23** 56 E3
Kilnwick **YO25** 59 G5
Kiloran **PA61** 72 B1
Kilpatrick **KA27** 66 D1
Kilpeck **HR2** 28 D5
Kilphedir **KW8** 104 E7
Kilpin **DN14** 58 D7
Kilrenny **KY10** 83 G7
Kilsby **CV23** 31 G1
Kilspindie **PH2** 82 D5
Kilstay **DG9** 64 B7
Kilsyth **G65** 75 F3
Kiltarlity **IV4** 96 C7
Kilton, *R. & C.* **TS13** 63 H5
Kilton, *Som.* **TA5** 7 K1
Kiltyre **FK21** 81 H4
Kilvaxter **IV51** 93 J5
Kilve **TA5** 7 K1
Kilverstone **IP24** 44 C7
Kilvington **NG13** 42 B1
Kilwinning **KA13** 74 B6
Kimberley, *Norf.* **NR18** 44 E5
Kimberley, *Notts.* **NG16** 41 H1
Kimble Wick **HP17** 22 B1
Kimblesworth **DH2** 62 D2
Kimbolton, *Cambs.* **PE28** 32 E2
Kimbolton, *Here.* **HR6** 28 E2
Kimcote **LE17** 41 H7
Kimmeridge **BH20** 9 J7
Kimmerston **NE71** 77 H7
Kimpton, *Hants.* **SP11** 21 F7
Kimpton, *Herts.* **SG4** 32 E7
Kinaldy **KY16** 83 G6
Kinblethmont **DD11** 83 H3
Kinbrace **KW11** 104 D5
Kinbreack **PH34** 87 G5
Kinbuck **FK15** 81 J7
Kincaldrum **DD8** 83 F3
Kincaple **KY16** 83 F6
Kincardine, *Fife* **FK10** 75 H2
Kincardine, *High.* **IV24** 96 D3
Kincardine O'Neil **AB34** 90 D5
Kinclaven **PH1** 82 C4
Kincorth **AB12** 91 H4
Kincraig, *Aber.* **AB41** 91 H2
Kincraig, *High.* **PH21** 89 F4
Kincraigie **PH8** 82 A3
Kindallachan **PH9** 82 A3
Kindrogan Field Centre **PH10** 82 B1
Kinellar **AB21** 91 G3
Kineton, *Glos.* **GL54** 30 B6
Kineton, *Warks.* **CV35** 30 E3
Kineton Green **B92** 40 D7
Kinfauns **PH2** 82 C5
King Sterndale **SK17** 50 C5
Kingarth **PA20** 73 J5
Kingcoed **NP15** 19 H1
Kingerby **LN8** 52 D3
Kingham **OX7** 30 D6
Kingholm Quay **DG1** 65 K3
Kinghorn **KY3** 76 A2
Kinglassie **KY5** 76 A1
Kingoodie **DD2** 82 E5
King's Bromley **DE13** 40 D4
Kings Caple **HR1** 28 E6
King's Cliffe **PE8** 42 D6
King's Coughton **B49** 30 B3
King's Green **WR13** 29 G5
Kings Heanton **EX31** 6 D2
King's Heath **B14** 40 C7
King's Hill **WS10** 40 B6
Kings Langley **WD4** 22 D1
King's Lynn **PE30** 44 A3
Kings Meaburn **CA10** 61 H4
Kings Muir **EH45** 76 A7
King's Newton **DE73** 41 F3
King's Norton, *Leics.* **LE7** 41 J5
King's Norton, *W.Mid.* **B38** 30 B1
King's Nympton **EX37** 6 E4
King's Pyon **HR4** 28 D3
Kings Ripton **PE28** 33 F1
King's Somborne **SO20** 10 E1
King's Stag **DT10** 9 G3
King's Stanley **GL10** 20 B1
King's Sutton **OX17** 31 F5
King's Walden **SG4** 32 E6
King's Worthy **SO23** 11 F1
Kingsand **PL10** 4 E5
Kingsbarns **KY16** 83 G6
Kingsbridge, *Devon* **TQ7** 5 H6
Kingsbridge, *Som.* **TA23** 7 H2
Kingsburgh **IV51** 93 J6
Kingsbury, *Gt.Lon.* **HA3** 22 E3
Kingsbury, *Warks.* **B78** 40 E6
Kingsbury Episcopi **TA12** 8 D2
Kingscavil **EH49** 75 J3
Kingsclere **RG20** 21 J6
Kingscote **GL8** 20 B2
Kingscott **EX38** 6 D4
Kingscross **KA27** 66 E1
Kingsdale **KY8** 82 E7
Kingsdon **TA11** 8 E2
Kingsdown **CT14** 15 J3
Kingseat **KY12** 75 K1
Kingsey **HP27** 22 A1
Kingsfold, *Pembs.* **SA71** 16 C5
Kingsfold, *W.Suss.* **RH12** 12 E3
Kingsford, *Aber.* **AB53** 99 F6
Kingsford, *Aber.* **AB33** 90 D3
Kingsford, *Aberdeen* **AB15** 91 G4
Kingsford, *E.Ayr.* **KA3** 74 C6
Kingsford, *Worcs.* **DY11** 40 A7
Kingsforth **DN18** 52 D1
Kingsgate **CT10** 25 K4
Kingshouse **FK19** 81 G5
Kingshouse Hotel **PH49** 80 D2
Kingskerswell **TQ12** 5 J4
Kingskettle **KY15** 82 E7
Kingsland, *Here.* **HR6** 28 D2
Kingsland, *I.o.A.* **LL65** 46 A4
Kingsley, *Ches.* **WA6** 48 E5
Kingsley, *Hants.* **GU35** 11 J1
Kingsley, *Staffs.* **ST10** 40 C1
Kingsley Green **GU27** 12 B3
Kingsmuir **DD8** 83 F3
Kingsnorth **TN23** 15 F4
Kingsnorth Power Station **ME3** 24 E4
Kingstanding **B44** 40 C6
Kingsteignton **TQ12** 5 J3
Kingsteps **IV12** 97 G6
Kingsthorne **HR2** 28 E5
Kingsthorpe **NN2** 31 J2
Kingston, *Cambs.* **CB3** 33 G3
Kingston, *Devon* **TQ7** 5 G6
Kingston, *Dorset* **DT10** 9 G4
Kingston, *Dorset* **BH20** 9 J7
Kingston, *E.Loth.* **EH39** 76 D2
Kingston, *Hants.* **BH24** 10 C4
Kingston, *I.o.W.* **PO38** 11 F6
Kingston, *Kent* **CT4** 15 G2
Kingston, *Moray* **IV32** 98 B4
Kingston, *W.Suss.* **BN16** 12 D6
Kingston Bagpuize **OX13** 21 H2
Kingston Blount **OX39** 22 A2
Kingston by Sea **BN43** 13 F6
Kingston Deverill **BA12** 9 H1
Kingston Lisle **OX12** 21 G3
Kingston near Lewes **BN7** 13 G6
Kingston on Soar **NG11** 41 H3
Kingston Russell **DT2** 8 E5
Kingston St. Mary **TA2** 8 B2
Kingston Seymour **BS21** 19 G5
KINGSTON UPON HULL HU 59 H7
KINGSTON UPON THAMES KT 22 E4
Kingston Warren **OX12** 21 G3
Kingstone, *Here.* **HR2** 28 D5
Kingstone, *Som.* **TA19** 8 C3
Kingstone, *Staffs.* **ST14** 40 C3
Kingstown **CA3** 60 E1
Kingswear **TQ6** 5 J5
Kingswell **KA3** 74 D6
Kingswells **AB15** 91 G4
Kingswinford **DY6** 40 A7
Kingswood, *Bucks.* **HP18** 31 H7
Kingswood, *Glos.* **GL12** 20 A2
Kingswood, *Kent* **ME17** 14 D2
Kingswood, *Powys* **SY21** 38 B5
Kingswood, *S.Glos.* **BS15** 19 K4
Kingswood, *Surr.* **KT20** 23 F6
Kingswood, *Warks.* **B94** 30 C1
Kingswood Common **HR5** 28 B3
Kingthorpe **LN8** 52 E5
Kington, *Here.* **HR5** 28 B3
Kington, *Worcs.* **WR7** 29 J3
Kington Langley **SN15** 20 C4
Kington Magna **SP8** 9 G2
Kington St. Michael **SN14** 20 B4
Kingussie **PH21** 88 E4
Kingweston **TA11** 8 E1
Kinharrachie **AB41** 91 H1
Kinharvie **DG2** 65 K4
Kinkell **G66** 74 E3
Kinkell Bridge **PH3** 82 A6
Kinknockie **AB42** 99 J6
Kinlet **DY12** 39 G7
Kinloch, *Fife* **KY15** 82 D6
Kinloch, *High.* **IV27** 103 F5
Kinloch, *High.* **IV16** 96 C4
Kinloch, *High.* **PH43** 85 K5
Kinloch, *High.* **PA34** 79 H2
Kinloch, *P. & K.* **PH10** 82 C3
Kinloch, *P. & K.* **PH12** 82 D3
Kinloch Hourn **PH35** 87 F4
Kinloch Laggan **PH20** 88 C6
Kinloch Rannoch **PH16** 81 H2
Kinlochan **PH37** 79 K1
Kinlochard **FK8** 81 F7
Kinlocharkaig **PH34** 87 F5
Kinlochbeoraid **PH38** 86 E6
Kinlochbervie **IV27** 102 E3
Kinlocheil **PH33** 87 F7
Kinlochetive **PH49** 80 C3
Kinlochewe **IV22** 95 G5
Kinlochlaich **PA38** 80 A3
Kinlochleven **PH50** 80 C1
Kinlochmoidart **PH36** 86 D7
Kinlochmorar **PH41** 86 E5
Kinlochmore **PH50** 80 C1
Kinlochspelve **PA63** 79 H5
Kinloss **IV36** 97 H5
Kinmel Bay (Bae Cinmel) **LL22** 47 H4
Kinmuck **AB51** 91 G3
Kinnadie **AB41** 99 H6
Kinnaird **PH14** 82 D5
Kinneff **DD10** 91 G7
Kinnelhead **DG10** 69 F3
Kinnell, *Angus* **DD11** 83 H2
Kinnell, *Stir.* **FK21** 81 G4
Kinnerley **SY10** 38 C3
Kinnersley, *Here.* **HR3** 28 C4
Kinnersley, *Worcs.* **WR8** 29 H4
Kinnerton **LD8** 28 B2
Kinnesswood **KY13** 82 C7
Kinnettles **DD8** 83 F3
Kinninvie **DL12** 62 B4
Kinnordy **DD8** 82 E2
Kinoulton **NG12** 41 J2
Kinrara **PH22** 89 F4
Kinross **KY13** 82 C7
Kinrossie **PH2** 82 C4
Kinsbourne Green **AL5** 32 E7
Kinsham **LD8** 28 C2
Kinsley **WF9** 51 G1
Kinson **BH11** 10 B5
Kintarvie **HS2** 100 E6
Kintbury **RG17** 21 G5
Kintessack **IV36** 97 G5
Kintillo **PH2** 82 C6
Kintocher **AB33** 90 D4
Kinton, *Here.* **SY7** 28 D1
Kinton, *Shrop.* **SY4** 38 C4
Kintore **AB51** 91 F3
Kintour **PA42** 72 C5
Kintra, *Arg. & B.* **PA66** 78 E5
Kintra, *Arg. & B.* **PA42** 72 B6
Kintradwell **KW9** 97 G1
Kintraw **PA31** 79 K7
Kinuachdrach **PA60** 73 F1
Kinveachy **PH24** 89 G3
Kinver **DY7** 40 A7
Kiplaw Croft **AB42** 91 J1
Kiplin **DL10** 62 D7
Kiplingcotes **YO43** 59 F5
Kipp **FK18** 81 G6
Kippax **LS25** 57 K6
Kippen, *P. & K.* **PH2** 82 B6
Kippen, *Stir.* **FK8** 74 E1
Kippenross Ho **FK15** 81 J7
Kippford or Scaur **DG5** 65 J5
Kipping's Cross **TN12** 23 K7
Kirbister, *Ork.* **KW17** 106 F5
Kirbister, *Ork.* **KW16** 107 C7
Kirbuster **KW17** 106 B5
Kirby Bedon **NR14** 45 G5
Kirby Cane **NR35** 45 H6
Kirby Corner **CV4** 30 D1
Kirby Cross **CO13** 35 G7
Kirby Grindalythe **YO17** 59 F3
Kirby Hill, *N.Yorks.* **DL11** 62 C6
Kirby Hill, *N.Yorks.* **YO51** 57 J3
Kirby Knowle **YO7** 57 K1
Kirby le Soken **CO13** 35 G6
Kirby Misperton **YO17** 58 D2
Kirby Muxloe **LE9** 41 H5
Kirby Row **NR35** 45 H6
Kirby Sigston **DL6** 63 F7
Kirby Underdale **YO41** 58 E4
Kirby Wiske **YO7** 57 J1
Kirdford **RH14** 12 D4
Kirk **KW1** 105 H3
Kirk Bramwith **DN7** 51 J1
Kirk Deighton **LS22** 57 J4
Kirk Ella **HU10** 59 G7
Kirk Hallam **DE7** 41 G1
Kirk Hammerton **YO26** 57 K4
Kirk Ireton **DE6** 50 E7
Kirk Langley **DE6** 40 E2
Kirk Merrington **DL16** 62 D3
Kirk Michael **IM6** 54 C4
Kirk of Shotts **ML7** 75 G4
Kirk Sandall **DN3** 51 J2
Kirk Smeaton **WF8** 51 H1
Kirk Yetholm **TD5** 70 D1
Kirkabister **ZE2** 109 D9
Kirkandrews **DG6** 65 G6
Kirkandrews-upon-Eden **CA5** 60 E1
Kirkbampton **CA5** 60 E1
Kirkbean **DG2** 65 K5
Kirkbride **CA7** 60 D1
Kirkbridge **DL8** 62 D7
Kirkbuddo **DD8** 83 G3
Kirkburn, *E.Riding* **YO25** 59 F4
Kirkburn, *Sc.Bord.* **EH45** 76 A7
Kirkburton **HD8** 50 D1
Kirkby, *Lincs.* **LN8** 52 D3
Kirkby, *Mersey.* **L32** 48 D3
Kirkby, *N.Yorks.* **TS9** 63 G6
Kirkby Bellars **LE14** 42 A4
Kirkby Fleetham **DL7** 62 D7
Kirkby Green **LN4** 52 D7
Kirkby in Ashfield **NG17** 51 G7
Kirkby la Thorpe **NG34** 42 E1
Kirkby Lonsdale **LA6** 56 B2
Kirkby Malham **BD23** 56 D3
Kirkby Mallory **LE9** 41 G5
Kirkby Malzeard **HG4** 57 H2
Kirkby Mills **YO62** 58 D1
Kirkby on Bain **LN10** 53 F6
Kirkby Overblow **HG3** 57 J5
Kirkby Stephen **CA17** 61 J6
Kirkby Thore **CA10** 61 H4
Kirkby Underwood **PE10** 42 D3
Kirkby Wharfe **LS24** 58 B5
Kirkbymoorside **YO62** 58 C1
KIRKCALDY KY 76 A1
Kirkcambeck **CA8** 70 A7
Kirkcolm **DG9** 64 A4
Kirkconnel **DG4** 68 C2
Kirkconnell **DG2** 65 K4
Kirkcowan **DG8** 64 D4
Kirkcudbright **DG6** 65 G5
Kirkdale **DG8** 65 F5
Kirkdean **EH46** 75 K6
Kirkfieldbank **ML11** 75 G6
Kirkgunzeon **DG2** 65 J4
Kirkham, *Lancs.* **PR4** 55 H6
Kirkham, *N.Yorks.* **YO60** 58 D3
Kirkhamgate **WF2** 57 H7
Kirkharle **NE19** 71 F5
Kirkhaugh **CA9** 61 H2
Kirkheaton, *Northumb.* **NE19** 71 F6
Kirkheaton, *W.Yorks.* **HD5** 50 D1
Kirkhill, *Angus* **DD10** 83 H1
Kirkhill, *High.* **IV5** 96 C7
Kirkhill, *Moray* **AB38** 98 B5
Kirkhope **TD7** 69 J1
Kirkibost, *High.* **IV49** 86 B3
Kirkibost, *W.Isles* **HS2** 100 D4
Kirkinch **PH12** 82 E3
Kirkinner **DG8** 64 E5
Kirkintilloch **G66** 74 E3
Kirkland, *Cumb.* **CA10** 61 H3
Kirkland, *Cumb.* **CA26** 60 B5
Kirkland, *D. & G.* **DG4** 68 C2
Kirkland, *D. & G.* **DG3** 68 D4
Kirkland, *D. & G.* **DG11** 69 F5
Kirkland of Longcastle **DG8** 64 D6
Kirkleatham **TS10** 63 G4
Kirklevington **TS15** 63 F5
Kirkley **NR33** 45 K6
Kirklington, *N.Yorks.* **DL8** 57 J1
Kirklington, *Notts.* **NG22** 51 J7
Kirklinton **CA6** 69 K7
Kirkliston **EH29** 75 K3
Kirkmaiden **DG9** 64 B7
Kirkmichael, *P. & K.* **PH10** 82 B1
Kirkmichael, *S.Ayr.* **KA19** 67 H3
Kirkmuirhill **ML11** 75 F6
Kirknewton, *Northumb.* **NE71** 70 E1
Kirknewton, *W.Loth.* **EH27** 75 K4
Kirkney **AB54** 90 D1
Kirkoswald, *Cumb.* **CA10** 61 G2
Kirkoswald, *S.Ayr.* **KA19** 67 G3
Kirkpatrick Durham **DG7** 65 H3
Kirkpatrick-Fleming **DG11** 69 H6
Kirksanton **LA18** 54 E1
Kirkstall **LS5** 57 H6
Kirkstead **LN10** 52 E6
Kirkstile, *Aber.* **AB54** 90 D1
Kirkstile, *D. & G.* **DG13** 69 J4
Kirkton, *Aber.* **AB53** 98 E5
Kirkton, *Aber.* **AB52** 90 E2
Kirkton, *Aber.* **AB33** 90 E3
Kirkton, *Angus* **DD8** 83 F3
Kirkton, *Arg. & B.* **PA31** 79 J7
Kirkton, *D. & G.* **DG1** 68 E5
Kirkton, *Fife* **DD6** 82 E5
Kirkton, *High.* **KW13** 104 D2
Kirkton, *High.* **KW10** 96 E2
Kirkton, *High.* **IV2** 96 E6
Kirkton, *High.* **IV3** 88 D1
Kirkton, *High.* **IV40** 86 E2
Kirkton, *P. & K.* **PH3** 82 A6
Kirkton, *Sc.Bord.* **TD9** 70 A2
Kirkton Manor **EH45** 76 A7
Kirkton of Airlie **DD8** 82 E2
Kirkton of Auchterhouse **DD3** 82 E4
Kirkton of Barevan **IV12** 97 F7
Kirkton of Bourtie **AB51** 91 G2
Kirkton of Collace **PH2** 82 C4
Kirkton of Craig **DD10** 83 J2
Kirkton of Culsalmond **AB52** 90 E1
Kirkton of Durris **AB31** 91 F5
Kirkton of Glenbuchat **AB36** 90 B3
Kirkton of Glenisla **PH11** 82 D1
Kirkton of Kingoldrum **DD8** 82 E2
Kirkton of Lethendy **PH1** 82 C3
Kirkton of Logie Buchan **AB41** 91 H2
Kirkton of Maryculter **AB12** 91 G5
Kirkton of Menmuir **DD9** 83 G1
Kirkton of Monikie **DD5** 83 G4
Kirkton of Skene **AB32** 91 G4
Kirkton of Strathmartine **DD3** 82 E4
Kirkton of Tealing **DD4** 83 F4
Kirktonhill **AB30** 83 H1
Kirktown **AB42** 99 J5
Kirktown of Alvah **AB45** 98 E4
Kirktown of Auchterless **AB53** 99 F6
Kirktown of Deskford **AB56** 98 D4
Kirktown of Fetteresso **AB39** 91 G6
Kirktown of Rayne **AB51** 90 E1
Kirktown of Slains **AB41** 91 J2
KIRKWALL KW 107 D6
Kirkwall Airport **KW15** 107 D7
Kirkwhelpington **NE19** 70 E5

Kirmington

Kirmington **DN39** 52 E1
Kirmond le Mire **LN8** 52 E3
Kirn **PA23** 73 K3
Kirriemuir **DD8** 82 E2
Kirstead Green **NR15** 45 G6
Kirtlebridge **DG11** 69 H6
Kirtling **CB8** 33 K3
Kirtling Green **CB8** 33 K3
Kirtlington **OX5** 31 F7
Kirtomy **KW14** 104 C2
Kirton, *Lincs.* **PE20** 43 G2
Kirton, *Notts.* **NG22** 51 J6
Kirton, *Suff.* **IP11** 35 G5
Kirton End **PE20** 43 F1
Kirton Holme **PE20** 43 F1
Kirton in Lindsey **DN21** 52 C3
Kiscadale **KA27** 66 E1
Kislingbury **NN7** 31 H3
Kismeblon Bridge **EX22** 6 B4
Kites Hardwick **CV23** 31 F2
Kitley **PL8** 5 F5
Kittisford **TA21** 7 J3
Kitwood **SO24** 11 H1
Kiveton Park **S26** 51 G4
Klibreck **IV27** 103 H5
Knabbygates **AB54** 98 D5
Knaith **DN21** 52 B4
Knap Corner **SP8** 9 H2
Knaphill **GU21** 22 C6
Knapp, *P. & K.* **PH14** 82 D4
Knapp, *Som.* **TA3** 8 B2
Knapton, *Norf.* **NR28** 45 H2
Knapton, *York* **YO26** 58 B4
Knapton Green **HR4** 28 D3
Knapwell **CB3** 33 G2
Knaresborough **HG5** 57 J4
Knarsdale **CA8** 61 H1
Knaven **AB42** 99 G6
Knayton **YO7** 57 K1
Knebworth **SG3** 33 F7
Knedlington **DN14** 58 D7
Kneesall **NG22** 51 K6
Kneesworth **SG8** 33 G4
Kneeton **NG13** 42 A1
Knelston **SA3** 17 H6
Knettishall **IP22** 34 D1
Knightacott **EX31** 6 E2
Knightcote **CV47** 31 F3
Knighton, *Devon* **PL9** 5 F6
Knighton, *Leic.* **LE2** 41 J5
Knighton, *Powys* **LD7** 28 B1
Knighton, *Som.* **TA5** 7 K1
Knighton, *Staffs.* **TF9** 39 G2
Knighton, *Staffs.* **ST20** 39 G3
Knighton, *Wilts.* **SN8** 21 F4
Knightwick **WR6** 29 G3
Knill **LD8** 28 B2
Knipoch **PA34** 79 K5
Knipton **NG32** 42 B2
Knitsley **DH8** 62 C2
Kniveton **DE6** 50 E7
Knock, *Arg. & B.* **PA71** 79 G4
Knock, *Cumb.* **CA16** 61 H4
Knock, *Moray* **AB54** 98 D5
Knock of Auchnahannet **PH26** 89 H1
Knockalava **PA31** 73 H1
Knockally **KW6** 105 G6
Knockaloe Moar **IM5** 54 B5
Knockan **IV27** 102 E7
Knockandhu **AB37** 89 K2
Knockando **AB38** 97 J7
Knockbain **IV8** 96 D6
Knockban **IV23** 95 J5
Knockbreck **IV19** 96 E3
Knockbrex **DG6** 65 F6
Knockdamph **IV26** 95 J2
Knockdee **KW12** 105 G2
Knockdow **PA23** 73 K3
Knockdown **GL8** 20 B3
Knockenkelly **KA27** 66 E1
Knockentiber **KA2** 74 C7
Knockfin **IV4** 87 J2
Knockgray **DG7** 67 K4
Knockholt **TN14** 23 H6
Knockholt Pound **TN14** 23 H6
Knockin **SY10** 38 C3
Knocklearn **DG7** 65 H3
Knocknaha **PA28** 66 A2
Knocknain **DG9** 66 D7
Knocknalling **DG7** 67 K5
Knockrome **PA60** 72 D3
Knocksharry **IM5** 54 B5
Knockville **DG8** 64 D3
Knockvologan **PA66** 78 E6
Knodishall **IP17** 35 J2
Knolls Green **WA16** 49 H5
Knolton **LL13** 38 C2
Knook **BA12** 20 C7
Knossington **LE15** 42 B5
Knott End-on-Sea **FY6** 55 G5
Knotting **MK44** 32 D2
Knotting Green **MK44** 32 D2
Knottingley **WF11** 58 B7
Knotty Ash **L14** 48 D3
Knotty Green **HP9** 22 C2
Knowbury **SY8** 28 E1
Knowe **DG8** 64 D3
Knowes of Elrick **AB54** 98 E5
Knowesgate **NE19** 70 E5
Knoweside **KA19** 67 G2
Knowetownhead **TD9** 70 A2
Knowhead **AB43** 99 H5
Knowl Green **CO10** 34 B4
Knowl Hill **RG10** 22 B4
Knowl Wall **ST4** 40 A2
Knowle, *Bristol* **BS4** 19 K4
Knowle, *Devon* **EX33** 6 C2
Knowle, *Devon* **EX17** 7 F5
Knowle, *Devon* **EX9** 7 J7
Knowle, *Shrop.* **SY8** 28 E1
Knowle, *W.Mid.* **B93** 30 C1
Knowle Green **PR3** 56 B6
Knowle Hall **TA7** 19 G7
Knowlton, *Dorset* **BH21** 10 B3
Knowlton, *Kent* **CT3** 15 H2
Knowsley **L34** 48 D3
Knowstone **EX36** 7 G3
Knucklas **LD7** 28 B1
Knutsford **WA16** 49 G5
Knypersley **ST8** 49 H7
Kuggar **TR12** 2 E7
Kyle of Lochalsh **IV40** 86 D2
Kyleakin **IV41** 86 D2
Kylerhea **IV40** 86 D2
Kyles Scalpay (Caolas Scalpaigh) **HS3** 93 H2
Kylesbeg **PH36** 86 C7
Kylesknoydart **PH41** 86 E5
Kylesmorar **PH41** 86 E5
Kylestrome **IV27** 102 E5
Kyloag **IV24** 96 D2
Kynnersley **TF6** 39 F4
Kyre Park **WR15** 29 F2

L

Labost **HS2** 100 E3
Lacasaigh **HS2** 101 F5
Lacasdal (Laxdale) **HS1** 101 G4
Laceby **DN37** 53 F2
Lacey Green **HP27** 22 B1
Lach Dennis **CW9** 49 G5
Lackford **IP28** 34 B1
Lacock **SN15** 20 C5
Ladbroke **CV47** 31 F3
Laddingford **ME18** 23 K7
Lade Bank **PE22** 53 G7
Ladock **TR2** 3 F3
Lady Hall **LA18** 54 E1
Ladybank **KY15** 82 D6
Ladycross **PL15** 6 B7
Ladyfield **PA32** 80 B6
Ladykirk **TD15** 77 G6
Lady's Green **CB8** 34 B3
Ladysford **AB43** 99 H4
Laga **PH36** 79 H1
Lagalochan **PA35** 79 K6
Lagavulin **PA42** 72 C6
Lagg, *Arg. & B.* **PA60** 72 D3
Lagg, *N.Ayr.* **KA27** 66 D1
Lagg, *S.Ayr.* **KA7** 67 G2
Laggan, *Arg. & B.* **PA43** 72 A5
Laggan, *High.* **PH34** 87 J5
Laggan, *High.* **PH20** 88 D5
Laggan, *Moray* **AB55** 90 B1
Laggan, *Stir.* **FK18** 81 G6
Lagganulva **PA73** 79 F3
Lagganvoulin **AB37** 89 J3
Laglingarten **PA25** 80 C7
Lagnalean **IV3** 96 D7
Lagrae **DG4** 68 C2
Laguna **PH1** 82 C4
Lahill **KY9** 83 F7
Laid **IV27** 103 G3
Laide **IV22** 94 E2
Laig **PH42** 85 K6
Laight **KA18** 68 B2
Lainchoil **PH25** 89 H3
Laindon **SS15** 24 C3
Lair **PH10** 82 C1
Lairg **IV27** 96 C1
Lairg Lo. **IV27** 96 C1
Lairigmor **PH33** 80 C1
Laithers **AB53** 98 E6
Laithes **CA11** 61 F3
Lake **SP4** 10 C1
Lakenham **NR1** 45 G5
Lakenheath **IP27** 44 B7
Lakesend **PE14** 43 J6
Lakeside **LA12** 55 G1
Laleham **TW18** 22 D5
Laleston **CF32** 18 B4
Lamancha **EH46** 76 A5
Lamarsh **CO8** 34 C5
Lamas **NR10** 45 G3
Lamb Corner **CO7** 34 E5
Lamberhurst **TN3** 13 K3
Lamberhurst Quarter **TN3** 13 K3
Lamberton **TD15** 77 H5
Lambeth **SW** 23 F4
Lambfell Moar **IM4** 54 B5
Lambley, *Northumb.* **CA8** 61 H1
Lambley, *Notts.* **NG4** 41 J1
Lambourn **RG17** 21 G4
Lambourn Woodlands **RG17** 21 G4
Lambourne End **RM4** 23 H2
Lambs Green **RH12** 13 F3
Lambston **SA62** 16 C3
Lamellion **PL14** 4 C4
Lamerton **PL19** 4 E3
Lamesley **NE11** 62 D1
Lamington, *High.* **IV18** 96 E4
Lamington, *S.Lan.* **ML12** 75 H7
Lamlash **KA27** 73 J7
Lamloch **DG7** 67 K4
Lamonby **CA11** 60 F3
Lamorran **TR2** 3 F4
Lampert **NE48** 70 B6
Lampeter **SA48** 26 E4
Lampeter Velfrey **SA67** 16 E3
Lamphey **SA71** 16 D4
Lamplugh **CA14** 60 B4
Lamport **NN6** 31 J1
Lamyatt **BA4** 9 F1
Lana **EX22** 6 B6
Lanark **ML11** 75 G6
LANCASTER LA 55 **H3**
Lanchester **DH7** 62 C2
Landbeach **CB4** 33 H2
Landcross **EX39** 6 C3
Landerberry **AB32** 91 F4
Landewednack **TR12** 2 E7
Landford **SP5** 10 D3
Landimore **SA3** 17 H5
Landkey **EX32** 6 D2
Landore **SA1** 17 K5
Landrake **PL12** 4 D4
Landscove **TQ13** 5 H4
Landshipping **SA67** 16 D3
Landulph **PL12** 4 E4
Landwade **CB8** 33 K2
Landywood **WS6** 40 B5
Lane End, *Bucks.* **HP14** 22 B2
Lane End, *Cumb.* **LA19** 60 C7
Lane End, *Derbys.* **DE55** 51 G6
Lane End, *Dorset* **BH20** 9 H5
Lane End, *Kent* **DA2** 23 J4
Lane Green **WV8** 40 A5
Lane Head, *Dur.* **DL11** 62 C5
Lane Head, *Gt.Man.* **WA3** 49 F3
Lane Head, *W.Yorks.* **HD8** 50 D2
Lane-end **PL30** 4 A4
Laneast **PL15** 4 C2
Laneham **DN22** 52 B5
Lanehead **NE48** 70 C5
Laneshawbridge **BB8** 56 E5
Langais **HS6** 92 D5
Langamull **PA75** 78 E2
Langar **NG13** 42 A2
Langbank **PA14** 74 B3
Langbar **LS29** 57 F4
Langcliffe **BD24** 56 D3
Langdale End **YO13** 63 J3
Langdon **EX23** 4 C1
Langdon Beck **DL12** 61 K3
Langdon Hills **SS16** 24 C3
Langdon House **EX7** 5 K3
Langdyke **KY8** 82 E7
Langenhoe **CO5** 34 E7
Langford, *Beds.* **SG18** 32 E4
Langford, *Devon* **EX15** 7 J5
Langford, *Essex* **CM9** 24 E1
Langford, *Notts.* **NG23** 52 B7
Langford, *Oxon.* **GL7** 21 F1
Langford Budville **TA21** 7 K3
Langham, *Essex* **CO4** 34 E5
Langham, *Norf.* **NR25** 44 E1
Langham, *Rut.* **LE15** 42 B4
Langham, *Suff.* **IP31** 34 D2
Langham Moor **CO4** 34 E5
Langho **BB6** 56 B6
Langholm **DG13** 69 J5
Langlands **DG6** 65 G5
Langlee **TD8** 70 B2
Langleeford **NE71** 70 E1
Langley, *Ches.* **SK11** 49 J5
Langley, *Derbys.* **DE75** 41 G1
Langley, *Essex* **CB11** 33 H5
Langley, *Hants.* **SO45** 11 F4
Langley, *Herts.* **SG4** 33 F6
Langley, *Kent* **ME17** 14 D2
Langley, *Slo.* **SL3** 22 D4
Langley, *W.Suss.* **GU33** 12 B4
Langley, *Warks.* **CV37** 30 C2
Langley Burrell **SN15** 20 C4
Langley Green **DE6** 40 E2
Langley Heath **ME17** 14 D2
Langley Marsh **TA4** 7 J3
Langley Mill **DE75** 41 G1
Langley Moor **DH7** 62 D2
Langley Park **DH7** 62 D2
Langley Street **NR14** 45 H5
Langney **BN23** 13 K6
Langold **S81** 51 H4
Langore **PL15** 6 B7
Langport **TA10** 8 D2
Langrick **PE22** 43 F1
Langridge, *B. & N.E.Som.* **BA1** 20 A5
Langridge, *Devon* **EX37** 6 D3
Langridgeford **EX37** 6 D3
Langrigg **CA7** 60 C2
Langrish **GU32** 11 J2
Langriville **PE22** 43 F1
Langsett **S36** 50 E2
Langshaw **TD1** 76 D7
Langshawburn **DG13** 69 H3
Langside **PH6** 81 J6
Langskaill **KW17** 106 D3
Langstone **PO9** 11 J4
Langthorne **DL8** 62 D7
Langthorpe **YO51** 57 J3
Langthwaite **DL11** 62 B6
Langtoft, *E.Riding* **YO25** 59 G3
Langtoft, *Lincs.* **PE6** 42 E4
Langton, *Dur.* **DL2** 62 C5
Langton, *Lincs.* **PE23** 53 G5
Langton, *Lincs.* **LN9** 53 F6
Langton, *N.Yorks.* **YO17** 58 D3
Langton by Wragby **LN8** 52 E5
Langton Green **TN3** 13 J3
Langton Herring **DT3** 9 F6
Langton Long Blandford **DT11** 9 J4
Langton Matravers **BH19** 10 B7
Langtree **EX38** 6 C4
Langwathby **CA10** 61 G3
Langwell **IV27** 96 B1
Langwell House **KW7** 105 G6
Langworth **LN3** 52 D5
Lanivet **PL30** 4 A4
Lanlivery **PL22** 4 A5
Lanner **TR16** 2 E4
Lanreath **PL13** 4 B5
Lansallos **PL13** 4 B5
Lansdown **BA1** 20 A5
Lanteglos **PL32** 4 A2
Lanton, *Northumb.* **NE71** 77 H7
Lanton, *Sc.Bord.* **TD8** 70 B1
Lapford **EX17** 7 F5
Laphroaig **PA42** 72 B6
Lapley **ST19** 40 A4
Lapworth **B94** 30 C1
Larach na Gaibhre **PA31** 73 F4
Larachbeg **PA34** 79 H3
Larbert **FK5** 75 G2
Larden Green **CW5** 48 E7
Larg **DG8** 64 D3
Largie **AB52** 90 E1
Largiemore **PA21** 73 H2
Largoward **KY9** 83 F7
Largs **KA30** 74 A5
Largue **AB54** 98 E6
Largybaan **PA28** 66 A2
Largybeg **KA27** 66 E1
Largymore **KA27** 66 E1
Lark Hall **CB1** 33 J3
Larkhall **ML9** 75 F5
Larkhill **SP4** 20 E7
Larling **NR16** 44 D7
Larriston **TD9** 70 A4
Lartington **DL12** 62 B5
Lary **AB35** 90 B4
Lasborough **GL8** 20 B2
Lasham **GU34** 21 K7
Lassington **GL2** 29 G6
Lassintullich **PH16** 81 J2
Lassodie **KY12** 75 K1
Lasswade **EH22** 76 B4
Lastingham **YO62** 63 J7
Latchford **WA4** 49 F4
Latchingdon **CM3** 24 E1
Latchley **PL18** 4 E3
Lately Common **WN7** 49 F3
Lathallan Mill **KY9** 83 F7
Lathbury **MK16** 32 B4
Latheron **KW5** 105 G5
Latheronwheel **KW5** 105 G5
Lathockar **KY16** 83 F6
Lathones **KY15** 83 F7
Lathrisk **KY15** 82 D7
Latimer **HP5** 22 D2
Latteridge **BS37** 19 K3
Lattiford **BA9** 9 F2
Latton **SN6** 20 D2
Lauchentyre **DG7** 65 F5
Lauchintilly **AB51** 91 F3
Lauder **TD2** 76 D6
Laugharne **SA33** 17 G3
Laughterton **LN1** 52 B5
Laughton, *E.Suss.* **BN8** 13 J5
Laughton, *Leics.* **LE17** 41 J7
Laughton, *Lincs.* **DN21** 52 B3
Laughton, *Lincs.* **NG34** 42 D2
Laughton en le Morthen **S25** 51 H4
Launcells **EX23** 6 A5
Launcells Cross **EX23** 6 A5
Launceston **PL15** 6 B7
Launde Abbey **LE7** 42 B5
Launton **OX26** 31 H6
Laurencekirk **AB30** 91 F7
Laurieston, *D. & G.* **DG7** 65 G4
Laurieston, *Falk.* **FK2** 75 H3
Lavendon **MK46** 32 C3
Lavenham **CO10** 34 D4
Laverhay **DG10** 69 G4
Lavernock **CF64** 18 E5
Laversdale **CA6** 69 K7
Laverstock **SP1** 10 C1
Laverstoke **RG28** 21 H7
Laverton, *Glos.* **WR12** 30 B5
Laverton, *N.Yorks.* **HG4** 57 H2
Laverton, *Som.* **BA2** 20 A6
Lavister **LL12** 48 C7
Law **ML8** 75 G5
Lawers, *P. & K.* **PH15** 81 H4
Lawers, *P. & K.* **PH6** 81 J5
Lawford **CO11** 34 E5
Lawhitton **PL15** 6 B7
Lawkland **LA2** 56 C3
Lawley **TF4** 39 F5
Lawnhead **ST20** 40 A3
Lawrenny **SA68** 16 D4
Laws **DD5** 83 F4
Lawshall **IP29** 34 C3
Lawton **HR6** 28 D3
Laxdale (Lacasdal) **HS1** 101 G4
Laxey **IM4** 54 D5
Laxfield **IP13** 35 G1
Laxfirth, *Shet.* **ZE2** 109 D7
Laxfirth, *Shet.* **ZE2** 109 D8
Laxford Bridge **IV27** 102 E4
Laxo **ZE2** 109 D6
Laxton, *E.Riding* **DN14** 58 D7
Laxton, *Northants.* **NN17** 42 C6
Laxton, *Notts.* **NG22** 51 K6
Laycock **BD22** 57 F5
Layer Breton **CO2** 34 D7
Layer de la Haye **CO2** 34 D7
Layer Marney **CO5** 34 D7
Layham **IP7** 34 E4
Laytham **YO42** 58 D6
Lazenby **TS6** 63 G4
Lazonby **CA10** 61 G3
Lea, *Derbys.* **DE4** 51 F7
Lea, *Here.* **HR9** 29 F6
Lea, *Lincs.* **DN21** 52 B4
Lea, *Shrop.* **SY5** 38 D5
Lea, *Shrop.* **SY9** 38 C7
Lea, *Wilts.* **SN16** 20 C3
Lea Marston **B76** 40 E6
Lea Town **PR4** 55 H6
Lea Yeat **LA10** 56 C1
Leac a' Li **HS3** 93 G2
Leachkin **IV3** 96 D7
Leack **PA27** 73 J1
Leadburn **EH46** 76 A5
Leaden Roding **CM6** 33 J7
Leadenham **LN5** 52 C7
Leadgate, *Cumb.* **CA9** 61 J2
Leadgate, *Dur.* **DH8** 62 C1
Leadgate, *T. & W.* **NE17** 62 C1
Leadhills **ML12** 68 D2
Leafield **OX29** 30 E7
Leagrave **LU4** 32 D6
Leake Common Side **PE22** 53 G7
Leake Hurn's End **PE22** 43 H1
Lealands **BN27** 13 J5
Lealholm **YO21** 63 J6
Lealt, *Arg. & B.* **PA60** 72 E1
Lealt, *High.* **IV51** 94 B5
Leamington Hastings **CV23** 31 F2
Leanach, *Arg. & B.* **PA27** 73 J1
Leanach, *High.* **IV2** 96 E7
Leanaig **IV6** 96 C6
Leanoch **IV30** 97 J6
Leargybreck **PA60** 72 D3
Leasgill **LA7** 55 H1
Leasingham **NG34** 42 D1
Leask **AB41** 91 J1
Leatherhead **KT22** 22 E6
Leathley **LS21** 57 H5
Leaton **SY4** 38 D4
Leaveland **ME13** 15 F2
Leavenheath **CO6** 34 D5
Leavening **YO17** 58 D3
Leaves Green **BR2** 23 H5
Lebberston **YO11** 59 G1
Lechlade **GL7** 21 F2
Lechuary **PA31** 73 G1
Leck **LA6** 56 B2
Leckford **SO20** 10 E1
Leckfurin **KW14** 104 C3
Leckgruinart **PA44** 72 A4
Leckhampstead, *Bucks.* **MK18** 31 J5
Leckhampstead, *W.Berks.* **RG20** 21 H4
Leckhampton **GL53** 29 J7
Leckie, *High.* **IV22** 95 G5
Leckie, *Stir.* **FK8** 74 E1
Leckmelm **IV23** 95 H2
Leckroy **PH31** 87 K5
Leckwith **CF11** 18 E4
Leconfield **HU17** 59 G5
Ledaig **PA37** 80 A4
Ledard **FK8** 81 F7
Ledbeg **IV27** 102 E7
Ledburn **LU7** 32 B6
Ledbury **HR8** 29 G5
Ledcharrie **FK20** 81 G5
Ledgemoor **HR4** 28 D3
Ledicot **HR6** 28 D2
Ledmore, *Arg. & B.* **PA72** 79 G3
Ledmore, *High.* **IV27** 102 E7
Lednagullin **KW14** 104 C2
Ledsham, *Ches.* **CH66** 48 C5
Ledsham, *W.Yorks.* **LS25** 57 K7
Ledston **WF10** 57 K7
Ledwell **OX7** 31 F6
Lee, *Arg. & B.* **PA67** 79 F5
Lee, *Devon* **EX34** 6 C1
Lee, *Hants.* **SO51** 10 E3
Lee, *Lancs.* **LA2** 55 J4
Lee, *Shrop.* **SY12** 38 D2
Lee Brockhurst **SY4** 38 E3
Lee Clump **HP16** 22 C1
Lee Mill Bridge **PL7** 5 F5
Lee Moor **PL7** 5 F4
Lee-on-the-Solent **PO13** 11 G4
Leebotten **ZE2** 109 D10
Leebotwood **SY6** 38 D6
Leece **LA12** 55 F3
Leeds, *Kent* **ME17** 14 D2
LEEDS, *W.Yorks.* LS 57 **H6**
Leeds Bradford International Airport **LS19** 57 H5
Leedstown **TR27** 2 D5
Leegomery **TF1** 39 F4
Leek **ST13** 49 J7
Leek Wootton **CV35** 30 D2
Leeming, *N.Yorks.* **DL7** 57 H1
Leeming, *W.Yorks.* **BD22** 57 F6
Leeming Bar **DL7** 62 D7
Lees, *Derbys.* **DE6** 40 E2
Lees, *Gt.Man.* **OL4** 49 J2
Leeswood **CH7** 48 B7
Legars **TD5** 77 F6
Legbourne **LN11** 53 G4
Legerwood **TD4** 76 D6
Legsby **LN8** 52 E4
LEICESTER LE 41 **H5**
Leideag **HS9** 84 B5
Leigh, *Dorset* **DT9** 9 F4
Leigh, *Glos.* **GL19** 29 H6

Llanarmon-yn-Ial

Leigh, *Gt.Man.* **WN7** 49 F2
Leigh, *Kent* **TN11** 23 J7
Leigh, *Shrop.* **SY5** 38 C5
Leigh, *Surr.* **RH2** 23 F7
Leigh, *Wilts.* **SN6** 20 D2
Leigh, *Worcs.* **WR6** 29 G3
Leigh Beck **SS8** 24 E3
Leigh Common **BA9** 9 G2
Leigh Delamere **SN14** 20 B4
Leigh Green **TN30** 14 E4
Leigh Sinton **WR13** 29 G3
Leigh upon Mendip **BA3** 19 K7
Leigh Woods **BS8** 19 J4
Leigh-on-Sea **SS9** 24 E3
Leighterton **GL8** 20 B2
Leighton, *N.Yorks.* **HG4** 57 G2
Leighton, *Powys* **SY21** 38 B5
Leighton, *Shrop.* **SY5** 39 F5
Leighton, *Som.* **BA11** 20 A7
Leighton Bromswold **PE28** 32 E1
Leighton Buzzard **LU7** 32 C6
Leinthall Earls **HR6** 28 D2
Leinthall Starkes **SY8** 28 D2
Leintwardine **SY7** 28 D1
Leire **LE17** 41 H7
Leirinmore **IV27** 103 G2
Leiston **IP16** 35 J2
Leitfie **PH11** 82 D3
Leith **EH6** 76 A3
Leitholm **TD12** 77 F6
Lelant **TR26** 2 C5
Lelley **HU12** 59 J6
Lem Hill **DY14** 29 G1
Lemington **NE15** 71 G7
Lemnas **AB43** 99 G4
Lempitlaw **TD5** 77 F7
Lemsford **AL8** 33 F7
Lenchwick **WR11** 30 B4
Lendalfoot **KA26** 67 F5
Lendrick **FK17** 81 G7
Lenham **ME17** 14 D2
Lenham Heath **ME17** 14 E3
Lenie **IV63** 88 C2
Lenimore **KA27** 73 G6
Lennel **TD12** 77 G6
Lennox Plunton **DG6** 65 G5
Lennoxtown **G66** 74 E3
Lenton **NG33** 42 D2
Lenwade **NR9** 45 F4
Lenzie **G66** 74 E3
Leoch **DD3** 82 E4
Leochel-Cushnie **AB33** 90 D3
Leominster **HR6** 28 D3
Leonard Stanley **GL10** 20 B1
Leorin **PA42** 72 B6
Lepe **SO45** 11 F5
Lephinchapel **PA27** 73 H1
Lephinmore **PA27** 73 H1
Leppington **YO17** 58 D3
Lepton **HD8** 50 E1
Lerags **PA34** 79 K5
Lerryn **PL22** 4 B5
LERWICK ZE 109 **D8**
Lesbury **NE66** 71 H2
Leschangie **AB51** 91 F3
Lescrow **PL23** 4 B5
Leslie, *Aber.* **AB52** 90 D2
Leslie, *Fife* **KY6** 82 D7
Lesmahagow **ML11** 75 G7
Lesnewth **PL35** 4 B1
Lessendrum **AB54** 98 D6
Lessingham **NR12** 45 H3
Lessonhall **CA7** 60 D1
Leswalt **DG9** 64 A4
Letchmore Heath **WD25** 22 E2
Letchworth **SG6** 33 F5
Letcombe Bassett **OX12** 21 G3
Letcombe Regis **OX12** 21 G3
Leth Meadhanach **HS8** 84 C3
Letham, *Angus* **DD8** 83 G3
Letham, *Fife* **KY15** 82 E6
Lethanhill **KA6** 67 J2
Lethendy **PH2** 82 C5
Lethenty **AB53** 99 G6
Letheringham **IP13** 35 G3
Letheringsett **NR25** 44 E2
Lettaford **TQ13** 7 F7
Letter Finlay **PH34** 87 J5
Letterewe **IV22** 95 F4
Letterfearn **IV40** 86 E2
Lettermorar **PH40** 86 D6
Lettermore, *Arg. & B.* **PA72** 79 G3
Lettermore, *High.* **IV27** 103 J4
Letters **IV23** 95 H3
Lettershaws **ML12** 68 D1
Letterston **SA62** 16 C2
Lettoch, *High.* **PH26** 89 H1
Lettoch, *High.* **PH25** 89 H3
Letton, *Here.* **SY7** 28 C1
Letton, *Here.* **HR3** 28 C4
Letty Green **SG14** 33 F7
Letwell **S81** 51 H4
Leuchars **KY16** 83 F5
Leumrabhagh **HS2** 101 F6
Levedale **ST18** 40 A4
Leven, *E.Riding* **HU17** 59 H5
Leven, *Fife* **KY8** 82 E7
Levencorroch **KA27** 66 E1
Levenhall **EH21** 76 B3
Levens **LA8** 55 H1
Levenshulme **M12** 49 H3
Levenwick **ZE2** 109 D10
Leverburgh (An T-òb) **HS5** 93 F3
Leverington **PE13** 43 H4
Leverstock Green **HP3** 22 D1
Leverton **PE22** 43 H1
Leverton Outgate **PE22** 43 H1
Levington **IP10** 35 G5
Levisham **YO18** 63 K7
Levishie **IV63** 88 B3
Lew **OX18** 21 G1
Lewannick **PL15** 4 C2
Lewdown **EX20** 6 C7
Lewes **BN7** 13 H5
Leweston **SA62** 16 C2
Lewisham **SE** 23 G4
Lewiston **IV63** 88 C2
Lewknor **OX49** 22 A2
Leworthy **EX32** 6 E2
Lewtrenchard **EX20** 6 C7
Ley, *Aber.* **AB33** 90 D3
Ley, *Cornw.* **PL14** 4 B4
Ley Green **SG4** 32 E6
Leybourne **ME19** 23 K6
Leyburn **DL8** 62 C7
Leycett **ST5** 39 G1
Leyland **PR25** 55 J7
Leylodge **AB51** 91 F3
Leys, *Aber.* **AB42** 99 J5
Leys, *Aber.* **AB34** 90 C4
Leys, *P. & K.* **PH13** 82 D4
Leys of Cossans **DD8** 82 E3
Leysdown-on-Sea **ME12** 25 G4
Leysmill **DD11** 83 H3
Leysters Pole **HR6** 28 E2
Leyton **E10** 23 G3
Lezant **PL15** 4 D3
Lhanbryde **IV30** 97 K5
Liatrie **IV4** 87 J1
Libanus **LD3** 27 J6
Libberton **ML11** 75 H6
Liberton **EH16** 76 A4
Liceasto **HS3** 93 G2
Lichfield **WS13** 40 D5
Lickey **B60** 29 J1
Lickey End **B60** 29 J1
Lickfold **GU28** 12 C4
Liddel **KW17** 107 D9
Liddesdale **PH33** 79 J2
Liddington **SN4** 21 F3
Lidgate, *Derbys.* **S18** 51 F5
Lidgate, *Suff.* **CB8** 34 B3
Lidlington **MK43** 32 C5
Lidsing **ME7** 24 D5
Lidstone **OX7** 30 E6
Lienassie **IV40** 87 F2
Lieurary **KW14** 105 F2
Liff **DD2** 82 E4
Lifton **PL16** 6 B7
Liftondown **PL15** 6 B7
Lighthorne **CV35** 30 E3
Lightwater **GU18** 22 C5
Lightwood **ST3** 40 B1
Lightwood Green, *Ches.* **CW3** 39 F1
Lightwood Green, *Wrex.* **LL13** 38 C1
Lilbourne **CV23** 31 G1
Lilburn Tower **NE66** 71 F1
Lilleshall **TF10** 39 G4
Lilley, *Herts.* **LU2** 32 E6
Lilley, *W.Berks.* **RG20** 21 H4
Lilliesleaf **TD6** 70 A1
Lillingstone Dayrell **MK18** 31 J5
Lillingstone Lovell **MK18** 31 J4
Lillington **DT9** 9 F3
Lilliput **BH14** 10 B5
Lilstock **TA5** 7 K1
Limbrick **PR6** 49 F1
Limbury **LU3** 32 D6
Limefield **BL9** 49 H1
Limehillock **AB55** 98 D5
Limekilnburn **ML3** 75 F5
Limekilns **KY11** 75 J2
Limerigg **FK1** 75 G3
Limerstone **PO30** 11 F6
Limington **BA22** 8 E2
Limpenhoe **NR13** 45 H5
Limpley Stoke **BA2** 20 A5
Limpsfield **RH8** 23 H6
Linbriggs **NE65** 70 D3
Linby **NG15** 51 H7
Linchmere **GU27** 12 B3
LINCOLN LN 52 **C5**
Lincomb **DY13** 29 H2
Lincombe **TQ9** 5 H5
Lindal in Furness **LA12** 55 F2
Lindale **LA11** 55 H1
Lindean **TD7** 76 C7
Lindertis **DD8** 82 E2
Lindfield **RH16** 13 G4
Lindford **GU35** 12 B3
Lindifferon **KY15** 82 E6
Lindley **HD3** 50 D1
Lindores **KY14** 82 D6
Lindridge **WR15** 29 F2
Lindsaig **PA21** 73 H3
Lindsell **CM6** 33 K6
Lindsey **IP7** 34 D4
Linford, *Hants.* **BH24** 10 C4
Linford, *Thur.* **SS17** 24 C4
Lingague **IM9** 54 B6
Lingdale **TS12** 63 H5
Lingen **SY7** 28 C2
Lingfield **RH7** 23 G7
Lingwood **NR13** 45 H5
Linhead **AB45** 98 E5
Linhope **TD9** 69 K3
Linicro **IV51** 93 J5
Linkenholt **SP11** 21 G6
Linkhill **TN18** 14 D5
Linkinhorne **PL17** 4 D3
Linklater **KW17** 107 D9
Linksness, *Ork.* **KW17** 107 E6
Linksness, *Ork.* **KW16** 107 B7
Linktown **KY1** 76 A1
Linley **SY9** 38 C6
Linley Green **WR6** 29 F3
Linlithgow **EH49** 75 H3
Linlithgow Bridge **EH49** 75 H3
Linn of Muick Cottage **AB35** 90 B6
Linnels **NE46** 70 E7
Linney **SA71** 16 B5
Linshiels **NE65** 70 D3
Linsiadar **HS2** 100 E4
Linsidemore **IV27** 96 C2
Linslade **LU7** 32 C6
Linstead Parva **IP19** 35 H1
Linstock **CA6** 60 F1
Linthwaite **HD7** 50 D1
Lintlaw **TD11** 77 G5
Lintmill **AB56** 98 D4
Linton, *Cambs.* **CB1** 33 J4
Linton, *Derbys.* **DE12** 40 E4
Linton, *Here.* **HR9** 29 F6
Linton, *Kent* **ME17** 14 C3
Linton, *N.Yorks.* **BD23** 56 E3
Linton, *Sc.Bord.* **TD5** 70 C1
Linton, *W.Yorks.* **LS22** 57 J5
Linton-on-Ouse **YO30** 57 K3
Lintzford **NE39** 62 C1
Linwood, *Hants.* **BH24** 10 C4
Linwood, *Lincs.* **LN8** 52 E4
Linwood, *Renf.* **PA3** 74 C4
Lionacleit **HS7** 92 C7
Lional **HS2** 101 H1
Liphook **GU30** 12 B3
Liscombe **TA22** 7 G2
Liskeard **PL14** 4 C4
Liss **GU33** 11 J2
Liss Forest **GU33** 11 J2
Lissett **YO25** 59 H4
Lissington **LN3** 52 E4
Liston **CO10** 34 C4
Lisvane **CF14** 18 E3
Liswerry **NP19** 19 G3
Litcham **PE32** 44 C4
Litchborough **NN12** 31 H3
Litchfield **RG28** 21 H6
Litherland **L21** 48 C3
Litlington, *Cambs.* **SG8** 33 G4
Litlington, *E.Suss.* **BN26** 13 J6
Little Abington **CB1** 33 J4
Little Addington **NN14** 32 C1
Little Alne **B95** 30 C2
Little Amwell **SG13** 33 G7
Little Assynt **IV27** 102 D6
Little Aston **B74** 40 C6
Little Atherfield **PO38** 11 F7
Little Ayton **TS9** 63 G5
Little Baddow **CM3** 24 D1
Little Badminton **GL9** 20 A3
Little Ballinluig **PH9** 82 A2
Little Bampton **CA7** 60 D1
Little Bardfield **CM7** 33 K5
Little Barford **PE19** 32 E3
Little Barningham **NR11** 45 F2
Little Barrington **OX18** 30 D7
Little Barugh **YO17** 58 D2
Little Bealings **IP13** 35 G4
Little Bedwyn **SN8** 21 F5
Little Bentley **CO7** 35 F6
Little Berkhamsted **SG13** 23 F1
Little Billing **NN3** 32 B2
Little Birch **HR2** 28 E5
Little Bispham **FY5** 55 G5
Little Blakenham **IP8** 35 F4
Little Bollington **WA14** 49 G4
Little Bookham **KT23** 22 E6
Little Bowden **LE16** 42 A7
Little Bradley **CB9** 33 K3
Little Brampton **SY7** 38 C7
Little Braxted **CM8** 34 C7
Little Brechin **DD9** 83 G1
Little Brickhill **MK17** 32 C5
Little Bridgeford **ST18** 40 A3
Little Brington **NN7** 31 H2
Little Bromley **CO11** 34 E6
Little Broughton **CA13** 60 B3
Little Budworth **CW6** 48 E6
Little Burstead **CM12** 24 C2
Little Burton **YO25** 59 H5
Little Bytham **NG33** 42 D4
Little Carlton, *Lincs.* **LN11** 53 H4
Little Carlton, *Notts.* **NG23** 51 K7
Little Casterton **PE9** 42 D5
Little Catwick **HU17** 59 H5
Little Cawthorpe **LN11** 53 G4
Little Chalfont **HP7** 22 C2
Little Chart **TN27** 14 E3
Little Chesterford **CB10** 33 J4
Little Cheverell **SN10** 20 C6
Little Chishill **SG8** 33 H5
Little Clacton **CO16** 35 F7
Little Clifton **CA14** 60 B4
Little Comberton **WR10** 29 J4
Little Common **TN39** 14 C7
Little Compton **GL56** 30 D5
Little Corby **CA4** 61 F1
Little Cowarne **HR7** 29 F3
Little Coxwell **SN7** 21 F2
Little Crakehall **DL8** 62 D7
Little Creich **IV24** 96 D3
Little Cressingham **IP25** 44 C6
Little Crosby **L23** 48 C2
Little Cubley **DE6** 40 D2
Little Dalby **LE14** 42 A4
Little Dens **AB42** 99 J6
Little Dewchurch **HR2** 28 E5
Little Downham **CB6** 43 J7
Little Driffield **YO25** 59 G4
Little Dunham **PE32** 44 C4
Little Dunkeld **PH8** 82 B3
Little Dunmow **CM6** 33 K6
Little Easton **CM6** 33 K6
Little Eaton **DE21** 41 F1
Little Ellingham **NR17** 44 E6
Little End **CM5** 23 J1
Little Eversden **CB3** 33 G3
Little Fakenham **IP24** 34 D1
Little Faringdon **GL7** 21 F1
Little Fencote **DL7** 62 D7
Little Fenton **LS25** 58 B6
Little Finborough **IP14** 34 E3
Little Fransham **NR19** 44 C4
Little Gaddesden **HP4** 32 C7
Little Garway **HR2** 28 D6
Little Gidding **PE28** 42 E7
Little Glemham **IP13** 35 H3
Little Gorsley **GL18** 29 F6
Little Gransden **SG19** 33 F3
Little Green **IP23** 34 E1
Little Grimsby **LN11** 53 G3
Little Gruinard **IV22** 95 F3
Little Habton **YO17** 58 D2
Little Hadham **SG11** 33 H6
Little Hale **NG34** 42 E1
Little Hallingbury **CM22** 33 H7
Little Hampden **HP16** 22 B1
Little Harrowden **NN9** 32 B1
Little Haseley **OX44** 21 K1
Little Hautbois **NR12** 45 G3
Little Haven **SA62** 16 B3
Little Hay **WS14** 40 D5
Little Hayfield **SK22** 50 C4
Little Haywood **ST18** 40 C3
Little Heath **CV6** 41 F7
Little Hereford **SY8** 28 E2
Little Holtby **DL8** 62 D7
Little Horkesley **CO6** 34 D5
Little Hormead **SG9** 33 H6
Little Horsted **TN22** 13 H5
Little Horwood **MK17** 31 J5
Little Houghton **NN7** 32 B3
Little Hucklow **SK17** 50 D5
Little Hulton **M38** 49 G2
Little Hungerford **RG18** 21 J4
Little Idoch **AB53** 99 F6
Little Kimble **HP22** 22 B1
Little Kineton **CV35** 30 E3
Little Kingshill **HP16** 22 B2
Little Langford **SP3** 10 B1
Little Laver **CM5** 23 J1
Little Lawford **CV23** 31 F1
Little Leigh **CW8** 49 F5
Little Leighs **CM3** 34 B7
Little Lever **BL3** 49 G2
Little Ley **AB51** 90 E3
Little Linford **MK19** 32 B4
Little London, *E.Suss.* **TN21** 13 J5
Little London, *Hants.* **RG26** 21 K6
Little London, *Hants.* **SP11** 21 G6
Little London, *I.o.M.* **IM6** 54 C5
Little London, *Lincs.* **LN9** 53 G5
Little London, *Lincs.* **PE12** 43 H3
Little London, *Lincs.* **PE11** 43 F3
Little London, *Norf.* **PE34** 43 J3
Little London, *Norf.* **IP26** 44 B6
Little Longstone **DE45** 50 D5
Little Malvern **WR13** 29 G4
Little Maplestead **CO9** 34 C5
Little Marcle **HR8** 29 F5
Little Marlow **SL7** 22 B3
Little Massingham **PE32** 44 B3
Little Melton **NR9** 45 F5
Little Mill **NP4** 19 G1
Little Milton **OX44** 21 K1
Little Missenden **HP7** 22 C2
Little Musgrave **CA17** 61 J5
Little Ness **SY4** 38 D4
Little Neston **CH64** 48 B5
Little Newcastle **SA62** 16 C2
Little Newsham **DL2** 62 C5
Little Oakley, *Essex* **CO12** 35 G6
Little Oakley, *Northants.* **NN18** 42 B7
Little Orton **CA5** 60 E1
Little Ouseburn **YO26** 57 K3
Little Parndon **CM20** 23 H1
Little Paxton **PE19** 32 E2
Little Petherick **PL27** 3 G1
Little Plumstead **NR13** 45 H4
Little Ponton **NG33** 42 C2
Little Raveley **PE28** 33 F1
Little Ribston **LS22** 57 J4
Little Rissington **GL54** 30 C6
Little Rogart **IV28** 96 E1
Little Ryburgh **NR21** 44 D3
Little Ryle **NE66** 71 F2
Little Salkeld **CA10** 61 G3
Little Sampford **CB10** 33 K5
Little Saxham **IP29** 34 B2
Little Scatwell **IV14** 95 K6
Little Shelford **CB2** 33 H3
Little Smeaton **WF8** 51 H1
Little Snoring **NR21** 44 D2
Little Sodbury **BS37** 20 A3
Little Somborne **SO20** 10 E1
Little Somerford **SN15** 20 C3
Little Stainton **TS21** 62 E4
Little Stanney **CH2** 48 D5
Little Staughton **PE19** 32 E2
Little Steeping **PE23** 53 H6
Little Stonham **IP14** 35 F3
Little Stretton, *Leics.* **LE2** 41 J6
Little Stretton, *Shrop.* **SY6** 38 D6
Little Strickland **CA10** 61 G4
Little Stukeley **PE28** 33 F1
Little Sutton **CH66** 48 C5
Little Swinburne **NE48** 70 E6
Little Tew **OX7** 30 E6
Little Tey **CO6** 34 C6
Little Thetford **CB6** 33 J1
Little Thirkleby **YO7** 57 K2
Little Thorpe **SR8** 63 F2
Little Thurlow **CB9** 33 K3
Little Thurrock **RM17** 24 C4
Little Torboll **IV25** 96 E2
Little Torrington **EX38** 6 C4
Little Totham **CM9** 34 C7
Little Town **CA12** 60 D5
Little Urswick **LA12** 55 F2
Little Wakering **SS3** 25 F3
Little Walden **CB10** 33 J4
Little Waldingfield **CO10** 34 D4
Little Walsingham **NR22** 44 D2
Little Waltham **CM3** 34 B7
Little Warley **CM13** 24 C2
Little Weighton **HU20** 59 F6
Little Welland **WR13** 29 H5
Little Welnetham **IP30** 34 C3
Little Wenham **CO7** 34 E5
Little Wenlock **TF6** 39 F5
Little Whittingham Green **IP21** 35 G1
Little Whittington **NE19** 70 E7
Little Wilbraham **CB1** 33 J3
Little Witcombe **GL3** 29 J7
Little Witley **WR6** 29 G2
Little Wittenham **OX14** 21 J2
Little Wolford **CV36** 30 D5
Little Woolstone **MK6** 32 B5
Little Wratting **CB9** 33 K4
Little Wymondley **SG4** 33 F6
Little Wyrley **WS3** 40 C5
Little Yeldham **CO9** 34 B5
Littlebeck **YO22** 63 K6
Littleborough, *Gt.Man.* **OL15** 49 J1
Littleborough, *Notts.* **DN22** 52 B4
Littlebourne **CT3** 15 G2
Littlebredy **DT2** 8 E6
Littlebury **CB11** 33 J5
Littlebury Green **CB11** 33 H5
Littledean **GL14** 29 F7
Littleferry **KW10** 97 F2
Littleham, *Devon* **EX39** 6 C3
Littleham, *Devon* **EX8** 7 J7
Littlehampton **BN17** 12 D6
Littlehempston **TQ9** 5 J4
Littlehoughton **NE66** 71 H2
Littlemill, *E.Ayr.* **KA6** 67 J2
Littlemill, *High.* **IV12** 97 G6
Littlemore **OX4** 21 J1
Littleover **DE23** 41 F2
Littleport **CB6** 43 J7
Littlestone-on-Sea **TN28** 15 F5
Littlethorpe **HG4** 57 J3
Littleton, *Ches.* **CH3** 48 D6
Littleton, *Hants.* **SO22** 11 F1
Littleton, *P. & K.* **PH14** 82 D4
Littleton, *Som.* **TA11** 8 D1
Littleton, *Surr.* **TW17** 22 D5
Littleton Drew **SN14** 20 B3
Littleton Panell **SN10** 20 C6
Littleton-on-Severn **BS35** 19 J3
Littletown **DH6** 62 E2
Littlewick Green **SL6** 22 B4
Littleworth, *Oxon.* **SN7** 21 G2
Littleworth, *Staffs.* **WS12** 40 C4
Littleworth, *Worcs.* **WR5** 29 H3
Littley Green **CM3** 33 K7
Litton, *Derbys.* **SK17** 50 D5
Litton, *N.Yorks.* **BD23** 56 E2
Litton, *Som.* **BA3** 19 J6
Litton Cheney **DT2** 8 E5
Liurbost **HS2** 101 F5
LIVERPOOL L 48 **C3**
Liverpool Airport **L24** 48 D4
Liversedge **WF15** 57 G7
Liverton, *Devon* **TQ12** 5 J3
Liverton, *R. & C.* **TS13** 63 J5
Liverton Street **ME17** 14 D3
Livingston **EH54** 75 J4
Livingston Village **EH54** 75 J4
Lixwm **CH8** 47 K5
Lizard **TR12** 2 D7
Llaingoch **LL65** 46 A4
Llaithddu **LD1** 37 K7
Llan **SY19** 37 H5
Llan-dafel **NP13** 18 E1
Llan-y-pwll **LL13** 48 C7
Llanaber **LL42** 37 F4
Llanaelhaearn **LL54** 36 C1
Llanaeron **SA48** 26 D2
Llanafan **SY23** 27 F1
Llanafan-fawr **LD2** 27 J3
Llanafan-fechan **LD4** 27 J3
Llanallgo **LL73** 46 C4
Llanarmon **LL53** 36 D2
Llanarmon Dyffryn Ceiriog **LL20** 38 A2
Llanarmon-yn-Ial **CH7** 47 K7

Llanarth

Llanarth, *Cere.* **SA47** 26 D3
Llanarth, *Mon.* **NP15** 28 C7
Llanarthney **SA32** 17 J2
Llanasa **CH8** 47 K4
Llanbabo **LL71** 46 B4
Llanbadarn Fawr **SY23** 36 E7
Llanbadarn Fynydd **LD1** 27 K1
Llanbadarn-y-garreg **LD2** 28 A4
Llanbadoc **NP15** 19 G1
Llanbadrig **LL67** 46 B3
Llanbeder **NP18** 19 G2
Llanbedr, *Gwyn.* **LL45** 36 E3
Llanbedr, *Powys* **LD2** 28 A4
Llanbedr, *Powys* **NP8** 28 B6
Llanbedr-Dyffryn-Clwyd **LL15** 47 K7
Llanbedr-y-cennin **LL32** 47 F6
Llanbedrgoch **LL76** 46 D4
Llanbedrog **LL53** 36 C2
Llanberis **LL55** 46 D6
Llanbethery **CF62** 18 D5
Llanbister **LD1** 28 A1
Llanblethian **CF71** 18 C4
Llanboidy **SA34** 17 F2
Llanbradach **CF83** 18 E2
Llanbrynmair **SY19** 37 H5
Llancarfan **CF62** 18 D4
Llancayo **NP15** 19 G1
Llancynfelyn **SY20** 37 F6
Llandaff **CF5** 18 E4
Llandaff North **CF14** 18 E4
Llandanwg **LL45** 36 E3
Llandawke **SA33** 17 F3
Llanddaniel Fab **LL60** 46 C5
Llanddarog **SA32** 17 J3
Llanddeiniol **SY23** 26 E1
Llanddeiniolen **LL55** 46 D6
Llandderfel **LL23** 37 J2
Llanddeusant, *Carmar.* **SA19** 27 G6
Llanddeusant, *I.o.A.* **LL65** 46 B4
Llanddew **LD3** 27 K5
Llanddewi **SA3** 17 H6
Llanddewi Rhydderch **NP7** 28 C7
Llanddewi Velfrey **SA67** 16 E3
Llanddewi Ystradenni **LD1** 28 A2
Llanddewi-Brefi **SY25** 27 F3
Llanddewi'r Cwm **LD2** 27 K4
Llanddoged **LL26** 47 G6
Llanddona **LL58** 46 D5
Llanddowror **SA33** 17 F3
Llanddulas **LL22** 47 H5
Llanddwywe **LL44** 36 E3
Llanddyfnan **LL77** 46 C5
Llandefaelog **SA17** 17 H3
Llandefaelog Fach **LD3** 27 K5
Llandefaelog-tre'r-graig **LD3** 28 A6
Llandefalle **LD3** 28 A5
Llandegfan **LL59** 46 D5
Llandegla **LL11** 47 K7
Llandegley **LD1** 28 A2
Llandegveth **NP18** 19 G2
Llandegwning **LL53** 36 B2
Llandeilo **SA19** 17 K2
Llandeilo Abercywyn **SA33** 17 G3
Llandeilo Graban **LD2** 27 K4
Llandeilo'r-Fan **LD3** 27 H5
Llandeloy **SA62** 16 B2
Llandenny **NP15** 19 H1
Llandevenny **NP26** 19 H3
Llandinabo **HR2** 28 E6
Llandinam **SY17** 37 K7
Llandissilio **SA66** 16 E2
Llandogo **NP25** 19 J1
Llandough, *V. of Glam.* **CF11** 18 E4
Llandough, *V. of Glam.* **CF71** 18 C4
Llandovery **SA20** 27 G5
Llandow **CF71** 18 C4
Llandre, *Carmar.* **SA19** 27 F4
Llandre, *Carmar.* **SA34** 16 E2
Llandre, *Cere.* **SY24** 37 F7
Llandrillo **LL21** 37 K2
Llandrillo-yn-Rhos **LL28** 47 G4
LLANDRINDOD WELLS LD 27 **K2**
Llandrinio **SY22** 38 B4
LLANDUDNO LL 47 **F4**
Llandudno Junction **LL31** 47 F5
Llandwrog **LL54** 46 C7
Llandybie **SA18** 17 K3
Llandyfriog **SA38** 26 C4
Llandyfrydog **LL71** 46 C4
Llandygai **LL57** 46 D5
Llandygwydd **SA43** 26 B4
Llandyrnog **LL16** 47 K6
Llandyry **SA17** 17 H4
Llandysilio **SY22** 38 B4
Llandyssil **SY15** 38 A6
Llandysul **SA44** 26 D4
Llanedeyrn **CF3** 19 F3
Llanegryn **LL36** 37 F5
Llanegwad **SA32** 17 J2
Llaneilian **LL68** 46 C3
Llanelian-yn-Rhôs **LL29** 47 G5
Llanelidan **LL15** 47 K7
Llanelieu **LD3** 28 A5
Llanellen **NP7** 28 C7
Llanelli **SA15** 17 J4
Llanelltyd **LL40** 37 G4
Llanelly **NP7** 28 B7
Llanelly Hill, *Mon.* **NP7** 28 B7
Llanelwedd **LD2** 27 K3
Llanelwy (St. Asaph) **LL17** 47 J5
Llanenddwyn **LL44** 36 E3
Llanengan **LL53** 36 B3
Llanerchymedd **LL71** 46 C4
Llanerfyl **SY21** 37 K5
Llanfachraeth **LL65** 46 B4
Llanfachreth **LL40** 37 G3
Llanfaelog **LL64** 46 B5
Llanfaelrhys **LL53** 36 B3
Llanfaes, *I.o.A.* **LL58** 46 E5
Llanfaes, *Powys* **LD3** 27 K6
Llanfaethlu **LL65** 46 B4
Llanfaglan **LL54** 46 C6
Llanfair **LL46** 36 E3
Llanfair Caereinion **SY21** 38 A5
Llanfair Clydogau **SA48** 27 F3
Llanfair Dyffryn Clwyd **LL15** 47 K7
Llanfair Talhaiarn **LL22** 47 H5
Llanfair Waterdine **LD7** 28 B1
Llanfair-Nant-Gwyn **SA41** 16 E1
Llanfair-Orllwyn **SA44** 26 C4
Llanfair-yn-Neubwll **LL65** 46 B5
Llanfairfechan **LL33** 46 E5
Llanfairpwllgwyngyll **LL61** 46 D5
Llanfairynghornwy **LL65** 46 B3
Llanfallteg **SA34** 16 E3
Llanfallteg West **SA66** 16 E3
Llanfaredd **LD2** 27 K3
Llanfarian **SY23** 26 E1
Llanfechain **SY22** 38 A3
Llanfechell **LL67** 46 B3
Llanfendigaid **LL36** 36 E5
Llanferres **CH7** 47 K6
Llanfflewyn **LL65** 46 B4
Llanfigael **LL65** 46 B4
Llanfihangel ar-arth **SA39** 17 H1
Llanfihangel Crucorney **NP7** 28 C6
Llanfihangel Glyn Myfyr **LL21** 37 J1
Llanfihangel Nant Bran **LD3** 27 J5
Llanfihangel Rhydithon **LD1** 28 A2
Llanfihangel Rogiet **NP26** 19 H3
Llanfihangel uwch-gwili **SA32** 17 H2
Llanfihangel-nant-Melan **LD8** 28 A3
Llanfihangel-Tal-y-llyn **LD3** 28 A6
Llanfihangel-y-Creuddyn **SY23** 27 F1
Llanfihangel-y-pennant, *Gwyn.* **LL49** 36 E1
Llanfihangel-y-pennant, *Gwyn.* **LL36** 37 F5
Llanfihangel-yng-Ngwynfa **SY22** 37 K4
Llanfilo **LD3** 28 A5
Llanfoist **NP7** 28 B7
Llanfor **LL23** 37 J2
Llanfrechfa **NP44** 19 G2
Llanfrothen **LL48** 37 F1
Llanfrynach **LD3** 27 K6
Llanfwrog, *Denb.* **LL15** 47 K7
Llanfwrog, *I.o.A.* **LL65** 46 B4
Llanfyllin **SY22** 38 A4
Llanfynydd, *Carmar.* **SA32** 17 J2
Llanfynydd, *Flints.* **LL11** 48 B7
Llanfyrnach **SA35** 17 F1
Llangadfan **SY21** 37 K4
Llangadog **SA19** 27 G6
Llangadwaladr, *I.o.A.* **LL62** 46 B6
Llangadwaladr, *Powys* **SY10** 38 A2
Llangaffo **LL60** 46 C6
Llangain **SA33** 17 G3
Llangammarch Wells **LD4** 27 J4
Llangan **CF35** 18 C4
Llangarron **HR9** 28 E6
Llangasty-Talyllyn **LD3** 28 A6
Llangathen **SA32** 17 J2
Llangattock **NP8** 28 B7
Llangattock Lingoed **NP7** 28 C6
Llangattock-Vibon-Avel **NP25** 28 D7
Llangedwyn **SY10** 38 A3
Llangefni **LL77** 46 C5
Llangeinor **CF32** 18 C3
Llangeitho **SY25** 27 F3
Llangeler **SA44** 17 G1
Llangelynin **LL36** 36 E5
Llangendeirne **SA17** 17 H3
Llangennech **SA14** 17 J4
Llangennith **SA3** 17 H5
Llangenny **NP8** 28 B7
Llangernyw **LL22** 47 G6
Llangian **LL53** 36 B3
Llangiwg **SA8** 18 A1
Llanglydwen **SA34** 16 E2
Llangoed **LL58** 46 E5
Llangoedmor **SA43** 26 A4
Llangollen **LL20** 38 B1
Llangolman **SA66** 16 E2
Llangorse **LD3** 28 A6
Llangorwen **SY23** 37 F7
Llangovan **NP25** 19 H1
Llangranog **SA44** 26 C3
Llangristiolus **LL62** 46 C5
Llangrove **HR9** 28 E7
Llangua **NP7** 28 C6
Llangunllo **LD7** 28 B1
Llangunnor **SA31** 17 H2
Llangurig **SY18** 27 J1
Llangwm, *Conwy* **LL21** 37 J1
Llangwm, *Pembs.* **SA62** 16 C4
Llangwm-isaf **NP15** 19 H1
Llangwnnadl **LL53** 36 B2
Llangwyfan **LL16** 47 K6
Llangwyllog **LL77** 46 C5
Llangwyryfon **SY23** 26 E1
Llangybi, *Cere.* **SA48** 27 F3
Llangybi, *Gwyn.* **LL53** 36 D1
Llangybi, *Mon.* **NP15** 19 G2
Llangyfelach **SA5** 17 K5
Llangynhafal **LL16** 47 K6
Llangynidr **NP8** 28 A7
Llangynin **SA33** 17 F3
Llangynog, *Carmar.* **SA33** 17 G3
Llangynog, *Powys* **SY10** 37 K3
Llangynwyd **CF34** 18 B3
Llangywer **LL23** 37 J2
Llanhamlach **LD3** 27 K6
Llanharan **CF72** 18 D3
Llanharry **CF72** 18 D3
Llanhennock **NP18** 19 G2
Llanhilleth **NP13** 19 F1
Llanidloes **SY18** 37 J7
Llaniestyn **LL53** 36 B2
Llanigon **HR3** 28 B5
Llanilar **SY23** 27 F1
Llanilid **CF35** 18 C3
Llanishen, *Cardiff* **CF14** 18 E3
Llanishen, *Mon.* **NP16** 19 H1
Llanllawddog **SA32** 17 H2
Llanllechid **LL57** 46 E6
Llanlleonfel **LD4** 27 J4
Llanllugan **SY21** 37 K5
Llanllwch **SA31** 17 G3
Llanllwchaiarn **SY16** 38 A6
Llanllwni **SA39** 26 D4
Llanllyfni **LL54** 46 C7
Llanllywel **NP15** 19 G2
Llanmadoc **SA3** 17 H5
Llanmaes **CF61** 18 C5
Llanmartin **NP18** 19 G3
Llanmerewig **SY15** 38 A6
Llanmihangel **CF71** 18 C4
Llanmiloe **SA33** 17 F4
Llanmorlais **SA4** 17 J5
Llannefydd **LL16** 47 H5
Llannerch **LL17** 47 J5
Llannerch-y-mor **CH8** 47 K5
Llannon **SA14** 17 J4
Llannor **LL53** 36 C2
Llanon **SY23** 26 E2
Llanover **NP7** 19 G1
Llanpumsaint **SA33** 17 H2
Llanreithan **SA62** 16 B2
Llanrhaeadr **LL16** 47 J6
Llanrhaeadr-ym-Mochnant **SY10** 38 A3
Llanrhian **SA62** 16 B1
Llanrhidian **SA3** 17 J5
Llanrhos **LL30** 47 F4
Llanrhyddlad **LL65** 46 B4
Llanrhystud **SY23** 26 E2
Llanrothal **NP25** 28 D7
Llanrug **LL55** 46 D6
Llanrumney **CF3** 19 F3
Llanrwst **LL26** 47 F6
Llansadurnen **SA33** 17 F3
Llansadwrn, *Carmar.* **SA19** 17 K1
Llansadwrn, *I.o.A.* **LL59** 46 D5
Llansaint **SA17** 17 G4
Llansamlet **SA7** 17 K5
Llansanffraid Glan Conwy **LL28** 47 G5
Llansannan **LL16** 47 H6
Llansannor **CF71** 18 C4
Llansantffraed **LD3** 28 A6
Llansantffraed-Cwmdeuddwr **LD6** 27 J2
Llansantffraed-in-Elvel **LD1** 27 K3
Llansantffraid **SY23** 26 E2
Llansantffraid-ym-Mechain **SY22** 38 B3
Llansawel, *Carmar.* **SA19** 17 K1
Llansawel (Briton Ferry), *N.P.T.* **SA11** 18 A2
Llansilin **SY10** 38 B3
Llansoy **NP15** 19 H1
Llanspyddid **LD3** 27 K6
Llanstadwell **SA73** 16 C4
Llanstephan, *Carmar.* **SA33** 17 G3
Llanstephan, *Powys* **LD3** 28 A4
Llantarnam **NP44** 19 G2
Llanteg **SA67** 16 E3
Llanthony **NP7** 28 B6
Llantilio Crossenny **NP7** 28 C7
Llantilio Pertholey **NP7** 28 C7
Llantood **SA43** 26 A4
Llantrisant, *Mon.* **NP15** 19 G2
Llantrisant, *R.C.T.* **CF72** 18 D3
Llantrithyd **CF71** 18 D4
Llantwit Fardre **CF38** 18 D3
Llantwit Major **CF61** 18 C5
Llantysilio **LL20** 38 A1
Llanuwchllyn **LL23** 37 H2
Llanvaches **NP26** 19 H2
Llanvair-Discoed **NP16** 19 H2
Llanvapley **NP7** 28 C7
Llanvetherine **NP7** 28 C7
Llanveynoe **HR2** 28 C5
Llanvihangel Gobion **NP7** 19 G1
Llanvihangel-Ystern-Llewern **NP25** 28 D7
Llanwarne **HR2** 28 E6
Llanwddyn **SY10** 37 K4
Llanwenog **SA40** 26 D4
Llanwern **NP18** 19 G3
Llanwinio **SA34** 17 F2
Llanwnda, *Gwyn.* **LL54** 46 C7
Llanwnda, *Pembs.* **SA64** 16 C1
Llanwnnen **SA48** 26 E4
Llanwnog **SY17** 37 K6
Llanwonno **CF37** 18 D2
Llanwrda **SA19** 27 G5
Llanwrin **SY20** 37 G5
Llanwrthwl **LD1** 27 J2
Llanwrtyd **LD5** 27 H4
Llanwrtyd Wells **LD5** 27 H4
Llanwyddelan **SY16** 37 K5
Llanyblodwel **SY10** 38 B3
Llanybri **SA33** 17 G3
Llanybydder **SA40** 26 E4
Llanycefn **SA66** 16 E2
Llanychaer Bridge **SA65** 16 C1
Llanycil **LL23** 37 J2
Llanycrwys **SA19** 27 F4
Llanymawddwy **SY20** 37 J4
Llanymynech **SY22** 38 B3
Llanynghenedl **LL65** 46 B4
Llanynys **LL16** 47 K6
Llanyre **LD1** 27 K2
Llanystumdwy **LL52** 36 D2
Llanywern **LD3** 28 A6
Llawhaden **SA67** 16 D3
Llawnt **SY10** 38 B2
Llawr-y-dref **LL53** 36 B3
Llawryglyn **SY17** 37 J6
Llay **LL12** 48 C7
Llechcynfarwy **LL65** 46 B4
Llechfaen **LD3** 27 K6
Llechryd, *Caerp.* **NP22** 18 E1
Llechryd, *Cere.* **SA43** 26 B4
Llechrydau **SY10** 38 B2
Lledrod, *Cere.* **SY23** 27 F1
Lledrod, *Powys* **SY10** 38 B2
Llethr **SA62** 16 B2
Llidiadnenog **SA32** 17 J1
Llidiardau **LL23** 37 H2
Llithfaen **LL53** 36 C1
Lloc **CH8** 47 K5
Llong **CH7** 48 B6
Llowes **HR3** 28 A4
Lloyney **LD7** 28 B1
Llwydcoed **CF44** 18 C1
Llwydiarth **SY21** 37 K4
Llwyn **SY7** 38 B7
Llwyn-Madoc **LD5** 27 J3
Llwyn-onn **SA45** 26 D3
Llwyn-y-brain, *Carmar.* **SA19** 27 G5
Llwyn-y-brain, *Carmar.* **SA34** 17 F3
Llwyncelyn **SA46** 26 D3
Llwyndafydd **SA44** 26 C3
Llwynderw **SY21** 38 B5
Llwyndyrys **LL53** 36 C1
Llwyngwril **LL37** 36 E5
Llwynhendy **SA14** 17 J5
Llwynmawr **LL20** 38 B2
Llwynypia **CF40** 18 C2
Llynclys **SY10** 38 B3
Llynfaes **LL77** 46 C5
Llys-y-fran **SA63** 16 D2
Llysfaen **LL29** 47 G5
Llyswen **LD3** 28 A5
Llysworney **CF71** 18 C4
Llywel **LD3** 27 H5
Loandhu **IV20** 97 F4
Loanhead, *Aber.* **AB41** 91 H1
Loanhead, *Midloth.* **EH20** 76 A4
Loans **KA10** 74 B7
Loch Baghasdail (Lochboisdale) **HS8** 84 C3
Loch Coire Lodge **KW11** 103 J5
Loch Eil Centre **PH33** 87 G7
Loch Head, *D. & G.* **KA6** 67 J4
Loch Head, *D. & G.* **DG8** 64 D6
Loch na Madadh (Lochmaddy) **HS6** 92 E5
Loch Sgioport **HS8** 84 D1
Lochailort **PH38** 86 D6
Lochaline **PA34** 79 H3
Lochans **DG9** 64 A5
Locharbriggs **DG1** 68 E5
Lochawe **PA33** 80 C5
Lochboisdale (Loch Baghasdail) **HS8** 84 C3
Lochbuie **PA62** 79 H5
Lochcarron **IV54** 86 E1
Lochdhu Hotel **KW12** 105 F4
Lochdon **PA64** 79 J4
Lochdrum **IV23** 95 J4
Lochearnhead **FK19** 81 G5
Lochee **DD2** 82 E4
Lochend, *High.* **KW14** 105 H2
Lochend, *High.* **IV3** 88 C1
Lochfoot **DG2** 65 K3
Lochgair **PA31** 73 H1
Lochgarthside **IV2** 88 C3
Lochgelly **KY5** 75 K1
Lochgilphead **PA31** 73 G2
Lochgoilhead **PA24** 80 D7
Lochgoin **KA3** 74 D6
Lochhill, *E.Ayr.* **KA18** 68 B2
Lochhill, *Moray* **IV30** 97 K5
Lochinch Castle **DG9** 64 B4
Lochinver **IV27** 102 C6
Lochlair **DD8** 83 G3
Lochlane **PH7** 81 K5
Lochlea **KA1** 67 J1
Lochluichart **IV23** 95 K5
Lochmaben **DG11** 69 F5
Lochmaddy (Loch na Madadh) **HS6** 92 E5
Lochore **KY5** 75 K1
Lochportain **HS6** 92 E4
Lochranza **KA27** 73 H6
Lochside, *Aber.* **DD10** 83 J1
Lochside, *High.* **KW14** 105 H2
Lochside, *High.* **IV27** 103 G3
Lochside, *High.* **KW11** 104 D5
Lochslin **IV20** 97 F3
Lochton **KA26** 67 G5
Lochty **KY10** 83 G7
Lochuisge **PH33** 79 J2
Lochurr **DG3** 68 C5
Lochussie **IV7** 96 B6
Lochwinnoch **PA12** 74 B5
Lockengate **PL26** 4 A4
Lockerbie **DG11** 69 G5
Lockeridge **SN8** 20 E5
Lockerley **SO51** 10 D2
Locking **BS24** 19 G6
Lockington, *E.Riding* **YO25** 59 G5
Lockington, *Leics.* **DE74** 41 G3
Lockleywood **TF9** 39 F3
Locks Heath **SO31** 11 G4
Locksbottom **BR6** 23 H5
Lockton **YO18** 63 K7
Loddington, *Leics.* **LE7** 42 A5
Loddington, *Northants.* **NN14** 32 B1
Loddiswell **TQ7** 5 H6
Loddon **NR14** 45 H6
Lode **CB5** 33 J2
Loders **DT6** 8 D5
Lodsworth **GU28** 12 C4
Lofthouse, *N.Yorks.* **HG3** 57 F2
Lofthouse, *W.Yorks.* **WF3** 57 J7
Loftus **TS13** 63 J5
Logan, *D. & G.* **DG9** 64 A6
Logan, *E.Ayr.* **KA18** 67 K1
Loganlea **EH55** 75 H4
Loggerheads **TF9** 39 G2
Loggie **IV23** 95 H2
Logie, *Angus* **DD10** 83 H1
Logie, *Angus* **DD8** 82 E2
Logie, *Fife* **KY15** 83 F5
Logie, *Moray* **IV36** 97 H6
Logie Coldstone **AB34** 90 C4
Logie Hill **IV18** 96 E4
Logie Newton **AB54** 90 E1
Logie Pert **DD10** 83 H1
Logierait **PH9** 82 A2
Login **SA34** 16 E2
Lolworth **CB3** 33 G2
Lonbain **IV54** 94 C6
Londesborough **YO43** 58 E5
London Beach **TN30** 14 D4
London City Airport **E16** 23 H3
London Colney **AL2** 22 E1
London Heathrow Airport **TW6** 22 D4
London Luton Airport **LU2** 32 E6
Londonderry **DL7** 57 H1
Londonthorpe **NG32** 42 C2
Londubh **IV22** 94 E3
Lonemore **IV25** 96 E3
Long Ashton **BS41** 19 J4
Long Bennington **NG23** 42 B1
Long Bredy **DT2** 8 E5
Long Buckby **NN6** 31 H2
Long Clawson **LE14** 42 A3
Long Common **SO32** 11 G3
Long Compton, *Staffs.* **ST18** 40 A3
Long Compton, *Warks.* **CV36** 30 D5
Long Crendon **HP18** 21 K1
Long Crichel **BH21** 9 J3
Long Ditton **KT10** 22 E5
Long Downs **TR10** 2 E5
Long Drax **YO8** 58 C7
Long Duckmanton **S44** 51 G5
Long Eaton **NG10** 41 G2
Long Gill **BD23** 56 C4
Long Hanborough **OX29** 31 F7
Long Itchington **CV47** 31 F2
Long Lawford **CV23** 31 F1
Long Load **TA10** 8 D2
Long Marston, *Herts.* **HP23** 32 B7
Long Marston, *N.Yorks.* **YO26** 58 B4
Long Marston, *Warks.* **CV37** 30 C4
Long Marton **CA16** 61 H4
Long Melford **CO10** 34 C4
Long Newnton **GL8** 20 C2
Long Preston **BD23** 56 D4
Long Riston **HU11** 59 H5
Long Stratton **NR15** 45 F6
Long Street **MK19** 31 J4
Long Sutton, *Hants.* **RG29** 22 A7
Long Sutton, *Lincs.* **PE12** 43 H3
Long Sutton, *Som.* **TA10** 8 D2
Long Thurlow **IP31** 34 E2
Long Waste **TF6** 39 F4
Long Whatton **LE12** 41 G3
Long Wittenham **OX14** 21 J2
Longbenton **NE7** 71 H7
Longborough **GL56** 30 C6
Longbridge, *W.Mid.* **B31** 30 B1
Longbridge, *Warks.* **CV34** 30 D2
Longbridge Deverill **BA12** 20 B7
Longburgh **CA5** 60 E1
Longburton **DT9** 9 F3
Longcliffe **DE4** 50 E7

M

Malleny Mills

Malleny Mills **EH14** 75 K4
Malletsheugh **G77** 74 D5
Malling **FK8** 81 G7
Malltraeth **LL62** 46 C6
Mallwyd **SY20** 37 H4
Malmesbury **SN16** 20 C3
Malmsmead **EX35** 7 F1
Malpas, *Ches.* **SY14** 38 D1
Malpas, *Cornw.* **TR1** 3 F4
Malpas, *Newport* **NP20** 19 G2
Maltby, *S.Yorks.* **S66** 51 H3
Maltby, *Stock.* **TS8** 63 F5
Maltby le Marsh **LN13** 53 H4
Maltman's Hill **TN27** 14 E3
Malton **YO17** 58 D2
Malvern Link **WR14** 29 G4
Malvern Wells **WR14** 29 G4
Mambeg **G84** 74 A2
Mamble **DY14** 29 F1
Mamhead **EX6** 7 H7
Mamhilad **NP4** 19 G1
Manaccan **TR12** 2 E6
Manafon **SY21** 38 A5
Manais **HS3** 93 G3
Manaton **TQ13** 7 F7
Manby **LN11** 53 G4
Mancetter **CV9** 41 F6
MANCHESTER M 49 H3
Manchester Airport **M90** 49 H4
Mancot Royal **CH5** 48 C6
Mandally **PH35** 87 J4
Manea **PE15** 43 H7
Maneight **KA18** 67 K3
Manfield **DL2** 62 D5
Mangaster **ZE2** 108 C5
Mangotsfield **BS16** 19 K4
Mangurstadh **HS2** 100 C4
Mankinholes **OL14** 56 E7
Manley **WA6** 48 E5
Manmoel **NP12** 18 E1
Mannel **PA77** 78 A3
Manningford Abbots **SN9** 20 E6
Manningford Bohune **SN9** 20 E6
Manningford Bruce **SN9** 20 E6
Mannings Heath **RH13** 13 F4
Mannington **BH21** 10 B4
Manningtree **CO11** 35 F5
Mannofield **AB15** 91 H4
Manorbier **SA70** 16 D5
Manordeifi **SA43** 26 B4
Manordeilo **SA19** 17 K2
Manorowen **SA65** 16 C1
Mansell Gamage **HR4** 28 C4
Mansell Lacy **HR4** 28 D4
Mansergh **LA6** 56 B1
Mansfield **NG18** 51 H6
Mansfield Woodhouse **NG19** 51 H6
Mansriggs **LA12** 55 F1
Manston, *Dorset* **DT10** 9 H3
Manston, *Kent* **CT12** 25 K5
Manswood **BH21** 9 J4
Manthorpe, *Lincs.* **NG31** 42 C2
Manthorpe, *Lincs.* **PE10** 42 D4
Manton, *N.Lincs.* **DN21** 52 C2
Manton, *Rut.* **LE15** 42 B5
Manton, *Wilts.* **SN8** 20 E5
Manuden **CM23** 33 H6
Maolachy **PA35** 79 K6
Maperton **BA9** 9 F2
Maple Cross **WD3** 22 D2
Maplebeck **NG22** 51 K6
Mapledurham **RG4** 21 K4
Mapledurwell **RG25** 21 K6
Maplehurst **RH13** 12 E4
Mapleton **DE6** 40 D1
Mapperley **DE7** 41 G1
Mapperton **DT8** 8 E5
Mappleborough Green **B80** 30 B2
Mappleton **HU18** 59 J5
Mapplewell **S75** 51 F2
Mappowder **DT10** 9 G4
Mar Lodge **AB35** 89 H5
Marazion **TR17** 2 C5
Marbury **SY13** 38 E1
March **PE15** 43 H6
Marcham **OX13** 21 H2
Marchamley **SY4** 38 E3
Marchington **ST14** 40 D2
Marchington Woodlands **ST14** 40 D3
Marchwiel **LL13** 38 C1
Marchwood **SO40** 10 E3
Marcross **CF61** 18 C5
Marcus **DD8** 83 G2
Marden, *Here.* **HR1** 28 E4
Marden, *Kent* **TN12** 14 C3
Marden, *T. & W.* **NE30** 71 J6
Marden, *Wilts.* **SN10** 20 D6
Marden Beech **TN12** 14 C3
Marden Thorn **TN12** 14 C3
Mardy **NP7** 28 C7
Mare Green **TA3** 8 C2
Marefield **LE15** 42 A5
Mareham le Fen **PE22** 53 F6
Mareham on the Hill **LN9** 53 F6
Maresfield **TN22** 13 H4
Marfleet **HU9** 59 H7
Marford **LL12** 48 C7
Margam **SA13** 18 A3
Margaret Marsh **SP7** 9 H3
Margaret Roding **CM6** 33 J7
Margaretting **CM4** 24 C1
Margate **CT9** 25 K4
Margnaheglish **KA27** 73 J7
Margreig **DG2** 65 J3
Margrove Park **TS12** 63 H5
Marham **PE33** 44 B5
Marhamchurch **EX23** 6 A5
Marholm **PE6** 42 E5
Marian Cwm **LL18** 47 J5
Marian-glas **LL78** 46 D4
Mariansleigh **EX36** 7 F3
Marishader **IV51** 93 K5
Maristow **PL6** 4 E4
Mark **TA9** 19 G7
Mark Causeway **TA9** 19 G7
Mark Cross **TN6** 13 J3
Markbeech **TN8** 23 H7
Markby **LN13** 53 H5
Markdhu **DG8** 64 B3
Market Bosworth **CV13** 41 G5
Market Deeping **PE6** 42 E4
Market Drayton **TF9** 39 F2
Market Harborough **LE16** 42 A7
Market Lavington **SN10** 20 D6
Market Overton **LE15** 42 B4
Market Rasen **LN8** 52 E4
Market Stainton **LN8** 53 F5
Market Street **NR12** 45 G3
Market Warsop **NG20** 51 H6
Market Weighton **YO43** 58 E5
Market Weston **IP22** 34 D1
Markethill **PH13** 82 D4
Markfield **LE67** 41 G4
Markham **NP12** 18 E1
Markham Moor **DN22** 51 K5
Markinch **KY7** 82 D7
Markington **HG3** 57 H3
Marks Gate **RM6** 23 H3
Marks Tey **CO6** 34 D6
Marksbury **BA2** 19 K5
Markwell **PL12** 4 D5
Markyate **AL3** 32 D7
Marlborough **SN8** 20 E5
Marldon **TQ3** 5 J4
Marlesford **IP13** 35 H3
Marley Green **SY13** 38 E1
Marley Hill **NE16** 62 D1
Marlingford **NR9** 45 F5
Marloes **SA62** 16 A4
Marlow **SL7** 22 B3
Marlpit Hill **TN8** 23 H7
Marlpool **DE75** 41 G1
Marnhull **DT10** 9 G3
Marnoch **AB54** 98 D5
Marple **SK6** 49 J4
Marr **DN5** 51 H2
Marrel **KW8** 105 F7
Marrick **DL11** 62 B7
Marrister **ZE2** 109 E6
Marros **SA33** 17 F4
Marsden, *T. & W.* **SR6** 71 K7
Marsden, *W.Yorks.* **HD7** 50 C1
Marsett **DL8** 56 E1
Marsh **EX14** 8 B3
Marsh Baldon **OX44** 21 J2
Marsh Benham **RG20** 21 H5
Marsh Chapel **DN36** 53 G3
Marsh Gibbon **OX27** 31 H6
Marsh Green, *Devon* **EX5** 7 J6
Marsh Green, *Kent* **TN8** 23 H7
Marsh Green, *Tel. & W.* **TF6** 39 F4
Marsh Lane **S21** 51 G5
Marsh Street **TA24** 7 H1
Marshall's Heath **AL4** 32 E7
Marshalsea **DT6** 8 C4
Marsham **NR10** 45 F3
Marshaw **LA2** 55 J4
Marshborough **CT13** 15 H2
Marshbrook **SY6** 38 D7
Marshfield, *Newport* **CF3** 19 F3
Marshfield, *S.Glos.* **SN14** 20 A4
Marshgate **PL32** 4 B1
Marshside **PR9** 48 C1
Marshwood **DT6** 8 C5
Marske **DL11** 62 C6
Marske-by-the-Sea **TS11** 63 H4
Marston, *Ches.* **CW9** 49 F5
Marston, *Here.* **HR6** 28 C3
Marston, *Lincs.* **NG32** 42 B1
Marston, *Oxon.* **OX3** 21 J1
Marston, *Staffs.* **ST18** 40 B3
Marston, *Staffs.* **ST20** 40 A4
Marston, *Warks.* **B76** 40 E6
Marston, *Wilts.* **SN10** 20 C6
Marston Green **B37** 40 D7
Marston Magna **BA22** 8 E2
Marston Meysey **SN6** 20 E2
Marston Montgomery **DE6** 40 D2
Marston Moretaine **MK43** 32 C4
Marston on Dove **DE65** 40 E3
Marston St. Lawrence **OX17** 31 G4
Marston Stannett **HR6** 28 E3
Marston Trussell **LE16** 41 J7
Marstow **HR9** 28 E7
Marsworth **HP23** 32 C7
Marten **SN8** 21 F5
Marthall **WA16** 49 H5
Martham **NR29** 45 J4
Marthig **HS2** 101 G6
Martin, *Hants.* **SP6** 10 B3
Martin, *Lincs.* **LN4** 52 E6
Martin Drove End **SP6** 10 B2
Martin Hussingtree **WR3** 29 H2
Martinhoe **EX31** 6 E1
Martinscroft **WA1** 49 F4
Martinstown **DT2** 9 F6
Martlesham **IP12** 35 G4
Martlesham Heath **IP5** 35 G4
Martletwy **SA67** 16 D3
Martley **WR6** 29 G2
Martock **TA12** 8 D3
Marton, *Ches.* **SK11** 49 H6
Marton, *Cumb.* **LA12** 55 F2
Marton, *E.Riding* **HU11** 59 H6
Marton, *Lincs.* **DN21** 52 B4
Marton, *Middbro.* **TS7** 63 G5
Marton, *N.Yorks.* **YO62** 58 D1
Marton, *N.Yorks.* **YO51** 57 K3
Marton, *Shrop.* **SY21** 38 B5
Marton, *Warks.* **CV23** 31 F2
Marton Abbey **YO61** 58 B3
Marton-le-Moor **HG4** 57 J2
Martyr Worthy **SO21** 11 G1
Martyr's Green **KT11** 22 D6
Maruig **HS3** 100 E7
Marwick **KW17** 106 B5
Marwood **EX31** 6 D2
Mary Tavy **PL19** 5 F3
Marybank **IV6** 96 B6
Maryburgh **IV7** 96 C6
Maryfield **ZE2** 109 D8
Marygold **TD11** 77 G4
Maryhill, *Aber.* **AB53** 99 G6
Maryhill, *Glas.* **G20** 74 D4
Marykirk **AB30** 83 H1
Marylebone, *Gt.Lon.* **W1G** 23 F3
Marylebone, *Gt.Man.* **WN1** 48 E2
Marypark **AB37** 89 J1
Maryport, *Cumb.* **CA15** 60 B3
Maryport, *D. & G.* **DG9** 64 B7
Marystow **PL16** 6 C7
Maryton **DD10** 83 H2
Marywell, *Aber.* **AB12** 91 H5
Marywell, *Aber.* **AB34** 90 D5
Marywell, *Angus* **DD11** 83 H3
Masham **HG4** 57 H1
Mashbury **CM1** 33 K7
Mastrick **AB16** 91 G4
Matching **CM17** 33 J7
Matching Green **CM17** 33 J7
Matching Tye **CM17** 33 J7
Matfen **NE20** 71 F6
Matfield **TN12** 23 K7
Mathern **NP16** 19 J2
Mathon **WR13** 29 G4
Mathry **SA62** 16 B1
Matlaske **NR11** 45 F2
Matlock **DE4** 51 F6
Matlock Bank **DE4** 50 E6
Matlock Bath **DE4** 50 E7
Matson **GL4** 29 H7
Matterdale End **CA11** 60 E4
Mattersey **DN10** 51 J4
Mattingley **RG27** 22 A6
Mattishall **NR20** 44 E4
Mattishall Burgh **NR20** 44 E4
Mauchline **KA5** 67 K1
Maud **AB42** 99 H6
Maugersbury **GL54** 30 C6
Maughold **IM7** 54 D4
Mauld **IV4** 87 K1
Maulden **MK45** 32 D5
Maulds Meaburn **CA10** 61 H5
Maunby **YO7** 57 J1
Maund Bryan **HR1** 28 E3
Maundown **TA4** 7 J3
Mautby **NR29** 45 J4
Mavesyn Ridware **WS15** 40 C4
Mavis Enderby **PE23** 53 G6
Maw Green **WS1** 40 C6
Mawbray **CA15** 60 B2
Mawdesley **L40** 48 D1
Mawdlam **CF33** 18 B3
Mawgan **TR12** 2 E6
Mawla **TR16** 2 D4
Mawnan **TR11** 2 E6
Mawnan Smith **TR11** 2 E6
Maxey **PE6** 42 E5
Maxstoke **B46** 40 E7
Maxton, *Kent* **CT17** 15 H3
Maxton, *Sc.Bord.* **TD6** 70 B1
Maxwellheugh **TD5** 77 F7
Maxwelltown **DG2** 65 K3
Maxworthy **PL15** 4 C1
Maybole **KA19** 67 H3
Mayen **AB54** 98 D6
Mayfield, *E.Suss.* **TN20** 13 J4
Mayfield, *Midloth.* **EH22** 76 B4
Mayfield, *Staffs.* **DE6** 40 D1
Mayford **GU22** 22 C6
Mayland **CM3** 25 F1
Maylandsea **CM3** 25 F1
Maynard's Green **TN21** 13 J5
Maypole, *I.o.S.* **TR21** 2 C1
Maypole, *Kent* **CT3** 25 H5
Maypole Green **NR14** 45 J6
Maywick **ZE2** 109 C10
Meabhag **HS3** 93 G2
Mead End **SP5** 10 B2
Meadle **HP17** 22 B1
Meadowhall **S9** 51 F3
Meadowmill **EH33** 76 C3
Meadowtown **SY5** 38 C5
Meal Bank **LA9** 61 G7
Mealabost **HS2** 101 G2
Mealasta **HS2** 100 B5
Meals **LN11** 53 H3
Mealsgate **CA7** 60 D2
Meanley **BB7** 56 C5
Mearbeck **BD23** 56 D3
Meare **BA6** 19 H7
Mearns **G77** 74 D5
Mears Ashby **NN6** 32 B2
Measham **DE12** 41 F4
Meathop **LA11** 55 H1
Meavy **PL20** 5 F4
Medbourne **LE16** 42 B6
Meddon **EX39** 6 A4
Meden Vale **NG20** 51 H6
Medmenham **SL7** 22 B3
Medomsley **DH8** 62 C1
Medstead **GU34** 11 H1
Meer End **CV8** 30 D1
Meerbrook **ST13** 49 J6
Meesden **SG9** 33 H5
Meeth **EX20** 6 D5
Meggethead **TD7** 69 G1
Meidrim **SA33** 17 F2
Meifod, *Denb.* **LL16** 47 J7
Meifod, *Powys* **SY22** 38 A4
Meigle **PH12** 82 D3
Meikle Earnock **ML3** 75 F5
Meikle Grenach **PA20** 73 J4
Meikle Kilmory **PA20** 73 J4
Meikle Rahane **G84** 74 A2
Meikle Strath **AB30** 90 E7
Meikle Tarty **AB41** 91 H2
Meikle Wartle **AB51** 91 F1
Meikleour **PH2** 82 C4
Meinciau **SA17** 17 H3
Meir **ST3** 40 B1
Meirheath **ST3** 40 B2
Melbost **HS2** 101 G4
Melbourn **SG8** 33 G4
Melbourne, *Derbys.* **DE73** 41 F3
Melbourne, *E.Riding* **YO42** 58 D5
Melbury **EX39** 6 B4
Melbury Abbas **SP7** 9 H3
Melbury Bubb **DT2** 8 E4
Melbury Osmond **DT2** 8 E4
Melbury Sampford **DT2** 8 E4
Melby **ZE2** 109 A7
Melchbourne **MK44** 32 D2
Melchet Court **SO51** 10 D2
Melcombe Bingham **DT2** 9 G4
Melcombe Regis **DT4** 9 F6
Meldon, *Devon* **EX20** 6 D6
Meldon, *Northumb.* **NE61** 71 G5
Meldreth **SG8** 33 G4
Melfort **PA34** 79 K6
Melgarve **PH20** 88 B5
Melgum **AB34** 90 C4
Meliden (Gallt Melyd) **LL19** 47 J4
Melin-y-coed **LL26** 47 G6
Melin-y-ddol **SY21** 37 K5
Melin-y-grug **SY21** 37 K5
Melin-y-Wig **LL21** 37 K1
Melincourt **SA11** 18 B1
Melincryddan **SA11** 18 A2
Melkinthorpe **CA10** 61 G4
Melkridge **NE49** 70 C7
Melksham **SN12** 20 C5
Melksham Forest **SN12** 20 C5
Melldalloch **PA21** 73 H3
Melling, *Lancs.* **LA6** 55 J2
Melling, *Mersey.* **L31** 48 C2
Melling Mount **L31** 48 D2
Mellis **IP23** 34 E1
Mellon Charles **IV22** 94 E2
Mellon Udrigle **IV22** 94 E2
Mellor, *Gt.Man.* **SK6** 49 J4
Mellor, *Lancs.* **BB2** 56 B6
Mellor Brook **BB2** 56 B6
Mells **BA11** 20 A7
Melmerby, *Cumb.* **CA10** 61 H3
Melmerby, *N.Yorks.* **DL8** 57 F1
Melmerby, *N.Yorks.* **HG4** 57 J2
Melplash **DT6** 8 D5
Melrose, *Aber.* **AB45** 99 F4
Melrose, *Sc.Bord.* **TD6** 76 D7
Melsetter **KW16** 107 B9
Melsonby **DL10** 62 C6
Meltham **HD9** 50 C1
Melton **IP12** 35 G3
Melton Constable **NR24** 44 E2
Melton Mowbray **LE13** 42 A4
Melton Ross **DN38** 52 D1
Meltonby **YO42** 58 D4
Melvaig **IV21** 94 D3
Melverley **SY22** 38 C4
Melverley Green **SY22** 38 C4
Melvich **KW14** 104 D2
Membury **EX13** 8 B4
Memsie **AB43** 99 H4
Memus **DD8** 83 F2
Menabilly **PL24** 4 A5
Menai Bridge (Porthaethwy) **LL59** 46 D5
Mendham **IP20** 45 G7
Mendlesham **IP14** 35 F2
Mendlesham Green **IP14** 34 E2
Menethorpe **YO17** 58 D3
Menheniot **PL14** 4 C4
Menie Ho. **AB41** 91 H2
Mennock **DG4** 68 D3
Menston **LS29** 57 G5
Menstrie **FK11** 75 G1
Mentmore **LU7** 32 C7
Meoble **PH40** 86 D6
Meole Brace **SY3** 38 D4
Meon **PO14** 11 G4
Meonstoke **SO32** 11 H3
Meopham **DA13** 24 C5
Meopham Green **DA13** 24 C5
Mepal **CB6** 43 H7
Meppershall **SG17** 32 E5
Merbach **HR3** 28 C4
Mercaston **DE6** 40 E1
Mere, *Ches.* **WA16** 49 G4
Mere, *Wilts.* **BA12** 9 H1
Mere Brow **PR9** 48 D1
Mere Green **B75** 40 D6
Mereworth **ME18** 23 K6
Mergie **AB39** 91 F6
Meriden **CV7** 40 E7
Merkland **DG7** 65 H3
Merlin's Bridge **SA61** 16 C3
Merridge **TA5** 8 B1
Merrifield **TQ7** 5 J6
Merrington **SY4** 38 D3
Merrion **SA71** 16 C5
Merriott **TA16** 8 D3
Merrivale **PL19** 5 F3
Merrow **GU1** 22 D6
Merry Hill, *Herts.* **WD23** 22 E2
Merry Hill, *W.Mid.* **DY5** 40 B7
Merrymeet **PL14** 4 C4
Mersham **TN25** 15 F4
Merstham **RH1** 23 F6
Merston **PO20** 12 B6
Merstone **PO30** 11 G6
Merther **TR2** 3 F4
Merthyr **SA33** 17 G2
Merthyr Cynog **LD3** 27 J5
Merthyr Dyfan **CF62** 18 E5
Merthyr Mawr **CF32** 18 B4
Merthyr Tydfil **CF47** 18 D1
Merthyr Vale **CF48** 18 D2
Merton, *Devon* **EX20** 6 D4
Merton, *Gt.Lon.* **SW** 23 F5
Merton, *Norf.* **IP25** 44 C6
Merton, *Oxon.* **OX25** 31 G7
Mertyn **CH8** 47 K5
Mervinslaw **TD8** 70 B2
Meshaw **EX36** 7 F4
Messing **CO5** 34 C7
Messingham **DN17** 52 B2
Metfield **IP20** 45 G7
Metheringham **LN4** 52 D6
Methil **KY8** 76 B1
Methlem **LL53** 36 A2
Methley **LS26** 57 J7
Methlick **AB41** 91 G1
Methven **PH1** 82 B5
Methwold **IP26** 44 B6
Methwold Hythe **IP26** 44 B6
Metrocentre **NE11** 71 H7
Mettingham **NR35** 45 H6
Metton **NR11** 45 F2
Mevagissey **PL26** 4 A6
Mexborough **S64** 51 G3
Mey **KW14** 105 H1
Meysey Hampton **GL7** 20 E1
Miabhag **HS3** 100 C7
Miabhig **HS2** 100 C4
Mial **IV21** 94 D4
Michaelchurch **HR2** 28 E6
Michaelchurch Escley **HR2** 28 C5
Michaelchurch-on-Arrow **HR5** 28 B3
Michaelston-le-Pit **CF64** 18 E4
Michaelston-y-Fedw **CF3** 19 F3
Michaelstow **PL30** 4 A3
Micheldever **SO21** 11 G1
Michelmersh **SO51** 10 E2
Mickfield **IP14** 35 F2
Mickle Trafford **CH3** 48 D6
Mickleby **TS13** 63 K5
Mickleham **RH5** 22 E6
Micklehurst **OL5** 49 J2
Mickleover **DE3** 41 F2
Micklethwaite **CA7** 60 D1
Mickleton, *Dur.* **DL12** 62 A4
Mickleton, *Glos.* **GL55** 30 C4
Mickletown **LS26** 57 J7
Mickley **HG4** 57 H2
Mickley Square **NE43** 71 F7
Mid Ardlaw **AB43** 99 H4
Mid Beltie **AB31** 90 E4
Mid Cairncross **DD9** 90 D7
Mid Calder **EH53** 75 J4
Mid Clyth **KW3** 105 H5
Mid Lavant **PO18** 12 B6
Mid Letter **PA27** 80 B7
Mid Lix **FK20** 81 G5
Mid Mossdale **DL8** 61 K7
Mid Sannox **KA27** 73 J6
Mid Yell **ZE2** 108 E3
Midbea **KW17** 106 D3
Middle Assendon **RG9** 22 A3
Middle Aston **OX25** 31 F6
Middle Barton **OX7** 31 F6
Middle Claydon **MK18** 31 J6
Middle Drums **DD9** 83 G2
Middle Handley **S21** 51 G5
Middle Harling **NR16** 44 D7
Middle Kames **PA31** 73 H2
Middle Littleton **WR11** 30 B4
Middle Maes-coed **HR2** 28 C5
Middle Mill **SA62** 16 B2
Middle Rasen **LN8** 52 D4
Middle Rigg **PH2** 82 B7
Middle Salter **LA2** 56 B3
Middle Town **TR25** 2 C1
Middle Tysoe **CV35** 30 E4
Middle Wallop **SO20** 10 D1
Middle Winterslow **SP5** 10 D1
Middle Woodford **SP4** 10 C1
Middlebie **DG11** 69 H6
Middleham **DL8** 57 G1
Middlehill, *Aber.* **AB53** 99 G6
Middlehill, *Cornw.* **PL14** 4 C4
Middlehope **SY7** 38 D7

Mountblairy

Middlemarsh DT9 9 F4
Middlesbrough TS1 63 F4
Middleshaw LA8 55 J1
Middlesmoor HG3 57 F2
Middlestone Moor DL16 62 D3
Middlestown WF4 50 E1
Middleton, Aber. AB21 91 G3
Middleton, Angus DD11 83 G3
Middleton, Cumb. LA6 56 B1
Middleton, Derbys. DE45 50 D6
Middleton, Derbys. DE4 50 E7
Middleton, Essex CO10 34 C4
Middleton, Gt.Man. M24 49 H2
Middleton, Hants. SP11 21 H7
Middleton, Lancs. LA3 55 H4
Middleton, Midloth. EH23 76 B5
Middleton, N.Yorks. YO18 58 D1
Middleton, Norf. PE32 44 A4
Middleton, Northants. LE16 42 B7
Middleton, Northumb. NE70 77 J7
Middleton, Northumb. NE61 71 F5
Middleton, P. & K. PH10 82 C3
Middleton, P. & K. KY13 82 C7
Middleton, Shrop. SY11 38 C3
Middleton, Shrop. SY15 38 B6
Middleton, Shrop. SY8 28 E1
Middleton, Suff. IP17 35 J2
Middleton, Swan. SA3 17 H6
Middleton, W.Yorks. LS29 57 G5
Middleton, W.Yorks. LS10 57 H7
Middleton, Warks. B78 40 D6
Middleton Bank Top NE61 71 F5
Middleton Cheney OX17 31 F4
Middleton Green ST10 40 B2
Middleton Hall NE71 70 E1
Middleton of Potterton AB23 91 H3
Middleton on the Hill SY8 28 E2
Middleton One Row DL2 62 E5
Middleton Park AB22 91 H3
Middleton Priors WV16 39 F7
Middleton Quernhow HG4 57 J2
Middleton St. George DL2 62 E5
Middleton Scriven WV16 39 F7
Middleton Stoney OX25 31 G6
Middleton Tyas DL10 62 D6
Middleton-in-Teesdale DL12 62 A4
Middleton-on-Leven TS15 63 F5
Middleton-on-Sea PO22 12 C7
Middleton-on-the-Wolds YO25 59 F5
Middletown, Cumb. CA22 60 A6
Middletown, Powys SY21 38 C4
Middlewich CW10 49 G6
Middlewood SK12 49 J4
Middlewood Green IP14 34 E2
Middleyard KA4 74 D7
Middlezoy TA7 8 C1
Middridge DL4 62 D4
Midfield IV27 103 H2
Midford BA2 20 A5
Midge Hall PR26 55 J7
Midgeholme CA8 61 H1
Midgham RG7 21 J5
Midgley, W.Yorks. HX7 57 F7
Midgley, W.Yorks. WF4 50 E1
Midhopestones S36 50 E3
Midhurst GU29 12 B4
Midlem TD7 70 A1
Midpark PA20 73 J5
Midsomer Norton BA3 19 K6
Midtown, High. IV27 103 H2
Midtown, High. IV22 94 E3
Midtown of Barras AB39 91 G6
Midville PE22 53 G7
Migdale IV24 96 D2
Migvie AB34 90 C4
Milarrochy G63 74 C1
Milber TQ12 5 J3
Milbethill AB54 98 E5
Milborne Port DT9 9 F3
Milborne St. Andrew DT11 9 H5
Milborne Wick DT9 9 F2
Milbourne NE20 71 G6
Milburn CA10 61 H4
Milbury Heath BS35 19 K2
Milcombe OX15 31 F5
Milden IP7 34 D4
Mildenhall, Suff. IP28 34 B1
Mildenhall, Wilts. SN8 21 F4
Mile Elm SN11 20 C5
Mile End, Essex CO4 34 D6
Mile End, Glos. GL16 28 E7
Milebrook LD7 28 C1
Milebush TN12 14 C3
Mileham PE32 44 D4
Milesmark KY12 75 J2
Milfield NE71 77 H7
Milford, Derbys. DE56 41 F1
Milford, Devon EX39 6 A3
Milford, Shrop. SY4 38 D3
Milford, Staffs. ST17 40 B3
Milford, Surr. GU8 22 C7
Milford Haven (Aberdaugleddau) SA73 16 C4
Milford on Sea SO41 10 D5
Milkwall GL16 19 J1
Mill Bank HX6 57 F7
Mill End, Bucks. RG9 22 A3
Mill End, Herts. SG9 33 G5
Mill End Green CM6 33 K6
Mill Green, Essex CM4 24 C1
Mill Green, Shrop. TF9 39 F3
Mill Hill NW7 23 F2
Mill Houses LA2 56 B3
Mill Lane GU10 22 A6
Mill of Colp AB53 99 F6
Mill of Elrick AB41 99 H6
Mill of Fortune PH6 81 J5
Mill of Kingoodie AB51 91 G2
Mill of Monquich AB39 91 G5
Mill of Uras AB39 91 G7
Mill Street NR20 44 E4
Milland Marsh GU30 12 B4
Millbank AB42 99 J6
Millbeck CA12 60 D4
Millbounds KW17 106 E4
Millbreck AB42 99 J6
Millbridge GU10 22 B7
Millbrook, Beds. MK45 32 D5
Millbrook, Cornw. PL10 4 E5
Millbrook, S'ham. SO15 10 E3
Millburn, Aber. AB54 90 E1
Millburn, Aber. AB33 90 D2
Millcombe TQ9 5 J6
Millcorner TN31 14 D5
Millden AB23 91 H3
Milldens DD8 83 G2
Millearn PH3 82 A6
Millenheath SY13 38 E2
Millerhill EH22 76 B4
Miller's Dale SK17 50 D5
Millholme LA8 61 G7
Millhouse, Arg. & B. PA21 73 H3
Millhouse, Cumb. CA7 60 E3
Millhousebridge DG11 69 G5
Millikenpark PA10 74 C4
Millington YO42 58 E4
Millmeece ST21 40 A2
Millness IV63 87 K1
Millom LA18 54 E1
Millport KA28 73 K5
Millthrop LA10 61 H7
Milltimber AB13 91 G4
Millton of Noth AB54 90 D2
Milltown, Aber. AB33 90 C3
Milltown, D. & G. DG14 69 J6
Milltown, Derbys. S45 51 F6
Milltown, Devon EX31 6 D2
Milltown, High. IV6 95 K6
Milltown, High. IV12 97 G7
Milltown of Aberdalgie PH2 82 B5
Milltown of Auchindoun AB55 98 B6
Milltown of Campfield AB31 90 E4
Milltown of Craigston AB53 99 F5
Milltown of Edinvillie AB38 97 K7
Milltown of Rothiemay AB54 98 D6
Milltown of Towie AB33 90 C3
Milnathort KY13 82 C7
Milngavie G62 74 D3
Milnrow OL16 49 J1
Milnsbridge HD4 50 D1
Milnthorpe LA7 55 H1
Milovaig IV55 93 G6
Milrig KA4 74 D7
Milson DY14 29 F1
Milstead ME9 14 E2
Milston SP4 20 E7
Milton, Angus DD8 82 E3
Milton, Cambs. CB4 33 H2
Milton, Cumb. CA8 70 A7
Milton, D. & G. DG2 68 D5
Milton, D. & G. DG2 65 J3
Milton, Derbys. DE65 41 F3
Milton, High. KW1 105 J3
Milton, High. IV18 96 E4
Milton, High. IV12 97 G6
Milton, High. IV6 96 C7
Milton, High. IV54 94 D7
Milton, High. IV63 88 B1
Milton, Moray AB56 98 D4
Milton, N.Som. BS22 19 G5
Milton, Newport NP19 19 G3
Milton, Notts. NG22 51 K5
Milton, Oxon. OX15 31 F5
Milton, Oxon. OX14 21 H2
Milton, P. & K. PH8 82 A4
Milton, Pembs. SA70 16 D4
Milton, Stir. FK17 81 G7
Milton, Stir. FK8 81 G7
Milton, Stir. G63 74 C1
Milton, Stoke ST2 49 J7
Milton, W.Dun. G82 74 C3
Milton Abbas DT11 9 H4
Milton Abbot PL19 4 E3
Milton Bridge EH26 76 A4
Milton Bryan MK17 32 C5
Milton Clevedon BA4 9 F1
Milton Coldwells AB41 91 H1
Milton Combe PL20 4 E4
Milton Damerel EX22 6 B4
Milton Ernest MK44 32 D3
Milton Green CH3 48 D7
Milton Hill OX13 21 H2
Milton Inveramsay AB51 91 F2
MILTON KEYNES MK 32 B5
Milton Keynes Village MK10 32 B5
Milton Lilbourne SN9 20 E5
Milton Lockhart ML8 75 G6
Milton Malsor NN7 31 J3
Milton Morenish FK21 81 H4
Milton of Auchinhove AB31 90 D4
Milton of Balgonie KY7 82 E7
Milton of Cairnborrow AB54 98 C6
Milton of Campsie G66 74 E3
Milton of Cullerlie AB32 91 F4
Milton of Cushnie AB33 90 D3
Milton of Dalcapon PH16 82 A2
Milton of Tullich AB35 90 B5
Milton on Stour SP8 9 G2
Milton Regis ME10 24 E5
Milton-under-Wychwood OX7 30 D7
Miltonduff IV30 97 J5
Miltonhill IV36 97 H5
Miltonise DG8 64 B3
Milverton TA4 7 K3
Milwich ST18 40 B2
Minard PA32 73 H1
Minard Castle PA32 73 H1
Minchington DT11 9 J3
Minchinhampton GL6 20 B1
Mindrum TD12 77 G7
Minehead TA24 7 H1
Minera LL11 48 B7
Minety SN16 20 D2
Minffordd, Gwyn. LL48 36 E2
Minffordd, Gwyn. LL40 37 G4
Mingearraidh HS8 84 C2
Miningsby PE23 53 G6
Minions PL14 4 C3
Minishant KA7 67 H2
Minley Manor GU17 22 B6
Minllyn SY20 37 H4
Minnes AB41 91 H2
Minnigaff DG8 64 E4
Minnonie AB45 99 F4
Minskip YO51 57 J3
Minstead SO43 10 D3
Minster, Kent ME12 25 F4
Minster, Kent CT12 25 K5
Minster Lovell OX29 30 E7
Minsterley SY5 38 C5
Minsterworth GL2 29 G7
Minterne Magna DT2 9 F4
Minting LN9 52 E5
Mintlaw AB42 99 J6
Minto TD9 70 A1
Minton SY6 38 D6
Minwear SA67 16 D3
Minworth B76 40 D6
Miodar PA77 78 B3
Mirbister KW17 106 C5
Mireland KW1 105 J2
Mirfield WF14 57 G7
Miserden GL6 20 C1
Miskin, R.C.T. CF45 18 D2
Miskin, R.C.T. CF72 18 D3
Misson DN10 51 J3
Misterton, Leics. LE17 41 H7
Misterton, Notts. DN10 51 K3
Misterton, Som. TA18 8 D4
Mitcham CR4 23 F5
Mitchel Troy NP25 28 D7
Mitcheldean GL17 29 F7
Mitchell TR8 3 F3
Mitchelland LA8 60 F7
Mitcheltroy Common NP25 19 H1
Mitford NE61 71 G5
Mithian TR5 2 E3
Mitton ST19 40 A4
Mixbury NN13 31 H5
Moar PH15 81 G3
Moat CA6 69 K6
Mobberley WA16 49 G5
Moccas HR2 28 C4
Mochdre, Conwy LL28 47 G5
Mochdre, Powys SY16 37 K7
Mochrum DG8 64 D6
Mockbeggar TN12 14 C3
Mockerkin CA13 60 B4
Modbury PL21 5 G5
Moddershall ST15 40 B2
Modsarie KW14 103 J2
Moelfre, I.o.A. LL72 46 D4
Moelfre, Powys SY10 38 A3
Moffat DG10 69 F3
Mogerhanger MK44 32 E4
Moin'a'choire PA44 72 B4
Moine Ho. IV27 103 H2
Moira DE12 41 F4
Mol-chlach PH41 85 K3
Molash CT4 15 F2
Mold (Yr Wyddgrug) CH7 48 B6
Molehill Green CM6 33 J6
Molescroft HU17 59 G5
Molesworth PE28 32 D1
Mollance DG7 65 H4
Molland EX36 7 G3
Mollington, Ches. CH1 48 C5
Mollington, Oxon. OX17 31 F4
Mollinsburn G67 75 F3
Monachty SY23 26 E2
Monachylemore FK19 81 F6
Moncreiffe PH2 82 C6
Monevechadan PA24 80 C7
Monewden IP13 35 G3
Moneydie PH1 82 B5
Moniaive DG3 68 C4
Monifieth DD5 83 F4
Monikie DD5 83 F4
Monimail KY15 82 D6
Monington SA43 26 A4
Monk Fryston LS25 58 B7
Monk Sherborne RG26 21 K6
Monk Soham IP13 35 G2
Monk Street CM6 33 K6
Monken Hadley EN5 23 F2
Monkhill CA5 60 E1
Monkhopton WV16 39 F6
Monkland HR6 28 D3
Monkleigh EX39 6 C3
Monknash CF71 18 C4
Monkokehampton EX19 6 D5
Monks Eleigh IP7 34 D4
Monk's Gate RH13 13 F4
Monks' Heath SK11 49 H5
Monks Kirby CV23 41 G7
Monks Risborough HP27 22 B1
Monkseaton NE25 71 J6
Monkshill AB53 99 F6
Monksilver TA4 7 J2
Monkstadt IV51 93 J5
Monkswood NP15 19 G1
Monkton, Devon EX14 7 K5
Monkton, Kent CT12 25 J5
Monkton, S.Ayr. KA9 67 H1
Monkton, T. & W. NE32 71 J7
Monkton Combe BA2 20 A5
Monkton Deverill BA12 9 H1
Monkton Farleigh BA15 20 A5
Monkton Heathfield TA2 8 B2
Monkton Up Wimborne BH21 10 B3
Monkwearmouth SR6 62 E1
Monkwood SO24 11 H1
Monmore Green WV1 40 B6
Monmouth (Trefynwy) NP25 28 E7
Monnington on Wye HR4 28 C4
Monreith DG8 64 D6
Monsale CM0 25 G2
Montacute TA15 8 D3
Monteach AB41 99 G6
Montford SY4 38 D4
Montford Bridge SY4 38 D4
Montgarrie AB33 90 D3
Montgomery (Trefaldwyn) SY15 38 B6
Montgreenan KA13 74 B6
Montrave KY8 82 E7
Montrose DD10 83 J2
Monxton SP11 21 G7
Monyash DE45 50 D6
Monymusk AB51 90 E3
Monzie PH7 81 K5
Moodiesburn G69 74 E3
Moonzie KY15 82 E6
Moor Allerton LS17 57 J6
Moor Cock LA2 56 B3
Moor Crichel BH21 9 J4
Moor End, Cumb. LA6 55 J2
Moor End, E.Riding YO43 58 E6
Moor Monkton YO26 58 B4
Moor Nook PR3 56 B6
Moor Row CA24 60 B5
Moor Side PE22 53 F7
Moorby PE22 53 F6
Moorcot HR5 28 C3
Moordown BH9 10 B5
Moore WA4 48 E4
Moorends DN8 51 J1
Moorgreen NG16 41 G1
Moorhall S18 51 F5
Moorhampton HR4 28 C4
Moorhouse, Cumb. CA5 60 E1
Moorhouse, Notts. NG23 51 K6
Moorland or Northmoor Green TA7 8 C1
Moorlinch TA7 8 C1
Moorsholm TS12 63 H5
Moorside OL4 49 J2
Moortown, I.o.W. PO30 11 F6
Moortown, Lincs. LN7 52 D3
Morangie IV19 96 E3
Morar PH40 86 C5
Morborne PE7 42 E6
Morchard Bishop EX17 7 F5
Morcombelake DT6 8 C5
Morcott LE15 42 C5
Morda SY10 38 B3
Morden, Dorset BH20 9 J5
Morden, Gt.Lon. SM4 23 F5
Mordiford HR1 28 E5
Mordington TD15 77 H5
Mordon TS21 62 E4
More SY9 38 C6
Morebath EX16 7 H3
Morebattle TD5 70 C1
Morecambe LA4 55 H3
Morefield IV26 95 H2
Moreleigh TQ9 5 H5
Morenish FK21 81 H4
Moresby CA28 60 A4
Morestead SO21 11 G2
Moreton, Dorset DT2 9 H6
Moreton, Essex CM5 23 J1
Moreton, Here. HR6 28 E2
Moreton, Mersey. CH46 48 B4
Moreton, Oxon. OX9 21 K1
Moreton Corbet SY4 38 E3
Moreton Jeffries HR1 29 F4
Moreton Morrell CV35 30 E3
Moreton on Lugg HR4 28 E4
Moreton Pinkney NN11 31 G4
Moreton Say TF9 39 F2
Moreton Valence GL2 20 A1
Moreton-in-Marsh GL56 30 D5
Moretonhampstead TQ13 7 F7
Morfa Bychan LL49 36 E2
Morfa Glas SA11 18 B1
Morfa Nefyn LL53 36 B1
Morgan's Vale SP5 10 C2
Mork GL15 19 J1
Morland CA10 61 G4
Morley, Derbys. DE7 41 F1
Morley, Dur. DL14 62 C4
Morley, W.Yorks. LS27 57 H7
Morley Green SK9 49 H4
Morley St. Botolph NR18 44 E5
Morningside, Edin. EH10 76 A3
Morningside, N.Lan. ML2 75 G5
Morningthorpe NR15 45 G6
Morpeth NE61 71 G5
Morphie DD10 83 J1
Morrey DE13 40 D4
Morriston, S.Ayr. KA19 67 G3
Morriston, Swan. SA6 17 K5
Morroch PH39 86 C6
Morston NR25 44 E1
Mortehoe EX34 6 C1
Mortimer RG7 21 K5
Mortimer West End RG7 21 K5
Mortimer's Cross HR6 28 D2
Mortlake SW14 23 F4
Morton, Derbys. DE55 51 G6
Morton, Lincs. DN21 52 B3
Morton, Lincs. PE10 42 E3
Morton, Norf. NR9 45 F4
Morton, Notts. NG25 51 K7
Morton, S.Glos. BS35 19 K2
Morton, Shrop. SY10 38 B3
Morton Bagot B80 30 C2
Morton-on-Swale DL7 62 E7
Morvah TR20 2 A5
Morval PL13 4 C5
Morvich, High. IV28 96 E1
Morvich, High. IV40 87 F2
Morvil SA62 16 D1
Morville WV16 39 F6
Morwellham PL19 4 E4
Morwenstow EX23 6 A4
Morwick Hall NE65 71 H3
Mosborough S20 51 G4
Moscow KA4 74 C6
Mosedale CA11 60 E3
Moselden Height HD3 50 C1
Moseley, W.Mid. B13 40 C7
Moseley, Worcs. WR2 29 H3
Moss, Arg. & B. PA77 78 A3
Moss, S.Yorks. DN6 51 H1
Moss, Wrex. LL11 48 C7
Moss Bank WA11 48 E3
Moss Nook M22 49 H4
Moss of Barmuckity IV30 97 K5
Moss Side PR4 55 G6
Moss-side, High. IV12 97 F6
Moss-side, Moray AB54 98 D5
Mossat AB33 90 C3
Mossbank ZE2 108 D5
Mossblown KA6 67 J1
Mossburnford TD8 70 B2
Mossdale DG7 65 G3
Mossend ML4 75 F4
Mossgiel KA5 67 J1
Mosshead AB54 90 D1
Mosside DD8 83 F2
Mossley OL5 49 J2
Mossley Hill L18 48 C4
Mosspaul Hotel DG13 69 K4
Mosstodloch IV32 98 B4
Mosston DD11 83 G3
Mosterton DT8 8 D4
Mostyn CH8 47 K4
Motcombe SP7 9 H2
Motherby CA11 60 F4
MOTHERWELL ML 75 F5
Mottingham SE9 23 H4
Mottisfont SO51 10 E2
Mottistone PO30 11 F6
Mottram in Longdendale SK14 49 J3
Mottram St. Andrew SK10 49 H5
Mouldsworth WA6 48 E5
Moulin PH16 82 A2
Moulsecoomb BN2 13 G6
Moulsford OX10 21 J3
Moulsham CM2 24 D1
Moulsoe MK16 32 C4
Moulton, Ches. CW9 49 F6
Moulton, Lincs. PE12 43 G3
Moulton, N.Yorks. DL10 62 D6
Moulton, Northants. NN3 31 J2
Moulton, Suff. CB8 33 K2
Moulton Chapel PE12 43 F4
Moulton St. Mary NR13 45 H5
Moulton Seas End PE12 43 G3
Mounie Castle AB51 91 F2
Mount, Cornw. PL30 4 B4
Mount, Cornw. TR8 2 E3
Mount, High. IV12 97 G7
Mount Bures CO8 34 D5
Mount Edgcumbe PL10 4 E5
Mount Hawke TR4 2 E4
Mount Manisty CH65 48 C5
Mount Oliphant KA6 67 H2
Mount Pleasant, Derbys. DE56 41 F1
Mount Pleasant, Suff. IP18 35 J1
Mount Tabor HX2 57 F7
Mountain Ash CF45 18 D2
Mountain Cross EH46 75 K6
Mountain Water SA62 16 C2
Mountbenger TD7 69 J1
Mountblairy AB45 98 E5

Norwick

Newham Hall **NE67** 71 G1
Newhaven **BN9** 13 H6
Newhey **OL16** 49 J1
Newholm **YO21** 63 K5
Newhouse **ML1** 75 F4
Newick **BN8** 13 H4
Newington, *Kent* **ME9** 24 E5
Newington, *Kent* **CT18** 15 G4
Newington, *Oxon.* **OX10** 21 K2
Newington Bagpath **GL8** 20 B2
Newland, *Glos.* **GL16** 19 J1
Newland, *N.Yorks.* **YO8** 58 C7
Newland, *Worcs.* **WR13** 29 G4
Newlandrig **EH23** 76 B4
Newlands, *Northumb.* **DH8** 62 B1
Newlands, *Sc.Bord.* **TD9** 70 A4
Newland's Corner **GU4** 22 D7
Newlands of Geise **KW14** 105 F2
Newlyn **TR18** 2 B6
Newlyn East **TR8** 3 F3
Newmachar **AB21** 91 G3
Newmains **ML2** 75 G5
Newmarket, *Suff.* **CB8** 33 K2
Newmarket, *W.Isles* **HS1** 101 G4
Newmill, *Aber.* **AB41** 99 G6
Newmill, *Aber.* **AB51** 91 G2
Newmill, *Moray* **AB55** 98 C5
Newmill, *Sc.Bord.* **TD9** 69 K2
Newmill of Inshewan **DD8** 83 F1
Newmills **IV7** 96 D5
Newmiln, *P. & K.* **PH2** 82 C4
Newmiln, *P. & K.* **PH1** 82 B5
Newmilns **KA16** 74 D7
Newnham, *Glos.* **GL14** 29 F7
Newnham, *Hants.* **RG27** 22 A6
Newnham, *Herts.* **SG7** 33 F5
Newnham, *Kent* **ME9** 14 E2
Newnham, *Northants.* **NN11** 31 G3
Newnham, *Worcs.* **WR15** 29 F2
Newnham Paddox **CV23** 41 G7
Newnoth **AB54** 90 D1
Newport, *Cornw.* **PL15** 6 B7
Newport, *Devon* **EX32** 6 D2
Newport, *E.Riding* **HU15** 58 E6
Newport, *Essex* **CB11** 33 J5
Newport, *Glos.* **GL13** 19 K2
Newport, *High.* **KW7** 105 G6
Newport, *I.o.W.* **PO30** 11 G6
NEWPORT (CASNEWYDD), *Newport* NP 19 G3
Newport, *Norf.* **NR29** 45 K4
Newport, *Pembs.* **SA42** 16 D1
Newport, *Tel. & W.* **TF10** 39 G4
Newport Pagnell **MK16** 32 B4
Newport-on-Tay **DD6** 83 F5
Newpound Common **RH14** 12 D4
Newquay **TR7** 3 F2
Newquay Cornwall Airport **TR8** 3 F2
Newseat **AB51** 91 F1
Newsham, *Lancs.* **PR3** 55 J6
Newsham, *N.Yorks.* **DL11** 62 C5
Newsham, *N.Yorks.* **YO7** 57 J1
Newsham, *Northumb.* **NE24** 71 H6
Newsholme, *E.Riding* **DN14** 58 D7
Newsholme, *Lancs.* **BB7** 56 D4
Newstead, *Northumb.* **NE67** 71 G1
Newstead, *Notts.* **NG15** 51 H7
Newstead, *Sc.Bord.* **TD6** 76 D7
Newthorpe **LS25** 57 K6
Newton, *Aber.* **AB54** 98 C6
Newton, *Aber.* **AB42** 99 J6
Newton, *Arg. & B.* **PA27** 73 J1
Newton, *Bridgend* **CF36** 18 B4
Newton, *Cambs.* **PE13** 43 H4
Newton, *Cambs.* **CB2** 33 H4
Newton, *Ches.* **WA6** 48 E5
Newton, *Ches.* **CH3** 48 D7
Newton, *Cumb.* **LA13** 55 F2
Newton, *D. & G.* **DG10** 69 G4
Newton, *Gt.Man.* **SK14** 49 J3
Newton, *Here.* **SY7** 28 C2
Newton, *High.* **KW1** 105 H3
Newton, *High.* **KW1** 105 J4
Newton, *High.* **IV27** 102 E5
Newton, *High.* **IV11** 96 E5
Newton, *High.* **IV6** 96 C6
Newton, *High.* **IV2** 96 E7
Newton, *Lancs.* **LA6** 55 J2
Newton, *Lancs.* **BB7** 56 B4
Newton, *Lincs.* **NG34** 42 D2
Newton, *Moray* **IV32** 98 B4
Newton, *N.Ayr.* **KA27** 73 H5
Newton, *Norf.* **PE32** 44 C4
Newton, *Northants.* **NN14** 42 B7
Newton, *Northumb.* **NE43** 71 F7
Newton, *Notts.* **NG13** 41 J1
Newton, *P. & K.* **PH8** 81 K4
Newton, *Pembs.* **SA62** 16 C2
Newton, *Pembs.* **SA71** 16 C4
Newton, *S.Lan.* **ML12** 75 H7
Newton, *Sc.Bord.* **TD8** 70 B1
Newton, *Staffs.* **WS15** 40 C3
Newton, *Suff.* **CO10** 34 D4
Newton, *Swan.* **SA3** 17 K6
Newton, *W.Loth.* **EH52** 75 J3
Newton, *W.Yorks.* **WF10** 57 K7
Newton, *Warks.* **CV23** 31 G1
Newton, *Wilts.* **SP5** 10 D2
Newton Abbot **TQ12** 5 J3
Newton Arlosh **CA7** 60 C1
Newton Aycliffe **DL5** 62 D4
Newton Bewley **TS22** 63 F4
Newton Blossomville **MK43** 32 C3
Newton Bromswold **MK44** 32 D2
Newton Burgoland **LE67** 41 F5
Newton by Toft **LN8** 52 D4
Newton Ferrers **PL8** 5 F6
Newton Flotman **NR15** 45 G6
Newton Harcourt **LE8** 41 J6
Newton Kyme **LS24** 57 K5
Newton Longville **MK17** 32 B5
Newton Mearns **G77** 74 D5
Newton Morrell **DL10** 62 D6
Newton Mountain **SA73** 16 C4
Newton Mulgrave **TS13** 63 J5
Newton of Ardtoe **PH36** 86 C7
Newton of Balcanquhal **PH2** 82 C6
Newton of Dalvey **IV36** 97 H6
Newton of Falkland **KY15** 82 D7
Newton of Leys **IV2** 96 D7
Newton on Trent **LN1** 52 B5
Newton Poppleford **EX10** 7 J7
Newton Purcell **MK18** 31 H5
Newton Regis **B79** 40 E5
Newton Reigny **CA11** 61 F3
Newton St. Cyres **EX5** 7 G6
Newton St. Faith **NR10** 45 G4
Newton St. Loe **BA2** 20 A5
Newton St. Petrock **EX22** 6 C4
Newton Solney **DE15** 40 E3
Newton Stacey **SO20** 21 H7
Newton Stewart **DG8** 64 E4
Newton Tony **SP4** 21 F7
Newton Tracey **EX31** 6 D3
Newton under Roseberry **TS9** 63 G5
Newton upon Derwent **YO41** 58 D5
Newton Valence **GU34** 11 J1
Newton-le-Willows, *Mersey.* **WA12** 48 E3
Newton-le-Willows, *N.Yorks.* **DL8** 57 H1
Newton-on-Ouse **YO30** 58 B3
Newton-on-Rawcliffe **YO18** 63 K7
Newton-on-the-Moor **NE65** 71 G3
Newtonairds **DG2** 68 D5
Newtongrange **EH22** 76 B4
Newtonhill **AB39** 91 H5
Newtonmill **DD9** 83 H1
Newtonmore **PH20** 88 E5
Newtown, *Aber.* **AB44** 99 F4
Newtown, *B.Gwent* **NP23** 28 A7
Newtown, *Bucks.* **HP5** 22 C1
Newtown, *Ches.* **CH3** 48 D7
Newtown, *Cumb.* **CA6** 70 A7
Newtown, *Derbys.* **SK23** 49 J4
Newtown, *Hants.* **RG20** 21 H5
Newtown, *Hants.* **SO51** 10 E2
Newtown, *Hants.* **SO32** 11 G3
Newtown, *Hants.* **PO17** 11 H3
Newtown, *Hants.* **SO43** 10 D3
Newtown, *Here.* **HR8** 29 F4
Newtown, *Here.* **HR8** 29 G5
Newtown, *High.* **PH35** 87 K4
Newtown, *I.o.M.* **IM4** 54 C6
Newtown, *I.o.W.* **PO30** 11 F5
Newtown, *Northumb.* **NE66** 71 F1
Newtown, *Northumb.* **NE65** 71 F3
Newtown, *Poole* **BH12** 10 B5
Newtown (Y Drenewydd), *Powys* **SY16** 38 A6
Newtown, *Shrop.* **SY4** 38 D2
Newtown, *Staffs.* **SK17** 50 C6
Newtown, *Staffs.* **ST8** 49 J6
Newtown, *Wilts.* **SP3** 9 J2
Newtown in St. Martin **TR12** 2 E6
Newtown Linford **LE6** 41 H4
Newtown St. Boswells **TD6** 76 D7
Newtown Unthank **LE9** 41 G5
Newtyle **PH12** 82 D3
Neyland **SA73** 16 C4
Nibley, *Glos.* **GL15** 19 K1
Nibley, *S.Glos.* **BS36** 19 K3
Nicholashayne **TA21** 7 K4
Nicholaston **SA3** 17 J6
Nidd **HG3** 57 J3
Niddrie **EH16** 76 A3
Nigg, *Aberdeen* **AB12** 91 H4
Nigg, *High.* **IV19** 97 F4
Nightcott **TA22** 7 G3
Nilig **LL15** 47 J7
Nine Ashes **CM4** 23 J1
Nine Elms **SN5** 20 E3
Nine Mile Burn **EH26** 75 K5
Ninebanks **NE47** 61 J1
Ninemile Bar or Crocketford **DG2** 65 J3
Ninfield **TN33** 14 C6
Ningwood **PO30** 11 F6
Nisbet **TD8** 70 B1
Niton **PO38** 11 G7
Nitshill **G53** 74 D4
Nizels **TN11** 23 J6
No Man's Heath, *Ches.* **SY14** 38 E1
No Man's Heath, *Warks.* **B79** 40 E5
Noak Hill **RM4** 23 J2
Noblehill **DG1** 65 K3
Nobottle **NN7** 31 H2
Nocton **LN4** 52 D6
Noddsdale **KA30** 74 A4
Noke **OX3** 31 G7
Nolton **SA62** 16 B3
Nomansland, *Devon* **EX16** 7 G4
Nomansland, *Wilts.* **SP5** 10 D3
Noneley **SY4** 38 D3
Nonington **CT15** 15 H2
Nook, *Cumb.* **CA6** 69 K6
Nook, *Cumb.* **LA6** 55 J1
Noonsbrough **ZE2** 109 B7
Noranside **DD8** 83 F1
Norbiton **KT2** 22 E5
Norbreck **FY5** 55 G5
Norbury, *Ches.* **SY13** 38 E1
Norbury, *Derbys.* **DE6** 40 D1
Norbury, *Shrop.* **SY9** 38 C6
Norbury, *Staffs.* **ST20** 39 G3
Norchard **DY13** 29 H2
Nordelph **PE38** 43 J5
Norden **BH20** 9 J6
Nordley **WV16** 39 F6
Norham **TD15** 77 H6
Norland Town **HX6** 57 F7
Norley **WA6** 48 E5
Norleywood **SO41** 10 E5
Norman Cross **PE7** 42 E6
Normanby, *N.Lincs.* **DN15** 52 B1
Normanby, *N.Yorks.* **YO62** 58 D1
Normanby, *R. & C.* **TS6** 63 G5
Normanby by Spital **LN8** 52 D4
Normanby by Stow **DN21** 52 B4
Normanby le Wold **LN7** 52 E3
Normandy **GU3** 22 C6
Normann's Ruh **PA74** 79 F3
Norman's Bay **BN24** 13 K6
Norman's Green **EX15** 7 J5
Normanton, *Derby* **DE23** 41 F2
Normanton, *Leics.* **NG13** 42 B1
Normanton, *Lincs.* **NG32** 42 C1
Normanton, *Notts.* **NG25** 51 K7
Normanton, *Rut.* **LE15** 42 C5
Normanton, *W.Yorks.* **WF6** 57 J7
Normanton le Heath **LE67** 41 F4
Normanton on Soar **LE12** 41 H3
Normanton on Trent **NG23** 51 K6
Normanton-on-the-Wolds **NG12** 41 J2
Normoss **FY3** 55 G6
Norrington Common **SN12** 20 B5
Norris Hill **DE12** 41 F4
North Anston **S25** 51 H4
North Ascot **SL5** 22 C5
North Aston **OX25** 31 F6
North Baddesley **SO52** 10 E2
North Ballachulish **PH33** 80 B1
North Balloch **KA26** 67 H4
North Barrow **BA22** 9 F2
North Barsham **NR22** 44 D2
North Benfleet **SS12** 24 D3
North Bersted **PO22** 12 C6
North Berwick **EH39** 76 D2
North Boarhunt **PO17** 11 H3
North Bogbain **AB55** 98 B5
North Bovey **TQ13** 7 F7
North Bradley **BA14** 20 B6
North Brentor **PL19** 6 C7
North Brewham **BA10** 9 G1
North Buckland **EX33** 6 C1
North Burlingham **NR13** 45 H4
North Cadbury **BA22** 9 F2
North Cairn **DG9** 66 D6
North Carlton, *Lincs.* **LN1** 52 C5
North Carlton, *Notts.* **S81** 51 H4
North Cave **HU15** 58 E6
North Cerney **GL7** 20 D1
North Chailey **BN8** 13 G4
North Charford **SP5** 10 D2
North Charlton **NE66** 71 G1
North Cheriton **BA8** 9 F2
North Cliffe **YO43** 58 E6
North Clifton **NG23** 52 B5
North Cockerington **LN11** 53 G3
North Coker **BA22** 8 E3
North Cornelly **CF33** 18 B3
North Cotes **DN36** 53 G2
North Cove **NR34** 45 J7
North Cowton **DL7** 62 D6
North Crawley **MK16** 32 C4
North Cray **DA14** 23 H4
North Creake **NR21** 44 C2
North Curry **TA3** 8 C2
North Dallens **PA38** 80 A3
North Dalton **YO25** 59 F4
North Dawn **KW17** 107 D7
North Deighton **LS22** 57 J4
North Duffield **YO8** 58 C6
North Elkington **LN11** 53 F3
North Elmham **NR20** 44 D3
North Elmsall **WF9** 51 G1
North End, *Bucks.* **LU7** 32 B6
North End, *Essex* **CM6** 33 K7
North End, *Hants.* **RG20** 21 H5
North End, *N.Som.* **BS19** 19 H5
North End, *Norf.* **NR16** 44 E6
North End, *Northumb.* **NE65** 71 G3
North End, *Ports.* **PO2** 11 H4
North End, *W.Suss.* **BN14** 12 E5
North Erradale **IV21** 94 D3
North Essie **AB42** 99 J5
North Ferriby **HU14** 59 F7
North Frodingham **YO25** 59 H4
North Gorley **SP6** 10 C3
North Green **IP21** 45 G7
North Grimston **YO17** 58 E3
North Hayling **PO11** 11 J4
North Hazelrigg **NE66** 77 J7
North Heasley **EX36** 7 F2
North Heath **RH20** 12 D4
North Hill **PL15** 4 C3
North Hinksey **OX2** 21 H1
North Holmwood **RH5** 22 E7
North Huish **TQ10** 5 H5
North Hykeham **LN6** 52 C6
North Johnston **SA62** 16 C3
North Kelsey **LN7** 52 D2
North Kessock **IV1** 96 D7
North Killingholme **DN40** 52 E1
North Kilvington **YO7** 57 K1
North Kilworth **LE17** 41 J7
North Kyme **LN4** 52 E7
North Lancing **BN15** 12 E6
North Lee **HP22** 22 B1
North Leigh **OX29** 30 E7
North Leverton with Habblesthorpe **DN22** 51 K4
North Littleton **WR11** 30 B4
North Lopham **IP22** 44 E7
North Luffenham **LE15** 42 C5
North Marden **PO18** 12 B5
North Marston **MK18** 31 J6
North Middleton **EH23** 76 B5
North Millbrex **AB53** 99 G6
North Molton **EX36** 7 F3
North Moreton **OX11** 21 J3
North Mundham **PO20** 12 B6
North Muskham **NG23** 51 K7
North Newbald **YO43** 59 F6
North Newington **OX15** 31 F5
North Newnton **SN9** 20 E6
North Newton **TA7** 8 B1
North Nibley **GL11** 20 A2
North Oakley **RG26** 21 J6
North Ockendon **RM14** 23 J3
North Ormesby **TS3** 63 G4
North Ormsby **LN11** 53 F3
North Otterington **DL7** 62 E7
North Owersby **LN8** 52 D3
North Perrott **TA18** 8 D4
North Petherton **TA6** 8 B1
North Petherwin **PL15** 4 C2
North Pickenham **PE37** 44 C5
North Piddle **WR7** 29 J3
North Poorton **DT6** 8 E5
North Queensferry **KY11** 75 K2
North Radworthy **EX36** 7 F2
North Rauceby **NG34** 42 D1
North Reston **LN11** 53 G4
North Rigton **LS17** 57 H5
North Rode **CW12** 49 H6
North Roe **ZE2** 108 C4
North Runcton **PE33** 44 A4
North Sandwick **ZE2** 108 E3
North Scale **LA14** 54 E3
North Scarle **LN6** 52 B6
North Seaton **NE63** 71 H5
North Shian **PA38** 80 A3
North Shields **NE30** 71 J7
North Shoebury **SS3** 25 F3
North Side **PE6** 43 F6
North Skelton **TS12** 63 H5
North Somercotes **LN11** 53 H3
North Stainley **HG4** 57 H2
North Stainmore **CA17** 61 K5
North Stifford **RM16** 24 C3
North Stoke, *B. & N.E.Som.* **BS30** 19 K5
North Stoke, *Oxon.* **OX10** 21 K3
North Stoke, *W.Suss.* **BN18** 12 D5
North Stoneham **SO50** 11 F3
North Street, *Hants.* **SO24** 11 H1
North Street, *Kent* **ME13** 15 F2
North Street, *W.Berks.* **RG7** 21 K4
North Sunderland **NE68** 77 K6
North Tamerton **EX22** 6 B6
North Tarbothill **AB23** 91 H3
North Tawton **EX20** 6 E5
North Third **FK7** 75 F2
North Thoresby **DN36** 53 F3
North Tidworth **SP9** 21 F7
North Togston **NE65** 71 H3
North Town, *Devon* **EX20** 6 D5
North Town, *Hants.* **GU12** 22 B6
North Tuddenham **NR20** 44 E4
North Walsham **NR28** 45 G2
North Waltham **RG25** 21 J7
North Warnborough **RG29** 22 A6
North Watten **KW1** 105 H3
North Weald Bassett **CM16** 23 H1
North Wheatley **DN22** 51 K4
North Whilborough **TQ12** 5 J4
North Wick **BS41** 19 J5
North Widcombe **BS40** 19 J6
North Willingham **LN8** 52 E4
North Wingfield **S42** 51 G6
North Witham **NG33** 42 C3
North Wootton, *Dorset* **DT9** 9 F3
North Wootton, *Norf.* **PE30** 44 A3
North Wootton, *Som.* **BA4** 19 J7
North Wraxall **SN14** 20 B4
North Wroughton **SN4** 20 E3
North Yardhope **NE65** 70 E3
Northacre **NR17** 44 D6
Northall Green **NR20** 44 E4
Northallerton **DL6** 62 E7
Northam, *Devon* **EX39** 6 C3
Northam, *S'ham.* **SO14** 11 F3
NORTHAMPTON NN 31 J2
Northaw **EN6** 23 F1
Northay **TA20** 8 B3
Northborough **PE6** 42 E5
Northbourne **CT14** 15 J2
Northbrook **OX5** 31 F6
Northburnhill **AB53** 99 G6
Northchapel **GU28** 12 C4
Northchurch **HP4** 22 C1
Northcote Manor **EX37** 6 E4
Northcott **PL15** 6 B6
Northdyke **KW16** 106 B5
Northend, *B. & N.E.Som.* **BA1** 20 A5
Northend, *Bucks.* **HP14** 22 A2
Northend, *Warks.* **CV47** 30 E3
Northfield, *Aber.* **AB45** 99 G4
Northfield, *Aberdeen* **AB16** 91 G4
Northfield, *High.* **KW1** 105 J4
Northfield, *Sc.Bord.* **TD14** 77 H4
Northfield, *W.Mid.* **B31** 30 B1
Northfleet **DA10** 24 C4
Northhouse **TD9** 69 K3
Northiam **TN31** 14 D5
Northill **SG18** 32 E4
Northington **SO24** 11 G1
Northlands **PE22** 53 G7
Northleach **GL54** 30 C7
Northleigh, *Devon* **EX32** 6 E2
Northleigh, *Devon* **EX24** 7 K6
Northlew **EX20** 6 D6
Northmoor **OX29** 21 H1
Northmoor Green or Moorland **TA7** 8 C1
Northmuir **DD8** 82 E2
Northney **PO11** 11 J4
Northolt **UB5** 22 E3
Northop **CH7** 48 B6
Northop Hall **CH7** 48 B6
Northorpe, *Lincs.* **DN21** 52 B3
Northorpe, *Lincs.* **PE11** 43 F2
Northorpe, *Lincs.* **PE10** 42 D4
Northover **BA22** 8 E2
Northowram **HX3** 57 G7
Northpunds **ZE2** 109 D10
Northrepps **NR27** 45 G2
Northton (Taobh Tuath) **HS3** 92 E3
Northtown **KW17** 107 D8
Northway **GL20** 29 J5
Northwich **CW8** 49 F5
Northwick **BS35** 19 J3
Northwold **IP26** 44 B6
Northwood, *Gt.Lon.* **HA6** 22 D2
Northwood, *I.o.W.* **PO31** 11 F5
Northwood, *Shrop.* **SY4** 38 D2
Northwood Green **GL14** 29 G7
Norton, *Glos.* **GL2** 29 H6
Norton, *Halton* **WA7** 48 E4
Norton, *Herts.* **SG6** 33 F5
Norton, *I.o.W.* **PO41** 10 E6
Norton, *N.Yorks.* **YO17** 58 D2
Norton, *Northants.* **NN11** 31 H2
Norton, *Notts.* **NG20** 51 H5
Norton, *Powys* **LD8** 28 C2
Norton, *S.Yorks.* **DN6** 51 H1
Norton, *S.Yorks.* **S8** 51 F4
Norton, *Shrop.* **SY4** 38 E5
Norton, *Shrop.* **TF11** 39 G5
Norton, *Shrop.* **SY7** 38 D7
Norton, *Stock.* **TS20** 63 F4
Norton, *Suff.* **IP31** 34 D2
Norton, *W.Mid.* **DY8** 40 A7
Norton, *W.Suss.* **PO20** 12 C6
Norton, *W.Suss.* **PO20** 12 B7
Norton, *Wilts.* **SN16** 20 B3
Norton, *Worcs.* **WR5** 29 H3
Norton, *Worcs.* **WR11** 30 B4
Norton Bavant **BA12** 20 C7
Norton Bridge **ST15** 40 A3
Norton Canes **WS11** 40 C5
Norton Canon **HR4** 28 C4
Norton Disney **LN6** 52 B7
Norton Ferris **BA12** 9 G1
Norton Fitzwarren **TA2** 7 K3
Norton Green **PO40** 10 E6
Norton Hawkfield **BS40** 19 J5
Norton Heath **CM4** 24 C1
Norton in Hales **TF9** 39 F2
Norton in the Moors **ST6** 49 H7
Norton Lindsey **CV35** 30 D2
Norton Malreward **BS39** 19 J5
Norton Mandeville **CM5** 23 J1
Norton St. Philip **BA2** 20 A6
Norton sub Hamdon **TA14** 8 D3
Norton Subcourse **NR14** 45 J6
Norton Wood **HR4** 28 C4
Norton-Juxta-Twycross **CV9** 41 F5
Norton-le-Clay **YO61** 57 J2
Norwell **NG23** 51 K6
Norwell Woodhouse **NG23** 51 K6
NORWICH NR 45 G5
Norwich Airport **NR6** 45 G4
Norwick **ZE2** 108 F1

Norwood Green

Norwood Green **UB2** 22 E4
Norwood Hill **RH6** 23 F7
Noseley **LE7** 42 A6
Noss Mayo **PL8** 5 F6
Nosterfield **DL8** 57 H1
Nostie **IV40** 86 E2
Notgrove **GL54** 30 C6
Nottage **CF36** 18 B4
Nottingham, *High.* **KW5** 105 H5
NOTTINGHAM, *Nott.* NG **41** **H1**
Notton, *W.Yorks.* **WF4** 51 F1
Notton, *Wilts.* **SN15** 20 C5
Nounsley **CM3** 24 D1
Noutard's Green **WR6** 29 G2
Nowton **IP29** 34 C2
Nox **SY5** 38 D4
Noyadd Trefawr **SA43** 26 B4
Nuffield **RG9** 21 K3
Nun Monkton **YO26** 58 B4
Nunburnholme **YO42** 58 E5
Nuneaton **CV11** 41 F6
Nuneham Courtenay **OX44** 21 J2
Nunney **BA11** 20 A7
Nunnington **YO62** 58 C2
Nunnington Park **TA4** 7 J3
Nunthorpe **TS7** 63 G5
Nunton **SP5** 10 C2
Nunwick, *N.Yorks.* **HG4** 57 J2
Nunwick, *Northumb.* **NE48** 70 D6
Nup End, *Bucks.* **HP22** 32 B7
Nup End, *Glos.* **GL19** 29 H6
Nursling **SO16** 10 E3
Nursted **GU31** 11 J2
Nurton **WV6** 40 A6
Nutbourne, *W.Suss.* **RH20** 12 D5
Nutbourne, *W.Suss.* **PO18** 11 J4
Nutfield **RH1** 23 G6
Nuthall **NG16** 41 H1
Nuthampstead **SG8** 33 H5
Nuthurst, *W.Suss.* **RH13** 12 E4
Nuthurst, *Warks.* **B94** 30 C1
Nutley, *E.Suss.* **TN22** 13 H4
Nutley, *Hants.* **RG25** 21 K7
Nutwell **DN3** 51 J2
Nyadd **FK9** 75 F1
Nybster **KW1** 105 J2
Nyetimber **PO21** 12 B7
Nyewood **GU31** 12 B4
Nymet Rowland **EX17** 7 F5
Nymet Tracey **EX17** 7 F5
Nympsfield **GL10** 20 B1
Nynehead **TA21** 7 K3
Nythe **TA7** 8 D1
Nyton **PO20** 12 C6

O

Oad Street **ME9** 24 E5
Oadby **LE2** 41 J5
Oak Cross **EX20** 6 D6
Oakamoor **ST10** 40 C1
Oakbank, *Arg. & B.* **PA64** 79 J4
Oakbank, *W.Loth.* **EH53** 75 J4
Oakdale **NP12** 18 E2
Oake **TA4** 7 K3
Oaken **WV8** 40 A5
Oakenclough **PR3** 55 J5
Oakengates **TF2** 39 F4
Oakenhead **IV31** 97 K5
Oakenshaw, *Dur.* **DL15** 62 D3
Oakenshaw, *W.Yorks.* **BD12** 57 G7
Oakford, *Cere.* **SA47** 26 D3
Oakford, *Devon* **EX16** 7 H3
Oakfordbridge **EX16** 7 H3
Oakgrove **SK11** 49 J6
Oakham **LE15** 42 B5
Oakhanger **GU35** 11 J1
Oakhill **BA3** 19 K7
Oakington **CB4** 33 H2
Oaklands, *Conwy* **LL26** 47 G7
Oaklands, *Herts.* **AL6** 33 F7
Oakle Street **GL2** 29 G7
Oakley, *Beds.* **MK43** 32 D3
Oakley, *Bucks.* **HP18** 31 H7
Oakley, *Fife* **KY12** 75 J2
Oakley, *Hants.* **RG23** 21 J6
Oakley, *Suff.* **IP21** 35 F1
Oakley Green **SL4** 22 C4
Oakley Park **SY17** 37 J7
Oakridge **GL6** 20 C1
Oaks **SY5** 38 D5
Oaksey **SN16** 20 C2
Oakshaw Ford **CA6** 70 A6
Oakthorpe **DE12** 41 F4
Oaktree Hill **DL6** 62 E7
Oakwoodhill **RH5** 12 E3
Oakworth **BD22** 57 F6
Oalinlongart **PA23** 73 K2
Oare, *Kent* **ME13** 25 G5
Oare, *Som.* **EX35** 7 G1
Oare, *Wilts.* **SN8** 20 E5
Oasby **NG32** 42 D2
Oatfield **PA28** 66 A2
Oathlaw **DD8** 83 F2
Oban **PA34** 79 K5
Obley **SY7** 28 C1
Oborne **DT9** 9 F3
Occlestone Green **CW10** 49 F6
Occold **IP23** 35 F1
Occumster **KW3** 105 H5
Ochiltree **KA18** 67 K1
Ochr-y-Mynydd **CF48** 18 D1
Ochtermuthill **PH5** 81 K6
Ochtertyre, *P. & K.* **PH7** 81 K5
Ochtertyre, *Stir.* **FK9** 75 F1
Ockbrook **DE72** 41 G2
Ockham **GU23** 22 D6
Ockle **PH36** 86 B7
Ockley **RH5** 12 E3
Ocle Pychard **HR1** 28 E4
Octon **YO25** 59 G3
Odcombe **BA22** 8 E3
Odd Down **BA2** 20 A5
Oddingley **WR9** 29 J3
Oddington **OX5** 31 G7
Oddsta **ZE2** 108 E3
Odell **MK43** 32 C3
Odie **KW17** 106 F5
Odiham **RG29** 22 A6
Odstock **SP5** 10 C2
Odstone **CV13** 41 F5
Offchurch **CV33** 30 E2
Offenham **WR11** 30 B4
Offerton **SK2** 49 J4
Offham, *E.Suss.* **BN8** 13 H5
Offham, *Kent* **ME19** 23 K6
Offord Cluny **PE19** 33 F2
Offord D'Arcy **PE19** 33 F2
Offton **IP8** 34 E4
Offwell **EX14** 7 K6
Ogbourne Maizey **SN8** 20 E4
Ogbourne St. Andrew **SN8** 20 E4
Ogbourne St. George **SN8** 20 E4
Ogden **HX2** 57 F6
Ogil **DD8** 83 F1
Ogle **NE20** 71 G6
Ogmore **CF32** 18 B4
Ogmore Vale **CF32** 18 C2
Ogmore-by-Sea **CF32** 18 B4
Oil Terminal **KW16** 107 C8
Okeford Fitzpaine **DT11** 9 H3
Okehampton **EX20** 6 D6
Okehampton Camp **EX20** 6 D6
Okraquoy **ZE2** 109 D9
Old **NN6** 31 J1
Old Aberdeen **AB24** 91 H4
Old Alresford **SO24** 11 G1
Old Arley **CV7** 40 E6
Old Basford **NG6** 41 H1
Old Basing **RG24** 21 K6
Old Belses **TD6** 70 A1
Old Bewick **NE66** 71 F1
Old Bolingbroke **PE23** 53 G6
Old Brampton **S42** 51 F5
Old Bridge of Urr **DG7** 65 H4
Old Buckenham **NR17** 44 E6
Old Burghclere **RG20** 21 H6
Old Byland **YO62** 58 B1
Old Cleeve **TA24** 7 J1
Old Colwyn **LL29** 47 G5
Old Craig **AB41** 91 H2
Old Craighall **EH22** 76 B3
Old Crombie **AB54** 98 D5
Old Dailly **KA26** 67 G4
Old Dalby **LE14** 41 J3
Old Deer **AB42** 99 H6
Old Ellerby **HU11** 59 H6
Old Felixstowe **IP11** 35 H5
Old Fletton **PE2** 42 E6
Old Glossop **SK13** 50 C3
Old Goginan **SY23** 37 F7
Old Goole **DN14** 58 D7
Old Gore **HR9** 29 F6
Old Grimsby **TR24** 2 B1
Old Hall **HU12** 53 F1
Old Heath **CO2** 34 E6
Old Hill **B64** 40 B7
Old Hutton **LA8** 55 J1
Old Kea **TR3** 3 F4
Old Kilpatrick **G60** 74 C3
Old Kinnernie **AB32** 91 F4
Old Knebworth **SG3** 33 F6
Old Leake **PE22** 53 H7
Old Leslie **AB52** 90 D2
Old Malton **YO17** 58 D2
Old Micklefield **LS25** 57 K6
Old Milverton **CV32** 30 D2
Old Netley **SO31** 11 F3
Old Newton **IP14** 34 E2
Old Philpstoun **EH49** 75 J3
Old Poltalloch **PA31** 79 K7
Old Portlethen **AB12** 91 H5
Old Radnor **LD8** 28 B3
Old Rattray **AB42** 99 J5
Old Rayne **AB52** 90 E2
Old Romney **TN29** 15 F5
Old Scone **PH2** 82 C5
Old Shields **G67** 75 G3
Old Sodbury **BS37** 20 A3
Old Somerby **NG33** 42 C2
Old Stratford **MK19** 31 J4
Old Sunderlandwick **YO25** 59 G4
Old Swarland **NE65** 71 G3
Old Swinford **DY8** 40 B7
Old Town, *Cumb.* **LA6** 55 J1
Old Town, *I.o.S.* **TR21** 2 C1
Old Town, *Northumb.* **NE19** 70 D4
Old Tupton **S42** 51 F6
Old Warden **SG18** 32 E4
Old Weston **PE28** 32 E1
Old Windsor **SL4** 22 C4
Old Wives Lees **CT4** 15 F2
Old Woking **GU22** 22 D6
Old Wolverton **MK12** 32 B4
Old Woods **SY4** 38 D3
Oldberrow **B95** 30 C2
Oldborough **EX17** 7 F5
Oldbury, *Kent* **TN15** 23 J6
Oldbury, *Shrop.* **WV16** 39 G6
Oldbury, *W.Mid.* **B69** 40 B6
Oldbury, *Warks.* **CV10** 41 F6
Oldbury Naite **BS35** 19 K2
Oldbury on the Hill **GL9** 20 B3
Oldbury-on-Severn **BS35** 19 K2
Oldcastle **NP7** 28 C6
Oldcastle Heath **SY14** 38 D1
Oldcotes **S81** 51 H4
Oldfield, *W.Yorks.* **BD22** 57 F6
Oldfield, *Worcs.* **WR9** 29 H2
Oldford **BA11** 20 A6
Oldhall, *Aber.* **AB34** 90 C5
Oldhall, *High.* **KW1** 105 H3
OLDHAM OL **49** **J2**
Oldhamstocks **TD13** 77 F3
Oldhurst **PE28** 33 F1
Oldland **BS30** 19 K4
Oldmeldrum **AB51** 91 G2
Oldmill **AB31** 90 D4
Oldpark **TF3** 39 F5
Oldridge **EX6** 7 G6
Oldshore Beg **IV27** 102 D3
Oldshore More **IV27** 102 E3
Oldstead **YO61** 58 B1
Oldtown of Aigas **IV4** 96 B7
Oldtown of Ord **AB45** 98 E5
Oldwalls **SA3** 17 H5
Oldways End **EX16** 7 G3
Oldwhat **AB53** 99 G5
Olgrinmore **KW12** 105 F3
Oliver **ML12** 69 G1
Oliver's Battery **SO22** 11 F2
Ollaberry **ZE2** 108 C4
Ollerton, *Ches.* **WA16** 49 G5
Ollerton, *Notts.* **NG22** 51 J6
Ollerton, *Shrop.* **TF9** 39 F3
Olmstead Green **CB1** 33 K4
Olney, *M.K.* **MK46** 32 B3
Olney, *Northants.* **NN12** 31 H4
Olrig House **KW14** 105 G2
Olton **B92** 40 D7
Olveston **BS35** 19 J3
Ombersley **WR9** 29 H2
Ompton **NG22** 51 J6
Onchan **IM3** 54 C6
Onecote **ST13** 50 C7
Ongar Hill **PE34** 43 J3
Ongar Street **HR6** 28 C2
Onibury **SY7** 28 D1
Onich **PH33** 80 B1
Onllwyn **SA10** 27 H7
Onneley **CW3** 39 G1
Onslow Village **GU2** 22 C7
Opinan, *High.* **IV22** 94 E2
Opinan, *High.* **IV21** 94 D4
Orange Lane **TD12** 77 F6
Orbliston **IV32** 98 B5
Orbost **IV55** 93 H7
Orby **PE24** 53 H6
Orcadia **PA20** 73 K4
Orchard **PA23** 73 K2
Orchard Portman **TA3** 8 B2
Orchard Wyndham **TA4** 7 J2
Orcheston **SP3** 20 D7
Orcop **HR2** 28 D6
Orcop Hill **HR2** 28 D6
Ord **IV46** 86 C3
Ordhead **AB51** 90 E3
Ordie **AB34** 90 C4
Ordiequish **IV32** 98 B5
Ordsall **DN22** 51 K5
Ore **TN35** 14 D6
Oreham Common **BN5** 13 F5
Oreston **PL9** 5 F5
Oreton **DY14** 39 F7
Orford, *Suff.* **IP12** 35 J4
Orford, *Warr.* **WA2** 49 F3
Orgreave **DE13** 40 D4
Orleton, *Here.* **SY8** 28 D2
Orleton, *Worcs.* **WR6** 29 F2
Orleton Common **SY8** 28 D2
Orlingbury **NN14** 32 B1
Ormacleit **HS8** 84 C1
Ormesby **TS3** 63 G5
Ormesby St. Margaret **NR29** 45 J4
Ormesby St. Michael **NR29** 45 J4
Ormiscaig **IV22** 94 E2
Ormiston **EH35** 76 C4
Ormsaigmore **PH36** 79 F1
Ormsdale **PA22** 73 J2
Ormskirk **L39** 48 D2
Ormwe **KW14** 105 G2
Orphir **KW17** 107 C7
Orpington **BR6** 23 H5
Orrell **WN5** 48 E2
Orrisdale **IM6** 54 C4
Orrok Ho. **AB23** 91 H3
Orroland **DG6** 65 H6
Orsett **RM16** 24 C3
Orslow **TF10** 40 A4
Orston **NG13** 42 A1
Orton, *Cumb.* **CA10** 61 H6
Orton, *Northants.* **NN14** 32 B1
Orton Longueville **PE2** 42 E6
Orton Waterville **PE2** 42 E6
Orton-on-the-Hill **CV9** 41 F5
Orwell **SG8** 33 G4
Osbaldeston **BB2** 56 B6
Osbaldwick **YO10** 58 C4
Osbaston, *Leics.* **CV13** 41 G5
Osbaston, *Tel. & W.* **TF6** 38 E4
Osborne **PO32** 11 G5
Osbournby **NG34** 42 D2
Oscroft **CH3** 48 E6
Ose **IV56** 93 J7
Osgathorpe **LE12** 41 G4
Osgodby, *Lincs.* **LN8** 52 D3
Osgodby, *N.Yorks.* **YO11** 59 G1
Osgodby, *N.Yorks.* **YO8** 58 C6
Oskaig **IV40** 86 B1
Osmaston, *Derby* **DE24** 41 F2
Osmaston, *Derbys.* **DE6** 40 D1
Osmington **DT3** 9 G6
Osmington Mills **DT3** 9 G6
Osmotherley **DL6** 63 F7
Osnaburgh or Dairsie **KY15** 83 F6
Osney **OX2** 21 J1
Ospringe **ME13** 15 F2
Ossett **WF5** 57 H7
Ossington **NG23** 51 K6
Ostend **CM0** 25 F2
Osterley **TW7** 22 E4
Oswaldkirk **YO62** 58 C2
Oswaldtwistle **BB5** 56 C7
Oswestry **SY11** 38 B3
Otford **TN14** 23 J6
Otham **ME15** 14 C2
Othery **TA7** 8 C1
Otley, *Suff.* **IP6** 35 G3
Otley, *W.Yorks.* **LS21** 57 H5
Otter **PA21** 73 H3
Otter Ferry **PA21** 73 H2
Otterbourne **SO21** 11 F2
Otterburn, *N.Yorks.* **BD23** 56 D4
Otterburn, *Northumb.* **NE19** 70 D4
Otterburn Camp **NE19** 70 D4
Otterden Place **ME13** 14 E2
Otterham **PL32** 4 B1
Otterhampton **TA5** 19 F7
Ottershaw **KT16** 22 D5
Otterswick **ZE2** 108 E4
Otterton **EX9** 7 J7
Ottery St. Mary **EX11** 7 J6
Ottinge **CT4** 15 G3
Ottringham **HU12** 59 J7
Oughterby **CA5** 60 D1
Oughtershaw **BD23** 56 D1
Oughtibridge **S35** 51 F3
Oulston **YO61** 58 B2
Oulton, *Cumb.* **CA7** 60 D1
Oulton, *Norf.* **NR11** 45 F3
Oulton, *Staffs.* **ST15** 40 B2
Oulton, *Suff.* **NR32** 45 K6
Oulton, *W.Yorks.* **LS26** 57 J7
Oulton Broad **NR33** 45 K6
Oulton Street **NR11** 45 F3
Oundle **PE8** 42 D7
Ousby **CA10** 61 H3
Ousdale **KW7** 105 F6
Ousden **CB8** 34 B3
Ousefleet **DN14** 58 E7
Ouston, *Dur.* **DH2** 62 D1
Ouston, *Northumb.* **NE18** 71 F6
Out Newton **HU19** 59 K7
Out Rawcliffe **PR3** 55 H5
Outertown **KW16** 107 B6
Outgate **LA22** 60 E7
Outhgill **CA17** 61 J6
Outlands **ST20** 39 G3
Outlane **HD3** 50 C1
Outwell **PE14** 43 J5
Outwood, *Surr.* **RH1** 23 G7
Outwood, *W.Yorks.* **WF1** 57 J7
Ovenden **HX2** 57 F7
Over, *Cambs.* **CB4** 33 G2
Over, *Ches.* **CW7** 49 F6
Over, *S.Glos.* **BS32** 19 J3
Over Compton **DT9** 8 E3
Over End **DE45** 50 E5
Over Haddon **DE45** 50 E6
Over Kellet **LA6** 55 J2
Over Kiddington **OX20** 31 F6
Over Norton **OX7** 30 E6
Over Peover **WA16** 49 G5
Over Rankeilour **KY15** 82 E6
Over Silton **YO7** 63 F7
Over Stowey **TA5** 7 K2
Over Stratton **TA13** 8 D3
Over Tabley **WA16** 49 G4
Over Wallop **SO20** 10 D1
Over Whitacre **B46** 40 E6
Over Worton **OX7** 31 F6
Overbister **KW17** 106 F3
Overbrae **AB53** 99 G5
Overbury **GL20** 29 J5
Overcombe **DT3** 9 F6
Overleigh **BA16** 8 D1
Overpool **CH66** 48 C5
Overscaig Hotel **IV27** 103 G6
Overseal **DE12** 40 E4
Oversland **ME13** 15 F2
Oversley Green **B49** 30 B3
Overstone **NN6** 32 B2
Overstrand **NR27** 45 G1
Overton, *Aber.* **AB51** 91 F3
Overton, *Aberdeen* **AB21** 91 G3
Overton, *Hants.* **RG25** 21 J7
Overton, *Lancs.* **LA3** 55 H4
Overton, *N.Yorks.* **YO30** 58 B4
Overton, *Shrop.* **SY8** 28 E1
Overton, *Swan.* **SA3** 17 H6
Overton, *Wrex.* **LL13** 38 C1
Overtown **ML2** 75 G5
Overy Staithe **PE31** 44 C1
Oving, *Bucks.* **HP22** 31 J6
Oving, *W.Suss.* **PO20** 12 C6
Ovingdean **BN2** 13 G6
Ovingham **NE42** 71 F7
Ovington, *Dur.* **DL11** 62 C5
Ovington, *Essex* **CO10** 34 B4
Ovington, *Hants.* **SO24** 11 G1
Ovington, *Norf.* **IP25** 44 D5
Ovington, *Northumb.* **NE42** 71 F7
Ower **SO51** 10 E3
Owermoigne **DT2** 9 G6
Owlswick **HP27** 22 A1
Owmby **DN38** 52 D2
Owmby by Spital **LN8** 52 D4
Owslebury **SO21** 11 G2
Owston **LE15** 42 A5
Owston Ferry **DN9** 52 B2
Owstwick **HU12** 59 J6
Owthorpe **NG12** 41 J2
Oxborough **PE33** 44 B5
Oxcliffe Hill **LA3** 55 H3
Oxcombe **LN9** 53 G5
Oxen End **CM7** 33 K6
Oxen Park **LA12** 55 G1
Oxenholme **LA9** 61 G7
Oxenhope **BD22** 57 F6
Oxenton **GL52** 29 J5
Oxenwood **SN8** 21 G6
OXFORD OX **21** **J1**
Oxhill **CV35** 30 E4
Oxley **WV10** 40 B5
Oxley Green **CM9** 34 D7
Oxley's Green **TN32** 13 K4
Oxnam **TD8** 70 B2
Oxnead **NR10** 45 G3
Oxnop Ghyll **DL8** 62 A7
Oxshott **KT22** 22 E5
Oxspring **S36** 50 E2
Oxted **RH8** 23 G6
Oxton, *Mersey.* **CH43** 48 C4
Oxton, *Notts.* **NG25** 51 J7
Oxton, *Sc.Bord.* **TD2** 76 C5
Oxwich **SA3** 17 J6
Oxwich Green **SA3** 17 J6
Oxwick **NR21** 44 D3
Oykel Bridge **IV27** 95 K1
Oyne **AB52** 90 E2
Ozleworth **GL12** 20 A2

P

Pabail Iarach **HS2** 101 H4
Pabail Uarach **HS2** 101 H4
Packington **LE65** 41 F4
Padanaram **DD8** 83 F2
Padbury **MK18** 31 J5
Paddington **W2** 23 F3
Paddlesworth **CT18** 15 G3
Paddock Wood **TN12** 23 K7
Paddockhaugh **IV30** 97 K6
Paddockhole **DG11** 69 H5
Paddolgreen **SY4** 38 E2
Padeswood **CH7** 48 B6
Padiham **BB12** 56 C6
Padside **HG3** 57 G4
Padstow **PL28** 3 G1
Padworth **RG7** 21 K5
Pagham **PO21** 12 B7
Paglesham Churchend **SS4** 25 F2
Paglesham Eastend **SS4** 25 F2
Paibeil **HS6** 92 C5
Paible **HS3** 93 F2
Paignton **TQ3** 5 J4
Pailton **CV23** 41 G7
Painscastle **LD2** 28 A4
Painshawfield **NE43** 71 F7
Painswick **GL6** 20 B1
PAISLEY PA **74** **C4**
Pakefield **NR33** 45 K6
Pakenham **IP31** 34 D2
Pale **LL23** 37 J2
Palestine **SP11** 21 F7
Paley Street **SL6** 22 B4
Palgowan **DG8** 67 H5
Palgrave **IP22** 35 F1
Pallinsburn House **TD12** 77 G7
Palmerscross **IV30** 97 K5
Palmerstown **CF63** 18 E5
Palnackie **DG7** 65 J5
Palnure **DG8** 64 E4
Palterton **S44** 51 G6
Pamber End **RG26** 21 K6
Pamber Green **RG26** 21 K6
Pamber Heath **RG26** 21 K5
Pamington **GL20** 29 J5
Pamphill **BH21** 9 J4
Pampisford **CB2** 33 H4
Pan **KW16** 107 C8
Panborough **BA5** 19 H7
Panbride **DD7** 83 G4
Pancrasweek **EX22** 6 A5
Pandy, *Gwyn.* **LL36** 37 F5
Pandy, *Mon.* **NP7** 28 C6
Pandy, *Powys* **SY19** 37 J5
Pandy, *Wrex.* **LL20** 38 A2
Pandy Tudur **LL22** 47 G6
Panfield **CM7** 34 B6
Pangbourne **RG8** 21 K4
Pannal **HG3** 57 J4
Panpunton **LD7** 28 B1
Pant, *Shrop.* **SY10** 38 B3
Pant, *Wrex.* **LL14** 38 B1
Pant Gwyn **LL40** 37 H3

Pityme

Pant Mawr SY18 37 H7
Pant-glas LL54 36 D1
Pant-lasau SA6 17 K4
Pant-pastynog LL16 47 J6
Pant-y-dwr LD6 27 J1
Pant-y-ffridd SY21 38 A5
Pantasaph CH8 47 K5
Pantglas SY20 37 G6
Pantgwyn SA43 26 B4
Panton LN8 52 E5
Pantperthog SY20 37 G5
Pantyffordd CH7 48 B7
Pantyffynnon SA18 17 K3
Panxworth NR13 45 H4
Papcastle CA13 60 C3
Papple EH41 76 D3
Papplewick NG15 51 H7
Papworth Everard CB3 33 F2
Papworth St. Agnes CB3 33 F2
Par PL24 4 A5
Parbold WN8 48 D1
Parbrook BA6 8 E1
Parc LL23 37 H2
Parcllyn SA43 26 B3
Parcrhydderch SY25 27 F3
Pardshaw CA13 60 B4
Parham IP13 35 H2
Parish Holm ML11 68 C1
Park AB45 98 D5
Park Corner RG9 21 K3
Park End NE48 70 D6
Park Gate SO31 11 G4
Park Lane LL13 38 D2
Park Street AL2 22 E1
Parkend, Cumb. CA7 60 D3
Parkend, Glos. GL15 19 K1
Parkeston CO12 35 G5
Parkford DD8 83 F2
Parkgate, Ches. CH64 48 B5
Parkgate, D. & G. DG1 69 F5
Parkgate, S.Yorks. S62 51 G3
Parkgate, Surr. RH5 23 F7
Parkham EX39 6 B3
Parkham Ash EX39 6 B3
Parkhill, Angus DD11 83 H3
Parkhill, P. & K. PH10 82 C3
Parkhouse NP25 19 J1
Parkhurst PO30 11 F5
Parkmill SA3 17 J6
Parkmore AB55 98 B6
Parkneuk AB30 91 F7
Parkstone BH14 10 B5
Parley Cross BH22 10 B5
Parracombe EX31 6 E1
Parrog SA42 16 D1
Parson Drove PE13 43 G5
Parsonby CA7 60 C3
Partick G11 74 D4
Partington M31 49 G3
Partney PE23 53 H6
Parton, Cumb. CA28 60 A4
Parton, D. & G. DG7 65 G3
Partridge Green RH13 12 E5
Parwich DE6 50 D7
Passenham MK19 31 J5
Passfield GU30 12 B3
Passingford Bridge RM4 23 H2
Paston NR28 45 H2
Patcham BN1 13 G6
Patching BN13 12 D6
Patchole EX31 6 E1
Patchway BS34 19 J3
Pateley Bridge HG3 57 G3
Path of Condie PH2 82 B6
Pathe TA7 8 C1
Pathfinder Village EX6 7 G6
Pathhead, Aber. DD10 83 J1
Pathhead, E.Ayr. KA18 68 B2
Pathhead, Fife KY1 76 A1
Pathhead, Midloth. EH37 76 B4
Patmore Heath SG11 33 H6
Patna KA6 67 J2
Patney SN10 20 D6
Patrick IM5 54 B5
Patrick Brompton DL8 62 D7
Patrington HU12 59 K7
Patrishow NP7 28 B6
Patrixbourne CT4 15 G2
Patterdale CA11 60 E5
Pattingham WV6 40 A6
Pattishall NN12 31 H3
Pattiswick CM7 34 C6
Paul TR19 2 B6
Paulerspury NN12 31 J4
Paull HU12 59 H7
Paulton BS39 19 K6
Pauperhaugh NE65 71 G4
Pavenham MK43 32 C3
Pawlett TA6 19 F7
Pawston TD12 77 G7
Paxford GL55 30 C5
Paxhill Park RH16 13 G4
Paxton TD15 77 H5
Payhembury EX14 7 J5
Paynes Hall SG12 33 G7
Paythorne BB7 56 D4
Peacehaven BN10 13 H6
Peacemarsh SP8 9 H2
Peachley WR2 29 H3
Peak Dale SK17 50 C5
Peak Forest SK17 50 D5
Peakirk PE6 42 E5
Pean Hill CT5 25 H5
Pearsie DD8 82 E2
Pease Pottage RH11 13 F3
Peasedown St. John BA2 20 A6
Peasemore RG20 21 H4
Peasenhall IP17 35 H2
Peaslake GU5 22 D7
Peasmarsh TN31 14 D5
Peaston EH35 76 C4
Peastonbank EH34 76 C4
Peat Inn KY15 83 F7
Peathill AB43 99 H4
Peatling Magna LE8 41 H6
Peatling Parva LE17 41 H7
Peaton SY7 38 E7
Pebble Coombe KT20 23 F6
Pebmarsh CO9 34 C5
Pebworth CV37 30 C4
Pecket Well HX7 56 E7
Peckforton CW6 48 E7
Peckleton LE9 41 G5
Pedmore DY9 40 B7
Pedwell TA7 8 D1
Peebles EH45 76 A6
Peel IM5 54 B5
Pegswood NE61 71 H5
Peighinn nan Aoireann HS8 84 C1
Peinchorran IV51 86 B1
Peinlich IV51 93 K6
Pelaw NE10 71 H7
Pelcomb Bridge SA62 16 C3
Pelcomb Cross SA62 16 C3
Peldon CO5 34 D7
Pelsall WS3 40 C5
Pelton DH2 62 D1
Pelutho CA7 60 C2
Pelynt PL13 4 C5
Pembrey SA16 17 H4
Pembridge HR6 28 C3
Pembroke (Penfro) SA71 16 C4
Pembroke Dock (Doc Penfro) SA72 16 C4
Pembury TN2 23 K7
Pen-bont Rhydybeddau SY23 37 F7
Pen-clawdd SA4 17 J5
Pen-ffordd SA66 16 D2
Pen-groes-oped NP7 19 G1
Pen-llyn LL65 46 B4
Pen-sarn, Gwyn. LL54 36 D1
Pen-sarn, Gwyn. LL45 36 E3
Pen-twyn NP25 19 J1
Pen-y-banc SA19 17 K2
Pen-y-bont, Carmar. SA20 27 G5
Pen-y-bont, Powys SY10 38 B3
Pen-y-bont, Powys SY21 37 K4
Pen-y-Bont ar Ogwr (Bridgend), Bridgend CF31 18 C4
Pen-y-bryn LL40 37 F4
Pen-y-cae SA9 27 H7
Pen-y-cae-mawr NP15 19 H2
Pen-y-cefn CH7 47 K5
Pen-y-clawdd NP25 19 H1
Pen-y-coedcae CF37 18 D3
Pen-y-fai CF31 18 B3
Pen-y-garn SA32 17 J1
Pen-y-garreg LD2 27 K4
Pen-y-Gwryd Hotel LL55 46 E7
Pen-y-Park HR3 28 B4
Pen-y-stryt LL11 47 K7
Pen-yr-hoel NP25 28 D7
Penallt NP25 28 E7
Penally SA70 16 E5
Penalt HR1 28 E6
Penare PL26 3 G4
Penarth CF64 18 E4
Penboyr SA44 17 G1
Penbryn SA44 26 B3
Pencader SA39 17 H1
Pencaenewydd LL53 36 D1
Pencaitland EH34 76 C4
Pencarreg SA40 26 E4
Pencelli LD3 27 K6
Pencoed CF35 18 C3
Pencombe HR7 28 E3
Pencoyd HR2 28 E6
Pencraig, Here. HR9 28 E6
Pencraig, Powys SY10 37 K3
Pendeen TR19 2 A5
Penderyn CF44 18 C1
Pendine SA33 17 F4
Pendlebury M27 49 G2
Pendleton BB7 56 C6
Pendock GL19 29 G5
Pendoggett PL29 4 A3
Pendomer BA22 8 E3
Pendoylan CF71 18 D4
Penegoes SY20 37 G5
Penfro (Pembroke) SA71 16 C4
Pengam NP12 18 E2
Penge SE20 23 G4
Pengenffordd LD3 28 A5
Pengorffwysfa LL68 46 C3
Pengover Green PL14 4 C4
Pengwern LL18 47 J5
Penhale TR12 2 D7
Penhallow TR4 2 E3
Penhalvean TR16 2 E5
Penhow NP26 19 H2
Penhurst TN33 13 K5
Peniarth LL36 37 F5
Penicuik EH26 76 A4
Penifiler IV51 93 K7
Peninver PA28 66 B1
Penisar Waun LL55 46 D6
Penisarcwn SY10 37 K4
Penistone S36 50 E2
Penjerrick TR11 2 E5
Penketh WA5 48 E4
Penkill KA26 67 G4
Penkridge ST19 40 B4
Penley LL13 38 D2
Penllech LL53 36 B2
Penllergaer SA4 17 K5
Penllyn CF71 18 C4
Penmachno LL24 47 F7
Penmaen SA3 17 J6
Penmaenmawr LL34 47 F5
Penmaenpool LL40 37 F4
Penmark CF62 18 D5
Penmon LL58 46 E4
Penmorfa LL49 36 E1
Penmynydd LL61 46 D5
Penn, Bucks. HP10 22 C2
Penn, W.Mid. WV4 40 A6
Penn Street HP7 22 C2
Pennal SY20 37 F5
Pennan AB43 99 G4
Pennance TR16 2 E4
Pennant, Cere. SY23 26 E2
Pennant, Powys SY19 37 H6
Pennant Melangell SY10 37 K3
Pennard SA3 17 J6
Pennerley SY5 38 C6
Penninghame DG8 64 D4
Pennington LA12 55 F2
Pennsylvania BS30 20 A4
Penny Bridge LA12 55 G1
Pennyfuir PA34 79 K4
Pennyghael PA70 79 G5
Pennyglen KA19 67 G2
Pennygown PA72 79 H3
Pennymoor EX16 7 G4
Penparc, Cere. SA43 26 B4
Penparc, Pembs. SA62 16 B1
Penparcau SY23 36 E7
Penperlleni NP4 19 G1
Penpillick PL24 4 A5
Penpol TR3 3 F5
Penpoll PL22 4 B5
Penpont, D. & G. DG3 68 D4
Penpont, Powys LD3 27 J6
Penrherber SA38 17 F1
Penrhiw-llan SA44 26 C4
Penrhiw-pal SA44 26 C4
Penrhiwceiber CF45 18 D2
Penrhiwgoch SA14 17 J3
Penrhos, Gwyn. LL53 36 C2
Penrhos, I.o.A. LL65 46 A4
Penrhos, Mon. NP15 28 D7
Penrhos, Powys SA9 27 H7
Penrhos-garnedd LL57 46 D5
Penrhyn Bay (Bae Penrhyn) LL28 47 G4
Penrhyn-coch SY23 37 F7
Penrhyn-side LL30 47 G4
Penrhyndeudraeth LL48 37 F2
Penrhys CF43 18 D2
Penrice SA3 17 H6
Penrith CA11 61 G3
Penrose PL27 3 F1
Penruddock CA11 60 F4
Penryn TR10 2 E5
Pensarn, Carmar. SA31 17 H3
Pensarn, Conwy LL22 47 H5
Pensax WR6 29 G2
Pensby CH61 48 B4
Penselwood BA9 9 G1
Pensford BS39 19 K5
Pensham WR10 29 J4
Penshaw DH4 62 E1
Penshurst TN11 23 J7
Pensilva PL14 4 C4
Pensnett DY5 40 B7
Pentewan PL26 4 A6
Pentir LL57 46 D6
Pentire TR7 2 E2
Pentireglaze PL27 3 G1
Pentlepoir SA69 16 E4
Pentlow CO10 34 C4
Pentney PE32 44 B4
Penton Mewsey SP11 21 G7
Pentraeth LL75 46 D5
Pentre, Powys SY10 37 K3
Pentre, Powys SY15 38 B6
Pentre, Powys SY16 37 K7
Pentre, Powys LD8 28 B2
Pentre, R.C.T. CF41 18 C2
Pentre, Shrop. SY4 38 C4
Pentre, Wrex. LL14 38 B1
Pentre Berw LL60 46 C5
Pentre Gwenlais SA18 17 K3
Pentre Gwynfryn LL45 36 E3
Pentre Halkyn CH8 48 B5
Pentre Isaf LL22 47 G6
Pentre Llanrhaeadr LL16 47 J6
Pentre Maelor LL13 38 C1
Pentre Saron LL16 47 J6
Pentre-bach LD3 27 J5
Pentre-bont LL25 47 F7
Pentre-bwlch LL11 38 A1
Pentre-celyn, Denb. LL15 47 K7
Pentre-celyn, Powys SY19 37 H5
Pentre-chwyth SA1 17 K5
Pentre-cwrt SA44 17 G1
Pentre-Dolau-Honddu LD3 27 J4
Pentre-Dwr SA7 17 K5
Pentre-galar SA41 16 E1
Pentre-Llwyn-Llwyd LD2 27 J3
Pentre-piod LL23 37 H2
Pentre-Poeth NP10 19 F3
Pentre-tafarn-y-fedw LL26 47 G6
Pentre-ty-gwyn SA20 27 H5
Pentrebach, M.Tyd. CF48 18 D1
Pentrebach, Swan. SA4 17 K4
Pentrecagal SA44 26 C4
Pentreclwydau SA11 18 B1
Pentredwr LL20 38 A1
Pentrefelin, Carmar. SA19 17 J2
Pentrefelin, Cere. SA48 27 F4
Pentrefelin, Conwy LL28 47 G5
Pentrefelin, Gwyn. LL52 36 E2
Pentrefelin, Powys SY10 38 A3
Pentrefoelas LL24 47 G7
Pentregat SA44 26 C3
Pentreheyling SY15 38 B6
Pentre'r beirdd SY21 38 A4
Pentre'r-felin LD3 27 J5
Pentrich DE5 51 F7
Pentridge SP5 10 B3
Pentwyn CF23 19 F3
Pentyrch CF15 18 E3
Penuwch SY25 26 E2
Penwithick PL26 4 A5
Penwortham PR1 55 J7
Penwyllt SA9 27 H7
Penybont LD1 28 A2
Penybontfawr SY10 37 K3
Penybryn CF82 18 E2
Penycae LL14 38 B1
Penycwm SA62 16 B2
Penyffordd CH4 48 C6
Penygarnedd SY10 38 A3
Penygraig CF40 18 C2
Penygroes, Carmar. SA14 17 J3
Penygroes, Gwyn. LL54 46 C7
Penysarn LL69 46 C3
Penywaun CF44 18 C1
Penzance TR18 2 B5
Penzance Heliport TR18 2 B5
Peopleton WR10 29 J3
Peover Heath WA16 49 G5
Peper Harow GU8 22 C7
Peplow TF9 39 F3
Perceton KA11 74 B6
Percie AB31 90 D5
Perham Down SP11 21 F7
Perivale UB6 22 E3
Perkhill AB31 90 D4
Perkins Beach SY5 38 C5
Perlethorpe NG22 51 J5
Perranarworthal TR3 2 E5
Perranporth TR6 2 E3
Perranuthnoe TR20 2 C6
Perranzabuloe TR4 2 E3
Perry Barr B42 40 C6
Perry Green SG10 33 H7
Perry Street DA11 24 C4
Persey PH10 82 C2
Pershall ST21 40 A3
Pershore WR10 29 J4
Pert AB30 83 H1
Pertenhall MK44 32 D2
PERTH PH 82 C5
Perthy SY12 38 C2
Perton WV6 40 A6
Peter Tavy PL19 5 F3
PETERBOROUGH PE 42 E6
Peterburn IV21 94 D3
Peterchurch HR2 28 C5
Peterculter AB14 91 G4
Peterhead AB42 99 K6
Peterlee SR8 63 F2
Peter's Green LU2 32 E7
Peters Marland EX38 6 C4
Petersfield GU32 11 J2
Peterston-super-Ely CF5 18 D4
Peterstone Wentlooge CF3 19 F3
Peterstow HR9 28 E6
Petham CT4 15 G2
Petrockstow EX20 6 D5
Pett TN35 14 D6
Pettaugh IP14 35 F3
Pettinain ML11 75 H6
Pettistree IP13 35 G3
Petton, Devon EX16 7 J3
Petton, Shrop. SY4 38 D3
Petty AB53 91 F1
Pettycur KY3 76 A2
Pettymuick AB41 91 H2
Petworth GU28 12 C4
Pevensey BN24 13 K6
Pevensey Bay BN24 13 K6
Pewsey SN9 20 E5
Phesdo AB30 90 E7
Philham EX39 6 A3
Philiphaugh TD7 69 K1
Phillack TR27 2 C5
Philleigh TR2 3 F5
Philpstoun EH49 75 J3
Phoenix Green RG27 22 A6
Phones PH20 88 E5
Phorp IV36 97 H6
Pibsbury TA10 8 D2
Pica CA14 60 B4
Piccadilly Corner IP20 45 G7
Piccotts End HP2 22 D1
Pickerells CM5 23 J1
Pickering YO18 58 E1
Picket Piece SP11 21 G7
Picket Post BH24 10 C4
Pickford Green CV5 40 E7
Pickhill YO7 57 J1
Picklescott SY6 38 D6
Pickletillem KY16 83 F5
Pickmere WA16 49 F5
Pickstock TF10 39 G3
Pickston PH1 82 A5
Pickwell, Devon EX33 6 C1
Pickwell, Leics. LE14 42 A4
Pickworth, Lincs. NG34 42 D2
Pickworth, Rut. PE9 42 C4
Picton, Ches. CH2 48 D5
Picton, N.Yorks. TS15 63 F6
Piddinghoe BN9 13 H6
Piddington, Northants. NN7 32 B3
Piddington, Oxon. OX25 31 H7
Piddlehinton DT2 9 G5
Piddletrenthide DT2 9 G5
Pidley PE28 33 G1
Piercebridge DL2 62 D5
Pierowall KW17 106 D3
Pigdon NE61 71 G5
Pikehall DE4 50 D7
Pilgrims Hatch CM15 23 J2
Pilham DN21 52 B3
Pill BS20 19 J4
Pillaton PL12 4 D4
Pillerton Hersey CV35 30 D4
Pillerton Priors CV35 30 D4
Pilleth LD7 28 B2
Pilley, Glos. GL53 29 J7
Pilley, Hants. SO41 10 E5
Pilley, S.Yorks. S75 51 F2
Pilling PR3 55 H5
Pilling Lane FY6 55 G5
Pillowell GL15 19 K1
Pilning BS35 19 J3
Pilsbury SK17 50 D6
Pilsdon DT6 8 D5
Pilsgate PE9 42 D5
Pilsley, Derbys. DE45 50 E5
Pilsley, Derbys. S45 51 G6
Piltdown TN22 13 H4
Pilton, Devon EX31 6 D2
Pilton, Northants. PE8 42 D7
Pilton, Rut. LE15 42 C5
Pilton, Som. BA4 19 J7
Pimperne DT11 9 J4
Pinchbeck PE11 43 F3
Pinchbeck Bars PE11 43 F3
Pinchbeck West PE11 43 F3
Pinchinthorpe TS14 63 G5
Pinfold L40 48 C1
Pinhay DT7 8 C5
Pinhoe EX1 7 H6
Pinkneys Green SL6 22 B3
Pinley Green CV35 30 D2
Pinminnoch KA26 67 F4
Pinmore KA26 67 G4
Pinn EX10 7 K7
Pinner HA5 22 E3
Pinner Green HA5 22 E2
Pinvin WR10 29 J4
Pinwherry KA26 67 F5
Pinxton NG16 51 G7
Pipe and Lyde HR1 28 E4
Pipe Gate TF9 39 G1
Pipe Ridware WS15 40 C4
Piperhall PA20 73 J5
Piperhill IV12 97 F6
Piper's Pool PL15 4 C2
Pipewell NN14 42 B7
Pippacott EX31 6 D2
Pipton LD3 28 A5
Pirbright GU24 22 C6
Pirnmill KA27 73 G6
Pirton, Herts. SG5 32 E5
Pirton, Worcs. WR8 29 H4
Pisgah FK15 81 J7
Pishill RG9 22 A3
Pistyll LL53 36 C1
Pitagowan PH18 81 K1
Pitblae AB43 99 H4
Pitcairngreen PH1 82 B5
Pitcairns PH2 82 B6
Pitcaple AB51 91 F2
Pitch Green HP27 22 A1
Pitch Place GU3 22 C6
Pitchcombe GL6 20 B1
Pitchcott HP22 31 J7
Pitchford SY5 38 E5
Pitcombe BA10 9 F1
Pitcot CF32 18 B4
Pitcox EH42 76 E3
Pitcur PH13 82 D4
Pitfichie AB51 90 E3
Pitgrudy IV25 96 E2
Pitinnan AB51 91 F1
Pitkennedy DD8 83 G2
Pitkevy KY6 82 D7
Pitlessie KY15 82 E7
Pitlochry PH16 82 A2
Pitmedden AB41 91 G2
Pitminster TA3 8 B3
Pitmuies DD8 83 G3
Pitmunie AB51 90 E3
Pitnacree PH9 82 A2
Pitney TA10 8 D2
Pitroddie PH2 82 D5
Pitscottie KY15 83 F6
Pitsea SS13 24 D3
Pitsford NN6 31 J2
Pitsford Hill TA4 7 J2
Pitstone LU7 32 C7
Pitstone Green LU7 32 C7
Pitt, Devon EX16 7 J4
Pitt, Hants. SO22 11 F2
Pittendreich IV30 97 J5
Pittentrail IV28 96 E1
Pittenweem KY10 83 G7
Pittington DH6 62 E2
Pittodrie Ho. AB51 90 E2
Pitton SP5 10 D1
Pity Me DH1 62 D2
Pityme PL27 3 G1

Queenzieburn **G65** 74 E3
Quemerford **SN11** 20 D4
Quendale **ZE2** 109 F9
Quendon **CB11** 33 J5
Queniborough **LE7** 41 J4
Quenington **GL7** 20 E1
Quernmore **LA2** 55 J3
Queslett **B44** 40 C6
Quethiock **PL14** 4 D4
Quholm **KW16** 107 B6
Quidenham **NR16** 44 E7
Quidhampton, *Hants.* **RG25** 21 J6
Quidhampton, *Wilts.* **SP2** 10 C1
Quilquox **AB41** 91 H1
Quina Brook **SY4** 38 E2
Quindry **KW17** 107 D8
Quine's Hill **IM4** 54 C6
Quinhill **PA29** 73 F5
Quinton, *Northants.* **NN7** 31 J3
Quinton, *W.Mid.* **B62** 40 B7
Quintrell Downs **TR8** 3 F2
Quoditch **EX21** 6 C6
Quoig **PH7** 81 K5
Quoigs **FK15** 81 K7
Quorn **LE12** 41 H4
Quothquan **ML12** 75 H7
Quoyloo **KW16** 106 B5
Quoys **ZE2** 108 F1
Quoys of Reiss **KW1** 105 J3

R

Raby **CH63** 48 C5
Rachan **ML12** 75 K7
Rachub **LL57** 46 E6
Rackenford **EX16** 7 G4
Rackham **RH20** 12 D5
Rackheath **NR13** 45 G4
Racks **DG1** 69 F6
Rackwick, *Ork.* **KW17** 106 D2
Rackwick, *Ork.* **KW16** 107 B8
Radbourne **DE6** 40 E2
Radcliffe, *Gt.Man.* **M26** 49 G2
Radcliffe, *Northumb.* **NE65** 71 H3
Radcliffe on Trent **NG12** 41 J2
Radclive **MK18** 31 H5
Radcot **OX18** 21 F2
Radford, *Oxon.* **OX7** 31 F6
Radford, *W.Mid.* **CV6** 41 F7
Radford Semele **CV31** 30 E2
Radipole **DT3** 9 F6
Radlett **WD7** 22 E1
Radley **OX14** 21 J2
Radstock **BA3** 19 K6
Radstone **NN13** 31 G4
Radway **CV35** 30 E4
Radway Green **CW1** 49 G7
Radwell, *Beds.* **MK43** 32 D3
Radwell, *Herts.* **SG7** 33 F5
Radwinter **CB10** 33 K5
Radyr **CF15** 18 E3
Raechester **NE19** 70 E5
Raemoir Ho. **AB31** 90 E5
Raffin **IV27** 102 C5
Rafford **IV36** 97 H6
Ragdale **LE14** 41 J4
Raglan **NP15** 19 H1
Ragnall **NG22** 52 B5
Rahoy **PA34** 79 H2
Rainford **WA11** 48 D2
Rainham, *Gt.Lon.* **RM13** 23 J3
Rainham, *Med.* **ME8** 24 E5
Rainhill **L35** 48 D3
Rainhill Stoops **L35** 48 E3
Rainow **SK10** 49 J5
Rainton **YO7** 57 J2
Rainworth **NG21** 51 H7
Raisbeck **CA10** 61 H6
Raise **CA9** 61 J2
Rait **PH2** 82 D5
Raithby, *Lincs.* **LN11** 53 G4
Raithby, *Lincs.* **PE23** 53 G6
Rake **GU33** 12 B4
Raleigh's Cross **TA23** 7 J2
Ram **SA48** 26 E4
Ram Lane **TN26** 14 E3
Ramasaig **IV55** 93 G7
Rame, *Cornw.* **PL10** 4 E6
Rame, *Cornw.* **TR10** 2 E5
Rampisham **DT2** 8 E4
Rampside **LA13** 55 F3
Rampton, *Cambs.* **CB4** 33 H2
Rampton, *Notts.* **DN22** 52 B5
Ramsbottom **BL0** 49 G1
Ramsbury **SN8** 21 F4
Ramscraigs **KW6** 105 G6
Ramsdean **GU32** 11 J2
Ramsdell **RG26** 21 J6
Ramsden **OX7** 30 E7
Ramsden Bellhouse **CM11** 24 D2
Ramsden Heath **CM11** 24 D2
Ramsey, *Cambs.* **PE26** 43 F7
Ramsey, *Essex* **CO12** 35 G6
Ramsey, *I.o.M.* **IM8** 54 D4
Ramsey Forty Foot **PE26** 43 G7
Ramsey Heights **PE26** 43 F7
Ramsey Island **CM0** 25 F1
Ramsey Mereside **PE26** 43 F7
Ramsey St. Mary's **PE26** 43 F7
Ramsgate **CT11** 25 K5
Ramsgate Street **NR24** 44 E2
Ramsgill **HG3** 57 G2
Ramsholt **IP12** 35 H4
Ramshorn **ST10** 40 C1
Ramsnest Common **GU8** 12 C3
Ranachan **PH36** 79 J1
Ranby, *Lincs.* **LN8** 53 F5
Ranby, *Notts.* **DN22** 51 J4
Rand **LN8** 52 E5
Randwick **GL6** 20 B1
Rangemore **DE13** 40 D3
Rangeworthy **BS37** 19 K3
Rankinston **KA6** 67 J2
Rank's Green **CM3** 34 B7
Rannoch School **PH17** 81 G2
Ranochan **PH38** 86 E6
Ranskill **DN22** 51 J4
Ranton **ST18** 40 A3
Ranworth **NR13** 45 H4
Rapness **KW17** 106 E3
Rascarrel **DG7** 65 J6
Raskelf **YO61** 57 K2
Rassau **NP23** 28 A7
Rastrick **HD6** 57 G7
Ratby **LE6** 41 H5
Ratcliffe Culey **CV9** 41 F6
Ratcliffe on Soar **NG11** 41 G3
Ratcliffe on the Wreake **LE7** 41 J4
Ratford Bridge **SA62** 16 C3
Rathen **AB43** 99 J4
Rathillet **KY15** 82 E5
Rathliesbeag **PH34** 87 J6
Rathmell **BD24** 56 D3
Ratho **EH28** 75 K3
Ratho Station **EH28** 75 K3
Rathven **AB56** 98 C4
Ratley **OX15** 30 E4
Ratlinghope **SY5** 38 D6
Rattar **KW14** 105 H1
Ratten Row **PR3** 55 H5
Rattery **TQ10** 5 H4
Rattlesden **IP30** 34 D3
Rattray **PH10** 82 C3
Raughton Head **CA5** 60 E2
Raunds **NN9** 32 D1
Ravenfield **S65** 51 G3
Ravenglass **CA18** 60 B7
Raveningham **NR14** 45 H6
Ravenscar **YO13** 63 J2
Ravensdale **IM7** 54 C4
Ravensden **MK44** 32 D3
Ravenshaw **BD23** 56 E5
Ravenshayes **EX5** 7 H5
Ravenshead **NG15** 51 H7
Ravensmoor **CW5** 49 F7
Ravensthorpe, *Northants.* **NN6** 31 H1
Ravensthorpe, *W.Yorks.* **WF13** 50 E1
Ravenstone, *Leics.* **LE67** 41 G4
Ravenstone, *M.K.* **MK46** 32 B4
Ravenstonedale **CA17** 61 J6
Ravenstruther **ML11** 75 H6
Ravensworth **DL11** 62 C6
Raw **YO22** 63 J2
Rawcliffe, *E.Riding* **DN14** 58 C7
Rawcliffe, *York* **YO30** 58 B4
Rawcliffe Bridge **DN14** 58 C7
Rawdon **LS19** 57 H6
Rawmarsh **S62** 51 G3
Rawreth **SS11** 24 D2
Rawridge **EX14** 7 K5
Rawtenstall **BB4** 56 D7
Rawyards **ML6** 75 F4
Raxton **AB41** 91 G1
Raydon **IP7** 34 E5
Raylees **NE19** 70 E4
Rayleigh **SS6** 24 E2
Raymond's Hill **EX13** 8 C5
Rayne **CM7** 34 B6
Reach **CB5** 33 J2
Read **BB12** 56 C6
READING RG 22 A4
Reading Street **TN30** 14 E4
Reagill **CA10** 61 H5
Rearquhar **IV25** 96 E2
Rearsby **LE7** 41 J4
Rease Heath **CW5** 49 F7
Reaster **KW1** 105 H2
Reaveley **NE66** 71 F2
Reawick **ZE2** 109 C8
Reay **KW14** 104 E2
Reculver **CT6** 25 J5
Red Dial **CA7** 60 D2
Red Hill, *Hants.* **PO9** 11 J3
Red Hill, *Warks.* **B49** 30 C3
Red Lodge **IP28** 33 K1
Red Oaks Hill **CB10** 33 J5
Red Post, *Cornw.* **EX23** 6 A5
Red Post, *Devon* **TQ9** 5 J4
Red Rock **WN2** 48 E1
Red Roses **SA34** 17 F3
Red Row **NE61** 71 H4
Red Street **ST5** 49 H7
Red Wharf Bay **LL75** 46 D4
Redberth **SA70** 16 D4
Redbourn **AL3** 32 E7
Redbourne **DN21** 52 C2
Redbridge **IG** 23 H3
Redbrook **NP25** 19 J1
Redbrook Street **TN26** 14 E4
Redburn, *High.* **IV16** 96 C5
Redburn, *High.* **IV12** 97 G7
Redcar **TS10** 63 H4
Redcastle, *Angus* **DD11** 83 H2
Redcastle, *High.* **IV6** 96 C7
Redcliff Bay **BS20** 19 H4
Redcloak **AB39** 91 G6
Reddish **SK5** 49 H3
Redditch **B97** 30 B2
Rede **IP29** 34 C3
Redenhall **IP20** 45 G7
Redesmouth **NE48** 70 D5
Redford, *Aber.* **AB30** 83 J1
Redford, *Angus* **DD11** 83 G3
Redford, *W.Suss.* **GU29** 12 B4
Redgrave **IP22** 34 E1
Redheugh **DD8** 83 F1
Redhill, *Aber.* **AB51** 90 E1
Redhill, *Aber.* **AB32** 91 F4
Redhill, *Moray* **AB54** 98 D6
Redhill, *N.Som.* **BS40** 19 H5
Redhill, *Notts.* **NG5** 41 H1
REDHILL, *Surr.* RH 23 F6
Redhill, *Tel. & W.* **TF2** 39 G4
Redhill Aerodrome & Heliport **RH1** 23 F7
Redhouse, *Aber.* **AB33** 90 D2
Redhouse, *Arg. & B.* **PA29** 73 G4
Redhouses **PA44** 72 B4
Redisham **NR34** 45 J7
Redland, *Bristol* **BS9** 19 J4
Redland, *Ork.* **KW17** 106 C5
Redlingfield **IP23** 35 F1
Redlynch, *Som.* **BA10** 9 F1
Redlynch, *Wilts.* **SP5** 10 D2
Redmarley D'Abitot **GL19** 29 G5
Redmarshall **TS21** 62 E4
Redmile **NG13** 42 B2
Redmire **DL8** 62 B7
Redmoor **PL30** 4 A4
Rednal, *Shrop.* **SY11** 38 C3
Rednal, *W.Mid.* **B45** 30 B1
Redpath **TD6** 76 D7
Redpoint **IV21** 94 D5
Redruth **TR15** 2 D4
Redscarhead **EH45** 76 A6
Redshaw **ML11** 68 D1
Redstone Bank **SA67** 16 E3
Redwick, *Newport* **NP26** 19 H3
Redwick, *S.Glos.* **BS35** 19 J3
Redworth **DL5** 62 D4
Reed **SG8** 33 G5
Reedham **NR13** 45 J5
Reedness **DN14** 58 D7
Reepham, *Lincs.* **LN3** 52 D5
Reepham, *Norf.* **NR10** 45 F3
Reeth **DL11** 62 B7
Regaby **IM7** 54 D4
Regil **BS40** 19 J5
Regoul **IV12** 97 F6
Reiff **IV26** 102 B7
Reigate **RH2** 23 F6
Reighton **YO14** 59 H2
Reinigeadal **HS3** 100 E7
Reisgill **KW3** 105 H5
Reiss **KW1** 105 J3
Rejerrah **TR8** 2 E3
Relubbus **TR20** 2 C5
Relugas **IV36** 97 G7
Remenham **RG9** 22 A3
Remenham Hill **RG9** 22 A3
Remony **PH15** 81 J3
Rempstone **LE12** 41 H3
Rendcomb **GL7** 30 B7
Rendham **IP17** 35 H2
Rendlesham **IP12** 35 H3
Renfrew **PA4** 74 D4
Renhold **MK41** 32 D3
Renishaw **S21** 51 G5
Rennington **NE66** 71 H2
Renton **G82** 74 B3
Renwick **CA10** 61 G2
Repps **NR29** 45 J4
Repton **DE65** 41 F3
Rescobie **DD8** 83 G2
Resipole **PH36** 79 J1
Resolis **IV7** 96 D5
Resolven **SA11** 18 B1
Resourie **PH37** 86 E7
Reston **TD14** 77 G4
Reswallie **DD8** 83 G2
Retew **PL26** 3 G3
Retford **DN22** 51 K4
Rettendon **CM3** 24 D2
Rettendon Place **CM3** 24 D2
Retyn **TR8** 3 F3
Revesby **PE22** 53 F6
Rew **TQ13** 5 H3
Rewe **EX5** 7 H6
Reydon **IP18** 35 J1
Reymerston **NR9** 44 E5
Reynalton **SA68** 16 D4
Reynoldston **SA3** 17 H6
Rezare **PL15** 4 D3
Rhandirmwyn **SA20** 27 G4
Rhaoine **IV28** 96 D1
Rhayader **LD6** 27 J2
Rhedyn **LL53** 36 B2
Rhegreanoch **IV27** 102 C7
Rheindown **IV4** 96 C7
Rhelonie **IV24** 96 C2
Rhemore **PA34** 79 G2
Rhes-y-cae **CH8** 47 K6
Rhewl, *Denb.* **LL15** 47 K6
Rhewl, *Denb.* **LL20** 38 A1
Rhewl, *Shrop.* **SY10** 38 C2
Rhian **IV27** 103 H7
Rhicarn **IV27** 102 C6
Rhiconich **IV27** 102 E3
Rhicullen **IV18** 96 D4
Rhidorroch **IV26** 95 H2
Rhifail **KW11** 104 C4
Rhigos **CF44** 18 C1
Rhilochan **IV28** 96 E1
Rhinduie **IV3** 96 C7
Rhireavach **IV23** 95 G2
Rhiroy **IV23** 95 H3
Rhiw **LL53** 36 B3
Rhiwargor **SY10** 37 J3
Rhiwbryfdir **LL41** 37 F1
Rhiwderin **NP10** 19 F3
Rhiwlas, *Gwyn.* **LL55** 46 D6
Rhiwlas, *Gwyn.* **LL23** 37 J2
Rhiwlas, *Powys* **SY10** 38 B2
Rhodes Minnis **CT4** 15 G3
Rhodesia **S80** 51 H5
Rhodiad **SA62** 16 A2
Rhodmad **SY23** 26 E1
Rhonadale **PA28** 73 F7
Rhonehouse or Kelton Hill **DG7** 65 H5
Rhoose **CF62** 18 D5
Rhos, *Carmar.* **SA44** 17 G1
Rhos, *N.P.T.* **SA8** 18 A1
Rhos Hill **SA43** 26 A4
Rhos-berse **LL11** 48 B7
Rhos-ddu **LL11** 48 C7
Rhos-fawr **LL53** 36 C2
Rhôs-on-Sea **LL28** 47 G4
Rhos-y-brwyner **CH4** 48 B6
Rhos-y-garth **SY23** 27 F1
Rhos-y-gwaliau **LL23** 37 J2
Rhos-y-llan **LL53** 36 B2
Rhos-y-mawn **LL22** 47 G6
Rhos-y-Meirch **LD7** 28 B2
Rhoscolyn **LL65** 46 A5
Rhoscrowther **SA71** 16 C4
Rhosesmor **CH7** 48 B6
Rhosgadfan **LL54** 46 D7
Rhosgoch, *I.o.A.* **LL66** 46 C4
Rhosgoch, *Powys* **LD2** 28 A4
Rhoshirwaun **LL53** 36 A3
Rhoslan **LL49** 36 D1
Rhoslefain **LL36** 36 E5
Rhosllanerchrugog **LL14** 38 B1
Rhosmaen **SA19** 17 K2
Rhosmeirch **LL77** 46 C5
Rhosneigr **LL64** 46 B5
Rhosnesni **LL13** 48 C7
Rhossili **SA3** 17 H6
Rhosson **SA62** 16 A2
Rhostryfan **LL54** 46 C7
Rhostyllen **LL14** 38 C1
Rhosybol **LL68** 46 C4
Rhu **G84** 74 A2
Rhualt **LL17** 47 J5
Rhubodach **PA20** 73 J3
Rhuddlan **LL18** 47 J5
Rhue **IV26** 95 G2
Rhulen **LD2** 28 A4
Rhumach **PH39** 86 C6
Rhunahaorine **PA29** 73 F6
Rhyd, *Gwyn.* **LL48** 37 F1
Rhyd, *Powys* **SY17** 37 J5
Rhyd-Ddu **LL54** 46 D7
Rhyd-rosser **SY23** 26 E2
Rhyd-uchaf **LL23** 37 J2
Rhyd-y-clafdy **LL53** 36 C2
Rhyd-y-foel **LL22** 47 H5
Rhyd-y-fro **SA8** 18 A1
Rhyd-y-meirch **NP7** 19 G1
Rhyd-yr-onnen **LL36** 37 F5
Rhydaman (Ammanford) **SA18** 17 K3
Rhydargaeau **SA33** 17 H2
Rhydcymerau **SA19** 17 J1
Rhydd **WR8** 29 H4
Rhydding **SA10** 18 A2
Rhydlanfair **LL24** 47 G7
Rhydlewis **SA44** 26 C4
Rhydlios **LL53** 36 A2
Rhydlydan, *Conwy* **LL24** 47 G7
Rhydlydan, *Powys* **SY16** 37 K6
Rhydolion **LL53** 36 B3
Rhydowen **SA44** 26 D4
Rhydspence **HR3** 28 B4
Rhydtalog **CH7** 48 B7
Rhydwyn **LL65** 46 B4
Rhydycroesau **SY10** 38 B2
Rhydyfelin, *Cere.* **SY23** 26 E1
Rhydyfelin, *R.C.T.* **CF37** 18 D3
Rhydymain **LL40** 37 G3
Rhydymwyn **CH7** 48 B6
Rhydywrach **SA34** 16 E3
Rhyl **LL18** 47 J4
Rhymney **NP22** 18 E1
Rhyn **SY11** 38 C2
Rhynd **PH2** 82 C5
Rhynie, *Aber.* **AB54** 90 C2
Rhynie, *High.* **IV20** 97 F4
Ribbesford **DY12** 29 G1
Ribbleton **PR1** 55 J6
Ribchester **PR3** 56 B6
Ribigill **IV27** 103 H3
Riby **DN37** 52 E2
Riccall **YO19** 58 C6
Riccarton **KA1** 74 C7
Richard's Castle **SY8** 28 D2
Richings Park **SL0** 22 D4
Richmond **DL10** 62 C6
Richmond upon Thames **TW** 22 E4
Rickarton **AB39** 91 G6
Rickford **BS40** 19 H6
Rickinghall **IP22** 34 E1
Rickling **CB11** 33 H5
Rickling Green **CB11** 33 J6
Rickmansworth **WD3** 22 D2
Riddell **TD6** 70 A1
Riddings **DE55** 51 G7
Riddlecombe **EX18** 6 E4
Riddlesden **BD20** 57 F5
Ridge, *Dorset* **BH20** 9 J6
Ridge, *Herts.* **EN6** 23 F1
Ridge, *Wilts.* **SP3** 9 J1
Ridge Green **RH1** 23 G7
Ridge Lane **CV9** 40 E6
Ridgebourne **LD1** 27 K2
Ridgeway **S12** 51 G4
Ridgeway Cross **WR13** 29 G4
Ridgewell **CO9** 34 B4
Ridgewood **TN22** 13 H4
Ridgmont **MK43** 32 C5
Riding Mill **NE44** 71 F7
Ridley **TN15** 24 C5
Ridleywood **LL13** 48 C7
Ridlington, *Norf.* **NR28** 45 H2
Ridlington, *Rut.* **LE15** 42 B5
Ridsdale **NE48** 70 E5
Riechip **PH8** 82 B3
Rievaulx **YO62** 58 B1
Rigg, *D. & G.* **DG16** 69 H7
Rigg, *High.* **IV51** 94 B6
Riggend **ML6** 75 F4
Rigmaden Park **LA6** 56 B1
Rigsby **LN13** 53 H5
Rigside **ML11** 75 G7
Rileyhill **WS13** 40 D4
Rilla Mill **PL17** 4 C3
Rillington **YO17** 58 E2
Rimington **BB7** 56 D5
Rimpton **BA22** 9 F2
Rimswell **HU19** 59 K7
Rinaston **SA62** 16 C2
Ringford **DG7** 65 G5
Ringland **NR8** 45 F4
Ringles Cross **TN22** 13 H4
Ringmer **BN8** 13 H5
Ringmore **TQ7** 5 G6
Ringorm **AB38** 97 K7
Ring's End **PE13** 43 G5
Ringsfield **NR34** 45 J7
Ringsfield Corner **NR34** 45 J7
Ringshall, *Herts.* **HP4** 32 C7
Ringshall, *Suff.* **IP14** 34 E3
Ringshall Stocks **IP7** 34 E3
Ringstead, *Norf.* **PE36** 44 B1
Ringstead, *Northants.* **NN14** 32 C1
Ringwood **BH24** 10 C4
Ringwould **CT14** 15 J3
Rinloan **AB35** 89 K4
Rinmore **AB33** 90 C3
Rinnigill **KW16** 107 C8
Rinsey **TR13** 2 C6
Ripe **BN8** 13 J6
Ripley, *Derbys.* **DE5** 51 G7
Ripley, *Hants.* **BH23** 10 C5
Ripley, *N.Yorks.* **HG3** 57 H3
Ripley, *Surr.* **GU23** 22 D6
Riplingham **HU15** 59 F6
Ripon **HG4** 57 J2
Rippingale **PE10** 42 E3
Ripple, *Kent* **CT14** 15 J2
Ripple, *Worcs.* **GL20** 29 H5
Ripponden **HX6** 50 C1
Risabus **PA42** 72 B6
Risbury **HR6** 28 E3
Risby **IP28** 34 B2
Risca **NP11** 19 F2
Rise **HU11** 59 H5
Risegate **PE11** 43 F2
Riseley, *Beds.* **MK44** 32 D2
Riseley, *W'ham* **RG7** 22 A5
Rishangles **IP23** 35 F2
Rishton **BB1** 56 C6
Rishworth **HX6** 50 C1
Risley, *Derbys.* **DE72** 41 G2
Risley, *Warr.* **WA3** 49 F3
Risplith **HG4** 57 H3
Rispond **IV27** 103 G2
Rivar **SN8** 21 G5
Rivenhall **CM8** 34 C7
Rivenhall End **CM8** 34 C7
River **GU28** 12 C4
River Bank **CB7** 33 J2
River Bridge **TA7** 19 G7
Riverford Bridge **TQ9** 5 H4
Riverhead **TN13** 23 J6
Rivington **BL6** 49 F1
Roa Island **LA13** 55 F3
Roade **NN7** 31 J3
Roadhead **CA6** 70 A6
Roadside, *High.* **KW12** 105 G2
Roadside, *Ork.* **KW17** 106 F3
Roadside of Kinneff **DD10** 91 G7
Roadwater **TA23** 7 J2
Roag **IV55** 93 H7
Roath **CF24** 19 F4
Roberton, *S.Lan.* **ML12** 68 E1
Roberton, *Sc.Bord.* **TD9** 69 K2
Robertsbridge **TN32** 14 C5
Robertstown **AB38** 97 K7
Roberttown **WF15** 57 G7
Robeston Cross **SA73** 16 B4
Robeston Wathen **SA67** 16 D3
Robin Hood, *Derbys.* **DE45** 50 E5
Robin Hood, *W.Yorks.* **LS26** 57 J7
Robin Hood's Bay **YO22** 63 J2
Robins **GU29** 12 B4
Roborough, *Devon* **EX19** 6 D4
Roborough, *Plym.* **PL6** 5 F4
Roby **L36** 48 D3

Roby Mill

Roby Mill WN8 48 E2
Rocester ST14 40 D2
Roch SA62 16 B2
Rochallie PH10 82 C2
Rochdale OL16 49 H1
Roche PL26 3 G2
Rochester, *Med.* ME1 24 D5
Rochester, *Northumb.* NE19 70 D4
Rochford, *Essex* SS4 24 E2
Rochford, *Worcs.* WR15 29 F2
Rock, *Caerp.* NP12 18 E2
Rock, *Cornw.* PL27 3 G1
Rock, *Northumb.* NE66 71 H1
Rock, *Worcs.* DY14 29 G1
Rock Ferry CH42 48 C4
Rockbeare EX5 7 J6
Rockbourne SP6 10 C3
Rockcliffe, *Cumb.* CA6 69 J7
Rockcliffe, *D. & G.* DG5 65 J5
Rockfield, *Arg. & B.* PA29 73 G5
Rockfield, *High.* IV20 97 G3
Rockfield, *Mon.* NP25 28 D7
Rockhampton GL13 19 K2
Rockhead PL33 4 A2
Rockingham LE16 42 B6
Rockland All Saints NR17 44 D6
Rockland St. Mary NR14 45 H5
Rockland St. Peter NR17 44 D6
Rockley SN8 20 E4
Rockside PA49 72 A4
Rockwell End RG9 22 A3
Rockwell Green TA21 7 K4
Rodborough GL5 20 B1
Rodbourne SN16 20 C3
Rodbridge Corner CO10 34 C4
Rodd LD8 28 C2
Roddam NE66 71 F1
Rodden DT3 9 F6
Rode BA11 20 B6
Rode Heath ST7 49 H7
Rodeheath CW12 49 H6
Rodel (Roghadal) HS5 93 F3
Roden TF6 38 E4
Rodhuish TA24 7 J2
Rodington SY4 38 E4
Rodley GL14 29 G7
Rodmarton GL7 20 C2
Rodmell BN7 13 H6
Rodmersham ME9 25 F5
Rodney Stoke BS27 19 H6
Rodsley DE6 40 E1
Rodway TA5 19 F7
Roe Green SG9 33 G5
Roecliffe YO51 57 J3
Roehampton SW15 23 F4
Roesound ZE2 109 C6
Roewen LL32 47 F5
Roffey RH12 12 E3
Rogart IV28 96 E1
Rogate GU31 12 B4
Rogerstone NP10 19 F3
Roghadal (Rodel) HS5 93 F3
Rogiet NP26 19 H3
Roker SR6 63 F1
Rollesby NR29 45 J4
Rolleston, *Leics.* LE7 42 A5
Rolleston, *Notts.* NG23 51 K7
Rolleston, *Staffs.* DE13 40 E3
Rollestone SP3 20 D7
Rolston HU18 59 J5
Rolvenden TN17 14 D4
Rolvenden Layne TN17 14 D4
Romaldkirk DL12 62 A4
Romanby DL7 62 E7
Romannobridge EH46 75 K6
Romansleigh EX36 7 F3
Romford, *Dorset* BH31 10 B4
ROMFORD, *Gt.Lon.* RM 23 J3
Romiley SK6 49 J3
Romney Street TN15 23 J5
Romsey SO51 10 E2
Romsley, *Shrop.* WV15 39 G7
Romsley, *Worcs.* B62 40 B7
Ronachan PA29 73 F5
Ronague IM9 54 B6
Ronnachmore PA43 72 B5
Rookhope DL13 62 A2
Rookley PO38 11 G6
Rooks Bridge BS26 19 G6
Rookwith HG4 57 H1
Roos HU12 59 J6
Roosecote LA13 55 F3
Rootpark ML11 75 H5
Ropley SO24 11 H1
Ropley Dean SO24 11 H1
Ropley Soke SO24 11 H1
Ropsley NG33 42 C2
Rora AB42 99 J5
Rorandle AB51 90 E3
Rorrington SY15 38 B5
Rosarie AB55 98 B5
Rose TR4 2 E3
Rose Ash EX36 7 F3
Rose Green CO6 34 C6
Roseacre PR4 55 H6
Rosebank ML8 75 G6
Rosebrough NE67 71 G1
Rosebush SA66 16 D2
Rosedale Abbey YO18 63 J7
Roseden NE66 71 F1
Rosehall IV27 96 B1
Rosehearty AB43 99 H4
Rosehill, *Aber.* AB34 90 D5
Rosehill, *Shrop.* TF9 39 F2
Roseisle IV30 97 J5
Rosemarket SA73 16 C4
Rosemarkie IV10 96 E6
Rosemary Lane EX15 7 K4
Rosemount, *P. & K.* PH10 82 C3
Rosemount, *S.Ayr.* KA9 67 H1
Rosepool SA62 16 B3
Rosewarne TR27 2 D5
Rosewell EH24 76 A4
Roseworthy TR14 2 D5
Rosgill CA10 61 G5
Roshven PH38 86 D7
Roskhill IV55 93 H7
Rosley CA7 60 E2
Roslin EH25 76 A4
Rosliston DE12 40 E4
Rosneath G84 74 A2
Ross, *D. & G.* DG6 65 G6
Ross, *Northumb.* NE70 77 K7
Ross, *P. & K.* PH6 81 J5
Ross Priory G83 74 C2
Ross-on-Wye HR9 29 F6
Rossdhu House G83 74 B2
Rossett LL12 48 C7
Rossie Farm School DD10 83 H2
Rossie Ochill PH2 82 B6
Rossie Priory PH14 82 D4
Rossington DN11 51 J3
Rosskeen IV18 96 D5
Roster KW3 105 H5
Rostherne WA16 49 G4
Rosthwaite, *Cumb.* CA12 60 D5
Rosthwaite, *Cumb.* LA20 55 F1
Roston DE6 40 D1
Rosyth KY11 75 K2
Rothbury NE65 71 F3
Rotherby LE14 41 J4
Rotherfield TN6 13 J4
Rotherfield Greys RG9 22 A3
Rotherfield Peppard RG9 22 A3
Rotherham S60 51 G3
Rothersthorpe NN7 31 J3
Rotherwick RG27 22 A6
Rothes AB38 97 K7
Rothesay PA20 73 J4
Rothiebrisbane AB53 91 F1
Rothienorman AB51 91 F1
Rothiesholm KW17 106 F5
Rothley, *Leics.* LE7 41 H4
Rothley, *Northumb.* NE61 71 F5
Rothwell, *Lincs.* LN7 52 E3
Rothwell, *Northants.* NN14 42 B7
Rothwell, *W.Yorks.* LS26 57 J7
Rotsea YO25 59 G4
Rottal DD8 82 E1
Rottingdean BN2 13 G6
Rottington CA28 60 A5
Roud PO38 11 G6
Roudham NR16 44 D7
Rough Close ST15 40 B2
Rough Common CT2 15 G2
Rougham, *Norf.* PE32 44 C3
Rougham, *Suff.* IP30 34 D2
Rougham Green IP30 34 D2
Roughburn PH31 87 K6
Roughlee BB9 56 D5
Roughley B75 40 D6
Roughton, *Lincs.* LN10 53 F6
Roughton, *Norf.* NR11 45 G2
Roughton, *Shrop.* WV15 39 G6
Roundhay LS8 57 J6
Roundstreet Common RH14 12 D4
Roundway SN10 20 D5
Rous Lench WR11 30 B3
Rousdon DT7 8 B5
Rousham OX25 31 F6
Rousham Gap OX25 31 F6
Routenburn KA30 74 A4
Routh HU17 59 G5
Row, *Cornw.* PL30 4 A3
Row, *Cumb.* CA10 61 H3
Row, *Cumb.* LA8 55 H1
Row Heath CO16 35 F7
Row Town KT15 22 D5
Rowanburn DG14 69 K6
Rowardennan Lodge G63 74 B1
Rowberrow BS25 19 H6
Rowchoish G63 80 E7
Rowde SN10 20 C5
Rowfoot NE49 70 B7
Rowhedge CO5 34 E6
Rowhook RH12 12 E3
Rowington CV35 30 D2
Rowington Green CV35 30 D1
Rowland DE45 50 E5
Rowland's Castle PO9 11 J3
Rowlands Gill NE39 62 C1
Rowledge GU10 22 B7
Rowley, *Devon* EX36 7 F4
Rowley, *Dur.* DH8 62 B2
Rowley, *E.Riding* HU20 59 F6
Rowley, *Shrop.* SY5 38 C5
Rowley Regis B65 40 B7
Rowlstone HR2 28 C6
Rowly GU5 22 D7
Rowner PO13 11 G4
Rowney Green B48 30 B1
Rownhams SO16 10 E3
Rowrah CA26 60 B5
Rowsham HP22 32 B7
Rowsley DE4 50 E6
Rowstock OX11 21 H3
Rowston LN4 52 D7
Rowthorne S44 51 G6
Rowton, *Ches.* CH3 48 D6
Rowton, *Shrop.* SY5 38 C4
Rowton, *Tel. & W.* TF6 39 F4
Roxburgh TD5 76 E7
Roxby, *N.Lincs.* DN15 52 C1
Roxby, *N.Yorks.* TS13 63 J5
Roxton MK44 32 E3
Roxwell CM1 24 C1
Royal British Legion Village ME20 14 C2
Royal Leamington Spa CV32 30 E2
ROYAL TUNBRIDGE WELLS TN 13 J3
Roybridge PH31 87 J6
Roydon, *Essex* CM19 33 H7
Roydon, *Norf.* PE32 44 B3
Roydon, *Norf.* IP22 44 E7
Roydon Hamlet CM19 23 H1
Royston, *Herts.* SG8 33 G4
Royston, *S.Yorks.* S71 51 F1
Royton OL2 49 J2
Ruabon LL14 38 C1
Ruaig PA77 78 B3
Ruan Lanihorne TR2 3 F4
Ruan Major TR12 2 D7
Ruan Minor TR12 2 E7
Ruanaich PA76 78 D5
Ruardean GL17 29 F7
Ruardean Woodside GL17 29 F7
Rubery B45 29 J1
Ruckcroft CA4 61 G2
Ruckinge TN26 15 F4
Ruckland LN11 53 G5
Ruckley SY5 38 E5
Rudbaxton SA62 16 C2
Rudby TS15 63 F6
Rudchester NE15 71 G7
Ruddington NG11 41 H2
Ruddlemoor PL26 4 A5
Rudford GL2 29 G6
Rudge BA11 20 B6
Rudgeway BS32 19 K3
Rudgwick RH12 12 D3
Rudhall HR9 29 F6
Rudheath CW9 49 F5
Rudley Green CM3 24 E1
Rudry CF83 18 E3
Rudston YO25 59 G3
Rudyard ST13 49 J7
Rufford L40 48 D1
Rufforth YO23 58 B4
Ruffside DH8 62 A1
Rugby CV21 31 G1
Rugeley WS15 40 C4
Ruilick IV4 96 C7
Ruishton TA3 8 B2
Ruisigearraidh HS6 92 E3
Ruislip HA4 22 D3
Rumbling Bridge KY13 75 J1
Rumburgh IP19 45 H7
Rumford PL27 3 F1
Rumney CF3 19 F4
Rumwell TA4 7 K3
Runacraig FK18 81 G6
Runcorn WA7 48 E4
Runcton PO20 12 B6
Runcton Holme PE33 44 A5
Rundlestone PL20 5 F3
Runfold GU9 22 B7
Runhall NR9 44 E5
Runham NR29 45 J4
Runnington TA21 7 K3
Runsell Green CM3 24 D1
Runswick TS13 63 K5
Runtaleave DD8 82 D1
Runwell SS11 24 D2
Ruscombe RG10 22 A4
Rush Green RM7 23 J3
Rushall, *Here.* HR8 29 F5
Rushall, *Norf.* IP21 45 F7
Rushall, *W.Mid.* WS4 40 C5
Rushall, *Wilts.* SN9 20 E6
Rushbrooke IP30 34 C2
Rushbury SY6 38 E6
Rushden, *Herts.* SG9 33 G5
Rushden, *Northants.* NN10 32 C2
Rushford IP24 44 D7
Rushlake Green TN21 13 K5
Rushmere NR33 45 J7
Rushmere St. Andrew IP5 35 F4
Rushmoor, *Surr.* GU10 22 B7
Rushmoor, *Tel. & W.* TF6 39 F4
Rushock WR9 29 H1
Rusholm M13 49 H3
Rushton, *Ches.* CW6 48 E6
Rushton, *Northants.* NN14 42 B7
Rushton, *Shrop.* TF6 39 F5
Rushton Spencer SK11 49 J6
Rushwick WR2 29 H3
Rushyford DL17 62 D4
Ruskie FK8 81 H7
Ruskington NG34 52 D7
Rusko DG7 65 F5
Rusland LA12 55 G1
Rusper RH12 13 F3
Ruspidge GL14 29 F7
Russel IV54 94 E7
Russell's Water RG9 22 A3
Rusthall TN3 23 J7
Rustington BN16 12 D6
Ruston YO13 59 F1
Ruston Parva YO25 59 G3
Ruswarp YO21 63 K6
Rutherend ML10 74 E5
Rutherford TD5 70 B1
Rutherglen G73 74 E4
Ruthernbridge PL30 4 A4
Ruthin (Rhuthun) LL15 47 K7
Ruthrieston AB10 91 H4
Ruthun (Ruthin) LL15 47 K7
Ruthven, *Aber.* AB54 98 D6
Ruthven, *Angus* PH12 82 D3
Ruthven, *High.* IV13 89 F1
Ruthven, *High.* PH21 88 E5
Ruthvoes TR9 3 G2
Ruthwaite CA7 60 D3
Ruthwell DG1 69 G7
Ruyton-XI-Towns SY4 38 C3
Ryal NE20 71 F6
Ryal Fold BB3 56 B7
Ryall DT6 8 D5
Ryarsh ME19 23 K6
Rydal LA22 60 E6
Ryde PO33 11 G5
Rydon EX22 6 B5
Rye TN31 14 E5
Rye Foreign TN31 14 D5
Rye Harbour TN31 14 E6
Rye Park EN11 23 G1
Ryhall PE9 42 D4
Ryhill WF4 51 F1
Ryhope SR2 63 F1
Ryland LN2 52 D4
Rylstone BD23 56 E4
Ryme Intrinseca DT9 8 E3
Ryther LS24 58 B6
Ryton, *Glos.* GL18 29 G5
Ryton, *N.Yorks.* YO17 58 D2
Ryton, *Shrop.* TF11 39 G5
Ryton, *T. & W.* NE40 71 G7
Ryton-on-Dunsmore CV8 30 E1

S

Sabden BB7 56 C6
Sackers Green CO10 34 D5
Sacombe SG12 33 G7
Sacriston DH7 62 D2
Sadberge DL2 62 E5
Saddell PA28 73 F7
Saddington LE8 41 J6
Saddle Bow PE34 44 A4
Sadgill LA8 61 F6
Saffron Walden CB10 33 J5
Sageston SA70 16 D4
Saham Toney IP25 44 C5
Saighdinis HS6 92 D5
Saighton CH3 48 D6
St. Abbs TD14 77 H4
St. Agnes TR5 2 E3
ST. ALBANS AL 22 E1
St. Allen TR4 3 F3
St. Andrews KY16 83 G6
St. Andrews Major CF64 18 E4
St. Anne's FY8 55 G7
St. Ann's DG11 69 F4
St. Ann's Chapel, *Cornw.* PL18 4 E3
St. Ann's Chapel, *Devon* TQ7 5 G6
St. Anthony, *Cornw.* TR2 3 F5
St. Anthony, *Cornw.* TR12 2 E6
St. Arvans NP16 19 J2
St. Asaph (Llanelwy) LL17 47 J5
St. Athan CF62 18 D5
St. Audries TA4 7 K1
St. Austell PL25 4 A5
St. Bees CA27 60 A5
St. Blazey PL24 4 A5
St. Blazey Gate PL24 4 A5
St. Boswells TD6 76 D7
St. Breock PL27 3 G1
St. Breward PL30 4 A3
St. Briavels GL15 19 J1
St. Brides SA62 16 B3
St. Brides Major CF32 18 B4
St. Brides Netherwent NP26 19 H3
St. Brides Wentlooge NP10 19 F3
St. Bride's-super-Ely CF5 18 D4
St. Budeaux PL5 4 E5
St. Buryan TR19 2 B6
St. Catherine BA1 20 A4
St. Catherines PA25 80 C7
St. Clears SA33 17 F3
St. Cleer PL14 4 C4
St. Clement TR1 3 F4
St. Clether PL15 4 C2
St. Columb Major TR9 3 G2
St. Columb Minor TR7 3 F2
St. Columb Road TR9 3 G3
St. Combs AB43 99 J4
St. Cross South Elmham IP20 45 G7
St. Cyrus DD10 83 J1
St. Davids KY11 75 K2
St. David's, *P. & K.* PH7 82 A5
St. David's (Tyddewi), *Pembs.* SA62 16 A2
St. Day TR16 2 E4
St. Decumans TA23 7 J1
St. Dennis PL26 3 G3
St. Dogmaels SA43 26 A4
St. Dogwells SA62 16 C2
St. Dominick PL12 4 E4
St. Donats CF61 18 C5
St. Edith's Marsh SN15 20 C5
St. Endellion PL29 3 G1
St. Enoder TR8 3 F3
St. Erme TR4 3 F4
St. Erth TR27 2 C5
St. Erth Praze TR27 2 C5
St. Ervan PL27 3 F1
St. Eval PL27 3 F2
St. Ewe PL26 3 G4
St. Fagans CF5 18 E4
St. Fergus AB42 99 K5
St. Fillans PH6 81 H5
St. Florence SA70 16 D4
St. Gennys EX23 4 B1
St. George LL22 47 H5
St. Georges BS22 19 G5
St. George's CF5 18 D4
St. Germans PL12 4 D5
St. Giles in the Wood EX38 6 D4
St. Giles on the Heath PL15 6 B6
St. Harmon LD6 27 J1
St. Helen Auckland DL14 62 C4
St. Helena NR10 45 F4
St. Helen's TN34 14 D6
St. Helens, *I.o.W.* PO33 11 H6
St. Helens, *Mersey.* WA10 48 E3
St. Hilary, *Cornw.* TR20 2 C5
St. Hilary, *V. of Glam.* CF71 18 D4
St. Hill RH19 13 G3
St. Illtyd NP13 19 F1
St. Ippollitts SG4 33 F6
St. Ishmael SA17 17 G4
St. Ishmael's SA62 16 B4
St. Issey PL27 3 G1
St. Ive PL14 4 D4
St. Ives, *Cambs.* PE27 33 G1
St. Ives, *Cornw.* TR26 2 C4
St. Ives, *Dorset* BH24 10 C4
St. James South Elmham IP19 45 H7
St. John, *Cornw.* PL11 4 E5
St. John's, *Dur.* DL13 62 B3
St. John's, *I.o.M.* IM4 54 B5
St. John's, *Surr.* GU21 22 C6
St. John's, *Worcs.* WR2 29 H3
St. John's Chapel, *Devon* EX31 6 D3
St. John's Chapel, *Dur.* DL13 61 K3
St. John's Fen End PE14 43 J4
St. John's Highway PE14 43 J4
St. John's Kirk ML12 75 H7
St. John's Town of Dalry DG7 68 B5
St. Judes IM7 54 C4
St. Just TR19 2 A5
St. Just in Roseland TR2 3 F5
St. Katherines AB51 91 F1
St. Keverne TR12 2 E6
St. Kew PL30 4 A3
St. Kew Highway PL30 4 A3
St. Keyne PL14 4 C4
St. Lawrence, *Cornw.* PL30 4 A4
St. Lawrence, *Essex* CM0 25 F1
St. Lawrence, *I.o.W.* PO38 11 G7
St. Leonards, *Bucks.* HP23 22 C1
St. Leonards, *Dorset* BH24 10 C4
St. Leonards, *E.Suss.* TN38 14 D7
St. Leonards Grange SO42 11 F5
St. Leonard's Street ME19 23 K6
St. Levan TR19 2 A6
St. Lythans CF5 18 E4
St. Mabyn PL30 4 A3
St. Margaret South Elmham IP20 45 H7
St. Margarets, *Here.* HR2 28 C5
St. Margarets, *Herts.* SG12 33 G7
St. Margaret's at Cliffe CT15 15 J3
St. Margaret's Hope KW17 107 D8
St. Mark's IM9 54 C6
St. Martin, *Cornw.* PL13 4 C5
St. Martin, *Cornw.* TR12 2 E6
St. Martins PH2 82 C4
St. Martin's SY11 38 C2
St. Mary Bourne SP11 21 H6
St. Mary Church CF71 18 D4
St. Mary Cray BR5 23 H5
St. Mary Hill CF35 18 C4
St. Mary in the Marsh TN29 15 F5
St. Marychurch TQ1 5 K4
St. Mary's KW17 107 D7
St. Mary's Airport TR21 2 C1
St. Mary's Bay TN29 15 F5
St. Mary's Croft DG9 64 A4
St. Mary's Grove BS48 19 H5
St. Mary's Hoo ME3 24 D4
St. Mawes TR2 3 F5
St. Mawgan TR8 3 F2
St. Mellion PL12 4 D4
St. Mellons CF3 19 F3
St. Merryn PL28 3 F1
St. Mewan PL26 3 G3
St. Michael Caerhays PL26 3 G4
St. Michael Penkevil TR2 3 F4
St. Michael South Elmham NR35 45 H7

Shawtonhill

St. Michaels, *Kent* **TN30** 14 D4
St. Michaels, *Worcs.* **WR15** 28 E2
St. Michael's on Wyre **PR3** 55 H5
St. Minver **PL27** 3 G1
St. Monans **KY10** 83 G7
St. Neot **PL14** 4 B4
St. Neots **PE19** 32 E3
St. Nicholas, *Pembs.* **SA64** 16 C1
St. Nicholas, *V. of Glam.* **CF5** 18 D4
St. Nicholas at Wade **CT7** 25 J5
St. Ninians **FK7** 75 F1
St. Osyth **CO16** 35 F7
St. Owen's Cross **HR2** 28 E6
St. Paul's Cray **BR5** 23 H5
St. Paul's Walden **SG4** 32 E6
St. Peter's **CT10** 25 K5
St. Petrox **SA71** 16 C5
St. Pinnock **PL14** 4 C4
St. Quivox **KA9** 67 H1
St. Stephen **PL26** 3 G3
St. Stephen's **PL12** 4 E5
St. Stephens, *Cornw.* **PL15** 6 B7
St. Stephens, *Herts.* **AL3** 22 E1
St. Teath **PL30** 4 A2
St. Tudy **PL30** 4 A3
St. Twynnells **SA71** 16 C5
St. Veep **PL22** 4 B5
St. Vigeans **DD11** 83 H3
St. Wenn **PL30** 3 G2
St. Weonards **HR2** 28 D6
Saintbury **WR11** 30 C4
Salachail **PA38** 80 B2
Salcombe **TQ8** 5 H7
Salcombe Regis **EX10** 7 K7
Salcott **CM9** 34 D7
Sale **M33** 49 G3
Sale Green **WR9** 29 J3
Saleby **LN13** 53 H5
Salehurst **TN32** 14 C5
Salem, *Carmar.* **SA19** 17 K2
Salem, *Cere.* **SY23** 37 F7
Salem, *Gwyn.* **LL54** 46 D7
Salen, *Arg. & B.* **PA72** 79 G3
Salen, *High.* **PH36** 79 H1
Salesbury **BB1** 56 B6
Salford, *Beds.* **MK17** 32 C5
Salford, *Gt.Man.* **M5** 49 H3
Salford, *Oxon.* **OX7** 30 D6
Salford Priors **WR11** 30 B3
Salfords **RH1** 23 F7
Salhouse **NR13** 45 H4
Saline **KY12** 75 J1
SALISBURY SP **10 C1**
Salkeld Dykes **CA11** 61 G3
Sall **NR10** 45 F3
Sallachan **PH33** 80 A1
Sallachry **PA32** 80 B6
Sallachy, *High.* **IV27** 96 C1
Sallachy, *High.* **IV40** 87 F1
Salmonby **LN9** 53 G5
Salmond's Muir **DD11** 83 G4
Salperton **GL54** 30 B6
Salph End **MK41** 32 D3
Salsburgh **ML7** 75 G4
Salt **ST18** 40 B3
Salt Hill **SL1** 22 C4
Saltash **PL12** 4 E5
Saltburn **IV18** 96 E4
Saltburn-by-the-Sea **TS12** 63 H4
Saltby **LE14** 42 B3
Saltcoats **KA21** 74 A6
Saltcotes **FY8** 55 G7
Saltdean **BN2** 13 G6
Salterforth **BB18** 56 D5
Salterhill **IV31** 97 K5
Salterswall **CW7** 49 F6
Saltfleet **LN11** 53 H3
Saltfleetby All Saints **LN11** 53 H3
Saltfleetby St. Clements **LN11** 53 H3
Saltfleetby St. Peter **LN11** 53 H4
Saltford **BS31** 19 K5
Salthaugh Grange **HU12** 59 J7
Salthouse **NR25** 44 E1
Saltley **B8** 40 C7
Saltmarshe **DN14** 58 D7
Saltney **CH4** 48 C6
Salton **YO62** 58 D1
Saltwick **NE20** 71 G5
Saltwood **CT21** 15 G4
Salvington **BN13** 12 E6
Salwarpe **WR9** 29 H2
Salwayash **DT6** 8 D5
Sambourne **B96** 30 B2
Sambrook **TF10** 39 G3
Samhla **HS6** 92 C5
Samlesbury **PR5** 55 J6
Samlesbury Bottoms **PR5** 56 B7
Sampford Arundel **TA21** 7 K4
Sampford Brett **TA4** 7 J1
Sampford Courtenay **EX20** 6 E5
Sampford Peverell **EX16** 7 J4
Sampford Spiney **PL20** 5 F3
Samuelston **EH41** 76 C3
Sanaigmore **PA44** 72 A4
Sancreed **TR20** 2 B6
Sancton **YO43** 59 F6
Sand **ZE2** 109 C8
Sand Hole **YO43** 58 E6
Sand Hutton **YO41** 58 C4
Sand Side **LA17** 55 F1
Sandaig, *High.* **IV40** 86 D3
Sandaig, *High.* **PH41** 86 D4
Sandbach **CW11** 49 G6
Sandbank **PA23** 73 K2
Sandbanks **BH13** 10 B6
Sandend **AB45** 98 D4
Sanderstead **CR2** 23 G5
Sandford, *Cumb.* **CA16** 61 J5
Sandford, *Devon* **EX17** 7 G5
Sandford, *Dorset* **BH20** 9 J5
Sandford, *I.o.W.* **PO38** 11 G6
Sandford, *N.Som.* **BS25** 19 H6
Sandford, *S.Lan.* **ML10** 75 F6
Sandford Orcas **DT9** 9 F2
Sandford St. Martin **OX7** 31 F6
Sandford-on-Thames **OX4** 21 J1
Sandfordhill **AB42** 99 K6
Sandgarth **KW17** 107 E6
Sandgate **CT20** 15 H4
Sandgreen **DG7** 65 F5
Sandhaven **AB43** 99 H4
Sandhead **DG9** 64 A5
Sandhills, *Dorset* **DT9** 9 F3
Sandhills, *Surr.* **GU8** 12 C3
Sandhoe **NE46** 70 E7
Sandholme, *E.Riding* **HU15** 58 E6
Sandholme, *Lincs.* **PE20** 43 G2
Sandhurst, *Brack.F.* **GU47** 22 B5
Sandhurst, *Glos.* **GL2** 29 H6
Sandhurst, *Kent* **TN18** 14 C5
Sandhutton **YO7** 57 J1
Sandiacre **NG10** 41 G2
Sandilands **LN12** 53 J4
Sandiway **CW8** 49 F5
Sandleheath **SP6** 10 C3
Sandleigh **OX13** 21 H1
Sandling **ME14** 14 C2
Sandness **ZE2** 109 A7
Sandon, *Essex* **CM2** 24 D1
Sandon, *Herts.* **SG9** 33 G5
Sandon, *Staffs.* **ST18** 40 B3
Sandown **PO36** 11 G6
Sandplace **PL13** 4 C5
Sandquoy **KW17** 106 G3
Sandridge, *Herts.* **AL4** 32 E7
Sandridge, *Wilts.* **SN12** 20 C5
Sandringham **PE35** 44 A3
Sandrocks **RH16** 13 G4
Sandsend **YO21** 63 K5
Sandside House **KW14** 104 E2
Sandsound **ZE2** 109 C8
Sandtoft **DN8** 51 K2
Sanduck **TQ13** 7 F7
Sandway **ME17** 14 D2
Sandwich **CT13** 15 J2
Sandwick, *Cumb.* **CA10** 60 F5
Sandwick, *Shet.* **ZE2** 109 D10
Sandwick (Sanndabhaig), *W.Isles* **HS1** 101 G4
Sandwith **CA28** 60 A5
Sandy **SG19** 32 E4
Sandy Haven **SA62** 16 B4
Sandy Lane, *W.Yorks.* **BD15** 57 G6
Sandy Lane, *Wilts.* **SN15** 20 C5
Sandycroft **CH5** 48 C6
Sandygate, *Devon* **TQ12** 5 J3
Sandygate, *I.o.M.* **IM7** 54 C4
Sandylands **LA3** 55 H3
Sandyway **HR2** 28 D6
Sangobeg **IV27** 103 G2
Sanna **PH36** 79 F1
Sannaig **PA60** 72 D4
Sanndabhaig (Sandwick) **HS1** 101 G4
Sanquhar **DG4** 68 C3
Santon Bridge **CA19** 60 C6
Santon Downham **IP27** 44 C7
Sapcote **LE9** 41 G6
Sapey Common **WR6** 29 G2
Sapiston **IP31** 34 D1
Sapperton, *Glos.* **GL7** 20 C1
Sapperton, *Lincs.* **NG34** 42 D2
Saracen's Head **PE12** 43 G3
Sarclet **KW1** 105 J4
Sardis **SA73** 16 C4
Sarisbury **SO31** 11 G4
Sarn, *Bridgend* **CF32** 18 C3
Sarn, *Powys* **SY16** 38 B6
Sarn Bach **LL53** 36 C3
Sarn-Meyllteyrn **LL53** 36 B2
Sarnau, *Carmar.* **SA33** 17 G3
Sarnau, *Cere.* **SA44** 26 C3
Sarnau, *Gwyn.* **LL23** 37 J2
Sarnau, *Powys* **SY22** 38 B4
Sarnesfield **HR4** 28 C3
Saron, *Carmar.* **SA44** 17 G1
Saron, *Carmar.* **SA18** 17 K3
Saron, *Gwyn.* **LL55** 46 D6
Sarratt **WD3** 22 D2
Sarre **CT7** 25 J5
Sarsden **OX7** 30 D6
Sarsgrum **IV27** 103 F2
Sartfield **IM7** 54 C4
Satley **DL13** 62 C2
Satterleigh **EX37** 6 E3
Satterthwaite **LA12** 60 E7
Sauchen **AB51** 90 E3
Saucher **PH2** 82 C4
Sauchieburn **AB30** 83 H1
Sauchrie **KA19** 67 H2
Saughall **CH1** 48 C6
Saughall Massie **CH47** 48 B4
Saughtree **TD9** 70 A4
Saul **GL2** 20 A1
Saundaig **PA77** 78 A3
Saundby **DN22** 51 K4
Saundersfoot **SA69** 16 E4
Saunderton **HP27** 22 A1
Saunton **EX33** 6 C2
Sausthorpe **PE23** 53 G6
Savalbeg **IV27** 96 C1
Savalmore **IV27** 96 C1
Sawbridgeworth **CM21** 33 H7
Sawdon **YO13** 59 F1
Sawley, *Derbys.* **NG10** 41 G2
Sawley, *Lancs.* **BB7** 56 C5
Sawley, *N.Yorks.* **HG4** 57 H3
Sawston **CB2** 33 H4
Sawtry **PE28** 42 E7
Saxby, *Leics.* **LE14** 42 B4
Saxby, *Lincs.* **LN8** 52 D4
Saxby All Saints **DN20** 52 C1
Saxelbye **LE14** 42 A3
Saxilby **LN1** 52 B5
Saxlingham **NR25** 44 E2
Saxlingham Green **NR15** 45 G6
Saxlingham Nethergate **NR15** 45 G6
Saxlingham Thorpe **NR15** 45 G6
Saxmundham **IP17** 35 H2
Saxon Street **CB8** 33 K3
Saxondale **NG13** 41 J2
Saxtead Green **IP13** 35 G2
Saxtead Little Green **IP13** 35 G2
Saxthorpe **NR11** 45 F2
Saxton **LS24** 57 K6
Sayers Common **BN6** 13 F5
Scackleton **YO62** 58 C2
Scadabhagh **HS3** 93 G2
Scaftworth **DN10** 51 J3
Scagglethorpe **YO17** 58 E2
Scalasaig **PA61** 72 B1
Scalby, *E.Riding* **HU15** 58 E7
Scalby, *N.Yorks.* **YO12** 59 G1
Scaldwell **NN6** 31 J1
Scale Houses **CA10** 61 G2
Scaleby **CA6** 69 K7
Scalebyhill **CA6** 69 K7
Scales, *Cumb.* **CA12** 60 E4
Scales, *Cumb.* **LA12** 55 F2
Scalford **LE14** 42 A3
Scaling **TS13** 63 J5
Scallasaig **IV40** 86 E3
Scallastle **PA65** 79 J4
Scalloway **ZE1** 109 C9
Scamadale **PA34** 79 K5
Scamblesby **LN11** 53 F5
Scamodale **PH37** 86 E7
Scampston **YO17** 58 E2
Scampton **LN1** 52 C5
Scaniport **IV2** 88 D1
Scapa **KW15** 107 D7
Scar **KW17** 106 F3
Scarborough **YO11** 59 G1
Scarcewater **TR2** 3 G3
Scarcliffe **S44** 51 G6
Scarcroft **LS14** 57 J5
Scardroy **IV6** 95 J6
Scarff **ZE2** 108 B4
Scarfskerry **KW14** 105 H1
Scargill **DL12** 62 B5
Scarinish **PA77** 78 B3
Scarisbrick **L40** 48 C1
Scarning **NR19** 44 D4
Scarrington **NG13** 42 A1
Scarth Hill **L40** 48 D2
Scartho **DN33** 53 F2
Scatraig **IV2** 88 E1
Scaur **DG2** 65 J3
Scaur or Kippford **DG5** 65 J5
Scawby **DN20** 52 C2
Scawton **YO7** 58 B1
Scayne's Hill **RH17** 13 G4
Scealascro **HS2** 100 D5
Scethrog **LD3** 28 A6
Schaw **KA5** 67 J1
Scholar Green **ST7** 49 H7
Scholes, *W.Yorks.* **LS15** 57 J6
Scholes, *W.Yorks.* **HD9** 50 D2
Sciberscross **IV28** 104 C7
Scleddau **SA65** 16 C1
Sco Ruston **NR12** 45 G3
Scofton **S81** 51 J4
Scole **IP21** 35 F1
Scolpaig **HS6** 92 C4
Scolton **SA62** 16 C2
Sconser **IV48** 86 B1
Scoor **PA67** 79 F6
Scopwick **LN4** 52 D7
Scoraig **IV23** 95 G2
Scorborough **YO25** 59 G5
Scorrier **TR16** 2 E4
Scorriton **TQ11** 5 H4
Scorton, *Lancs.* **PR3** 55 J5
Scorton, *N.Yorks.* **DL10** 62 D6
Scotby **CA4** 60 F1
Scotch Corner **DL10** 62 D6
Scotforth **LA1** 55 H4
Scothern **LN2** 52 D5
Scotland Gate **NE62** 71 H5
Scotlandwell **KY13** 82 C7
Scotnish **PA31** 73 F2
Scots' Gap **NE61** 71 F5
Scotsburn **IV18** 96 E4
Scotston, *Aber.* **AB30** 91 F7
Scotston, *P. & K.* **PH8** 82 A3
Scotstown **PH36** 79 K1
Scotter **DN21** 52 B2
Scotterthorpe **DN21** 52 B2
Scottlethorpe **PE10** 42 D3
Scotton, *Lincs.* **DN21** 52 B3
Scotton, *N.Yorks.* **DL9** 62 C7
Scotton, *N.Yorks.* **HG5** 57 J4
Scottow **NR10** 45 G3
Scoulton **NR9** 44 D5
Scourie **IV27** 102 D4
Scourie More **IV27** 102 D4
Scousburgh **ZE2** 109 F9
Scrabster **KW14** 105 F1
Scrainwood **NE65** 70 E3
Scrane End **PE22** 43 G1
Scraptoft **LE7** 41 J5
Scratby **NR29** 45 K4
Scrayingham **YO41** 58 D3
Scredington **NG34** 42 D1
Scremby **PE23** 53 H6
Scremerston **TD15** 77 J6
Screveton **NG13** 42 A1
Scriven **HG5** 57 J4
Scrooby **DN10** 51 J3
Scropton **DE6** 40 D2
Scrub Hill **LN4** 53 F7
Scruton **DL7** 62 D7
Sculthorpe **NR21** 44 C2
Scunthorpe **DN15** 52 B1
Scurlage **SA3** 17 H6
Sea Palling **NR12** 45 J3
Seabank **PA37** 80 A3
Seaborough **DT8** 8 D4
Seacombe **CH41** 48 B3
Seacroft, *Lincs.* **PE25** 53 J6
Seacroft, *W.Yorks.* **LS14** 57 J6
Seafield, *Arg. & B.* **PA31** 73 F2
Seafield, *S.Ayr.* **KA7** 67 H1
Seafield, *W.Loth.* **EH47** 75 J4
Seaford **BN25** 13 H7
Seaforth **L22** 48 C3
Seagrave **LE12** 41 J4
Seaham **SR7** 63 F2
Seahouses **NE68** 77 K6
Seal **TN15** 23 J6
Sealand **CH1** 48 C6
Seale **GU10** 22 B7
Seamer, *N.Yorks.* **TS9** 63 F5
Seamer, *N.Yorks.* **YO12** 59 G1
Seamill **KA23** 74 A6
Searby **DN38** 52 D2
Seasalter **CT5** 25 G5
Seascale **CA20** 60 B6
Seathwaite, *Cumb.* **CA12** 60 D5
Seathwaite, *Cumb.* **LA20** 60 D7
Seatoller **CA12** 60 D5
Seaton, *Cornw.* **PL11** 4 D5
Seaton, *Cumb.* **CA14** 60 B3
Seaton, *Devon* **EX12** 8 B5
Seaton, *Dur.* **SR7** 63 F2
Seaton, *E.Riding* **HU11** 59 H5
Seaton, *Northumb.* **NE26** 71 J6
Seaton, *Rut.* **LE15** 42 C6
Seaton Burn **NE13** 71 H6
Seaton Carew **TS25** 63 G3
Seaton Delaval **NE25** 71 J6
Seaton Junction **EX13** 8 B5
Seaton Ross **YO42** 58 D5
Seaton Sluice **NE26** 71 J6
Seatown, *Aber.* **AB42** 99 K5
Seatown, *Dorset* **DT6** 8 D5
Seatown, *Moray* **AB56** 98 D4
Seatown, *Moray* **AB56** 98 C4
Seave Green **TS9** 63 G6
Seaview **PO34** 11 H5
Seaville **CA7** 60 C1
Seavington St. Mary **TA19** 8 D3
Seavington St. Michael **TA19** 8 D3
Seawick **CO16** 35 F7
Sebastopol **NP4** 19 F2
Sebergham **CA5** 60 E2
Seckington **B79** 40 E5
Second Coast **IV22** 95 F2
Sedbergh **LA10** 61 H7
Sedbury **NP16** 19 J2
Sedbusk **DL8** 61 K7
Sedgeberrow **WR11** 30 B5
Sedgebrook **NG32** 42 B2
Sedgefield **TS21** 62 E4
Sedgeford **PE36** 44 B2
Sedgehill **SP7** 9 H2
Sedgley **DY3** 40 B6
Sedgwick **LA8** 55 J1
Sedlescombe **TN33** 14 C6
Sedlescombe Street **TN33** 14 C6
Seend **SN12** 20 C5
Seend Cleeve **SN12** 20 C5
Seer Green **HP9** 22 C2
Seething **NR15** 45 H6
Sefton **L29** 48 C2
Seghill **NE23** 71 H6
Seighford **ST18** 40 A3
Seilebost **HS3** 93 F2
Seion **LL55** 46 D6
Seisdon **WV5** 40 A6
Seisiadar **HS2** 101 H4
Selattyn **SY10** 38 B2
Selborne **GU34** 11 J1
Selby **YO8** 58 C6
Selham **GU28** 12 C4
Selkirk **TD7** 69 K1
Sellack **HR9** 28 E6
Sellafield **CA20** 60 B6
Sellafirth **ZE2** 108 E3
Sellindge **TN25** 15 F4
Selling **ME13** 15 F2
Sells Green **SN12** 20 C5
Selly Oak **B29** 40 C7
Selmeston **BN26** 13 J6
Selsdon **CR2** 23 G5
Selsey **PO20** 12 B7
Selsfield Common **RH19** 13 G3
Selside **BD24** 56 C2
Selstead **CT15** 15 H3
Selston **NG16** 51 G7
Selworthy **TA24** 7 H1
Semblister **ZE2** 109 C7
Semer **IP7** 34 D4
Semington **BA14** 20 B5
Semley **SP7** 9 H2
Send **GU23** 22 D6
Send Marsh **GU23** 22 D6
Senghenydd **CF83** 18 E2
Sennen **TR19** 2 A6
Sennen Cove **TR19** 2 A6
Sennybridge **LD3** 27 J6
Senwick **DG6** 65 G6
Sequer's Bridge **PL21** 5 G5
Sessay **YO7** 57 K2
Setchey **PE33** 44 A4
Setley **SO42** 10 E4
Setter, *Shet.* **ZE2** 109 C7
Setter, *Shet.* **ZE2** 109 E8
Settiscarth **KW17** 107 C6
Settle **BD24** 56 D3
Settrington **YO17** 58 E2
Seven Bridges **SN6** 20 E2
Seven Kings **IG3** 23 H3
Seven Sisters **SA10** 18 B1
Seven Springs **GL53** 29 J7
Sevenhampton, *Glos.* **GL54** 30 B6
Sevenhampton, *Swin.* **SN6** 21 F2
Sevenoaks **TN13** 23 J6
Sevenoaks Weald **TN14** 23 J6
Severn Beach **BS35** 19 J3
Severn Stoke **WR8** 29 H4
Sevington **TN24** 15 F3
Sewards End **CB10** 33 J5
Sewardstone **E4** 23 G2
Sewerby **YO15** 59 J3
Seworgan **TR11** 2 E5
Sewstern **NG33** 42 B3
Sexhow **TS15** 63 F6
Sgarasta Mhòr **HS3** 93 F2
Sgiogarstaigh **HS2** 101 H1
Sgodachail **IV24** 96 B2
Shabbington **HP18** 21 K1
Shackerley **WV7** 40 A5
Shackerstone **CV13** 41 F5
Shackleford **GU8** 22 C7
Shadfen **NE61** 71 H5
Shadforth **DH6** 62 E2
Shadingfield **NR34** 45 J7
Shadoxhurst **TN26** 14 E4
Shadwell **IP24** 44 D7
Shaftesbury **SP7** 9 H2
Shafton **S72** 51 F1
Shalbourne **SN8** 21 G5
Shalcombe **PO41** 11 F6
Shalden **GU34** 21 K7
Shaldon **TQ14** 5 K3
Shalfleet **PO30** 11 F6
Shalford, *Essex* **CM7** 34 B6
Shalford, *Surr.* **GU4** 22 D7
Shalford Green **CM7** 34 B6
Shallowford **EX31** 7 F1
Shalmsford Street **CT4** 15 F2
Shalmstry **KW14** 105 G2
Shalstone **MK18** 31 H5
Shalunt **PA20** 73 J3
Shambellie **DG2** 65 K4
Shamley Green **GU5** 22 D7
Shandon **G84** 74 A2
Shandwick **IV20** 97 F4
Shangton **LE8** 42 A6
Shankend **TD9** 70 A3
Shankhouse **NE23** 71 H6
Shanklin **PO37** 11 G6
Shannochie **KA27** 66 D1
Shantron **G83** 74 B2
Shantullich **IV8** 96 D6
Shanzie **PH11** 82 D2
Shap **CA10** 61 G5
Shapwick, *Dorset* **DT11** 9 J4
Shapwick, *Som.* **TA7** 8 D1
Shardlow **DE72** 41 G2
Shareshill **WV10** 40 B5
Sharlston **WF4** 51 F1
Sharnbrook **MK44** 32 D3
Sharnford **LE10** 41 G6
Sharoe Green **PR2** 55 J6
Sharow **HG4** 57 J2
Sharpenhoe **MK45** 32 D5
Sharperton **NE65** 70 E3
Sharpham House **TQ9** 5 J5
Sharpness **GL13** 19 K1
Sharpthorne **RH19** 13 G3
Sharrington **NR24** 44 E2
Shatterford **DY12** 39 G7
Shaugh Prior **PL7** 5 F4
Shavington **CW2** 49 F7
Shaw, *Gt.Man.* **OL2** 49 J2
Shaw, *Swin.* **SN5** 20 E3
Shaw, *W.Berks.* **RG14** 21 H5
Shaw, *Wilts.* **SN12** 20 B5
Shaw Mills **HG3** 57 H3
Shawbury **SY4** 38 E3
Shawclough **OL12** 49 H1
Shawell **LE17** 41 H7
Shawford **SO21** 11 F2
Shawforth **OL12** 56 D7
Shawhead **DG2** 65 J3
Shawtonhill **ML10** 74 E6

Staxigoe

Somersham, *Cambs.* **PE28** 33 G1
Somersham, *Suff.* **IP8** 34 E4
Somerton, *Oxon.* **OX25** 31 F6
Somerton, *Som.* **TA11** 8 D2
Somerton, *Suff.* **IP29** 34 C3
Sompting **BN15** 12 E6
Sonning **RG4** 22 A4
Sonning Common **RG4** 22 A3
Sonning Eye **RG4** 22 A4
Sopley **BH23** 10 C5
Sopworth **SN14** 20 B3
Sorbie **DG8** 64 E6
Sordale **KW12** 105 G2
Sorisdale **PA78** 78 D1
Sorn **KA5** 67 K1
Sornhill **KA4** 74 D7
Soroba **PA34** 79 K5
Sortat **KW1** 105 H2
Sotby **LN8** 53 F5
Sots Hole **LN4** 52 E6
Sotterly **NR34** 45 J7
Soudley **TF9** 39 G3
Soughton **CH7** 48 B6
Soulbury **LU7** 32 B6
Soulby **CA17** 61 J5
Souldern **OX27** 31 G5
Souldrop **MK44** 32 C2
Sound, *Ches.* **CW5** 39 F1
Sound, *Shet.* **ZE2** 109 C7
Sound, *Shet.* **ZE1** 109 D8
Soundwell **BS16** 19 K4
Sourhope **TD5** 70 D1
Sourin **KW17** 106 D4
Sourton **EX20** 6 D7
Soutergate **LA17** 55 F1
South Acre **PE32** 44 C4
South Allington **TQ7** 5 H7
South Alloa **FK7** 75 G1
South Ambersham **GU29** 12 C4
South Anston **S25** 51 H4
South Ascot **SL5** 22 C5
South Ballachulish **PH49** 80 B2
South Balloch **KA26** 67 H4
South Bank **TS6** 63 G4
South Barrow **BA22** 9 F2
South Beddington **SM6** 23 F5
South Benfleet **SS7** 24 D3
South Bersted **PO22** 12 C7
South Blackbog **AB51** 91 F1
South Bowood **DT6** 8 D5
South Brent **TQ10** 5 G4
South Brentor **PL19** 6 C7
South Brewham **BA10** 9 G1
South Broomhill **NE61** 71 H4
South Burlingham **NR13** 45 H5
South Cadbury **BA22** 9 F2
South Cairn **DG9** 66 D7
South Carlton **LN1** 52 C5
South Cave **HU15** 59 F6
South Cerney **GL7** 20 D2
South Chard **TA20** 8 C4
South Charlton **NE66** 71 G1
South Cheriton **BA8** 9 F2
South Cliffe **YO43** 58 E6
South Clifton **NG23** 52 B5
South Cockerington **LN11** 53 G4
South Common **BN8** 13 G5
South Cornelly **CF33** 18 B4
South Corrygills **KA27** 73 J7
South Cove **NR34** 45 J7
South Creagan **PA35** 80 A3
South Creake **NR21** 44 C2
South Croxton **LE7** 41 J4
South Dalton **HU17** 59 F5
South Darenth **DA4** 23 J5
South Duffield **YO8** 58 C6
South Elkington **LN11** 53 F4
South Elmsall **WF9** 51 G1
South End, *Bucks.* **LU7** 32 B6
South End, *Cumb.* **LA14** 55 F3
South End, *N.Lincs.* **DN19** 52 E1
South Erradale **IV21** 94 D4
South Fambridge **SS4** 24 E2
South Fawley **OX12** 21 G3
South Ferriby **DN18** 59 F7
South Flobbets **AB51** 91 F1
South Garth **ZE2** 108 E3
South Godstone **RH9** 23 G7
South Gorley **SP6** 10 C3
South Green, *Essex* **CM12** 24 C2
South Green, *Norf.* **NR20** 44 E4
South Hall **PA22** 73 J3
South Hanningfield **CM3** 24 D2
South Harting **GU31** 11 J3
South Hayling **PO11** 11 J5
South Hazelrigg **NE66** 77 J7
South Heath **HP16** 22 C1
South Heighton **BN9** 13 H6
South Hetton **DH6** 62 E2
South Hiendley **S72** 51 F1
South Hill **PL17** 4 D3
South Hinksey **OX1** 21 J1
South Hole **EX39** 6 A4
South Holmwood **RH5** 22 E7
South Hornchurch **RM13** 23 J3
South Hourat **KA24** 74 A5
South Huish **TQ7** 5 G6
South Hykeham **LN6** 52 C6
South Hylton **SR4** 62 E1
South Kelsey **LN7** 52 D3
South Kessock **IV3** 96 D7
South Killingholme **DN40** 52 E1
South Kilvington **YO7** 57 K1
South Kilworth **LE17** 41 J7
South Kirkby **WF9** 51 G1
South Kirkton **AB32** 91 F4
South Kyme **LN4** 42 E1
South Lancing **BN15** 12 E6
South Ledaig **PA37** 80 A4
South Leigh **OX29** 21 G1
South Leverton **DN22** 51 K4
South Littleton **WR11** 30 B4
South Lopham **IP22** 44 E7
South Luffenham **LE15** 42 C5
South Malling **BN7** 13 H5
South Marston **SN3** 20 E3
South Milford **LS25** 57 K6
South Milton **TQ7** 5 H6
South Mimms **EN6** 23 F1
South Molton **EX36** 7 F3
South Moor **DH9** 62 C1
South Moreton **OX11** 21 J3
South Mundham **PO20** 12 B6
South Muskham **NG23** 51 K7
South Newbald **YO43** 59 F6
South Newington **OX15** 31 F5
South Newton **SP2** 10 B1
South Normanton **DE55** 51 G7
South Norwood **SE25** 23 G5
South Nutfield **RH1** 23 G7
South Ockendon **RM15** 23 J3
South Ormsby **LN11** 53 G5
South Otterington **DL7** 57 J1
South Oxhey **WD19** 22 E2
South Park **RH2** 23 F7
South Perrott **DT8** 8 D4
South Petherton **TA13** 8 D3
South Petherwin **PL15** 6 B7
South Pickenham **PE37** 44 C5
South Pool **TQ7** 5 H6
South Queensferry **EH30** 75 K3
South Radworthy **EX36** 7 F2
South Rauceby **NG34** 42 D1
South Raynham **NR21** 44 C3
South Redbriggs **AB53** 99 F6
South Reston **LN11** 53 H4
South Runcton **PE33** 44 A5
South Scarle **NG23** 52 B6
South Shian **PA37** 80 A3
South Shields **NE33** 71 J7
South Skirlaugh **HU11** 59 H6
South Somercotes **LN11** 53 H3
South Stainley **HG3** 57 J3
South Stoke, *Oxon.* **RG8** 21 K3
South Stoke, *W.Suss.* **BN18** 12 D6
South Street, *E.Suss.* **BN8** 13 G5
South Street, *Kent* **DA13** 24 C5
South Tawton **EX20** 6 E6
South Thoresby **LN13** 53 H5
South Tidworth **SP9** 21 F7
South Town **GU34** 11 H1
South Upper Barrack **AB41** 99 H6
South View **ZE2** 109 C8
South Walsham **NR13** 45 H4
South Warnborough **RG29** 22 A7
South Weald **CM14** 23 J2
South Weston **OX9** 22 A2
South Wheatley, *Cornw.* **PL15** 4 C1
South Wheatley, *Notts.* **DN22** 51 K4
South Widcombe **BS40** 19 J6
South Wigston **LE18** 41 H6
South Willesborough **TN24** 15 F3
South Willingham **LN8** 52 E4
South Wingate **TS27** 63 F3
South Wingfield **DE55** 51 F7
South Witham **NG33** 42 C4
South Wonston **SO21** 11 F1
South Woodham Ferrers **CM3** 24 E2
South Wootton **PE30** 44 A3
South Wraxall **BA15** 20 B5
South Yardley **B26** 40 D7
South Zeal **EX20** 6 E6
SOUTHALL UB 22 E4
Southam, *Glos.* **GL52** 29 J6
Southam, *Warks.* **CV47** 31 F2
SOUTHAMPTON SO 11 F3
Southampton International Airport **SO18** 11 F3
Southbar **PA4** 74 C4
Southborough **TN4** 23 J7
Southbourne, *Bourne.* **BH6** 10 C5
Southbourne, *W.Suss.* **PO10** 11 J4
Southburgh **IP25** 44 E5
Southburn **YO25** 59 F4
Southchurch **SS1** 25 F3
Southcott **EX20** 6 D6
Southdean **TD9** 70 B3
Southease **BN7** 13 H6
Southend, *Aber.* **AB53** 99 F6
Southend, *Arg. & B.* **PA28** 66 A3
Southend, *W.Berks.* **RG7** 21 K4
SOUTHEND-ON-SEA SS 24 E3
Southerndown **CF32** 18 B4
Southerness **DG2** 65 K5
Southery **PE38** 44 A6
Southfleet **DA13** 24 C4
Southgate, *Gt.Lon.* **N14** 23 F2
Southgate, *Norf.* **PE31** 44 A2
Southgate, *Norf.* **NR10** 45 F3
Southgate, *Swan.* **SA3** 17 J6
Southill **SG18** 32 E4
Southington **RG25** 21 J7
Southleigh **EX24** 8 B5
Southminster **CM0** 25 F2
Southmuir **DD8** 82 E2
Southoe **PE19** 32 E2
Southolt **IP23** 35 F2
Southorpe **PE9** 42 D5
Southowram **HX3** 57 G7
Southport **PR8** 48 C1
Southrepps **NR11** 45 G2
Southrey **LN3** 52 E6
Southrop **GL7** 20 E1
Southrope **RG25** 21 K7
Southsea, *Ports.* **PO4** 11 H5
Southsea, *Wrex.* **LL11** 48 B7
Southstoke **BA2** 20 A5
Southtown, *Norf.* **NR31** 45 K5
Southtown, *Ork.* **KW17** 107 D8
Southwaite, *Cumb.* **CA4** 61 F2
Southwaite, *Cumb.* **CA17** 61 J6
Southwark **SE** 23 G4
Southwater **RH13** 12 E4
Southway **BA5** 19 J7
Southwell, *Dorset* **DT5** 9 F7
Southwell, *Notts.* **NG25** 51 K7
Southwick, *Hants.* **PO17** 11 H4
Southwick, *Northants.* **PE8** 42 D6
Southwick, *T. & W.* **SR5** 62 E1
Southwick, *W.Suss.* **BN42** 13 F6
Southwick, *Wilts.* **BA14** 20 B6
Southwold **IP18** 35 K1
Southwood, *Norf.* **NR13** 45 H5
Southwood, *Som.* **BA6** 8 E1
Sowerby, *N.Yorks.* **YO7** 57 K1
Sowerby, *W.Yorks.* **HX6** 57 F7
Sowerby Bridge **HX6** 57 F7
Sowerby Row **CA4** 60 E2
Sowton **EX5** 7 H6
Soyal **IV24** 96 C2
Spa Common **NR28** 45 G2
Spadeadam **CA8** 70 A6
Spalding **PE11** 43 F3
Spaldington **DN14** 58 D6
Spaldwick **PE28** 32 E1
Spalefield **KY10** 83 G7
Spalford **NG23** 52 B6
Spanby **NG34** 42 D2
Sparham **NR9** 44 E4
Spark Bridge **LA12** 55 G1
Sparkford **BA22** 9 F2
Sparkwell **PL7** 5 F5
Sparrowpit **SK23** 50 C4
Sparrow's Green **TN5** 13 K3
Sparsholt, *Hants.* **SO21** 11 F1
Sparsholt, *Oxon.* **OX12** 21 G3
Spartylea **NE47** 61 K2
Spaunton **YO62** 63 J7
Spaxton **TA5** 8 B1
Spean Bridge **PH34** 87 J6
Speddoch **DG2** 68 D5
Speen, *Bucks.* **HP27** 22 B1
Speen, *W.Berks.* **RG14** 21 H5
Speeton **YO14** 59 H2
Speke **L24** 48 D4
Speldhurst **TN3** 23 J7
Spellbrook **CM23** 33 H7
Spelsbury **OX7** 30 E6
Spen Green **CW11** 49 H6
Spencers Wood **RG7** 22 A5
Spennithorne **DL8** 57 G1
Spennymoor **DL16** 62 D3
Spetchley **WR5** 29 H3
Spetisbury **DT11** 9 J4
Spexhall **IP19** 45 H7
Spey Bay **IV32** 98 B4
Speybridge **PH26** 89 H2
Speyview **AB38** 97 K7
Spilsby **PE23** 53 H6
Spindlestone **NE70** 77 K7
Spinkhill **S21** 51 G5
Spinningdale **IV24** 96 D2
Spirthill **SN11** 20 C4
Spital, *High.* **KW1** 105 G3
Spital, *W. & M.* **SL4** 22 C4
Spital in the Street **LN8** 52 C3
Spitalbrook **EN11** 23 G1
Spithurst **BN8** 13 H5
Spittal, *D. & G.* **DG8** 64 E4
Spittal, *D. & G.* **DG8** 64 D5
Spittal, *E.Loth.* **EH32** 76 C3
Spittal, *Northumb.* **TD15** 77 J5
Spittal, *Pembs.* **SA62** 16 C2
Spittal of Glenmuick **AB35** 90 B6
Spittal of Glenshee **PH10** 82 C1
Spittalfield **PH1** 82 C3
Spixworth **NR10** 45 G4
Spofforth **HG3** 57 J4
Spondon **DE21** 41 G2
Spooner Row **NR18** 44 E6
Spoonley **TF9** 39 F2
Sporle **PE32** 44 C4
Sportsman's Arms **LL22** 47 H7
Spott **EH42** 76 E3
Spratton **NN6** 31 J2
Spreakley **GU10** 22 B7
Spreyton **EX17** 6 E6
Spridlington **LN8** 52 D4
Springburn **G21** 74 E4
Springfield, *Arg. & B.* **PA22** 73 J3
Springfield, *D. & G.* **DG16** 69 J7
Springfield, *Fife* **KY15** 82 E6
Springfield, *Moray* **IV36** 97 H6
Springfield, *P. & K.* **PH13** 82 C4
Springfield, *W.Mid.* **B13** 40 C7
Springholm **DG7** 65 J4
Springkell **DG11** 69 H6
Springleys **AB51** 91 F1
Springside **KA11** 74 B7
Springthorpe **DN21** 52 B4
Springwell **NE9** 62 D1
Sproatley **HU11** 59 H6
Sproston Green **CW4** 49 G6
Sprotbrough **DN5** 51 H2
Sproughton **IP8** 35 F4
Sprouston **TD5** 77 F7
Sprowston **NR7** 45 G4
Sproxton, *Leics.* **LE14** 42 B3
Sproxton, *N.Yorks.* **YO62** 58 C1
Spurstow **CW6** 48 E7
Square Point **DG7** 65 H3
Squires Gate **FY4** 55 G6
Sròn Doire **PA30** 73 G3
Sronphadruig Lodge **PH18** 88 E7
Stableford **ST5** 40 A2
Stackhouse **BD24** 56 D3
Stackpole **SA71** 16 C5
Stacksteads **OL13** 56 D7
Staddiscombe **PL9** 5 F5
Staddlethorpe **HU15** 58 E7
Stadhampton **OX44** 21 K2
Stadhlaigearraidh **HS8** 84 C1
Staffield **CA10** 61 G2
Staffin **IV51** 93 K5
Stafford **ST16** 40 B3
Stagden Cross **CM1** 33 K7
Stagsden **MK43** 32 C4
Stagshaw Bank **NE46** 70 E7
Stain **KW1** 105 J2
Stainburn **LS21** 57 H5
Stainby **NG33** 42 C3
Staincross **S75** 51 F2
Staindrop **DL2** 62 C4
Staines **TW18** 22 D4
Stainfield, *Lincs.* **LN3** 52 E5
Stainfield, *Lincs.* **PE10** 42 D3
Stainforth, *N.Yorks.* **BD24** 56 D3
Stainforth, *S.Yorks.* **DN7** 51 J1
Staining **FY3** 55 G6
Stainland **HX4** 50 C1
Stainsacre **YO22** 63 J2
Stainton, *Cumb.* **CA11** 61 F4
Stainton, *Cumb.* **LA8** 55 J1
Stainton, *Dur.* **DL12** 62 B5
Stainton, *Middbro.* **TS8** 63 F5
Stainton, *N.Yorks.* **DL11** 62 B7
Stainton, *S.Yorks.* **S66** 51 H3
Stainton by Langworth **LN3** 52 D5
Stainton le Vale **LN8** 52 E3
Stainton with Adgarley **LA13** 55 F2
Staintondale **YO13** 63 J3
Stair, *Cumb.* **CA12** 60 D4
Stair, *E.Ayr.* **KA5** 67 J1
Staithes **TS13** 63 J5
Stake Pool **PR3** 55 H5
Stakeford **NE62** 71 H5
Stalbridge **DT10** 9 G3
Stalbridge Weston **DT10** 9 G3
Stalham **NR12** 45 H3
Stalham Green **NR12** 45 H3
Stalisfield Green **ME13** 14 E2
Stalling Busk **DL8** 56 E1
Stallingborough **DN41** 53 F1
Stalmine **FY6** 55 G5
Stalybridge **SK15** 49 J3
Stambourne **CO9** 34 B5
Stamford, *Lincs.* **PE9** 42 D5
Stamford, *Northumb.* **NE66** 71 H2
Stamford Bridge **YO41** 58 D4
Stamfordham **NE18** 71 F6
Stanborough **AL8** 33 F7
Stanbridge, *Beds.* **LU7** 32 C6
Stanbridge, *Dorset* **BH21** 10 B4
Stanbridge Earls **SO51** 10 E2
Stanbury **BD22** 57 F6
Stand **ML6** 75 F4
Standburn **FK1** 75 H3
Standeford **WV10** 40 B5
Standen **TN27** 14 D3
Standford **GU35** 12 B3
Standish **WN6** 48 E1
Standlake **OX29** 21 G1
Standon, *Hants.* **SO21** 11 F2
Standon, *Herts.* **SG11** 33 G6
Standon, *Staffs.* **ST21** 40 A2
Stane **ML7** 75 G5
Stanfield **NR20** 44 D3
Stanford, *Beds.* **SG18** 32 E4
Stanford, *Kent* **TN25** 15 G4
Stanford Bishop **WR6** 29 F3
Stanford Bridge **WR6** 29 G2
Stanford Dingley **RG7** 21 J4
Stanford in the Vale **SN7** 21 G2
Stanford on Avon **NN6** 31 G1
Stanford on Soar **LE12** 41 H3
Stanford on Teme **WR6** 29 G2
Stanford Rivers **CM5** 23 J1
Stanford-le-Hope **SS17** 24 C3
Stanghow **TS12** 63 H5
Stanground **PE2** 43 F6
Stanhoe **PE31** 44 C2
Stanhope, *Dur.* **DL13** 62 A3
Stanhope, *Sc.Bord.* **ML12** 69 G1
Stanion **NN14** 42 C7
Stanley, *Derbys.* **DE7** 41 G1
Stanley, *Dur.* **DH9** 62 C1
Stanley, *P. & K.* **PH1** 82 C4
Stanley, *Staffs.* **ST9** 49 J7
Stanley, *W.Yorks.* **WF3** 57 J7
Stanley, *Wilts.* **SN15** 20 C4
Stanley Common **DE7** 41 G1
Stanmer **BN1** 13 G6
Stanmore, *Gt.Lon.* **HA7** 22 E2
Stanmore, *W.Berks.* **RG20** 21 H4
Stannersburn **NE48** 70 C5
Stanningfield **IP29** 34 C3
Stannington, *Northumb.* **NE61** 71 H6
Stannington, *S.Yorks.* **S6** 51 F4
Stansbatch **HR6** 28 C2
Stansfield **CO10** 34 B3
Stanstead **CO10** 34 C4
Stanstead Abbotts **SG12** 33 G7
Stansted **TN15** 24 C5
Stansted Airport **CM24** 33 J6
Stansted Mountfitchet **CM24** 33 J6
Stanton, *Derbys.* **DE15** 40 E4
Stanton, *Glos.* **WR12** 30 B5
Stanton, *Northumb.* **NE65** 71 G4
Stanton, *Staffs.* **DE6** 40 D1
Stanton, *Suff.* **IP31** 34 D1
Stanton by Bridge **DE73** 41 F3
Stanton by Dale **DE7** 41 G2
Stanton Drew **BS39** 19 J5
Stanton Fitzwarren **SN6** 20 E2
Stanton Harcourt **OX29** 21 H1
Stanton Hill **NG17** 51 G6
Stanton in Peak **DE4** 50 E6
Stanton Lacy **SY8** 28 D1
Stanton Long **TF13** 38 E6
Stanton Prior **BA2** 19 K5
Stanton St. Bernard **SN8** 20 D5
Stanton St. John **OX33** 21 J1
Stanton St. Quintin **SN14** 20 C3
Stanton Street **IP31** 34 D2
Stanton under Bardon **LE67** 41 G4
Stanton upon Hine Heath **SY4** 38 E3
Stanton Wick **BS39** 19 K5
Stanton-on-the-Wolds **NG12** 41 J2
Stanwardine in the Fields **SY4** 38 D3
Stanway, *Essex* **CO3** 34 D6
Stanway, *Glos.* **GL54** 30 B5
Stanwell **TW19** 22 D4
Stanwell Moor **TW19** 22 D4
Stanwick **NN9** 32 C1
Stanwix **CA3** 60 F1
Stanydale **ZE2** 109 B7
Staoinebrig **HS8** 84 C1
Stape **YO18** 63 J7
Stapehill **BH21** 10 B4
Stapeley **CW5** 39 F1
Staple **CT3** 15 H2
Staple Cross **TN32** 14 C5
Staple Fitzpaine **TA3** 8 B3
Staplefield **RH17** 13 F4
Stapleford, *Cambs.* **CB2** 33 H3
Stapleford, *Herts.* **SG14** 33 G7
Stapleford, *Leics.* **LE14** 42 B4
Stapleford, *Lincs.* **LN6** 52 B7
Stapleford, *Notts.* **NG9** 41 G2
Stapleford, *Wilts.* **SP3** 10 B1
Stapleford Abbotts **RM4** 23 H2
Stapleford Tawney **RM4** 23 J2
Staplegrove **TA2** 8 B2
Staplehurst **TN12** 14 C3
Staplers **PO30** 11 G6
Stapleton, *Bristol* **BS7** 19 J4
Stapleton, *Cumb.* **CA6** 70 A6
Stapleton, *Here.* **LD8** 28 C2
Stapleton, *Leics.* **LE9** 41 G6
Stapleton, *N.Yorks.* **DL2** 62 D5
Stapleton, *Shrop.* **SY5** 38 D5
Stapleton, *Som.* **TA12** 8 D2
Stapley **TA3** 7 K4
Staploe **PE19** 32 E2
Staplow **HR8** 29 F4
Star, *Fife* **KY7** 82 E7
Star, *Pembs.* **SA35** 17 F1
Star, *Som.* **BS25** 19 H6
Starbotton **BD23** 56 E2
Starcross **EX6** 7 H7
Starkigarth **ZE2** 109 D10
Starling's Green **CB11** 33 H5
Starr **KA6** 67 J4
Starston **IP20** 45 G7
Startforth **DL12** 62 B5
Startley **SN15** 20 C3
Statham **WA13** 49 F4
Stathe **TA7** 8 C2
Stathern **LE14** 42 A2
Station Town **TS28** 63 F3
Staughton Green **PE19** 32 E2
Staughton Highway **PE19** 32 E2
Staunton, *Glos.* **GL19** 29 G6
Staunton, *Glos.* **GL16** 28 E7
Staunton Harold Hall **LE65** 41 F3
Staunton on Arrow **HR6** 28 C2
Staunton on Wye **HR4** 28 C4
Staveley, *Cumb.* **LA8** 61 F7
Staveley, *Derbys.* **S43** 51 G5
Staveley, *N.Yorks.* **HG5** 57 J3
Staveley-in-Cartmel **LA12** 55 G1
Staverton, *Devon* **TQ9** 5 H4
Staverton, *Glos.* **GL51** 29 H6
Staverton, *Northants.* **NN11** 31 G2
Staverton, *Wilts.* **BA14** 20 B5
Staverton Bridge **GL51** 29 H6
Stawell **TA7** 8 C1
Stawley **TA21** 7 J3
Staxigoe **KW1** 105 J3

Upper Inglesham

Trawsfynydd **LL41** 37 G2
Tre-ddiog **SA62** 16 B2
Tre-groes, *Bridgend* **CF35** 18 C3
Tre-groes, *Cere.* **SA44** 26 D4
Tre-Rhys **SA43** 26 A4
Tre-vaughan **SA31** 17 H2
Trealaw **CF40** 18 C2
Treales **PR4** 55 H6
Trearddur **LL65** 46 A5
Treaslane **IV51** 93 J6
Trebanog **CF39** 18 D2
Trebanos **SA8** 18 A1
Trebarrow **EX22** 4 C1
Trebartha **PL15** 4 C3
Trebarwith **PL33** 4 A2
Trebetherick **PL27** 3 G1
Treborough **TA23** 7 J2
Trebudannon **TR8** 3 F2
Trebullett **PL15** 4 D3
Treburley **PL15** 4 D3
Trebyan **PL30** 4 A4
Trecastle **LD3** 27 H6
Trecwn **SA62** 16 C1
Trecynon **CF44** 18 C1
Tredavoe **TR20** 2 B6
Tredegar **NP22** 18 E1
Tredington, *Glos.* **GL20** 29 J6
Tredington, *Warks.* **CV36** 30 D4
Tredinnick, *Cornw.* **PL27** 3 G1
Tredinnick, *Cornw.* **PL14** 4 C5
Tredomen **LD3** 28 A5
Tredrissi **SA42** 26 A4
Tredunnock **NP15** 19 G2
Treen **TR19** 2 A6
Treeton **S60** 51 G4
Trefaldwyn (Montgomery) **SY15** 38 B6
Trefasser **SA64** 16 B1
Trefdraeth **LL62** 46 C5
Trefecca **LD3** 28 A5
Trefeglwys **SY17** 37 J6
Trefenter **SY23** 27 F2
Treffgarne **SA62** 16 C2
Treffynnon (Holywell), *Flints.* **CH8** 47 K5
Treffynnon, *Pembs.* **SA62** 16 B2
Trefgarn Owen **SA62** 16 B2
Trefil **NP22** 28 A7
Trefilan **SA48** 26 E3
Treflach **SY10** 38 B3
Trefnanney **SY22** 38 B4
Trefnant **LL16** 47 J5
Trefonen **SY10** 38 B3
Trefor, *Gwyn.* **LL54** 36 C1
Trefor, *I.o.A.* **LL65** 46 B4
Treforest **CF37** 18 D3
Treforest Ind. Est. **CF37** 18 E3
Trefriw **LL27** 47 F6
Trefynwy (Monmouth) **NP25** 28 E7
Tregadillett **PL15** 6 B7
Tregaian **LL77** 46 C5
Tregare **NP15** 28 D7
Tregaron **SY25** 27 F3
Tregarth **LL57** 46 E6
Tregavethan **TR4** 2 E4
Tregear **TR2** 3 F3
Tregeare **PL15** 4 C2
Tregeiriog **LL20** 38 A2
Tregele **LL68** 46 B3
Tregidden **TR12** 2 E6
Treglemais **SA62** 16 B2
Tregolds **PL28** 3 F1
Tregole **EX23** 4 B1
Tregonetha **TR9** 3 G2
Tregony **TR2** 3 G4
Tregoyd **LD3** 28 A5
Treguff **CF71** 18 D4
Tregurrian **TR8** 3 F2
Tregynon **SY16** 37 K6
Trehafod **CF37** 18 D2
Treharris **CF46** 18 D2
Treherbert **CF42** 18 C2
Trekenner **PL15** 4 D3
Trelash **PL15** 4 B1
Trelassick **TR2** 3 F3
Trelawnyd **LL18** 47 J5
Trelech **SA33** 17 F1
Trelech a'r Betws **SA33** 17 G2
Treleddyd-fawr **SA62** 16 A2
Trelewis **CF46** 18 E2
Treligga **PL33** 4 A2
Trelights **PL29** 3 G1
Trelill **PL30** 4 A3
Trelissick **TR3** 3 F5
Trelleck **NP25** 19 J1
Trelleck Grange **NP16** 19 H1
Trelogan **CH8** 47 K4
Trelystan **SY21** 38 B5
Tremadog **LL49** 36 E1
Tremail **PL32** 4 B2
Tremain **SA43** 26 B4
Tremaine **PL15** 4 C2
Tremar **PL14** 4 C4
Trematon **PL12** 4 D5
Tremeirchion **LL17** 47 J5
Tremethick Cross **TR20** 2 B5
Trenance **TR8** 3 F2
Trenarren **PL26** 4 A6
Trench, *Tel. & W.* **TF2** 39 F4
Trench, *Wrex.* **LL13** 38 C2
Treneglos **PL15** 4 C2
Trenewan **PL13** 4 B5
Trent **DT9** 8 E3
Trentham **ST4** 40 A1
Trentishoe **EX31** 6 E1
Treoes **CF35** 18 C4
Treorchy **CF42** 18 C2
Tre'r-ddol **SY20** 37 F6
Trerule Foot **PL12** 4 D5
Tresaith **SA43** 26 B3
Trescott **WV6** 40 A6
Trescowe **TR20** 2 C5
Tresham **GL12** 20 A2
Treshnish **PA75** 78 E3
Tresillian **TR2** 3 F4
Tresinney **PL32** 4 B2
Tresinwen **SA64** 16 C1
Treskinnick Cross **EX23** 4 C1
Tresmeer **PL15** 4 C2
Tresparrett **PL32** 4 B1
Tresparrett Posts **PL32** 4 B1
Tressait **PH16** 81 K1
Tresta, *Shet.* **ZE2** 108 F3
Tresta, *Shet.* **ZE2** 109 C7
Treswell **DN22** 51 K5
Trethurgy **PL26** 4 A5
Tretio **SA62** 16 A2
Tretire **HR2** 28 E6
Tretower **NP8** 28 A6
Treuddyn **CH7** 48 B7
Trevalga **PL35** 4 A2
Trevalyn **LL12** 48 C7
Trevanson **PL27** 3 G1
Trevarren **TR9** 3 G2
Trevarrick **PL26** 3 G4
Trevaughan **SA34** 17 F3
Trevellas **TR5** 2 E3
Trevelmond **PL14** 4 C4
Treverva **TR11** 2 E5
Trevescan **TR19** 2 A6
Trevethin **NP4** 19 F1
Trevigro **PL17** 4 D4
Trevine, *Arg. & B.* **PA35** 80 B5
Trevine, *Pembs.* **SA62** 16 B1
Treviscoe **PL26** 3 G3
Trevone **PL28** 3 F1
Trevor **LL20** 38 B1
Trewalder **PL33** 4 A2
Trewarmett **PL34** 4 A2
Trewarthenick **TR2** 3 G4
Trewassa **PL32** 4 B2
Trewellard **TR19** 2 A5
Trewen **PL15** 4 C2
Trewern **SY21** 38 B4
Trewidland **PL14** 4 C5
Trewilym **SA41** 26 A4
Trewint **EX23** 4 B1
Trewithian **TR2** 3 F5
Trewoon **PL25** 3 G3
Treworнan **PL27** 3 G1
Treyarnon **PL28** 3 F1
Treyford **GU29** 12 B5
Triangle **HX6** 57 F7
Trickett's Cross **BH22** 10 B4
Trimdon **TS29** 62 E3
Trimdon Colliery **TS29** 62 E3
Trimdon Grange **TS29** 62 E3
Trimingham **NR27** 45 G2
Trimley St. Martin **IP11** 35 G5
Trimley St. Mary **IP11** 35 G5
Trimpley **DY12** 29 G1
Trimsaran **SA17** 17 H4
Trimstone **EX34** 6 D1
Trinafour **PH18** 81 J1
Trinant **NP11** 19 F2
Tring **HP23** 32 C7
Trinity **DD9** 83 H1
Trislaig **PH33** 87 G7
Trispen **TR4** 3 F3
Tritlington **NE61** 71 H4
Trochry **PH8** 82 A3
Troedyraur **SA38** 26 C4
Troedyrhiw **CF48** 18 D1
Trondavoe **ZE2** 108 C5
Troon, *Cornw.* **TR14** 2 D5
Troon, *S.Ayr.* **KA10** 74 B7
Trosaraidh **HS8** 84 C3
Troston **IP31** 34 C1
Troswell **PL15** 4 C1
Trottiscliffe **ME19** 23 K6
Trotton **GU31** 12 B4
Troughend **NE19** 70 D4
Troustan **PA22** 73 J3
Troutbeck **LA23** 60 F6
Troutbeck Bridge **LA23** 60 F6
Trow Green **GL15** 19 J1
Trowbridge **BA14** 20 B6
Trowle Common **BA14** 20 B6
Trowley Bottom **AL3** 32 D7
Trows **TD5** 76 E7
Trowse Newton **NR14** 45 G5
Trudernish **PA42** 72 C5
Trudoxhill **BA11** 20 A7
Trull **TA3** 8 B2
Trumaisge Arraidh **HS6** 92 D4
Trumpan **IV55** 93 H5
Trumpet **HR8** 29 F5
Trumpington **CB2** 33 H3
Trunch **NR28** 45 G2
Trunnah **FY5** 55 G5
TRURO TR 3 F4
Trusham **TQ13** 7 G7
Trusley **DE6** 40 E2
Trusthorpe **LN12** 53 J4
Truthan **TR4** 3 F3
Trysull **WV5** 40 A6
Tubney **OX13** 21 H2
Tuckenhay **TQ9** 5 J5
Tuckingmill **TR14** 2 D4
Tuddenham, *Suff.* **IP28** 34 B1
Tuddenham, *Suff.* **IP6** 35 F4
Tudeley **TN11** 23 K7
Tudhoe **DL16** 62 D3
Tudweiliog **LL53** 36 B2
Tuffley **GL4** 29 H7
Tufton, *Hants.* **RG28** 21 H7
Tufton, *Pembs.* **SA63** 16 D2
Tugby **LE7** 42 A5
Tugford **SY7** 38 E7
Tughall **NE67** 71 H1
Tuirnaig **IV22** 94 E3
Tulchan **PH1** 82 A5
Tullibody **FK10** 75 G1
Tullich, *Arg. & B.* **PA32** 80 B6
Tullich, *Arg. & B.* **PA34** 79 K6
Tullich, *High.* **IV20** 97 F4
Tullich, *High.* **IV2** 88 D2
Tullich, *Moray* **AB55** 98 B6
Tullich, *Stir.* **FK21** 81 G4
Tullich Muir **IV18** 96 E4
Tulliemet **PH9** 82 A2
Tulloch, *Aber.* **AB51** 91 G1
Tulloch, *High.* **IV24** 96 D2
Tulloch, *Moray* **IV36** 97 H6
Tullochgorm **PA32** 73 H1
Tullochgribban High **PH26** 89 G2
Tullochvenus **AB31** 90 D4
Tulloes **DD8** 83 G3
Tullybannocher **PH6** 81 J5
Tullybelton **PH1** 82 B4
Tullyfergus **PH11** 82 D3
Tullymurdoch **PH11** 82 C2
Tullynessle **AB33** 90 D3
Tumble **SA14** 17 J3
Tumby **PE22** 53 F7
Tumby Woodside **PE22** 53 F7
Tummel Bridge **PH16** 81 J2
Tundergarth Mains **DG11** 69 G5
Tunga **HS2** 101 G4
Tunstall, *E.Riding* **HU12** 59 K6
Tunstall, *Kent* **ME10** 24 E5
Tunstall, *Lancs.* **LA6** 56 B2
Tunstall, *N.Yorks.* **DL10** 62 D7
Tunstall, *Norf.* **NR13** 45 J5
Tunstall, *Stoke* **ST6** 49 H7
Tunstall, *Suff.* **IP12** 35 H3
Tunstead **NR12** 45 H3
Tunworth **RG25** 21 K7
Tupsley **HR1** 28 E4
Tupton **S42** 51 F6
Tur Langton **LE8** 42 A6
Turbiskill **PA31** 73 F2
Turclossie **AB43** 99 G5
Turgis Green **RG27** 21 K6
Turin **DD8** 83 G2
Turkdean **GL54** 30 C7
Turnastone **HR2** 28 C5
Turnberry **KA26** 67 G3
Turnchapel **PL9** 4 E5
Turnditch **DE56** 40 E1
Turner's Green **CV35** 30 C1
Turners Hill **RH10** 13 G3
Turners Puddle **DT2** 9 H5
Turnford **EN10** 23 G1
Turnworth **DT11** 9 H4
Turret Bridge **PH31** 87 K5
Turriff **AB53** 99 F5
Turton Bottoms **BL7** 49 G1
Turvey **MK43** 32 C3
Turville **RG9** 22 A2
Turville Heath **RG9** 22 A2
Turweston **NN13** 31 H5
Tutbury **DE13** 40 E3
Tutnall **B60** 29 J1
Tutshill **NP16** 19 J2
Tuttington **NR11** 45 G3
Tuxford **NG22** 51 K5
Twatt, *Ork.* **KW17** 106 B5
Twatt, *Shet.* **ZE2** 109 C7
Twechar **G65** 74 E3
Tweedmouth **TD15** 77 H5
Tweedsmuir **ML12** 69 F1
Twelveheads **TR4** 2 E4
Twenty **PE10** 42 E3
Twerton **BA2** 20 A5
TWICKENHAM TW 22 E4
Twigworth **GL2** 29 H6
Twineham **RH17** 13 F4
Twinhoe **BA2** 20 A6
Twinstead **CO10** 34 C5
Twiss Green **WA3** 49 F3
Twitchen, *Devon* **EX36** 7 F2
Twitchen, *Shrop.* **SY7** 28 C1
Twizell House **NE70** 71 G1
Two Bridges **PL20** 5 G3
Two Dales **DE4** 50 E6
Two Gates **B77** 40 E5
Twycross **CV9** 41 F5
Twyford, *Bucks.* **MK18** 31 H6
Twyford, *Derbys.* **DE73** 41 F3
Twyford, *Dorset* **SP7** 9 H3
Twyford, *Hants.* **SO21** 11 F2
Twyford, *Leics.* **LE14** 42 A5
Twyford, *Norf.* **NR20** 44 E3
Twyford, *Oxon.* **OX17** 31 F5
Twyford, *W'ham* **RG10** 22 A4
Twyford Common **HR2** 28 E5
Twyn-y-Sheriff **NP15** 19 H1
Twyn-yr-odyn **CF5** 18 E4
Twynholm **DG6** 65 G5
Twyning **GL20** 29 H5
Twyning Green **GL20** 29 H5
Twynllanan **SA19** 27 G6
Twywell **NN14** 32 C1
Ty-hen **LL53** 36 A2
Ty-mawr, *Conwy* **LL21** 37 J1
Ty-mawr, *Denb.* **LL21** 38 A1
Ty-nant, *Conwy* **LL21** 37 J1
Ty-nant, *Gwyn.* **LL23** 37 J3
Ty-uchaf **SY10** 37 J3
Tyberton **HR2** 28 C5
Tyburn **B24** 40 D6
Tycroes **SA18** 17 K3
Tycrwyn **SY22** 38 A4
Tydd Gote **PE13** 43 H4
Tydd St. Giles **PE13** 43 H4
Tydd St. Mary **PE13** 43 H4
Tyddewi (St. David's) **SA62** 16 A2
Tye Common **CM12** 24 C2
Tye Green **CM7** 34 B6
Tyldesley **M29** 49 F2
Tyle-garw **CF72** 18 D3
Tyler Hill **CT2** 25 H5
Tylers Green, *Bucks.* **HP10** 22 C2
Tylers Green, *Essex* **CM16** 23 J1
Tylorstown **CF43** 18 D2
Tylwch **LD6** 27 J1
Tyn-y-cefn **LL21** 37 K1
Tyn-y-Cwm **SY18** 37 H7
Tyn-y-ffridd **SY10** 38 A2
Tyn-y-graig **LD2** 27 K4
Ty'n-y-groes **LL32** 47 F5
Tyndrum **FK20** 80 E4
Tyneham **BH20** 9 H6
Tynehead **EH37** 76 B5
Tynemouth **NE30** 71 J7
Tynewydd **CF42** 18 C2
Tyninghame **EH42** 76 E3
Tynribbie **PA38** 80 A3
Tynron **DG3** 68 D4
Tynygraig **SY25** 27 F2
Tyringham **MK16** 32 B4
Tythegston **CF32** 18 B4
Tytherington, *Ches.* **SK10** 49 J5
Tytherington, *S.Glos.* **GL12** 19 K3
Tytherington, *Som.* **BA11** 20 A7
Tytherington, *Wilts.* **BA12** 20 C7
Tytherleigh **EX13** 8 C4
Tytherton Lucas **SN15** 20 C4
Tywardreath **PL24** 4 A5
Tywardreath Highway **PL24** 4 A5
Tywyn **LL36** 36 E5

U

Uachdar **HS7** 92 D6
Uags **IV54** 86 D1
Ubbeston Green **IP19** 35 H1
Ubley **BS40** 19 J6
Uckerby **DL10** 62 D6
Uckfield **TN22** 13 H4
Uckinghall **GL20** 29 H5
Uckington **GL51** 29 J6
Uddingston **G71** 74 E4
Uddington **ML11** 75 G7
Udimore **TN31** 14 D6
Udny Green **AB41** 91 G2
Udny Station **AB41** 91 H2
Udstonhead **ML10** 75 F6
Uffcott **SN4** 20 E4
Uffculme **EX15** 7 J4
Uffington, *Lincs.* **PE9** 42 D5
Uffington, *Oxon.* **SN7** 21 G3
Uffington, *Shrop.* **SY4** 38 E4
Ufford, *Peter.* **PE9** 42 D5
Ufford, *Suff.* **IP13** 35 G3
Ufton **CV33** 30 E2
Ufton Nervet **RG7** 21 K5
Ugborough **PL21** 5 G5
Uggeshall **NR34** 35 J1
Ugglebarnby **YO22** 63 K6
Ugley **CM22** 33 J6
Ugley Green **CM22** 33 J6
Ugthorpe **YO21** 63 J5
Uig, *Arg. & B.* **PA78** 78 C2
Uig, *Arg. & B.* **PA23** 73 K2
Uig, *High.* **IV51** 93 J5
Uig, *High.* **IV55** 93 G6
Uigen **HS2** 100 C4
Uiginish **IV55** 93 H7
Uigshader **IV51** 93 K7
Uisgebhagh **HS7** 92 D7
Uisken **PA67** 78 E6
Ulbster **KW2** 105 J4
Ulcat row **CA11** 60 F4
Ulceby, *Lincs.* **LN13** 53 H5
Ulceby, *N.Lincs.* **DN39** 52 E1
Ulceby Cross **LN13** 53 H5
Ulcombe **ME17** 14 D3
Uldale **CA7** 60 D3
Uldale House **CA17** 61 J7
Uley **GL11** 20 A2
Ulgham **NE61** 71 H4
Ullapool **IV26** 95 H2
Ullenhall **B95** 30 C2
Ullenwood **GL53** 29 J7
Ulleskelf **LS24** 58 B5
Ullesthorpe **LE17** 41 H7
Ulley **S26** 51 G4
Ullingswick **HR1** 28 E4
Ullinish **IV56** 85 J1
Ullock **CA14** 60 B4
Ulpha **LA20** 60 C7
Ulrome **YO25** 59 H4
Ulsta **ZE2** 108 D4
Ulting **CM9** 24 E1
Uluvalt **PA70** 79 G5
Ulverston **LA12** 55 F2
Ulwell **BH19** 10 B6
Ulzieside **DG4** 68 C3
Umberleigh **EX37** 6 E3
Unapool **IV27** 102 E5
Underbarrow **LA8** 61 F7
Underhoull **ZE2** 108 E2
Underriver **TN15** 23 J6
Underwood, *Newport* **NP18** 19 G3
Underwood, *Notts.* **NG16** 51 G7
Undy **NP26** 19 H3
Unifirth **ZE2** 109 B7
Union Croft **AB39** 91 G5
Union Mills **IM4** 54 C6
Unstone **S18** 51 F5
Unthank **CA11** 61 F3
Up Cerne **DT2** 9 F4
Up Exe **EX5** 7 H5
Up Hatherley **GL51** 29 J6
Up Holland **WN8** 48 E2
Up Marden **PO18** 11 J3
Up Nately **RG27** 22 A6
Up Somborne **SO20** 10 E1
Up Sydling **DT2** 9 F4
Upavon **SN9** 20 E6
Upchurch **ME9** 24 E5
Upcott, *Devon* **EX21** 6 C6
Upcott, *Here.* **HR3** 28 C3
Upend **CB8** 33 K3
Uphall, *Dorset* **DT2** 8 E4
Uphall, *W.Loth.* **EH52** 75 J3
Uphall Station **EH54** 75 J3
Upham, *Devon* **EX17** 7 G5
Upham, *Hants.* **SO32** 11 G2
Uphampton **WR9** 29 H2
Uphill **BS23** 19 G6
Uplawmoor **G78** 74 C5
Upleadon **GL18** 29 G6
Upleatham **TS11** 63 H4
Uplees **ME13** 25 G5
Uploders **DT6** 8 E5
Uplowman **EX16** 7 J4
Uplyme **DT7** 8 C5
Upminster **RM14** 23 J3
Upottery **EX14** 7 K5
Upper (Over) Winchendon **HP18** 31 J7
Upper Affcot **SY6** 38 D7
Upper Ardroscadale **PA20** 73 J4
Upper Arley **DY12** 39 G7
Upper Arncott **OX25** 31 H7
Upper Aston **WV5** 40 A6
Upper Astrop **OX17** 31 G5
Upper Basildon **RG8** 21 K4
Upper Beeding **BN44** 12 E5
Upper Benefield **PE8** 42 C7
Upper Bighouse **KW13** 104 D3
Upper Boat **CF37** 18 E3
Upper Boddington **NN11** 31 F3
Upper Borth **SY24** 37 F7
Upper Boyndlie **AB43** 99 H4
Upper Brailes **OX15** 30 E4
Upper Breinton **HR4** 28 D4
Upper Broughton **LE14** 41 J3
Upper Bucklebury **RG7** 21 J5
Upper Burgate **SP6** 10 C3
Upper Burnhaugh **AB39** 91 G5
Upper Caldecote **SG18** 32 E4
Upper Camster **KW3** 105 H4
Upper Catshill **B61** 29 J1
Upper Chapel **LD3** 27 K4
Upper Chute **SP11** 21 F6
Upper Clatford **SP11** 21 G7
Upper Coberley **GL53** 29 J7
Upper Cound **SY5** 38 E5
Upper Cwmbran **NP44** 19 F2
Upper Dallachy **IV32** 98 B4
Upper Dean **PE28** 32 D2
Upper Denby **HD8** 50 E2
Upper Derraid **PH26** 89 H1
Upper Diabaig **IV22** 94 E5
Upper Dicker **BN27** 13 J5
Upper Dovercourt **CO12** 35 G6
Upper Dunsforth **YO26** 57 K3
Upper Eastern Green **CV5** 40 E7
Upper Eathie **IV11** 96 E5
Upper Elkstone **SK17** 50 C7
Upper End **SK17** 50 C5
Upper Farringdon **GU34** 11 J1
Upper Framilode **GL2** 29 G7
Upper Froyle **GU34** 22 A7
Upper Gills **KW1** 105 J1
Upper Glendessarry **PH34** 87 F5
Upper Godney **BA5** 19 H7
Upper Gornal **DY3** 40 B6
Upper Gravenhurst **MK45** 32 E5
Upper Green, *Essex* **CB11** 33 H5
Upper Green, *Mon.* **NP7** 28 C7
Upper Green, *W.Berks.* **RG20** 21 G5
Upper Gylen **PA34** 79 K5
Upper Hackney **DE4** 50 E6
Upper Halliford **TW17** 22 D5
Upper Halling **ME2** 24 C5
Upper Hambleton **LE15** 42 C5
Upper Hardres Court **CT4** 15 G2
Upper Hartfield **TN7** 13 H3
Upper Hawkhillock **AB42** 91 J1
Upper Hayton **SY8** 38 E7
Upper Heath **SY7** 38 E7
Upper Helmsley **YO41** 58 C4
Upper Hergest **HR5** 28 B3
Upper Heyford **OX25** 31 F6
Upper Hill **HR6** 28 D3
Upper Hopton **WF14** 50 D1
Upper Horsebridge **BN27** 13 J5
Upper Hulme **ST13** 50 C6
Upper Inglesham **SN6** 21 F2

Upper Kilchattan

212

Wettenhall Green

Wednesfield **WV11** 40 B5
Weedon **HP22** 32 B7
Weedon Bec **NN7** 31 H3
Weedon Lois **NN12** 31 H4
Weeford **WS14** 40 D5
Week **EX18** 7 F4
Week Orchard **EX23** 6 A5
Week St. Mary **EX22** 4 C1
Weekley **NN16** 42 B7
Weeley **CO16** 35 F6
Weeley Heath **CO16** 35 F7
Weem **PH15** 81 K3
Weeping Cross **ST17** 40 B3
Weethley **B49** 30 B3
Weeting **IP27** 44 B7
Weeton, *E.Riding* **HU12** 59 K7
Weeton, *Lancs.* **PR4** 55 G6
Weeton, *N.Yorks.* **LS17** 57 H5
Weir, *Essex* **SS6** 24 E3
Weir, *Lancs.* **OL13** 56 D7
Weirbrook **SY11** 38 C3
Welbeck Abbey **S80** 51 H5
Welborne **NR20** 44 E5
Welbourn **LN5** 52 C7
Welburn **YO60** 58 D3
Welbury **DL6** 62 E6
Welby **NG32** 42 C2
Welches Dam **PE16** 43 H7
Welcombe **EX39** 6 A4
Weldon **NN17** 42 C7
Welford, *Northants.* **NN6** 41 J7
Welford, *W.Berks.* **RG20** 21 H4
Welford-on-Avon **CV37** 30 C3
Welham, *Leics.* **LE16** 42 A6
Welham, *Notts.* **DN22** 51 K4
Welham Green **AL9** 23 F1
Well, *Hants.* **RG29** 22 A7
Well, *Lincs.* **LN13** 53 H5
Well, *N.Yorks.* **DL8** 57 H1
Well End **SL8** 22 B3
Well Hill **BR6** 23 H5
Well Town **EX16** 7 H5
Welland **WR13** 29 G4
Wellbank **DD5** 83 F4
Wellesbourne **CV35** 30 D3
Wellhill **IV36** 97 G5
Welling **DA16** 23 H4
Wellingborough **NN8** 32 B2
Wellingham **PE32** 44 C3
Wellingore **LN5** 52 C7
Wellington, *Cumb.* **CA20** 60 B6
Wellington, *Here.* **HR4** 28 D4
Wellington, *Som.* **TA21** 7 K3
Wellington, *Tel. & W.* **TF1** 39 F4
Wellington Heath **HR8** 29 G4
Wellington Marsh **HR4** 28 E4
Wellow, *B. & N.E.Som.* **BA2** 20 A6
Wellow, *I.o.W.* **PO41** 10 E6
Wellow, *Notts.* **NG22** 51 J6
Wells **BA5** 19 J7
Wells-Next-The-Sea **NR23** 44 D1
Wellsborough **CV13** 41 F5
Wellwood **KY12** 75 J2
Welney **PE14** 43 J6
Welsh Bicknor **GL17** 28 E7
Welsh End **SY13** 38 E2
Welsh Frankton **SY11** 38 C2
Welsh Hook **SA62** 16 C2
Welsh Newton **NP25** 28 E7
Welsh St. Donats **CF71** 18 D4
Welshampton **SY12** 38 D2
Welshpool (Y Trallwng) **SY21** 38 B5
Welton, *B. & N.E.Som.* **BA3** 19 K6
Welton, *Cumb.* **CA5** 60 E2
Welton, *E.Riding* **HU15** 59 F7
Welton, *Lincs.* **LN2** 52 D4
Welton, *Northants.* **NN11** 31 G2
Welton le Marsh **PE23** 53 H6
Welton le Wold **LN11** 53 F4
Welwick **HU12** 59 K7
Welwyn **AL6** 33 F7
Welwyn Garden City **AL8** 33 F7
Wem **SY4** 38 E3
Wembdon **TA6** 8 B1
Wembley **HA0** 22 E3
Wembury **PL9** 5 F6
Wembworthy **EX18** 6 E5
Wemyss Bay **PA18** 73 K4
Wenallt, *Gwyn.* **LL21** 37 J1
Wenallt, *Gwyn.* **LL40** 37 H3
Wendens Ambo **CB11** 33 J5
Wendlebury **OX25** 31 G7
Wendling **NR19** 44 D4
Wendover **HP22** 22 B1
Wendron **TR13** 2 D5
Wendy **SG8** 33 G4
Wenhaston **IP19** 35 J1
Wenlli **LL22** 47 G6
Wennington, *Cambs.* **PE28** 33 F1
Wennington, *Gt.Lon.* **RM13** 23 J3
Wennington, *Lancs.* **LA2** 56 B2
Wensley, *Derbys.* **DE4** 50 E6
Wensley, *N.Yorks.* **DL8** 62 B7
Went Hill **BN20** 13 J7
Wentbridge **WF8** 51 G1
Wentnor **SY9** 38 C6
Wentworth, *Cambs.* **CB6** 33 H1
Wentworth, *S.Yorks.* **S62** 51 F3
Wentworth Castle **S75** 51 F2
Wenvoe **CF5** 18 E4
Weobley **HR4** 28 C3
Weobley Marsh **HR4** 28 D3
Wepham **BN18** 12 D6
Wepre **CH5** 48 B6
Wereham **PE33** 44 A5
Wergs **WV6** 40 A5
Wernyrheolydd **NP15** 28 C7
Werrington, *Cornw.* **PL15** 6 B7
Werrington, *Peter.* **PE4** 42 E5
Werrington, *Staffs.* **ST9** 40 B1
Wervil Brook **SA44** 26 C3
Wervin **CH2** 48 D5
Wesham **PR4** 55 H6
Wessington **DE55** 51 F7
West Aberthaw **CF62** 18 D5
West Acre **PE32** 44 B4
West Allerdean **TD15** 77 H6
West Alvington **TQ7** 5 H6
West Amesbury **SP4** 20 E7
West Anstey **EX36** 7 G3
West Ashby **LN9** 53 F5
West Ashling **PO18** 12 B6
West Ashton **BA14** 20 B6
West Auckland **DL14** 62 C4
West Ayton **YO13** 59 F1
West Bagborough **TA4** 7 K2
West Barkwith **LN8** 52 E4
West Barnby **YO21** 63 K5
West Barns **EH42** 76 E3
West Barsham **NR21** 44 D2
West Bay **DT6** 8 D5
West Beckham **NR25** 45 F2
West Benhar **ML7** 75 G4
West Bergholt **CO6** 34 D6
West Bexington **DT2** 8 E6
West Bilney **PE32** 44 B4
West Blatchington **BN3** 13 F6
West Boldon **NE36** 71 J7
West Bradenham **IP25** 44 D5
West Bradford **BB7** 56 C5
West Bradley **BA6** 8 E1
West Bretton **WF4** 50 E1
West Bridgford **NG2** 41 H2
West Bromwich **B70** 40 C6
West Buckland, *Devon* **EX32** 6 E2
West Buckland, *Som.* **TA21** 7 K3
West Burrafirth **ZE2** 109 B7
West Burton, *N.Yorks.* **DL8** 57 F1
West Burton, *W.Suss.* **RH20** 12 C5
West Butterwick **DN17** 52 B2
West Byfleet **KT14** 22 D5
West Cairncake **AB53** 99 G6
West Caister **NR30** 45 K4
West Calder **EH55** 75 J4
West Camel **BA22** 8 E2
West Cauldcoats **ML10** 74 E6
West Challow **OX12** 21 G3
West Charleton **TQ7** 5 H6
West Chelborough **DT2** 8 E4
West Chevington **NE61** 71 H4
West Chiltington **RH20** 12 D5
West Chinnock **TA18** 8 D3
West Chisenbury **SN9** 20 E6
West Clandon **GU4** 22 D6
West Cliffe **CT15** 15 J3
West Clyne **KW9** 97 F1
West Coker **BA22** 8 E3
West Compton, *Dorset* **DT2** 8 E5
West Compton, *Som.* **BA4** 19 J7
West Cross **SA3** 17 K6
West Curry **PL15** 4 C1
West Curthwaite **CA7** 60 E2
West Dean, *W.Suss.* **PO18** 12 B5
West Dean, *Wilts.* **SP5** 10 D2
West Deeping **PE6** 42 E5
West Derby **L12** 48 C3
West Dereham **PE33** 44 A5
West Ditchburn **NE66** 71 G1
West Down **EX34** 6 D1
West Drayton, *Gt.Lon.* **UB7** 22 D4
West Drayton, *Notts.* **DN22** 51 K5
West Dullater **FK17** 81 G7
West Dunnet **KW14** 105 H1
West Edington **NE61** 71 G5
West Ella **HU14** 59 G7
West End, *Beds.* **MK43** 32 C3
West End, *E.Riding* **YO25** 59 G3
West End, *Hants.* **SO30** 11 F3
West End, *Kent* **CT6** 25 H5
West End, *Lancs.* **LA4** 55 H3
West End, *Lincs.* **DN36** 53 G3
West End, *N.Som.* **BS48** 19 H5
West End, *N.Yorks.* **HG3** 57 G4
West End, *Norf.* **NR30** 45 J4
West End, *Oxon.* **OX29** 21 H1
West End, *S.Lan.* **ML11** 75 H6
West End, *Suff.* **NR34** 45 J7
West End, *Surr.* **KT10** 22 E5
West End, *Surr.* **GU24** 22 C5
West End Green **RG7** 21 K5
West Farleigh **ME15** 14 C2
West Farndon **NN11** 31 G3
West Felton **SY11** 38 C3
West Firle **BN8** 13 H6
West Fleetham **NE67** 71 G1
West Garforth **LS25** 57 J6
West Ginge **OX12** 21 H3
West Glen **PA21** 73 J3
West Grafton **SN8** 21 F5
West Green **RG27** 22 A6
West Grimstead **SP5** 10 D2
West Grinstead **RH13** 12 E4
West Haddlesey **YO8** 58 B7
West Haddon **NN6** 31 H1
West Hagbourne **OX11** 21 J3
West Hagley **DY9** 40 B7
West Hall **CA8** 70 A7
West Hallam **DE7** 41 G1
West Halton **DN15** 59 F7
West Ham **E15** 23 H3
West Handley **S21** 51 F5
West Hanney **OX12** 21 H2
West Hanningfield **CM2** 24 D2
West Hardwick **WF4** 51 G1
West Harptree **BS40** 19 J6
West Harting **GU31** 11 J2
West Hatch **TA3** 8 B2
West Heath, *Hants.* **GU14** 22 B6
West Heath, *W.Mid.* **B38** 30 B1
West Helmsdale **KW8** 105 F7
West Hendred **OX12** 21 H3
West Heslerton **YO17** 59 F2
West Hill, *Devon* **EX11** 7 J6
West Hill, *N.Som.* **BS20** 19 H4
West Hoathly **RH19** 13 G3
West Holme **BH20** 9 H6
West Horndon **CM13** 24 C3
West Horrington **BA5** 19 J7
West Horsley **KT24** 22 D6
West Horton **NE71** 77 J7
West Hougham **CT15** 15 H3
West Huntspill **TA9** 19 G7
West Hyde **WD3** 22 D2
West Hythe **CT21** 15 G4
West Ilsley **RG20** 21 H3
West Itchenor **PO20** 11 J4
West Keal **PE23** 53 G6
West Kennett **SN8** 20 E5
West Kilbride **KA23** 74 A6
West Kingsdown **TN15** 23 J5
West Kington **SN14** 20 B4
West Kirby **CH48** 48 B4
West Knapton **YO17** 58 E2
West Knighton **DT2** 9 G6
West Knoyle **BA12** 9 H1
West Kyloe **TD15** 77 J6
West Lambrook **TA13** 8 D3
West Langdon **CT15** 15 J3
West Langwell **IV28** 96 D1
West Lavington, *W.Suss.* **GU29** 12 B4
West Lavington, *Wilts.* **SN10** 20 D6
West Layton **DL11** 62 C5
West Leake **LE12** 41 H3
West Lexham **PE32** 44 C4
West Lilling **YO60** 58 C3
West Lingo **KY9** 83 F7
West Linton **EH46** 75 K5
West Littleton **SN14** 20 A4
West Lockinge **OX12** 21 H3
West Looe **PL13** 4 C5
West Lulworth **BH20** 9 H6
West Lutton **YO17** 59 F3
West Lydford **TA11** 8 E1
West Lyng **TA3** 8 C2
West Lynn **PE34** 44 A4
West Mains **TD15** 77 J6
West Malling **ME19** 23 K6
West Malvern **WR14** 29 G4
West Marden **PO18** 11 J3
West Markham **NG22** 51 K5
West Marsh **DN31** 53 F2
West Marton **BD23** 56 D4
West Melton **S63** 51 G2
West Meon **GU32** 11 H2
West Meon Hut **GU32** 11 H2
West Mersea **CO5** 34 E7
West Milton **DT6** 8 E5
West Minster **ME12** 25 F4
West Molesey **KT8** 22 E5
West Monkton **TA2** 8 B2
West Moors **BH22** 10 B4
West Mostard **LA10** 61 J7
West Muir **DD9** 83 G1
West Ness **YO62** 58 C2
West Newton, *E.Riding* **HU11** 59 J6
West Newton, *Norf.* **PE31** 44 A3
West Norwood **SE27** 23 G4
West Ogwell **TQ12** 5 J3
West Orchard **SP7** 9 H3
West Overton **SN8** 20 E5
West Park, *Aber.* **AB31** 91 F5
West Park, *Mersey.* **WA10** 48 E3
West Parley **BH22** 10 B5
West Peckham **ME18** 23 K6
West Pennard **BA6** 8 E1
West Pentire **TR8** 2 E2
West Perry **PE28** 32 E2
West Porlock **TA24** 7 G1
West Putford **EX22** 6 B4
West Quantoxhead **TA4** 7 K1
West Rainton **DH4** 62 E2
West Rasen **LN8** 52 D4
West Raynham **NR21** 44 C3
West Rounton **DL6** 63 F6
West Row **IP28** 33 K1
West Rudham **PE31** 44 C3
West Runton **NR27** 45 F1
West Saltoun **EH34** 76 C4
West Sandwick **ZE2** 108 D4
West Scrafton **DL8** 57 F1
West Shinness Lodge **IV27** 103 H7
West Somerton **NR29** 45 J3
West Stafford **DT2** 9 G6
West Stockwith **DN10** 51 K3
West Stoke **PO18** 12 B6
West Stonesdale **DL11** 61 K6
West Stoughton **BS28** 19 H7
West Stour **SP8** 9 G2
West Stourmouth **CT3** 25 J5
West Stow **IP28** 34 C1
West Stowell **SN8** 20 E5
West Stratton **SO21** 21 J7
West Street **ME17** 14 E2
West Tanfield **HG4** 57 H2
West Taphouse **PL22** 4 B4
West Tarbert **PA29** 73 G4
West Tarring **BN13** 12 E6
West Thorney **PO10** 11 J4
West Thurrock **RM20** 23 J4
West Tilbury **RM18** 24 C4
West Tisted **SO24** 11 H2
West Tofts, *Norf.* **IP26** 44 C6
West Tofts, *P. & K.* **PH1** 82 C4
West Torrington **LN8** 52 E4
West Town, *Hants.* **PO11** 11 J5
West Town, *N.Som.* **BS48** 19 H5
West Tytherley **SP5** 10 D1
West Walton **PE14** 43 H4
West Walton Highway **PE14** 43 H4
West Wellow **SO51** 10 D2
West Wemyss **KY1** 76 B1
West Wick **BS24** 19 G5
West Wickham, *Cambs.* **CB1** 33 K4
West Wickham, *Gt.Lon.* **BR4** 23 G5
West Williamston **SA68** 16 D4
West Winch **PE33** 44 A4
West Winterslow **SP5** 10 D1
West Wittering **PO20** 11 J5
West Witton **DL8** 57 F1
West Woodburn **NE48** 70 D5
West Woodhay **RG20** 21 G5
West Woodlands **BA11** 20 A7
West Worldham **GU34** 11 J1
West Worlington **EX17** 7 F4
West Worthing **BN11** 12 E6
West Wratting **CB1** 33 J3
West Wycombe **HP14** 22 B2
West Yell **ZE2** 108 D4
Westbere **CT2** 25 H5
Westborough **NG23** 42 B1
Westbourne, *Bourne.* **BH4** 10 B5
Westbourne, *W.Suss.* **PO10** 11 J4
Westbrook **RG20** 21 H4
Westbury, *Bucks.* **NN13** 31 H5
Westbury, *Shrop.* **SY5** 38 C5
Westbury, *Wilts.* **BA13** 20 B6
Westbury Leigh **BA13** 20 B6
Westbury on Trym **BS9** 19 J4
Westbury-on-Severn **GL14** 29 G7
Westbury-sub-Mendip **BA5** 19 J7
Westby **PR4** 55 G6
Westcliff-on-Sea **SS0** 24 E3
Westcombe **BA4** 9 F1
Westcote **OX7** 30 D6
Westcott, *Bucks.* **HP18** 31 J7
Westcott, *Devon* **EX5** 7 J5
Westcott, *Surr.* **RH4** 22 E7
Westcott Barton **OX7** 31 F6
Westdean **BN25** 13 J7
Westdowns **PL33** 4 A2
Wester Aberchalder **IV2** 88 C2
Wester Badentyre **AB53** 99 F5
Wester Culbeuchly **AB45** 98 E4
Wester Dechmont **EH52** 75 J3
Wester Fintray **AB51** 91 G3
Wester Gruinards **IV24** 96 C2
Wester Lealty **IV17** 96 D4
Wester Lonvine **IV18** 96 E4
Wester Newburn **KY8** 83 F7
Wester Ord **AB32** 91 G4
Wester Quarff **ZE2** 109 D9
Wester Skeld **ZE2** 109 B8
Westerdale, *High.* **KW12** 105 G3
Westerdale, *N.Yorks.* **YO21** 63 H6
Westerfield, *Shet.* **ZE2** 109 C7
Westerfield, *Suff.* **IP1** 35 F4
Westergate **PO20** 12 C6
Westerham **TN16** 23 H6
Westerleigh **BS37** 19 K4
Westerton, *Aber.* **AB31** 91 F5
Westerton, *Angus* **DD10** 83 H2
Westerton, *Dur.* **DL14** 62 D3
Westerton, *P. & K.* **PH5** 81 K6
Westerwick **ZE2** 109 B8
Westfield, *Cumb.* **CA14** 60 A4
Westfield, *E.Suss.* **TN35** 14 D6
Westfield, *High.* **KW14** 105 F2
Westfield, *Norf.* **NR19** 44 D5
Westfield, *W.Loth.* **EH48** 75 H3
Westfield Moor **TN35** 14 D6
Westgate, *Dur.* **DL13** 62 A3
Westgate, *N.Lincs.* **DN9** 51 K2
Westgate, *Norf.* **NR21** 44 D1
Westgate, *Northumb.* **NE20** 71 G6
Westgate Hill **BD4** 57 H7
Westgate on Sea **CT8** 25 K4
Westhall, *Aber.* **AB52** 90 E2
Westhall, *Suff.* **IP19** 45 J7
Westham, *Dorset* **DT4** 9 F7
Westham, *E.Suss.* **BN24** 13 K6
Westham, *Som.* **TA7** 19 G7
Westhampnett **PO18** 12 B6
Westhay **BA6** 19 H7
Westhead **L40** 48 D2
Westhide **HR1** 28 E4
Westhill, *Aber.* **AB32** 91 G4
Westhill, *High.* **IV2** 96 E7
Westhope, *Here.* **HR4** 28 D3
Westhope, *Shrop.* **SY7** 38 D7
Westhorpe, *Lincs.* **PE11** 43 F2
Westhorpe, *Suff.* **IP14** 34 E2
Westhoughton **BL5** 49 F2
Westhouse **LA6** 56 B2
Westhouses **DE55** 51 G7
Westhumble **RH5** 22 E6
Westing **ZE2** 108 E2
Westlake **PL21** 5 G5
Westleigh, *Devon* **EX39** 6 C3
Westleigh, *Devon* **EX16** 7 J4
Westleigh, *Gt.Man.* **WN7** 49 F2
Westleton **IP17** 35 J2
Westley, *Shrop.* **SY5** 38 C5
Westley, *Suff.* **IP33** 34 C2
Westley Heights **SS16** 24 C3
Westley Waterless **CB8** 33 K3
Westlington **HP17** 31 J7
Westlinton **CA6** 69 J7
Westloch **EH45** 76 A5
Westmarsh **CT3** 25 J5
Westmeston **BN6** 13 G5
Westmill **SG9** 33 G6
Westmuir **DD8** 82 E2
Westness **KW17** 106 C5
Westnewton, *Cumb.* **CA7** 60 C2
Westnewton, *Northumb.* **NE71** 77 G7
Weston, *B. & N.E.Som.* **BA1** 20 A5
Weston, *Ches.* **CW2** 49 G7
Weston, *Devon* **EX12** 7 K7
Weston, *Dorset* **DT5** 9 F7
Weston, *Halton* **WA7** 48 E4
Weston, *Hants.* **GU32** 11 J2
Weston, *Herts.* **SG4** 33 F5
Weston, *Lincs.* **PE12** 43 F3
Weston, *Moray* **AB56** 98 C4
Weston, *N.Yorks.* **LS21** 57 G5
Weston, *Northants.* **NN12** 31 G4
Weston, *Notts.* **NG23** 51 K6
Weston, *Shrop.* **SY4** 38 E3
Weston, *Shrop.* **TF13** 38 E6
Weston, *Staffs.* **ST18** 40 B3
Weston, *W.Berks.* **RG20** 21 H4
Weston Beggard **HR1** 28 E4
Weston by Welland **LE16** 42 A6
Weston Colville **CB1** 33 K3
Weston Corbett **RG25** 21 K7
Weston Coyney **ST3** 40 B1
Weston Favell **NN3** 31 J2
Weston Green, *Cambs.* **CB1** 33 K3
Weston Green, *Norf.* **NR9** 45 F4
Weston Green, *Surr.* **KT10** 22 E5
Weston Heath **TF11** 39 G4
Weston Hills **PE12** 43 F3
Weston Jones **TF10** 39 G3
Weston Longville **NR9** 45 F4
Weston Lullingfields **SY4** 38 D3
Weston Patrick **RG25** 21 K7
Weston Point **WA7** 48 D4
Weston Rhyn **SY10** 38 B2
Weston Subedge **GL55** 30 C4
Weston Turville **HP22** 32 B7
Weston under Penyard **HR9** 29 F6
Weston under Wetherley **CV33** 30 E2
Weston Underwood, *Derbys.* **DE6** 40 E1
Weston Underwood, *M.K.* **MK46** 32 B4
Weston-in-Gordano **BS20** 19 H4
Weston-on-the-Green **OX25** 31 G7
Weston-on-Trent **DE72** 41 G3
Weston-super-Mare **BS23** 19 G5
Weston-under-Lizard **TF11** 40 A4
Westonbirt **GL8** 20 B3
Westoning **MK45** 32 D5
Westonzoyland **TA7** 8 C1
Westow **YO60** 58 D3
Westport, *Arg. & B.* **PA28** 66 A1
Westport, *Som.* **TA10** 8 C3
Westrigg **EH48** 75 H4
Westruther **TD3** 76 E5
Westry **PE15** 43 G6
Westside **AB12** 91 G5
Westward **CA7** 60 D2
Westward Ho! **EX39** 6 C3
Westwell, *Kent* **TN25** 14 E3
Westwell, *Oxon.* **OX18** 30 D7
Westwell Leacon **TN27** 14 E3
Westwick, *Cambs.* **CB4** 33 H2
Westwick, *Dur.* **DL12** 62 B5
Westwick, *Norf.* **NR10** 45 G3
Westwood, *Devon* **EX5** 7 J6
Westwood, *Wilts.* **BA15** 20 B6
Westwood Heath **CV4** 30 D1
Westwoodside **DN9** 51 K3
Wether Cote Farm **YO62** 58 C1
Wetheral **CA4** 61 F1
Wetherby **LS22** 57 K5
Wetherden **IP14** 34 E2
Wetheringsett **IP14** 35 F2
Wethersfield **CM7** 34 B5
Wethersta **ZE2** 109 C6
Wetherup Street **IP14** 35 F2
Wetley Rocks **ST9** 40 B1
Wettenhall **CW7** 49 F6
Wettenhall Green **CW7** 49 F6

Wetton

Wetton DE6 50 D7
Wetwang YO25 59 F4
Wetwood ST21 39 G2
Wexcombe SN8 21 F6
Weybourne NR25 45 F1
Weybread IP21 45 G7
Weybridge KT13 22 D5
Weycroft EX13 8 C4
Weydale KW14 105 G2
Weyhill SP11 21 G7
Weymouth DT4 9 F7
Whaddon, Bucks. MK17 32 B5
Whaddon, Cambs. SG8 33 G4
Whaddon, Glos. GL4 29 H7
Whaddon, Wilts. SP5 10 C2
Whaddon Gap SG8 33 G4
Whale CA10 61 G4
Whaley NG20 51 H5
Whaley Bridge SK23 50 C4
Whaligoe KW2 105 J4
Whalley BB7 56 C6
Whalton NE61 71 G5
Wham BD24 56 C3
Whaplode PE12 43 G3
Whaplode Drove PE12 43 G4
Whaplode St. Catherine PE12 43 G4
Wharfe LA2 56 C3
Wharles PR4 55 H6
Wharncliffe Side S35 51 F3
Wharram le Street YO17 58 E3
Wharram Percy YO17 58 E3
Wharton, Ches. CW7 49 F6
Wharton, Here. HR6 28 E3
Whashton DL11 62 C6
Whatcote CV36 30 D4
Whatfield IP7 34 E4
Whatley BA11 20 A7
Whatlington TN33 14 C6
Whatstandwell DE4 51 F7
Whatton NG13 42 A2
Whauphill DG8 64 E6
Whaw DL11 62 A6
Wheatacre NR34 45 J6
Wheatenhurst GL2 20 A1
Wheathampstead AL4 32 E7
Wheathill WV16 39 F7
Wheatley, Hants. GU34 11 J1
Wheatley, Oxon. OX33 21 K1
Wheatley Hill DH6 62 E3
Wheatley Lane BB12 56 D6
Wheaton Aston ST19 40 A4
Wheddon Cross TA24 7 H2
Wheedlemont AB54 90 C2
Wheelerstreet GU8 22 C7
Wheelock CW11 49 G7
Wheelton PR6 56 B7
Wheen DD8 90 B7
Wheldrake YO19 58 C5
Whelford GL7 20 E2
Whelpley Hill HP5 22 D1
Whelpo CA7 60 E3
Whenby YO61 58 C3
Whepstead IP29 34 C3
Wherstead IP9 35 F4
Wherwell SP11 21 G7
Wheston SK17 50 D5
Whetley Cross DT8 8 D4
Whetsted TN12 23 K7
Whetstone LE8 41 H6
Whicham LA18 54 E1
Whichford CV36 30 E5
Whickham NE16 71 H7
Whiddon Down EX6 6 E6
Whifflet ML5 75 F4
Whigstreet DD8 83 F3
Whilton NN11 31 H2
Whim EH46 76 A5
Whimple EX5 7 J6
Whimpwell Green NR12 45 H2
Whin Lane End PR3 55 G5
Whinburgh NR19 44 E5
Whinnyfold AB42 91 J1
Whippingham PO32 11 G5
Whipsnade LU6 32 D7
Whipton EX1 7 H6
Whisby LN6 52 C6
Whissendine LE15 42 B4
Whissonsett NR20 44 D3
Whistley Green RG10 22 A4
Whiston, Mersey. L35 48 D3
Whiston, Northants. NN7 32 B2
Whiston, S.Yorks. S60 51 G4
Whiston, Staffs. ST10 40 C1
Whiston, Staffs. ST19 40 A4
Whitbeck LA19 54 E1
Whitbourne WR6 29 G3
Whitburn, T. & W. SR6 71 K7
Whitburn, W.Loth. EH47 75 H4
Whitby, Ches. CH65 48 C5
Whitby, N.Yorks. YO21 63 K5
Whitchurch, B. & N.E.Som. BS14 19 K5
Whitchurch, Bucks. HP22 32 B6
Whitchurch, Cardiff CF14 18 E4
Whitchurch, Devon PL19 4 E3
Whitchurch, Hants. RG28 21 H7
Whitchurch, Here. HR9 28 E7
Whitchurch, Oxon. RG8 21 K4
Whitchurch, Pembs. SA62 16 B2
Whitchurch, Shrop. SY13 38 E1
Whitchurch Canonicorum DT6 8 C5
Whitchurch Hill RG8 21 K4
Whitcombe DT2 9 G6
Whitcott Keysett SY7 38 B7
White Colne CO6 34 C6
White Coppice PR6 49 F1
White Cross, Cornw. TR8 3 F3
White Cross, Devon EX5 7 J6
White Cross, Here. HR4 28 D4
White End GL19 29 H6
White Lackington DT2 9 G5
White Ladies Aston WR7 29 J3
White Mill SA32 17 H2
White Moor DE56 41 F1
White Notley CM8 34 B7
White Pit LN13 53 G5
White Roding CM6 33 J7
White Waltham SL6 22 B4
Whiteacen AB38 97 K7
Whiteash Green CO9 34 B5
Whitebog AB43 99 H5
Whitebridge, High. KW14 105 H1
Whitebridge, High. IV2 88 B3
Whitebrook NP25 19 J1
Whiteburn TD2 76 D6
Whitecairn DG8 64 C5
Whitecairns AB23 91 H3
Whitecastle ML12 75 J6
Whitechapel PR3 55 J5
Whitechurch SA41 16 E1
Whitecraig EH22 76 B3
Whitecroft GL15 19 K1
Whitecrook DG9 64 B5
Whitecross TR20 2 C5
Whiteface IV25 96 E3
Whitefield, Aber. AB51 91 F2
Whitefield, Gt.Man. M45 49 H2
Whitefield, High. KW1 105 H3
Whitefield, High. IV2 88 C2
Whitefield, P. & K. PH13 82 C4
Whiteford AB51 91 F2
Whitegate CW8 49 F6
Whitehall KW17 106 F5
Whitehaven CA28 60 A5
Whitehill, Hants. GU35 11 J1
Whitehill, Kent ME13 14 E2
Whitehill, N.Ayr. KA24 74 A5
Whitehills AB45 98 E4
Whitehouse, Aber. AB33 90 E3
Whitehouse, Arg. & B. PA29 73 G4
Whitekirk EH39 76 D2
Whitelackington TA19 8 C3
Whitelaw TD11 77 G5
Whiteleen KW2 105 J4
Whitelees KA1 74 B7
Whiteley PO15 11 G4
Whiteley Bank PO38 11 G6
Whiteley Village KT12 22 D5
Whiteleys DG9 64 A5
Whitemans Green RH17 13 G4
Whitemire IV36 97 G6
Whiteparish SP5 10 D2
Whiterashes AB21 91 G2
Whiterow KW1 105 J4
Whiteshill GL6 20 B1
Whiteside, Northumb. NE49 70 C7
Whiteside, W.Loth. EH48 75 H4
Whitesmith BN8 13 J5
Whitestaunton TA20 8 B3
Whitestone, Aber. AB31 90 E5
Whitestone, Arg. & B. PA28 73 F7
Whitestone, Devon EX4 7 G6
Whitestripe AB43 99 H5
Whiteway GL6 29 J7
Whitewell, Aber. AB43 99 H4
Whitewell, Lancs. BB7 56 B5
Whiteworks PL20 5 G3
Whitewreath IV30 97 K6
Whitfield, Here. HR2 28 D5
Whitfield, Kent CT16 15 H3
Whitfield, Northants. NN13 31 H4
Whitfield, Northumb. NE47 61 J1
Whitfield, S.Glos. GL12 19 K2
Whitford, Devon EX13 8 B5
Whitford (Chwitffordd), Flints. CH8 47 K5
Whitgift DN14 58 E7
Whitgreave ST18 40 A3
Whithorn DG8 64 E6
Whiting Bay KA27 66 E1
Whitkirk LS15 57 J6
Whitlam AB21 91 G2
Whitland SA34 17 F3
Whitland Abbey SA34 17 F3
Whitletts KA8 67 H1
Whitley, N.Yorks. DN14 58 B7
Whitley, Read. RG2 22 A5
Whitley Bay NE26 71 J6
Whitley Chapel NE47 62 A1
Whitley Lower WF12 50 E1
Whitley Row TN14 23 H6
Whitlock's End B90 30 C1
Whitminster GL2 20 A1
Whitmore, Dorset BH21 10 B4
Whitmore, Staffs. ST5 40 A1
Whitnage EX16 7 J4
Whitnash CV31 30 E2
Whitney HR3 28 B4
Whitrigg, Cumb. CA7 60 D1
Whitrigg, Cumb. CA7 60 D3
Whitsbury SP6 10 C3
Whitsome TD11 77 G5
Whitson NP18 19 G3
Whitstable CT5 25 H5
Whitstone EX22 4 C1
Whittingham NE66 71 F2
Whittingslow SY6 38 D7
Whittington, Derbys. S41 51 F5
Whittington, Glos. GL54 30 B6
Whittington, Lancs. LA6 56 B2
Whittington, Norf. PE33 44 B6
Whittington, Shrop. SY11 38 C2
Whittington, Staffs. WS14 40 D5
Whittington, Staffs. DY7 40 A7
Whittington, Worcs. WR5 29 H3
Whittle-le-Woods PR6 55 J7
Whittlebury NN12 31 H4
Whittlesey PE7 43 F6
Whittlesford CB2 33 H4
Whitton, N.Lincs. DN15 59 F7
Whitton, Northumb. NE65 71 F3
Whitton, Powys LD7 28 B2
Whitton, Shrop. SY8 28 E1
Whitton, Stock. TS21 62 E4
Whitton, Suff. IP1 35 F4
Whittonditch SN8 21 F4
Whittonstall DH8 62 B1
Whitway RG20 21 H6
Whitwell, Derbys. S80 51 H5
Whitwell, Herts. SG4 32 E6
Whitwell, I.o.W. PO38 11 G7
Whitwell, N.Yorks. DL10 62 D7
Whitwell, Norf. NR10 45 F3
Whitwell, Rut. LE15 42 C5
Whitwell-on-the-Hill YO60 58 D3
Whitwick LE67 41 G4
Whitwood WF10 57 K7
Whitworth OL12 49 H1
Whixall SY13 38 E2
Whixley YO26 57 K4
Whorlton, Dur. DL12 62 C5
Whorlton, N.Yorks. DL6 63 F6
Whygate NE48 70 C6
Whyle HR6 28 E2
Whyteleafe CR3 23 G6
Wibdon NP16 19 J2
Wibsey BD6 57 G6
Wibtoft LE17 41 G7
Wichenford WR6 29 G2
Wichling ME9 14 E2
Wick, Bourne. BH6 10 C5
Wick, High. KW1 105 J3
Wick, S.Glos. BS30 20 A4
Wick, V. of Glam. CF71 18 C4
Wick, W.Suss. BN17 12 D6
Wick, Wilts. SP5 10 C2
Wick, Worcs. WR10 29 J4
Wick Airport KW1 105 J3
Wick Hill, Kent TN27 14 D3
Wick Hill, W'ham RG40 22 A5
Wick St. Lawrence BS22 19 G5
Wicken, Cambs. CB7 33 J1
Wicken, Northants. MK19 31 J5
Wicken Bonhunt CB11 33 H5
Wickenby LN3 52 D4
Wickerslack CA10 61 H5
Wickersley S66 51 G3
Wickford SS12 24 D2
Wickham, Hants. PO17 11 G3
Wickham, W.Berks. RG20 21 G4
Wickham Bishops CM8 34 C7
Wickham Heath RG20 21 H5
Wickham Market IP13 35 G3
Wickham St. Paul CO9 34 C5
Wickham Skeith IP23 34 E2
Wickham Street, Suff. IP23 34 E2
Wickham Street, Suff. CB8 34 B3
Wickhambreaux CT3 15 H2
Wickhambrook CB8 34 B3
Wickhamford WR11 30 B4
Wickhampton NR13 45 J5
Wicklewood NR18 44 E5
Wickmere NR11 45 F2
Wickwar GL12 20 A3
Widdington CB11 33 J5
Widdop HX7 56 E6
Widdrington NE61 71 H4
Wide Open NE13 71 H6
Widecombe in the Moor TQ13 5 H3
Widegates PL13 4 C5
Widemouth Bay EX23 6 A5
Widewall KW17 107 D8
Widford, Essex CM2 24 C1
Widford, Herts. SG12 33 H7
Widmerpool NG12 41 J3
Widnes WA8 48 E4
Widworthy EX14 8 B5
WIGAN WN 48 E2
Wiggaton EX11 7 K6
Wiggenhall St. Germans PE34 44 A4
Wiggenhall St. Mary Magdalen PE34 44 A4
Wiggenhall St. Mary the Virgin PE34 43 J4
Wiggenhall St. Peter PE34 44 A4
Wiggington YO32 58 C4
Wigginton, Herts. HP23 32 C7
Wigginton, Oxon. OX15 30 E5
Wigginton, Staffs. B79 40 E5
Wigglesworth BD23 56 D4
Wiggonby CA7 60 D1
Wiggonholt RH20 12 D5
Wighill LS24 57 K5
Wighton NR23 44 D2
Wightwizzle S36 50 E3
Wigmore, Here. HR6 28 D2
Wigmore, Med. ME8 24 E5
Wigsley NG23 52 B5
Wigsthorpe NN14 42 D7
Wigston LE18 41 J6
Wigston Parva LE10 41 G6
Wigthorpe S81 51 H4
Wigtoft PE20 43 F2
Wigton CA7 60 D2
Wigtown DG8 64 E5
Wilbarston LE16 42 B7
Wilberfoss YO41 58 D4
Wilburton CB6 33 H1
Wilby, Norf. NR16 44 E6
Wilby, Northants. NN8 32 B2
Wilby, Suff. IP21 35 G1
Wilcot SN9 20 E5
Wilcott SY4 38 C4
Wilcrick NP26 19 H3
Wildboarclough SK11 49 J6
Wilden, Beds. MK44 32 D3
Wilden, Worcs. DY13 29 H1
Wildhern SP11 21 G6
Wildhill AL9 23 F1
Wildsworth DN21 52 B3
Wilford NG11 41 H2
Wilkesley SY13 39 F1
Wilkhaven IV20 97 G3
Wilkieston EH27 75 K4
Willand EX15 7 J4
Willaston, Ches. CH64 48 C5
Willaston, Ches. CW5 49 F7
Willen MK15 32 B4
Willenhall, W.Mid. WV13 40 B6
Willenhall, W.Mid. CV3 30 E1
Willerby, E.Riding HU10 59 G7
Willerby, N.Yorks. YO12 59 G2
Willersey WR12 30 C4
Willersley HR3 28 C4
Willesborough TN24 15 F3
Willesborough Lees TN24 15 F3
Willesden NW10 23 F3
Willesley GL8 20 B3
Willett TA4 7 K2
Willey, Shrop. TF12 39 F6
Willey, Warks. CV23 41 G7
Williamscot OX17 31 F4
Williamthorpe S42 51 G6
Willian SG6 33 F5
Willimontswick NE47 70 C7
Willingale CM5 23 J1
Willingdon BN20 13 J6
Willingham, Cambs. CB4 33 H2
Willingham, Lincs. DN21 52 B4
Willington, Beds. MK44 32 E4
Willington, Derbys. DE65 40 E3
Willington, Dur. DL15 62 C3
Willington, T. & W. NE28 71 J7
Willington, Warks. CV36 30 D5
Willington Corner CW6 48 E6
Willisham IP8 34 E3
Willitoft YO8 58 D6
Williton TA4 7 J1
Willoughby, Lincs. LN13 53 H5
Willoughby, Warks. CV23 31 G2
Willoughby Waterleys LE8 41 H6
Willoughby-on-the-Wolds LE12 41 J3
Willoughton DN21 52 C3
Willows Green CM3 34 B7
Willsworthy PL19 6 D7
Wilmcote CV37 30 C3
Wilmington, Devon EX14 8 B4
Wilmington, E.Suss. BN26 13 J6
Wilmington, Kent DA2 23 J4
Wilmslow SK9 49 H4
Wilnecote B77 40 E5
Wilpshire BB1 56 B6
Wilsden BD15 57 F6
Wilsford, Lincs. NG32 42 D1
Wilsford, Wilts. SN9 20 D6
Wilsford, Wilts. SP4 20 E7
Wilsill HG3 57 G3
Wilsley Green TN17 14 C4
Wilson DE73 41 G3
Wilstead MK45 32 D4
Wilsthorpe PE9 42 D4
Wilstone HP23 32 C7
Wilton, Cumb. CA22 60 B5
Wilton, N.Yorks. YO18 58 E1
Wilton, R. & C. TS10 63 G4
Wilton, Sc.Bord. TD9 69 K2
Wilton, Som. TA1 8 B2
Wilton, Wilts. SN8 21 F5
Wilton, Wilts. SP2 10 B1
Wimbish CB10 33 J5
Wimbish Green CB10 33 K5
Wimblebury WS12 40 C4
Wimbledon SW19 23 F4
Wimblington PE15 43 H6
Wimborne Minster BH21 10 B4
Wimborne St. Giles BH21 10 B3
Wimbotsham PE34 44 A5
Wimpstone CV37 30 D4
Wincanton BA9 9 G2
Wincham CW9 49 F5
Winchburgh EH52 75 J3
Winchcombe GL54 30 B6
Winchelsea TN36 14 E6
Winchelsea Beach TN36 14 E6
Winchester SO23 11 F2
Winchet Hill TN17 14 C3
Winchfield RG27 22 A6
Winchmore Hill, Bucks. HP7 22 C2
Winchmore Hill, Gt.Lon. N21 23 G2
Wincle SK11 49 J6
Wincobank S9 51 F3
Windermere LA23 60 F7
Winderton OX15 30 E4
Windhill IV6 96 C7
Windlesham GU20 22 C5
Windley DE56 41 F1
Windley Meadows DE56 41 F1
Windmill Hill, E.Suss. BN27 13 K5
Windmill Hill, Som. TA19 8 C3
Windrush OX18 30 C7
Windsor SL4 22 C4
Windy Yet KA3 74 C5
Windygates KY8 82 E7
Wineham BN5 13 F4
Winestead HU12 59 K7
Winewall BB8 56 E5
Winfarthing IP22 45 F7
Winford BS40 19 J5
Winforton HR3 28 B4
Winfrith Newburgh DT2 9 H6
Wing, Bucks. LU7 32 B6
Wing, Rut. LE15 42 B5
Wingate TS28 63 F3
Wingates, Gt.Man. BL5 49 F2
Wingates, Northumb. NE65 71 F4
Wingerworth S42 51 F6
Wingfield, Beds. LU7 32 D6
Wingfield, Suff. IP21 35 G1
Wingfield, Wilts. BA14 20 B6
Wingham CT3 15 H2
Wingmore CT4 15 G3
Wingrave HP22 32 B7
Winkburn NG22 51 K7
Winkfield SL4 22 C4
Winkfield Row RG42 22 B4
Winkhill ST13 50 C7
Winkleigh EX19 6 E5
Winksley HG4 57 H2
Winksley Banks HG4 57 H2
Winkton BH23 10 C5
Winlaton NE21 71 G7
Winlaton Mill NE39 71 G7
Winless KW1 105 H3
Winmarleigh PR3 55 H5
Winnards Perch TR9 3 G2
Winnersh RG41 22 A4
Winscombe BS25 19 H6
Winsford, Ches. CW7 49 F6
Winsford, Som. TA24 7 H2
Winsham TA20 8 C4
Winshill DE15 40 E3
Winskill CA10 61 G3
Winslade RG25 21 K7
Winsley BA15 20 A5
Winslow MK18 31 J6
Winson GL7 20 D1
Winsor SO40 10 E3
Winster, Cumb. LA23 60 F7
Winster, Derbys. DE4 50 E6
Winston, Dur. DL2 62 C5
Winston, Suff. IP14 35 F2
Winstone GL7 20 C1
Winswell EX38 6 C4
Winterborne Came DT2 9 G6
Winterborne Clenston DT11 9 H4
Winterborne Houghton DT11 9 H4
Winterborne Kingston DT11 9 H5
Winterborne Monkton DT2 9 F6
Winterborne Stickland DT11 9 H4
Winterborne Whitechurch DT11 9 H4
Winterborne Zelston DT11 9 H5
Winterbourne, S.Glos. BS36 19 K3
Winterbourne, W.Berks. RG20 21 H4
Winterbourne Abbas DT2 9 F5
Winterbourne Bassett SN4 20 D4
Winterbourne Dauntsey SP4 10 C1
Winterbourne Earls SP4 10 C1
Winterbourne Gunner SP4 10 C1
Winterbourne Monkton SN4 20 D4
Winterbourne Steepleton DT2 9 F6
Winterbourne Stoke SP3 20 D7
Winterburn BD23 56 E4
Wintercleugh ML12 68 E2
Winteringham DN15 59 F7
Winterley CW11 49 G7
Wintersett WF4 51 F1
Wintershill SO32 11 G3
Winterslow SP5 10 D1
Winterton DN15 52 C1
Winterton-on-Sea NR29 45 J4
Winthorpe, Lincs. PE25 53 J6
Winthorpe, Notts. NG24 52 B7
Winton, Bourne. BH3 10 B5
Winton, Cumb. CA17 61 J5
Wintringham YO17 58 E2
Winwick, Cambs. PE28 42 E7
Winwick, Northants. NN6 31 H1
Winwick, Warr. WA2 49 F3

Yiewsley

Wirksworth **DE4** 50 E7
Wirswall **SY13** 38 E1
Wisbech **PE13** 43 H5
Wisbech St. Mary **PE13** 43 H5
Wisborough Green **RH14** 12 D4
Wiseton **DN10** 51 K4
Wishaw, *N.Lan.* **ML2** 75 F5
Wishaw, *Warks.* **B76** 40 D6
Wisley **GU23** 22 D6
Wispington **LN9** 53 F5
Wissett **IP19** 35 H1
Wissington **CO6** 34 D5
Wistanstow **SY7** 38 D7
Wistanswick **TF9** 39 F3
Wistaston **CW2** 49 F7
Wiston, *Pembs.* **SA62** 16 D3
Wiston, *S.Lan.* **ML12** 75 H7
Wistow, *Cambs.* **PE28** 43 F7
Wistow, *N.Yorks.* **YO8** 58 B6
Wiswell **BB7** 56 C6
Witcham **CB6** 33 H1
Witchampton **BH21** 9 J4
Witchburn **PA28** 66 B2
Witchford **CB6** 33 J1
Witcombe **TA12** 8 D2
Witham **CM8** 34 C7
Witham Friary **BA11** 20 A7
Witham on the Hill **PE10** 42 D4
Withcote **LE15** 42 B5
Witherenden Hill **TN19** 13 K4
Witherhurst **TN19** 13 K4
Witheridge **EX16** 7 G4
Witherley **CV9** 41 F6
Withern **LN13** 53 H4
Withernsea **HU19** 59 K7
Withernwick **HU11** 59 J5
Withersdale Street **IP20** 45 G7
Withersfield **CB9** 33 K4
Witherslack **LA11** 55 H1
Witherslack Hall **LA11** 55 H1
Withiel **PL30** 3 G2
Withiel Florey **TA24** 7 H2
Withington, *Glos.* **GL54** 30 B7
Withington, *Gt.Man.* **M20** 49 H3
Withington, *Here.* **HR1** 28 E4
Withington, *Shrop.* **SY4** 38 E4
Withington, *Staffs.* **ST10** 40 C2
Withington Green **SK11** 49 H5
Withleigh **EX16** 7 H4
Withnell **PR6** 56 B7
Withybrook **CV7** 41 G7
Withycombe **TA24** 7 J1
Withycombe Raleigh **EX8** 7 J7
Withyham **TN7** 13 H3
Withypool **TA24** 7 G2
Witley **GU8** 12 C3
Witnesham **IP6** 35 F3
Witney **OX28** 30 E7
Wittering **PE8** 42 D5
Wittersham **TN30** 14 D5
Witton **DD9** 83 G1
Witton Bridge **NR28** 45 H2
Witton Gilbert **DH7** 62 D2
Witton Park **DL14** 62 C3
Witton-le-Wear **DL14** 62 C3
Wiveliscombe **TA4** 7 J3
Wivelsfield **RH17** 13 G4
Wivelsfield Green **RH17** 13 G5
Wivenhoe **CO7** 34 E6
Wiveton **NR25** 44 E1
Wix **CO11** 35 F6
Wixford **B49** 30 B3
Wixoe **CO10** 34 B4
Woburn **MK17** 32 C5
Woburn Sands **MK17** 32 C5
Wokefield Park **RG7** 21 K5
Woking **GU22** 22 D6
Wokingham **RG40** 22 B5
Wolborough **TQ12** 5 J3
Wold Newton, *E.Riding* **YO25** 59 G2
Wold Newton, *N.E.Lincs.* **LN8** 53 F3
Woldingham **CR3** 23 G6
Wolfelee **TD9** 70 A3
Wolferlow **WR15** 29 F2
Wolferton **PE31** 44 A3
Wolfhampcote **CV23** 31 G2
Wolfhill **PH2** 82 C4
Wolfpits **LD8** 28 B3
Wolf's Castle **SA62** 16 C2
Wolfsdale **SA62** 16 C2
Woll **TD7** 69 K1
Wollaston, *Northants.* **NN29** 32 C2
Wollaston, *Shrop.* **SY5** 38 C4
Wollaston, *W.Mid.* **DY8** 40 A7
Wollerton **TF9** 39 F3
Wolsingham **DL13** 62 B3
Wolstenholme **OL12** 49 H1
Wolston **CV8** 31 F1
Wolvercote **OX2** 21 H1
WOLVERHAMPTON WV 40 B6
Wolverley, *Shrop.* **SY4** 38 D2
Wolverley, *Worcs.* **DY11** 29 H1
Wolverton, *Hants.* **RG26** 21 J6
Wolverton, *M.K.* **MK12** 32 B4
Wolverton, *Warks.* **CV35** 30 D2
Wolvesnewton **NP16** 19 H2
Wolvey **LE10** 41 G7
Wolviston **TS22** 63 F4
Wombleton **YO62** 58 C1
Wombourne **WV5** 40 A6
Wombwell **S73** 51 G2
Womenswold **CT4** 15 H2
Womersley **DN6** 51 H1
Wonastow **NP25** 28 D7
Wonersh **GU5** 22 D7
Wonson **EX20** 6 E7
Wonston **SO21** 11 F1
Wooburn **HP10** 22 C3
Wooburn Green **HP10** 22 C3
Wood Burcote **NN12** 31 H4
Wood Dalling **NR11** 44 E3
Wood End, *Beds.* **MK43** 32 D4
Wood End, *Herts.* **SG2** 33 G6
Wood End, *Warks.* **CV9** 40 E6
Wood End, *Warks.* **B94** 30 C1
Wood Enderby **PE22** 53 F6
Wood Green **N22** 23 G2
Wood Hayes **WV11** 40 B5
Wood Norton **NR20** 44 E3
Wood Street **GU3** 22 C6
Woodale **DL8** 57 F2
Woodbastwick **NR13** 45 H4
Woodbeck **DN22** 51 K5
Woodbine **SA61** 16 C3
Woodborough, *Notts.* **NG14** 41 J1
Woodborough, *Wilts.* **SN9** 20 E5
Woodbridge **IP12** 35 G4
Woodbury **EX5** 7 J7
Woodbury Salterton **EX5** 7 J7
Woodchester **GL5** 20 B1
Woodchurch, *Kent* **TN26** 14 E4
Woodchurch, *Mersey.* **CH49** 48 B4
Woodcote, *Oxon.* **RG8** 21 K3
Woodcote, *Tel. & W.* **TF10** 39 G4
Woodcott **RG28** 21 H6
Woodcroft **NP16** 19 J2
Woodcutts **SP5** 9 J3
Woodditton **CB8** 33 K3
Woodeaton **OX3** 31 G7
Woodend, *Aber.* **AB51** 90 E3
Woodend, *Cumb.* **CA18** 60 C7
Woodend, *High.* **IV13** 88 E2
Woodend, *High.* **PH36** 79 J1
Woodend, *Northants.* **NN12** 31 H4
Woodend, *P. & K.* **PH15** 81 J3
Woodend, *W.Suss.* **PO18** 12 B6
Woodfalls **SP5** 10 D2
Woodford, *Cornw.* **EX23** 6 A4
Woodford, *Glos.* **GL13** 19 K2
Woodford, *Gt.Lon.* **IG8** 23 H2
Woodford, *Gt.Man.* **SK7** 49 H4
Woodford, *Northants.* **NN14** 32 C1
Woodford Bridge **IG8** 23 H2
Woodford Green **IG8** 23 H2
Woodford Halse **NN11** 31 G3
Woodgate, *Norf.* **NR20** 44 E4
Woodgate, *W.Mid.* **B32** 40 B7
Woodgate, *W.Suss.* **PO20** 12 C6
Woodgate, *Worcs.* **B60** 29 J2
Woodgreen **SP6** 10 C3
Woodhall **DL8** 62 A7
Woodhall Spa **LN10** 52 E6
Woodham, *Dur.* **DL17** 62 D4
Woodham, *Surr.* **KT15** 22 D5
Woodham Ferrers **CM3** 24 D2
Woodham Mortimer **CM9** 24 E1
Woodham Walter **CM9** 24 E1
Woodhaven **DD6** 83 F5
Woodhead **AB53** 91 F1
Woodhill **WV16** 39 G7
Woodhorn **NE64** 71 H5
Woodhouse, *Cumb.* **LA7** 55 J1
Woodhouse, *Leics.* **LE12** 41 H4
Woodhouse, *S.Yorks.* **S13** 51 G4
Woodhouse Eaves **LE12** 41 H4
Woodhouses **DE13** 40 D4
Woodhuish **TQ6** 5 K5
Woodhurst **PE28** 33 G1
Woodingdean **BN2** 13 G6
Woodland, *Devon* **TQ13** 5 H4
Woodland, *Dur.* **DL13** 62 B4
Woodlands, *Dorset* **BH21** 10 B4
Woodlands, *Hants.* **SO40** 10 E3
Woodlands, *Shrop.* **WV16** 39 G7
Woodlands Park **SL6** 22 B4
Woodleigh **TQ7** 5 H6
Woodlesford **LS26** 57 J7
Woodley **RG5** 22 A4
Woodmancote, *Glos.* **GL52** 29 J6
Woodmancote, *Glos.* **GL7** 20 D1
Woodmancote, *W.Suss.* **BN5** 13 F5
Woodmancote, *W.Suss.* **PO10** 11 J4
Woodmancott **SO21** 21 J7
Woodmansey **HU17** 59 G6
Woodmansterne **SM7** 23 F6
Woodminton **SP5** 10 B2
Woodmoor **SY15** 38 B5
Woodnesborough **CT13** 15 H2
Woodnewton **PE8** 42 D6
Woodplumpton **PR4** 55 J6
Woodrising **NR9** 44 D5
Woodseaves, *Shrop.* **TF9** 39 F2
Woodseaves, *Staffs.* **ST20** 39 G3
Woodsend **SN8** 21 F4
Woodsetts **S81** 51 H4
Woodsford **DT2** 9 G5
Woodside, *Aberdeen* **AB21** 91 H4
Woodside, *Brack.F.* **SL4** 22 C4
Woodside, *D. & G.* **DG1** 69 F6
Woodside, *Fife* **KY8** 83 F7
Woodside, *Fife* **KY7** 82 D7
Woodside, *Herts.* **AL9** 23 F1
Woodside, *N.Ayr.* **KA15** 74 B5
Woodside, *P. & K.* **PH13** 82 C4
Woodside, *Shrop.* **SY7** 28 C1
Woodside, *W.Mid.* **DY5** 40 B7
Woodstock **OX20** 31 F7
Woodstock Slop **SA63** 16 D2
Woodston **PE2** 42 E6
Woodthorpe, *Derbys.* **S43** 51 G5
Woodthorpe, *Leics.* **LE12** 41 H4
Woodton **NR35** 45 G6
Woodtown, *Aber.* **DD9** 90 E7
Woodtown, *Devon* **EX39** 6 C3
Woodville **DE11** 41 F4
Woodwalton **PE28** 43 F7
Woodyates **SP5** 10 B3
Woofferton **SY8** 28 E2
Wookey **BA5** 19 J7
Wookey Hole **BA5** 19 J7
Wool **BH20** 9 H6
Woolacombe **EX34** 6 C1
Woolaston **GL15** 19 J2
Woolavington **TA7** 19 G7
Woolbeding **GU29** 12 B4
Wooler **NE71** 70 E1
Woolfardisworthy, *Devon* **EX39** 6 B3
Woolfardisworthy, *Devon* **EX17** 7 G5
Woolfords Cottages **EH55** 75 J5
Woolhampton **RG7** 21 J5
Woolhope **HR1** 29 F5
Woollage Green **CT4** 15 H3
Woolland **DT11** 9 G4
Woollard **BS39** 19 K5
Woollaton **EX38** 6 C4
Woolley, *B. & N.E.Som.* **BA1** 20 A5
Woolley, *Cambs.* **PE28** 32 E1
Woolley, *W.Yorks.* **WF4** 51 F1
Woolmer Green **SG3** 33 F7
Woolmere Green **B60** 29 J2
Woolmersdon **TA5** 8 B1
Woolpit **IP30** 34 D2
Woolscott **CV23** 31 F2
Woolstaston **SY6** 38 D6
Woolsthorpe, *Lincs.* **NG32** 42 B2
Woolsthorpe, *Lincs.* **NG33** 42 C3
Woolston, *S'ham.* **SO19** 11 F3
Woolston, *Shrop.* **SY10** 38 C3
Woolston, *Shrop.* **SY6** 38 D7
Woolston, *Warr.* **WA1** 49 F4
Woolston Green **TQ13** 5 H4
Woolstone **SN7** 21 F3
Woolton **L25** 48 D4
Woolton Hill **RG20** 21 H5
Woolverstone **IP9** 35 F5
Woolverton **BA2** 20 A6
Woolwich **SE18** 23 H4
Woonton **HR3** 28 C3
Wooperton **NE66** 71 F1
Woore **CW3** 39 G1
Wootton, *Beds.* **MK43** 32 D4
Wootton, *Hants.* **BH25** 10 D5
Wootton, *Kent* **CT4** 15 H3
Wootton, *N.Lincs.* **DN39** 52 D1
Wootton, *Northants.* **NN4** 31 J3
Wootton, *Oxon.* **OX20** 31 F7
Wootton, *Oxon.* **OX1** 21 H1
Wootton, *Shrop.* **SY7** 28 D1
Wootton, *Staffs.* **DE6** 40 D1
Wootton, *Staffs.* **ST21** 40 A3
Wootton Bassett **SN4** 20 D3
Wootton Bridge **PO33** 11 G5
Wootton Common **PO33** 11 G5
Wootton Courtenay **TA24** 7 H1
Wootton Fitzpaine **DT6** 8 C5
Wootton Green **MK43** 32 D4
Wootton Rivers **SN8** 20 E5
Wootton St. Lawrence **RG23** 21 J6
Wootton Wawen **B95** 30 C2
WORCESTER WR 29 H3
Worcester Park **KT4** 23 F5
Wordsley **DY8** 40 A7
Wordwell **IP28** 34 C1
Worfield **WV15** 39 G6
Work **KW15** 107 D6
Workington **CA14** 60 B4
Worksop **S80** 51 H5
Worlaby **DN20** 52 D1
Worlds End **PO7** 11 H3
World's End **RG20** 21 H4
Worle **BS22** 19 G5
Worleston **CW5** 49 F7
Worlingham **NR34** 45 J6
Worlington **IP28** 33 K1
Worlingworth **IP13** 35 G2
Wormbridge **HR2** 28 D5
Wormegay **PE33** 44 A4
Wormelow Tump **HR2** 28 D5
Wormhill **SK17** 50 D5
Wormiehills **DD11** 83 H4
Wormingford **CO6** 34 D5
Worminghall **HP18** 21 K1
Wormington **WR12** 30 B5
Worminster **BA4** 19 J7
Wormistone **KY10** 83 H7
Wormit **DD6** 82 E5
Wormleighton **CV47** 31 F3
Wormley, *Herts.* **EN10** 23 G1
Wormley, *Surr.* **GU8** 12 C3
Wormshill **ME9** 14 D2
Wormsley **HR4** 28 D4
Worplesdon **GU3** 22 C6
Worrall **S35** 51 F3
Worsbrough **S70** 51 F2
Worsley **M28** 49 G2
Worstead **NR28** 45 H3
Worsted Lodge **CB1** 33 J3
Worsthorne **BB10** 56 D6
Worston **BB7** 56 C5
Worswell **PL8** 5 F6
Worth, *Kent* **CT14** 15 J2
Worth, *W.Suss.* **RH10** 13 G3
Worth Matravers **BH19** 9 J7
Wortham **IP22** 34 E1
Worthen **SY5** 38 C5
Worthenbury **LL13** 38 D1
Worthing, *Norf.* **NR20** 44 E4
Worthing, *W.Suss.* **BN11** 12 E6
Worthington **LE65** 41 G3
Wortley, *Glos.* **GL12** 20 A2
Wortley, *S.Yorks.* **S35** 51 F3
Worton **SN10** 20 C6
Wortwell **IP20** 45 G7
Wotherton **SY15** 38 B5
Wotton **RH5** 22 E7
Wotton Underwood **HP18** 31 H7
Wotton-under-Edge **GL12** 20 A2
Woughton on the Green **MK6** 32 B5
Wouldham **ME1** 24 D5
Wrabness **CO11** 35 F5
Wrae **AB53** 99 F5
Wrafton **EX33** 6 C2
Wragby **LN8** 52 E5
Wragholme **LN11** 53 G3
Wramplingham **NR18** 45 F5
Wrangham **AB52** 90 E1
Wrangle **PE22** 53 H7
Wrangle Lowgate **PE22** 53 H7
Wrangway **TA21** 7 K4
Wrantage **TA3** 8 C2
Wrawby **DN20** 52 D2
Wraxall, *N.Som.* **BS48** 19 H4
Wraxall, *Som.* **BA4** 9 F1
Wray **LA2** 56 B3
Wray Castle **LA22** 60 E6
Wraysbury **TW19** 22 D4
Wrea Green **PR4** 55 G6
Wreay, *Cumb.* **CA4** 60 F2
Wreay, *Cumb.* **CA11** 60 F4
Wrecclesham **GU10** 22 B7
Wrecsam (Wrexham) **LL13** 38 C1
Wrekenton **NE9** 62 D1
Wrelton **YO18** 58 D1
Wrenbury **CW5** 38 E1
Wreningham **NR16** 45 F6
Wrentham **NR34** 45 J7
Wrenthorpe **WF2** 57 J7
Wrentnall **SY5** 38 D5
Wressle **YO8** 58 D6
Wrestlingworth **SG19** 33 F4
Wretham **IP24** 44 D7
Wretton **PE33** 44 A6
Wrexham (Wrecsam) **LL13** 38 C1
Wrexham Industrial Estate **LL13** 38 C1
Wribbenhall **DY12** 29 G1
Wrightington Bar **WN6** 48 E1
Wrightpark **FK8** 74 E1
Wrinehill **CW3** 39 G1
Wrington **BS40** 19 H5
Writhlington **BA3** 19 K6
Writtle **CM1** 24 C1
Wrockwardine **TF6** 39 F4
Wroot **DN9** 51 K2
Wrotham **TN15** 23 K6
Wrotham Heath **TN15** 23 K6
Wrotham Hill **TN15** 24 C5
Wrotham Park **EN5** 23 F2
Wroughton **SN4** 20 E3
Wroxall **PO38** 11 G7
Wroxeter **SY5** 38 E5
Wroxhall **CV35** 30 D1
Wroxham **NR12** 45 H4
Wroxton **OX15** 31 F4
Wstrws **SA44** 26 C4
Wyaston **DE6** 40 D1
Wyberton **PE21** 43 G1
Wyboston **MK44** 32 E3
Wybunbury **CW5** 39 F1
Wych Cross **RH18** 13 H3
Wychbold **WR9** 29 J2
Wyck **GU34** 11 J1
Wyck Rissington **GL54** 30 C6
Wycliffe **DL12** 62 C5
Wycoller **BB8** 56 E6
Wycomb **LE14** 42 A3
Wycombe Marsh **HP11** 22 B2
Wyddial **SG9** 33 G5
Wye **TN25** 15 F3
Wyke, *Dorset* **SP8** 9 G2
Wyke, *Shrop.* **TF13** 39 F5
Wyke, *W.Yorks.* **BD12** 57 G7
Wyke Regis **DT4** 9 F7
Wykeham, *N.Yorks.* **YO13** 59 F1
Wykeham, *N.Yorks.* **YO17** 58 E2
Wyken **WV15** 39 G6
Wykey **SY4** 38 C3
Wylam **NE41** 71 G7
Wylde Green **B72** 40 D6
Wyllie **NP11** 18 E2
Wylye **BA12** 10 B1
Wymering **PO6** 11 H4
Wymeswold **LE12** 41 J3
Wymington **NN10** 32 C2
Wymondham, *Leics.* **LE14** 42 B4
Wymondham, *Norf.* **NR18** 45 F5
Wyndham **CF32** 18 C2
Wynford Eagle **DT2** 8 E5
Wynnstay **LL14** 38 C1
Wynyard **TS22** 63 F4
Wyre Piddle **WR10** 29 J4
Wyresdale Tower **LA2** 56 B4
Wysall **NG12** 41 J3
Wyson **SY8** 28 E2
Wythall **B47** 30 B1
Wytham **OX2** 21 H1
Wythburn **CA12** 60 E5
Wyton **PE28** 33 F1
Wyverstone **IP14** 34 E2
Wyverstone Street **IP14** 34 E2
Wyville **NG32** 42 B3
Wyvis Lodge **IV16** 96 B4

Y

Y Bryn **LL23** 37 H3
Y Drenewydd (Newtown) **SY16** 38 A6
Y Fan **SY18** 37 J7
Y Felinheli (Port Dinorwig) **LL56** 46 D6
Y Felint (Flint) **CH6** 48 B5
Y Fenni (Abergavenny) **NP7** 28 C7
Y Ffôr **LL53** 36 C2
Y Trallwng (Welshpool) **SY21** 38 B5
Yaddlethorpe **DN17** 52 B2
Yafford **PO30** 11 F6
Yafforth **DL7** 62 E7
Yalding **ME18** 23 K7
Yanworth **GL54** 30 B7
Yapham **YO42** 58 D4
Yapton **BN18** 12 C6
Yarburgh **LN11** 53 G3
Yarcombe **EX14** 8 B4
Yardley **B25** 40 D7
Yardley Gobion **NN12** 31 J4
Yardley Hastings **NN7** 32 B3
Yardro **LD8** 28 B3
Yarkhill **HR1** 29 F4
Yarlet **ST18** 40 B3
Yarley **BA5** 19 J7
Yarlington **BA9** 9 F2
Yarm **TS15** 63 F5
Yarmouth **PO41** 10 E6
Yarnacott **EX32** 6 E2
Yarnbrook **BA14** 20 B6
Yarnfield **ST15** 40 A2
Yarnscombe **EX31** 6 D3
Yarnton **OX5** 31 F7
Yarpole **HR6** 28 D2
Yarrow **TD7** 69 J1
Yarrow Feus **TD7** 69 J1
Yarrowford **TD7** 69 K1
Yarsop **HR4** 28 D4
Yarwell **PE8** 42 D6
Yate **BS37** 20 A3
Yateley **GU46** 22 B5
Yatesbury **SN11** 20 D4
Yattendon **RG18** 21 J4
Yatton, *Here.* **HR6** 28 D2
Yatton, *N.Som.* **BS19** 19 H5
Yatton Keynell **SN14** 20 B4
Yaverland **PO36** 11 H6
Yaxham **NR19** 44 E4
Yaxley, *Cambs.* **PE7** 42 E6
Yaxley, *Suff.* **IP23** 35 F1
Yazor **HR4** 28 D4
Yeading **UB4** 22 E3
Yeadon **LS19** 57 H5
Yealand Conyers **LA5** 55 J2
Yealand Redmayne **LA5** 55 J2
Yealmpton **PL8** 5 F5
Yearby **TS11** 63 H4
Yearsley **YO61** 58 B2
Yeaton **SY4** 38 D4
Yeaveley **DE6** 40 D1
Yedingham **YO17** 58 E2
Yelford **OX29** 21 G1
Yelland, *Devon* **EX31** 6 C2
Yelland, *Devon* **EX20** 6 D6
Yelling **PE19** 33 F2
Yelvertoft **NN6** 31 G1
Yelverton, *Devon* **PL20** 5 F4
Yelverton, *Norf.* **NR14** 45 G5
Yenston **BA8** 9 G2
Yeo Vale **EX39** 6 C3
Yeoford **EX17** 7 F6
Yeolmbridge **PL15** 6 B7
Yeomadon **EX22** 6 B5
Yeovil **BA20** 8 E3
Yeovil Marsh **BA21** 8 E3
Yeovilton **BA22** 8 E2
Yerbeston **SA68** 16 D4
Yesnaby **KW16** 107 B6
Yetlington **NE65** 71 F2
Yetminster **DT9** 8 E3
Yettington **EX9** 7 J7
Yetts o'Muckhart **FK14** 82 B7
Yielden **MK44** 32 D2
Yiewsley **UB7** 22 D4

Ynys

INDEX TO NORTHERN IRELAND

Administrative Area Abbreviations

Arma.	Armagh	London.	Londonderry
Down	Down	Tyr.	Tyrone
Ferm.	Fermanagh		